Native American Major Leaguers

Edited by Rob Daugherty and Bill Nowlin
Associate editors Len Levin and Carl Riechers

Society for American Baseball Research, Inc.
Phoenix, AZ

Native American Major Leaguers
Copyright © 2025 Society for American Baseball Research, Inc.

Edited by Rob Daugherty and Bill Nowlin
Associate editors Len Levin and Carl Riechers
Design: Rachael Sullivan

Front cover baseball card images are from the collection of Rob Daugherty.
Card images are public domain, with the exception of the Ellsbury, McLish, Conley, Reynolds, Lohse, Willoughby, and Adams cards, which are courtesy of Topps.
Topps® trading cards used courtesy of The Topps Company, Inc.

ISBN 978-1-960819-48-2 ebook
ISBN 978-1-960819-49-9 paper

Library of Congress Control Number: 9781960819499

Cronkite School at ASU
555 N. Central Ave., #406-C
Phoenix, AZ 85004
Phone: (602) 496-1460
www.sabr.org

CONTENTS

INTRODUCTION

In the early days of baseball, Native players were often identified not by their actual heritage but by perceived facial features or stereotypes. The label "Chief" was frequently used by opponents, fans, management, teammates, and coaches alike. Far from honoring the players, the term was an appropriation and caricature, and was perpetuated by the sportswriters to garner sensationalized headlines. This practice was not meant to respect Native Americans; rather it reduced them to stereotypes.

I encountered similar attitudes firsthand while playing college ball in the early 1970s. Fortunately, the open name-calling has diminished over time, but the use of monikers and caricatures still continues. At a community leaders conference hosted by the Cherokee Nation, I had the privilege of introducing my friend and fellow Haskell alumnus Mr. Billy Mills – a proud Citizen of the Lakota Sioux from Pine Ridge, South Dakota. Billy Mills was a gold medalist in the 10,000-meter race in the 1964 Olympics in Japan. I asked him in a conversation about the use of the term "Chief" and other stereotypical names our Native athletes have been called over the years. Billy, with his characteristic grace, smiled and replied, "You don't mind being known as an Indian, but you don't want it to be your whole identity." I had come across that quote in a book before, but having Billy say it in person made the moment – and the message – all the more meaningful.

I have always known that several Native ballplayers made their mark in major-league baseball, and over the years I casually sought out their cards and memorabilia. Whenever I was asked to speak or emcee at Native events, I'd share a bit about my collection and research, highlighting players from the Tribe or Nation connected to the community I was visiting. To my surprise, very few were familiar with the names I would mention. It quickly became clear to me that this history wasn't being shared – and it needed to be.

What began as a personal interest to correct a misnomer in baseball turned into a focused mission. By that I mean to make the sports world aware that the very first person to break the color barrier in the major leagues was in fact a Native American named Louis Sockalexis from the Penobscot Tribe in Maine. That was in 1897 with the Cleveland Spiders. The requests for presentations started increasing, and soon media inquiries followed. When asked to provide proof for my talks, I began organizing my collection into a formal exhibit, showcasing the 28 Native men who made it to the major leagues 50 years prior to Mr. Jackie Robinson. I continue to travel across the country searching for more cards and photos, and artifacts tied to these Indigenous icons. This journey has been more than a hobby; it's a deeply rewarding experience – one that only those driven by passion for history and heritage can truly understand. Sadly, many of those 28 Native players are overlooked by sports media and rarely mentioned. Some played for many seasons but many played for a season, a month, or, in some cases, just a single game. When people questioned the legitimacy of these players, it only fueled my determination to shine the light on these sports heroes whose stories have long gone untold. This is why it matters to me. Someone needs to tell their story. And I intend to make sure it's heard.

– Rob Daugherty / Cherokee Nation Oklahoma

After becoming aware of the Society for American Baseball Research and eventually joining the organization, I began exploring research conducted by other SABR members, specifically Native and those who played between 1897 and 1947. I discovered that some research had already been done. I was fortunate to connect with Mr. Bill Nowlin, a sitting board member of SABR. He was very helpful and encouraging as I delved deeper into my effort to document and research Native major-league baseball players. Our correspondence quickly became regular and it eventually led to co-editing a book – this book – that focused on Native Americans in major-league baseball. As my research expanded beyond 1947, I remained committed to verifying tribal affiliations of these players using the same application process I had applied to the earlier group of players. This application ensures that the consistency and the integrity and accuracy of the research are maintained throughout.

CRITERIA

From the very start of my research, the established process to verify and authenticate the identities of Native ballplayers was by contacting the enrollment and registration offices of their respective Tribes. The initial publication of this project was made possible through a grant from two Tribes, the Cherokee Nation and the Chickasaw Nation, both from Oklahoma. The grant involved the use of federal funding; as a result, it was necessary to include only those players who were enrolled citizens of federally recognized Tribes, as listed by the Office of Federal Acknowledgement in the Bureau of Indian Affairs, part of the US Department of the Interior.

There are former major-league players whose names are associated with Native heritage, but do not meet the established criteria for inclusion in this book. One example is Hall of Fame catcher Johnny Bench of the Cincinnati Reds. While Bench is Choctaw by blood, he is not officially enrolled, but is certainly eligible. As such, he does not meet the enrollment-based standards required for inclusion. There are Dwight Lowry, a former player for the Tigers and the Twins, and Gene Locklear, a former player for the Reds, Padres, and the Yankees. Both are from the Lumbee Tribe in North Carolina. The Lumbee are actively seeking full federal recognition. Currently, the Lumbee are recognized in North Carolina as a state recognized Tribe. In 1956 the US Congress passed the Lumbee Act, recognizing Lumbees as being Native Americans, but denying the benefits of a federally recognized Tribe.

ACKNOWLEDGMENT

Throughout this project, I was fortunate to receive support from many individuals – far too many to name them all. However, there are several whose special contributions kick-started my work. First and foremost, my family. Kelly, with her computer navigation skills, and to BC and Jay who always from the beginning helped me sort and catalog my collection. You each tolerated the countless boxes of cards lining the hallways and into your closets. Special thanks to Catherine Foreman Gray, who was the first to ask me to make a presentation on this work. To Dr. Gourd, for the idea of an exhibit. Deep gratitude to Tonya Hogner-Weavel, who took charge to curate my entire collection at the Cherokee Heritage Center that brought my vision to life. I am also grateful to Nathan Rueckert and Ethan Bryan for selecting my story for their publication and connecting me with Matt Strahm of the Philadelphia Phillies, who kindly featured me on his show on Bally Sports, a national syndicated production.

A heartfelt thanks to Bill Nowlin, whose guidance and encouragement have been instrumental throughout this project. And finally, to many friends, colleagues, and supporters who discussed this work with me or offered kind words to keep me going forward – I say WaDo!

To Bo, Callie, Cassidy, Uncle Curt, Dave, Donetta, Hunter, James, Jason, Joaquin, Joe, John, Lin, Matt, Molly, Paul, Ron, Tammy, Thomas, Todd, Travis, Cherokee Nation, Cherokee Phoenix, Chickasaw Nation, NCAI, 97.1 Sports Animal, the Tulsa Drillers and the *Tulsa World*.

WADO, SGI, THANK YOU!!!

LANE ADAMS

By Will Hyland

Born in Talihina, Oklahoma, on November 13, 1989, Lane Weston Adams is a child of the Heartland, raised in his hometown of Red Oak, Oklahoma. He is of Choctaw heritage and a member of the Choctaw Nation.[1] It is thus only fitting that he made his major-league debut with the nearby Kansas City Royals in neighboring Missouri.

But well before Adams found his way to Kauffman Stadium on the night of September 1, 2014, he made news as a young multisport superstar in Red Oak.

The son of Shelly and older brother to Chance, Lane was likely known better to locals as a basketball star. As an eighth-grader, he believed he could play pro basketball.[2] There was even a time when Adams wanted to quit baseball, but his mother told him he would have to get a job at Sonic fast-food instead, so he stayed with it despite being a basketball-focused teenager.[3][4] While at Red Oak High School, he played guard for the basketball team and scored 3,251 points in his interscholastic career, making him the fifth-highest scorer in Oklahoma high-school basketball. His 93.7 percent

Lane Adams

(Courtesy of ESPN)

free-throw percentage as a junior led all of Oklahoma.[5] Adams told the *McAlester News Capital* that 300 people lined up outside the gym before one of their home games.[6] (According to the 2010 Census, only 549 people resided in Red Oak) His team won a state championship during his senior season in 2009. He was not heavily recruited to play collegiate baseball and committed to play basketball for Missouri State University in Springfield, Missouri.[7] The 6-foot-4, 190-pound player did receive an invitation to work out with the New York Yankees, but turned it down because he was primarily focusing on basketball.[8] He also received offers from numerous other college basketball programs, though interest waned as it became clear that Adams was garnering interest as a baseball prospect and could sign with a major-league baseball team.[9]

Aside from his talents on the hardwood, Adams was also known for his overall quickness and speed, a trait that served him well as a right-handed throwing and batting outfielder. He never competed in track and field as a result of Red Oak High School not having a team, but perhaps it was unlikely that he would have anyway since he was a baseball standout in the spring. In the spring of 2008, Adams led Red Oak to a state championship in baseball and then another baseball title in the fall. Small schools in Oklahoma like his did not have football programs, so many talented players like Adams had the opportunity to refine their baseball skills in the fall as well. That ultimately played a huge role in the baseball exposure Adams received growing up.[10]

The Royals drafted Adams in the 13th round of the June 2009 amateur draft.

Adams was faced with a major decision. He was forced to either forgo his opportunity with Missouri State and sign with the Royals, or stay in school and likely not play baseball professionally again. As someone who was a basketball standout, the decision was a hard one. Adams did not want to give up basketball, but he also did not want to have regrets about passing up the opportunity to play professional sports.[11] With strong counsel from his mother, who handled his negotiations,[12] Adams chose to sign with Kansas City and later informed Missouri State and head basketball coach Cuonzo Martin of his decision. Martin told Adams he would have the opportunity to come back and play basketball if he wished, but it never came to be. Martin eventually left to coach at the University of Tennessee, and Adams was destined for the major leagues.[13]

NATIVE AMERICAN MAJOR LEAGUERS

First on Adams's journey to Kauffman were brief stops in rookie ball during 2009 with the Arizona League and for Idaho Falls in the Pioneer League in 2010. Over those two seasons, Adams batted .264 in 70 games. For the 2011 season, Adams began with Burlington in the rookie Appalachian League before moving on to play with Kane County in the Class-A Midwest League. He finished that season with a .261 cumulative batting average in 90 games. In 2012, after hitting .298 with 44 RBIs, 5 home runs, and 11 stolen bases in 67 games with Kane County, Adams was promoted to Wilmington, in the high Class-A Carolina League. He finished the season there with six more home runs and was named a Midwest League All-Star.

In 2013, Adams was being noticed more as a prospect by the Royals' brass and by Kansas City fans. He was named the Wilmington Blue Rocks player of the year. His .276 batting average, 7 home runs, and 39 RBIs were enough to earn a call-up to the Northwest Arkansas Naturals of the Double-A Texas League. In 44 games with the Naturals, Adams added 5 homers, 26 RBIs, and 15 steals to his tally.[14]

By season's end, he was promoted again to Triple-A Omaha during the Pacific Coast League playoffs, where the Storm Chasers won the 2013 Triple-A championship. The 2013 season was Adams's best as a minor leaguer, and it didn't go unnoticed. The club named him the co-Minor League Player of the Year, alongside the late Yordano Ventura.[15] After the season, the Royals added Adams to their 40-man roster.

Adams began the 2014 campaign with Northwest Arkansas, and slashed .269/.352/.427 with 36 RBIs and 38 stolen bases. His encore performance was strong enough to propel him to a Texas League All-Star selection. When major-league rosters expanded in September, Adams was called up to the Royals. He had been told in July that he might be called up because of his speed.[16] On September 1, 2014, Adams made his major-league debut, against the Texas Rangers at Kansas City.

Adams entered the contest in the eighth inning, running at first base for designated hitter Raúl Ibañez. He moved to second on a wild pitch but did not advance further. Kansas City defeated the Rangers, 4-3. The Royals went on to win the American League pennant, but Adams was not on the postseason roster.

By the time 2015 spring training ended and the regular season began, Adams found himself back in the minors with Northwest Arkansas. The season turned out to be one of his strongest minor-league campaigns; he hit .298 with 29 stolen bases. He was not promoted again to Kansas City, though, and after the season he was released.[17]

Within a few months, Adams was claimed off waivers by the Yankees.[18] He spent the early part of the 2016 season with the Trenton Thunder of the Double-A Eastern League. During that stint Adams batted .253 with 31 stolen bases. He was released in late July, and it was at this time that Adams, turning 27 in November, again contemplated

leaving the sport, but persevered and found his way to a new opportunity.[19]

Adams completed the 2016 season with the Double-A Tennessee Smokies, as part of the Chicago Cubs organization, compiling a strong .325 average over the remainder of the minor-league campaign. He elected free agency after the season and was determined to find a path back to the majors.[20]

A month later, Adams signed a minor-league contract with the Atlanta Braves, in what would prove to be a pivotal turning point in his journey back to the majors. His agent's assistant pitched the idea of going to Atlanta instead of the San Francisco Giants, the other team that Adams was considering.[21] Adams acquiesced and only a little under a month into the following season, he was called up to Atlanta from the Gwinnett Braves. It had been over two years since he last appeared in a big-league game with the Royals. On April 28, 2017, Adams got his first big-league base hit, a pinch-hit single to right field off Milwaukee Brewers pitcher Jacob Barnes. The next batter, Ender Inciarte, doubled in two runs, Dansby Swanson and Adams. Atlanta went on to win the game, 10-8.

On June 22, Adams recorded his first major-league home run, off San Francisco Giants hurler Bryan Morris. It was a "no-doubter" deep to left field that had a 107 MPH exit velocity according to Statcast.[22] When asked about the experience, Adams told MLB.com that the feeling of hitting his first home run was "probably better than [he had] ever thought." What made the moment even more special was that his nieces were in attendance that day. They had driven from Oklahoma all the way to the Braves' SunTrust Park to see Adams play in Atlanta. Adams went on to recall the journey back to the big leagues, telling MLB.com, "It's a grind getting up here, I'm just taking it day by day and trying to make the most of the opportunity the Braves have given me."[23]

Toward the end of the season, Adams twice came to bat against the Miami Marlins with the game on the line. On September 10, with the Braves trailing 8-6, Adams came to bat with two outs in the bottom of the ninth, and Nick Markakis on second base. He drew a walk from Marlins pitcher Jarlín García and advanced to second on a single by Johan Camargo. Next, Rio Ruiz singled to left; Marlins outfielder Ichiro Suzuki was unable to make a quick play, allowing Markakis to cross home plate and Adams to score the tying run, sending the game to extra innings.

Two innings later, in the bottom of the 11th, Adams came to bat again for Atlanta with the game still tied. With one out and Tyler Flowers on first base, Adams deposited a first-pitch fastball from Vance Worley into the left-field stands, securing the win for Atlanta and providing what was likely the highlight of his major-league career.

After the game, Adams told MLB.com once again that he valued the opportunity, saying, "It all comes with opportunity and timing, being at the right place at the right time. I was fortunate to be given an opportunity at the right place and the right time." Flowers echoed the sentiment by complimenting his readiness, "He's got an upbeat attitude and he's a tremendous worker. He's ready [to pinch-hit] the third inning sometimes."[24]

To that point in the season, Adams had hit .281 with 3 home runs and an .839 OPS in 74 plate appearances. By season's end a few weeks later, he finished the season with a final batting average of .275 and an OPS of .807 to go along with 5 home runs. The 2017 season was his most successful to date.

Adams began 2018 with the big-league club after breaking camp, but was designated for assignment on April 18 to create a roster spot for pitcher Matt Wisler. At the time, his skipper was hopeful that Adams would go unclaimed on waivers. "He's done a really good job," manager Brian Snitker said. "Hopefully, everything works out [so] that we can keep him. It's unfortunate, but it's just one of those moves we had to make."[25]

Snitker's wishes were not met. Adams went unclaimed; he declined an assignment to Triple-A Gwinnett and became a free agent.[26] In May 2018 he signed a minor-league deal with the Chicago Cubs. With the Triple-A Iowa Cubs, he hit .136 in 32 games and was released by the end of June.

After his release by the Cubs, Adams signed another minor-league contract, returning to the Braves organization for the second time in his career. With Gwinnett, Adams struggled offensively and batted .192 in 30 games.

However, Adams was still a part of the September call-ups in late 2018, as the Braves were in the thick of a National League East division race. By season's end, Adams had compiled a .250 batting average during his final 11 big-league games, including a home run in the fifth inning on September 23 against Philadelphia Phillies Aaron Nola, who was an All-Star that season.

Adams was not brought back to Atlanta at the end of 2018 season and instead signed with the Phillies in January 2019. Through the first three months of the 2019 season, Adams had 271 at-bats and drove in 29 runs with 12 home runs for the Triple-A Lehigh Valley IronPigs. Despite the strong performance, he was released on July 1, 2019.

For the rest of 2019, Adams appeared in only 18 more games in the minor leagues, returning once again to the Braves organization and playing all of those 18 games with Double-A Mississippi. He spent the 2020 pandemic-shortened season as a taxi-squad member of the Minnesota Twins, but his appearances with Mississippi were his last in affiliated professional baseball. Adams's post-pandemic time on the diamond came during 2021 in the Mexican League, where he played for the Acereros de Monclova and the Tigres de Quintana Roo.

After his playing career, one could still find Lane Adams in the baseball conversation on X, where he engaged with fans and other former players on all of the game's latest topics, including hitting mechanics, player movement, and analytics.[27] He also privately coaches and instructs young hitters at his facility in Norman, Oklahoma, focusing on both the mental and physical side of the game.[28]

For a ballplayer who began his career as a high school basketball star, Adams's journey through the challenges of professional baseball is an admirable one. He is a player and teammate who the State of Oklahoma and the Choctaw Nation can proudly call one of their own.

SOURCES

In addition to the sources cited in the Notes, the author consulted numerous websites such as Baseball-Reference.com, baseballalmanac.com, and MiLB.com.

NOTES

1   David O'Brien, "5 Things You Might Not Know about Braves Rookie Lane Adams," *Atlanta Journal-Constitution*, September 16, 2017. https://www.ajc.com/sports/baseball/things-you-might-not-know-about-braves-rookie-lane-adams/kdP2fdl6v6vGVWof5krL4M/.

2   Kyle Bandujo, "Lane Adams on Approaching Baseball as a Multi-Sport Athlete," *From Phenom to Farm*, June 16, 2020. Accessed November 26, 2024. https://podcasts.apple.com/us/podcast/lane-adams-on-approaching-baseball-as-a-multi-sport/id1497327828?i=100478222718.

3   Gaurav Vedek, "An Interview with Former Braves Outfielder Lane Adams," *Talking Chop*, August 20, 2020. Accessed October 22, 2024. https://podcasts.apple.com/us/podcast/battery-power-for-atlanta-braves-fans/id1082214582?i=1000488640090.

4   Jeff Stanek, "Lane Adams – High-Level Experiences from a Former MLB Outfielder," *Figure It Out Baseball*. December 13, 2024. Accessed January 24, 2025. https://youtube.com/watch?v=XkJ2PBj-x8Y.

5   "Arizona Fall League Profiles: Lane Adams and Malcom Culver." MLB Blogs. Royal Rundown, November 7, 2016. https://royals.mlblogs.com/arizona-fall-league-profiles-lane-adams-and-malcom-culver-a1c6748e7680.

6   Adrian O'Hanlon, "Legends: Lane Adams – Red Oak Grad Working Back toward Majors," *McAlester* (Oklahoma) *News*, July 6, 2015. https://www.mcalesternews.com/sports/legends-lane-adams---red-oak-grad-working-back-toward-majors/article_4b0dda74-2399-11e5-ad43-c70143ec0015.html.

7   Bandujo.

8   Stanek.

9   Vedek.

10   Vedek.

11   Bandujo.

12   Bandujo.

13   O'Hanlon.

14   Paul Boyd, "Naturals' Adams Made Right Choice," *Northwest Arkansas Democrat Gazette* (Fayetteville, Arkansas), April 3, 2014. https://www.nwaonline.com/news/2014/apr/03/naturals-adams-made-right-choice-20140403/.

15   SI Wire, "Yordano Ventura: Royals Pitcher Killed in Car Crash," *Sports Illustrated*, January 22, 2017. https://www.si.com/mlb/2017/01/22/royals-yordano-ventura-dead-car-crash

16   Bandujo.

17   Associated Press, "Tuesday's Sports Transactions," *San Diego Union-Tribune*, November 3, 2015. https://www.sandiegouniontribune.com/sdut-tuesdays-sports-transactions-2015nov03-story.html.

18 Steve Adams, "Yankees Claim Lane Adams from Royals, Designate Ronald Torreyes," MLB Trade Rumors, January 15, 2016. https://www.mlbtraderumors.com/2016/01/yankees-claim-lane-adams-dfa-ronald-torreyes.html.

19 Gabriel Burns, "A Year after Almost Retiring, Lane Adams Finds New Life with Braves," *Atlanta Journal-Constitution,* August 26, 2017. https://www.ajc.com/sports/baseball/year-after-almost-retiring-lane-adams-finds-new-life-with-braves/gd3WGg2JtfWBtXBFgHUTKO/; Stanek, "Lane Adams – High-Level Experiences from a Former MLB Outfielder.".

20 Bandujo.

21 Bandujo.

22 Mark Bowman, "L. Adams on First MLB HR: 'A Great Feeling,'" MLB.com, June 23, 2017. https://www.mlb.com/news/braves-lane-adams-hits-first-homer-in-majors-c238224684.

23 Bowman, "L. Adams on First MLB HR: 'A Great Feeling,'"

24 Mark Bowman, "L. Adams Goes from No Invite to Walk-Off Hero," MLB.com, September 10, 2017. https://www.mlb.com/news/braves-lane-adams-hits-walk-off-homer-c253607634.

25 Mark Bowman, "Freeman in Fine Form Night after HBP Scare," MLB.com, April 19, 2018. https://www.mlb.com/news/braves-freddie-freeman-back-after-clean-mri-c272923376.

26 David O'Brien, "Lane Adams Opts for Free Agency; Acuna Call-Up Clogs Outfield," *Atlanta Journal-Constitution*, April 27, 2018. https://www.ajc.com/sports/baseball/lane-adams-opts-for-free-agency/dih7x19GNP3pMDX7BUVjEL/.

27 Lane Adams, "Situational Hitting. Nobody On Get 'Em In. It's the Little Things," Twitter, October 19, 2022. Accessed December 2, 2022. https://twitter.com/LA_Swiftness/status/1587622514364227584.

28 Stanek.

BRANDON BAILEY

By Carter Cromwell

In this day and age, an athlete sporting tattoos is nothing unusual. Brandon Bailey's tattoos, though, are not usual.

On his left arm, the former major-league pitcher sports a grizzly bear surrounded by various symbols, a depiction of a Native American warrior, a bison, and a chain of triangles. On the other, he has a tattoo of a woman wearing a bear headdress and painted mask, along with a howling wolf. The difference is that these are not just random pieces of artwork; instead, they reference Native American culture and act as a tribute to Bailey's Chickasaw ancestry.

In a video, Bailey said, "Basically, this represents seven generations of native family. I need to honor the people that came before me. ... And anything I do will impact the people that come after me."[1]

"It's something we are very, very proud of," said Bailey, who is enrolled as a citizen of the tribe and wants to use his position in the game as a platform to support Native American issues. "For me, it's trying to keep my family heritage alive, but it's also trying to give back to the people, who, over the course of time, were told their background was wrong."[2]

"It doesn't matter if you're one-sixteenth, one-eighth [Chickasaw] or whatever. This is who we are as a family," he said. "This is where we came from, and we should be proud of that."[3]

Bailey, a pitcher who was part of three major-league organizations and appeared briefly in the big leagues with Houston in 2020, is one-eighth Chickasaw. According to family oral history, his great-great-great-grandmother, Matahoya, walked the Trail of Tears.[4] Her son George, Bailey's great-grandfather, was full-blooded Chickasaw. He was born and raised in Oklahoma and attended boarding schools there to become "Americanized." He served in World War II, married a non-native, and later moved the family to Colorado.

Bailey's father, Brad, began looking to connect with his roots not long before Brandon was born in 1994. Though he raised his family far from Chickasaw Nation's headquarters in Ada, Oklahoma, Brad Bailey made it a point to continually expose Brandon and his sister Bri to native culture.

"When my grandfather [George] left Oklahoma, he was 18 years old, and he said he would never go back," Brad Bailey said. "[But] it was important for me because the traditions were kind of lost between my dad [Keith] and me. ... Now, it's coming full circle [with Brandon]."[5]

Cultural identity, though, wasn't the only thing imbued in Bailey from an early age. There were also sports, particularly baseball. Brandon David Keith Bailey was born to Brad and Antoinette Bailey on October 19, 1994, in the Denver suburb of Westminster, Colorado. His father was a software engineer, and his mother worked for grocery stores. He was given the native name of Nita' Iskanno'si, which translates to Little Bear, because he had hair from the start. He recalled that his "very first memory was of a ball in my hand."[6] Another of his earliest recollections is when his father took him to a Colorado Rockies game for the first time. "I fell in love with the game then. I wanted to be just like them."[7]

And it was clear early on that he might be able to do that.

"When he was three years old, we'd get out in the yard and play catch," father Brad recalled. "He'd watch something on TV, then go outside and do it ... exactly like what he saw. He'd have a correct windup, over the top, and hit what he was aiming at."

"For his entire career, since T-ball, I've never seen a ball come to him that he didn't go to the right bag with," Brad said. "A lot of kids, especially that young, don't know where to throw it. It was always natural to him. By the time he was 11, he knew more about the game than I ever did."[8]

As a high-school junior in 2012, Bailey was 11-0 with a 1.02 earned-run average and led Broomfield High School to the Colorado Class 4A state championship. He was a first-team all-state selection, was named player of the year in Colorado Class 4A, and was tabbed state player of the year by BoCoPreps.com. All that brought Bailey some national recognition: Under Armour included him on a preseason All-America team for the following year.

"I was definitely coming off a high and feeling on top of the world going into summer ball with my travel team," he said. "I had just committed to Gonzaga University on a baseball scholarship and was feeling pretty confident about where things were going. Things couldn't get much better."[9]

But, in fact, they initially got worse.

His elbow started bothering him in summer ball, but he pitched through it. Then, in July 2012, he went to a show-case event in which a good performance could have gotten him an invitation to the Under Armour All-America game to be held at Chicago's Wrigley Field.

"Playing in that game was a big goal because I wanted to show that guys from Colorado can really play, and that short athletes like myself [he's officially 5-feet-9] can compete at the highest level with some of the most elite prospects," Bailey said. However, his velocity – as high as 95 mph during his junior season – was significantly off.

"I was throwing 86 or 87 and getting hit around pretty badly," he recalled. "I went back out and threw a pitch and felt a pop. I knew deep down what had happened, but I tried to throw one more pitch, and it went like 50 feet at like 65 miles an hour."[10]

Hello, Tommy John surgery. Goodbye, senior season.

On July 26, 2012, Dr. David Schneider, formerly the head surgeon for the Los Angeles Dodgers, Lakers, and Kings, performed the procedure.

"When I found out I needed the surgery, I broke down crying," Bailey said. "Our high school team had 10 of 16 guys coming back and was fully geared to make another run, so it was really hard not to be able to help us defend our championship. And you hear the horror stories about high school guys getting injured and colleges taking their scholarships away."

Luckily, that did not happen in Bailey's case – "I was very scared when I had to call the coach at Gonzaga and tell him the news, but everyone on the coaching staff from Coach [Marc] Machtolf on down told me to just do everything I could to get healthy and be as close to 100 percent as I could by the time I stepped on campus. That says a lot about the type of people they are."[11]

The doctors grafted a ligament from Bailey's left hamstring, the recovery from which was more difficult than from the elbow procedure. "I couldn't walk even two weeks after the surgery. After that, I was on a crutch with my left arm, and I couldn't use my right elbow. Getting around school was a struggle, and I couldn't write with my right arm. I went to physical therapy every day after school."[12]

But it worked. It can take as much as 18 months for a pitcher to come back from Tommy John surgery, but Bailey said he "started tossing a ball around" six months after the procedure and made 20 pitches in a game – "all fastballs" – 11 months after surgery. Working with his trainers, he slowly increased his pitch count over the summer and "felt really good ... heading into my freshman year at Gonzaga."

That wasn't false optimism, as Bailey posted a 6-7 record and a 3.69 earned-run average over 102⅓ innings and made the All-West Coast Conference first team. He got stronger as the season went on, posting a 6-2 mark with a 2.85 ERA in conference play.

"The initial speculation had been that I might redshirt since I was coming off Tommy John surgery, but I went into my freshman year and earned the Friday night starting job," he said. "That was extremely exciting because your ace is the one who usually pitches on Friday nights. There was really no gap in my performance from high school to college."[13]

He later recalled that "as I got older, I started to realize that there was something that separated me – the ability to throw hard and put the ball where I wanted it to go. As I

started to develop in my freshman year, I began to think that ... maybe I could be dominant."[14]

And Bailey's performance steadily improved over the next two seasons. As a sophomore in 2015, he was 8-3 with a 3.72 ERA and significantly improved his hits- and strike-outs-to-innings-pitched ratios. He also earned honorable mention all-academic recognition. That summer, Bailey played for Yarmouth-Dennis in the prestigious Cape Cod League, posting a 2-4 mark and a 3.03 ERA.

Bailey really broke out in his junior year at Gonzaga, winning 10 of 13 decisions with a 2.42 ERA and 125 strike-outs in 100⅓ innings. He was first-team all-conference, second-team all-West Region, and academic all-region. He struck out 17 batters in a complete-game victory over Brigham Young in the West Coast Conference championship tournament.[15]

That set Bailey up for the 2016 major-league draft. He had been worried that his history of Tommy John surgery might give some clubs pause, but that was not an issue. There was some concern about his height, as Bailey was listed at 5-feet-10, which may have been generous. In fact, one Colorado Rockies scout used a tape measure to record his height and then rejected him on the spot.[16]

In a March 2020 tweet, Bailey revealed that "HS teammates told me I'd never achieve my dream of playing pro ball. Travel coaches told me to go to a JC b/c I wasn't a D-1 talent. Scouts told me I was too small & I would never be considered a prospect."[17]

Nonetheless, the Oakland Athletics selected Bailey in the sixth round,[18] setting up a major decision. Though his dream had been to play baseball professionally, he had shortly before the draft been chosen over thousands of applicants for an internship with Nike's N7 Fund, which raises funds to promote health and disease-prevention programs among Native tribes. He said he would have taken the job if the Athletics had not agreed to his $300,000 asking price.

"Something like 11,000 people applied for about a hundred internships," Bailey said, "so it was a real opportunity that I debated for a long time."[19]

Bailey's father acknowledged that "all of us were torn, but we also knew Brandon had dreamed of playing pro ball since he was three years old."[20]

After signing with Athletics scout Jeff Coffman, Bailey began living out the dream in 2016 with the Athletics' team in the Arizona Complex League, starting two games and putting up a 1.80 ERA in five innings. He then moved up to the Vermont affiliate in the low-A New York-Pennsylvania League. In 38 innings there, he was 3-1 with a 3.08 ERA while striking out 42 batters and walking just 9.

"I was definitely nervous as I transitioned from college to the professional ranks," Bailey said. "You don't truly understand [what is necessary] until you immerse yourself in it. The minor-league experience helped establish who I was as a competitor. You have to have that internal flame."[21]

The next season Bailey advanced to Beloit (Wisconsin) in the Class A Midwest League. Appearing in 15 games (11 starts), he was 1-1 with a 2.68 ERA and struck out 73 batters in 57 innings. That earned him a boost to Stockton of the high-A California League. There, he was 2-1 with an ERA of 4.24, not a bad mark in a very hitter-friendly league. He struck out 47 batters in 34 innings.

Despite his positive results, Bailey got a brush with the business side of baseball when the Athletics traded him to the Houston Astros on November 20, 2017, for outfielder Ramon Laureano. According to Bailey, Oakland general manager David Forst regretted losing him but said, "[T]he Astros were dead set on me. They said, 'Either Bailey, or no deal'"[22]

Bailey reached a milestone in a February 26, 2018, preseason matchup against the New York Mets when he made his first appearance for and against a major-league team. He entered the game with two out in the fourth inning and pitched 1⅓ scoreless innings.[23]

Bailey split the 2018 season between Buies Creek (North Carolina) in the high-A Carolina League and Corpus Christi of the Double-A Texas League. He was 5-8 with a 2.49 earned-run average in 20 games (16 starts) at Buies Creek and got a big boost after a heart-to-heart talk with manager Morgan Ensberg.

Ensberg asked him, "Why are you still here? In my opinion, you should be in Double-A or Triple-A, dominating those hitters, or potentially knocking on the door of the big leagues, right now." Bailey later called that discussion "a turning point," as he reaffirmed a commitment to improvement, pitched 30 consecutive scoreless innings, and cut down on his walks allowed. A month and a half later, he was promoted to Double-A Corpus Christi, where he got into five games (one start), going 1-0 with a 4.01 ERA.[24]

Bailey spent the entire 2019 season at Corpus Christi (4-5, 3.30). After that season, the Astros made him available in the Rule 5 draft, and he was chosen by the Baltimore Orioles.

Bailey at the time was considered the most big-league ready of the three prospects Houston lost in the draft. His changeup was considered a "plus" pitch.[25]

Since Baltimore had hit rock bottom with just 54 victories in 2019 and 47 the year before, it seemed like a good opportunity for Bailey. "We're excited about the pitch mix he has. He has five really good weapons," Orioles manager Brandon Hyde said, alluding to Bailey's fastball with good spin rate, changeup, spike curve, slider, and cutter.[26]

Nonetheless, Bailey failed to make the club in spring training and was returned to Houston on March 6, 2020.[27] That actually turned out well for him.

Covid-19 restrictions, put in place shortly after he went back to Houston, forced cancellation of the 2020 minor-league season and shortened the major-league season to 60 games. But while the pandemic cast a pall over so much of daily life, the year proved to be the brightest part of Bailey's baseball career, as the Astros put the 25-year-old on the July 23 Opening Day roster.[28]

"When Covid hit, I went home to Colorado and continued to train and be ready," Bailey said. "I then got a call in June that I was on the 60-man roster and needed to be in Houston, so I went with zero expectations of getting onto the active roster. But I pitched really well in the alternative camp against a lot of major-league hitters like Yuli Gurriel, Martin Maldanado, and others and caught the attention of [manager] Dusty Baker and pitching coach Brent Strom."

A Tweet from a beat writer said Bailey had a chance to be on the roster, but he didn't pay much attention to it. Soon after, he was awakened by a call at 7:30 in the morning and told he needed to be at the ballpark. After a half-hour wait, he was ushered into Baker's office and encountered pitcher Blake Taylor, who had just been told he'd made the Opening Day roster.

"So I was kind of holding my breath," Bailey said. "I knew this meeting could either be really good or really bad."

It was the former. He had made the club.

"I just lost it then," he said. "I started crying. I walked out of the office, and Justin Verlander and Lance McCullers – who probably didn't know me from Adam – congratulated me."[29]

Bailey made his debut three days later by pitching a scoreless ninth inning in a 7-6 loss to the Seattle Mariners at Houston's Minute Maid Park.[30] That appearance made him one of only four people with Chickasaw heritage to play in the major leagues. (The others are catcher Wyatt Toregas, who appeared briefly for Cleveland in 2009 and Pittsburgh in 2011; pitcher Dallas Beeler of the Chicago Cubs in 2014-2015; and Euel Moore, who pitched for the Philadelphia Phillies and New York Giants from 1934 to 1936.[31])

There were no fans in the stands that day because of Covid restrictions, so Bailey's family members couldn't be there in person. Nonetheless, the thrill was there.

"I was definitely nervous – sweating bullets," he said. "I was thinking, 'I am a major-league baseball player. I've accomplished my dream, and no one can take that away from me.'"[32]

A few years later, he recalled, "The only way I can describe it is that time [seemed to be] moving in slow motion. I was handed the ball and started fixing the dirt. I turned around and looked at the people behind me – George Springer, Jose Altuve, Josh Reddick, Michael Brantley, and others. I tried to soak up every moment."[33]

Then Bailey turned back to the plate. He retired the Mariners' Evan White on a groundout, then gave up a single to José Marmolejos, who was thrown out trying to stretch the hit into a double. Tim Lopes then singled, but Mallex Smith grounded out to first base to end the inning. It was an efficient, 13-pitch effort.

Bailey pitched in four more games, all in relief. He appeared against the Los Angeles Angels on August 1, the Arizona Diamondbacks on August 5, Oakland on August

9, and Seattle again on August 14. Overall, he was 0-0 with a 2.45 earned-run mark in 7⅓ innings. He allowed six hits, three walks, and one home run while striking out four batters.

Those were the only games in which Bailey pitched. Rosters were trimmed from 30 players to 28 on August 6 and were set to go to 26 on August 20. On August 15, the Astros activated pitcher Joe Biagini and optioned Bailey to the alternate training site,[34] where he remained for the rest of the regular season.

"I had known that when some of the veterans came off the injured list that I'd at least be a candidate to be cut," he said. "It's one of those things when you're on the low rungs and fighting to keep a roster spot. After that, I always pitched in workouts following the games, just to be ready if an opportunity presented itself. That's something I preach to all players now – you have to be ready."[35]

Though eligible, Bailey was not placed on the active roster for the playoffs, in which the Astros advanced to the American League Championship Series before losing to Tampa Bay. And he never again appeared in a major-league game, as arm trouble continually played the bogeyman role.

Not long after the playoffs, on November 20, 2020, Bailey was traded to the Cincinnati Reds for cash.[36] But he never threw a pitch for Cincinnati; instead, he had to undergo a second Tommy John surgery just a few months later, on February 26, 2021.

"I was already on a throwing program in late November [of 2020] and preparing for spring training 2021 [and] felt a little tweak in my forearm," Bailey said. "I went to Dr. Schneider, and he informed me that there was just a bit of fluid buildup in the elbow and a slight strain of the pronator muscle. So I thought I'd just rehab in December and return to throwing in January."

He showed up early at the Reds training facility in Goodyear, Arizona, but didn't feel right as he started to increase the intensity of his throws. "Something was off," he said. After a two-week shutdown, he went for another MRI, which showed a partial tear of the UCL. The doctor recommended that he get surgery as soon as possible.[37]

Bailey missed the entire 2021 season. The Reds then dropped him from the 40-man roster on November 30, 2021 and re-signed him to a minor-league contract with an invitation to 2022 spring training.

"As a competitor, this one stings," Bailey wrote on Twitter. "But I'm thankful the Reds are giving me the opportunity to prove I'm healthy and show what I can do on an MiLB deal. Adversity shows one's true character, and my first instinct is to get back to work!"[38]

On January 2, 2022, Bailey posted a video of himself working out in Phoenix and reaching 90-plus mph on a couple of throws. He said in his tweet, "It's been over 450 days since I last threw a baseball 90 mph. It's been exactly 310 days since my 2nd Tommy John surgery. Words can't describe how much this moment meant to me. But I'm just getting started."[39]

But Bailey did not appear in a game and elected free agency on November 10, 2022. He then went to the Dominican Winter League but tore the flexor tendon in his arm on his very first pitch for Escogido. That necessitated yet another surgery, which took place December 1.[40]

Still, he wasn't through trying. In a video posted on April 29, 2023, he said, "[I] don't know if I can make it back to MLB, but let's find out."[41]

(Courtesy Brandon Bailey)

Brandon Bailey and his sister, Bri, on their family visit to the Chickasaw Cultural Center in Sulphur, Oklahoma

Bailey's prospects got a boost when he signed a minor-league contract with the Chicago White Sox in June 2023. In a tweet, he said, "The past seven months have been the most challenging time of my life. ... There were days when I thought my playing career was over. ... [But] I never gave up. I'm back in the game."[42]

But not for long. Bailey made just two short appearances, pitching just one-third of an inning for the White Sox entry in the Arizona Complex League and another third of an inning for Winston-Salem in the high-A South Atlantic League. He allowed two hits, one walk, and three earned runs. Bailey was released by the White Sox on November 1, 2023.

"In May of that year, I'd thrown for some [Colorado] Rockies' scouts and was back up to 95 mph," he said. "They didn't sign me, but then the White Sox stepped in. They knew my medical background and that I needed to rehab, so there was no pressure to perform right out of the gate."

"The goal was to get to [Triple-A] Charlotte by the end of the season, but I strained a bicep on the very first batter I faced in Winston-Salem, so I went back to the Complex League. By then, there was a new regime in Chicago, and I had a gut feeling that I was going to be released."[43]

Then, in a sometimes emotional video posted on February 2, 2024, Bailey announced his retirement as a player.

"While my MLB career was very short, I'm blessed to have those experiences," he said. "It was extremely hard being hurt the entire 2021, 2022, and 2023 seasons [and] trying to do everything I could think of to heal my arm. It's tough to walk away from something that has been my entire life – my entire identity. I'm going to miss it. [But I] accomplished something that so many kids dream about."[44]

But while Bailey's playing career is over, his baseball career is not. In February 2024 he signed to be a pitching coach for the Orioles' Sarasota entry in the Florida Complex League.

"When the White Sox released me, I had to think long and hard about whether to continue pushing toward my dream of playing," Bailey said. "Some teams were interested in me as a player but were reluctant to take a chance on me because of the health issues. I talked with several teams about coaching opportunities, but the Orioles showed the most interest, and this has turned out to be a great fit."

"I would have preferred to go out on my own terms, but I also wanted more consistency and certainty in my life, so I decided to focus on coaching," he added. "I'd always wanted to do that anyway. I'd worked on my master's degree in sports coaching while I was in the minor leagues, and then had an internship at Driveline in 2019 and realized that working with other players was really enjoyable. From that point, coaching became something I wanted to pursue. I'm now looking at my baseball career through a different lens – trying to turn a negative into a positive."[45]

NOTES

1   "Brandon Bailey on His Tattoos," YouTube video, February 24, 2020: https://www.mlb.com/video/brandon-bailey-on-his-tattoos.

2   Joe Trezza, "Chickasaw Heritage Helps Drive Orioles Pitcher; Bailey Plans to Use Platform to Advocate for Native American Issues," mlb.com, February 26, 2020. https://www.mlb.com/news/orioles-brandon-bailey-native-american-heritage.

3   Infield Chatter Player Profile: Brandon Bailey 2021, YouTube video: https://www.youtube.com/watch?v=qMzyT7NQbmc

4   "Trail of Tears," history.com, https://www.history.com/topics/native-american-history/trail-of-tears, November 9, 2009.

5   Trezza.

6   "Brandon Bailey Retirement," YouTube Video, February 2, 2024: https://www.youtube.com/watch?v=kOEz6aDyqto

7   "Brandon Bailey Retirement."

8   Stanley Nelson, "Mound Builder: Being Chickasaw Is a Part of Pro Pitcher Brandon Bailey's Game," *Chokma Chickasaw Magazine,* Spring 2019: 56.

9   Scott Bolohan, "Interview: Reds Pitcher Brandon Bailey on Tommy John Surgery," thetwinbill.com, no date shown. https://thetwinbill.com/interview-reds-pitcher-brandon-bailey-on-tommy-john-surgery/.

10 Bolohan.

11 Bolohan.

12 Bolohan.

13 Bolohan.

14 "Brandon Bailey Retirement."

15 https://gozags.com/sports/baseball/roster/brandon-bailey/199#:~:text=Had%20a%20team%2Dbest%206,Coast%20Conference%20Freshman%20first%20team…

16 Trezza. He is listed on Baseball-Reference.com as weighing 195 pounds.

17 Twitter, March 20, 2020: https://twitter.com/BBailey_19/status/1235279437404557313.

18 Bailey had thought the Chicago Cubs would take him in the fifth round, but they took Duke pitcher Bailey Clark instead. "A Cubs' area scout had asked me if I would sign for slot value, and I said absolutely. After the draft, the scout called me and apologized. Whoever was calling the shots had decided to go with the other guy. But Oakland still took me in the next round, so things worked out." Brandon Bailey telephone interview, April 13, 2024.

19 Bailey telephone interview.

20 Trezza.

21 "Brandon Bailey Retirement."

22 Nelson, 60.

23 ESPN.com, February 26, 2020. https://www.espn.com/mlb/boxscore/_/gameId/380226118.

24 Nelson, 64.

25 "Astros Lose Three Players in Rule 5 Draft," *Houston Chronicle,* December 12, 2019. https://www.houstonchronicle.com/sports/astros/article/Astros-lose-three-players-in-Rule-5-draft-14902086.php.

26 Trezza.

27 "Orioles to Return Rule 5 Pick Brandon Bailey to Astros," *Houston Chronicle,* March 6, 2020. https://www.houstonchronicle.com/sports/astros/article/Ex-Astros-prospect-Ramon-Laureano-finds-home-with-13165301.php.

28 Jeff Todd, "Astros Select Brandon Bailey," mlbtraderumors.com, July 23, 2020. https://www.mlbtraderumors.com/2020/07/astros-select-brandon-bailey.html.

29 Bailey telephone interview.

30 "Brandon Bailey's 9th-Inning Debut," YouTube video, July 26, 2020. https://www.mlb.com/video/brandon-bailey-s-9th-inning-debut.

31 Nelson, "The Trailblazer," *Chokma Chickasaw Magazine,* Spring 2019: 65.

32 "Profiles of a Nation: Brandon Bailey," Chickasaw TV, September 21, 2022. https://www.chickasaw.tv/episodes/profiles-of-a-nation-season-17-episode-1-brandon-bailey.

33 "Brandon Bailey Retirement."

34 Associated Press, "Christian Javier Gives Up 1 Hit in 6 Innings as Astros Beat Mariners," *Houston Chronicle,* August 15, 2020. https://www.houstonchronicle.com/sports/astros/article/Ex-Astros-prospect-Ramon-Laureano-finds-home-with-13165301.php.

35 Bailey telephone interview.

36 Steve Adams, "Reds Acquire Brandon Bailey from Astros," mlbtraderumors.com, November 20, 2020. https://www.mlbtraderumors.com/2020/11/astros-trade-brandon-bailey-reds.html.

37 Bolohan.

38 Bobby Nightengale, "Cincinnati Reds Take Brandon Bailey off 40-Man Roster at MLB Deadline to Tender Contracts," *Cincinnati Enquirer,* November 30, 2021. https://www.cincinnati.com/story/sports/mlb/reds/2021/11/30/cincinnati-reds-roster-brandon-bailey-cut-40-man-roster/8797998002/.

39 Twitter, January 2, 2022. https://twitter.com/BBailey_19/status/1477788059366084609.

40 Bailey telephone interview.

41 TikTok, April 29, 2023. https://www.tiktok.com/@bbailey_1994/video/7223773849664392491.

42 Twitter, June 6, 2023. https://twitter.com/BBailey_19/status/1666237871148404736.

43 Bailey telephone interview.

44 "Brandon Bailey Retirement."

45 Bailey telephone interview.

MIKE BALENTI

By Jack V. Morris

The Carlisle Indian Industrial School from 1893-1917 churned out athletes that fascinated the American public. Two in particular, Jim Thorpe and Charles Bender, better known in the press as "Chief" Bender, dominated sports pages during their athletic years. In addition to the more famous athletes, Carlisle also produced a number of graduates, while not household names, that made an impact in sports. One of those was Mike Balenti.

Balenti was a great football player for Carlisle but was overshadowed by teammate Thorpe on their powerful team. Playing quarterback in the backfield, he combined with Thorpe to give Carlisle a one-two punch that overwhelmed

(Public domain)

Mike Balenti with the 1913 St. Louis Browns.

opponents with their incredible speed. But it was Thorpe who captured most of the headlines with his staggering athleticism. Transferring to Texas A&M in 1909, Balenti moved briefly out of Thorpe's shadow by leading the football team to an undefeated season, including two wins over its bitter interstate rival, the University of Texas.

Yet while football may have been Balenti's best sport, he also starred at track and field and baseball while at Carlisle. And it was in baseball that he carved out a career including two stints in the major leagues. Possessing tremendous speed and a strong throwing arm, attributes highly valued in the Deadball Era, Balenti, a right-hander who stood 5-feet-11 and weighed 175 pounds, quickly ascended to the major leagues after his year at Texas A&M. But it was his bat that kept him from staying at that level. First with the 1911 Cincinnati Reds, then with the 1913 St. Louis Browns, Balenti was unable to stick in the majors. But he stuck with baseball, playing regularly in the minors until 1918, then appearing sporadically as he moved from the minors to semipro teams and back again until 1926.

Michael Richard Balenti Jr. was born on July 3, 1886, in Calumet, Indian Territory, the third of six children, to Hungarian-born Mike Balenti and his wife, Belle Rath, or as she was also known, Cheyenne Belle.[1] Cheyenne Belle was only half Cheyenne, the product of a marriage between a Cheyenne woman, Roadmaker, and Wild West legend Charles Rath. Rath eventually divorced Roadmaker, also known as Making-Out-Roads, when tensions rose between settlers and the Cheyenne. He had two more wives after Roadmaker. With his third wife he had a son, Morris Charles "Morrie" Rath, who went on to play major-league baseball. Rath and his nephew Balenti played against each other in 1913 in the American League. It's unclear if Rath and Balenti knew they were related but chances are likely they didn't.

Mike Sr. immigrated to America at the age of 20 and joined the Army, eventually finding himself at Fort Reno, where he met Cheyenne Belle. They married in 1879. In 1885, a year before Mike Jr. was born, Cheyenne Belle served as an interpreter for General Philip Sheridan during the Stone Calf uprising of the Cheyenne in Western Oklahoma.[2] A government report in 1887 described Cheyenne Belle as "an intelligent half-breed married to a white man."[3] After they were married, Balenti left the Army and become a tailor at Fort Reno.

NATIVE AMERICAN MAJOR LEAGUERS

In 1904 Mike Jr. was sent to the Carlisle Indian Industrial School in central Pennsylvania. Starting in 1905, and for the next four years, he played both football (quarterback) and baseball (outfielder) and found time to participate on the track team. In 1907 he moved to second base. That summer, he played semipro baseball for the Hagerstown, Maryland, town team where he was "one of the stars of the Hagerstown Baseball Club."[4]

In 1908 Balenti was elected captain of the Carlisle baseball team. He moved over to shortstop to take advantage of his strong arm. The following summer, he played semipro baseball for the Bridgeton, New Jersey town team. His manager was Charles "Pop" Kelchner, the Albright College baseball coach and a future scout for Connie Mack and the Philadelphia Athletics. Playing under the name "Mike Ball," Balenti had an excellent summer.[5]

Back at Carlisle for the 1908 football season, Balenti took over the quarterback position from Frank Mount Pleasant, who had graduated. Mount Pleasant not only was an All-American football player, he was a two-time US Olympian on the track team. Balenti had big shoes to fill but he more than held his own.

Carlisle won its first five games, then tied powerful University of Pennsylvania. The following week Carlisle traveled to Annapolis to play the Naval Academy, a perennial powerhouse. With Thorpe unable to dropkick for the game due to injury, Balenti led his team to a 16-6 victory, kicking four field goals and causing one sportswriter to claim that it was "the most notable performance in this line against a strong team in the history of the game."[6]

Injuries took their toll on Carlisle as the team lost two of its next three games. However, Carlisle ended the season with a three-game winning streak, leading to a 10-2-1 record with all but three of the games played away from Carlisle.

Toward the end of the football season it was revealed that Balenti had signed with the Philadelphia Athletics. He had promised Charles Bender, the Athletics pitching ace, that he would sign with the Athletics.[7] Kelchner, his coach during the summer, signed him to the contract.[8]

But Balenti didn't report to the Athletics until after the Carlisle baseball season. He was again elected captain and played shortstop. In June after the college season, the Athletics sent him to the Milwaukee Brewers of the American Association. The Brewers in turn sent him to the Dayton Veterans of the Class-B Central League.[9] Balenti, playing center field, started out quickly with the bat but soon cooled off.[10] By early July he was benched and a couple of weeks later he was released, having played in only 20 games while batting just .213.

A week later Balenti caught on with El Reno of the Class-C Western Association.[11] He played well for the Packers and stuck for the rest of the season with the team. The *Dallas Morning News* remarked that Balenti was "making good as a heavy hitter and swift man on the bases."[12]

After the season, Balenti enrolled in Texas A&M University, taking an agricultural course.[13] He quarterbacked the A&M football team, playing for coach Charlie Moran, a former major leaguer for the St. Louis Cardinals. Despite protestations of playing professionals by several opponents, Balenti led A&M to a 7-0-1 record, including two wins over archrival University of Texas, and was named to the All-Southwestern team.[14]

In 1910 Balenti was signed by Savannah of the Class-C South Atlantic League. By June he was having such a good year that he attracted the attention of Washington Senators scout Dick Padden.[15] On June 25 his considerable speed helped break up future major leaguer Roy Radebaugh's bid for a no-hitter when he beat out an infield single with two out in the ninth.[16] For the season Balenti batted .254, playing 97 games at third base and 12 at shortstop.[17] Though the Senators didn't sign Balenti, the Atlanta Crackers of the Class-A Southern Association were impressed, drafting him in November from Savannah.[18]

Balenti held out and didn't sign with Atlanta until April 6, 1911, as a utility infielder.[19] Eleven days later, Atlanta sold Balenti to Macon of the South Atlantic League.[20]

Playing in the South Atlantic League for a second straight year, Balenti had a great season. The *Charleston News & Courier* wrote, "That Balenti is certainly a beautiful ball player. He starred on a team which, in this circuit, is scintillating with baseball stuff."[21] In late May, when he was batting .371, Chattanooga of the Southern Association tried to purchase him.[22] Macon, however, held onto Balenti.

Finally, on July 13, on the recommendation of scout Hugh Nicol, the Cincinnati Reds bought Balenti from Macon for $12,500.[23] He reported immediately to Philadelphia, where the Reds were playing. His first major-league appearance came on July 19 in New York against the Giants. He entered the game in the bottom of the second after Reds shortstop Tom Downey was thrown out for arguing balls and strikes. Balenti showed his great speed by stealing a base in the sixth, then got his first major-league base hit, off Red Ames, in the eighth. His successful debut earned him his only start of the season, two days later. But Balenti got into only six more games, five as a pinch-runner, before the Reds sold Balenti to Chattanooga of the Southern Association after his final appearance of the season on September 13.[24]

While there had been a handful of Native Americans who had played in the major leagues, Balenti was still a novelty based on his looks – not because he looked like a Native American but the opposite. One sportswriter wrote that "Balenti, the new Indian outfielder of the Cincinnati club, isn't as dark as [Charles] Bender or [Jack] Meyers, and is hardly to be taken as an Indian even on close inspection."[25]

After the season Balenti married his college sweetheart, Cecilia Baronovitch, a Hydah Indian from Alaska, in Cincinnati on October 10.[26] Balenti's younger brother, John, who also attended Carlisle, joined him in Organized

Baseball in 1912. John pitched for Asheville in the Appalachian League for a handful of games before being released.[27]

Balenti played the entire 1912 season with Chattanooga, batting .288 in 139 games. In July Cincinnati waived its option on Balenti and he was sold outright to Chattanooga for $750.[28] Chattanooga turned its $750 investment into $1,200 when it sold Balenti to the St. Louis Browns on September 16.[29]

In the offseason Mike lived in Kasaan, Alaska, on Prince of Wales Island with his wife's tribe. Newspapers reported that it cost nearly $200 for Balenti to travel to the Browns spring-training camp in Dallas, Texas. He left on March 11 and arrived in Dallas on March 23 and was a holdout. Balenti claimed that Chattanooga was offering him more than the Browns. Eventually he signed with the Browns and found himself in a competition for the starting shortstop job with Dee Walsh and Bobby Wallace.

Balenti had a good camp. He was in excellent condition when he reported, telling reporters that he had rowed an average of 15 miles a day in a canoe while fishing for salmon in the offseason.[30] He was described in camp as "a rare combination of phenomenal fielding and hard-hitting infielder at the same time."[31] Based on his camp, he made the Browns team.

The first game he played for the Browns on April 13 was unremarkable in all aspects except one – his uncle, Morrie Rath, was leading off for the opposing team, the Chicago White Sox. No mention was made of the fact in newspapers and it was probable that neither knew they were related.

Balenti's excellent spring training didn't transfer to the regular season. In 70 games, he batted only .180. And equally disappointing, he stole only three bases the entire season – the same total he had in eight games in 1911 for the Reds. In October the Browns sent Balenti back to Chattanooga. He never played in another major-league game.

Balenti's original plans for the offseason were to work as an assistant football coach at the University of St. Louis.[32] Instead, he decided to winter in Alaska again.[33]

The following season, Balenti played in only 40 games for Chattanooga before breaking his leg sliding into second base on May 25. He was in the midst of another poor season, batting only .157 and was dead last in the league in fielding percentage for shortstops.[34] In July Balenti was appointed athletic director at the University of Chattanooga. His duties included coaching the football team.[35]

Not only was Balenti busy with his duties with the university but he also found time to develop an apparatus to help measure jumping heights in the high jump and pole vault. He submitted a patent with his brother George on April 14, 1915, to the US Patent and Trademark Office. It was approved in August 1916.[36] The apparatus was used by the Southwestern Conference for its track meet at College Station, Texas, in May 1916.[37]

Meanwhile, Chattanooga sold Balenti to San Antonio of the Class-B Texas League for the 1915 season where he was paid $150 per month.[38] In 148 games, he batted .259 for the Bronchos. In September he accepted a position as the backfield coach for Baylor University. The Baylor head coach was C.P. Mosley, a minor-league baseball player as well.[39]

Balenti was back with San Antonio for the 1916 season but he got off to a slow start. By May 2 he was batting only .219. Later in the month, he was benched in favor of Shorty Dee. On June 1 San Antonio sold Balenti to league rival Galveston. Balenti found his hitting stroke and was batting .262 in July. He finished the season with Galveston batting .242.

In addition to his football coaching duties at Baylor, Balenti also helped out with the baseball team in the spring of 1917. In the meantime, he signed with Galveston after threatening to retire from baseball. While Balenti was leading the league in steals, he was batting only .181 in 39 games before he was let go.[40] He caught on with Tulsa of the Class-D Western Association. He played well enough that he was selected to the Western Association all-stars, who played Texas League champion Dallas in a postseason series.

Balenti was out of Organized Baseball in 1918 and didn't return to it until 1922. After not coaching at Baylor in 1918, he was brought back for one more season as an assistant football coach in 1919.

He did patent another invention in 1920. This time, with brother John, he patented a design for a pancake machine for commercial restaurants.[41]

After playing for a semipro team in Jackson, Tennessee, in 1921, Balenti returned to Organized Baseball in the Class-D Oklahoma State League in 1922. He started out as the manager of Guthrie and then moved to Clinton as a player-manager later in the season.[42] The following year Balenti played a few games for Sioux City in the Class-A Western League, then moved to Henryetta of the Class-C Western Association.[43] He played 39 games for Henryetta, batting .265.

Balenti played one more year in Organized Baseball. In 1926, at the age of 40, while playing for the powerful Tonkawa Comar semipro team, he was asked to step in as player-manager of Blackwell in the Class-D Southwestern League.[44] He took over the club on June 26 and held the position for a month before he was released.[45] Balenti went back to Tonkawa Comar in time to play in the prestigious Denver Post Tournament.[46] For the next few years, he played for the semi-pro Lone Wolf, Oklahoma town team.

With his playing career behind him, Balenti kept his hand in sports. He refereed high-school football games and managed a semipro team in his hometown of Altus, Oklahoma.

When he wasn't busy with sports, Balenti farmed his 160 acres in Oklahoma.[47] In the 1930 US Census, he listed his occupation as bookkeeper at a garage. Ten years later, he was a foreman for a highway construction firm. He eventually found employment at the Altus Air Force Base in the 1950s.[48]

In 1950 Balenti consented to let himself be portrayed in the movie *Jim Thorpe – All American*.[49] It's unclear who portrayed him or even if his character made it into the movie, since there is no one credited as portraying Mike Balenti.

On August 4, 1955, Balenti died, at the age of 69, in Jackson County Memorial Hospital in Altus after having a heart attack at home.[50] He was buried in Altus Cemetery. Balenti was survived by his wife, Cecilia, three sons, and two daughters.

NOTES

1 Calumet is now in the State of Oklahoma.

2 Muriel H. Wright, "A Cheyenne Peace Pipe Smoked and Betrayed by Custer," *Chronicles of Oklahoma*, Vol. 36, No. 1, Spring 1958, 89-92.

3 U.S. Government, *A Brief Statement of the Object, Achievements and Needs of the Indian Rights Association*, Philadelphia, 1887.

4 "Indian Villanova Contest," *Hagerstown* (Maryland) *Mail*, September 13, 1907: 7.

5 "Bridgeton Shut Out Diamond Field Club," *Bridgeton* (New Jersey) *Evening News*, June 22, 1908: 1.

6 "Mike Balenti's Seven-League Boots," *Boston Herald*, September 15, 1925: 20; Arthur P. Young, "The Big Eight," *Baseball Magazine*, December 1908: 21-23.

7 "Balenti To Join Mack," *Boston Herald*, November 11, 1908: 4.

8 "Kelchner Brings Learned Mind To Scouting," *The Sporting News*, January 3, 1935: 2.

9 "Notes of Central League," *Fort Wayne Sentinel*, June 18, 1909: 11.

10 "Around the Circuit," *Evansville Courier*, July 11, 1909: 7.

11 "Questionable Decision Gives Game to Midgets," *Daily Oklahoman*, July 23, 1909: 7.

12 "Football Star Playing Baseball," *Dallas Morning News*, August 1, 1909: 28.

13 "Farmers to Play Oklahoma Here," *Dallas Morning News*, November 14, 1909: 28.

14 "Big Football Elevens Will Meet at Dallas," *Dallas Morning News*, November 10, 1909: 28; "Moran Picks Players for All-Southwestern," *Fort Worth Star-Telegram*, December 1, 1909: 13.

15 "Scout Padden on Job," *Washington Post*, June 2, 1910: 8.

16 "Robbed Radabaugh of 'No-Hit' Honors," *State* (Columbia, South Carolina), June 26, 1910: 5.

17 "South Atlantic League," *Sporting Life*, November 26, 1910: 13.

18 "Magoon Is Planning for Savannah Team," *Charleston* (South Carolina) *Evening Post*, November 28, 1910: 3.

19 "Columbia Squad Begins Practice," *Charleston* (South Carolina) *Evening Post*, March 8, 1911: 3; "Balenti Signs, Reports Soon," *Atlanta Constitution*, April 7, 1911: 5.

20 "Balenti Bought for Macon Team," *Macon Telegraph*, April 18, 1911: 6.

21 "Snappy Sporting Paragraphs," *Charleston* (South Carolina) *News & Courier*, May 25, 1911: 8.

22 "How the Menafee Deal Went Through," *Augusta Chronicle*, May 22, 1911: 5.

23 "Balenti Sold to Cincinnati," *Columbus Ledger*, July 13, 1911, *Boston Post*, August 6, 1911.

24 "Balenti to Chattanooga," *Charleston* (South Carolina) *Evening Post*, September 13, 1911: 3.

25 Clyde H. Hoss, *Spitting on Diamonds* (Columbia, Missouri: University of Missouri Press, 2005), 27.

26 "Balenti Takes Wife," *Daily Oklahoman*, October 11, 1911: 8.

27 "Further Changes in Baseball Team," *Asheville Gazette News*, May 27, 1912: 7.

28 "Secretary Bruce's Bulletin," *Sporting Life*, July 20, 1912: 6; "National Agreements Approved," *Sporting Life* August 24, 1912: 3.

29 "Wagner Drafted by Brooklyn Team," *New Orleans Item*, September 16, 1912: 1; "Drafted Players," *Sporting Life*, November 23, 1912: 8.

30 "Balenti Reports to Browns," *Dallas Morning News*, March 26, 1913: 9.

31 "Balenti Seems to be Lost to Lookouts, Stays with Browns," *Montgomery Advertiser*, April 11, 1913: 10.

32 "Mike Balenti to Coach," *Cincinnati Post*, September 6, 1913: 6.

33 "To Go to Alaska," *Syracuse Herald*, October 18, 1913: 10.

34 "The Southern League," *Sporting Life*, January 2, 1915: 18.

35 "Sport Salad," *Cincinnati Post*, July 13, 1914: 7; "Mike Balenti Rapidly Recovering from Hurt," *Macon Telegraph*, July 31, 1914: 8; "Mercer Meets Balenti's Eleven at Central City," *Macon Telegraph*, September 30, 1914: 9.

36 US Patent number 1,193,972.

37 "Mike Balenti Invents an Athletic Device," *San Antonio Light*, May 5, 1916: 12.

38 "Sport Lights," *San Antonio Light*, February 16, 1933: 13.

39 Balenti coached at Baylor in 1915-1917 and again in 1919.

40 "Watson Leads Texas League Curvers and James Sets Pace for Batsmen," *Dallas Morning News*, May 6, 1917: Section 4, 8.

41 US Patent number 1,363,706.

42 "Oklahoma State League," *The Sporting News*, July 13, 1922: 8.

43 "Oilers Win Slugfest," *Omaha World-Herald*, May 6, 1923: 2.

44 "Oilers Capture," *Perry* (Oklahoma) *Daily Journal*, May 20, 1926: 4.

45 "Kromer Resigns as Manager of Baseball Team," *Appleton* (Wisconsin) *Post-Crescent*, June 26, 1926: 6, and "Kromer Puts Grabby in Charge of Team," *Appleton* (Wisconsin) *Post-Crescent*, July 31, 1926: 6; "The S.W. Batting Averages," *Kansas City Star*, July 24, 1926: 7.

46 "Lamesa Defeats Tonkawa Oklahoma With Score of 8-7," *Lubbock Morning Avalanche*, September 7, 1926: 5.

47 1920 U.S. Census.

48 "Ex-Grid Star Dies at Altus," *Wichita Daily Times*, August 6, 1955: 9.

49 "Grid Greats to be Seen by Proxy," *Long Beach Press-Telegram*, April 25, 1950: B-7; "Jim Thorpe Asks Mike Balenti for Film Rights," *Grove* (Oklahoma) *Sun*, April 6, 1950: 1.

50 "Ex-Grid Star Dies at Altus," *Wichita Daily Times*, August 6, 1955: 9; Bill Lee, *The Baseball Necrology* (Jefferson, North Carolina: McFarland & Co, 2003), 18.

DALLAS BEELER

By Kelly Bennett

In his debut for the Chicago Cubs, right-handed pitcher Dallas Beeler checked off more "career goal" boxes than some other pitchers manage in their entire major-league careers. As the starting pitcher in the first game of a doubleheader against the Washington Nationals, Beeler tallied six strikeouts, picked off a player, and singled his first at-bat – a trifecta that prompted Cubs announcer Pat Hughes to bellow, "Dallas Beeler, you're my hero!"[1]

That first game as a major-league player, being in the bullpen and on the field with players he'd previously only seen in televised games, is etched in Beeler's memory. As is his first time stepping up to the plate. "When I was on deck, I just kept thinking, 'Man, I'm not going to let a pitch go by. I'm swinging first pitch,'" he recalled. "I just put bat on ball like we're taught to do in BP. ... It's another moment you'll have for your lifetime."[2]

That game, that day, June 28, 2014, also shines as the highlight of Beeler's time pitching professionally, which included seven seasons with the Cubs organization. From July of 2010 through his release in March of 2017, Beeler appeared as a starting pitcher for the Cubs five times in two seasons (2014 and 2015). In 19⅓ innings and 92 major-league batters faced, he tallied 13 strikeouts and 14 walks to finish with a major-league career ERA of 6.05.

"The question for Dallas Beeler has always been when, not if," sportswriter Tommy Birch wrote in a 2015 article.[3] As demonstrated time and time again over decades on the mound, including 10 years playing at the professional level, when the 6-foot-5, 225-pound fastball-hurling Beeler was on, he was on! Over eight seasons pitching in the minors, primarily as a starting pitcher, Beeler tallied 368 strikeouts and 156 walks in 559 innings pitched, and a minor-league career ERA of 3.88.

Dallas James Beeler was born on June 12, 1989, in Tulsa, Oklahoma, and was raised in Jenks, a suburb of Tulsa, surrounded by family on all sides. His father, Darrell, one of three children, likewise grew up in Jenks. Beeler's mother, Susan, also one of three siblings, grew up in Tulsa. On his

Dallas Beeler

mother's side, Beeler is part Choctaw and Chickasaw and his family, especially his grandmother and aunts, is active in the tribe and community.

In the Beeler household, the question was never whether to play sports, it was which sport to play. Theirs is an athletic family. Susan, a retired schoolteacher, ran track at Hale High School, and in college, at Arkansas and Northeastern State University. Darrell, a Tulsa firefighter, played baseball for Jenks High School (the same school Dallas and his siblings attended) and college ball before making a name for himself in competitive slow-pitch softball. Dallas's older brother, Chase, a star football player went to Stanford and then the NFL as a practice squad player. And their younger sister Lacy, excelled at volleyball and soccer.

Beeler can't remember a time when he didn't play baseball. Among his earliest memories is a photo of himself at about 2 years old, posing with a bat. He started with T-ball, then Coach Pitch, Little League, and on. Those early baseball years were truly a family affair. Darrell helped coach both Dallas and Chase's teams. And when he wasn't coaching, he was playing. Darrell is a USSSA hall of famer with a career batting average of .715.[4] Dallas Beeler said watching the highly competitive athletes in action during his father's slow-pitch softball games taught him about teamwork and the game.

Following in their father's footsteps, Dallas and his siblings attended Jenks High School, where he and his older brother Chase excelled at baseball and football. By his sophomore year, however, Dallas – then 6-feet-5 and 200 pounds, long and lean – realized that his football future was limited. "I wasn't fast enough, couldn't jump high enough, I wasn't quite big enough," he said.[5] But that didn't stop him giving it his all. As a starting wide receiver, Beeler helped the Jenks Trojans bring home a pair of state football championships.

Beeler hyperfocused on baseball and his hard work paid off. During his senior season, he posted a 4-1 record and a 1.09 ERA with 34 strikeouts in 38⅔ innings pitched and batted .385 with 4 home runs and 17 stolen bases. Beeler earned All-Conference, All-Metro, and All-State honors with the Jenks Trojans. It was no surprise that he caught the attention of Toronto Blue Jays area scout Ty Nichols. Beeler was drafted by the Blue Jays in the 37th round of the June 2008 amateur draft. "I was tempted [to sign]," Beeler said. "As a high schooler it's hard to turn down a chance to play baseball – get paid for it?" In the end, after lengthy family discussions, Beeler turned down the offer in favor of going to college. "I had a good feeling that getting some more playing time against better competition would benefit me."

In the fall of 2008, Beeler began his freshman year at Seminole State College in Seminole, Oklahoma, a Division I junior college "known for turning out good ballplayers."[6] Support offered by the Chickasaw Nation was a key factor in Beeler's opting for college at that point. The tribe helped defray Beeler's tuition, books, clothing, and housing costs.

In addition, he participated in the work-study program. And he played ball. Beeler called playing ball at Seminole "a game changer." He credited the Seminole coaching staff, especially Mark Allen, for helping hone his competitive edge or, as he put it "find that killer instinct" pitchers need. Find it he did. But three-quarters of the way through the season, he injured his elbow. Facing surgery on his right elbow, after finishing out his freshman year at Seminole, he returned home to Jenks.

That summer Beeler underwent Tommy John ligament replacement surgery. Wanting to continue his education and eagerly anticipating his return to baseball, he enrolled at nearby Oral Roberts University, where he majored in business administration. "This is where support from the Chickasaw really helped with tuition, books, even clothing and living expenses," Beeler said. As part of ORU's work-study program, he also served as the locker room "clubbie," and put in the work needed to rehabilitate his elbow.

Beeler recovered faster than expected and as is often the case after Tommy John surgery, came back stronger. Under the tutelage of ORU coach Rob Walton, Beeler matured as a pitcher. Walton, Beeler said, "taught me the importance of throwing a fastball for a strike and about pitch sequencing. How pitching is actually a chess game. It's not just throwing pitches out there; it's attacking a batter with a plan." Walton's coaching style included having players study and emulate successful pitchers' style. Beeler, Walton observed, had a similar body type, arm slot, and pitch arsenal as Hall of Famer Roy Halladay, who "blended a blistering sinking fastball with pinpoint control."[7] Beeler studied film of Halladay in action and mirrored his technique. Additionally, Walton worked with Beeler to develop new pitches.

By the end of the 2010 season, Beeler proved himself to be one of the team's standout players, going 2-0 in two starts and earning two saves.[8] Scout Ty Nichols once again put out the word. Beeler was picked up by the Cubs in the 41st round of the 2010 draft.

That summer, Beeler played college ball in South Carolina with the Florence Flamingos for whom, he recalled, "I pitched some of the best games I ever had." That's when the call from the Cubs organization came. "It was decision time," Beeler recalled. "Do I stay in college or sign? ... It happens fast. One day you're a college kid, two days later you report to spring training."

After signing, Beeler headed to Mesa, Arizona, to play Rookie ball with the Arizona Cubs. At 21, with two years of college under his belt, in comparison to the 16- and 17-year-old high-schoolers, he was one of the older guys, which, in terms of maturity, may have been to his advantage. Rookie ball was super-competitive. "I remember telling myself to enjoy it," Beeler said of the experience, "because I had prepared for this." Shortly after his arrival, Beeler got the first strikeout of his professional career. As is the way in rookie ball. he only pitched the one inning against maybe four batters, still, "That strikeout felt good." So did moving up to the Boise Hawks, the Cubs' short-season team, a month later. And a week after that, moving up again to the Peoria Chiefs of the Class-A Midwest League.

Beeler started the 2011 season with Peoria and was quickly promoted to Tennessee (Knoxville) of the Double-A Southern League. In his Double-A debut, on June 7, 2011, "throwing what he estimated to be 90-95 percent two-seam fastballs, the 21-year-old right-hander struck out four without walking a batter" to lead the Smokies to a 6-0 victory over the Jackson Generals.[9]

He stayed with the Smokies the rest of that season, all of 2012, and the first part of the 2013 season. Beeler recalled those early years fondly. "Some of your best friends and best memories are made in the minor leagues," he said. "Because everyone is going through the grind together, whether it's the bus rides, whether it's long travel, whether it's the locker rooms that are worse than any small-town high school you've been to or peanut butter and jelly sandwiches five times a day … that's where bonds are made." Among the bonds Beeler forged in the minors were those with fellow pitchers Kyle Hendricks and Eric Jokisch, with whom he shared similar pitch arsenals and approach to the game.

Having quickly worked his way up in the minor-league system, January of 2013, Beeler was selected to take part in the Cubs' inaugural Rookie Development Program, a "joint venture between the Major League Baseball Players Association and the commissioner's office.[10] Beeler found that participating in the program "gives you a glimpse of what goes into being in the big leagues, how to manage your days and the season. Mostly it made me feel like I was ready for the next level." But toward the end of the season, a sprained finger on Beeler's right hand kept him in the Smokies dugout for the rest of 2013.

Beeler was assigned to the Mesa Solar Sox of the Arizona Fall League. He made six starts and went 4-1 with a 2.49 ERA, a performance that earned him a promotion to the Triple-A Pacific Coast League. *Baseball America* ranked him the number-24 prospect in the Cubs organization, noting, "He can touch 94 mph with the fastball and has a slurvy slider as his main breaking ball, working to get early contact with both pitches. He uses both forkball-type of splitter that he can use in the strike zone and a more conventional split-finger pitch that he tries to bury out of the zone."[11]

That November Beeler was added to the Cubs' 40-man roster. "I think he's a kid that everybody's looking forward to having an opportunity to come out here and show what he can do," Cubs manager Rich Renteria said. "We're glad to have him."[12]

At the start of 2014 spring training, the 24-year-old, commenting on the sprained finger that had curtailed the previous season, said, "It happened, I got over it, I worked hard, and now I'm here and now I'm just trying to stay healthy and pitch well."[13]

Beeler observed that at every step of his baseball career, coaches guided him to the next level. With the Triple-A Iowa Cubs, two coaches were instrumental in his getting a shot at the majors. Bruce "Pap" Walton, had been the bullpen coach for the Blue Jays when Beeler's role model, Roy Halladay, played for Toronto. "To be able to pick Pap's brain on what made Halladay successful, his work ethic, pitch grips, pitch sequencing, what he was trying to accomplish and how, was fantastic." And pitching coordinator David Johnson taught Beeler the pitch that got him his shot.

"It was a cutter," Beeler said. "Honestly, I think that pitch is what got me to the big leagues. Two-seam is good, but it's great to have a pitch that goes the opposite direction at basically the same speed." For Beeler, a groundball pitcher, adding the cutter to his arsenal was a huge advantage, because groundball pitchers try to get early swings and early contact so they can pitch longer into the game and save bullpen arms. "I could pepper the same spot," Beeler explained. "If I was facing a lefty, I could throw a fastball in the outside corner and I could make it run away from the guy, make it run back on the plate, or I could freeze them. I could go through a whole at bat and throw the same pitch."

On Sunday, June 8, 2014, in a game against Colorado Springs, Beeler pitched seven shutout innings, during which he gave up five hits, struck out five and walked two to lead the Iowa Cubs to a 3-0 win. It was, sportswriter Tommy Birch noted, his "fourth consecutive quality start and fifth of the season."[14] Birch wasn't the only one who noticed. A few weeks later, Beeler was at Wrigley Field making his major-league debut with the Chicago Cubs.

When asked to name one best memory of his time in the pros, Beeler didn't hesitate. "My debut, definitely." Called up for a spot start in the June 28 doubleheader at Wrigley Field, he recalled running out to center field prior to the start of the game. "Everyone's cheering for you, they don't know who you are, but they're still rooting for you." He was especially impressed with how knowledgeable the fans were. While he was warming up in the outfield before the game, the fans – who had most likely never even seen him play – called out stats about him and the other players they themselves didn't even know. "Then, of course, running out for the first inning, picking up the ball, standing on the mound and taking everything in. That was one of the bigger moments of my career … and my hit." Beeler's first time batting in a big-league game, he swung at the first pitch Gio González threw and singled. His debut performance didn't go unnoticed by Cubs management. In a postgame interview, Rich Renteria told reporters, "Beel showed really good stuff today. He's a Cubbie now."[15]

That was the first of two starts with the Cubs in 2014. He made 20 starts for Iowa, where he went 9-6 with a 3.40 ERA.[16] But by the end of the season Beeler was plagued with shoulder issues. In a postseason newspaper interview, Beeler described the 2014 season in one word: "Maturing."

He added that he was "trying to pick up little things that I can improve mentally and physically on the mound."[17]

In 2015 Beeler missed all of spring training after suffering biceps tendinitis with a shoulder impingement. He went to extended spring training before rejoining the Iowa Cubs on a rehab assignment. Rebounding wasn't easy. He struggled to find the strike zone. "I had about five starts in those 30 days and I never pitched more than three innings in one game," Beeler said of that frustrating time. "And in all those five starts I didn't give up less than seven runs. I was so low after one game I remember sitting in the batting cages with the lights off thinking, 'What am I doing? I need to quit. I need to retire.'"

Again, coaching, this time from Cubs mental skills coach Josh Lifrak, helped turn things around. Lifrak told Beeler he was trying too hard. "Go out there and clear your mind," Beeler recalled Lifrak telling him. "You can only worry about what you do when the ball comes out of your hand. You can't control much after that." His next outing, Beeler took Lifrak's advice. "I tried not to throw so hard, but to relax into it."

What followed was, in Beeler's words, "The start of the best three months of my career." He was feeling good, pitching well, and it didn't go unnoticed. July 7 found him back in Wrigley Field for another spot start in the second game of a day-night doubleheader against the St. Louis Cardinals. In five innings, he struck out six, walked two, and allowed four hits and two runs. That was the first of three major-league starts. Beeler finished 2015 with an ERA of 4.07, enough to once again earn a spot on the Cubs' 40-player 2016 roster, assigned to Iowa, his third stint with the club.

Beeler said he felt especially fortunate to have been part of the Cubs organization when, as he put it, it was all coming together.

Although lingering injuries kept Beeler on the disabled list for much of the 2016 season (after 21 starts for Iowa in 2015, he managed only eight in 2016), being part of the Cubs, "with its history and incredible fans," when they won the 2016 World Series was indescribable. He said his World Series ring, emblazoned with 108 round diamonds to commemorate the 108 years between World Series championships, is one of his prized possessions, still in the lighted case in which it was delivered.

Released by the Cubs on March 30, 2017, Beeler signed with the Kansas City T-Bones of the independent American Association. However, because of persistent shoulder issues, he soon doubted the wisdom of his decision. Rather than cause further damage, he opted to sit out the 2017 season and focus instead on healing. The decision proved to be a good one. The next season, 2018, he signed with the Sugar Land Skeeters of the independent Atlantic League. Beeler quickly proved himself a valuable addition to the team. In his June 3 start against the York Revolution, Beeler struck out 10 batters, to set a single-game high for a Skeeters

pitcher that season. Five days later, in a home game against the Lancaster Barnstormers, he pitched eight no-hit innings.[18] After going 5-0 with a 1.61 ERA in June, Beeler was named the Atlantic League's Pitcher of the Month.

His pitching performance didn't go unnoticed. On July 9, 2018, the Kansas City Royals purchased Beeler's contract from the Skeeters. He was sent to the Northwest Arkansas Naturals of the Double-A in the Texas League. Beeler struggled, losing two starts. On July 23 he was released by the Royals and re-signed by the Skeeters.

Beeler helped the Skeeters win the division and league titles in 2018, and in 2019 he helped them win a division title again. Beeler spent both the 2018 and 2019 offseasons in the Mexican Pacific Winter League playing for the Tomateros de Culiacan, which he thoroughly enjoyed and would have returned to but for the Covid pandemic.

Careerwise, the Covid shutdown came at the worst possible time for Beeler. In January of 2020 he signed with the Lincoln Saltdogs of the American Association as a player-coach. The Covid shutdown in March put an end to that plan as the Saltdogs were not one of the teams selected to compete in the condensed 2020 season. That, as it turned out, was the end of his professional pitching career. "Guys that are done playing always talk about how a ballplayer never knows what the last pitch will be," said Beeler. "Mine was a friggin' curveball I threw in Sugar Land to get me out of an inning."

With his playing days over, Beeler and his wife, Bayle, whom he's met in Des Moines while playing with the Iowa Cubs, settled in Broken Arrow, Oklahoma, a suburb of Tulsa, not far from where he grew up. As of 2025, Bayle worked in educational tech and the couple have two sons, Stellan and Graeme. Unlike many big-leaguers who stay in the game in some capacity, Beeler pivoted. His interest in business coupled with his own familiarity with sports-related injuries led to a job with RX Medical, providing technical support and guidance to health-care providers for patients with spinal injuries.

Beeler thought he'd put baseball – except as a fan – behind him. A call from his former high-school coach, Jeff Owens, in 2021 changed that. Owens had been offered a coaching position at Cassia Hall Preparatory School in Tulsa and Beeler's father, Darrell, was going as assistant coach. Did Dallas want to join them as pitching coach? After the possibility of becoming a player-coach for the Lincoln Saltdogs fell through, Beeler hadn't given coaching another thought. Now, perhaps because a few years had passed since he'd been a player, he became part of a coaching team with his father and Owens, two coaches who had been instrumental in his success as a ballplayer. Coaching seemed like the right next step.

Beeler said he enjoyed being on the coaching side of the game. "It's addicting," he said. "I learned more about pitching from coaching than I ever did as a player." Well aware of the impact knowledgeable, patient coaches had on his career, Beeler is grateful to have a chance to give back. "What seems like common knowledge to a 30-year-old is brand new to kids and can make all the difference to their game." After three years at Cassia Hall, Beeler, along with his father and Coach Owens, moved with head coach Dean Wilson to Bixby High School.

The motto that was written all over the Cubs' facilities during his time with the organization, "It's not if it happens, it's when it happens" also became Beeler's personal motto. He credits that "if not when" attitude with his being able to rebound from setbacks throughout his career. Now that he was coaching, he tried to foster that same supportive attitude among his players. "Teams ebb and flow. No matter how good a team you are, every season there are low points. And especially during those low points there can be friction in the dugout, issues with personalities, frayed nerves, and the like. I try to teach my players you've got to have each other's backs, be each other's best friends and at the same time toughest competitors, and also to understand we are all trying to be our best."

In 2024 Beeler said that if his sons chose to play baseball (and he couldn't help hoping they did) he would do just as his father did by assisting with their teams. In the meantime, he intended to continue coaching, with a goal of helping young pitchers achieve their goals the way coaches and many others at every step of his career supported him. "I'm blessed to have the career I've had – five or six starts in the big leagues," said Beeler. "I battled with injuries here and there but I was fortunate to play and do I all got to do."

SOURCES

In addition to the sources cited in the Notes, the author consulted Baseball-Reference.com, baseball-almanac.com, and MLB.com.

NOTES

1   YouTube highlights from Beeler's major-league debut on June 28, 2014: "WSH@CHC: Beeler Allows No Earned Runs in MLB Debut," YouTube. com. https://www.youtube.com/watch?v=VyXpPJrRYwY, accessed September 25, 2024.

2   Jacob Unruh, "Q&A: Iowa Cubs' Dallas Beeler Talks Major League Debut, Keeping Up with Jenks," the *Oklahoman* (Oklahoma City), July 6, 2014. https://www.oklahoman.com/story/sports/columns/2014/07/06/qa-iowa-cubs-dallas-beeler-talks-major-league-debut-keeping-up-with-jenks/60813609007/.

3   Tommy Birch, "Dallas Beeler Battles Through Rehab Start for I-Cubs," *Des Moines Register*, May 11, 2015. https://www.desmoinesregister.com/story/sports/baseball/iowa-cubs/2015/05/11/dallas-beeler-iowa-chicago-cubs-colorado-springs-sky-sox-pcl/27144547/.

4   USSSA was the United States Slowpitch Softball Association. It has since been renamed: The United States Specialty Sports Association.

5   Author interview with Dallas Beeler on September 5, 2024. Unless otherwise indicated, all direct quotations from Beeler come from either this interview or in interviews on September 26 and 27, 2024.

6   Beeler interview.

7   https://baseballhall.org/hall-of-famers/halladay-roy.

8   "Oral Roberts Golden Eagles - 2011 Baseball, 18 – Dallas Beeler,"

9   David Heck, "Beeler Tosses Gem in Double-A Debut," June 8, 2011, https://www.milb.com/news/gcs-20191636.

10 "Rookie Career Development," mlbpplayers.com. https://www.mlbplayers.com/rookie-career-development#:~:text=The%20RCDP%20is%20joint%20venture,leagues%20in%20the%20upcoming%20season.

11 Baseballamerica.com, https://www.baseballamerica.com/players/671871-dallas-beeler/.

12 Bruce Miles. "Cubs Add 2 Players to Roster," *Arlington Heights* (Illinois) *Daily Herald,* November 20, 2013. https://www.dailyherald.com/20131120/pro-sports/cubs-add-2-players-to-roster/.

13 Tommy Birch, "Dallas Beeler Shines Again for Iowa Cubs in Strong Start," *Des Moines Register,* June 8, 2014. https://www.desmoinesregister.com/story/sports/baseball/iowa-cubs/2014/06/08/dallas-beeler-iowa-cubs-chicago-cubs-baseball-america/10204471/.

14 "Dallas Beeler Shines Again for Iowa Cubs in Strong Start."

15 Bruce Miles, "Cubs Come Away with 7-2 Win on Strange Day at Wrigley," *Arlington Heights Daily Herald,* June 29, 2014. https://www.dailyherald.com/sports/20170725/cubs-come-away-with-7-2-win-on-strange-day-at-wrigley/

16 Dallas Beeler stats, https://www.mlb.com/player/dallas-beeler-542923.

17 "Jokisch, Beeler Hoping to Pitch at Some Point," *Arlington Heights Daily Herald,* February 28, 2015.

18 Carrie Muskat, "Cubs Make Adjustments to 40-Man Roster," MLB.com, November 7, 2016. https://www.mlb.com/news/cubs-add-rosario-mullee-to-40-man-roster-c208325178.

CHARLES BENDER

By Tom Swift

American Indian. Innovator. Renaissance man. Charles Albert "Chief" Bender lived a unique American life, fashioned a Hall of Fame career, and was an important member of modern baseball's first dynasty. He silently struggled against racial prejudice, became a student of the game, and was a lifetime baseball man. His legacy, however, is less nuanced than all of that. Bender is known foremost for a rare ability to pitch under pressure. "If I had all the men I've ever handled, and they were in their prime, and there was one game I wanted to win above all others," said Philadelphia Athletics icon Connie Mack, who managed fellow all-time pitching greats Lefty Grove, Herb Pennock, Eddie Plank, and Rube Waddell, "Albert would be my man."[1]

For nearly the entire second half of the twentieth century Bender was the lone Minnesota representative in the National Baseball Hall of Fame. That he is no longer a household name in the North Star State is in part because he spent so little time in Minnesota and because some details about that time remain unclear. Bender's birthday, for one, is not certain. His birth certificate, registered decades after the fact, says May 3, 1883. Other sources list May 5, 1883. Based on the federal Indian census and on Bender's school records, the correct year, almost certainly, is 1884. Many sources list his birthplace as Brainerd but that is likely inaccurate. According to research on Bender's early years conducted by researcher Robert Tholkes, within a year of Charley's birth the family lived in an area close to Partridge Lake, 20 miles east of Brainerd. No town existed on the site at the time. So it is most accurate to say that Bender was born in Crow Wing County.

Not long after Charles's birth, the Bender family moved to the White Earth Reservation in the northwest section of the state. Bender's father, Albertus Bliss Bender (often referred to as William), was an early white settler in Minnesota, a homesteader-farmer of German-American descent. Charley's mother, Mary Razor Bender, was believed a member of the Mississippi Band of the Ojibwe. Mary, whose Indian name was "Pay shaw de o quay," gave birth to at least 11 children, perhaps as many as 14. Charley was the fourth child born and the third son. His troubled older brother, John Charles Bender, was an outfielder who bounced from team to team in the minor leagues.

At White Earth, the family lived in a log house on a small farm. The Benders had to be self-sufficient and they were not the only ones. As scholar Melissa Meyer chronicles in *The White Earth Tragedy*, during the early years

of Charley's childhood White Earth was destitute.[2] Things were so meager that as a young boy Charley supposedly went to work, taking a job as a farmhand for a dollar a week. At the time reservation families such as the Benders often sent their kids to boarding schools. There were four on-reservation boarding schools, and Charley attended one of them for a short time, but at age 7 he was sent to the Educational Home, which was under the auspices of the Lincoln Institution, an off-reservation boarding school for American Indian children near Philadelphia.

Bender was at the Educational Home for five years before he went back to White Earth not long after he turned 12 in June of 1896. He had been out of touch with his family for those years and he returned to a situation that had not improved and possibly regressed. During his time away, too, the Bender family had continued to grow; Charley was then one of nine children in the modest Bender home. A few months after he returned to White Earth, according to a story Bender told *The Sporting News* as an adult, he and his older brother Frank ran away from home. The two went to

Charles Bender with the 1909 A's

another White Earth farm and got jobs in the fields. While there, a teacher from the Carlisle Indian School, a boarding school in Carlisle, Pennsylvania, later made famous by Jim Thorpe-led powerhouse football teams, came through and recruited Frank and Charley to Carlisle.

In many respects, Charley Bender's life was shaped during five years at Carlisle, which was run by Richard Henry Pratt, a military man who strictly drove his pupils to assimilate into the dominant white culture. At Carlisle, Bender continued to develop his sharp mind—during his career, teammates, and sportswriters often attributed Bender's success to his mental approach—and he met his first real baseball coach, legendary football maven Pop Warner. After becoming a rare Carlisle Indian School graduate in 1902, the right-handed pitcher signed with the semi-pro Harrisburg Athletic Club. While playing for that team in the summer of 1902—not long after he held his own in an exhibition loss to the National League's Chicago Cubs—Bender was discovered by one of Connie Mack's birddogs.

Bender joined the Philadelphia Athletics in 1903 and, as chronicled in *Chief Bender's Burden,* had one of the great seasons in history for someone aged 19.[3] After an impressive debut in which he pitched six innings in relief for a

(SABR – The Rucker Archive)

Charles Bender won 212 major-league games and was voted into the National Baseball Hall of Fame by the Veterans Committee in 1953.

victory over Boston's Cy Young, Bender earned his first complete-game shutout victory on April 27, defeating New York Highlanders pitcher and future Hall of Famer Clark Griffith. By the end of the 1903 season the rookie had 17 wins and a 3.07 earned-run average (ERA), which was about league average. His control was impressive from the start as he walked just 2.17 batters per nine innings.

Compared to his peers, Bender did not have an inordinate level of pitching stamina as he was plagued by poor health during several seasons. (Bender battled a number of physical ailments and, later in his career, drank heavily.) He never pitched more than 270 innings in any season, a feat regularly attained by top-tier starters of the Deadball Era. Near the end of the 1905 season, however, Bender showed he could labor long if given the chance. The Athletics needed to win two games against Washington to all but secure the pennant. Bender won the first game 8-0 and came on as a relief pitcher in the second game to win that one as well. It was an incredible one-day performance. Bender pitched 15 innings, won two games, and struck out 14 Senators. What's more, he was the hitting hero. A right-handed hitter who posted a lifetime .212 batting average, he made five hits in six official at-bats, including two triples and a two-run double in the fourth inning of the second game that pushed Philadelphia ahead. On the day he drove in seven runs.

Bender's poise in big games was most evident during the World Series, and he received his first such opportunity in 1905. Starting the second game against John McGraw's New York Giants, he delivered a masterful, four-hit, 3-0 shutout in the Athletics' only victory of the series. Following the 1905 season, and after studying New York's Christy Mathewson up close, Bender worked to further develop his control. He threw a well-directed fastball and a sharp-breaking curve—a man named Bender has to have one—that was a precursor to the slider, a pitch he may have invented.[4] He also threw a submarine fadeaway—a pitch that moved like the contemporary screwball, away from a left-handed hitter. "I use fast curves, pitched overhand and sidearm, fastballs, high and inside, and an underhand fadeaway pitch with the hand almost down to the level of the knees," Bender told *Baseball Magazine* in 1911. "They are my most successful deliveries, though a twisting slow one mixed up with them helps at times."[5]

Bender was exceptionally bright. His intelligence was recognized by teammates, opponents, and umpires, such as Billy Evans, who believed Bender was one of the smartest pitchers in the game. "He takes advantage of every weakness," Evans said in his *Atlanta Constitution* column, "and once a player shows him a weak spot he is marked for life by the crafty Indian."[6] Bender possessed a keen ability to focus on the task at hand, attributes that won the admiration of legendary sportswriter Grantland Rice, who once called Bender one of "the greatest competitors I ever knew." Rice and Bender often played golf together, and Rice sometimes quoted Bender in his syndicated column. "Tension is the greatest curse in sport," said Bender, according to Rice. "I've never had any tension. You give the best you have—you win or lose. What's the difference if you give all you've got to give?"[7]

During his first eight years in the major leagues, Bender continued to hone his craft. Though his win-loss record fluctuated, his ERA dropped every year, to a career-best 1.58 in 1910. That year he also won 20 games for the first time, notching 23 victories against only five defeats, which gave him the league's best winning percentage (.821). Among his victories that season was a no-hitter, thrown May 12 against the Cleveland Indians. Bender was nearly perfect; he faced just 27 hitters as the lone man to reach, shortstop Terry Turner, was caught stealing after a walk. Bender won the opening game of the 1910 World Series, and the Athletics beat the Chicago Cubs in five games—Philadelphia's first world championship.

The following year, Bender helped the A's win a second title, as his 17-5 record again led the league in winning percentage (.773). Facing the New York Giants in the World Series, Bender pitched brilliantly, winning two of three starts, posting a 1.04 ERA, and striking out 20 batters in 26 innings. Philadelphia failed to win a third straight pennant in 1912 as injuries, illness, and a team suspension for alcohol use limited Bender to a 13-8 record in just 171 innings.[8] But the following year the A's were again the premier team, as Bender won 20 games and also led the league with 13 saves (retroactively calculated). In that year's World Series—the A's and Giants squared off one more time—Bender won two games and the Athletics captured their third world championship in four years.

Bender's World Series career line was blemished in 1914, as the favored Philadelphia Athletics were swept by the so-called "Miracle" Boston Braves. Bender had put up a fine regular season record, winning 14 straight games during one stretch, finishing the year with a 17-3 mark and a league-leading .850 winning percentage. But, in his only appearance in the World Series, Bender started the opening game and surrendered six earned runs in 5⅓ innings. It was his last appearance in an A's uniform.

The next year, Bender signed with the Federal League and was assigned to Baltimore. Pitching for the last-place Terrapins, he went 4-16 and was released by the team in September. After the 1915 season, Bender was picked up by the Philadelphia Phillies, where, pitching mostly in relief, he had a 7-7 record in 1916. In 1917, he showed flashes of his previous level of performance with an 8-2 mark and a 1.67 ERA but nonetheless was released by the Phillies at the end of the season. During the 1918 season Bender went to work in the Philadelphia shipyards to contribute to the war effort.

His life in baseball did not end, however. When the war was over, Bender began a successful career as a minor-league player and manager. He was offered opportunities to return to the big leagues but enjoyed managing so much—and probably earned as much money in the minors

as he would have in the majors—that he declined. Bender managed Richmond of the Virginia League in 1919 and also dominated the league as a pitcher, winning 29 games against two defeats. Subsequently, he pitched and managed at New Haven in the Eastern League (1920-21); Reading (1922) and Baltimore (1923) in the International League; and Johnstown, Pennsylvania, in the Mid-Atlantic League in 1927. During that period he also spent several years as a baseball coach for the U.S. Naval Academy.

Bender pitched once more in the major leagues. In 1925, while employed as a coach for his friend, Chicago White Sox manager Eddie Collins, he worked a gimmicky frame in a game against the Boston Red Sox—the club he had beaten for his first major-league victory 22 years prior. Bender, 42 at the time, allowed two runs on a walk and a home run but did manage to retire the side.

During the 1930s, Bender managed the Eastern team of the independent House of David. He also managed Erie in the Continental League in 1932, Wilmington of the Inter-State League in 1940, Newport News of the Virginia League in 1941, and Savannah of the Southern Association in 1946. Thereafter he was associated with the New York Yankees, Chicago White Sox, New York Giants, and Philadelphia Athletics as a coach or scout. At 61 he began pitching batting practice to the Athletics and years later served as the A's de facto pitching coach.

Over a 16-year major-league career, Bender won 212 games and posted a .625 winning percentage. He pitched to avoid the bats of American League hitters, and every time he did he stared into the face of racism. Though he often exhibited a calm, levelheaded demeanor, he was seldom portrayed in newspapers, cartoons, or words on the street without references—many of them demeaning, few of them subtle—to his race. Though proud of his American Indian heritage Bender resented the bigotry and the moniker he and nearly every other Indian ballplayer of the time received. "I do not want my name to be presented to the public as an Indian, but as a pitcher," he told *Sporting Life* in 1905.[9] The writers didn't listen. Though his manager called him Albert, prevailing stereotypes rarely were absent from baseball coverage and bench jockeying. Bender didn't publicly protest, but he signed his autograph as "Charles" or some derivative. Eventually, he was called "Chief" so often (and so often with affection) that he allowed the name to be etched into his tombstone. But the tacit racism never went away. Even decades after his retirement, Bender's obituary in *The Sporting News* carried the headline, "Chief Bender Answers Call to Happy Hunting Grounds."[10]

As noted in *Chief Bender's Burden,* as a way to keep his mind occupied, Bender engaged in an inordinate number of sports and hobbies outside of baseball, and he was exceptional at many of them. He was often referred to as one of the top trap shooters (he shot live bird and clay pigeons) in the country. He loved to hunt and fish and was an outstanding golfer. Bender's favorite hobbies were gardening, playing billiards, and painting oil landscapes. He also occasionally served as a consultant to people in the diamonds and textiles trades. He had a long post-major-league career in retail, selling, among other things, sporting goods and men's clothing.

Bender's life partner was Marie (Clement) Bender, whom he married in 1904. The couple's marriage, which lasted nearly 50 years, did not produce any children. In 1953, Bender became the first Minnesota-born player enshrined in the Hall of Fame, and he remained the only one until Dave Winfield joined him in 2001. On May 22, 1954, the year following the vote, Bender died, a few weeks shy of his 71st birthday and a few weeks before his induction ceremony. He had previously suffered a heart attack and was receiving treatments for prostate cancer. Bender is buried in Hillside Cemetery in Roslyn, Pennsylvania.

A version of this biography appeared in the book Minnesotans in Baseball, *edited by Stew Thornley (Nodin, 2009).*

SOURCES

Portions of this biography are drawn from the author's book *Chief Bender's Burden* (Lincoln: University of Nebraska Press, 2008).

Research conducted by Robert Tholkes, written in an excellent article called "Chief Bender: The Early Years," published in the 1983 edition of the *Baseball Research Journal* of the Society for American Baseball Research, was the solid foundation upon which I conducted further exploration about the rough details of Bender's first years, his family, and life at White Earth. Beverly Hermes provided additional genealogical research assistance. The Charles Albert Bender file at the United States Department of the Interior, Bureau of Indian Affairs, Bemidji, Minnesota, was useful. Facts about the Bender family were also found in the federal Indian census and the U.S. census.

Paulette Fairbanks Molin's article, "Training the Hand, the Head, and the Heart: Indian Education at Hampton Institute," published in the fall 1988 issue of *Minnesota History,* revealed facts about the Bender family.

Articles in a multiple-part series about Bender's life published in *The Sporting News,* December 24-31, 1942, were used for information about Bender's childhood, including the story of how Bender and his brother ran away.

NOTES

1   The Connie Mack quote that if he could pick one pitcher for a big game, "Albert would be my man," has been included in nearly every biographical profile ever written about Bender, including David Pietrusza, Matthew Silverman, and Michael Gershman, editors, *Baseball: The Biographic Encyclopedia* (Total Sports, 2000), 80. Mack made the statement often in his later years.

2   Melissa L. Meyer, *The White Earth Tragedy: Ethnicity and Dispossession at a Minnesota Anishinaabe Reservation, 1889-1920* (Lincoln: University of Nebraska Press, 1994).

3   Tom Swift, *Chief Bender's Burden* (Lincoln: University of Nebraska Press, 2008).

4   There is no one agreed-upon inventor of the slider. One source among several sources consulted on this topic was *The Neyer/James Guide to Pitchers: An Historical Compendium of Pitching, Pitchers, and Pitches* by Rob Neyer and Bill James (Fireside, 2004). E-mail correspondences with Bill James were also useful.

5   "Big Chief Bender," *Baseball,* Vol. 7, August 1911: 64.

6   Billy Evans, "Chief Bender Discusses Pitchers and Pitching; Control greatest Asset," *Atlanta Constitution,* December 28, 1913: 5. There is no one agreed-upon inventor of the slider. One source among several sources consulted on this topic was *The Neyer/James Guide to Pitchers: An Historical Compendium of Pitching, Pitchers, and Pitches* by Rob Neyer and Bill James (Fireside, 2004). E-mail correspondences with Bill James were also useful.

7   Grantland Rice wrote about Bender in several columns during and after Bender's major-league career, including a column that appeared in the September 2, 1915 *Boston Daily Globe.*

8   Regarding Bender's alcohol use, Connie Mack discussed problems he had with Bender and a teammate in the March 6, 1950 *New York Times.* Bender's drinking habits in the 1912 season were discussed most prominently in the *Philadelphia North American's* coverage that year, from September 12 on. Other useful information was found in an article under the headline "The Fallen Stars of the 1912 Season" in the September 21, 1912 *Philadelphia Evening Telegraph.* One of Bender's contracts, according to his salary history card at the National Baseball Hall of Fame (thanks to Gabriel Schechter for providing a copy), stated that he must "[refrain] from intoxicating liquors."

9   Francis C. Richter, "Philadelphia News," *Sporting Life,* August 5, 1905: 25.

10 "Chief Bender Answers Call to Happy Hunting Grounds," *The Sporting News,* June 2, 1954: 32.

JIM BLUEJACKET

By Bill Lamb

The World War I-era right-hander who played under the name Jim Bluejacket possessed key perquisites for pitching success – intimidating size, good stuff, and the ability to change speeds effectively. But he also had to contend with a ruinous shortcoming: the weakness for alcohol that pervaded his career. In the end, intemperance won out, precipitating Bluejacket's departure from the major league scene in what should have been his pitching prime. Notwithstanding that unfulfilled potential, it appears that Bluejacket led a happy and productive life in his later years, particularly while living on the Dutch Antilles island of Aruba. There, Jim worked for Standard Oil of Indiana for 15 years and spent untold hours of his free time imparting baseball instruction to local youth. In appreciation, a street in the capital city Oranjestad was later named in his honor. His life story follows.

Jim Bluejacket was born William Lincoln Smith[1] in Adair, Indian Territory (now Oklahoma) on July 8, 1887.[2] He was the second of five children born to William F. Smith (born 1852), a farmer of Irish descent originally from Tennessee, and his wife, the former Lucy Daugherty (b. 1859), a Shawnee Indian born in Kansas.[3] Young William grew up on reservation lands and was educated at the National Cherokee Male Seminary, an academically rigorous tribal school open to members of all tribes. There are various anecdotes, ranging from the improbable to the inane, regarding how he acquired the name Jim Bluejacket. Among other things, it has been published that Smith adopted the name Bluejacket while still at school in order to be accepted at play by Indian youth.[4] Or that the name derived from the Navy uniform (bluejacket) that he wore to a baseball tryout.[5] Or that he took the name Bluejacket early in his pro career because mail addressed to his common surname Smith never reached him as he traveled the country.[6] To the published accounts, the writer would add that Chief Jim Blue Jacket fought alongside Tecumseh at the Battle of the Thames (1813), and that the name Blue Jacket was long revered among the Shawnee, often signifying a tribal chieftain. At this late date, it is unlikely that the origin of the William Lincoln Smith to Jim Bluejacket name change will ever be established with certainty. Suffice it to say that our subject played his baseball career as Bluejacket, not Smith.

Large (eventually 6'2½" and well over 200 lbs.) and athletic, Jim began playing baseball while still in school, but the mists of time handicap inerrant exposition of his early pro years. Contemporary news reports related that upon finishing his four years at tribal school, Bluejacket returned to the reservation and began farming, his father's occupation.[7] In February 1906, the young man who would become Jim Bluejacket enlisted in the United States military. He lasted a mere six weeks, mustered out honorably on eyesight disability grounds.[8] Some sources assert that Bluejacket got his baseball start around 1907 with Bartlesville in the Class-D Oklahoma-Arkansas-Kansas League.[9] Another report has Bluejacket beginning his playing days as a member of a travelling Indian team called the Kickapoos, before settling down to play with a semipro team in Pittsfield, Illinois.[10] In 1909, however, the Jim Bluejacket trail finally becomes traceable. He spent that season pitching for the Keokuk (Iowa) Indians of the Class-D Central Association, going 14-12 in 257 innings for a third-place (80-57) club. The following year, Jim returned to Keokuk,

Jim Bluejacket broke in with the Federal League's Brooklyn Tip-Tops.

but neither the club (67-70) nor Bluejacket (15-17) improved their performance over the previous campaign.

After getting off to a 4-4 start for Keokuk in 1911, Bluejacket was optioned to the Pekin (Illinois) Celestials of the Class-D Illinois-Missouri League. Here, his fortunes improved – both on and off the diamond. Professionally, Jim yielded barely one run per game in going 15-11 for his new club. Personally, he began courting Jennie Piro, the Pekin teenager who would become Mrs. Bluejacket the following year. Still in Pekin for 1912, Jim posted a 19-13 mark before being sold to the Bloomington (Illinois) Bloomers of the Class-B Three-I League in August. Five late-season wins there boosted his combined record to an eye-catching 24-16 in 359 1/3 innings, prompting the Los Angeles Angels of the Class-A Pacific Coast League to draft Bluejacket from the Bloomington roster. It appears, however, that Jim saw no action with the Angels before he was returned to Bloomington in early December.[11] The year concluded with William L. Smith, aka Jim Bluejacket, and Jennie Piro tying the knot in Carthage, Missouri, on December 23, 1912. In time, the birth of sons Fred (1913) and James Louis (1918) completed the family.

Back in a Bloomington uniform for the 1913 season, Bluejacket turned in an excellent 23-13 record that attracted little notice; *Sporting Life,* an assiduous coverer of minor league baseball, did not publish his name even once during the year. Nor did Bluejacket receive attention in the off-season. Even Federal League recruiters in search of the manpower needed to launch the circuit as a major league paid him no heed. That would change in the months to come, but for the time being, Bluejacket remained stuck in Bloomington. With age 27 coming into view, the big right-hander overpowered the Three-I League, combining a newly developed slow ball with his natural speed and good control to great effect. By the time a 12-game winning streak was halted,[12] Bluejacket was under contract to the New York Giants and scheduled to report to manager John McGraw at the close of the Bloomington season on August 27.[13] But shortly thereafter, it was discovered that Bluejacket had jumped his new Giants contract to sign with the Brooklyn Tip-Tops of the Federal League for better salary terms, plus a $1,000 signing bonus.[14] In defense of the signing, Brooklyn owner Robert B. Ward, a principled man who had publicly foresworn the signing of any player under contract to another club, maintained that he possessed documentary proof that "Bluejacket had accepted our terms long before the Giants ever heard of him."[15] Given the priority of this commitment, Ward intended to keep him. Bluejacket would play for Brooklyn.

While both clubs consulted their lawyers, Jim Bluejacket made his major league debut against the Kansas City Packers on August 6, 1914. Unable to resist a matchup of "aborigines," the clubs arranged for Bluejacket to face right-hander George "Chief" Johnson, a Winnebago Indian. Both men pitched well, with a two-run Brooklyn first inning

providing the only scoring in the 2-0 outcome. Over seven innings – the game had been shortened by prearrangement so that the Packers could catch a train – Bluejacket scattered six hits, striking out three while walking only one. Jim pitched well again in his second outing against the St. Louis Terriers, the only concern being a ninth-inning liner back through the box that Bluejacket batted down with his pitching hand. Thereafter hampered by the resultant aching hand, Bluejacket's pitching was not nearly as effective for the remainder of his maiden major-league season. But in the second game of a September 7 doubleheader against the Pittsburgh Stogies, Jim was able to put something else in his repertoire to good use: an exceptional pick-off move. Entering the game in the top of the ninth with enemy runners on base and Brooklyn down a run, Bluejacket immediately picked Steve Yerkes off first, retiring the side. He then adjourned to the bench as his teammates took their last at-bats. A two-run rally later and Jim Bluejacket was in the record books – the first major-league pitcher to receive credit for a victory without having thrown a pitch. In all, Bluejacket made a respectable start, going 4-5, with a 3.76 ERA in 17 games.

Although New York did not pursue threatened litigation, the Bluejacket controversy did not abate in the offseason. In November, various newspapers published reports alleging that Bluejacket had come to regret not honoring his Giants contract and that he was attempting to reconcile with the club.[16] These reports drew a swift and unequivocal denial from the hurler himself. In a letter to sportswriter Henry Lipman published in *Sporting Life,* Bluejacket expressed "disgust with the false stories printed in the newspapers," denied any contact whatever with the Giants, and proclaimed his loyalty to Brooklyn. He believed himself lucky to be on a team owned by men as "honest" and "courteous" as the Ward brothers, with his only regret being that "my work for them was not better."[17] With that settled, the controversy died.

The 1915 season saw the return of Bluejacket to the Tip-Tops, and the first publicized manifestation of the erratic behavior that would stunt his playing career. Expected to be a mainstay in manager Lee Magee's rotation, Bluejacket was put on the sidelines by a leg sprain in an early season start against Buffalo, an injury that Bluejacket blamed on Magee's "insistence that the pitcher change the angle of his delivery."[18] Bluejacket was given time off to allow the leg to heal, but when club management checked in on him, Bluejacket's hotel room had been vacant for days. Neither his wife in Illinois nor the Smith family back in Oklahoma had had contact with the hurler, and he remained AWOL in parts unknown for six weeks.[19] He finally returned to the club on June 15 – and was promptly restored to the pitching-strapped Brooklyn rotation by Magee, just as if he had never been gone.[20] The remainder of the season proceeded uneventfully, as the Tip-Tops finished out a non-contending 70-82 season. Bluejacket's work was about on par. He went

10-11, with a 3.15 ERA, but had been wild, surrendering 75 walks (as compared to only 48 strikeouts) in 162 2/3 innings pitched.

On October 18, 1915, the untimely death of Brooklyn owner Robert B. Ward dealt a catastrophic blow to the financially ailing Federal League. Soon thereafter, the circuit succumbed. These events, in turn, had a derivative effect on Jim Bluejacket's fortunes. In addition to signing Jim to a major league baseball contract, Ward had taken a kindly personal interest in Bluejacket's welfare, supplying the mechanically inclined hurler off-season employment repairing the Tip-Top bakery trucks.[21] Now with his employer/benefactor gone, Jim would have to find work elsewhere. He attempted to mend fences with Giants manager McGraw.[22] But however willing McGraw may have been to take a chance on Bluejacket, stiff-necked club president Harry Hempstead was having none of it. As he had vowed earlier, there would be no "deserters" wearing a Giants uniform.[23] Given the surplus of pitching made available by the Federal League demise, the mediocrity of Bluejacket's 1915 performance, and his growing reputation for unreliability, no other major league clubs offered Jim a contract, either. With Bluejacket thus "left out in the cold," he was obliged to sign with Bloomington, his former minor league employer.[24]

The 1916 season would prove a tumultuous one for Bluejacket. He got off to a fine start, and his record stood at 11-4, with a 2.75 ERA in 132 innings pitched,[25] when the pitching-poor Cincinnati Reds came to Bloomington to scout Bluejacket in early July. Unfortunately, Bluejacket was then on suspension, having just returned from a seven-day "spree" with fellow Bloomington hurler Dan Marion.[26] The Reds signed Bluejacket anyway, conditionally.[27] Without his having pitched in some 20 days, Bluejacket was handed the ball in the second game of a doubleheader against Brooklyn, but was driven from the mound early in a slugfest that the Reds eventually won. Two more ineffective appearances left the Bluejacket log at 0-1, with a 7.71 ERA in three games. He drew his release on July 20. Bluejacket's stint with his second and final major league team had lasted two weeks. In a post-mortem on the Bluejacket tenure with the Reds, *Sporting Life* observed that "Cincinnati had picked up big Jim Bluejacket some days after he had fallen off the water wagon in [Bloomington, … and that] Cincinnati is a tough town to invite any guy with a thirst."[28]

Although he would pitch professionally into the early 1920s, the big leagues career of 29-year-old Jim Bluejacket was now over. In parts of three seasons, he had posted a 14-17 record, with a 3.46 ERA in 236 2/3 innings pitched, striking out 78 while walking 97. Upon his release by the Reds, Bluejacket refused to return to Bloomington. His contract was therefore assigned, again on condition, to the Milwaukee Brewers of the Class-A American Association. After Jim had gone 1-2 in a "brief but stormy trial, the Brewers had no use for the redskin and shipped him back to Bloomington."[29] Bloomington, in turn, promptly

dispatched Bluejacket to the Dallas Giants of the Class-B Texas League, where it was hoped that he would benefit from the supervision of manager Joe Gardner, a tough disciplinarian.[30] Bluejacket pitched well in his no-decision Dallas debut, but was apparently set adrift at season's end by the tail-end (61-84) Texas League club.

In March 1917, Bluejacket sought reinstatement with Bloomington. The Bloomers took him back, if only to sell Bluejacket, again on condition, to the Lincoln Links of the Class-A Western League. Bluejacket was shelled 7-0 by Denver in his Western League debut, and immediately returned to Bloomington. Thereafter, it appears that Bluejacket descended to the Central Association, the bottom-tier minor league where he had gotten his professional start, pitching briefly for the Clinton (Iowa) Pilots.[31] But by mid-May, Jim was back in the Three-I League, on loan from Bloomington to the Alton (Illinois) Blues. He did not stay there long, abandoning Alton within days of his arrival to join the Nebraska Indians, an itinerant semipro nine. Reaction to his departure was adverse, with one local newspaper sneering that Bluejacket's new situation would afford him the liberty to "indulge his inclination for absorbing brewery products."[32] A month later, Bluejacket returned home to Adair to register for the World War I draft under his birth name: William Lincoln Smith. Where, if anywhere, he pitched after that is unknown, as many professional leagues suspended play during the latter half of the 1917 season.

Bluejacket benefited from circumstances as roster-depleted professional baseball leagues struggled to launch a 1918 season. Soon to be 31 years old, with dependents and a prior discharge on disability grounds, Jim was unlikely to be called to military service. And he had major league pitching experience. All in all, he was an attractive prospect for many clubs, his erratic performance in seasons past notwithstanding. On 1918 Opening Day in the American Association, Bluejacket was on the mound for the Columbus Senators. He was released two appearances later, and then latched on back in the Western League, signing with the St. Joseph (Missouri) Saints.[33] This time, he pitched effectively in that circuit, going 6-1 in spot starter/relief duty before the league suspended play on July 7. From there, Jim's baseball engagements grew sporadic. He was briefly a member of the Western League Oklahoma City Indians in 1919. The following year, he pitched for Greybull (Wyoming) in the unrecognized Midwest League. Bluejacket returned to Greybull in 1921, after having had a short stint with the Enid (Oklahoma) Harvesters of the Class-D Western Association.[34] It appears that Jim finished his professional career in 1922, punctuating another year on the mound for Greybull with a three-week posting with the Anaconda Anodes of the Montana Mining League.[35] After that, he pitched some semipro ball in and around Greybull through 1925.[36]

Although the surviving evidence is largely circumstantial, it appears that as Bluejacket's baseball days receded, the positive aspects of his persona came to the fore. Jim had always been intelligent and well spoken, and now he became increasingly more responsible, as well. A skilled welder, he traveled extensively in the employ of Standard Oil of Indiana. About 1929, he and his family relocated to Aruba, where he served as a Standard Oil foreman in the [then] largest oil refinery in the world. A large, amiable man with an outgoing personality, Jim did much to popularize baseball on the island. He spent innumerable hours of his off-work time teaching the game to local youth, and was instrumental in the construction of the Lago Sports Park in Oranjestad.[37] Although it would take decades to flower, the seed for the Aruba baseball talent that began arriving in the major leagues late in the 1980s was planted by Jim Bluejacket.

Upon retiring from Standard Oil in 1944, Bluejacket returned to Greybull, where he was received warmly by those who remembered him from his local playing days of 20 years before.[38] Sadly, within two years, his health began to fail. Suffering from hypertensive heart disease, Jim spent his final days in Pekin, Illinois, his wife's hometown. He died there on March 26, 1947, the immediate cause of death being a gastric hemorrhage suffered a week earlier.[39] Jim Bluejacket was 59. Following a Funeral Mass at St. Joseph's Church in Pekin, he was laid to rest in the parish cemetery. Survivors included his wife Jennie, sons Fred and James, and his brothers Louis Smith and David Smith. Aside from a handsome headstone in St. Joseph's Cemetery (where Jennie, who died in 1987, lies next to him), *Jim Bluejacket Straat* (street) in Oranjestad, Aruba commemorates his memory. Jim Bluejacket also has a living memorial: former pitcher Bill Wilkinson. When the Seattle Mariners reliever made his major league debut on June 13, 1985, he and Jim Bluejacket became the first great grandfather-great grandson duo in major-league history.

SOURCES

Sources for the biographical data presented herein include the Jim Bluejacket file with questionnaire maintained at the Giamatti Research Center, National Baseball Hall of Fame and Museum, Cooperstown, New York: US Census and family data accessed via Ancestry.com; a brief portrait of Bluejacket posted on-line by an unidentified niece; a Jim Bluejacket biographical profile authored by Carole Hill Martin, accessible on-line via http://www.illinoisancestors.org/tazewell/ Biographies-b.htm; and certain of the newspaper articles cited in the endnotes, particularly the Bluejacket obituaries published in the *Pekin* (Illinois) *Times*, March 26, 1947, and *Greybull* (Wyoming) *Standard and Tribune*, April 3, 1947. Unless otherwise specified, stats have been taken from Baseball-Reference.

NOTES

1. Although he appears in the 1900 US Census as William L. Smith, age 13 and living with his family in Adair, Indian Territory, our subject lived his adult life as Jim Bluejacket – except when dealing with officialdom. His 1912 Missouri marriage license application recorded his name as William L. Smith, and he himself filled out his World War I draft registration card as William Lincoln Smith. The oft-published notion that Bluejacket's birth name was James Smith is erroneous.

2. The siblings of William Lincoln Smith/Jim Bluejacket were Hattie June Smith (born 1877), Lola Smith (1882), Louis E. Smith (1886), and David C. Smith (1901).

3. See "Indian Bluejacket Is a Deserter," *Sporting Life*, August 8, 1914: 1. Sources have long been in conflict regarding whether our subject was of partial Cherokee or partial Shawnee blood. But circumstances suggest that his mother Lucy Daugherty Smith was Shawnee, among the so-called Loyal Shawnee expelled from Kansas and accepted into the Cherokee Nation in 1869.

4. According to the (Springfield) *Illinois State Journal*, April 2, 1947: 13.

5. This yarn is memorialized on Bluejacket's *TSN* player contract card.

6. See the Bullpen section of the Baseball-Reference entry for Jim Bluejacket.

7. Per "Pitcher Bluejacket Is Genuine Indian," *Charleston* (South Carolina) *News and Courier*, August 23, 1914: 6; "Jim Bluejacket, Indian Hurler," *Watertown* (New York) *Times*, August 12, 1914: 6.

8. A playing rival claimed that Bluejacket had briefly been in the US Navy. See "Jim Bluejacket Smith of Federals Is Prized 'Nut,' Says Tiger Infielder," *New Orleans Times-Picayune*, March 29, 1915: 10. But the posthumous player questionnaire completed by wife Jennie Bluejacket indicated that Jim had been in the Army. Moreover, the World War I draft registration card filled out by William Lincoln Smith (aka Jim Bluejacket) states that he was a recruit discharged on disability from Jefferson Barracks, a US Army installation near St. Louis.

9. Per "Jim Bluejacket Smith," *New Orleans Times-Picayune*, March 29, 1915: 10. See also, the Bluejacket obituary in *The Sporting News*, April 9, 1947: 18.

10. See "Jim Bluejacket, Bloomer Pitcher, Not an Indian," (Springfield) *Illinois State Register*, April 5, 1914: 21.

11. Per "News Items Gathered from All Quarters," *Sporting Life*, November 30, 1912: 8, and "Farrell Facts," *Sporting Life*, December 7, 1912: 12.

12. Baseball-Reference gives Bluejacket a 17-10 record for Bloomington in 1914, but years later a local newspaper put the Bluejacket record at 20-4. See Fred Young, "Bluejacket Would Stump Today's Hitters – Syfert," *Bloomington* (Illinois) *Pantagraph*, March 26, 1947.

13. As reported in "Giants Get Another Indian," *New Orleans Times-Picayune*, July 25, 1914: 7; "Giants Purchase Bluejacket," *Philadelphia Inquirer*, July 25, 1914: 10; and elsewhere. The terms of the two-year pact covered the 1915 and 1916 seasons at $1,800 per year.

14. Per William J. Granger, "Brooklyn Tip Tops," *Sporting Life*, August 15, 1914: 13; "Tip-Tops Outbid Giants and Sign Jim Bluejacket," *Brooklyn Citizen*, August 4, 1914: 4.

15. Per "'Bluejacket Ours' Insists Brookfeds," *Pawtucket* (Rhode Island) *Times*, August 7, 1914: 14; "Can Have Bluejacket If Claim Is Proved," *Washington Times*, August 7, 1914: 11.

16. See e.g., "Jim Bluejacket Repents Too Late," *New York Times*, November 3, 1914: 12. See also, Harry Dix Cole, "New York Giants," *Sporting Life*, November 14, 1914: 8.

17. Henry Lipman, "Lines from Lipman," *Sporting Life*, November 21, 1914: 7.

18. Robert Peyton Wiggins, *The Federal League of Base Ball Clubs: The History of an Outlaw Major League, 1914-1915* (Jefferson, North Carolina: McFarland, 2009), 234.

19. As reported in Wm. J. Granger, "Brooklyn Budget," *Sporting Life*, May 15, 1915: 13, and "Tip Top Topics," *Sporting Life*, June 12, 1915: 12.

20. Per William T. McCollough, "The Pittsburgh Rebels," *Sporting Life*, June 26, 1915: 7.

21. As reported in "M'Graw Absolutely Off Red-Skin Tribe," *Jackson* (Michigan) *Citizen Press*, April 15, 1916: 11. See also, William J. Granger, "The Brooklyn Tip Tops," *Sporting Life*, November 6, 1915: 3, and "Brooklyn Brief," November 27, 1915: 6.

22 Per "Baseball Briefs," *Springfield* (Massachusetts) *Republican,* February 1, 1916: 10.

23 See again, "Jim Bluejack Repents Too Late," *New York Times,* November 3, 1914: 12.

24 As reported in "Jim Bluejacket Back in League," (Davenport, Iowa) *Times,* March 21, 1916: 11; "Bloomington Signs Pitcher," *Rockford* (Illinois) *Register-Gazette,* March 21, 1916: 2; and elsewhere.

25 Per the *1917 Reach Official American League Guide,* 175. Baseball-Reference has only 1916 batting stats for Bluejacket in Bloomington.

26 See "Close Decisions," *Rockford* (Illinois) *Morning Star,* July 7, 1916: 11. See also, "Suspends Jim Bluejacket," *Elkhart* (Indiana) *Review,* July 7, 1916: 6: Bloomington manager Howard Darringer has suspended Bluejacket for "Disobeying rules," and "Reds Pass Up J. Bluejacket," *Cincinnati Post,* July 7, 1916: 10: "Jim failed to stick to the straight and narrow ... and was under suspension for being out of condition."

27 See "Federals Coming Back," *Baltimore Sun,* July 7, 1916: 8; "Reds Buy Pitcher Bluejacket," *Washington Post,* July 7, 1916: 8.

28 "Frost Bitten Hopes," *Sporting Life,* July 29, 1916: 3.

29 Per "Bluejacket Goes Down," *New Britain* (Connecticut) *Herald,* August 8, 1916: 8, and *Washington* (DC) *Evening Star,* August 8, 1916: 11.

30 As reported in "Sports by Sports," *Watertown Times,* August 15, 1916: 8; "Bluejacket Lands with Joe Gardner at Dallas," *Omaha Bee,* August 13, 1916: 27; and elsewhere.

31 Per "Bluejacket Grasshopper," *Muskegon* (Michigan) *Chronicle,* May 18, 1917: 22.

32 "Close Decisions," *Rockford Morning Star,* May 18, 1917: 9.

33 See "Bluejacket Released, Signs with St. Joseph," *Duluth* (Minnesota) *News-Tribune,* June 16, 1918: 7.

34 For the Enid engagement, see "Jim Bluejacket Is Still Playing Game," *Rockford Register-Gazette,* January 28, 1921: 15, and Larry Dailey, "Cleveland Lines Up Strong Team," *Tulsa* (Oklahoma) *World,* January 11, 1921: 8; for Greybull, see "Midwest League Is All Ready for Season to Open Wednesday," *Denver Post,* April 24, 1921: 12, and Frank Farley, "Greybull to Meet Broncos in First Clash Tomorrow," (Denver) *Rocky Mountain News,* April 26, 1921: 10.

35 Per the *Anaconda* (Montana) *Standard,* September 8, 1922: 8, and September 10, 1922: 1.

36 According to the *Greybull* (Wyoming) *Standard and Tribune,* April 3, 1947.

37 Per an undated 1968 *Pekin* (Illinois) *Times* article incorporated into Carole Hill Martin's profile of Jim Bluejacket.

38 As reflected in a 1944 *Casper* (Wyoming) *Tribune Herald* article attached to the Martin profile of Bluejacket.

39 Per the death certificate contained in the Jim Bluejacket file at the Giamatti Research Center.

EMMETT BOWLES

By Chad Moody

Emmett Bowles' story was once characterized as "the type that leaves the baseball fan choking back salty tears."[1] Indeed, the small-town Oklahoman's first decade in the game was primarily spent toiling in obscurity as a semipro, accentuated by a failed cup of coffee in the major leagues. He even unsuccessfully resorted to written correspondence with Cincinnati Reds President Garry Herrmann in a desperate plea to "get someplace in baseball."[2] But after years of moving from team to team and town to town, the Native American pitcher finally achieved "legendary" status – in a most unlikely desert outpost.[3]

Any understanding of Bowles' background would be incomplete without some discussion of the history of the Potawatomi in Oklahoma. Following a series of treaties signed from the 1820s through '40s, the Potawatomi in the Great Lakes region – whose descendants had "developed close political, economic, and consanguine ties to the French" – were forced to relocate west.[4] Many eventually settled outside Topeka, Kansas, near St. Mary's Mission, a Jesuit-run institution that served tribe members. In the 1870s, the Citizen Potawatomi, a band of the tribe that had

accepted US citizenship and a land allotment process in the prior decade, began relocating at their own expense from Kansas to the Indian Territory (Oklahoma) per stipulations of an 1867 treaty. This chronology closely follows Bowles' own ancestral story.

The Citizen Potawatomi Nation's website reports this of Bowles' maternal grandmother: "Mary Margaret (Mack) McWinnery, a full-blood Potawatomi, was born in 1844 in Michigan. She was orphaned at a young age, and a non-Indian couple named McWinnery adopted her. Mary traveled to Kansas to study at St. Mary's [Mission], where she eventually met [and married] Amable Toupin, a French-Canadian who looked to make a fortune on the early American frontier."[5] Being "among the more affluent Potawatomi families," the couple had the wherewithal to become early settlers in Pottawatomie County, Oklahoma, where one of their children, Adele, eventually wed Michael Bowles, a Southern farmer of English heritage.[6] In the early 1890s, Adele and Michael received a land allotment (which divvied up commonly held reservation lands to individual tribal members) in Wanette, Oklahoma, a cotton-based small community about 60 miles southeast of Oklahoma City.[7] It was there on August 2, 1898, that the two brought Emmett Jerome Bowles into the world. Census information indicates that Bowles was the second youngest of his six known siblings: Lillie, Mary Elizabeth, Martha Louise, Grace, Andrew, and Alberta. An unidentified brother or sister reportedly died as a youngster (as did Lillie). Bowles was only 7 years old when his father passed away, leaving the clan's matriarch to raise the family on her "own income" in Wanette.[8] The rural area traces its formative period to the 1870s, when the noted French Benedictine monk Father Isidore Robot obtained nearby land from the Potawatomi in exchange for building a mission and school for the tribe members. The resulting formation of the Sacred Heart Mission became the "first center of Catholicism" in what was then Indian Territory.[9]

During his youth, Bowles cultivated his diamond skills by running "barefooted over the sandburrs on the vacant lots of Wanette playing ball."[10] After graduating from Wanette Grade School around 1916, he attended Sacred Heart College (later renamed St. Gregory's University) in Shawnee, Oklahoma, for one year. In November 1917 Bowles enlisted in the US Army. Serving overseas in World War I, he was a bugler in the 20th Engineers Regiment. Dubbed the Fighting Foresters, these soldiers "operated

Emmett Bowles pitched in 1925 for the Florence, Colorado club.

in various areas of France's forestlands, managing forest growth, felling and logging timber, and operating sawmills" to produce wood for American forces throughout Europe used for "building roads and railroads, constructing barracks, erecting telephone poles, supporting trenches, and various other building and construction projects."[11] The 20-year-old headed stateside in May 1919 and received his honorable discharge from the service a month later.

Immediately after returning from war, Bowles headed to south central Kansas, where he "pitched winning ball" for the semipro Larned club during the summer of 1919.[12] The right-hander also moonlighted for the Hoisington team, located in an adjacent county.[13] Despite possessing the nickname "Gravy" in his home area, contemporaneous newspaper articles indicate that he was becoming more widely known by the moniker Chief, an epithet that was commonly foisted upon Native Americans back in that day.[14]

The 1920 campaign found Bowles much closer to home in Oklahoma toeing the slab for independent clubs in Asher and Byars; both small towns were neighboring to his birthplace.[15] Census information reported that Bowles worked as a farmer when not hitting the diamond. He lived alone in Eason, another rural community near Wanette.

After two years of laboring in anonymity, Bowles had a watershed season in 1921 – despite still not yet appearing in Organized Baseball. Back in the Sunflower State with his old Larned team, Bowles had "not lost a single contest to a strong club" well into August.[16] The *Hutchinson* (Kansas) *Gazette* offered this scouting report of the hurler: "His broad smile and very peculiar delivery baffles opposing batters."[17] Featuring "perfect control" and a "strike out reputation," Bowles reportedly fanned a remarkable 21 batters in an early August contest against Ellinwood.[18] Particularly in the latter part of the campaign, the "husky" pitcher also loaned his services to the nearby Great Bend club, where his success continued.[19] Less than two weeks after outdueling Ellinwood's former big-league moundsman Claude Hendrix in early September, Bowles again victimized the rival club – this time with a no-hitter.[20] His strong performance did not go unnoticed. Great Bend offered Bowles $50 per game plus a $1,500 year-end bonus to stay on for the 1922 season.[21] Rumors also were circulating that a scout from the Kansas City Blues of the Double-A[22] American Association had been giving the "bright" prospect the "once over."[23] And most significantly, the American League's Chicago White Sox reportedly agreed to give Bowles a future tryout at the behest of Father Edward Cryne, a former collegiate athlete with Windy City roots and important baseball connections who had recently relocated to Larned. "When [Cryne] came West, [White Sox owner Charles] Comiskey, realizing our newly made Kansan's judgment was good, requested Father Cryne to keep his eye open for big league timber," reported the *Kinsley* (Kansas) *Mercury*.[24] Finally ending any further speculation, in November the "sturdy" pitcher with "quite an assortment of stuff" signed with the Little Rock Travelers

of the Class-A Southern Association after piquing the interest of the club's manager, Kid Elberfeld.[25]

The frenzied activity at the end of the prior year continued into the 1922 campaign for Bowles. Reportedly on the spring camp roster in Seguin, Texas, for his promised tryout with the White Sox, the 6-foot, 180-pounder soon developed a sore arm and was farmed out to Little Rock, where the nagging ailment lingered.[26] After getting hammered there in a preseason intrasquad exhibition in which he "was as wild as the proverbial March," Bowles was demoted to the Joplin Miners of the Class-C Western Association.[27] Because this proposed move "didn't meet with his approval," he decided instead to return to his old Great Bend club in the semipro ranks as a player-manager to open the regular season.[28] The musical chairs resumed in mid-May, when Bowles was picked up by the Hutchinson Wheat Shockers of the Class-C Southwestern League. In his first regular-season appearance in Organized Baseball, Bowles "was pounded at a lively clip" by the Independence Producers in suffering an 8-3 complete-game loss.[29] He was promptly released by Hutchinson and returned to Great Bend, where he tossed a no-hitter in recapturing his status as one of the "ranking independent right-handers of the state."[30]

Despite the unevenness of his 1922 season to that point, Bowles was nonetheless summoned to report to the White Sox in August.[31] Waiting until September 12 to finally make an appearance for the middling Chicago club, he was "hit hard" at Comiskey Park by the Cleveland Indians in his big-league debut.[32] After rookie starter Cecil Duff gave up three consecutive hits to start the third inning, Bowles entered the game with one runner aboard and his team down 3-0. Although able to close out the frame, the 24-year-old was touched for two earned runs, two hits, and a walk in his one inning of work. First up to bat for the White Sox in the bottom half of the third, Bowles was replaced by pinch-hitter Augie Swentor, who was also making his premiere in "The Show." Chicago went on to lose the contest 8-2, and Bowles was released shortly thereafter. The hurler described as dark-complexioned with black hair and blue eyes never appeared in another major-league game. (Neither did Swentor.)

Disappointedly returning to his familiar south central Kansas stamping grounds, Bowles capped his year with a modicum of consolation when he took the mound on October 27 for the independent Belpre club in a barnstorming exhibition tilt against Pratt. The Belpre squad that day included major-league star outfielder Bob Meusel, while Pratt featured none other than Silent Bob's Yankee teammate Babe Ruth. In "arguably the most infamous case of barnstormers being penalized," Meusel and Ruth had both been fined and suspended that spring by Commissioner Kenesaw Landis for wrongfully participating in postseason exhibition contests in 1921; this incident led to a loosening of barnstorming restrictions in the summer of 1922.[33] Striking out six Pratt batters – including the Bambino – Bowles "shared the biggest honors of the day" with the slugging Meusel in Belpre's 13-2 victory.[34] Prior to his guest spot with Belpre, Bowles had earlier in the month plied his trade with the Little River and Great Bend semipro teams.

Although reportedly under contract with either the Portland Beavers or the Seattle Indians of the Double-A Pacific Coast League for the 1923 season, Bowles "didn't want to go."[35] Instead, he remained in Kansas playing semipro ball for his old Larned squad. At some point during the year the Wichita Izzies of the Class-A Western League picked up Bowles' contract, but it does not appear that he ever played for the team.

Continuing to call Kansas home in 1924, Bowles "pitched winning ball" after opening the campaign with the Independence Producers of the Class-D Southwestern League.[36] The team ceased operations in early July; shortly thereafter he joined the Topeka Senators of the Class-C Western Association. Despite being awarded the victory in his first start (and appearance) with the team, Bowles was "pounded" and "knocked out of the box" in the high-scoring contest.[37] And after being tagged with two losses while pitching poorly in a handful of outings over the subsequent two-week period, he was quickly released by the Senators. At the end of July, Bowles headed back the Southwestern League upon being picked up by the Eureka Oilers, with whom he finished the hectic season.[38] All told during his time in the Southwestern loop with Independence and Eureka, the 26-year-old tossed 223 innings in 31 games and posted a 15-12 record with a respectable 4.32 RA9 (total runs, both earned and unearned, allowed per nine innings).

In February 1925 Bowles signed with the Denver Bears of the Class-A Western League for a salary of $300 per month. However, with his old Independence and Eureka clubs both believing they held claims to his services, a contract dispute was ignited. "I do not care with whom I play, but I do wish to make sure of a position," Bowles said of the predicament.[39] Denver ultimately prevailed but released the journeyman hurler toward the end of spring training. Back in the mix, Independence (now a member of the Class-C Western Association) quickly added Bowles to its regular-season roster; however, he "failed to make the grade" and was released after only two weeks without appearing in a game.[40] Heading west, Bowles spent the season as the "big ace" of the local semipro club in Florence, Colorado, a town a little over 100 miles south of Denver, where he boasted that he had "as good a curve ball as anybody" that he could throw in a "knothole."[41]

Moving about 30 miles east for the 1926 campaign, Bowles signed on as a slabman for the independent Pueblo Fords.[42] Late that summer, he also moonlighted for the Wyoming-based Green River club in the Denver Post Tournament.[43] Eventually becoming popularly known as the "Little World Series of the West," this prominent competition (sponsored by its namesake newspaper) drew some of the nation's best semipro teams.

After a 1927 season spent with the independent club in Rushville, Nebraska, Bowles returned to Pueblo – and Organized Baseball – in 1928, signing with the Steelworkers, the city's new entry in the Class-A Western League.[44] Upon posting an 0-2 record after pitching abysmally in his only two outings, he was released. Bowles remained in Colorado and spent the balance of the campaign tossing for the Leadville club, with which he competed again in that year's Denver Post Tournament.[45]

After 10 nomadic seasons, Bowles settled down in Madrid, New Mexico, a booming coal-mining company town located between Albuquerque and Santa Fe. There, the "old master" excelled for the semipro Madrid Miners from 1929 to 1938 before finally hanging up his spikes.[46] Although the team was made up primarily of miners from the Albuquerque and Cerrillos Coal Company, some "ringers" employed by the business – including Bowles – were "given special privileges" and not required to work underground.[47] Behind the "stellar" veteran hurler's mound exploits, the Miners – whose historic ballpark is said to be the first in the West to have been equipped with lights – became "one of the most feared teams in the Central New Mexico League" in the 1930s.[48] Consistently drawing "nearly the entire town" of over 3,000 denizens to home games along with "crowds from around the state," the team, with Bowles its "legendary" star, became an "institution" in central New Mexico.[49] And despite their remote desert locale, the widely popular Miners drew barnstorming opponents of note such as the Detroit Colored Giants, the House of David, and the Zulu Cannibal Giants.[50]

With World War II pulling many miners into military service and the country simultaneously beginning to decrease its dependence on coal, the flagging mining industry began to suffer. Madrid began a decline to almost ghost-town status by the mid-1950s. It was at that time that Bowles, who had remained in Madrid as a miner until its near bitter end, relocated to the much more vibrant Albuquerque. There, the adopted New Mexican held memberships in the Catholic Church and the American Legion.[51] Bowles shared his life with Nora (née Kirkham), a homemaker from his hometown whom he had wed in 1921 in a "seemingly sudden event" that "rather surprised" their friends.[52] The union produced three daughters: Wilma Jean, Betty Jo, and Mickie Ann.

On September 3, 1959, Bowles died in Flagstaff, Arizona, where he had been working. Just prior to making a speech at the Flagstaff chapter of Alcoholics Anonymous, the 61-year-old "dropped dead" at the podium of a heart attack.[53] Funeral services were held at St. Therese Catholic Church in Albuquerque, with interment nearby at Mount Calvary Cemetery.[54]

NATIVE AMERICAN MAJOR LEAGUERS

ACKNOWLEDGMENTS

The author wishes to thank Kelly Boyer Sagert for her research assistance.

SOURCES

In addition to the sources listed in the Notes, the author accessed Bowles' file from the library of the National Baseball Hall of Fame and Museum in Cooperstown, New York; Bowles' player contract card from *The Sporting News* collection; Ancestry.com; Baseball-Reference.com; Chronicling America; Fold3.com; GenealogyBank.com; NewspaperArchive.com; Newspapers.com; Paper of Record; Retrosheet.org; and Stathead.com.

NOTES

1   L.M. Sutter, *New Mexico Baseball: Miners, Outlaws, Indians and Isotopes, 1880 to the Present* (Jefferson, North Carolina: McFarland & Company, 2010), 65.

2   Kelly Boyer Sagert, untitled biographical profile from Bowles' file at the library of the National Baseball Hall of Fame and Museum.

3   Sutter, *New Mexico Baseball: Miners, Outlaws, Indians and Isotopes, 1880 to the Present*, 68.

4   Mary B. Davis, *Native America in the Twentieth Century: An Encyclopedia* (New York: Routledge, 2014), 469.

5   "CPN Family Reunion Festival: Honored Families of 2018," Citizen Potawatomi Nation, June 25, 2018, potawatomi.org/blog/2018/06/25/honored-families-of-2018, accessed May 27, 2022.

6   "Moving to Indian Territory," Citizen Potawatomi Nation Cultural Heritage Center, potawatomiheritage.com/history, accessed June 3, 2022.

7   Sagert, untitled biographical profile from Bowles' file at the library of the National Baseball Hall of Fame and Museum.

8   1910 US Federal Census.

9   "Wanette," Oklahoma Historical Society, okhistory.org/publications/enc/entry.php?entry=WA017, accessed May 30, 2022; "Benedictine Beginning: 1875-1891," Archdiocese of Oklahoma City, archokc.org/history/1875-1891, accessed May 30, 2022.

10 Kate R. Snider, "Wanette," Shawnee (Oklahoma) *Morning News*, October 30, 1921: 6.

11 "WWI: The 20th Engineers Regiment ('Fighting Foresters')," US Forest Service Southern Research Station, srs.fs.usda.gov/video/fightingforesters, accessed May 30, 2022; "World War I: 10th and 20th Forestry Engineers," Forest History Society, foresthistory.org/digital-collections/world-war-10th-20th-forestry-engineers, accessed May 30, 2022.

12 "Local Jottings," Larned (Kansas) *Chronoscope*, October 9, 1919: 12.

13 "Beloit Was Too Good," Hoisington (Kansas) *Dispatch*, September 4, 1919: 1.

14 Kate R. Snider, "Wanette," *Shawnee Morning News*, April 7, 1921: 7.

15 Kate R. Snyder, "Asher," *Shawnee Morning News*, June 30, 1920: 5; Kate R. Snyder, "Asher," *Shawnee Morning News*, July 4, 1920: 5.

16 "Larned Will Meet Grain Club Today," Hutchinson (Kansas) *Gazette*, August 14, 1921: 8.

17 "Larned Will Meet Grain Club Today."

18 "Larned, With Indian Pitcher, Coming to Play Grain Club," *Hutchinson Gazette*, August 13, 1921: 2; "Mound Battle Is Certainty," *Hutchinson News*, August 13, 1921: 10.

19 "Chief Bowles May Get League Tryout," *Hutchinson News*, September 20, 1921: 13.

20 "Locals Defeated Ellinwood," Great Bend (Kansas) *Daily Tribune*, September 6, 1921: 6; "A No-Hit Game for Bowles," *Great Bend Daily Tribune*, September 19, 1921: 2.

21 "Big Offer for 'Chief' Bowles," Larned (Kansas) *Tiller and Toiler*, September 15, 1921: Second Section-1.

22 Double A then was the equivalent of today's Triple A.

23 "Chief Bowles May Get League Tryout."

24 "Scouting for Big League," Kinsley (Kansas) *Mercury*, October 20, 1921: 5.

25 "Elberfield Signs an Indian Pitcher," *Arkansas Gazette* (Little Rock), November 20, 1921: 18.

26 "Local Happenings," *Great Bend Daily Tribune*, July 31, 1922: 3.

27 "Tutweiler and Sturdy Join Travelers' Training Camp; Kidlets Trim Streeties," *Arkansas Democrat* (Little Rock), March 14, 1922: 7.

28 "Local Happenings," *Great Bend Daily Tribune*, March 25, 1922: 3; "Bowles to Manage Team," *Great Bend Tribune*, May 8, 1922: 1.

29 "Bowles Is Hit Hard and Loses," *Hutchinson News*, May 19, 1922: 3.

30 "A No-Hit, No-Run Game," *Great Bend Daily Tribune*, June 12, 1922: 3; "Pitchers' Battle Likely Tomorrow," *Hutchinson News*, June 17, 1922: 3.

31 "Local Happenings," *Great Bend Daily Tribune*, July 31, 1922: 3.

32 "Cleveland Takes 8 to 2 Game from White Sox," Wilmington (North Carolina) *Morning Star*, September 13, 1922: 5.

33 Bill Francis, "At Home on the Road," National Baseball Hall of Fame and Museum, baseballhall.org/discover-more/history/barnstorming-tours, accessed June 16, 2022.

34 "Local Happenings," *Great Bend Daily Tribune*, October 28, 1922: 3.

35 "'Rusty' Pitched Two-Hit Game," *Ness County News* (Ness City, Kansas), May 5, 1923: 1; "Chief Bowles Reports to Wichita," *Larned Tiller and Toiler*, September 20, 1923: 2.

36 "The Fanning Bee Hive," *Hutchinson News*, July 14, 1924: 3.

37 "The Fanning Bee Hive."

38 "Eureka Hires New Pitchers," Emporia (Kansas) *Daily Gazette*, July 30, 1924: 8.

39 "Fight Over Contract," *Wichita Daily Eagle*, February 14, 1925: 3.

40 "Same Old Faces and Many New Ones in Western Association This Year," Ardmore (Oklahoma) *Daily Press*, April 16, 1925: 2; "The Fanning Bee Hive."

41 "Florence, Colorado, Enters Post's Tenth Annual Baseball Tournament," *Denver Post*, July 28, 1925: 17; Sagert, untitled biographical profile from Bowles' file at the library of the National Baseball Hall of Fame and Museum.

42 Leo Hoban, "North Denver Merchants Down Knights of Columbus, 10-8, in Elitch League," *Denver Post*, May 10, 1926: 15.

43 C.L. Parsons, "Cheyenne and Woodmen Win Wednesday Afternoon Games in Post Tourney," *Denver Post*, September 2, 1926: 22.

44 "Bats Will Swing at Hemingford," Alliance (Nebraska) *Times and Herald*, April 26, 1927: 1.

45 "Leadville Wins From Rifle, 6-5," *Denver Post*, July 17, 1928: 18; "Boulder and Texon Post Tourney Winners," *Denver Post*, August 5, 1928: Section 5-3.

46 "Bowles Yields But 5 Hits to Local Ball Club," *Albuquerque Journal*, August 11, 1930: 2.

47 Levi Weaver, "Miner Leagues: Discovering a Hidden Baseball Treasure in Madrid, New Mexico," The Athletic, January 15, 2019, theathletic.com/756090/2019/01/15/miner-leagues-discovering-a-hidden-baseball-treasure-in-madrid-new-mexico, accessed June 19, 2022; Laurie Evans

Frantz, *The Turquoise Trail* (Charleston, South Carolina: Arcadia Publishing, 2013), 59.

48   Sutter, *New Mexico Baseball: Miners, Outlaws, Indians and Isotopes, 1880 to the Present*, 68; William M. Simons, *The Cooperstown Symposium on Baseball and American Culture, 2005-2006* (Jefferson, North Carolina: McFarland & Company, 2007), 135.

49   Weaver, "Miner Leagues: Discovering a Hidden Baseball Treasure in Madrid, New Mexico"; Sutter, *New Mexico Baseball: Miners, Outlaws, Indians and Isotopes, 1880 to the Present*, 68.

50   Simons, *The Cooperstown Symposium on Baseball and American Culture, 2005-2006*, 140-141.

51   "Emmett J. Bowles Dies in Arizona," *Albuquerque Tribune*, September 4, 1959: A-2.

52   Kate R. Snider, "Wanette," *Shawnee Morning News*, April 29, 1921: 6.

53   "Albuquerque Man Dies at Meeting," *Arizona Daily Sun* (Flagstaff), September 4, 1959: 10.

54   "Bowles Rites Set," *Albuquerque Tribune*, September 7, 1959: B-1.

LOU BRUCE

By Rory Costello

Full-blooded Mohawk Louis Bruce was one of the earlier Native Americans to reach the majors. He got into 30 games with the Philadelphia Athletics in 1904, during a pro career that ran from 1900 to 1907. He was small (5'5" and 145 pounds) but hit for good averages in the minors while playing numerous positions. He was also a good little pitcher, though he made just two relief appearances for Philadelphia. His teammate with the A's, the great Ojibwa pitcher Chief Bender, had looked up to him when both were at the Lincoln Institute for Indians some years before.[1]

Bruce was a serious and intelligent man. His baseball career helped finance his education; before joining the A's, he graduated from the University of Pennsylvania School of Dentistry. Bruce went on to obtain another degree in theology from Syracuse University and became a Methodist minister. He served 11 different churches (including tribal congregations) in central and upstate New York over a 38-year period.

In addition, Bruce sought to help indigenous peoples in secular life. He was an active proponent of the Indian Citizenship Act of 1924, which granted Indians suffrage. His son, Louis Rooks Bruce, carried on this tradition as an organizer of the National Congress of American Indians (founded in 1944) and U.S. Commissioner of Indian Affairs from 1969 to 1972.

Louis Bruce was born in St. Regis, New York, on January 16, 1877.[2] This is part of the St. Regis Mohawk Reservation in Franklin County. It is way upstate, lying on the St. Lawrence River across from Cornwall, Ontario. Some sources show Bruce as being born in the neighboring village of Hogansburg, New York. Hogansburg is the location of the Akwesasne Cultural Center. ("Akwesasne" is the Mohawks' name for their nation.)

Bruce's parents were John Bruce and Christine Benedict. Further detail on siblings is scanty, though the 1887 census of the St. Regis Mohawk Reservation shows John Bruce as the head of a household of seven. John was a Mohawk chief, although his basic occupation was farming. Louis eventually inherited the family property and later passed it on to his son. One of John Bruce's most remarkable accomplishments, however, was fighting on behalf of the British crown in Africa in the mid-1880s. He was part of a contingent of about 60 Mohawks in the expedition that attempted to rescue General Charles Gordon when he was besieged in Khartoum, Sudan. Bruce served as a boatman, won two medals, and was taken on visits to Asia and Australia.[3]

At the age of seven, Louis Bruce went to live and study at the Lincoln Institute in Philadelphia, which was founded in 1866.[4] According to his grandson, Don Bruce, "Grampa was one of the few Indians who wasn't taken away to school – he wanted to go. He always wanted to further himself in life." In addition to his studies and athletic pursuits, at Lincoln Louis met a girl named Noresta Rooks, who was born in Nebraska to a mixed-blood Sioux mother and a Caucasian father from Missouri.[5] Their friendship later blossomed into marriage in 1904.[6]

Bruce went from Lincoln to Philadelphia's Central High School, "where he excelled as a student and as an athlete before graduating with an A.B. degree in 1899."[7] According to a 1903 article in *Sporting Life*, he "played with Westchester, Atlantic City, and Morristown, semi-amateur teams. He started out as an outfielder, and began pitching in 1899 for Morristown." He was discovered by Ed Barrow, who later attained fame as manager of the Boston Red Sox

Lou Bruce played six positions with the 1904 Philadelphia Athletics.

and then as business manager of the New York Yankees.[8] Barrow became manager of the Toronto Maple Leafs in the Eastern League in 1900, and Bruce was one of his first signings.[9]

As Barrow biographer Daniel Levitt wrote, "Players like Bruce who could both pitch and play the field offered important versatility when competing for minimal roster spots."[10] For the Maple Leafs in 1900, the Mohawk batted .275 in 60 games, while going 6-5 on the mound. Bruce spent time in Toronto during the winter, and as *Sporting Life* wrote, "made many friends by his quiet behavior." The news snippet quoted him as saying, "This is the way I am."[11]

In 1901, Bruce lifted his average to .322 in 101 games. Baseball-reference.com shows no records for him as a pitcher that season; a May account in *Sporting Life* showed that Ed Barrow had focused him on left field, though there was "talk of putting Bruce on the rubber again."[12] Indeed, he did pitch at least once that year, a complete-game 4-2 win on May 28.[13] In the fall of 1901, Bruce began attending dental school at Penn. By that time, his family was living on Cornwall Island, Ontario, on the St. Lawrence River, very close to his birthplace.

Bruce excelled with Toronto in 1902, in particular as a pitcher. He was 18-2 in his 20 appearances for the Eastern League champions, allowing just 38 runs and pitching five shutouts.[14] As *Sporting Life* wrote that June, "the Toronto Indian is pitching a wonderful article of ball for Ed Barrow. Bruce is one of the most valuable men in the league, all positions appearing the same to him."[15] He batted .313 in 88 games overall, as his season did not begin until May 15 owing to his school commitment.[16]

Sporting Life reported in October 1902 that the Cincinnati Reds invited Bruce to spring training for 1903.[17] No further news on this topic surfaced in the paper, though, and he continued to do it all for the Maple Leafs that year, batting .356 in 100 games and going 12-4 as a pitcher. According to the *Toronto Mail*, "Not even the redoubtable Jimmy Casey, in the heyday of his popularity in Toronto, was ever as warm a favorite as Louis Bruce, the clever twirler and utility man of the Toronto Club. Bruce is a natural ball player. While small in stature, he has tremendous strength and stamina, and unquestioned ability. His remarkable pitching since he played with the Toronto Club has created a sensation. He is also one of the leading batsmen of the Eastern League, and probably without a peer as an emergency hitter."[18]

That year, Arthur Irwin – the Toronto native and former big-leaguer who succeeded Ed Barrow as manager of the Leafs – hung a $5,000 price tag on Bruce.[19] That reportedly scared away some clubs, but not the Philadelphia Athletics. Connie Mack purchased Bruce's rights that September, later turning over pitcher Connie McGeehan (who was 1-0 in his only three big-league appearances for the A's in 1903) as partial consideration.[20]

Bruce married Noresta Rooks, also known as Nellie, on February 20, 1904. Shortly thereafter, he finished dental school. He was vice president of his class in his senior year, captain of the class baseball team, and manager of the class football team in 1903.

Bruce did not report to the A's until after they finished their "western" swing – St. Louis, Chicago, Cleveland, and Detroit – on June 18.[21] He made his debut on June 22 and appeared in 30 games altogether for Connie Mack, batting .267 in 112 plate appearances with no homers and 8 RBIs. He had three extra-base hits, all doubles, out of his 27 safeties. Of his two pitching appearances, one was a strong effort in long relief on July 6. On the road in New York, he allowed one run on three hits in six innings after the Highlanders took an early 6-0 lead (the final was 7-1). In the other, on July 21 at Philadelphia, he entered in the fifth inning as Cleveland led 8-1. This time he was hit hard, giving up six runs (five earned) in five innings. As a result, his final ERA in the majors was 4.91.

In late July, *Sporting Life* wrote, "Bruce is available as a pinch hitter and all around substitute, but apparently not quite the real thing, either as outfielder or as a pitcher."[22] On August 16, the *Hartford Courant* added, "Connie Mack does not think as much of Bruce as he did in the spring. He has sent the little bronze-faced pitcher to the Toronto club for more experience."[23] Philadelphia loaned Bruce to Toronto, which badly wanted him back. He got into 16 games for the Maple Leafs (.171, 4-3 as pitcher) and rejoined the A's in mid-September. His final game in the majors came on the season's last day, October 10.

Right around then, *Sporting Life* reiterated, "Manager Mack seems to have little confidence in the Indian, either as fielder or pitcher."[24] Nonetheless, Bruce was with the A's at their 1905 spring training camp in Shreveport, Louisiana. He was apparently suffering from a sore arm.[25] He bounced back, however; as the *Chicago Tribune* wrote on April 9, "Bruce, the Indian pitcher, has done remarkably well in the practice and Manager Mack probably will use him in some of the big games before the close of [the exhibition season]."[26]

On May 6, however, *Sporting Life* reported, "Louis Bruce has been disposed of by the Athletic Club to the [Indianapolis] Hoosiers. . .The lad's hitting was not up to Manager Mack's requirements."[27] The manager in Indianapolis was old friend Ed Barrow. Bruce got into 132 games that year in the American Association, batting .252 and posting a 1-2 record on the mound. His career trailed off after that, as he played just 30 games for Columbus (also in the AA) in 1906. He turned down a deal to become manager-captain of Newark that June, as he hoped to return to Toronto.[28]

Bruce's last professional action came with the Binghamton Bingoes of the New York State League (Class B) in 1907. Statistics are lacking, but that August, *Sporting Life* wrote, "Lou Bruce, of whom great things were expected, proved a positive failure."[29]

Bruce then returned to family life. He and Nellie welcomed their other child, a daughter also named Noresta, in 1908. Son Louis had arrived near the end of 1906. "By 1910, Bruce had finished his degree in theology, gave up his job as a mechanic in a typewriter company and began his Methodist ministry on the Onondaga Indian Reservation."[30] He also established a dental practice in Syracuse at that time.

Bruce believed strongly in the value of education. In 1918, he issued the following statement with regard to his people:

"The reservation blocks the progress of the Indian. Present conditions make it impossible to succeed there. I do not think I would ever return to make it my home again. We Indians must think of the future. We have a duty to perform which our ancestors shirked when they sold all the ancient lands. They did not think of us who were to come after them. They gave up their broad domains for a mess of pottage. They thought only of themselves, but we are thinking of our children and we must provide for them, and strive that they obtain an education which will fit them for the struggle of life in competition to-day."[31]

Bruce, a "stern but loving" father, instilled this value in his son. He sent young Louis to Cazenovia Seminary, a Methodist school in Cazenovia, New York, where the lad was the only Indian student.[32] Bruce was also strongly against drinking alcohol, the scourge of so many Indian nations.[33]

"The great battle of [Bruce's] life was for Indian citizenship and he campaigned on all the New York reservations."[34] In 1921, *The Southern Workman* identified him as "among the noteworthy leaders of the citizenship movement."[35] There was a serious debate among the six Iroquois Nations on this topic, though. In May 1919, the New York Indian Welfare Society met to confer on "their present and future needs. . .The temporary chairman was Jesse Lyon, the courier of the Six Nations. Mr Lyon is a stalwart exponent of the old regime and is bitterly opposed to citizenship, preferring the citizenship of his tribe to that of the United States." Even so, at that meeting Bruce was elected an officer of the society.[36]

One wonders what Bruce would have thought of developments in the Mohawk nation in more recent years: casinos, tax-free cigarette and gasoline sales, and outbreaks of violence on the St. Regis Reservation. It's probably safe to conclude that his beliefs in religion and citizenship would have led him to deplore all these things.

Bruce retired from his ministry in 1949. Six years before, his wife Nellie had died. The widower survived her for a quarter-century; among other things, he instructed his grandson when Don played baseball as a youth. He died at the age of 91 on February 9, 1968, at his daughter's home in Ilion, New York. Although his big-league career was brief and took place over a hundred years ago, Louis Bruce's conduct off the field remains his enduring accomplishment. As a 1922 Methodist publication observed, "he was said by Connie Mack to be 'one of the best influences he ever had on the team.'"[37]

With thanks to Don Bruce for memories of his grandfather.

SOURCES

In addition to the sources cited in the Notes, the author also consulted www.ancestry.com, www.baseball-reference.com, www.retrosheet.org, and 1904 University of Pennsylvania Yearbook (http://dla.library.upenn.edu/dla/archives/image.html?id=ARCHIVES_20051102003&)

Richardson, Jane. *Chief of the Chiefs* (biography of Bruce's son, Louis Rooks Bruce). (Colorado Springs, Colorado: Thistle Publishing, 2008). Abstracts from this book are available at the author's website: http://www.janerichardson.com/chiefofthechiefs/default.asp.

NOTES

1   Tom Swift, *Chief Bender's Burden* (Lincoln: University of Nebraska Press, 2008), 23.

2   Baseball references list Bruce as having the middle initial R., but according to grandson Don Bruce, there was no middle name.

3   Carl Benn, *Mohawks on the Nile* (Toronto, Ontario: Natural Heritage Books, 2009). Marion Eleanor Gridley, *Contemporary American Indian Leaders* (New York: Dodd, Mead, 1972).

4   Marion Eleanor Gridley, *Indians of Today* (Chicago, Illinois: Indian Council Fire, 1960), 35.

5   *Descendants of John Rooks*, online family tree (http://familytreemaker.genealogy.com/users/c/o/f/Harold-E-Coffman/GENE4-0004.html). Supported by various other genealogies.

6   "Pitcher Bruce Married," *Sporting Life*, February 27, 1904: 5.

7   "Louis R. Bruce (1877-1968)." Biographical sketch in the University of Pennsylvania online archives. In 1849, an Act of Assembly gave Central High the power to confer academic degrees in the arts upon its graduates – a distinction that was rare, perhaps unique, among American high schools. https://archives.upenn.edu/exhibits/penn-people/biography/louis-r-bruce/

8   "The Athletics' New Pitcher," *Sporting Life*, October 17, 1903: 10.

9   Daniel R. Levitt, *Ed Barrow* (Lincoln: University of Nebraska Press, 2008), 38.

10   Levitt, 44.

11   "Toronto Tips," *Sporting Life*, March 2, 1901: 8.

12   Frank Miley, "Toronto topics," *Sporting Life*, May 11, 1901: 15.

13   *Sporting Life*, June 8, 1901: 8.

14   *Sporting Life*, October 4, 1902: 12.

15   "News and Gossip," *Sporting Life*, June 28, 1902: 13.

16   "Toronto Topics," *Sporting Life*, April 12, 1902: 12.

17   "National News." *Sporting Life*, October 11, 1902: 7.

18   "The Athletics' New Pitcher."

19   Ren Mulford Jr., "Balldom's Capital," *Sporting Life*, September 5, 1903: 9.

20   F.C. Richter, "Local Jottings," *Sporting Life*, November 14, 1903: 5.

21   Francis C. Richter, "Quakers' Quiver," *Sporting Life*, June 4, 1904: 5.

22   Francis C. Richter, "Quaker Quips." *Sporting Life*, July 30, 1904: 2.

23   "Baseball Notes," *Hartford Courant*, August 16, 1904.

24   "Quakers Quail," *Sporting Life*, October 8, 1904: 1.

25 Francis C. Richter, "Philadelphia Points," *Sporting Life*, March 18, 1905: 3.

26 "Pennant Races Begin This Week," *Chicago Tribune*, April 9, 1905: A1.

27 Francis C. Richter, "Philadelphia Points," *Sporting Life*, May 6, 1905: 18.

28 "Ohio-Pennsylvania League," *Sporting Life*, June 16, 1906: 8.

29 "Binghamton Briefs," *Sporting Life*, August 17, 1907: 15.

30 Denise A. Raymo, "Major presence." *Plattsburgh* (New York) *Press-Republican*, September 4, 2011.

31 Arthur Caswell Parker, *A Prehistoric Iroquoian Site on the Reed Farm, Richmond Mills, Ontario* (Rochester, New York: The New York State Archeological Association, Morgan Chapter, 1918), 93.

32 Gridley, *Contemporary American Indian Leaders*, 41.

33 C. Richard King, editor, *Native Americans in Sports, Volume 1 (A-L)* (Armonk, New York: M.E. Sharpe, Inc: 2003), 63.

34 Gridley, *Contemporary American Indian Leaders*, 41.

35 Arthur C. Parker, "The New York Indians," *The Southern Workman*, Volume 50, 1921: 159.

36 *New York State Museum Bulletin* (Albany: University of the State of New York, November-December 1919), 16.

37 *Woman's Home Missions*, October 1922: 12.

DYLAN BUNDY

By Bill Nowlin

Dylan Matthew Bundy was a right-handed pitcher with eight years of major-league experience and with 54 wins to his credit. He is Cherokee, born to Lori and Denver Bundy on November 15, 1992, in Tulsa, Oklahoma. Lori Bundy worked as a plumber and pipefitter for the Ford Motor Co. and later at Home Depot in Owasso, Oklahoma. When Lori met Denver Bundy, he was a mechanic and also ran a gym. The two later both worked together at the Ford Motor Company's auto glass plant in Tulsa, she as a plumber and pipefitter, then later at Home Depot in Owasso.[1] Denver Bundy also coached high-school baseball in Owasso.

Dylan's older brother, Bobby Bundy (b. January 13, 1990), was also a pitcher and had been an eighth-round draft pick of the Baltimore Orioles in the June 2008 draft.[2] The boys grew up under the tutelage of their father, and when Dylan was only 8 years old, he "helped his father and brother build a mound and a batting cage in the backyard."[3]

Mother Lori was often the one who urged the boys on. Dylan recalled, "Huge baseball fan. Huge. Dad would be gone on a hunting trip or something, and I'd be like 14 or 15 years old and I'd have to play long toss. Well, Mom would get a glove and say, 'Let's go. You've got work to do.'"[4]

A graduate of Owasso High School in the Tulsa suburb of Sperry, Dylan was selected as *Baseball America*'s 2011 High School Player of the Year.[5] It was no wonder: it was reported that he struck out 158 batters in 71 innings while allowing just five walks and two earned runs. He won all 11 of his starts and also earned a save.[6] His four-year pitching record was 44-3. He recorded 595 strikeouts and had an earned-run average of 0.20. He reportedly clocked 100-mph pitches on radar guns.[7]

Scouted by Ernie Jacobs, Bundy was selected by the Baltimore Orioles in the first round of the June 2011 draft, the fourth overall pick, and was signed to a five-year contract set to begin the following year for $6.25 million.[8] Orioles scouting director Joe Jordan said, "This kid looked me right in the eye and said, 'Joe, I want to be drafted by the Orioles and I want to pitch in a major league rotation with my brother.'"[9]

He cited both his father and brother Bobby as key supporters. "Me, my dad and brother, we've prepared our whole lives for this whole year, everything. It's finally coming to reality that I was picked by the Orioles, the same team my brother is on. It's pretty amazing I get the opportunity to be on the same team as my brother. We'll see what happens here in August."[10]

Bobby had excelled himself, winning the 2008 Small School Tulsa World Player of the Year Award and being named Gatorade Oklahoma Player of the Year. Bobby – then a minor leaguer in the Orioles organization – said, "Having me as an older brother, he's got goals and things to look forward to and up to. I'm really proud of Dylan. He's worked his butt off to become a better player. He does things the right way." Dylan said, "Bobby has always been my inspiration. He taught me how to work hard. He's someone I have always looked up to and will forever. … I kept track of his accomplishments in high school and it gives me something to shoot for in my career."[11]

Hard work was nothing new to Dylan Bundy. A profile in *Sports Illustrated* said, "As a young teenager Bundy flipped truck tires, threw 75-pound sandbags over his shoulder, pushed wheelbarrows full of dirt around the family's 15-acre plot in northeast Oklahoma, dug four-foot holes and refilled them purely for the exercise."[12]

(courtesy of Keith Allison Photo)

Dylan Bundy

Dylan Bundy is listed as 6-feet-1, weighing 225 pounds. He started his professional career in the 2012 season – with the Single-A Delmarva Shorebirds (1-0 in eight starts, throwing 30 innings and striking out 40 batters without yielding an earned run), the Class A+ Frederick Keys (he was 6-3 in 12 starts with a 2.84 ERA and 66 strikeouts in 57 innings), and then in in August with the Double-A Bowie Baysox (2-0, with a 3.24 ERA). Bobby Bundy was with the Baysox as well in 2012, but less successfully. (Starting 17 games, he was 2-11 with a 6.25 ERA.) Bobby's final game with the Baysox that season was on July 8; Dylan's debut with the team was on August 14. Dylan was called up to the Orioles in mid-September.

On September 23, 2012, Dylan Bundy had his major-league debut, working the final two-thirds of an inning in a 2-1 Orioles loss to the Red Sox at Fenway Park in Boston. With a runner on second base and one out, he induced outfield flies from the only two batters he faced. Two days later, at Oriole Park at Camden Yards, he worked the top of the ninth inning in a game the visiting Toronto Blue Jays were winning, 4-0. He walked the first batter, gave up a single, then got a fly ball and a double play.

Bundy didn't return to the majors until 2016. He was held back by injuries in 2013, and underwent Tommy John surgery on June 27. Bobby himself had surgery for bone chips in 2012 and his own Tommy John surgery in 2013 within three months of Dylan's.[13]

In the 2014 season, the two brothers again both wore the same uniform for a while – that of the Aberdeen IronBirds (low Class A) – but not at the same time. They each worked in three games, Dylan in the second half of June and Bobby in the second half of August.

For 2015, the Orioles were content to bide their time and wait in hopes that Dylan would "dominate in the minors again."[14]

Bobby Bundy was 1-0 in eight games for the Baysox in 2015. Dylan Bundy likewise appeared in eight games (in his case, all starts) for Bowie, but was 0-3 and required medical treatment in July for calcification in his shoulder.[15] This time they enjoyed being teammates for a while. They had both pitched in the same spring-training game on March 12, against the St. Louis Cardinals in Jupiter, Florida.[16] With the Baysox, Bobby's first game was on April 9; Dylan's was four days later, on April 13. They were both on the team into May, even appearing three times in the same game: April 24 and 29 and May 5. In the April 24 game, Akron batters jumped on starter Dylan Bundy early and scored two runs. He worked three innings. Bobby Bundy pitched two scoreless innings at the end.[17] Against Erie on April 29, Dylan Bundy "pitched his allotted three innings" and "threw three perfect frames," striking out five.[18] He was just getting some work in, rather than put too much stress on his shoulder.[19] On May 5, Dylan started and worked the first inning before rain delayed the game. When play resumed, Bobby took the mound and worked 3⅓ innings of scoreless relief.[20] Later

in the month, Dylan was shut down with shoulder stiffness due to the calcium deposits, and Bobby suffered a tear to his ACL.[21] Bobby Bundy played for Bowie again in 2016 and 2017.

It was in 2016 that Dylan Bundy finally made it back to the majors, able to work. He was on the Opening Day roster for the Orioles and he earned a hold in both of his first two appearances, on April 7 and 12. His first 22 appearances were all in relief and he had a cumulative 3.08 earned-run average, with a record of 2-1. His first win had been on May 27, when he worked in a tie game in Cleveland and his teammates came through with three runs in the top of the seventh and gave the Orioles a lead, which held.

Manager Buck Showalter gave Bundy his first start on July 17. Though he lost that one, 5-2, he won the next start and finished the 2016 season with a record of 10-6 (4.02 ERA). He had worked a total of 109⅔ innings and struck out 104 batters.

Working exclusively as a starter in 2017, Bundy pitched in 28 games and compiled a record of 13-9 (4.24) for the last-place Orioles. He added another 152 strikeouts to his total, in 169⅔ innings. The gem of his season was a one-hit shutout on August 29 against visiting Seattle, the one hit a fourth-inning bunt by Kyle Seager.

The 2018 Orioles finished the year 47-115. Bundy's 5.45 ERA represented a lack of success, but his eight wins led the team. (He was 8-16 for the season.) Though he struck out 184 batters (with a career-high 14 on May 25 against the Chicago White Sox), he also surrendered a majors-worst 41 home runs. The 16 losses also led both leagues.[22]

Bundy's 2019 was similar – with the Orioles in last place again. Bundy was 7-14 (4.79). Strikeouts dropped in number to 162, and homers allowed to 29.

In December 2019 he was traded to the Los Angeles Angels for four minor-league players.[23]

The year 2020 was abbreviated due to the COVID-19 pandemic. The team played 60 games and Bundy started 11 of them, leading the staff in wins with a record of 6-3 and a distinctly improved ERA of 3.29. He struck out 72 in 65⅔ innings. On August 6 he threw a complete-game 6-1 win in Seattle.

Bundy's 2021 season went upside-down, with a 6.06 ERA and a record of 2-9. He became a free agent after the season and was signed by the Minnesota Twins to a one-year, $5 million deal, for what became his last season in the majors. The Twins finished third in the AL Central Division, and Bundy's record was of a middling nature as well – 8-8 (4.89). Only Joe Ryan had more wins for the Twins that year. Sonny Gray (8-5) matched Bundy.

Late in March 2023, Bundy signed as a free agent with the New York Mets, but was assigned to Triple-A Syracuse, where he was 0-2 in six games, with a 10.08 ERA, and was released in July. His career as a pitcher was over.

All in all, he had won 54 major-league games with a career ERA of 4.74 and had struck out 852 opponents. He had worked 910 2/3 innings and – except in 2016 almost always playing for teams with losing records – had borne 65 losses.[24]

Bundy was a switch-hitter and, despite working exclusively in the American League, he nonetheless accumulated 14 plate appearances. He singled twice. On June 23, 2018, he led off the fifth inning in Atlanta with a single and scored what was the fifth run in a 7-5 win over the Atlanta Braves. On May 31, 2021, he singled in the second inning. All told, he was 2-for-14 with nine strikeouts, one run scored, and no runs batted in.

He had married Caitlin Smith in November 2020. She had seven years of experience as a lieutenant with the Owasso Fire Department. They may have bonded a bit through art. Both took a painting class and – along with hunting – it proved to be a diversion that helped provide Bundy some relaxation.[25]

In early 2024, Dylan Bundy left professional baseball to work as a real estate agent with the Ary Land Co. in Broken Arrow, Oklahoma. The couple has welcomed a first child into the family.

He remained active in baseball, though, and in early 2025 was a clinic instructor – with his brother, Bobby – at the Sperry (Oklahoma) Baseball Academy.

SOURCES

Thanks to Jake Bell, Anne Keene, Bob Lemoine, and Rod Nelson.

NOTES

1   Mike Brown, "Bundy Family Mourns Death of Wife, Mother Lori," *Tulsa World*, December 9, 2013: 1. See also Don Connolly, "'Life's Experiences Always Shape You, and That One Was Pretty Devastating': How Dylan Bundy's World Exploded, and How He Pushed Through," *The Athletic*, September 12, 2018. https://www.nytimes.com/athletic/512816/2018/09/12/lifes-experiences-always-shape-you-and-that-one-was-pretty-devastating-how-dylan-bundys-world-exploded-and-how-he-pushed-through/.

2   The Orioles gave him a $4 million signing bonus. John McNamara, "Baysox, Bundy Taking It Slow for Now," *Bowie* (Maryland) *Blade-News*, April 9, 2015: A6.

3   Tom Verducci, "The Bundy Project," *Sports Illustrated*, July 30, 2012.

4   Connolly.

5   Nathan Rode, "Dylan Bundy's Stats, Stuff Turns Heads," *Baseball America*. June 27, 2011. https://www.baseballamerica.com/stories/dylan-bundys-stats-stuff-turns-heads/. Accessed August 10, 2025.

6   The article by Rode provides effusive quotes from Bundy's coach, Larry Turner, and teammates. A *Tulsa World* article credited him with an 11-1 record (1.58 ERA) with 164 strikeouts in 79⅔ innings. Lynn Jacobsen, "Brotherly competition," *Tulsa World*, June 10, 2010: B6. Jacobsen wrote that Dylan also ranked second on the team in batting average (.442). The Associated Press's David Ginsburg had him batting .467 with 11 home runs and 57 RBIs, and agreed with Rode's reported statistics for pitching. David

Ginsburg, "Baltimore Takes Pitcher Bundy with Fourth Pick," *Delaware State News*, June 7, 2011: 15.

7   Dylan played shortstop and reportedly drew interest from the Tampa Bay Rays as such, but the Orioles had a higher pick in the 2001 draft and selected him as a pitcher. Bill Haisten, "Bundy's Standout Career Ends," *Tulsa World*, May 15, 2011: B9.

8   Ronald Blum (Associated Press), "Top Pick Gerrit Cole and Pirates Agree to Deal," *Poplar Bluff* (Missouri) *Daily American Republic*, August 16, 2011: 2B.

9   David Ginsburg (Associated Press), "Bundy Joins Brother's Organization," *Oklahoman* (Oklahoma City), June 8, 2011: 7C.

10 Rode, "Dylan Bundy's Stats, Stuff Turns Heads." Bobby Bundy (born January 13, 1990, also in Tulsa) was a right-hander selected in the eighth round of the June 2008 draft. He was 11-5 in Class A+ ball with the Frederick Keys during the 2011 season. He worked nine seasons in the minor leagues, primarily in Double A, in the Baltimore system, through the 2017 season.

11 Jacobsen, "Brotherly Competition." Bobby won the Gatorade Player of the Year Award in 2008 and 2009, both times with the state champion Sperry High School team, and Dylan won it in 2010 at Owasso High School.

12 Verducci noted that Bundy "swore off hamburgers" and maintained a disciplined diet. For three summers starting at age 15, he left home alone to pitch for a team in Texas. Denver Bundy said, "I've been criticized for working the boys that hard. I wasn't hard because I was doing every bit of it too. I never broke 'em or anything. Most of the time they were laughing."

13 Jon Meoli, "Orioles' Family Affair," *Baltimore Sun*, August 6, 2016: 1. See also Mike Brown, "Bundy Family Mourns Death of Wife, Mother Lori."

14 Dan Connolly, "Roster Has Share of Questions," *Annapolis* (Maryland) *Sunday Capital*, February 15, 2015: C4.

15 Jeff Todd, "Dylan Bundy Shut Down Indefinitely," MLBtraderumors.com, June 29, 2015. https://www.mlbtraderumors.com/2015/06/dylan-bundy-shut-down-indefinitely.html.

16 "Spring Special; Bundy Brothers Pitch in Same Game for Orioles," *Tulsa World*, March 14, 2015: B11. Both worked in relief, Dylan first – allowing one run while retiring six of the eight batters he faced. Another Orioles pitcher appeared in between the brothers but Bobby worked in the seventh and retired two batters on a total of four pitches. Dylan was apparently in the clubhouse and did not see Bobby pitch but said it was "definitely special" that they had both pitched in the same game and requested that the box score be framed and sent to their father.

17 "Baysox Win Streak Halted," *Annapolis Capital*, April 25, 2015: B12.

18 "Bundy Perfect in Baysox Sweep," *Annapolis Capital*, April 30, 1990: B7. Neither article noted the unusual situation of the pitchers being brothers.

19 Don Connolly, *Baltimore Sun*, "Dylan Bundy Could Get to Majors This Year," *Carroll County Times* (Westminster, Maryland), May 21, 2015: B2.

20 Barry Lewis, "Dodgers Official Has '60s Connection to Tulsa," *Tulsa World*, May 10, 2015: 27.

21 Meoli, "Orioles' Family Affair."

22 James Shields of the Chicago White Sox also had 16 losses.

23 Subsequently, both Kyle Bradish and Isaac Mattson made it to the majors.

24 During 2012, when he worked in his first two games, the Orioles had a winning record.

25 Jon Meoli, "Birds' Bundy – Painting More Than Corners," *Annapolis Capital*, March 27, 2016: 2C.

WILLIAM CADREAU, AKA CHIEF CHOUNEAU

By Stew Thornley

A pitcher for one game in the major leagues, appearing under the name Chief Chouneau, William "Nitchie" Cadreau was a member of the Fond du Lac Band, Lake Superior Ojibwe in northeastern Minnesota.

Cadreau grew up on the Fond du Lac Reservation, to the west of Cloquet, Minnesota, approximately 20 miles west-southwest of Duluth. The reservation was established in 1854 by a treaty between the Lake Superior Chippewa and the United States government.

Baseball records show Cadreau's birth date as September 2, 1889 in Cloquet, Minnesota. His death certificate lists his birth date as September 2, 1888, and his birthplace as Knife Falls Township, which is now part of Cloquet. The death certificate identifies his parents as Antoine Cadreau and

William Cadreau's 1913 Zee-Nut baseball card

Louise Nahgahub. Cadreau was a descendent (probably the grandson) of Chief Joseph Naganub (Sits Ahead), one of the last of the Ojibwe chiefs in that territory. Sits Ahead had become the foremost spokesman for the Lake Superior bands of Ojibwe, representing his people in numerous treaty negotiations in Washington, D. C. The negotiations included the 1866 Treaty of Bois Forte that ceded the iron lands, which encompassed the Vermilion and Mesabi ranges in northeastern Minnesota, to the United States.

Beyond his ancestry, little is known about Cadreau's life on Fond du Lac Reservation. Some information comes from two men with the Fond du Lac Tribal and Community Center—LeRoy DeFoe, the band's cultural resources specialist, and Russ DuFault, its multi-media assistant. Neither had a great deal of first-hand knowledge of Cadreau although they were able to provide insights into the setting of Cadreau's youth. In addition, DuFault had been in the hospital at the same time as Cadreau, shortly before the latter's death.

DuFault was 11 years old in 1946 when he was in the old government hospital, also known as the old Indian hospital, on the reservation and recalled "Nitchie" as being "well known in the hospital. During the time that I remember, the nurses used to come in the morning and ask him [Cadreau] how he was doing. He always said the same thing: 'I'm in the pink.' I just took it that he was feeling good. I didn't pay a lot of attention to what was going on [with Cadreau] because I spent a lot of time outside."[1]

Asked about Cadreau's appearance and health, DuFault said, "As far as I remember he didn't really make any kind of commotion about anything I could remember. He was just there, laying *[sic]* in bed like the other guys who were in there." DuFault never talked to Cadreau directly but was aware of him. As far as Cadreau's baseball career, DuFault said, "I heard that he did play, but I really wasn't in to the subject very far."

DeFoe recalled that there had been a lot of Indian baseball teams on the reservation. Near the Holy Family Cemeteries, where Cadreau is buried, is a small baseball diamond that DeFoe says has been used for baseball for 50 to 80 years and that Cadreau probably had pitched on that diamond. "That generation there seemed like there was a lot of them, good baseball players from up here," said DeFoe.[2]

Besides baseball, log rolling was a major activity on the reservation during Cadreau's time. "You gotta understand this river [St. Louis River] here," DeFoe said. "At one time it was the White Pine capital of the world. That river used to be full of logs all the way up almost to Brookston, which is about 10 miles straight up north from here. That whole area was full of log jams, and a lot of these Indian people used to work for the lumber companies as, what do they call those guys who used to fix those log jams, tear them apart."

"You could go down there and meet guys running all over out there with picks and running on the logs, sending them up the chutes on conveyors that would go up into the mills," DuFault added. "A matter of fact, there are still pools of dead heads in the river right now with the ends sticking up. You have to kind of watch when you go up there so you don't run into them with boats. They used to have special guys—dead-head picking skulls, I guess they called them. They'd tow them up the river so far by power boat, and they'd leave them up there and then guys would migrate down the river again, picking up dead heads. Then they'd bring them over, let them dry out, cut them up. That had a saw mill up there by the double islands just north of town."

Skilled at working on the logs, the Indians had log-rolling competitions. DeFoe said, "My great-grandfather—his name was Joe Medweiosh—we used to live up by near the church. Right behind his house, it was kind of like a swamp, but he went out and dug himself a practice pool so he could practice his log rolling."

Much about Cadreau's life remains a mystery, including his full baseball career and how he came about the name Chouneau ("Chief," of course, was usually attached to Native American players in the early part of the twentieth century).

Marc Okkonen, a member of the Society for American Baseball Research who researches players who had brief major-league careers, says he found a player named Chouteau (a possible misspelling of Chouneau) with two Michigan teams—Grand Rapids in 1911 and Muskogee in 1916. Okkonen adds, "After originally looking for Chouneau on the reserve lists I went back and found him under Cadreau for Vancouver (Class-B Northwestern League) in October 1913 and under Spokane (Class B-Northwestern League) in October 1912."[3] He also says that Cadreau played for the famed Cherokee travel team of Kingsville, Ontario, but he doesn't know which years.

Cadreau's obituary, in the September 20, 1946 *Cloquet Pine Knot,* says that he "made an outstanding name for himself as a member of organized baseball at Vancouver, Spokane, and Portland and finally as the property of the Chicago White Sox baseball team. About 1910, Cadreau sought an opportunity to play with the Cloquet baseball team. The local manager felt that he did not have the necessary qualifications as a pitcher. That year he left Cloquet for the Iron Range [probably the Mesabi Iron Range, about 50 miles north of Cloquet], played there a short time, moved into North Dakota, pitched at Minot, N. D., then moved on to Ashland, Wis., where he made such an outstanding showing that he was brought into Chicago by the Chicago

American league baseball team. He pitched one of the closing games against Detroit and seemed to have assured himself a place in the Chicago team. The next year he disappeared and later turned up in the Western Canada league."[4]

Regarding his one appearance in the major leagues, an item in the *Cloquet Pine Knot* of October 8, 1910, noted, "Will Cadreau, former pitcher of the Ashland baseball team now wears the uniform of the Chicago White Sox. Cadreau left Ashland last Monday for Chicago, accompanied by J. B. Carlin, who acted as agent for Charles Comiskey, owner of the White Sox. Cadreau has without doubt one of the best records as a strikeout pitcher in the northwest. In the last three games he pitched for Ashland he struck out nearly 50 men, and in one game struck out 17 and walked no one. This is the game that attracted the attention of the big leaguers, and he was accordingly signed."[5]

Cadreau's lone game came on Sunday, October 9, 1910, as he started for the White Sox against the visiting Detroit Tigers, the final game of the season for both teams. Listed as Chouneau in all the newspapers of the following day, the right-hander held the Tigers scoreless through the first five innings. "Chief Bill looked the part of a promising pitcher, after he has acquired the beef and experience necessary to enable him to go the route," wrote I. E. Sanborn in the *Chicago Daily Tribune.* "For five innings he had speed and curves enough to stall off the past champions successfully, allowing them only three hits in that time. Once a three base hit put a Tiger on third base with nobody out and the little chief did not appear to mind that any more than nothing at all, minus six. He disposed of the next three batsman without letting in the runs. His control was perfect and he never was in the hole to the batsman."[6]

However, another three-base hit, by Sam Crawford, led to a rally that put Detroit into the lead and knocked Cadreau out of the game. With Chicago holding a 1-0 lead in the top of the sixth, Crawford tripled off Cadreau and scored on a single by Jay Kirke. Tom Jones followed with a single, and George Mullin doubled to score Kirke. Manager Hugh Duffy then called for Frank Lange to relieve Cadreau. Cadreau was charged with the loss as the Tigers won the game, 2-1. Cadreau did not walk a batter and struck out one. (Ty Cobb did not play for Detroit, having already left the team. In Cleveland, Napoleon Lajoie recorded eight hits in a doubleheader against St. Louis to apparently take the league's batting-average title from Cobb. However, the batting race of 1910 remains shrouded in controversy because of how Lajoie got his hits—seven were bunts—and later record-keeping errors that were discovered.)

In addition to the information cited by Marc Okkonen above, researcher Gary Ashwill has found Cadreau back in Ashland, Wisconsin, and also playing for independent and minor-league teams in Michigan, Minnesota, North Dakota, and Montana. "In the spring of 1917," writes Ashwill, "this veteran of outsider baseball took an extremely unusual career move, even for him. He joined a black baseball team."

In 1917, Cadreau pitched for the Chicago Union Giants, an all-Black baseball team. Cadreau was gone from the Union Giants within two months, but, according to Ashwill, "Cadreau was the only non-Latin between Fleet Walker and Jackie Robinson to play for both a major league team and an all-black team."[7]

Cadreau's grave marker notes military service as a private during World War I. Cadreau died September 17, 1946 (although in some baseball record books, Cadreau's death date has been listed as September 17, 1948. His death certificate lists his occupation as laborer, his marital status as divorced (with Eliza Neveaux Couture as his wife), and his cause of death as "Cirrhosis of the liver due to tertiary syphilis."

SOURCES

In addition to the sources cited in the Notes, the author consulted:

"A Famous Chief," *The Mail and Empire* (Toronto), October 17, 1895.

An Annotated Listing of Ojibwa Chiefs, 1690-1890, compiled by John A. Ilko (Troy, New York: Whitson Publishing Company, 1995).

Mark Diedrich, *Ojibway Chiefs: Portraits of Anishinaabe Leadership* (Rochester, Minnesota: Coyote Books, 1999).

NOTES

1   Interview with Russell DuFault, Multi-Media Assistant, Fond du Lac Reservation, Fond du Lac Band, Lake Superior Chippewa, June 13, 2002. Other quotations attributed to DuFault come from this interview.

2   Interview with LeRoy DeFoe, Cultural Resources Specialist, Fond du Lac Reservation, Fond du Lac Band, Lake Superior Chippewa, June 13, 2002. Other quotations attributed to DeFoe come from this interview.

3   E-mail correspondence with Marc Okkonen, May 10, 2002.

4   "'Nitchie' Cadreau, Pitcher, Dies," *Cloquet Pine Knot,* Friday September 20, 1946.

5   "Cadreau Making Good: Indian from Local Reservation Joins the Chicago White Sox as Pitcher. Will Have Try-out Tomorrow," *Cloquet Pine Knot,* Saturday, October 8, 1910: 1.

6   I. E. Sanborn, "Final Act of Sox Story of Defeat: Redskin in Spotlight," *Chicago Daily Tribune,* October 10, 1910: 21.

7   Gary Ashwill, "Between Blackball and the Major Leagues: The Unusual Baseball Resume of Bill Cadreau, aka 'Chief Chouneau,'" *Outsider Baseball Bulletin* (https://outsiderbaseball.com/), Vol. 1, Issue 19 (October 13, 2010): 2, 5-7.

JOBA CHAMBERLAIN

By Alan Raylesberg

The lasting image of Joba Chamberlain is that of him swatting midges away from his face on an unseasonably warm night in Cleveland in Game Two of the 2007 American League Division Series. Chamberlain had an electric start to his career and was so tremendous as a New York Yankees rookie that the team instituted the "Joba Rules" to try to maintain his effectiveness for the long haul. While Chamberlain pitched 10 seasons in the majors, his career was plagued by injuries, and he never recaptured the magic of his rookie season, when he excited the city of New York with his dominant fastball and a dramatic life story that took him from a tough childhood in Nebraska to pitching in the postseason at the age of 21.

Justin Louis "Joba" Chamberlain was born on September 23, 1985, in Lincoln, Nebraska. He was born Justin Louis Heath and ultimately took the surname of his father, Harlan Chamberlain. Joba's parents were never married and split up when Joba was an infant.[1] His father raised him and his sister as a single parent. Born on the Winnebago Indian Reservation,[2] Harlan was stricken with polio as an infant and became permanently disabled as a result. When he was 9 months old, Harlan had to leave the reservation to live in a children's hospital. He was there for over six years before growing up in a series of foster homes.[3] Despite needing a motorized scooter to move around, Harlan worked full time at a state penitentiary for 27 years while also working a second job as the manager of a local bar. He also managed to go to college and earn a degree in social work.[4] After retiring, Harlan worked as a substitute teacher and as a ticket taker at Nebraska Cornhuskers' football games.[5]

Chamberlain got his nickname when a 2-year-old cousin, whose brother's name was Joshua, was unable to pronounce it correctly, pronouncing Joshua as Joba. Harlan liked the nickname and began calling his son by that name. The name stuck and Justin eventually changed his name legally to Joba.[6]

Although Joba, his sister, and Harlan did not live in a "palatial house," they "always had what [they] needed and

Joba Chamberlain pitching for Trenton in the New York Yankees organization.

there was always love in [the] house."[7] As Joba recalled, "All we had was each other. And we never took that lightly. It's not just father and son. We were best friends."[8] It was Harlan who instilled in Joba a love of baseball. Father and son would play catch in their front yard, even though Harlan did not have use of his left arm. "He'd throw it left, right, short, long," Joba recalled.[9] Joba wasn't raised on the reservation "but he was raised knowing what his culture was and being proud of that," Harlan recalled in 2007, adding that Joba "identifies and can function on the reservation."[10]

Chamberlain graduated from Lincoln Northeast High School, where he starred on the baseball team. He did not make the team until his junior year and was not in the starting rotation until his senior year.[11] He then earned second team "Super State" honors, going 2-2 with a 3.35 ERA with 29 strikeouts in 31⅓ innings.[12]

After graduating from high school, and without a college scholarship, Chamberlain worked as a maintenance employee for the Parks Department in Lincoln. He played American Legion ball and the University of Nebraska-Kearney offered him a scholarship.[13] As a freshman he pitched and led the team in various categories before transferring to the University of Nebraska-Lincoln for his sophomore year. In Lincoln, Chamberlain was a member of the 2005 Cornhuskers team that went to the College World Series. His performance was "one of the most dominant pitching years in school history" and he was named the 2005 Big 12 Newcomer Pitcher of the Year, the first team All-Big 12, and a third-team All-American by *Collegiate Baseball*.[14] In 2006 he was named a first-team Preseason All-American by *Collegiate Baseball* and second-team Preseason All-American by the National College Baseball Writers' Association as he pitched to a 6-5 record in 14 starts with a 3.93 ERA and a team-leading 102 strikeouts in 89⅓ innings.[15]

Chamberlain was selected by the Yankees as a supplemental pick in the first round (41st overall) of the June 2006 amateur player draft.[16] He was the second-highest drafted Native American in baseball history.[17] He received a $1,150,000 bonus to sign with the Yankees and debuted, in 2006, with the West Oahu Cane Fires in the Hawaiian Winter League, where he had an ERA of 2.63 and ranked second in the league in strikeouts with 46 in 37⅔ innings.

Before the 2007 season, *Baseball America* ranked Chamberlain as the fourth-best prospect in the Yankees organization and 75th of all major-league prospects.[18] His first full season in professional baseball began in 2007 with the Tampa Yankees in the Class-A Florida State League. After excelling there (4-0, 2.03 ERA), he was promoted to Trenton in the Double-A Eastern League, where he continued to excel (4-2, 3.35) and was named to the United States team for the 2007 All-Star Futures game. Later that year, Chamberlain was promoted again, to Triple-A Scranton/Wilkes-Barre (1-0, 0.00), where he continued to dominate

with a fastball that *Baseball America* ranked as the best in the Yankees farm system.

Although Chamberlain projected as a major-league starting pitcher, his meteoric rise through the Yankees organization in his first professional season resulted in the Yankees moving him to the Scranton/Wilkes-Barre bullpen in anticipation of a possible call-up to the big-league club. With the Yankees in the thick of a pennant race, the team did indeed bring Chamberlain up to the majors, in August.[19] He was 21 years old. On August 7 Chamberlain made his debut, in Toronto, against the Blue Jays. Pitching in relief, he pitched two scoreless innings, striking out two. He quickly became a fan favorite as the result of his youth, his meteoric rise through the system and an electric fastball. When he pitched, "he rocked [old Yankee Stadium] like few pitchers ever had."[20] His father, disabled and in his motorized scooter, often attended his games and was frequently shown in the stands during local telecasts of the games. All of this added to the growing legend for the young right-hander.

Mindful of his youth and limited professional experience, the Yankees placed certain highly publicized restrictions on how often Chamberlain would be allowed to pitch. In what became known as the "Joba Rules," Chamberlain was not allowed to pitch on consecutive days and was to be given an additional day of rest for each inning pitched when he did appear in a game.[21]

As a dominant reliever, Chamberlain was an important part of the Yankees' 2007 pennant chase. In 19 regular season games, Chamberlain allowed only 12 hits and one earned run in 24 innings for an ERA of 0.38 while striking out 34 batters. The Yankees were 17-2 in games in which he pitched, as he held opponents to a .145 batting average. His performance was nothing short of phenomenal.[22] The future as well as the present looked bright, and the fans were eating it up.

Adding to the excitement surrounding Chamberlain was the feel-good story about father and son. When the Yankees traveled to Kansas City in September 2007, Harlan was able to make the trip from Nebraska and was in the stands to watch his son pitch in the major leagues. It was an emotional night for father and son, as tears streamed down Harlan's face. Harlan told the *New York Times,* "I'm just as proud as I can be for him to be a part of such a storied organization. … The thing that touches me the most, when he's in the dugout, to think he can be with Jeter and Cano and all these people. This is where Babe Ruth played and Joe DiMaggio. I grew up on Mantle and Maris. My son is a part of that."[23]

Chamberlain had an opportunity to write his own chapter in Yankees history in the 2007 postseason. But the chapter had a bad ending. In Game Two of the ALDS in Cleveland, with the Yankees trailing in the series one game to none, Chamberlain was called upon for the biggest appearance of his young career. He was on the mound in the bottom of the eighth inning with the Yankees clinging to a

1-0 lead.[24] And that's when the midges came out. The tiny flies were everywhere, including on his arms and neck, and Chamberlain was clearly bothered by them. The Yankees trainers sprayed him repeatedly with insect repellant, but the midges would not be stopped. Plainly bothered by the disruption, Chamberlain walked two batters, hit another, and threw two wild pitches, allowing the tying run to score. Despite not allowing a hit in the inning, Chamberlain had blown the save and the lead. The Indians went on to win the game 2-1 in 12 innings and to defeat the Yankees in four games.[25]

Looking back on that game years later, longtime Yankees broadcaster John Sterling recalled it vividly, telling the *New York Post* that "Joe [Torre] should have pulled his team off the field. They would never have touched Chamberlain. The Yankees would have won that game."[26] Torre had a similar thought, telling the *Post* in 2017, "I second guessed myself for not pulling the team off the field. … I knew [Joba] couldn't see. … Little did we know that the stuff Gino [Yankee trainer Gene Monahan] was spraying on Joba's face was like chateaubriand for those bugs."[27]

When the 2008 season started, the excitement around Chamberlain continued. The Yankees announced he would begin the season in the bullpen and that the Joba Rules would no longer apply. Chamberlain started off well, not allowing a run in his first four relief appearances. On April 13 his father collapsed at home and was hospitalized. Chamberlain was placed on the bereavement list and left the team for a week to be with him. When he arrived at the hospital, his father's first thoughts were about how much time Chamberlain was going to miss from the team. "Before he could talk he asked the doctor how long it was going to take and he pointed at me," Joba said.[28] The relationship between father and son continued to captivate the New York fans as well as his teammates. When he returned to the team on April 19, he was hugged on the field by many of his teammates, with the *New York Post* noting that "many Yankees treat [Chamberlain] like a kid brother."[29]

Upon his return, Chamberlain picked up right where he left off, pitching another scoreless inning in relief in his first game back. His effective pitching continued through the end of May. In 20 relief appearances, Chamberlain had a 1-2 record and a 2.28 ERA. Enthralled by his electric stuff and in need of a starter, the Yankees transitioned Chamberlain to a new role. He made his first major-league start against Toronto on June 3 and walked four before being replaced in the third inning. He pitched well after that, including throwing seven shutout innings against the Red Sox on July 25 in a game the Yankees won 1-0. In 11 starts through July 30, Chamberlain was 3-1 and he had lowered his ERA for the season to 2.24.

Chamberlain's 12th start, on August 4, was when the bubble began to burst. Pitching against Texas, he injured his shoulder and was placed on the 15-day disabled list with rotator-cuff tendinitis. Despite the Joba Rules and the care

the Yankees took with him in his first full season, the worst had happened as Chamberlain sustained an arm injury at the age of 22. While he pitched five more seasons with the Yankees (through 2013) before ending his career in 2016 after short stints with Detroit, Kansas City, and Cleveland, Chamberlain never duplicated the effectiveness of his debut season or his first full season in 2008.[30]

The saga of Joba Chamberlain took another negative hit during the 2008 offseason when he was arrested back home in Lincoln for driving under the influence. Writing in the *New York Times*, the week after his arrest and concerned what the charges meant for Chamberlain's career and life, columnist Harvey Araton noted that "few athletes [took] a city the way Joba Chamberlain stormed New York in the late summer of 2007… a one- time phenomenon, the fantasy of a B-movie screenwriter with his broad shoulders, immediate swagger and pugnacious face that might have landed him the role of a young Babe Ruth."[31] Chamberlain was sentenced to probation in April 2009. The sentencing judge told him in words that would prove prophetic: "You probably worked long and hard to get where you are today. … It takes about 10 seconds to wipe that all out."[32]

In the Yankees' World Series championship season of 2009, an apparently healthy Chamberlain was mediocre as a full-time starter, pitching 157⅓ innings (31 starts) with a 4.75 ERA. When the postseason came around, the Yankees did not need Chamberlain to start and returned him to the bullpen. He made 10 appearances in the postseason, pitching 6⅓ innings, allowing only two runs. He made three

(Aspenphotos / Dreamstime)

Joba Chamberlain.

one-inning appearances in the World Series against the Phillies, and was the winning pitcher in Game Four. The Yankees won the Series in six games and Chamberlain received a much-deserved World Series ring.[33]

Believing that his ability to throw at maximum velocity for short stints was better suited for the bullpen, the Yankees made Chamberlain a reliever again in 2010. He was not able to duplicate the phenomenal start he had to his career. And the injuries began to multiply. Midway through the 2011 season, he injured his elbow, leading to Tommy John surgery. Before the 2012 season began, he seriously injured his ankle in the offseason when jumping on a trampoline with his young son. Recovering from both the elbow surgery and the ankle injury, Chamberlain did not return to the mound until August 2012. The injuries continued to mount as he was hit in the elbow by a broken bat in Game Four of the 2012 ALDS,[34] followed by a stint on the DL in early 2013 with an oblique strain. The 2013 season was his last with the Yankees and he became a free agent, signing with the Tigers. In 2014 Chamberlain pitched 63 innings for Detroit, all in relief, with a 3.57 ERA. He pitched briefly in 2015 for Detroit and two other teams before his major-league career came to an end during the 2016 season.[35]

Joba Chamberlain burst on the baseball scene in 2007 like a bolt of lightning. Despite the Yankees' efforts to protect his arm, the excitement of 2007 was not repeated in his career. Chamberlain always kept perspective about his career, remembering how his disabled father never complained and, by example, taught him "not to feel sorry for myself."[36] Looking back in 2012, Chamberlain appreciated how few ballplayers make it to the major leagues, adding: "You come up and make a splash like [I did,] that's what everybody's going to remember, but that's also the standard you're going to be held to. I've had my ups and downs, my good, my bad and my awful. Now I just try to get better every day, just stay balanced, respect the game, but most of all respect myself."[37] As his Yankees career was coming to an end in 2013, Chamberlain reflected in the same positive way: "Your time in this league is so short, but I'll always be Joba the person and Joba the dad. This game has taught me a lot; it's taught me patience and taught me to keep everything in perspective. … [A]t the end of the day you have to be accountable to yourself and your son and be an example to him."[38]

Chamberlain's son, Karter, was born out of wedlock when Joba was a junior in college. Given the relationship Joba had with his own father, he wanted to be as good a father to his son as his dad had been to him. In 2014, after joining the Tigers, Chamberlain spoke with MLB reporter Jason Buck about what it was like to be a dad. "You don't really realize it or understand it until you become a father yourself," Chamberlain said. "I didn't really like all the things that [my father] did when I was that age. Looking back, he was always just looking out for the best and making

sure that I did everything that I could to be the person that he wanted me to be."[39]

Chamberlain found his father intimidating, partly from the fact that he worked in a prison for so long. His father's "tough love" taught Joba how to do things the right way and made him appreciate what his father meant in his life. Despite his disability and his stressful job at the prison, Harlan always had time for his son and taught him not to make excuses. As Joba said about his father, "He drives, he walks. He just does it with crutches and a scooter. … It's just different. That's just the way he did it. I learned to do a lot of things with one hand, because that was the only way he knew how to teach me: Tie a tie one-handed, break an egg one-handed. I still can't do a button one-handed. It still takes me forever. Your parents teach you ways that they know. For my father, that was the only way he knew."[40] As Buck wrote, "It's also helped make Joba Chamberlain who he is. He's trying to do the same for his son."[41]

After retiring from baseball, Chamberlain was involved in various business ventures, including ownership of bars and restaurants.[42] In 2018 he opened a bar, aptly named Chamberlain's, in his hometown of Lincoln.[43] The restaurant closed, and Chamberlain reportedly had financial problems. In 2020 he left an expensive house he had purchased in Lincoln and had some of his baseball memorabilia sold at auction.[44]

From the time he retired, Chamberlain has been, and still was, as of December 2024, extensively involved with social and other media. He has appeared on television as a baseball analyst, including appearances on the MLB Network and MLB.com.[45] He does multiple podcasts, is frequently interviewed online and has a YouTube channel known as "Joba and the Mouth," which he co-hosts.[46] As of 2025, Chamberlain maintained a very active presence on Twitter (now X) where he had more than 118,000 followers. He was listed with the All American Speakers Bureau and available as a keynote speaker and industry expert on sports.[47]

In November 2024 Chamberlain was inducted into the Nebraska Baseball Hall of Fame. He acknowledged that it was an "honor and a privilege" to be inducted and he was especially proud "to share this [honor]with my son and my dad, those are the two that have built me into this game, and I'm just so grateful for that."[48]

The main focus of Chamberlain's post-baseball life remained his son, Karter. His X page is titled "The official twitter of pitcher Joba Chamberlain and very proud father of my main man Karter." Shortly after his retirement, in 2017, Chamberlain spoke about his son in a conversation with the *New York Post*. At the time, Karter was 11 and Chamberlain remarked that "it's time to be a dad" and spoke about how he now had time to watch his son play baseball, including in a tournament in Cooperstown.[49]

Fast-forward five years to 2022, and Karter was a high-school sophomore, playing the first of his three seasons of varsity baseball. Playing shortstop and pitcher for Lincoln

Southwest High School, Karter played on Sherman Field, the same field that his father had played on years earlier. The memories came flooding back on a Friday night in April, when Joba and his father, Harlan, sat in the stands to watch their son and grandson. "It was kind of a moment where I was taken back as a father, because my dad was watching his grandson and I was watching my son like he did with me," Chamberlain said that night. "It was one of those moments where you just kind of stop and be thankful that as a family we've gotten to share some pretty cool moments on this field. Hopefully, Karter will give us many more of those."[50] After graduating from high school in 2024, Karter in December 2024 was a freshman at Hutchinson Community College in Hutchinson, Kansas, where he was a member of the baseball team as a right-handed pitcher, just like his dad.

Summing up Chamberlain's star-crossed career, sports columnist Mike Lupica wrote in the *New York Daily News*, "Before there was Jeremy Lin and Tim Tebow, there was … a kid with a colorful name and backstory and fastball" who made Yankee Stadium "go mad with excitement." "Joba came at us with a rush with that name and Native American in him and … [his] father in a wheelchair, and even though it wasn't all a happy story … it really was like some colorful character out of the past, as if [he] had walked out of some old baseball novel before he walked through those doors in the outfield." The story started to unravel that night in Cleveland and things were never the same. Yet, as Lupica wrote, in 2012, "Even now, you can see Harlan Chamberlain, those pictures of him at the old Stadium watching his son pitch for the Yankees, the dad in his Yankees warmup jacket."[51]

SOURCES

In addition to the sources cited in the Notes, the author relied on Baseball-Reference.com and *Baseball America*. The author thanks the National Baseball Hall of Fame Library for supplying some of the sources, as referenced in those instances where the source material may not otherwise be readily available.

NOTES

1   His mother, Jackie Standley, began abusing drugs when Chamberlain was a child, and they are largely estranged.   Museum of Nebraska Major League Baseball, http://www.nebraskabaseballmuseum.com/spotlight3. html#:~:text=Now%20retired%20from%20his%20job,living%20on%20 American%20Indian%20reservations.

2   The Winnebago Reservation is in Thurston County, Nebraska, in the northeast corner of the state about 90 miles from Omaha.

3   Kevin Kernan, "Joba the Hot," *New York Post*, June 24, 2007, https://nypost. com/2007/06/24/joba-the-hot/; Barbara Barker, "Road to Yankees Wasn't the Norm for Joba," Newsday.com, August 6, 2007, http://www.newsday.com/ sports/baseball/Yankees/ny-spjoba0817,0,4431401.story (National Baseball Hall of Fame Library, player file for Joba Chamberlain).

4   Barker.

5   Museum of Nebraska Major League Baseball. Harlan Chamberlain died on March 2, 2025 at the age of 73. Alyssa Johnson, "Harlan Chamberlain, Father and Supporter of Ex-Husker Joba, Dies at 73," *Lincoln Journal-*

Star, March 22, 2025, https://journalstar.com/sports/huskers/baseball/ article_5dbe5ff8-f8f3-4c61-886d-d5e3d60bc6ae.html.

6   Museum of Nebraska Major League Baseball.

7   Barker.

8   Barker.

9   Barker.

10   Kernan.

11   Chamberlain was overweight in high school (5-feet-8, 230 pounds as a freshman) before losing weight and standing 6-3, 225 pounds when he entered college. Barker.

12   Huskers.com, Joba Chamberlain, https://huskers.com/sports/baseball/roster/ player/joba-chamberlain.

13   Huskers.com; Barker.

14   Huskers.com. He was 10-2 with a 2.81 ERA and second in the Big 12 with 130 strikeouts.

15   Huskers.com.

16   The Yankees obtained the pick as compensation for the loss of Tom Gordon as a free agent.

17   Jacoby Ellsbury was the highest drafted Native American, selected in the first round (23rd overall) by the Boston Red Sox in the 2005 Draft. See Baseball Almanac for a list of Native American Major League Baseball Players, https://www.baseball-almanac.com/legendary/american_indian_ baseball_players.shtml.

18   The Yankees had another pitching prospect, Phil Hughes, who was more highly regarded and better known than Chamberlain. Hughes was the Yankees' number-one prospect and fourth among all major-league prospects, according to *Baseball America*.

19   After going to the World Series six times in eight years, from 1996 to 2003, the Yankees were trying to get back there. Having won the AL East for nine straight seasons, the Yankees found themselves trailing the Boston Red Sox throughout the 2007 season. While trying to catch the Red Sox, the Yankees were also trying to take what was then the one and only AL wild-card spot. In the end, the 2007 Yankees finished second and made the playoffs as the wild card.

20   Mike Lupica, "Joba Chamberlain, Who Was Once Thought to Be the Next Mariano Rivera, Is Yankees' Fallen Star," *New York Daily News*, March 24, 2012.

21   Tyler Kepner, "The Joba Rules," *New York Times*, August 19, 2007, https://archive.nytimes.com/bats.blogs.nytimes.com/2007/08/19/the- joba-rules/.

22   Chamberlain retired 16 of 19 first batters he faced. He struck out an average of 12.75 per 9 innings pitched and pitched more than one inning in 8 of his 19 appearances. He did not allow a run in his first 15⅓ innings. According to the Elias Sports Bureau, it was the second-longest scoreless-inning streak for any pitcher in Yankees history to begin his major-league career. MLB.com, Joba Chamberlain, https://www.mlb.com/player/joba- chamberlain-501955.

23   Pat Borzi, 'Chamberlain's Effort Brings His Father to Tears," *New York Times*, September 8, 2007, https://www.nytimes.com/2007/09/08/sports/ baseball/08yankees.html?_r=1&ref=sports&oref=login.

24   Chamberlain had entered the game in the bottom of the seventh and struck out two batters with two men on to preserve the Yankees' lead.

25   Joseph Wancho, "October 5, 2007: Midges Invade Jacobs Field, Attack Yankees' Joba Chamberlain in ALDS," SABR Games Project, https://sabr. org/gamesproj/game/october-5-2007-midges-invade-jacobs-field-attack- yankees-joba-chamberlain-in-alds/.

26   Steve Serby, "John Sterling Opens Up to Post about Yankees Career, Retirement Plans," *New York Post*, April 20, 2024, https://nypost.com/2024/04/20/sports/john-sterling-on-yankees-career-retirement-plans-return-chance/#:~:text=A:%20Oh%20my%20God.%20Joe%20should%20have,the%20Yankees%20would%20have%20won%20that%20game.

27   George A. King III, "Stunning Rise and Stunning Fall of Joba Chamberlain, a Major Torre Regret," *New York Post*, August 5, 2017, https://nypost.com/2017/08/05/the-joba-chamberlain-story-a-meteoric-rise-and-hard-fall/.

28   King, "He's Back On the Joba," *New York Post*, April 20, 2008, https://nypost.com/2008/04/20/hes-back-on-the-joba/.

29   King. The tests done on Chamberlain's father showed that he had respiratory issues and would need a machine at night to breathe. Joba remarked, "Hopefully he isn't too stubborn to use it."

30   Chamberlain returned to the mound, in 2008 after his stint on the DL. His 2008 season was a good one. In 42 appearances (12 starts), he had a 2.60 ERA with 118 strikeouts in 100⅓ innings. The 2008 Yankees missed the postseason, ending a streak of 13 straight years in the playoffs.

31   Harvey Araton, "Five Years Later, Yankees' Chamberlain Hopes to Write Another Feel-Good Story," *New York Times*, March 14, 2012, https://www.nytimes.com/2012/03/15/sports/baseball/yankees-joba-chamberlain-hoping-to-write-another-feel-good-story.html.

32   Associated Press, "Chamberlain Gets Probation for DUI," April 1, 2009. https://www.espn.com/mlb/news/story?id=4032927. Chamberlain said in a statement, "I made a mistake and hope over time to turn this into a positive learning experience for me and others."

33   He received a second World Series ring in 2015 as a member of the World Series champion Kansas City Royals, even though he did not pitch in the postseason.

34   In a game that lasted 13 innings, Chamberlain was the fifth of eight pitchers used by the Yankees, pitching the 11th inning and facing one batter in the 12th. That batter, Matt Wieters, broke his bat and the shard hit Chamberlain on the elbow, forcing him to leave the game. The Yankees lost the game, 2-1, but went on to win the Series, three games to two. The Yankees were swept in four games by the Tigers in the ALCS.

35   As a free agent after the 2014 season, Chamberlain signed once again with the Tigers for 2015. He was released in July and signed first with Toronto and then with Kansas City. He did not play for Toronto and finished the 2015 season playing for Detroit and Kansas City, with an ERA of 4.88 in 27⅔ innings pitched. A free agent again after the 2015 season, Chamberlain signed with Cleveland. He pitched 20 innings for the 2016 Indians, with a 2.25 ERA, before being released in July. That was the end of his major-league career. Chamberlain attempted a comeback in 2017, signing with the Milwaukee Brewers, but was released in spring training.

36   Araton.

37   Araton.

38   David Waldstein, "Losing Support, Chamberlain Keeps Composure," *New York Times*, September 6, 2013.

39   Jason Buck, "Joba Trying to Be the Father His Dad Was," MLB.com, June 12, 2014, https://www.mlb.com/news/joba-chamberlain-trying-to-be-the-father-his-father-was/c-79169622.

40   Buck.

41   Buck.

42   In 2013, his final year with the Yankees, Chamberlain got involved with a group that owned American Whiskey, a restaurant in New York City. The restaurant was still operating as of December 2024. King, "Joba Chamberlain Sounds Content as He Quietly Quits Baseball," *New York Post*, October 4, 2017, https://nypost.com/2017/10/04/joba-chamberlain-sounds-content-as-he-quietly-quits-baseball/.

43   Chamberlain's 2008 DUI conviction, as well as a second DUI case that occurred in Lincoln in 2018, proved to be an obstacle in his efforts to open the restaurant. Post Wire Report, "Joba Chamberlain's Two Duis Are Haunting Him," *New York Post*, August 8, 2018, https://nypost.com/2018/08/08/joba-chamberlains-two-duis-are-haunting-him/. Chamberlain was nevertheless able to obtain a state liquor license, on the condition that he not have any more alcohol-related violations for a year. "Chamberlain's Bar Up and Running," 1011 NOW, October 22, 2018, https://www.1011now.com/content/news/Chamberlains-bar-up-and-running-498233891.html.

44   Jake Elman, "Ex-Yankees Phenom Joba Chamberlain Earned $13 Million in the Majors but Lost Everything," *Sportscasting*, August 10, 2020, https://www.sportscasting.com/news/ex-yankees-phenom-joba-chamberlain-earned-13-million-in-the-majors-but-just-lost-everything/; Peter Salter, "Joba Chamberlain's Belongings, Baseball History to Be Auctioned Saturday," *Lincoln Journal-Star*, August 7, 2020, https://journalstar.com/news/local/joba-chamberlains-belongings-baseball-history-to-be-auctioned-saturday/article_459e1349-95a8-5b14-a481-e6ada6384e9e.html; (National Baseball Hall of Fame Library, player file). According to the reports, Chamberlain kept his 2009 World Series ring.

45   Elman, "Whatever Happened to Yankee Phenom Joba Chamberlain," *Sportscasting*, March 27, 2020, https://www.sportscasting.com/news/whatever-happened-to-yankees-phenom-joba-chamberlain/. In 2018 Chamberlain provided commentary for a short MLB.com video about the "midge game," "31 Days of October: Chamberlain," MLB.com, October 5, 2018, .https://www.mlb.com/video/31-days-of-october-chamberlain-c2513531583#:~:text=Joba%20Chamberlain%20recalls%20his%20bout%20with%20the%20midges%20%7C%2010/05/2018%20%7C%20MLB.com

46   *Joba and the Mouth* is an award-winning show on the World Wide Sports Radio Network (https://kkloiber7.podbean.com/). Chamberlain has also co-hosted *The Triple Play Podcast* on Hurrdat Sports (https://podcasts.apple.com/us/podcast/the-triple-play-podcast-with-joba-chamberlain/id1712368066) and has appeared on, among others, *Yanks Go Yard* (https://yanksgoyard.com/podcast/) and "Catching Up With Joba Chamberlain" (https://www.youtube.com/watch?v=6md8Dc7jdgc).

47   All American Speakers Bureau, Joba Chamberlain, https://www.allamericanspeakers.com/speakers/431780/Joba-Chamberlain.

48   Jake Bartecki, "Joba Chamberlain Inducted into Nebraska Baseball Hall of Fame," News Channel Nebraska, November 18, 2024, https://southeast.newschannelnebraska.com/story/51818028/joba-chamberlain-inducted-into-nebraska-baseball-hall-of-fame. Chamberlain's father and son were in attendance to share the honor with him.

49   King, "Joba Chamberlain Sounds Content as He Quietly Quits Baseball."

50   Luke Mullin, "From Yankee Stadium to Sherman Field, Baseball Shapes Father-Son Connection for Joba and Karter Chamberlain," *Husker Extra*, April 23, 2022, https://huskerextra.com/news/baseball/from-yankee-stadium-to-sherman-field-baseball-shapes-father-son-connection-for-joba-and-karter/article_2927942e-75a5-52e3-9785-e55cc9d00f2b.html; (National Baseball Hall of Fame Library, player file).

51   Mike Lupica, "Joba Chamberlain, Who Was Once Thought to Be the Next Mariano Rivera, Is Yankees' Fallen Star."

GENE CONLEY

By John R. Husman

Gene Conley excelled at the major-league level of two sports and is the only athlete to own dual-sport championships in major-league baseball and the NBA. Besides pitching for the World Series champion Milwaukee Braves in 1957, he was a member of three NBA championship teams with the Boston Celtics. He was the first player to earn Minor League Player of the Year honors twice and appeared in three major-league All-Star Games. His 15-year career as a professional athlete totaled 23 seasons that included 11 in baseball's major leagues and six in the NBA. At one point he packed 12 major-league seasons into six years with not a day off between those seasons.

The middle of three children of Raymond Leslie "Les" Conley and Eva Beatrice Brewer Conley, Donald Eugene Conley was born on November 10, 1930, in Muskogee, Oklahoma. His heritage includes Irish, German, English, and Cherokee. His eldest child, Dr. Gene R. Conley, explained a bit more about his heritage. "Gene's Native American, specifically Cherokee, heritage comes from his mother whose father, Richard Taylor Brewer, was half Cherokee and half White. Gene was proud of his Native American heritage and was a citizen of the Cherokee Nation. He had learned some Cherokee words and phrases from his mother and, every once in a while, would interject them in a conversation to kind of mix it up. He encouraged his eldest child, Gene R. Conley, to be proud of his heritage and he joined his father as a Citizen of Cherokee Nation."[1]

Gene was introduced to sports as a boy in Muskogee. He participated in swimming, football, and basketball and was a knothole gang member of the Class-D Muskogee RedsWhen Gene was 12 the family moved to Richland, Washington. There at Columbia High School, he earned letters in baseball, basketball, and track. He enjoyed a productive senior year in all three sports. In baseball he lost only one of 10 starts (to the eventual state champions) and batted at a nearly .500 clip. In basketball he averaged more than 15 points per game, led the Richland Bombers to their first-ever state tournament berth, and was selected to the all-state team. He was runner-up in the state track meet in the high jump with a leap of 6 feet 3 inches. He has been made a member of the Richland Bomber Hall of Fame.

As an 18-year-old and near his mature height of 6-feet-8, Conley chose Washington State University from the many prominent basketball schools that had offered him scholarships. At WSU he was also afforded an automobile and expenses by a grateful alumnus. Conley captained the freshman basketball team and as a sophomore led the varsity to the Northern Division championship of the Pacific Coast Conference. He was the top scorer for the Cougars, who lost to UCLA for the overall conference championship on a buzzer-beater. Conley represented the Northwest in the 1949 Hearst All-Star (baseball) Game, which pitted all-stars from the greater New York area against the top players from the rest of the country. Gene was named the United States All-Stars captain for the game, played at the Polo Grounds. He was the starting and winning pitcher, besting Frank Torre of the New York team. Conley called the experience of the preliminary games in Seattle, practice in Yankee Stadium, and game itself "as much fun as I ever had in my life." During the spring of 1950, Conley starred for the Washington State baseball team that finished 32-6 and was runner-up for the national championship. He pitched in 16 games, winning five, including two shutouts, saving two more and averaging .417 at the plate. He was inducted into Washington State University's Hall of Fame in 1979.

Conley's pitching attracted scouts from most of the major-league teams. He initially resisted, citing his desire to finish college, but signed with Bill Marshall of the Braves, then in Boston, in October of 1950. He began both his professional sports career and his marriage in the spring of 1951. He married Kathryn Dizney, whom he had met the previous fall.

The Braves assigned Conley to their Class-A team at Hartford of the Eastern League for 1951. His debut season was outstanding, with 20 wins, an earned-run average of 2.16, and a strikeout-to-walk ratio well over three to one. He was honored as the league's Most Valuable Player and

Gene Conley with the Boston Braves

named Minor League Player of the Year by *The Sporting News*. Conley's success came because of only two pitches – a fastball and a curve – which was his complete repertoire for his entire career.

Basketball re-entered Conley's life late in the 1951 baseball season. Kathryn R. "Katie" Conley told the story in her biography of her husband, *One of a Kind*. She related that during the Hartford club's last trip to Wilkes-Barre, Pennsylvania, Gene was invited to suit up for a scrimmage with the Wilkes-Barre Barons of the American Basketball Association. The Barons' head coach and owner, Eddie White, was impressed and offered him a contract for $5,000. When the Braves learned that Gene was considering playing professional basketball, he was summoned to a meeting with general manager John Quinn. At the meeting, Katie Conley wrote, Gene "had been given a $1,000 check in return for his promise never to play basketball again."[2] Conley honored the deal and labored as an ironworker during the offseason.

Conley's 1951 season earned him a serious look by the Braves, who promoted him to the big-league club as the fourth starter for 1952. His stay was short because of three dismal and winless starts, after which he was assigned to the Braves' top farm club, Milwaukee of the American Association. He did not get his first start there until the season was well into June but still finished with 11 victories for the pennant-winning Brewers. He chipped in with a .338 batting average, aided by a 5-for-5 day against the Indianapolis Indians. Earlier in the 1952 season, on April 26, Conley was the 90th overall pick in the NBA draft, selected by the Boston Celtics. Katie and Gene decided, for financial reasons, that he should try to make the club. He did so and, surprisingly, secured Quinn's permission to play. He played sparingly for Red Auerbach's Celtics, but established that he had the ability to play in the league. The Celtics made the NBA playoffs and were eliminated in the second round. As a consequence, Conley was late in reporting for spring training in 1953.

The year of 1953 was one of promise for Conley as he fully expected to make the big-league baseball club. But he did not. He was again sent to the Braves' top minor club, which had been displaced to Toledo when the Braves moved from Boston to Milwaukee. Conley started fast and kept up the pace until late in the season, when he was sidelined by a troublesome back. He won 23 games before his early exit and was named the American Association's Most Valuable Player. For the second time *The Sporting News* selected him as the Minor League Player of the Year. He was the first player to be so honored more than once. After a week's stay in a Toledo hospital, Conley was fitted with a back brace that he was told to wear for six weeks and then begin a therapy regimen. He immediately discarded the brace and after a couple of weeks his back was feeling fine, enough that he again made the Celtics for the 1953-1954 season. Once again Quinn intervened but this time matched the Celtics' offer

of $5,000 to induce Gene not to play basketball. Conley accepted and spent the winter working in Toledo.

En route to Florida for 1954 spring training the Conleys were involved in a serious auto accident. Though their car was demolished, they sustained only minor injuries, and Katie's pregnancy was not compromised. Conley, now well-prepared by his three years and 54-22 record in the minors, made the Braves' Opening Day roster. However, because of the Braves' solid and deep pitching staff, headed by Warren Spahn and Lew Burdette, Gene was not initially placed in manager Charlie Grimm's four-man starting rotation. After he recorded a few solid starts, Grimm revised his plans and went to a five-man rotation. The rookie responded and was selected for the 1954 All-Star Game in Cleveland but was the losing pitcher. By the end of August he had notched 14 wins, but his season was cut short again because of back problems. Conley finished third in an outstanding class for Rookie of the Year honors in 1954. Wally Moon and Ernie Banks finished in the top two spots while Hank Aaron rounded out the group.

As he had the previous summer, Conley recovered quickly from the back ailment with treatment and rest. Once again he tried out for and made the Celtics, but shocked the team by resigning on the eve of the season's opening game. He said he wanted to spend more time with his family and was not sure he would be able to continue as a two-sport athlete. Conley made a difficult decision that he hoped would prolong his baseball career.

Conley went to the Braves' spring training in 1955 without a contract – he was a holdout. Once in camp, he was able to negotiate a $20,000 contract with John Quinn, double his rookie salary. He started the campaign very well and was 8-3 going into a June 15 game against Philadelphia. During that game, according to Kathryn Conley, there was a "horrible sound of something popping or cracking, as he delivered a pitch to Granny Hamner that even our catcher, Del Crandall, heard from his crouched position."[3] This injury to Conley's rotator cuff would plague him for the rest of his career and would have ended it except for regular cortisone injections. He estimated that he had more than 100 injections.

Conley left that game but took his next regular turn five days later and beat the Pirates. He was struck on the injured shoulder by a batted ball in his next start, against Brooklyn, and was forced to leave the game. He missed only a single start before resuming his spot in the rotation, but his pitching arm was still hurting. For the second time in as many years, Conley was selected for the NL All-Star team, but was not slated to pitch as he had only one day's rest. He was forced into action when the NL came back from a 5-0 deficit to send the game into extra innings. Gene was called in to pitch the 12th inning in his home County Stadium and struck out Al Kaline, Mickey Vernon, and Al Rosen in order. Stan Musial slammed a home run leading off the bottom of the 12th to hand the win to the NL and to Conley. Gene did not win another game that season. He lost two starts after the All-Star Game and was rested for three weeks before he went on the disabled list for the balance of the season. He was sent to the Mayo Clinic, where he was prescribed exercises, but he self-imposed complete rest.

The shoulder problems were still with Conley at the start of the 1956 season and he was once again on the disabled list. Therapy promoted healing and he returned to the team and won for the first time, in relief, on May 28. Conley was used sparingly by new Braves manager Fred Haney over the remainder of the season. He won only eight times in yet another injury-shortened season as Milwaukee finished in second place, one game behind the Dodgers. The following season, 1957, Gene again alternated between starting and the bullpen, avoided the disabled list for the first time, and won nine games. The Braves continued their fine play and won both the National League pennant and the World Series. Lew Burdette beat the Yankees three times, while Conley had a single lackluster relief appearance, giving up two runs in Game Three.

The pitching career that had been so promising just a few years earlier came unraveled in 1958. Conley's shoulder was still a bother and the Braves' pitching was stronger than ever. Conley, when used, saw mostly relief action and became frustrated, began drinking heavily, and was constantly at odds with manager Haney. He finished the season 0-6 and did not appear in the World Series, again against the Yankees.

After the horrible and disappointing season of 1958, Conley decided to give basketball another try. He called Red Auerbach and was told that Boston did not need him and that Red did not think that he could make the team anyway. Auerbach gave in to Gene's demands for a tryout, but refused to pay the expenses for his trip to Boston. By his sheer determination Conley made the Celtics and signed a contract over the objections of the Braves. On the court he was strong, hustled, could outjump most anyone in the league, and excelled on defense and in rebounding. He would prove that he had staying power as he played three seasons with the Celtics, who were NBA champions all three seasons.

The Celtics' playoff run was cause for Conley not to report to the Braves in the spring of 1959. As a result he was traded to the Philadelphia Phillies on March 31, 1959. The six-player deal was made by the Phillies' new general manager, John Quinn, who had just moved over from Milwaukee. The Celtics wrapped up the NBA championship on April 7 and Conley had his second championship ring. He was the first athlete to play on championship teams in two professional sports.

A few days later Conley was in Florida, albeit late, for spring training. It was near the end of April before he made an appearance. He began in relief but was soon moved to the starting rotation and finished with 12 wins for the last-place Phillies. His last win came on August 19, a three-hitter against the Cubs. In the third inning he was hit on the pitching hand while batting against Glen Hobbie. The resulting fracture ended what was Conley's finest season in the making, but not before he completed the game while allowing only a single over the last six innings. He was picked by his former manager, Fred Haney, for the second 1959 All-Star Game in Los Angeles, where he pitched two perfect innings that included strikeouts of Ted Williams and Yogi Berra. He was also named Comeback Player of the Year by the Baseball Writers' Association of America. After the season he signed two contracts, one with the Phillies and another with the Celtics.

The 1960 baseball season was not much different from the previous one, but Conley's wins dropped off to eight. The Phillies offered him $20,000 to forgo basketball the next winter. He made a counter-offer that ended the negotiations and resulted in his being traded to the Boston Red Sox on December 15, 1960. Conley called it the "biggest trade in baseball" because at 6-feet-8-inches he was swapped for Frank Sullivan, who stood 6-feet-6.[4]

Including his previous appearances with the Boston Braves, Conley was about to become the only athlete to appear for three major-league teams in the same city. On April 11, 1961, the Celtics wrapped up another NBA championship, against the St. Louis Hawks at the Boston Garden. Conley was quickly off to Florida for an abbreviated spring training and came back to Boston to start for the Red Sox against the Washington Senators on April 25. Just two weeks removed from the basketball court, he made his first appearance in a Red Sox uniform and pitched eight shutout innings. But after just a few games the pain returned to Conley's pitching shoulder. He kept the recurrence of the rotator cuff injury to himself and continued through the season, pitching lust shy of 200 innings and winning 11 games for the sixth-place Red Sox.

Conley had been left unprotected by the Celtics when the NBA held an expansion draft in the spring of 1961. He was selected by the Chicago Packers but did not report, intending to take the winter off. Instead he signed with the Washington/New York Tapers in the fledgling American Basketball League. While with the Tapers, he often accompanied team owner Paul Cohen on sales calls for his Tuck Tape Company. The experience would prove to be valuable when Conley established his own company after his playing days.

The Tapers' season ended in time for Conley to participate in most of spring training with the Red Sox in Arizona. He parlayed a productive spring and a resolve to control his alcohol use into a productive 1962 season. He recorded career highs in wins and innings. The season was not without incident, however, as the shoulder pain returned along with his drinking. After a 13-3 shellacking on July 26 in Yankee Stadium in which he gave up eight runs in two-plus innings, Conley embarked on a venture that has remained signature to him. When the team bus became mired in New

York City traffic on the way to the airport, Conley and teammate Pumpsie Green stepped off to find a restroom. This was later dubbed Conley's "intentional walk" by the press.[5] When the players returned, the bus was gone. Left in New York, the pair did some drinking before Green realized he was in trouble and decided to return to the club. Conley continued his binge for a few days and at some point decided to go to Jerusalem. He went so far as to buy a ticket and went to Idlewild Airport (later renamed JFK), but was denied access to the flight because he had no passport. The bizarre incident was well covered by the press and resulted in a substantial fine by the Red Sox, but Conley eventually returned to the good graces of the club.

Before the 1962 baseball season had ended, Conley's NBA rights were traded from Chicago to the New York Knicks. He signed on and played center for what turned out to be the NBA's worst team that year. Two injuries ended his basketball season prematurely, a broken index finger on his pitching hand and a severely sprained ankle.

Because of his early exit from basketball in 1963, Conley was able to participate in an entire spring training. The basketball injuries proved to be a major issue, as was the chronic shoulder injury. He was unable to pitch smoothly and without pain during the exhibition season. He struggled during the early going of the regular season but came back late in the year. He did not know it at the time but when he started and won against the Twins on September 21, 1963, it would be his last major-league appearance. He had started nine games, and finished the season 3-4, with a 6.64 ERA.

As was now usual, Conley picked up basketball, again with New York. He was of little use to the Knicks because of injuries and exhaustion. The team was going nowhere and let him leave early to attend spring training. Just after the 1964 baseball season got under way and before he made an appearance, the Red Sox released Conley on April 21. Gabe Paul of the Cleveland Indians signed him the next day for $1 and offered him a trial with the Indians' Burlington (North Carolina) team. Conley pitched in only two games

there before becoming convinced that his shoulder would not come around and he could no longer be effective. He retired from baseball.

Gene and Katie made their home in Foxboro, Massachusetts, for 40 years. They established and operated together, for 35 years, the Foxboro Paper Company, which dealt in industrial packaging supplies. Gene had his last drink in 1966. Katie Conley related that a baseball fan told Gene that he was too good to be drinking and that he (the fan) did not like to see him that way. Gene later said, "That was it. I haven't had a drink since." Also in 1966 Conley was asked to try professional basketball again and played and coached in the Eastern League for Hartford and New Haven on weekends for two years.

After his professional sports career, Conley continued to be active with skiing and golf. He never had his rotator cuff repaired. The Conleys were instrumental in gaining pensions for the NBA's pre-1965 players. Conley credited Katie as the catalyst for forming the NBA Old Timers Association, which lobbied their commissioner, David Stern, to provide pensions for players who retired before 1965. Their initiative proved successful in 1988 when the NBA and the Players Association agreed to extend benefits to early players. In 1989 Gene helped Katie through a life-threatening surgery to remove a brain tumor. Together they reared three children who gave them seven grandchildren.

Following the sale of the Foxboro Paper Company, Gene and Katie retired to Florida and lived on a golf course which he frequented. They returned to Massachusetts in 2010 to be near family.[6]

Gene Conley died in Foxboro, Massachusetts of congestive heart failure on July 4, 2017, at the age of 86.[7] Katie died in Norwood, Massachusetts on January 10, 2020.[8]

A version of this biography is included in the book *"Thar's Joy in Braveland! The 1957 Milwaukee Braves"* (SABR, 2014), edited by Gregory H. Wolf.

SOURCES

In addition to the sources cited in the Notes, the author consulted Baseball-Reference.com, Basketball-Reference.com, nba.com, Retrosheet.org, and the following:

Husman, John, interviews with Gene Conley by telephone on May 17, 1988; June 4, 2002; January 3, 2010; and February 26, 2013; in Orlando, Florida, on February 14, 2005.

Crehan, Herbert F., *Red Sox Heroes of Yesteryear* (Cambridge, Massachusetts: Rounder Books, 2005).

Hilton, Michael, "Doubling His Pleasure," *Sports Illustrated*, April 2, 1979.

Paschke, Jim, "Two-Sporters." *Bucks Beat*, April 12, 2002. http://www.nba.com/bucks/news/paschke_020411.html.

Riley, Jim, "Richland's Conley Set Standard Yet Unequalled For 2-Sport Athlete,"

Tri-City Herald, Kennewick, Washington, December 30, 1999.

Greensboro (North Carolina) *Daily News*, August 19, 1949.

Seattle Daily Times, July 26, 1949.

Witter, Greg. "Cougar Baseballers Wake the Echoes of a Legend." Posted atwashingtonstate.scout.com/2/867723.html.

apbr.org/pension.html. Congressional Hearings on "Pension Fairness for NBA Pioneers," July 15, 1998.

richlandbombers.1948.tripod.com/Conley/1999-12-30TCHtop100.htm.

NOTES

1 John R. Husman telephone interview with Gene R. Conley M.D. on February 4 and 27, 2025.

2 Kathryn R. Conley, *One of a Kind* (Altamonte, Florida: Advantage Books, 2004), 105.

3 Conley, *One of a Kind*, 155.

4 Telephone interview with Gene Conley by author, May 17, 1988.

5 Conley, *One of a Kind*, 321.

6 John R. Husman telephone interview with Gene R. Conley M.D. on February 4 and 27, 2025.

7 *Boston Globe*, July 9, 2017: B13.

8 John R. Husman telephone interview with Gene R. Conley M.D. on February 4 and 27, 2025

LEE DANEY

By Frederick C. Bush

Baseball fans have become acquainted with the story of outfielder Archibald "Moonlight" Graham, whose major-league career consisted of playing two innings of one game without an at-bat for the New York Giants in 1905, primarily via the 1989 film *Field of Dreams*. In the history of America's national pastime, there have been many players whose major-league tenures were so short as to be a mere sip of coffee rather than the cup used as a metaphor for most brief careers. Pitcher Lee Daney, a member of the Choctaw Nation, became the mound equivalent to Graham when he pitched one inning in the second game of a doubleheader for the Philadelphia Athletics in 1928.

Daney's May 25 debut occurred in a low-leverage situation, with the A's trailing 9-2 in the top of the ninth. Nonetheless, it was a baptism of fire in which the 23-year-old hurler faced four members of the 1927 Murderer's Row New York Yankees – Babe Ruth, Lou Gehrig, Bob Meusel, and Tony Lazzeri. Far from quaking with fear, though, Daney acquitted himself splendidly, allowing only a leadoff

Lee Daney

(Courtesy Choctaw Spirit)

double to Ruth. However, he was a member of a team with seven future Hall of Famers of its own that also had World Series aspirations, and he soon found himself sold to the Bloomington (Illinois) Bloomers of the Three-I League. The A's finished in second place behind the Yankees in the American League in 1928, but the team made three consecutive trips to the World Series from 1929 to 1931, winning two championships. Meanwhile, Daney toiled in the minors and for semipro teams until 1941, but never pitched for a major-league squad again.

Arthur Lee Daney was born on July 9, 1904, in Talihina, Oklahoma, as the seventh of Daniel Daney and Rebecca (Anderson) Daney's nine children. Lee, as he was called, also had five half-siblings from his father's first marriage, who were all at least 18 years older than he was. Daniel Daney was a full-blooded Choctaw who owned a large farm that he leased to sharecroppers while he preached as a minister in the Methodist Church. Daney recalled that his father could not speak English well and preached in his native Choctaw. However, his mother, who was half-Choctaw and half-Irish, did not want Daniel to speak his native language with their children because she thought it would make it difficult for Lee and his siblings to learn English.[1] The conflict over which language to speak in the home foreshadowed the prejudices and stereotypes that Daney had to deal with as a Native American in the early twentieth century, though he maintained an indomitable spirit that empowered him to enjoy his long life.

Daney developed an interest in baseball by watching the Talihina town team play. He became determined to play ball himself, and recounted, "One day I was fooling around the house, and I came across a brand-new pair of Dad's socks. I unraveled one of the socks and had enough string to wind a good tight ball. When Dad found the sock put to this use, it wasn't any fun – but I still had the ball."[2] Daney and his brother Joe, who was two years older, attended Jones Academy in Hartshorne, Oklahoma, and formed the school's battery for a time. He remembered learning how to doctor a baseball – an act that was not illegal at the time – from an opposing pitcher who had played professional ball and asserted that his "hopping pitches ... worked out all right for me."[3]

In 1923 Daney enrolled at Haskell Institute in Lawrence, Kansas, one of the schools that the US government had built to educate and assimilate Native Americans into the majority White culture. The school was known nationwide for its successful football team, which Daney wanted to join. However, after the coach, Dick Handley, told him that he was too small – 5-feet-11 and 165 pounds – he pitched for the baseball team instead.[4]

Daney not only honed his pitching skills at Haskell, but his time there also provides insight into some aspects of Native American life during that period. He was 19 years old when he enrolled at the school in 1923, but he was only in the eighth grade. In early February 1924, it was reported that Daney, still 19, and two classmates, ages 18 and 17, had run away from the school. The trio had been heading to Wichita by foot, and they were apprehended in Pomona, Kansas, while "hanging around the railroad station apparently waiting for a freight to come along."[5] Although he was a 19-year-old adult, as a Native American he did not have the same freedom of movement that non-Natives had since he was still a citizen of the Choctaw Nation. That circumstance soon changed when the federal government passed the Indian Citizenship Act on June 2, 1924, which stipulated that all Natives were now American citizens without having to meet the previous requirements of either joining a branch of the US armed forces or giving up tribal citizenship/affiliation and assimilating into mainstream culture.[6]

Shortly after the passage of the Indian Citizenship Act, on June 15, Daney again left Haskell Institute on foot. This time, however, he was one of eight students who had agreed to walk home "[i]n order that they might donate the sum that otherwise might be used for railroad fare" to Haskell's fund-raising drive for "the erection of a modern athletic field and Stadium at the Indian School."[7] The distance Daney had to walk was approximately 377 miles.

In 1925 Daney returned to the school and its baseball team. On April 30, against St. Mary's College, "Daney started on the mound for Haskell, and pitched very good ball for four and a half innings, when he became troubled with a lame arm."[8] Haskell won the game 4-1, but Daney did not pitch again until May 11. On that date, he "went the full route, allowing seven hits"[9] in a 6-2 triumph over William Jewell College, demonstrating that his arm was healed. After Haskell's season ended, Daney pitched for the semipro Nebraska Indians team that played games throughout the Midwest. In an August 18 game preview, a newspaper article noted that "[n]ine full blood Indians comprise [the] lineup of [the] visiting aggregation. Among them are several from Haskell Institute. Their two pitching mainstays are Curtis Riko, an Ottawomie [sic], and Chief Whitehorn, a Choctaw."[10] Chief Whitehorn was none other than Lee Daney, who pitched under both names from this point forward in his baseball career.

In the summer of 1926, Daney plied his pitching trade for the Wetumka Drillers[11] and Quinton Indians, two semipro squads from Oklahoma. Even though Oklahoma consisted primarily of Native American lands, the hometown *Quinton Times* nevertheless referred to the Indians team as "[manager] Phil Fronkier's Savages"[12] in an article about

a three-game series the squad had just played against the Muskogee Veterans Hospital Team. The names and stereotypes became more prevalent in the newspapers as Daney's career progressed.

Daney was with the Nebraska Indians in 1927 when the team was merged into the All-Nations squad from Kansas City, Missouri. The team had the same name and multicultural lineup as Kansas City Monarchs owner J.L. Wilkinson's former All-Nations teams, but Wilkinson had disbanded his group at the conclusion of the 1925 season. This new All-Nations squad "feature[d] 'shadow ball' and many clown antics,"[13] and thus was a precursor to Black teams such as the Zulu Cannibal Giants and Indianapolis Clowns that became better known for combining baseball with such "entertainment" activities. On May 1 "Chief Whitehorn of the All Nations struck out fourteen men and allowed but four hits" in a 2-1 victory against the Crick Lumber Company of Independence, Missouri.[14]

Regarding his time with the All-Nations team in 1927, Daney recollected, "We had a good season, but the team wound up broke."[15] However, Daney's pitching had gained notice and he became a member of the Concordia (Kansas) Travelers team, which won that year's prestigious Denver Post Tournament, a top semipro competition. Daney made his debut in relief, under his Chief Whitehorn name, in a 9-0 shutout against Denver's own Powers-Behen team. The *Denver Post* noted, "The Chief breezed thru five innings and showed a variety of slants. Nine of the locals were third-strike victims and only three bingles, one an infield scratch, were made off Whitehorn."[16] Ray Quincey [sic], who had attended spring training with the St. Louis Cardinals that year but had been "farmed" to Vicksburg (Mississippi), won the championship game for the Travelers, 10-6.[17] Concordia was the first and, as it turned out after the final tourney in 1947, the only team from Kansas ever to win the event.[18] Decades later, Daney proudly, but also humbly, reflected on the fact that "[his] pitching had something to do with it."[19]

Another event that had brought Daney joy was his marriage to Marguerite Anna Ridling. As Daney recalled, "The year before, I met a schoolteacher in Quinton, Oklahoma. Before we left for Denver, I wrote her and told her I now had good prospects and if she would say yes, I was willing to say yes, too."[20] The couple married on June 23, 1927, and their union endured until Marguerite's death in January 1984.[21] They had three children – two daughters, Wanda Lee and Drucilla, and a son, Donald.

Daney's prospects became even better after he impressed Philadelphia Athletics scout and coach Ira Thomas so much that he signed Daney during the tournament.[22] Connie Mack had been looking for a replacement for Charles Albert "Chief" Bender, the future Hall of Famer, ever since the Native American had thrown his last pitch for the Athletics in 1917,[23] and Thomas thought he had found Mack's man in Daney. As spring training began in 1928, one news article heralded Daney's arrival with every stereotype available:

"All Indians may be chiefs in baseball[,] but Daney has the stature and the mien that one associates with the tribal head of a redskin nation. High cheek bones, an aquiline nose, straight, blue-black hair, skin the color of dull copper, makes his face an unmistakable one. The heritage of the Choctaw nation is in his build, the lithe grace of his carriage, the frankness of his eye. It would be easy to picture him stamping a war dance around a campfire clearing in a forest and framing his lips as he emitted a blood-curdling whoop of the warpath."[24]

Ty Cobb, who was playing out the final season of his career with the Athletics, indulged the "all Indians may be chiefs in baseball" attitude when he gave Daney the nickname "Chief Cool 'Em Off." At that time, the "Chief" part of the moniker was largely ignored, and the "Cool 'Em Off" name was intended to be complimentary as Cobb intimated that was what Daney would do to opposing hitters. Daney had fond memories of Cobb and stated that the legendary batsman "continually asked [him] to tell stories about Indians."[25]

Daney experienced an up-and-down spring training in Florida. In his debut, on March 8 against the International League's Baltimore Orioles, he pitched the fourth through sixth innings and surrendered six hits and two walks that resulted in six Baltimore tallies in a 14-4 loss.[26]

Four days later, during an Athletics practice session, the *Philadelphia Inquirer* asserted:

"Although he said nothing about it, Daney has had a sore arm and was unable to let loose out on the mound. But today was different.

"He flashed a 'Sinker,' a ball that started for the batters [sic] head, then shot downward, at the same time breaking over the corner of the plate. [Tris] Speaker, [Joe] Hauser, [Sammy] Hale and others fell prey to this puzzler which is similar to the famous 'Sinker' thrown by Wilcy Moore of the Yankees."[27]

Daney's "Sinker" did not fool the Orioles in a March 21 rematch any more than it had done the first time. He was tagged for two hits, gave up a walk, and uncorked a wild pitch as Baltimore scored two runs against him in 1⅔ innings of work. After the Orioles' 10-2 triumph, one reporter mocked Mack's team, writing, "The Athletics did not look like major leaguers or play like them."[28]

On April 10, one day before Opening Day, the Athletics played an exhibition game against the National League's Philadelphia Phillies at Shibe Park. Daney pitched the final three innings of the Athletics' 2-1 win, and allowed the Phillies to score their lone run in the eighth inning.[29] Another six weeks passed before Mack sent Daney to the mound in a game again.

Daney's lone regular-season appearance in a major-league game took place on May 25 at Shibe Park. The Yankees had defeated the A's, 4-2, in the first game of a doubleheader and now had a 9-2 lead entering the ninth inning of the nightcap. The *Philadelphia Inquirer* described Daney's simultaneous debut and coda:

"The Yanks were blanked in the ninth. Lee Daney, Choctaw Indian[,] had his Major League christening as a pitcher and his first opponent was no other than Babe Ruth, who dropped a double in short centre.

"[Center fielder Mule] Haas crashed into the scoreboard to catch Gehrig's long liner. Daney stopped Meusel's savage shot and threw him out. Then Lazzeri lined to [shortstop Joe] Boley."[30]

Ruth's double notwithstanding, Daney had put on a fine performance and surely thought that he had earned further appearances as the season continued.

On June 1 Daney was the starting pitcher for the Athletics in an exhibition game against the International League champion Buffalo Bisons in Buffalo. He threw the first four innings and allowed two runs, departing with a 5-2 lead in a game that Philadelphia won, 11-3.[31] Three days later, he was sold to the Bloomington (Illinois) Bloomers of the Class-B Illinois-Indiana-Iowa (Three-I) League.[32]

As Daney looked back on his short tenure with the A's over 40 years later, he conceded, "I did not succeed Chief Bender. It was too big and too fast a jump."[33] The press, too, commented on Daney's departure from Philadelphia and on the lack of Native Americans in baseball:

"In writing about the big Indians of baseball[,] you have to reminisce a bit. Their glory is all in the past. Louis Sockalexis, Chief Meyers, Charles Albert Bender, even Jim Thorpe have folded their blankets and stolen away from the big league tepee. And there are none to take their vacant places.

"We would almost have forgotten them ourself [sic] if the Athletics hadn't tried out an Indian pitcher this spring. He was scarcely a ghost of the mighty Bender of the same team and has disappeared in the direction of the bush. But Bender is still pitching in the minors."[34]

Bender was managing in Johnstown, Pennsylvania, and Richmond, Virginia, in 1928. Daney was the Native American player who continued to pitch in the minors for another decade-plus.

Daney spent the remainder of the 1928 season with Bloomington until he was loaned to the Springfield Senators in mid-August when the Bloomers had to make a roster cut to get down to the player limit.[35] He finished with a cumulative 3-9 record for the two Three-I squads.

In 1929 Daney's 15-10 record and 2.79 ERA for the Bloomers gained him acknowledgment as the "ace of the Bloomington staff."[36] Then, in early September, a headline announced, "Indian Goes to Indians," as he joined the American Association's Indianapolis Indians. Not only did the press tend to indulge in stereotypes about Native Americans, but now the papers did not bother to discover Daney's correct tribal affiliation and identified him as Cherokee rather than Choctaw.[37] He found less success in the Hoosier State as he posted a 0-4 record and an inflated 7.50 ERA.

The 1930 season found Daney leading a nomadic existence as he began the year with Indianapolis, spent most of July with the Chattanooga Lookouts, and then finished the season with the Springfield Senators. Perhaps due in part to the extensive travel, success eluded Daney that year. He was 2-4 with an 8.33 ERA with Indianapolis, 4-5 with a 5.82 ERA with Springfield, and spent such a brief time with Chattanooga that no official statistics are available.

Daney's almost-forgotten stint with Chattanooga came about when the Lookouts' manager, Joe Engel, who had recently scouted Daney, purchased him from Indianapolis. As was ever the case, the press engaged in stereotypes about Daney's heritage with the headline, "Engel Buys Cherokee [sic] Indian Hurler to Help in Scalping Memphis Tribe."[38] News articles show that, in his brief time in Tennessee, Daney pitched to a 1-2 record for the Lookouts before he was returned to Indianapolis.[39] Soon thereafter, he was back in Springfield.

In his memoir, Daney noted that, after the Great Depression began, "baseball, especially in the smaller leagues, was hard hit."[40] The Depression's deleterious effect on attendance already was in evidence when Daney started for Springfield in a game at Terre Haute, Indiana, on August 30. A Springfield reporter provided a humorous description of the "crowd":

"Danny Clark's Solons presented a private showing of their wares yesterday afternoon, turning back the Tots from Terre Haute in a brisk 8 to 3 encounter before a grandstand jammed almost to capacity with empty seats.

"In fact, the athletes were actually lonesome and conversed freely with the multitude – all three of them – in the boxes back of third base."

"Lee Daney was the Solon flinger yesterday and a real flinger, too, after the first canto. Apparently self conscious before the mob of vacant chairs, the athletes started out as if to kick the game all over the place. Two hits, two walks, an error, a passed ball and some other bits of bum baseball netted two runs."[41]

As the Depression continued, there was no longer any humor in the effects it had on American society, including the national pastime, and it greatly limited the opportunities for minor-league ballplayers.

Daney persevered and went to spring training in Florida with Indianapolis in 1931. He got to test his mettle against top competition once more as the Indians played numerous exhibition games against major-league teams. Although Daney performed well in both starting and relief roles,[42] none of the opposing squads gave him a second chance at a career in the majors. Thus, he spent the first two months of the season with Indianapolis, where he was 2-6 with a 4.50 ERA. On June 4, it was reported that the Indians had purchased infielder Frank Sigafoos from the Cincinnati Reds and that Daney was being sent to the Peoria Tractors, a Reds farm team in the Three-I League, as part of the deal.[43]

Daney did not fare any better with Peoria than he had with Indianapolis as he pitched to a 7-11 record with a 4.33 ERA. He did victimize the Terre Haute Tots again as he struck out 13 batters in a 7-5 complete-game triumph on July 13.[44] Three days later, in a game against Danville, "A near riot resulted in the third inning when Umpire Davis ejected Pitcher Daney of Peoria because of a heated protest over a changed decision. Fans swarmed out on the field, but none was hurt."[45] Later in life, Daney reflected upon his temper, writing, "[W]hen I started out, I was known as a hot head. Whenever something happened that didn't seem just right, I would blow my stack. But it didn't take the umpires long to catch on and after a while, every time I opened my mouth, I was either fined or run out of the ball park. So I toned down."[46]

Prior to the 1932 season, Daney was once again under contract with Indianapolis. However, the Indians sent him to the Knoxville (Tennessee) Smokies in February.[47] It ended up being a short stay. After spending spring training with Knoxville, Daney was returned to Indianapolis prior to Opening Day so that the Smokies would be down to the roster limit required by the Southern League.[48] It was the same scenario he had encountered with Bloomington toward the end of the 1928 season, but this time there was one notable difference: as soon as Daney was returned to Indianapolis, the Indians released him.[49] He found employment with Springfield for the first part of May before that team released him as well. He then was picked up by the Quincy Indians, an affiliate of the Cleveland Indians, toward the end of the month, but his time there was as brief as his stay with Springfield had been.[50]

As the season progressed, so did Daney's travels and travails. In July, he moved to northeastern Pennsylvania, where he joined the Hazelton Mountaineers, with the local press noting that he was being "accompanied here by his wife and little papoose [Wanda Lee]."[51] Daney had "a most impressive debut" for Hazelton in a 6-3 victory against the Elmira Red Wings on July 5; however, as the team's fortunes took a downturn, so did Daney's, and he was released yet again before the end of the month.[52]

Believing his days in professional baseball to be at an end, Daney took his family back to his home state of Oklahoma, where he now moved back into semipro ball. In 1933 he still led a peripatetic existence, but it was confined to one state rather than large swaths of the country. Daney played for teams from Wetumka (the Harjoche Indians, as player-manager), Wilburton, McAlester, and Quinton (where he had met his wife a few years earlier).[53] The next season he settled in with the Hugo (Oklahoma) team, first as a pitcher-right fielder and later as player-manager.[54]

In 1935 Daney pitched for the Pampa (Texas) Roadrunners, sponsored by the Danciger Oil & Refining Company. The Roadrunners were a powerful semipro squad, and Daney made his return to the Denver Post Tournament with the team. The competition began inauspiciously for

NATIVE AMERICAN MAJOR LEAGUERS

Daney on August 5 as he surrendered six runs in 4⅔ innings in a 6-5 loss to the Colorado Ice team.[55] Six days later, however, Daney turned in the finest of all his tournament appearances in a game against the Denver White Elephants, a formidable all-Black team. The *Denver Post* extolled Daney's stellar performance:

"White Elephants' week in Wonderland was over Monday, their dream shattered by two tornados from Texas. ...

"The Pachyderms, the toast of Denver's Negro colony after their triumphs over Enid, Okla., and Los Angeles, came into the tourney like elephants and went out like mice. They started their ups-and-downs by trampling Gering, Neb., 26-3, and bowed out with a coating of whitewash.

"The wielder of the calcimine brush was Lee Daney, 30-year-old [sic] Indian chief, who had his day of days Sunday.

"Chief Whitehorn, as he is known on the reservation, weaved a spell of impotency around the black bats with a medicine man mixture of speed, change of pace, control and headwork."[56]

The Roadrunners' 7-0 triumph over the White Elephants was the high point for Pampa, which posted a strong third-place finish in the 1935 tournament.[57]

Daney was back with Pampa in 1936, and the Roadrunners again competed in the Denver Post Tournament in August. Pampa finished in fifth place,[58] which still earned the team's players a share of the cash prizes, but, as the *Pampa Daily News* noted, "Loss of Lee Daney in the first game probably cost the Road Runners a place higher in the money." Daney had "pulled the muscles on his left side between the lower ribs and Denver physicians expressed doubt if he would pitch again this season."[59]

Daney not only recovered within a month, but he was on the mound and scored victories against some of Pampa's most prominent opponents. On September 2, in his first start since the Denver tourney, he hurled a 13-8 victory over the Mexico City Aztecas. Daney had weakened as the game progressed and, although he took the mound in the top of the ninth, he called for relief help after having allowed the final two Aztecas runs.[60] After this game there was great fanfare about coming visits from the Kansas City Monarchs and the Denver Post Tournament champion Negro League All-Stars in mid-September. Daney was expected to pitch one of the two games against the Monarchs, but heavy rain caused their cancellation.[61] Daney grew stronger as the month progressed and on September 21 he led Pampa to a 14-2 triumph over the Hawaiian All Stars. After Pampa's starting pitcher, Childers, threw his first six pitches for balls, Daney entered the game and went the distance for the win.[62]

In 1937 Daney found employment with the Blackwell Oil Company and played semipro ball for the Seminole (Oklahoma) Redbirds. It was a low-key summer on the baseball diamond for Daney, but in the fall he had an unusual off-field incident. On November 18, it was reported that

Marguerite Daney had asked the county sheriff and highway patrol to search for Lee, who had disappeared after leaving for Muskogee on business six days earlier. According to the press, "Fears that Daney may have become an amnesia victim were believed possible because of an accident he suffered a short time ago. He was struck on the head while engaged in oil field duties."[63] Although there were no further reports regarding Daney's whereabouts, he turned up again, was fine, and picked up where he had left off in business and baseball.

The next major change in Daney's life occurred in 1938. On July 11, it was announced that "Lee Daney, coach and pitcher for the Holdenville [Oklahoma] baseball club, leaves tomorrow for Kanapolis [sic], N.C., where he will join the fast Kanapolis semi-pro club. Daney, Mrs. Daney and their two children [Wanda Lee and Donald] will make their home in Kanapolis where he will have steady employment in addition to pitching for the baseball club."[64] At 34 years of age, it is doubtful that Daney imagined going east to play ball might result in his being rediscovered by a major-league team. Instead, the job that he was offered in the textile industry,[65] and the opportunity to continue to play baseball likely were more appealing than the potential dangers of the oil fields that he had already experienced. Thus, Daney finished the 1938 season with the Kannapolis team.[66] A few months later, on November 16, the Daneys' third child, Drucilla, was born.

Daney pitched for the team in Landis, a town five miles north of Kannapolis, in the spring of 1939.[67] However, at the beginning of July, he joined the Statesville Owls, a member team of the Class D Tar Heel League, which was starting its inaugural season. On July 3, in his first appearance with the Owls, Daney hurled a complete game – called after eight innings because of rain – in a 9-5 win against the Shelby Nationals.[68] In an example of the maxim "the more things change, the more they stay the same," Daney's move to North Carolina did not change the stereotypes of Native Americans that he had to endure everywhere he went. On July 6 the Statesville newspaper wrote, "Now if we can just persuade Chief Daney to bring along his tomahawk and scalp Manager Tuck McWilliams of Hickory[,] the fans' joy will be complete. How about it, Chief?"[69] Statesville finished third in the six-team league with a 56-51 record. The top four teams made the playoffs, and Statesville defeated Lenoir (61-46) before falling to first-place Gastonia (72-36) in the finals.[70]

The first incarnation of the Tar Heel League folded in 1940, so Daney went back to semipro baseball. He played for the Kannapolis team again in 1940 and 1941 while continuing to work as a weaver in the textile industry.[71]

Soon thereafter, Daney decided to follow in his father's footsteps and, before the 1940s were over, he entered the clergy. He moved his family across the country to Tucson, Arizona, where he became a minister in the Southside Presbyterian Church.[72] The fact that the church interacted with Arizona's large Native American population no doubt held additional appeal for Daney.[73]

A final move brought the Daney family to the Phoenix suburb of Scottsdale. Marguerite Daney died on January 15, 1984, and Lee Daney died on March 11, 1988.[74] The couple are buried together in Green Acres Memorial Park in Scottsdale.

Regarding his life's experiences, Daney reflected, "The one thing I will never forget was when I had to quit playing baseball – my only life and occupation up to that time – and to work to earn a living. ... My first paycheck was $11 and the world seemed to stand still. ... But my wife and I worked things out. ... And through it all I have that great memory of playing with Connie Mack's Philadelphia Athletics in the days of their great glory. And of playing with that team as Chief Whitehorn."[75]

SOURCES

Unless otherwise indicated in the notes below, Ancestry.com was consulted for Native American enrollment and census information, US Census information, and birth and death records.

Baseball-reference.com was consulted for player statistics and team records.

NOTES

1   Arthur Lee Daney with an Introduction by Dru Paine (Arthur's daughter), "Chief Whitehorn Threw a Fastball," in *Scottsdale Progress*, March 17, 1979, reprinted on https://www.baseball-almanac.com/players/Arthur_Lee_Daney. shtml, accessed May 16, 2023.

2   Daney.

3   Daney.

4   Daney.

5   "Eastern Kansas Happenings," *Parker* (Kansas) *Message,* February 7, 1924: 1.

6   See the following for information about this legislation: https://www. archives.gov/files/historical-docs/doc-content/images/indian-citizenship-act-1924.pdf and http://digital.library.okstate.edu/kappler/vol4/html_files/ v4p1165.html, both accessed on May 17, 2023.

7   "Boys Due to Arrive Today," *Osage Journal* (Pawhuska, Oklahoma), June 19, 1924: 1.

8   "Haskell's Baseball Team Making a Good Record," *Indian Leader* (Lawrence, Kansas), May 8-15, 1925: 8.

9   "Haskell's Baseball Team Making a Good Record."

10 "Rochelle Giants Win Sunday Game; Prime for Indians," *Rockford* (Illinois) *Morning Star,* August 18, 1925: 11. Curtis Riko was most likely a member of the Pottawatomie tribe, which had a significant population in states like Kansas and Oklahoma and is the only tribe with a name that is spelled close to what the news article printed.

11 "Wetumka Drillers 6 – Carter Oil Team 1," *Wetumka* (Oklahoma) *Gazette,* July 2, 1926: 2; "Drillers 7 – Shawnee 2," *Wetumka Gazette*, August 13, 1926: 4.

12 "Muskogee Vets Drop 2 to Quinton Indians," *Quinton* (Oklahoma) *Times,* September 2, 1926: 1.

13 "Colorful Club Faces Beaches Here Tuesday," *La Crosse* (Wisconsin) *Tribune*, June 5, 1927: 21.

14 "All Nations Win," *Des Moines Register*, May 2, 1927: 9; "Defeat the Cricks in Ninth," *Kansas City Times*, May 2, 1927: 10.

15 Daney.

16 Leonard Cahn, "Kansas Team Defeats Powers-Behen, 9 to 0," *Denver Post*, September 3, 1927: 13.

17 "Ray Quincey Wins More Laurels by Playing on Championship Team in Tournament," *Neligh* (Nebraska) *News*, September 15, 1927: 1.

18 Jay Sanford, *The Denver Post Tournament* (Cleveland: Society for American Baseball Research, 2003), 28.

19 Daney.

20 Daney.

21 "Mr. and Mrs. A.L. Daney," *Arizona Republic* (Phoenix), July 3, 1977: K-15; "Marguerite A. Daney," *Arizona Republic*, January 17, 1984: D2.

22 "Indian Pitcher to Tryout [*sic*] with Macks [*sic*] Athletics/Arthur Lee Daney Is Real Name of Choctaw Brave to Succeed Bender," *Wilkes-Barre Times Leader*, February 24, 1928: 26.

23 Bender was out of the major leagues from 1918 to 1924. In 1925 he made one appearance for the Chicago White Sox in which he allowed two runs in one inning pitched.

24 "Indian Pitcher to Tryout with Macks Athletics."

25 Daney.

26 "Orioles Wallop Athletics, 14 to 4, in Opener of Exhibition Schedule/Birds Batter Mack Rookies," *Baltimore Sun*, March 9, 1928: 14.

27 "'Chief' Daney, Choctaw, Dazzles with 'Sinker,' Lyons Also Looks Good," *Philadelphia Inquirer*, March 13, 1928: 23.

28 "Birds Topple A's by Heavy Hitting," *Wilmington* (Delaware) *News Journal*, March 22, 1928: 19.

29 "Athletics Take Final Game of Series from Phillies/Misjudged Fly, Going for Triple Results in Quakers' Defeat," *Reading* (Pennsylvania) *Times*, April 11, 1928: 13. An erroneous subheadline for the article states, "Jing Johnson Goes Entire Route for Mackians, Winning by 2 to 1," but the game article and box score clearly indicate that Daney pitched the final three innings of the game for the Athletics.

30 James C. Isaminger, "Babe Hits 15th and 16th, Dugan Socks Pair as Yanks Trip A's in Twin Bill," *Philadelphia Inquirer*, May 26, 1928: 20.

31 "Athletics Wallop 17 Hits to Overwhelm Buffalo Nine by 11-3/Jimmy Foxx Hits Home Run in Exhibition Tilt; Daney and Powers Hurl Well," *Reading Times*, June 2, 1928: 17.

32 "Mack Releases Powers, Daney/Pitchers Farmed Out to Bloomington; A's Roster Down to 24 Players," *Atlantic City Daily Press*, June 5, 1928: 12.

33 Daney.

34 Harold C. Burr, "Chief Bender, Great Indian Ball Player, Still in National Game," *Brooklyn Daily Eagle*, July 11, 1928: 22.

35 "Senators Take on Lee Daney, Indian, Release Lefty Dill," *Daily Illinois State Journal* (Springfield, Illinois), August 15, 1928: 12.

36 "Lee Daney Bests Roxy [sic] Lawson in Tight Pitching Duel to Give Bloomers Three in Row Over Huts," *Bloomington* (Illinois) *Pantagraph,* June 30, 1929: 17.

37 "Indian Goes to Indians," *Lafayette* (Indiana) *Journal and Courier,* September 4, 1929: 10.

38 "Engel Buys Cherokee [*sic*] Indian Hurler to Help in Scalping Memphis Tribe," *Chattanooga Daily Times*, July 9, 1930: 8.

39 "Decatur Weakens After Great Start, Daney Fails in Debut and Barons Win, 6 to 5," *Chattanooga Daily Times*, July 10, 1930: 11; "Chattanooga Gets Only Two Runs on Eleven Hits, Crackers Take Contest, 11 to 2/Lookouts Drop

Third Conflict to Dobbs Crew/Daney Gets Off to Fine Start, Then Blows Up," *Chattanooga Daily Times*, July 14, 1930: 7; "Charlie Bates Blasts Homer With One On as Chattanooga Noses Out Pebbles, 5-4," *Chattanooga Daily Times*, July 19, 1930: 9; "Dick Ludolph Holds Chattanooga as Birmingham Takes First of Series, 8 to 4," *Chattanooga Daily Times*, July 29, 1930: 8.

40   Daney.

41   R.A. Drysdale, "Solons Beat Tots 8-3; Swift Hurls Today/Clark Also Due to Play in Outfield/Daney Pitches Great Ball in Opening Game of Series," *Daily Illinois State Journal,* August 31, 1930: 17.

42   "Indianapolis Beats Phillies," *Jacksonville* (Florida) *Daily Journal*, March 20, 1931: 9; "Indians Defeat Yankees in 11 Innings and Play Ruth's Gang Again Today," *Sarasota Herald-Tribune*, March 24, 1931: 6; "Defeat the Cards, 12 to 3/The Indianapolis Indians Get Fourteen Hits in Victory," *Kansas City Times*, March 30, 1931: 12; "Indianapolis 4; Red Sox 1," *Wisconsin State Journal* (Madison), April 6, 1931: 14.

43   "Tribe Buys Sigafoos for Job on Infield/Second Baseman, Who Batted .305 for Angels Last Year, Is Bought from Reds; Daney Goes to Peoria; Wednesday Game Dropped," *Indianapolis Times*, June 4, 1931: 10.

44   "Tractors Win Over Tots, 7-5, to Take Lead/Daney Holds Terre Haute to Six Hits and Strikes Out 13," *Decatur* (Illinois) *Herald*, July 14, 1931: 8.

45   "Peoria Rallies to Tighten Lead with Win Over Danville, 12-7/Fraser's Nine Scores Eight Runs in Rally/Daney Ejected for Argument with Umpire Davis in Third Frame/Crossley Shines," *Decatur Herald*, July 17, 1931: 20.

46   Daney.

47   Bob Murphy, "Smoky Owner Leaves Last Part of Month; New Deals Pending/Indianapolis Sends Six Players to Knoxville; Thompson and Bass Come from Louisville; Allen Enthused Over Florida Trip," *Knoxville Journal*, February 6, 1932: 8.

48   Bob Wilson, "Smokies Ready to Go, Says Joe Schepner/Burns Opposes Liska in Opening Battle at Chattanooga Park," *Knoxville News-Sentinel*, April 11, 1932: 11.

49   "Indians Release Daney," *Indianapolis News*, April 12, 1932: 16.

50   Howard V. Millard, "Ladies Free Tonight as Commies End Home Stand/Thad Campbell Will Hurl for Locals – Daney Pitches 6 to 2 Victory," *Decatur Daily Review*, May 27, 1932: 32.

51   "Mountaineers Get Indian Flinger," *Hazelton* (Pennsylvania) *Standard-Sentinel*, July 2, 1932: 25.

52   "Lee Daney Joins Mountaineers and Beat [sic] Elmira Red Wings 6-3," *Hazelton Standard-Sentinel*, July 6, 1932: 8; "Pitchers Released," *Hazelton Plain Speaker*, July 25, 1932: 11.

53   "Independents Lost Hard Fought Game to Redskins," *Holdenville* (Oklahoma) *Daily News*, May 19, 1933: 3; "McAlester Runs Wild Over Wilburton Team," *Latimer County News-Democrat* (Wilburton, Oklahoma), June 30, 1933: 4; "McAlester Beats Heavener's Crew by Score of 5-2," *McAlester* (Oklahoma) *News-Capital*, July 10, 1933: 5; "Quinton Baseball Fans Have Enjoyed Games/Home Club Climbs as Daney Pitches Allowing Four Hits," *Quinton Times*, September 21, 1933: 1.

54   "Tentative Lineup Is Announced by Beaty," *Hugo* (Oklahoma) *Daily News*, April 6, 1934: 1; "Hugo Will Play Antlers Sunday/Daney Slated to Face Winford as Game Begins," *Hugo Daily News*, May 13, 1934: 1; "Cato Lost to Hugo Tigers Saturday/Johnson May Face Bohannon in Game at Antlers," *Hugo Daily News*, June 17, 1934: 1.

55   Leonard Cahn, "Icemen Upset Pampa, Tex, 6-5; Cabble Again Stars in Box," *Denver Post*, August 6, 1935: 23.

56   Robert Gamzey, "Roadrunners and United Fuel Win Sunday/White Elephants Eliminated by Pampa, Texas Team, 7 to 0/Lee Daney Pitches Great Game, Allowing Colored Club Only Five Hits – Summers Turns in Sensational Fielding Plays," *Denver Post*, August 12, 1935: 17.

57   Sanford, 55, 89.

58   Sanford, 89.

59   "Cox Leads Road Runners in Hitting for Denver Games," *Pampa* (Texas) *Daily News*, August 11, 1936: 5.

60   "Road Runners Pound Out 13 to 8 Victory Over Aztecas/Daney Hurls Game as Bailey Leads in Hitting," *Pampa Daily News*, September 3, 1936: 5.

61   "Daney or Stewart to Hurl Against Kansas City Negroes Tonight/Another Tilt to Be Played on Wednesday," *Pampa Daily News*, September 15, 1936: 5; "Texas Floods Damage Roads and Bridges," *Lawton* (Oklahoma) *Constitution*, September 17, 1936: 2.

62   "Road Runners Crush Hawaii Nine 14 to 2," *Pampa Daily News*, September 23, 1936: 5.

63   "Sheriff, Patrol Asked to Search for Missing Man/Lee Daney, Seminole, Has Not Been Seen Since Leaving Here for Muskogee Last Friday," *Wewoka* (Oklahoma) *Times-Democrat*, November 18, 1937: 1.

64   "Daney Leaving for New Club/Holdenville Coach Is Given Place With North Carolina Club," *Holdenville Daily News*, July 11, 1938: 4.

65   Daney.

66   "Kannapolis Tops Gastonia, 5 to 3," *Greensboro* (North Carolina) *Daily News*, July 16, 1938:13; "Kannapolis Tops Hickory by 5 to 0," *Greensboro Daily News*, August 13, 1938: 11.

67   "Kannapolis 7 Landis 2," *Winston-Salem* (North Carolina) *Journal*, May 6, 1939: 9; "Landis 2 Concord 1," *Winston-Salem Journal*, May 10, 1939: 8.

68   "Rally Enables Owls to Defeat Nats, 9-5," *Charlotte Observer*, July 4, 1939: 19.

69   "Reflections on Sports," *Statesville* (North Carolina) *Record and Landmark*," July 6, 1939: 2.

70   Lloyd Johnson and Miles Wolff, eds., *Encyclopedia of Minor League Baseball*, Third Edition (Durham, North Carolina: Baseball America, 2007), 368.

71   "Landis Indians Top Kannapolis, 10 to 3," *Greensboro Daily News*, August 10, 1940: 5; "Hosiery Advances in Semipro Play," *Winston-Salem Journal*, August 29, 1941: 9.

72   "Topics of Tucson," *Arizona Daily Star* (Tucson), May 3, 1949: 15.

73   "Indian Choirs to Sing Here," *Arizona Daily Star*, March 4, 1951: 30.

74   "Marguerite A. Daney"; "Arthur Lee Daney, 83, Scottsdale," *Arizona Republic*, March 14, 1988: 8.

75   Daney.

JACOBY ELLSBURY

By Oliver George Tapaha

Driven by the excitement of his teammates in the *nidaanéhé nahâaztánígí*[1](dugout) and *joоł yikalí* (baseball) fans in the stadium, rookie Boston Red Sox center fielder Jacoby Ellsbury had one mission during Game Two of the 2007 World Series against the Colorado Rockies – steal second base and earn free tacos for everyone across the country.[2] Ellsbury, with his lightning-speed agility, stole second base in the bottom of the fourth inning and was celebrated as the first "Taco Hero." Thanks in part to Taco Bell's "Steal a Base, Steal a Taco" promotion,[3] from that moment on, millions of people around the world knew the name, Jacoby Ellsbury. And they recognized his face, too. In American Indian[4] communities, particularly among the Diné/Navajo, pride and hope flowed into the hearts of many tribal youth and adults because Ellsbury was the first *joоł yikalí naanéhé* (baseball player) of Navajo descent to play in major-league baseball.

The Confederated Tribes of Warm Springs reservation in central Oregon was the place Ellsbury called home. Born on September 11, 1983, in Madras, Oregon, Jacoby McCabe Ellsbury is the eldest son of Jim and Margie Ellsbury and has three brothers, Matt, Tyler, and Spencer. Ellsbury is a citizen of the Colorado River Indian Tribes. His mother is Navajo and was a special-education teacher in early childhood for the Tribe's education department most of her career. She speaks the *Diné bizaad* (Diné/Navajo language) fluently and would teach her sons Navajo words as often as possible. His father, who grew up in Seattle, is of English and German descent and worked as a forester for the Bureau of Indian Affairs.[5]

Ellsbury spent the first few years of his childhood on the Warm Springs reservation, living the life of any boy his age – playing video games, hitting balls off a tee, play-ing ping-pong, and watching sports on television, drawing inspiration from notable athletes like Ken Griffey, Jr. and Michael Jordan.[6] Warm Springs, Wasco, and Paiute tribes make up the Confederated Tribes. The reservation covers roughly 1,010 square miles and occupies parts of Wasco and Jefferson County on the Cascade Range near Mount Hood National Forest. Growing up there, he carried a competitive spirit on his shoulders when he engaged in sports or games and developed a passion for *joоł yikalí* early on.

In 1990 Ellsbury moved to nearby Madras with his family. At 10 years old, he already had his eyes set on great things. According to his mother, Ellsbury wanted to be a major-league player, be in the "hot box," win the World

Series, and be on a baseball card.[7] His journey to the majors was determined at a young age. Outside of elementary school, he participated in several Little League all-star teams. His father organized practice sessions at home and coached him and his younger brothers, Matt and Tyler, at local ball fields. On weekends, the family traveled to games and tournaments all over the Pacific Northwest. Ever his guide and constant supporter, Jacoby's mother videotaped the games and he would review and critique his skills and performance to prepare for coming games. His father was a "soft-spoken, hardworking, [and a] fair-minded guy" off the field, but on the field, he was verbally tough on the boys. Matt struggled to measure up to his father's high standards and strident tone, choosing often to ride the bus after games so as to avoid critique in the family car. Jacoby, on the other hand, "accept[ed] criticism and use[d] it to his advantage."[8]

When Ellsbury entered middle school, he moved with his mother and brothers to Parker, Arizona, to live near his grandmother, Alice McCabe, who was battling an illness.[9]

(Courtesy Cindy M. Lou / Boston Red Sox)

Jacoby Ellsbury with the 2012 Red Sox

NATIVE AMERICAN MAJOR LEAGUERS

Alice's husband, Franklin McCabe, Sr., died before Jacoby was born, and Alice had no one in Parker who could provide the care she needed; so, Margie stepped up to lend a hand. In addition to helping her mother, Margie held a minimum-wage job to cover basic living expenses in the low-income housing where they lived.

Parker is a town on the Colorado River Indian Tribes reservation, which lies next to the Arizona-California border in La Paz County, along the shoreline of Colorado River and US Highway 95. The reservation rests on 300,000 acres of land and has been the homeland for the Mohave and Chemehuevi tribes since 1865. In the mid-1940s, some Hopi and Navajo people moved to the Colorado River Indian Tribes as part of the relocation project. Ellsbury's grandparents were among the few who were forced to relocate to Parker, a place that once served as an internment camp for Japanese Americans at the start of World War II.[10] Alice and Franklin spent their lives in Parker harvesting alfalfa, cotton, and watermelon and raising their 13 children. Significantly, Ellsbury's mother designed the Tribe's flag in 1979.[11]

The Ellsbury boys made frequent trips to Parker growing up, so reorienting themselves to reservation life happened effortlessly. Jacoby cherished all the time he spent living with his grandmother and had deep respect for his cultural heritage. He helped care for *dibé* (a flock of sheep), ate his favorite food – *dahdíníilghaazh* (fry bread) – and watched his grandmother weave distinct *dah'iistł'ó* (Navajo rugs). The boys attended Le Pera Elementary School in Poston, Arizona, 15 miles from Parker. At school, Jacoby always had a *jooł* (ball) in his hands and was close to his friends. After school and on weekends, the boys played in Parker's Little League.[12]

ADEISHŁÍíŁ NÍZIN: CHASING SUCCESS TO LIVE A DREAM

For high school, Ellsbury returned to Oregon and enrolled at Madras High School, a school with even enrollment of Native, Latine, and White students. Impressively, he played *jooł yikalí*, basketball, football, soccer, and ran cross-country for the White Buffaloes. It is uncommon for high-school students to participate in five sports, but Ellsbury balanced his schedule and responsibilities to make this work. In the fall season, he played football and soccer or ran cross-country. During the winter and spring seasons, he devoted his time and energy to basketball and *jooł yikalí*, respectively. From his freshman year, he was a varsity-level athlete in nearly every sport he participated in but became a rising star basketball and *jooł yikalí* player his junior year.

The competitive nature that Ellsbury grew into as a child stayed with him throughout his high-school years. In his senior year, he achieved an impressive record in *jooł yikalí* with 65 stolen bases and a batting average of .537. He was named Oregon Player of the Year, Tri-Valley League co-player of the year, and first-team all-state. In basketball he averaged 23.6 points per game as a shooting guard and helped his team to a third-place finish in the 2002 Oregon

4A state tournament. He earned the first-team all-state selection his junior and senior years. In football, he was a double threat. He ran the ball on the offense side as a quarterback and then switched over to the defensive side and played as a defensive back. He ended the football season with nine interceptions and six kickoff returns for touchdowns.[13] When it came to cross-country, he "never lost a race."[14]

Ellsbury was impossible to defeat in cross-country races because he was told by his mother since he was a youngster that if he "rubbed the feet of a dragonfly on the bottom of [his] bare feet [he] would have the ability to run faster."[15] This was his grandfather's teaching retold to him in his memory and as a source of resilience – and he valued it, believed it, and lived it. He ran each race guided by the values his grandfather left behind coupled with the strength of the dragonfly that pushed him to produce more speed in his strides.

While basketball is the most popular sport at Madras, Ellsbury's legacy is still remembered and honored. In one of the entryways of the school building, adjacent to the Buffalo Dome gymnasium, is an Athletic Hall of Fame. It displays a line of commemorative plaques on each inductees' accomplishments. Near the center of the gallery wall is a plaque paying tribute to Ellsbury, the only American Indian in the school's athletic history to receive this meritorious recognition. His notable achievements from 1998 to 2002 are etched on a wooden plaque for fans and visitors to see and admire. Inside the Buffalo Dome is a vinyl poster of Ellsbury endorsing a *jooł yikalí* gear with the following tagline, "Gear Up or Shut Up. The Advantage of Superior Gear." And on the baseball field, Ellsbury's jersey number (2) is permanently stamped on the right-field wall. He shares this stardom with Darrell Ceciliani, also a center fielder, whose jersey number (8) is featured on the left-field wall. Ceciliani was drafted by the New York Mets in 2009.

As a five-sport standout athlete who was quick, disciplined, and committed to winning, Ellsbury was noticed by scouts. Colleges and professional *jooł yikalí* leagues quickly spotted his willpower and versatility. Before he graduated from Madras in 2002, he was offered numerous athletic scholarships. He was even drafted by the Tampa Bay Devil Rays in the 2002 draft but chose not to sign with them. Instead, he prioritized his education and enrolled at Oregon State University on a *jooł yikalí* scholarship.[16]

While enrolled at Oregon State University from 2002 to 2005, Ellsbury achieved academically while pursuing double majors in business and communication. In 2004 and 2005, he earned the PAC-10 All-Academic Honorable Mention. This recognition is awarded to noteworthy student-athletes who completed their freshman year of college with a grade-point average over 3.2. These consecutive honors gestured to Ellsbury's dual commitment to getting a quality education and thriving on the diamond.

Ellsbury had an exceptional *jooł yikalí* career at Oregon State. In 2003 he batted .330 and was named a second-team freshman NCAA All-American as an outfielder. In 2004 he batted .352 and was selected as the PAC-10 Conference All-Star.[17] In 2005, as co-captain of the *jooł yikalí* team, his batting average reached .406, he had 26 stolen bases, and he was once again honored as the PAC-10 First Team NCAA All-American and named Co-MVP. The Oregon State Beavers won the NCAA Regional and the Corvallis Super Regional playoffs in 2005. However, they lost to Baylor, 4-3, in the first round of the College World Series. This was Oregon State's first appearance in the College World Series since 1952. And Ellsbury's stellar performance during the championship games did not go unnoticed by major-league teams. He ended his junior year with a .365 batting average, 37 doubles, 8 triples, 16 home runs, 101 RBIs, and 60 stolen bases.

In the years that Ellsbury was at Oregon State, he was one of the less than 1 percent of American Indian/Alaska Native students to attend college and one of the rare few Native athletes to play at the Division-I level. During the 2004-05 academic year, when Ellsbury was a junior, only 51 AI/AN student-athletes played for D-I teams. Kelvin Sampson, an enrolled member of the Lumbee Tribe, was the only American Indian to serve as a coach for a D-I school that year.[18] But the number of Native students recruited to play in college sports substantially increased in recent years thanks to former college athletes like Ellsbury, Bronson Koenig (Ho-Chunk Nation; University of Wisconsin men's basketball standout), and Alissa Pili (Samoan and Inupiaq Alaska Native; University of Utah women's lead basketball player), for paving the way for the next generations of Native youth to follow. In 2023-24, around 500 AI/AN students participated in a sport at a Division-I level, and over 2,300 AI/AN student-athletes competed in sports at the collegiate level (D-I, II, and III).[19] It is without question that more Native athletes will demonstrate their academic and athletic excellence in the years to come, but will colleges take a chance on those Native student-athletes?

The Boston Red Sox were particularly interested in Ellsbury, a left-handed, 6-foot-1 player. With all the attention Ellsbury was receiving his junior year, he agreed to explore professional *jooł yikalí*. On June 7, 2005, Ellsbury, his younger brother Matt (a freshman at OSU at the time), and his friends all anxiously watched the draft online and listened for Ellsbury's name to be called.[20] Their wait was short-lived when the Boston Red Sox selected him in the first round, making him the 23rd overall pick. In a cheerful mood, Ellsbury immediately jumped on the phone to call his mother to share the news. She cried with joy, and they spread the news to the rest of the family and close friends. Within a month's time, he moved to Boston, and then on July 1, signed a $1.4 million contract and began his professional *jooł yikalí* career as the first Navajo to play in the major leagues.

YÁʼÁTʼÉÉHÍJÍ DÓÓ NÍNÁÁYIIŁBAʼ: TRIUMPHS AND SETBACKS WITH THE RED SOX

At the tender age of 21, Ellsbury felt the weight of expectations to be the top prospect for the Red Sox. His entrance to the minor leagues started with the Lowell Spinners in the short-season New York-Penn League. He batted .317 in 35 games and stole 23 bases.[21] At Class-A Wilmington in 2006, he appeared in 61 games, swiped 25 bases, and posted a batting average of .299. At midseason, Ellsbury was promoted to Double-A Portland and garnered 16 steals in 50 games and batted .308. The following year, 2007, he began again with Portland and after batting .452 in 17 games he was promoted to the Triple-A Pawtucket Red Sox at midseason; he hit .298 in 87 games. Ellsbury ended his 2007 season with Boston with a .353 batting average and nine stolen bases in 33 games.

Ellsbury made his major-league debut on June 30, 2007, when the Red Sox hosted the Texas Rangers. His first major-league base hit was a single; he was 1-for-4. The Red Sox lost the game, 5-4, but for him it tasted like victory. He lived what he had dreamed about since childhood. After his initial appearance in the big leagues, his mission was to show up to each game, mentally and physically ready to help turn his team into a championship team. His performance drew some praise, but the month of September was particularly important. He batted .361 in 105 plate appearances and earned a spot on the playoff roster.[22]

From the bench in the first few games of the postseason, Ellsbury observed and learned each hitter's posture and swing and then tracked where they batted the *jooł*. He was a pinch-runner or defensive replacement when called upon and carried out those tasks with confidence.[23] On October 20, manager Terry Francona inserted Ellsbury in the starting lineup in Game Six of the League Championship Series against the Cleveland Indians, replacing Coco Crisp in the *ałníigi sizínígíí* (center field) position.

In the Red Sox' sweep of the Colorado Rockies in the World Series, Ellsbury was 7-for-16 (.438), four hits (three of them doubles) in Game Three, the first rookie to achieve this since Joe Garagiola in 1946.

In 2008, his first full season with the Red Sox, Ellsbury appeared in 145 games and played all three outfield positions, mainly as an *ałníigi sizínígíí* and *nishʼnáájígo sizínígíí* (left fielder).[24] He batted a respectable .280 and had 50 stolen bases in 61 attempts, leading the American League in steals.

When Ellsbury got on an *azis béédazhdiltałígíí* (a base), he was a force to be reckoned with. During the 2009 season, he set a new team record with 70 steals[25] and led the AL in stolen bases for the second year in a row. He ended the season with a .301 batting average, had 10 triples, and scored 94 runs.

Ellsbury's 2010 season was marked by a recurrence of an injury that was not properly assessed. Playing left field on April 11, in the Red Sox' sixth game of the season, he took a knee to the left ribs and suffered hairline fractures when he collided with third baseman Adrian Beltré as they chased a foul ball on the left-field line. This critical hit was severe enough that it immediately caused sharp pain to his back and he had difficulty breathing.[26]

Ellsbury received medical treatment, and an X-ray revealed that he had bruised ribs. Several medications were prescribed to him, and he took them, but the intense pains persisted in the front and back of his torso. He requested the Red Sox for an MRI only to be told, "We aren't going to MRI a bruise."[27] When he returned home, he endured sleepless nights and had trouble getting out of bed due to excruciating pains he felt. He finally asked his agent to help him get an MRI done. The organization approved the request, and the MRI showed fractured ribs.

After what appeared to be adequate healing time, Ellsbury returned on May 22 and played in three games, only to reinjure the same ribs. Another visit to a medical specialist revealed a fifth fractured rib that caused additional damage to his nerves and back muscle.[28] He was returned to the disabled list, not to return until August 4. And nearly a week later, he reinjured his ribs once again and his season ended. He was heavily criticized by media analysts for being too soft.[29] For the season, Ellsbury played in 18 games, hit .192, stole 7 bases, and scored 10 runs.[30]

After spending some time at the Athletes' Performance Institute in Arizona, rehabbing and recovering from his rib and back injuries, Ellsbury had a strong 2011 season, batting .321 with 46 doubles, 32 home runs and 39 steals. He became the first Red Sox player to join the 30-30 club.[31] He earned four major accolades: the American League Comeback Player of the Year Award, the Rawlings Gold Glove Award, the Silver Slugger Award, and being named to the All-Star Game.[32] He was second in the AL MVP balloting. In Navajo, when a person overcomes great adversity, they are characterized with the term, *ha'óólní* (resilient/ce). Ellsbury's *ha'óólní* led him to signing an $8.05 million deal with the Red Sox for another year.[33]

But in 2012 Ellsbury's performance plummeted and he missed nearly half the season with a right-shoulder injury.[34] A week into the season, in the fourth inning of a game against Tampa Bay, Rays shortstop Reid Brignac fell on Ellsbury at *naaki góné azis béédazhdiltałígíí* (second base) and dislocated his shoulder. Ellsbury missed three months of playing time and his worth and contributions to the Red Sox team was questioned. One writer wrote that Ellsbury's value "isn't low, it just already sunk."[35] Indeed, Ellsbury had a terrible season, as did the entire team. They finished last in the AL with 69 wins and 93 losses. Ellsbury played in 74 games and finished with a .271 average, 4 home runs, and 14 steals.[36] Although Ellsbury had a rough season and was a possible trade candidate, Boston gave him another chance to showcase his talents. They offered him a $9 million, one-year contract.

Going into the 2013 season, Ellsbury was hopeful about helping his team win the championship trophy again. Early in the season, his optimism was quickly overshadowed by the struggles he faced. An *iikałígíí's* (a batter's) stance at the *ninádajiilyeedígí* (home plate), preparing to hit a *jooł*, is crucial. A slight shift in a player's posture while at bat can impact the direction of a *jooł's* flight. Such was the case with Ellsbury. His hip was out when at bat, which caused him to hit groundballs to the right side of the field.[37] Notwithstanding this minor mishap, his overall season performance in the majors was his second-best, and he helped his team win the World Series against the St. Louis Cardinals in six games. He played in all 16 playoff games. For the season, he appeared in 134 games, stole 52 bases, hit .298, had a slugging percentage of .426 and 53 RBIs.

Celebrating a second World Series win was bittersweet for Ellsbury. On the one hand, he knew his teammates functioned cohesively during the 2013 season and the thought of another exceptional season together in 2014 looked promising. On the other hand, in early December he signed a seven-year, $153 million contract with the New York Yankees.

T'ÁÁBITA'ÍGII NAAZNE': AN IN-BETWEEN PLAYER WITH THE YANKEES

Ellsbury started his season with the Yankees in spring 2014. He was in Toronto with his new team when his former Red Sox teammates received their championship rings in the same city. Ellsbury missed the celebration but received congratulatory messages from his former teammates.

Ellsbury's transition to the Yankees was not so pleasant. There was an outcry from fans and the media asking why the Yankees spent a massive amount of money on a player who had a history of injuries.[38] Amid the criticisms, he stayed healthy most of the season, minus the nine final games he missed because of a thigh strain. In total, he played 149 games, batted .271, had 39 stolen bases, and added 16 home runs.

The 2015 season was a below-par season for Ellsbury. He played reasonably well the first month of the season, but then sustained a knee sprain in May, which resulted in losing two months of playing time.[39] Then in the postseason Ellsbury was benched in favor of Chris Young in a wild-card game against the Houston Astros. Ellsbury, 32 at the time, was viewed as "brittle" and "not a quick healer."[40] The Yankees worried about the deterioration of his athleticism, but they had committed to him until 2020, one of the longest contractual agreements the Yankees had ever made with a position player. Ellsbury concluded the season with a batting average of .257 in 111 games.

Known for being one of the top baserunners in professional *jooł yikalí*, Ellsbury consistently held a steady track record for reaching nearly every *azis béédazhdiltałígíí* and stealing them with ease. However, during the 2016 season, he stole only 20 bases in 148 games. From the time he cut ties with the Red Sox, his stolen-base rate decreased each year. A Yankees fan blogger noted that Ellsbury had aged and the "lingering hip problem could easily explain any hesitation on the bases."[41]

Ellsbury's mindset at the start of each new season was to play his best and get better as the season progressed. But achieving this was challenging for him the last couple of seasons with the Yankees. He was not terrible and not useless, but he was not great either – he was stuck somewhere in the middle – as an in-between player.[42] He hit .264 in 2017 and stole 22 bases. He played his last game on October 17, 2017, and missed all of 2018 and 2019 because of lower back issues and a torn hip. With a year to go on his contract, he was released by the Yankees on November 20, 2019.[43]

After releasing him, the Yankees filed a grievance against Ellsbury, seeking to recover the $26 million remaining on his contract because he sought an outside facility, without permission, to rehab injuries he sustained the past two seasons.[44] The matter was settled with the amount awarded to Ellsbury kept confidential. He never signed with another major-league team.

While Ellsbury's deal may be viewed as the worst in Yankees history, many fans remained loyal to him, particularly American Indian/Alaska Native communities. They considered him an example to follow. Among the Navajo, the youth called him a hero; they cared about what children thought about someone or something.[45] To them, Ellsbury mattered.

BIDÁÁH NA'ÍÍDZA DÓÓ KÉK'EHASHCHIIN: GIVING BACK AND CREATING PATHWAYS

Ellsbury married Kelsey Hawkins in 2012; they had spent six years together as a couple. They met at Oregon State University. They live in Scottsdale, Arizona, have four children, and stay connected to their relatives 2½ hours away in Parker, Arizona.

Giving back has always been one of Ellsbury's life missions. During his time with the Red Sox, he donated to two charities, The Navajo Relief Fund and Project Bread: The Walk for Hunger. In 2011 he partnered with Nike N7 to host baseball camps for Native youth from multiple Tribal Nations on the Salt River Pima-Maricopa Indian Community in Scottsdale. He held these camps throughout his time with the Yankees. He also gave $1 million to the Oregon State baseball program in 2014. The funds were used to expand the locker-room facilities in the university's Goss Stadium. The locker room was named in his honor.

When he was starting out as a professional *jooł yikalí naanéhé* in 2005, Ellsbury was recognized at the Warm Springs Pi-Ume-Sha Treaty Days Pow Wow during the 150th celebration of the Treaty of 1855. He showed up there with his family and they gave him an Honor Dance. A tribal citizen stated, "Our elders shared with him that he is not only a role model for his tribe, but for all tribal children and people and we are all so proud of his accomplishments. He made the community feel so special. That is the kind of man this young man is – so respectful."[46]

Ellsbury is undeniably a respectful man, but he is also strong-minded, quiet, and humble. Each season, his fight never left him. He showed up to each game *bidziilgo* (with strength) and *ha'óólníi*go even when many people were not in his corner. In Native communities, he was highly admired for leaving his footprints behind for other Natives to follow, such as Anthony Seigler, who on July 1, 2025, with the Milwaukee Brewers, became the second Navajo *jooł yikalí naanéhé* to compete in the major leagues.[47]

In 2024 Jacoby McCabe Ellsbury, the first *jooł yikalí naanéhé* of Navajo descent to play in the majors, was inducted into the Oregon State University Hall of Fame, the first American Indian athlete in the university's history to receive the honor.

SOURCES

In addition to the sources cited in the Notes, the author consulted Baseball-Reference.com.

NOTES

1   Navajo terms, particularly baseball-related terms translated into the Navajo language, are used in this article to honor the Tribe's language and encourage their use among Navajo tribal citizens. See M. Yellowhair & E.C. Parnell, eds., *The New Oxford Picture Dictionary: Navajo-English Edition* (New York: Oxford University Press, 1989).

2   David Lefort, "Tacoby Bellsbury," Boston.com, October 26, 2007. https://www.boston.com/sports/boston-red-sox/2007/10/26/tacoby_bellsbur/.

3   Janey Murray, "World Series History and 'Taco Heroes' Collide in Cooperstown," National Baseball Hall of Fame, October 2021. https://baseballhall.org/discover/baseball-history/world-series-history-and-taco-heroes-collide-in-cooperstown.

4   The terms American Indian, American Indian/Alaska Native, and Native are general terms used to describe Indigenous Peoples of North America. They are used interchangeably throughout this article.

5   Bob Sherwin, "Yankees' Ellsbury Has Reputation as 'Dirt Rat' (It's Praise)," *New York Times*, June 11, 2014. https://www.nytimes.com/2014/06/12/sports/baseball/ellsbury-has-respect-of-yankees-and-rivals.html#:~:text=An%20article%20in%20some%20editions,%E2%80%9D%20not%20a%20%E2%80%9Cdirtbag.%E2%80%9D.

6   Beverly Bidney, "Indian Country Profile: Jacoby Ellsbury," *Seminole Tribune* (Hollywood, Florida), April 29, 2014. https://seminoletribune.org/indian-country-profile-jacoby-ellsbury/.

7   Bryan Hoch, "Ellsbury's Tireless Work Ethic Traces to Mother," MLB.com, May 8, 2015. https://www.mlb.com/news/jacoby-ellsburys-tireless-work-ethic-traces-to-mother/c-123016810

8   Neil Swidey, "The Jacoby Factor," *Boston Globe*, March 30, 2008: 3. https://archive.boston.com/bostonglobe/magazine/articles/2008/03/30/the_jacoby_factor/?page=full.

9   Joan M. Travis, "McCabe Family Supports Their Baseball Superhero – Jacoby Ellsbury," ParkerPioneer.net, April 30, 2008. https://www.parkerpioneer.net/news/article_6f1a7211-47fb-53e9-a0d2-7166ee312ad4.html.

10   Jon Schwartz, "In His Blood: Jacoby Ellsbury's Commitment to Navajo Youth Will Be Felt by Generations to Come," MLB.com, April 3, 2017. https://www.linkedin.com/pulse/his-blood-jacoby-ellsburys-commitment-navajo-youth-felt-jon-schwartz/.

NATIVE AMERICAN MAJOR LEAGUERS

11 Colorado River Indian Tribes, 2009: Retrieved from https://www.crit-nsn.gov/ on March 15, 2025.

12 Joan M. Travis, "McCabe Family Supports Their Baseball Superhero – Jacoby Ellsbury."

13 Emanuela Samwel, "Jacoby Ellsbury Biography: Life, Legacy and Achievements," *Mabumbe*, January 23, 2025. https://mabumbe.com/people/jacoby-ellsbury-biography-life-legacy-and-achievements/.

14 Neil Swidey, "The Jacoby Factor."

15 Bryan Hoch, "Ellsbury's Tireless Work Ethic Traces to Mother."

16 Tony Ahern, "Jacoby Ellsbury on the Hall of Fame Ballot," *Madras* (Oregon) *Pioneer*, November 23, 2022.

17 Joan M. Travis, "McCabe Family Supports Their Baseball Superhero – Jacoby Ellsbury."

18 Mary Annette Pember, "'Rez Ball' Gains NCAA Certification Thanks to Native American Basketball Invitational (NABI)," *Diverse Issues in Higher Education*, April 9, 2007. https://www.diverseeducation.com/students/article/15083347/rez-ball-gains-ncaa-certification-thanks-to-native-american-basketball-invitational-nabi.

19 Corbin McGuire, "NCAA Native American Student-Athlete by the Numbers," NCAA, November 1, 2024. https://www.ncaa.org/news/2024/11/1/media-center-ncaa-native-american-student-athletes-by-the-numbers.aspx.

20 Gale Courey Toensing, "Boston Red Sox Select Ellsbury," *Indian Country Times*, July 28, 2005. https://ictnews.org/archive/boston-red-sox-select-ellsbury/.

21 "Jacoby Ellsbury Biography," *Mudville Megaphone*, October 27, 2007. https://thethunderchild.com/themudvillemegaphone/NewsFiles/Ellsburybio.html.

22 Matt Collins, "Remembering the 2007 Red Sox: Jacoby Ellsbury," *SB Nation Over the Monster*, April 24, 2017. https://www.overthemonster.com/2017/4/24/15402680/2007-red-sox-jacoby-ellbury.

23 Collins.

24 Associated Press, "Red Sox: Ellsbury Front and Center," *Cape Cod Times* (Hyannis, Massachusetts), February 25, 2009. https://www.capecodtimes.com/story/sports/2009/02/25/red-sox-ellsbury-front-center/52085343007/.

25 Benjamin Klein, "Jacoby Ellsbury Breaks Boston Red Sox Single-Game Stolen Base Record," MLB, May 31, 2018. https://bleacherreport.com/articles/1657319-jacoby-ellsbury-breaks-all-time-franchise-single-game-stolen-base-record.

26 Joe McDonald, "Ellsbury Said Team Backed Time in Arizona," ESPN, July 10, 2010. https://www.espn.com/boston/mlb/news/story?id=5369440.

27 McDonald.

28 Gordon Edes, "Jacoby Ellsbury Out at Least 4-6 Weeks," ESPN, August 17, 2010. https://www.espn.com/boston/mlb/news/story?id=5472158 .

29 Jackie MacMillan, "It's Time to Embrace Jacoby Ellsbury," ESPN, October 10, 2013.https://www.espn.com/boston/mlb/story/_/id/9804639/embrace-jacoby-ellsbury

30 "Jacoby Ellsbury Officially Ruled Out for Rest of 2010 Season," NESN, October 10, 2010. https://nesn.com/2010/09/jacoby-ellsbury-officially-ruled-out-for-rest-of-2010-season/#:~:text=Jacoby%20Ellsbury%20will%20not%20resume,scored%20in%20just%2018%20games.

31 Benjamin Klein, "Boston Red Sox: Jacoby Ellsbury Wins Comeback Player of the Year," MLB, June 7, 2018. https://bleacherreport.com/articles/892463-boston-red-sox-jacoby-ellsbury-wins-comeback-player-of-the-year-award.

32 Emanuela Samwel, "Jacoby Ellsbury Biography: Life, Legacy and Achievements."

33 Gordon Edes, "Jacoby Ellsbury Gets 9M Deal," ESPN, January 18, 2013. https://www.espn.com/mlb/story/_/id/8857840/jacoby-ellsbury-boston-red-sox-agree-one-year-9-million-deal.

34 Tyler Kepner, "Of Red Sox' Many Problems, Injuries Have Hurt the Most," *New York Times*, August 18, 2012: D3. https://www.nytimes.com/2012/08/18/sports/baseball/valentine-takes-blame-but-red-sox-woes-go-deeper.html.

35 Ben Buchanan, "Season Review: Jacoby Ellsbury," SB Nation Over the Monster, November 12, 2012. https://www.overthemonster.com/2012/11/12/3635730/season-review-jacoby-ellsbury.

36 "Injury Plagued Ellsbury in 2012," *Bend* (Oregon) *Bulletin*, October 6, 2012. https://bendbulletin.com/2012/10/06/injuries-plagued-ellsbury-in-2012/.

37 Matt Sullivan, "Jacoby Ellsbury's Resurgence," SB Nation Over the Monster, August 22, 2013. https://www.overthemonster.com/2013/8/22/4646868/jacoby-ellsbury-resurgence-red-sox-free-agent.

38 Andrew Mearns, "Yankees 2014 Roster Report Card: Jacoby Ellsbury," SB Nation Pinstripe Alley, October 6, 2014. https://www.pinstripealley.com/yankees-analysis-sabermetrics/2014/10/6/6917101/yankees-2014-player-report-card-jacoby-ellsbury-season-review#:~:text=Ellsbury%20also%20quickly%20made%20a,an%20excellent%2088.6%25%20success%20rate.

39 Scott Davis, "Yankees 2015 Report Card: Jacoby Ellsbury," SB Nation Pinstripe Alley, October 24, 2015. https://www.pinstripealley.com/2015/10/24/9603210/yankees-2015-roster-report-card-jacoby-ellsbury.

40 Joel Sherman, "The Bitter Reality of Yankees' $153M Ties to Jacoby Ellsbury," *New York Post*, October 6, 2015. https://nypost.com/2015/10/06/the-bitter-reality-of-yankees-153m-ties-to-jacoby-ellsbury/.

41 Mike Axisa, "The Underwhelming Jacoby Ellsbury 2016 Season Review," River Ave Blues, November 1, 2016: https://riveraveblues.com/2016/11/the-underwhelming-jacoby-ellsbury-2016-season-review-146714/#:~:text=330%2F.,average%20offensive%20production%20in%202016.

42 Brad Kelly, "Yankees Jacoby Ellsbury Time to Turn the Page: Fantasy Value in 2017," Fox News, March 4, 2020. https://www.foxsports.com/stories/mlb/yankees-jacoby-ellsbury-time-to-turn-the-page-fantasy-value-in-2017.

43 Emanuela Samwel, "Jacoby Ellsbury Biography: Life, Legacy and Achievements."

44 Mike Axisa, "Yankees Settle Contract Dispute with Jacoby Ellsbury and Avoid Grievance Hearing, Per Report," *CBS Sports*, April 22, 2022. https://www.cbssports.com/mlb/news/yankees-settle-contract-dispute-with-jacoby-ellsbury-and-avoid-grievance-hearing-per-report/.

45 Sunnie R. Clahchischiligi, "Reporter's Notebook: Does Jacoby Deserve the Rank of Hero?," *Navajo Times*, October 31, 2013: A-7. https://navajotimes.com/opinion/notebook/jacoby-deserve-rank-hero/.

46 Gale Courey Toensing, "Boston Red Sox Select Ellsbury," *Indian Country Today*, 2005. https://ictnews.org/archive/boston-red-sox-select-ellsbury/#:~:text=By%20all%20accounts%2C%20Jacoby%20is,and%20third%2Dbest%20defensive%20outfielder.

47 Kiali Berg, "Anthony Seigler Becomes Second Navajo Player in MLB History After Brewers Call-Up," *Native News Online*, July 3, 2025. https://nativenewsonline.net/currents/anthony-seigler-becomes-second-navajo-player-in-mlb-history-after-brewers-call-up.

BILL HARRELSON

By Jason Scheller

William "Wee Willy" Harrelson had an intriguing albeit short major-league baseball career. Harrelson was a rarity for a pitcher because he was a switch-hitter. He stood 6-foot-5 and was listed at 215 pounds during his playing career, which made him an imposing presence on the mound. He appeared in only 10 games in one season with the California Angels in 1968. In 1970 he was part of a trade in which none of the players who were involved ever played professional baseball again. Despite his brief career, Harrelson played in several memorable games against many future Hall of Famers.

William Charles Harrelson was born in Tahlequah, Oklahoma, on November 17, 1945, to William Harrelson, Sr. and Margaret Harrelson. His father was an auto parts salesman, and his mother was a waitress. He is a full-blooded Cherokee. He attended Bakersfield (California) High School, where he wrestled and played football and baseball. Pitching in one game, he struck out 12 for the Drillers. Harrelson was a wrestling and football champion and was twice named to the All-Valley baseball team. Harrelson's one ambition was "to become one of the greatest pitchers in baseball."[1] After high school he attended Bakersfield Junior College in 1963.

Before the 1964 season, Harrelson was signed by the Los Angeles Angels as an amateur free agent by scout Bert Niehoff. With the San Jose Bees of the Class-A California League, Harrelson appeared in seven games, starting three of them. His time with the Bees was short: After compiling an 0-2 record and a 15.00 ERA, he was sent to the Idaho Falls Angels of the Pioneer League (Rookie), where he got off to a much better start. In 15 games (10 starts), he pitched 66 innings, threw two complete games, and finished the season with a 4-5 record and an ERA of 5.59.

In 1965 Harrelson moved on to Davenport, Iowa, home of the Quad Cities Angels of the Class-A Midwest League. With Davenport, Harrelson pitched in 16 games, starting 12 while throwing two complete games, going 3-9 and recording an ERA of 4.99.

In 1966 Harrelson pitched for the Batavia Trojans of the Class-A New York-Pennsylvania League. Harrelson started 22 of his 24 games, hurling eight complete games, one a shutout. He finished the season with an 8-11 record and an ERA of 3.31. He finished second in the league in strikeouts (181).

Harrelson returned to San Jose in 1967. He started 10 of the 22 games he appeared in, throwing two complete games

(one a shutout). He finished with a record of 7-4 and a better ERA of 2.48.

In 1968 Harrelson moved up to Double-A, the El Paso Sun Kings of the Texas League. There he threw four complete games in seven starts. Harrelson finished his short stint with the Sun Kings with a 3-2 record and 3.60 ERA before moving up to the Seattle Angels of the Triple-A Pacific Coast League. There he pitched in 10 games (nine starts) and threw four complete games, two of them shutouts, and went 4-3 with a 4.17 ERA.

In June of 1968, Harrelson's contract was purchased by the California Angels. The Angels had been an expansion

1968 Seattle Angels Popcorn card

BILL HARRELSON

Bill Harrelson

team, purchased for $2.5 million in 1960 by Gene Autry.[2] Autry was an ever-present figure at the ballpark, mingling with the crowd and watching the games. His Angels made the playoffs three times during his tenure and lost each time.[3]

Some baseball records show Bill Harrelson's first major-league appearance as occurring in the nightcap of a doubleheader with the Boston Red Sox that had begun on June 13, 1968. However, Angels third baseman Paul Schaal was beaned in the left ear in the top of the fourth inning by Red Sox pitcher José Santiago, and was sent to Sancta Maria Hospital with a fractured skull. The Angels won that game 4-2. The Red Sox, led by Carl Yastrzemski, donned plastic batting helmets with ear flaps for game two. Spurred by the memory of Tony Conigliaro who was beaned by California Angels pitcher Jack Hamilton in 1967, Yastrzemski said, "It makes you realize you could be next."[4]

The Angels and Red Sox got in a half game in the second game of the doubleheader before the game was suspended in the bottom of the sixth inning because the Angels needed to make their 5:55 P.M. flight back to Los Angeles. The game was completed on August 4, 1968, when the Angels returned to Fenway Park.[5] When the game resumed that day, the score was tied, 1-1.

In his major-league debut, against the Oakland A's on July 31, 1968, at Oakland, Harrelson faced off against future Hall of Famer Catfish Hunter. He scattered four singles over the first seven innings. Then in the eighth inning Harrelson walked Ted Kubiak and gave up a single to Sal Bando. With two on and two out, Harrelson gave up a three-run home run to Mike Hershberger that put the A's ahead 3-0. Harrelson wound up pitching a complete-game six-hitter and losing, 4-1.[6]

The suspended game on June 13, 1968 resumed on August 4 with the score tied, 1-1. Harrelson was brought on in the bottom of the sixth inning and pitched well until the bottom of the ninth. Mike Andrews singled to left field and then Joe Foy and Carl Yastrzemski walked to load the bases. Andy Messersmith replaced Bill Harrelson after he loaded the bases and began pitching to Ken Harrelson.[7] Messersmith quickly ran up the count to 3-1 and Ken Harrelson blasted his next pitch into deep left field for the first grand slam of his career. "I was charged up," the batter said. "I just wanted to hit the ball hard to the outfield."[8] His grand slam put the Red Sox up 5-1 to win the game. Bill Harrelson was given the loss making him winless in his first two appearances at 0-2.

The defeat made Bill Harrelson's record 0-2. Under major-league rules, the game was "played" in its entirety on June 13. So, Harrelson's first defeat officially came on June 13, and his defeat on July 31 put his record at 0-2.

Harrelson made his second start on August 9, 1968, against Baltimore Orioles hurler Dave McNally at Baltimore's Memorial Stadium. In the bottom of the third inning, a Frank Robinson single scored Don Buford to give the Orioles a 1-0 lead. Then with one man on base in the seventh inning, Buford took a Harrelson offering deep for a two-run homer. The Angels, plagued by poor run support and wildness, lost the game. To make matters worse, the pitchers in the game hit four different batters including Brooks Robinson.[9] No matter the cause, the Angels lost 3-0 and Harrelson's record sank to a dismal 0-3.[10]

Harrelson faced another challenge on August 16, 1968, when he dueled Washington Senators pitcher Joe Coleman. Harrelson gave up three hits in five innings and struck out seven. The Senators capitalized on shoddy Angels fielding to score four runs off Harrelson, all unearned.[11]

Rookie third baseman Winston Llenas made his second error in as many games during the fourth inning, giving the Senators a two-run lead. Errors by shortstop Jim Fregosi and catcher Tom Satriano in the fifth inning contributed two more unearned runs to the Senators' lead. Harrelson did himself no favors, throwing wild pitches in the fourth and fifth innings as the Angels lost 4-2. Over the course of his first five games, Harrelson had pitched 22 innings and received one run of support. Speaking of Harrelson after the game, Angels manager Bill Rigney said, "We sure didn't give that kid much support, at bat or in the field."[12] "I'll have to admit this is shaking my confidence a little," Harrelson said. "When I go out there, I feel like I can't give up a run, earned or unearned." Harrelson added that he was "due to get some runs."[13]

The next game gave Harrelson everything he had asked for. On August 27 the Angels played the New York Yankees in a doubleheader at Yankee Stadium. In the first game the Yankees took the win, 2-0, behind clutch hitting from Mickey Mantle and Bobby Cox. In the nightcap, Harrelson pitched a no-hitter into the sixth inning before Joe Pepitone looped a one-out single to left field. Harrelson then walked Andy Kosco and Rocky Colavito. Then, out of the dugout came Mickey Mantle to pinch-hit to the delight of the 21,419 fans in attendance. As Mantle strolled to the plate, Angels shortstop Jim Fregosi walked to the pitcher's mound to talk to Harrelson. "Do you know who that is?" Fregosi asked Harrelson. The Angels rookie hurler stood there silently. Fregosi continued, "That's Mickey Mantle," and Harrelson replied, "That's who I thought it was."[14] Whether Harrelson recognized Mantle or not, Angels manager Rigney pulled Harrelson out of the game in favor of Andy Messersmith, who struck out Mantle. Even though Harrelson did not get to face Mantle, he got the first and only win of his major-league career.

Harrelson's next appearance came against the Oakland Athletics on September 1 at Anaheim Stadium. Things got off to a bad start for the Angels starter, Clyde Wright, who threw a wild pitch in the top of the fifth to score Sal Bando and give the A's a 1-0 lead. With one on and two out in the sixth inning Wright gave up a 489-foot home run to Reggie Jackson. Wright gave up a single to Danny Cater before allowing Sal Bando to smash a 400-foot home run to give the A's a 5-0 lead. In the top of the eighth, Harrelson came into the game and got the first batter to fly out to center field and struck out Jackson. Angels catcher Tom Satriano threw out Cater trying to steal second base to end the inning. In the ninth, Harrelson retired the A's on two fly outs and a groundout. The Angels scored two runs in the sixth inning, but that was all the offense they could muster, losing 5-2.[15]

On September 4 Harrelson started against the Cleveland Indians and Luis Tiant who was 18-9 at that point. Harrelson was in trouble from the beginning giving up four runs in 1⅓ innings before Clyde Wright replaced him. Wright fared no better. Tiant meanwhile pitched 5⅔ innings, and the Indians won, 9-5. Harrelson's record dropped to 1-5.[16]

On September 10 at Anaheim Stadium, Harrelson faced a Detroit Tigers team primed to win the pennant and their ace Denny McLain, who was looking for his 29th win of the season. Harrelson entered the game in the top of the sixth inning and coaxed Don Wert into a fly out to center field for the first out of the inning. He struck out McLain looking but walked Dick McAuliffe and gave up a single to Mickey Stanley. With runners in scoring position, Harrelson retired Jim Northrup on a fly ball to left field to end the inning. Harrelson was removed for a pinch-hitter in the bottom of the inning as the Tigers won, 7-2.[17]

In the rubber match the next day, Harrelson had a repeat performance of game two. He entered the game in the second inning and allowed a run to score on a sacrifice fly. Then in the third inning, Harrelson gave up two solo home runs in a row before leaving the game in the third inning. The Angels lost, 8-2.[18]

Harrelson endured his sixth loss of the season in game one of a road doubleheader against the Minnesota Twins on September 18. Entering a 1-1 game in the bottom of the fourth inning, he gave up three runs on four walks, two singles and a run-scoring balk. The final score, 4-3, pushed his won-lost record to 1-6.[19]

After the season the Angels returned Harrelson to the minors. He began 1969 with the Hawaii Islanders of the Pacific Coast League, appearing in four games, starting two of them, and going 1-0. Then he moved on to the El Paso Sun Kings of the Double-A Texas League. For El Paso he pitched 94 innings and had two complete games (one a shutout), finishing with a 4-9 record and a 4.40 ERA. Harrelson married Jane Sisson on February 8, 1969.

On January 14, 1970, the Angels traded Harrelson and utilityman Daniel Loomer to the Cincinnati Reds for pitcher Jack Fisher. None of the men in the trade would play in majors again. Loomer toiled for five more years in the minors, last playing for the Double-A Arkansas Travelers of the Texas League in 1974. Fisher pitched eight games for the Rochester Red Wings of the Triple-A International League, where he threw five complete games and finished with a 4-4 record before being moved to the Tulsa Oilers of the Texas League, where he appeared in nine games. In that nine-game span he pitched a shutout and was credited with two saves. Fisher never saw the majors again.

Harrelson was also relegated to the minors for the remainder of his career. He appeared in 22 games for the Indianapolis Indians of the Triple-A American Association, where he went 3-8 with a 5.48 ERA. Over 22 games he pitched one complete game (a shutout) and recorded one save. He continued pitching for Indianapolis in 1971, appearing in nine games, starting three, and recording one save. Harrelson moved down to the Trois-Rivieres Aigles (Eagles) of the Double-A Eastern League. He appeared in 16 games (started eight) and finished with a 2-3 record while recording one save.

In 1972 Harrelson played for Charros de Jalisco of the Mexican League. He appeared in 18 games, 17 of which he started for the Charros. He finished the 1972 season with a 5-7 record and a 5.55 ERA. Harrelson finished the season with three complete games for the Charros. He retired from the game after the 1972 season.

As of 2025, Harrelson lived in Ada, Oklahoma. Despite repeated attempts to reach him, the author was unable to obtain any information about his life since 1972. We understand that he and his family prefer to remain private.

SOURCES

In addition to the sources cited in the Notes, the author consulted Baseball-Reference, Retrosheet, Baseball Almanac, Stats Crew, and the Bill Harrelson player file at the National Baseball Hall of Fame.

Thanks to Anne R. Keene, who tried to help me track down Bill Harrelson. Thanks to Rachel Wells at the National Baseball Hall of Fame and Bill Nowlin for tracking down newspaper articles for Harrelson's first major-league appearance. Special thanks to Pat and Holly Scheller.

Written in memory of Greg Fowler.

NOTES

1   "William J. Weiss Baseball Questionnaire," June 22, 1964. Ancestry.com, https://www.ancestry.com/search/collections/61599/records/94023, accessed June 18, 2024.

2   Myrna Oliver, "From the Archives: Cowboy Tycoon Gene Autry Dies," *Los Angeles Times*, October 3, 1988. https://www.latimes.com/local/la-me-gene-autry-19981003-story.html, accessed June 18, 2024. Known as the Singing Cowboy, Autry is the only actor to have five stars on the Hollywood Walk of Fame, the first actor to star in both movies and television series, and to have his number 26 (representing his symbolic standing as the 26th man on a 25-man roster) retired by the Angels as team owner. He is most famous for the songs "Back in the Saddle Again," "Yellow Rose of Texas," "Frosty the Snowman," and "Rudolph the Red-Nosed Reindeer."

3   Scott Martelle, "'Win One for the Cowboy' is Still a Battle Cry in Anaheim," *Los Angeles Times*, October 10, 2002. https://www.latimes.com/archives/la-xpm-2002-oct-10-me-autry10-story.html, accessed June 18, 2024.

4   At the time of Conigliaro's beaning the batting helmet did not have the protective earpieces that are standard today. Conigliaro was struck in the left cheek fracturing his cheekbone and severely damaging the retina in his left eye. He missed the entire 1968 season and was eventually traded by the Red Sox to the Angels in 1970. Conigliaro retired after the 1970 season and tried to make a comeback with the Red Sox in 1975. Despite being only 30 years old, his eyesight had deteriorated, and he played in only 21 games.

Conigliaro retired for good after the 1975 season. Will McDonough, "Pitch Fractures Schaal's Skull," *Boston Globe*, June 14, 1968: 29.

5   Bob Sales, "Red Sox Lose, 4-2, Tie," *Boston Globe*, June 14, 1968: 29.

6   "Angels Lose Two Games to Athletics," *Lodi* (California) *News Sentinel*, August 1, 1968: 11.

7   Bill Harrelson has no known relation to Ken Harrelson.

8   Leigh Montville, "Hawk Slam in 9th Gives Sox Split," *Boston Globe*, August 5, 1968: 21.

9   The Angels hit four different batters in the game including Don Buford (hit by Bill Harrelson), Mark Belanger (hit by Marty Pattin), Frank Robinson (hit by Marty Pattin), and Brooks Robinson (hit by Dennis Bennett).

10   "O's Spank Angels, 3-0," *Eureka* (California) *Times Standard,* August 10, 1968: 7.

11   Dave Distel, "'Comedy of Errors' Gives Nats Victory," *Santa Ana* (California) *Register,* August 17, 1968: 13.

12   Fred Claire, "Angels Give Bats, Balls to Fans, Game to Nats," *Long Beach* (California) *Press-Telegram,* August 17, 1968: 18.

13   Claire.

14   "McLain Bids for 26 Again," *Redwood City* (California) *Tribune,* August 28, 1968: 9.

15   "Homers Win for A's, 5-2," *Fremont* (California) *Argus,* September 2, 1968: 9.

16   "Tribe Tees Off on Halo Hurlers as Tiant Gets 19th," *San Bernardino County Sun* (San Bernardino, California), September 5, 1968: 48.

17   Dave Distel, "McLain Notches No. 29 With 7-2 Win Over Angels," *Santa Ana Register,* September 11, 1968: 35. The win was McLain's 29th of the season. It made him the first Tigers pitcher to accomplish that feat since Hal Newhouser won 29 games in 1944.

18   "Tigers Bomb Angels, Reduce Number to 8," *Oklahoma City Times,* September 12, 1968: 33.

19   "Spencer Shocks Twins with Play," *Pomona* (California) *Progress Bulletin,* September 19, 1968: 85.

SLADE HEATHCOTT

By Mark S. Sternman

A first-round draft choice of the New York Yankees, Slade Heathcott had just a cup of coffee in the majors. He hit two home runs – one an especially memorable blast – but problems with alcohol curtailed his career.

Heathcott has Cherokee heritage. "A Cherokee is who I am," he said. "That's what I stand for. I always have a deep tie to it. … I have been to a point in my career where I was told my career might be over and to realize the mental side of it. With the right process and with the right mentality, we can do anything we want."[1]

Born in Texarkana, Texas, on September 28, 1990, Heathcott attended Texas High in Texarkana. After batting .457 with 4 home runs and 28 RBIs, he initially committed to Louisiana State University.[2] New York drafted Heathcott 29th overall in 2009, a draft most notable for the selections of Stephen Strasburg as the first overall pick and Mike Trout as the 25th. "Heathcott had a rough childhood," a journalist wrote. "Homeless for a brief period of his senior year of high school, Heathcott lived in his truck … [He] developed a drinking problem by age 19, but the Yankees helped him … through Alcoholics Anonymous meetings."[3]

The lack of male role models may help explain Heathcott's substance-use disorder. "Maybe he was looking for a little bit of guidance," said Barry Norton, Texas High's athletic director and its football coach. "I know that after every single practice he told me he loved me."[4]

Slade never met his biological father and once "pulled a shotgun on his stepfather" Jeff, who also had substance-use issues and died at the age of 47.[5] In a 2011 interview, his mother, Kimberly Johnson, said, "We had already split up and gone our separate ways by the time [Slade] got in trouble with the law. [He] got addicted to painkillers."[6] Slade also has a younger brother named Zane.

As an 18-year-old, Heathcott, a left-handed batter and outfielder, got one hit in three games for the Yankees' Gulf Coast League rookie league team in 2009. In 2010 he played 76 games for the Class-A Charleston RiverDogs, striking out 101 times in 298 at-bats. "I've never been a big strikeout guy," Heathcott said. "That was frustrating."[7]

Heathcott started with Charleston again in 2011 before advancing to the Tampa Yankees, where he homered in his first plate appearance[8] before hurting his left shoulder and missing the rest of the season.[9]

Heathcott had a .307 batting average in his full season (2012) with Tampa. The Yankees invited him to spring training for the first time before the 2013 season.[10] Heathcott played 103 games in 2013 for the Double-A Trenton Thunder where hitting coach Justin Turner touted his potential. "He's a tremendous athlete and a tremendous ballplayer, and I think we're just scratching the surface at age 22," Turner said. "Once the kid starts clicking, he's going to be a special player."[11]

After knee injuries limited Heathcott to just nine games with Trenton in 2014, the Yankees dropped him from the 40-man roster but invited him to spring training in 2015. He responded by winning the James P. Dawson Award as the best Yankee rookie in camp. The Yankees sent Heathcott to the Triple-A Scranton/Wilkes-Barre RailRiders and then recalled him in May to replace the injured Jacoby Ellsbury. "I think the kid's had to overcome a lot, not only growing up but even here," Yankees manager Joe Girardi said. "I think it's a great story where he's been and where he's come from, and he's got a chance to make it really good."[12]

By the time he got to the majors, Heathcott had a family of his own, with wife Jessica and son Kysen.[13] He debuted on May 20, 2015, as a pinch-runner and remained in the game to play center field. Heathcott started his first game on May 22. Batting ninth, he had two hits and scored a run in a 10-9 loss to Texas. Facing Colby Lewis, Heathcott hit a gapper into medium left-center that he ran into a double for his first big-league hit in his first Yankee Stadium at-bat.[14] On the same homestand, Heathcott had two hits again on May 25, including a two-run homer off Kansas City's Greg Holland into the short porch in right field[15] for the final runs in a 14-1 New York rout. "Is this real?" Heathcott said of his reaction to the homer. "I come back to the dugout, and I see

Slade Heathcott

a lot of the veteran guys. [Brian] McCann, CC [Sabathia], guys like that, congratulating me. It's awesome."[16]

Off to a .353 start through May 27, Heathcott injured his right quadriceps and went on the disabled list.[17] "Heathcott said he believed he aggravated the injury, which has troubled him on and off since spring training, chasing a Prince Fielder home run against the Yankees in a game on May 22."[18] Heathcott did not play again for the Yankees until September 14, in a game that would serve as the highlight of his baseball career.

Heathcott entered a scoreless contest at Tampa in the bottom of the eighth to play right field. The Rays scored a run in the frame to take a 1-0 lead into the ninth inning. Tampa closer Brad Boxberger pitched in relief. With two outs, Brett Gardner walked and stole second base. Álex Rodríguez doubled to score Gardner and tie the game. Boxberger intentionally walked McCann to get to Heathcott for his first plate appearance in a Yankees uniform in more than 3½ months. "I was just trying to pretend that this game is the same everywhere I play," Heathcott said. "Stay calm, get a good pitch to hit and hit it. That's all you can do." Still, he admitted, "I was trying to crush a ball."[19]

Not quite crushing it, Heathcott took Boxberger the other way with a homer just over the wall in left field[20] that proved decisive in New York's 4-1 win. Rodríguez most enthusiastically celebrated Heathcott's hit by coming off the bench to congratulate his teammate. "It's a moment he will never forget," Rodríguez said. "What a story."[21]

After his debut season in 2015, Heathcott never played in the majors again.

Heathcott had a splendid spring training in 2015 but a horrible one in 2016. Slated to start a Grapefruit League game, he missed the bus and got pulled from the lineup. "It was an immature decision that was disrespectful to not only this team but all the fans, people who have to wake up and go to work every day," Heathcott told the press.[22]

New York sent Heathcott to Triple A. In 23 games, he hit just .230 with no homers, and the Yanks released him in May. The White Sox signed him in June, and he hit .258 with two home runs in 34 games for Triple-A Charlotte. Heathcott signed with the Giants as a free agent before the 2017 season. San Francisco had "a good track record of not caring where their players come from, but when guys are producing moving them up," Heathcott said. "Ultimately I just needed an opportunity to play again and have fun and take advantage of that opportunity."[23]

Heathcott split his season between the San Francisco Double-A and Triple-A affiliates, batting .267 with 14 homers in 119 games. Oakland signed him as a free agent for 2018, but Heathcott played only 31 Triple-A games with one home run before getting released again. At the age of 27, he concluded his baseball career in 2018 with the Sugar Land Skeeters of the Atlantic League.

Heathcott has dabbled in a variety of ventures since he stopped playing, including going to school to become a commercial pilot[24] and serving as director of business development for More Than Baseball, which works to improve the living conditions of minor leaguers.[25] In June 2022 his LinkedIn profile listed four positions. On the social-media site, Heathcott described himself as "specializing in curating sustainable relationships while maximizing existing partnerships to increase revenue and brand storytelling. Passionately obsessive servant and perspective shifter. Purpose driven business development, influencer and ambassador marketing, and 501c3 strategy / partnership consultant."[26]

Fans may view first-round picks who last less than one year in the majors as disappointments, but in terms of Wins Above Replacement the Yankees did well by selecting Heathcott. New York picked him 29th overall, and as of May 2025 he ranked 25th in WAR among 2009 draftees.

Heathcott's brief big-league career serves as a compelling tale of someone who admirably combatted adversity and shined for a moment under the brightest lights for baseball's most successful franchise.

NOTES

1 Mark Dreadfulwater, "Heathcott Overcomes Injuries to Fulfill MLB Dream," www.cherokeephoenix.org/news/heathcott-overcomes-injuries-to-fulfill-mlb-dream/article_d697b894-9e49-50a5-bd47-eb25e43d862b.html, March 18, 2016 (accessed June 10, 2022).

2 Tim Bontemps, "Slade Heathcott on Slade Heathcott," *New York Post*, June 10, 2009.

3 Brendan Kuty, "Who Is Yankees' Slade Heathcott?" NJ.com, May 20, 2015. https://www.nj.com/yankees/2015/05/who_is_yankees_slade_heathcott.html

4 Gene Sapakoff, "Tale of Salvation: Formerly a Tormented Teen, Riverdogs Star and Top Yankee Prospect Slade Heathcott Has Turned His Life Around," *Charleston* (South Carolina) *Post and Courier*, May 12, 2011.

5 Brendan Kuty, "Former Top Yankees Prospect Who Overcame Demons Just Wants to Be the Father He Didn't Have," NJ.com, March 27, 2019. https://www.nj.com/yankees/2019/03/former-top-yankees-prospect-who-battled-demons-just-wants-to-be-the-father-he-didnt-have.html

6 Travis G., "Interview With Slade Heathcott's Mother: Part 1 of 2," www.pinstripealley.com/2011/6/21/2234557/interview-with-slade-heathcotts-mother-part-1-of-2, June 21, 2011 (accessed June 10, 2022).

7 Erik Boland, "Prospect Heathcott Hitting His Stride," *Newsday* (Long Island, New York), April 28, 2011.

8 David Heck, "Heathcott Homers in Debut with Tampa," MLB.com, June 29, 2011.

9 Marc Carig, "The Yankees This Week: Derek Jeter, Jorge Posada Set Mark, Bartolo Colon Implodes," *Newark Star-Ledger*, July 17, 2011.

10 Andrew Marchand, "Get to Know: Slade Heathcott," ESPN.com, February 27, 2013.

11 Steven Braid, "Slade Heathcott Showing Hustle in Minors," *Newsday*, May 25, 2013.

12 Daniel Barbarisi, "Uncertain Return for Jacoby Ellsbury Means a Chance for Slade Heathcott," *Wall Street Journal*, May 20, 2015.

13 George A. King III, "Yankees Once Feared Alcohol Would Kill Call-Up Slade Heathcott," *New York Post*, May 20, 2015.

14 www.youtube.com/watch?v=lUxHYg9M3FM (accessed May 20, 2022).

15   www.youtube.com/watch?v=5M4OdzauXEE (accessed May 20, 2022).

16   Ryan Hatch, "Yankees' Slade Heathcott on 1st Career Home Run: 'Is This Real?'" NJ.com, May 25, 2015. https://www.nj.com/yankees/2015/05/yankees_slade_heathcott_on_1st_career_home_run_is.html

17   George A. King III, "Yanks' Heathcott DL-Bound after MRI Exam Worse Than Expected," *New York Post*, May 29, 2015.

18   Wallace Matthews, "Slade Heathcott put on DL with quad injury," ESPN.com, May 29, 2015.

19   Wallace Matthews, "On Brink of Disaster, Heathcott Delivers Yankees' 'Biggest Win of the Year,'" ESPN.com, September 15, 2015.

20   www.youtube.com/watch?v=f7GafAXiVa4 (accessed May 20, 2022).

21   Kevin Kernan, "From Alcohol Struggles to Yankees Hero: Slade Heathcott's Journey," *New York Post*, September 15, 2015.

22   Anthony Rieber, "Yankees' Slade Heathcott Apologetic, Regretful About Missing Bus to Bradenton," *Newsday*, March 19, 2016.

23   Kyle Glaser, "Slade Heathcott Starts Fresh in Giants System," *BA Newsletter*, May 10, 2017. https://www.baseballamerica.com/stories/slade-heathcott-starts-fresh-in-giants-system/.

24   Mark W. Sanchez, "Former Troubled Yankees Top Prospect Slade Heathcott Becoming Pilot," *New York Post*, January 14, 2019.

25   Scott Ortega, "'More Than Baseball' Aims to Help Minor Leaguers with Food, Housing, Equipment and Other Services," *Forbes*, February 20, 2019, www.forbes.com/sites/scottorgera/2019/02/20/more-than-baseball-aims-to-help-minor-leaguers-with-food-housing-equipment-and-more/?sh=2b360e951279 (last accessed June 10, 2022).

26   www.linkedin.com/in/sladeheathcott/ (last accessed June 14, 2022).

BOB JOHNSON

By Bill Nowlin

Because he was born on an Indian reservation, Bob Johnson was considered a ward of the government. He and his older brother Roy Johnson, whose career began in 1929 with the Detroit Tigers, were both born in Pryor, Oklahoma (some 35 miles east of Tulsa) – before Oklahoma became a state.[1] Roy was the eldest of the two, born in 1903. Robert Lee Johnson was born on November 26, 1905.[2] They had six siblings, two other boys and four girls. Their father was also named Robert Lee Johnson; he'd moved to the area from Missouri. Anna B. Downing was half-French, half-Cherokee. Bob came to be widely known as "Indian Bob" Johnson. When he was asked his nationality, Bob replied, "American."[3]

There are different stories suggesting why the family moved to Tacoma, Washington, but move there they did.[4] Both brothers enrolled in Irving School and played sandlot ball. It's said they attended Tacoma High School, but biographers Patrick J. and Terrence K. McGrath report, "Nobody remembers the boys ever attending high school."[5] Roy reported going to school through eighth grade; Bob said he went to the Irving School through fifth grade and

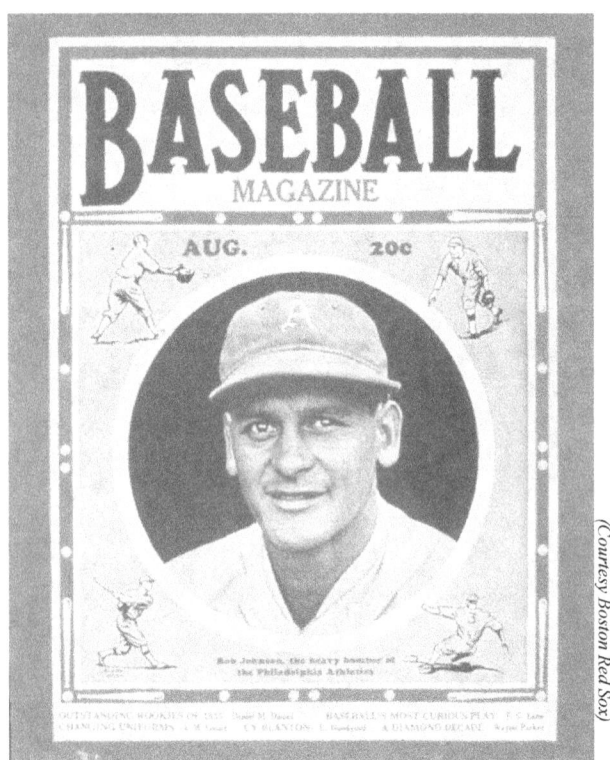

Bob Johnson, 1944

(Courtesy Boston Red Sox)

no further.[6] In fact, it seems that Bob may have run away from home at age 13 and gone to Southern California.[7] Roy began playing ball there, in the City League around 1922 and eventually came to the attention of scouts. Sonny Bailey, a former classmate of both Roy and Bob, saw them as opposites: "Roy was a hot-headed guy; Bob was real quiet. Roy could run like a rabbit. He was actually a natural right-handed hitter but his coaches always had him bat left-handed to take advantage of that great speed. Years later, when he made the big leagues, they made motion pictures of him running and bunting."[8]

Bob Johnson is listed as batting and throwing right-handed, standing an even six feet tall and weighing 180 pounds. He was an outfielder throughout his 13-year big-league career (three more than his elder brother). Bob hit for more power (288 HR to Roy's 58, for instance) but, remarkably, both brothers wound up with identical .296 averages. If they really wanted to get down to it, though, Roy could lord it over his brother just a bit in batting average: Roy hit .2963982 and Bob came in second with .2963872.

Bob held a very significant edge, being named seven times to the American League All-Star team. Roy was never so honored.

As the younger Johnson, Bob followed Roy into baseball. He got married five years earlier, however, and married Caroline Stout on August 15, 1924. They had three children — Roberta Louise, Beverly, and a son, Robert Lee Johnson III, who died before the age of 1.

Bob had been playing some semipro ball in Glendale, California, and he took a position as a firefighter serving in the ladder company as a pump engineer. Both he and Roy had played for the Miner Bldg. Co. team in Los Angeles, Roy as a pitcher and Bob at shortstop. They won the Industrial League pennant in 1925.

In 1931, he told sportswriters in Philadelphia, "I'd probably be chief of my company by now if that brother of mine, Roy, hadn't kidded himself that he was a ball player. I was always better than Roy. When he stuck with Detroit, I knew I was good enough for the big leagues. That's why I'm here."[9] Roy's ragging on his brother may have blurred the timeline a little. Roy's first year with the Tigers was in 1929, the same year Bob began his career with Portland in the Pacific Coast League. But Roy had been playing baseball for pay for several years, though one could say he started his own fulltime career the year before, with the San Francisco Seals.

Roy wowed followers of the game that year, hitting .360 with 22 homers, and making the Pacific Coast League All-Star team. The Detroit Tigers paid the Seals $75,000 for him.[10] As one of the highest amounts ever paid for a player, it made headlines and certainly showed Bob Johnson there might be more lucrative opportunities for him than firefighting, particular if he did indeed believe he was a better player than his brother. Henry P. Edwards of the American League Service Bureau quoted Bob: "By all the gods of the Cherokee, if Brother Roy can get away with it in the big leagues, so can I."[11]

While Roy was due to break in during 1929, Bob continued to play semipro ball. In fact, he'd saved some vacation time and in the spring of 1928 had visited any Coast League training camp he could get to. "He was rejected by every team he approached."[12] Even after Roy's $75,000 purchase was so widely publicized, Bob was again "turned down by virtually every club in the circuit. But Lady Luck was riding with Bob this time around. A Wichita (Western League) scout spotted Bob during one of his futile attempts with a Coast League club."[13] The "scout" in question was Art Griggs, manager of the Wichita Aviators.[14] Griggs had first heard of Johnson from Marty Krug of the Angels, who saw Bob hit five balls over the left-field fence during a workout, but the Angels had too many outfielders at the time and no place to farm out Johnson.[15] Henry Edwards told another story about the tryout for the Angels. He wrote that Bob had shown up in shoes that were too big for him, resulting in his coming across as very awkward and an L.A. writer calling him a "big-footed Swede." Bob, the Glendale firefighter, later said, "If I knew that writer's house were burning, I would have let it burn. Me, a big-footed Swede. Me through whose veins the blood of the Cherokee warriors flowed."[16] Bob signed with Wichita in February 1929.

Even with Krug's recommendation, he had difficulty getting established. Wichita, unimpressed, even loaned him out to the Pueblo club at one point. At Pueblo, "they decided someone had pulled a fast one of them and they sent me back. The Wichita manager grunted and made room for me on the bench. Then the regular center fielder [Forrest Jensen] broke an ankle and I was placed out there. Suddenly, I began to hit and after that they couldn't get me out. Portland bought me."[17] They could have signed him a few months earlier. Now it cost Portland $12,500.[18] He had begun to hit for sure. The *Chicago Tribune* says he had hit 16 homers in three weeks.[19] In all he hit .273 with those 16 homers for Wichita. It took him a while to get going with the higher-classification Portland, but in 81 games he hit a respectable .254 with five more homers. Portland's president Tom Turner predicted, "You'll hear from this fellow in the majors in another season, or so."[20]

It was three seasons later. Bob Johnson played 1930 through 1932 for Portland. In 1930, he hit .265 in 157 games but showed some power, with 21 home runs, though he was inconsistent and a little streaky. After the 1930 season, the

Philadelphia Athletics purchased his contract on November 10. He'd been personally recommended to Connie Mack by Athletics VP John D. Shibe, who'd been particularly impressed with his fielding.[21] He kept in shape playing winter ball with the Shell Oil team in Los Angeles.

Bob had a very good spring training at Fort Myers with the Athletics, but it was a tough outfield to crack. The absence of Al Simmons, holding out, gave Bob an opening. Bob even played in the city series with the Phillies in April, and Mack had decided to keep him. But at the last minute, Simmons signed, and Mack optioned Johnson back to Portland, admitting he'd changed his mind. In the 1931 season, Johnson hit .337 with 22 home runs for Portland despite being moved around in the field. He played every infield position at one time or another, though largely played outfield. The Beavers had been last in 1930 but finished in third place in 1931.

The Athletics had won the American League pennant three years in a row, 1929-1931. They'd won the World Series in 1929 and 1930, and took the 1931 Series to Game Seven before falling to the Cardinals. Arguably, they didn't need Bob Johnson yet, and Mack optioned him to Portland yet again, well before spring training – in December 1931.[22] Johnson was disappointed, and perhaps surprised by Mack being quoted as saying, "Johnson still does not hit the curve ball well enough." The McGraths suggest that there were "whispers throughout the league about Roy Johnson's flirtation with firewater [and that in spring training 1931 there had been] reports of Bob roaming the streets of Fort Myers chanting war whoops into the small wee hours of the morning."[23] It took another year before Bob could make the Athletics. He hit .330 in 149 games for Portland, with 29 home runs, and the Beavers won the Pacific Coast League pennant.

Johnson was pretty much a lock for 1933, and if there was any doubt he may have secured it with back-to-back games against the Dodgers in late March exhibition play in which he cracked four doubles and a home run, and drove in six.[24] He debuted with Philadelphia on April 12, collecting his first base hit, a double, on a 1-for-4 day. He got one or more hits, including his first home run, in each of his first 19 games, save one (and in that one, he drove in a run). He was batting .348 with 18 RBIs after his first 20 games. That made an impression.

It was less than two weeks into the season when the two brothers – Bob and Roy – first faced each other in major-league play on April 23, 1933 when the Athletics visited Fenway Park. Bob played right field for Philadelphia and batted fifth in the order, following Jimmie Foxx. He was 0-for-5 on the day, batting against an unrelated Johnson, Red Sox pitcher Hank. Roy Johnson batted second for the Red Sox, playing center field. He had a 2-for-5 day, with one RBI and one run scored. He committed two errors. The Red Sox won. Both Johnsons had two RBIs the next day, with Roy enjoying another 3-for-5 day, and Bob settling for a double and three runs scored. (Jimmie Foxx overshadowed them both; he drove in seven runs with three doubles and a homer; the Athletics held on to win, 12-11.)

There were numerous other times in the four seasons they both played American League ball when both brothers played in the same game, but being on opposing teams didn't affect their closeness. The two often spent time together in the offseason hunting and fishing. They never played for the same team at the same time, but after the June 17, 1933, doubleheader in Boston, the two teams shared the same train west — the Red Sox heading to Cleveland and the Athletics to Detroit.

Bob played right field in April, then switched over and played left field from that point forward. He had a .952 fielding percentage and recorded 16 assists. At the plate, he drove in 93 runs and scored 103; his batting average was .290.

Where brother Roy had slumped a bit in his sophomore season, Bob bumped his average up to .307 in 1934; he remained steady with 92 RBIs and 111 runs scored. He hit 34 homers, one of which was a May 2 pinch-hit homer at Fenway that gave the Athletics the lead in a game they won, 12-11. The four RBIs that Roy drove in kept the Red Sox close, but it was Bob's hit that made the difference. He had 27 home runs when he wrenched his back spearing a ball off the wall of the bleachers at Comiskey Park on July 15, and hit none for more than a month. He could still play, but he was hampered as to power. Up to that point, he'd battled teammate Jimmie Foxx back and forth for the league lead in home runs, but after the 15th he hit only seven more. He still finished fourth in the league and had a very good year. His best day had to have been the June 16 doubleheader against the White Sox. Johnson was 2-for-5 in the first game, with a run scored, but the Athletics lost, 9-7. So he poured it on in the second game, going 6-for-6 with a double and two home runs, driving in four runs in an 11-inning 7-6 win. Over the winter, Johnson worked as a carpenter at Paramount Studios in Los Angeles.

In his third year – 1935 – he was named to the All-Star team for the first time. As late as June 8, he was still batting over .400. From June 10 on, he hit at a .259 pace, ceding first place on the 26th and winding up with a .299 average, but he drove in 109 runs. He was a legitimate slugger. Each of his first three seasons, he ranked third in the league in home runs.

Presumably, he earned a nice bonus. He had argued for more money after his exceptional second season, but Connie Mack was apparently still concerned that Johnson could get a little too rowdy. One Philadelphia headline read, "Bob Johnson Learns He Will Get Bonus If He Conducts Himself Beyond Reproach."[25] In 1936, when he seemed prepared to hold out yet again, he told newspapers that he wanted $12,000 for the year, and that he'd gotten $2,500 the year before by holding out (perhaps not the wisest thing to say.)[26] Matters were worked out quickly and he joined the team for spring training.

Contrary to the prior years, Johnson got off to a slow start in 1936 and didn't approach .300 until late June. His wife had a serious illness that required hospitalization and it had been weighing on his mind. By season's end, he hit .292. There was a stretch in mid-July where he played 22 games at second base (and turned 20 double plays), but otherwise he was in his accustomed left field. At the plate, he drove in a career-best 121 runs. The Athletics had slipped badly; they finished in last place. Johnson's 25 homers were more than double anyone else on the team.

In 1937, six of the 108 runs he batted in all came in one inning, an American League record at the time. It was in the first inning of the first game on August 29 against the White Sox at Chicago, and accounted for half of the 12 runs the Athletics put on the board before the White Sox ever got to bat. He drove in two with a single his first time up and hit a grand slam the next time up. Johnson drove in another run later in the game. The final score was 16-0. Another run he drove in that year had been the June 30 fifth-inning homer he hit off the Yankees' Lefty Gomez, the only hit of the game off Gomez.

In terms of runs batted in, one would be hard-pressed to find someone with more consistent production over the seven-year stretch from 1935 through 1941: 109, 121, 108, 113, 114, 103, 107. By 1938, it was safe to say that Johnson had become Connie Mack's franchise player. Many of the others – Foxx, Lefty Grove, and more – Mack had sold off, mostly to Tom Yawkey of the Red Sox.

The Athletics held a "Bob Johnson Day" on September 17, 1939. Bob was 3-for-7 on the day. In ceremonies, he was presented "a set of silver, two bird dogs, and numerous gifts."[27]

Mack continued to sell off players when he had to, but he always held back Bob Johnson. In preparing for the winter meetings in December 1939, for instance, he declared that the whole team was "on the auction block," except for catcher Frankie Hayes and Bob Johnson.[28] Johnson had been an All-Star once again in 1939, and this time maintained his hitting throughout the full year, ending with a .338 batting average, best of his career, topped only by Joe DiMaggio and Jimmie Foxx. His 114 RBIs also placed him third; only Ted Williams and Joe DiMaggio drove in more. The Athletics were a seventh-place team in 1939, but Bob Johnson placed eighth in the MVP balloting.

Before the 1940 season, Mack took the unusual step of signing Johnson to a two-year contract. Johnson had a mixed year in 1940; with a bad ankle, his average dropped to its lowest, .268, but he hit 31 home runs, drove in 103 runs, and played well in the field. The team finished in last place again.

For a while, heading into August 1941, it looked like the Athletics might get out of the cellar; they were in fourth place as late as August 3. Bob Johnson drove in 107, homered 22 times, and improved his average, though only slightly, to .275.

Bob was not likely to be called to military service in the immediate aftermath of Pearl Harbor. He was 35, married, and with two children. Fellow outfielder Wally Moses was no longer with the team, though, traded to the White Sox. The McGraths write, "One player who would definitely miss Moses was none other than Bob Johnson. It was no coincidence that with the arrival of Wally, Bob started his consecutive 100 RBI streak, and it would be no mere happenstance that with the departure of Moses, Bob's streak would come to an end. Wally was one of the few guys at the top of the order who proved to be of great assistance to Indian Bob."[29] He hit .291 but drove in only 80 (the entire team drove in 517), and homered 13 times (no one else homered more than five times.) Johnson had one of his best years on defense, with a .990 fielding percentage and 17 outfield assists.

After the season, and before September was over, Johnson announced that he would not play again for the Athletics. There was a bitter disagreement between him and Connie Mack over the second threshold of the attendance bonus Johnson believed he should have received, based on the announced attendance for the season. "Mack held to his position that the attendance figures announced daily had been inflated," and that they had actually drawn more than 116,000 fewer (or more than 20% less than announced.)[30] Naturally, Johnson was suspicious and felt aggrieved. He said he would work in a shipyard instead. At least one headline in November read, "A's Want To Get Rid of Bob."[31] Mack announced that Johnson was available.

Spring training started later in 1943, and the two were still at loggerheads, neither willing to bend.[32] The day pitchers and catchers were due to report was March 21 and on that day, Mack traded Johnson to the Washington Senators for outfielder Bobby Estalella, infielder Jimmy Pofahl, and that ever-helpful commodity, cash. The McGraths say that not only did Mack deny Johnson the $2,500 bonus but he offered him $4,000 less in base salary for 1943 and did away with attendance bonuses completely. They also say that "Mack's pique got in the way of his judgment" and he had turned down better offers that had been available earlier.[33]

Red Smith wrote, "The Athletics lost the finest ball player they have had since championship days."[34]

Naturally, Johnson wanted to do well against his former team. He didn't have a very good year overall. He got into 117 games (his previous low was 138) and hit a career-low .265 for the year, with only 63 RBIs, also the fewest of any year to date. Of the 63 RBIs, 19 of them were against the Athletics, far more than against any other team. His batting average was .320 against the Athletics; only the .306 he hit against the Red Sox exceeded .300. And he hit only seven home runs all year long, attributable perhaps to the softer "balata ball" used during World War II to help conserve rubber for the war effort. (The entire Washington team hit 47 home runs in 1943, and yet finished in second place.)

Part of the reason for his relatively poor performance can be traced to a hand injury on July 17. He had a 3-for-4 day and was hitting .296 at the time, but hurt his hand. "How the hand was injured was open to conjecture," report the McGraths. "The story given by the club was that Bob had sprained the hand making a sliding catch against the Red Sox. Later it was strongly hinted that Bob had dented the hand on the head of [teammate] Alex Carrasquel for the big right-hander's lack of competitive fire."[35] He also had a serious fever that had him out from August 25 to September 4.

Johnson also played 19 games at third base and 10 at first, and was glad for the opportunity. For years, he had said he wanted to play infield and finally got his chance.[36] For all his talk, he made eight errors in 76 chances, an .895 fielding percentage.

Despite his offensive stats being much lower than other years, the baseball writers noted his importance to the second-place Senators and voted Bob Johnson fifth place in league MVP voting. It was the highest he ever placed.

The Boston Red Sox offered cash and bought Johnson from Washington on December 4, reportedly for $10,000.[37] He played his next two seasons for the team that had once employed his brother Roy. Burt Whitman of the *Boston Herald* wrote, "Johnson's no paragon. In fact, he's earned himself quite a rep with the old fire-water, second only to that enjoyed by brother Roy."[38] Whitman also reported that Bob had never had a run-in with Washington manager Ossie Bluege.

Johnson played left field for the Red Sox and had a very good year. He hit .324, and his .431 on-base percentage led the American League. He hit for the cycle on June 6 in Detroit. Johnson drove in 106 runs, the eighth time he'd exceeded 100 RBIs. He was named to the All-Star team, and placed 10th for MVP. The Red Sox made a legitimate run for the pennant, but when September arrived (and Bobby Doerr and a couple of others left for military service), they slid back to fourth place, solidified by a 10-game losing streak.

He came close to perishing on his way to spring training in 1945. He traveled across country from Oregon to Philadelphia, then caught a connecting train to Atlantic City, near where the Red Sox were holding spring training. The train was packed and there was no room to sit, but it was only an hour's ride so he stood in between two cars, one foot on each side of the gap. Somehow the cars became uncoupled and he "found himself doing a split" but held onto one of the railings and pulled himself onto that car.[39]

Johnson's last year in the majors was 1945, and his .280 average cost him the chance to finish with a career average over .300. He finished at .296. He added another 72 runs batted in, and 12 more homers boosted his career total to 288. Two days after Christmas, knowing that most of their prewar team – Ted Williams, Dominic DiMaggio, Bobby

Doerr, Johnny Pesky, etc. – would be rejoining them for the 1946 season, the Red Sox released Bob Johnson. On July 26, he had passed the 2,000-hit mark and he finished with 2,051 base hits. He realized he might have put up even higher totals on offense if he had played on better teams. "When you're playing for a weak team, it's a lot tougher… Just for my own satisfaction, I would have liked to have been playing for the Yankees when they were good. Pitchers couldn't have afforded to concentrate on me – they would have been busy worrying about other guys in the lineup. Besides, when you're with a winning team, you can't help but be a better ball player."[40]

Hall of Famer Bucky Harris agreed: "That guy should have led the league both in hitting and runs batted in. But with the Athletics there was rarely anybody on base to drive home, and because there was nobody behind him in the lineup with any batting power, Bob had to keep hitting at bad balls."[41]

Only three times did he play for a team that finished above .500.

Johnson was already thinking about life after baseball. "I know this game. I am confident I could do a good job as a manager. But then again – that's all of baseball's breaks, too. Somebody's got to give you a chance. And there aren't that many managerial jobs floating around."[42]

He wasn't ready to hang up his playing career, however. Apparently, more than one big-league team made him an offer, but the American Association's Milwaukee Brewers offered $10,000, outbidding them all.[43] He got off to a good start, but injured his leg on July 3, toughed it out but felt he was adding nothing to the team, and decided to quit on July 31. He'd been in 94 games, batting .270 at the end.

Johnson came back in 1947, playing for the Seattle Rainiers in the Pacific Coast League. He hit .295 in 130 games, though with only seven home runs. The team released him on September 30 and it looked as though his time in baseball may be done. But on July 14, 1948, a need developed and the Rainiers added him to their roster. He got into 83 games and hit .283.

In 1949 he was presented the managerial opportunity he had sought, with the Tacoma Tigers of the Class-B Western International League. He didn't have the strongest personnel. The best player on the team was himself, and he assigned himself to play wherever needed – six positions in May alone, including pitching. It wasn't just a stunt. He actually pitched 99 innings in 27 games, with a 5-7 record but a telltale 7.00 earned run average. On September 4, the team held a Bob Johnson Day in Tacoma. In December, Jim Brillheart was named manager for 1950.

Bob's marriage to Caroline Stout ended around this time, and he married Betty Pastore on September 20, 1950. He gave up his ranch in the divorce from Caroline, but the marriage to Betty lasted for the rest of his life. Betty also gave birth to Robert Lee Johnson III in 1951. Two years later, Bob lost his daughter Beverly Jean to lupus.

For years, Johnson had run a tavern in Tacoma. He had been driving an oil truck from the late 1940s, making fuel deliveries to homes in the area.

Bob played City League ball in Tacoma for a few years, and played games against the maximum security prison team on McNiel Island all the way until 1967.[44] After working for the oil company, he began driving for the George Scofield Company, which dealt in ready-mix concrete, sand, and gravel. Lastly, he worked driving a beer truck for the Heidelberg Brewery and as a worker in the Carling Brewery Co. bottling plant.

His work in the beer industry stands in juxtaposition to the demons with which brother Roy struggled. Accounts indicate that Bob took care of his brother Roy, who battled alcoholism and didn't hold a regular job. Roy died on September 10, 1973, his death attributed to "chronic alcoholism."[45] Bob Johnson was later named to the Pierce County Hall of Fame and the Washington State Hall of Fame. None other than Ted Williams once spoke, in 1975, about Bob's accomplishment with the Philadelphia Athletics: "Bob drove in over one hundred runs in seven of his first nine seasons with that rag-tag outfit. There weren't that many runners on base than that when he came to the plate in those years, let alone guys in scoring position."[46]

Bob Johnson died of heart failure on July 6, 1982, in Tacoma.

SOURCES

In addition to the sources cited in the Notes, the author also accessed Johnson's player file and player questionnaire from the National Baseball Hall of Fame, the *Encyclopedia of Minor League Baseball*, Retrosheet.org, Baseball-Reference.com, and the SABR Minor Leagues Database, accessed online at Baseball-Reference.com.

NOTES

1   Roy Johnson reported being "farm born" on his Hall of Fame player questionnaire. Other accounts locate the ranch at Spavinaw, Oklahoma, about 24 miles from Pryor. Spavinaw itself is the birthplace of Mickey Mantle. Bob wrote "on a farm near Pryor, Oklahoma."

2   On an American League questionnaire he appears to have completed around 1940, Bob wrote that he was born on that date in 1906. On his Hall of Fame player questionnaire, which he completed in the early 1960s, he made himself yet another year younger, saying he's been born in 1907.

3   *Chicago Tribune*, June 22, 1934: 25. Some of the newspapers, of course, played up the Indian angle. John Drohan of a Boston newspaper wrote about approaching Roy in the Red Sox dugout and holding up his right hand and saying, "How?" Then he asked, "How many base hits you ketchum today?" Roy, playing along (and it was in play), responded, "Injun no know, but him keep swingin' just the same. He like white man pitcher, but if white man pitcher get 'um mad, just too bad. Injun know you can't get 'em hit with tomahawk on shoulder. But if Injun swing 'em, ketchum base hit." How do we know this was all said in jest? After two more paragraphs of this farcical language, Drohan quoted wrote: "'Say cut it out,' said Roy breaking into United States, 'you'll have me talking that way permanently." John Drohan, "Cherokee-Swede Smote Ball for .571 Against St. Louis and Chicago Teams," unattributed, undated newspaper clipping,

4   Most of the information about the Johnson family, and Bob's post-baseball career, comes from the exhaustively researched book by Patrick J. and

Terrence K. McGrath, *Bright Star in a Shadowy Sky: The Story of Indian Bob Johnson* (Pittsburgh: Dorrance Publishing, 2002).

5   McGrath & McGrath, 3.

6   Bob Johnson player questionnaire at the National Baseball Hall of Fame.

7   Red Smith, *Philadelphia Record*, n.d., September 1939. See McGrath & McGrath, 361.

8   McGrath & McGrath, 2, 3.

9   McGrath & McGrath, 4.

10   Associated Press, "Tigers Sign Harris, Former Washington Leader, As Manager," *New York Times*, October 20, 1928: 15.

11   American League press release, dated December 1933. Roy added, "I'm a better player than Roy…if he can make good in the big show, what's to stop me."

12   McGrath & McGrath, 10.

13   McGrath & McGrath, 15.

14   James C. Isaminger, "Under the Spotlight," *Philadelphia Inquirer*, June 10, 1934: 4S.

15   "Youngster Shows Power," *Los Angeles Times*, February 15, 1929: A9.

16   American League press release dated December 1933.

17   McGrath & McGrath, 15, 16.

18   L. H. Gregory, "Angels Got Started Too Late to Save Krug After Hollywood Passed," *Oregonian*, July 11, 1929: 15.

19   "Johnson Is Just As Handy at Bat as at Fire Pump," *Chicago Tribune*, June 22, 1934: 25.

20   McGrath & McGrath, 17.

21   James C. Isaminger, "Under the Spotlight," *Philadelphia Inquirer*, June 10, 1934: 4S. See also *Philadelphia Record*, January 9, 1931, and James C. Isaminger, "Under the Spotlight," *Philadelphia Inquirer*, January 25, 1931: 4S.

22   Associated Press, "Johnson Goes Back to Portland Team," *San Diego Union*, December 31, 1931: 13.

23   McGrath & McGrath, 84, 87.

24   Roscoe McGowen, "Athletics' Long Hits Beat Dodgers, 7-4," *New York Times*, March 31, 1933: 24.

25   McGrath & McGrath, 205.

26   McGrath & McGrath, 239.

27   "Feller Bows, 4-2, Then Indians Win," *New York Times*, September 18, 1937: 26.

28   Associated Press, "Auction Block," *Christian Science Monitor*, November 1, 1939: 15.

29   McGrath & McGrath, 446.

30   McGrath & McGrath, 471.

31   *Evening Post* (Charleston, South Carolina), November 28, 1942: 37.

32   See, for instance, Associated Press, "Johnson Rejects A'S Offer, Still Wants To Be Traded," *Washington* (DC) *Evening Star* of January 24, 1943.

33   McGrath & McGrath, 478.

34   *Philadelphia Record*, March 24, 1943.

35   McGrath & McGrath, 491.

36   Shirley Povich, "Senators' Homers Check Browns, 6-4," *Washington Post*, July 4, 1943: S3.

37   Staff Correspondent, "Red Sox Pay $10,000 for Outfielder," *Washington Post*, December 4, 1943: 10.

38   Burt Whitman, "Red Sox Purchase Indian Bob Johnson From Nats for Cash," *Boston Herald*, December 4, 1943: 4.

39   "Bob Johnson of Red Sox Had Close Call on Train," unidentified March 29, 1945 news clipping in Johnson's Hall of Fame player file.

40   Vincent X. Flaherty, "Belting Bob Looks Back at the 'Breaks'," *The Sporting News*, August 16, 1945: 11.

41   Shirley Povich, "Bob Johnson, Seldom in Headlines, Always 'Carried Load'," *Washington Post*, March 23, 1943: 14.

42   Povich, "Bob Johnson, Seldom in Headlines, Always 'Carried Load'."

43   McGrath & McGrath, 566.

44   McGrath & McGrath, 598.

45   State of Washington certificate of death.

46   Cited in McGrath & McGrath, 614.

GEORGE JOHNSON

By Steven Schmitt

Chief Johnson was a strong-armed pitcher who had great beginnings to his professional baseball career but met a tragic, untimely end. Johnson was known for hurricane speed and a slippery-elm-laced spitball that baffled batters at all levels of competition. He pitched a shutout in his first major-league start and became a controversial figure when he jumped to the Federal League. Yet Johnson, whom sportswriters described as "sturdy" and "muscular," endured racial taunts throughout his career, and became alcoholic and overweight. His weakness for drink ultimately led to his demise from a fatal shooting at a Des Moines, Iowa, cabin on the morning of June 12, 1922.

George Howard Johnson was born on March 30, 1886, in Winnebago Village, Thurston County, Nebraska, to a Civil War veteran of Irish descent named Murphy and his mother, Louisa Johnson, who raised him and a sister with another man named Joe Johnson.[1] A Winnebago Indian and member of the Ho-Chunk nation, George Johnson (nicknamed "Murphy" or "Big Murph" after his Irish-bred biological father) attended Carlisle Indian Institute in Carlisle, Pennsylvania, and Haskell Institute in Lawrence, Kansas.[2] The US Army had created more than 100 such boarding schools by the time of Johnson's birth to force the assimilation of Great Plains Native Americans into Western society and culture, thereby losing their own tribal language and traditions in the process.[3] Johnson ran away from both schools, choosing to preserve his culture and heritage. His desire to prove himself as a Native American in a white man's world carried on to his baseball career.[4]

Johnson played outfield for a semipro team in Oakland, Nebraska, then became a pitcher for Guy W. Green's Nebraska Indians, a nationally recognized barnstorming team, in 1906 and 1907. He won 32 of 38 games in '07. "He is a husky young lad of (21) years, standing six feet m his stockings and weighing 190 pounds," *Sporting Life* reported. "He has terrific speed and lots of curves. The signing of an Indian player on the local team has recalled the successful careers of Indian players such as Soxalexis [*sic*], Bender and Jude. Johnson will have a chance to climb the ladder."[5] When Green bought the Class-A Lincoln (Nebraska) franchise in the Western League from Howard "Ducky" Holmes in September 1907, Green recruited Johnson, future Reds teammate Frank Jude, and other Nebraska Indian players for the team he renamed the Greenbackers.[6] The team took a two-month tour of Florida, Mexico, and Cuba with an all-American team in the fall of 1907, playing 12 games in Havana.[7] Johnson made his Western League debut on March 31, 1908, with three scoreless innings against the Chicago White Sox number 2 squad. The Greenbackers won, 2-1.[8]

Johnson lasted only three innings in his next start, against the Omaha Rourkes, but then shut out the Sioux City Packers and avenged the Omaha loss with a three-hit victory on July 13.[9] Five days later, Johnson lost, 4-0, to Des Moines before a raucous crowd. "War whooping from the bleachers and good old American rooting from the grandstand was not enough to bring victory to Lincoln," the *Lincoln Star* reported. A gray-haired Mexican War veteran yelled so loudly as Lincoln loaded the bases in the bottom of the ninth that his $25 gold-rimmed set of false teeth fell out and under the bleachers. The last batter lined out to shortstop.[10]

Johnson brought out the best and the worst in the Western League crowds. Home fans cheered him because he was clearly the team's best pitcher. Yet Indian epithets

George Johnson - 1913 Cincinnati Reds

were directed at Johnson from the stands and in the sports pages. "Numerous local humorists have started what they imagine to be Indian war cries; others have yelled, 'Back to the reservation,' and the third variety of town jester has shrieked, 'Dog soup! Dog soup!,'" Green told the *Sioux City Journal.* "You would think people would get all that kind of patent inside stuff out of their systems after a while, wouldn't you? But they never do."[11] Sports headlines referred to Johnson as "the Winnebago" or "the Big Indian." Even after Johnson (19-16) beat Denver, 3-1, the *Nebraska State Journal* called it "another exhibition of very nifty pitching which, by the way, has become quite the habit with the husky scion of the aborigines."[12] When he blanked the visiting Pueblo (Colorado) Indians on April 23, 1909, the *Lincoln Star* headline read, "Have Hard Time Getting Hip to Redskin Slang," referring to Johnson's dominance.[13]

On May 12 Nebraska Gov. George L. Sheldon joined 4,500 fans at M Street Park to see Johnson beat Pueblo, 6-3, and collect two hits.[14] For the next month, Johnson struggled with control and lost three straight games before beating Omaha. He was back in form on June 14, beating first-place Des Moines, 7-1. Left fielder Frank Jude, who also attended Carlisle Institute, had three hits.[15] Struggles with wildness and allowing double-digit hits resurfaced until July 5, when Johnson homered and beat Topeka, 7-1. Fans showered Johnson with coins as he circled the bases wearing a wide grin.[16] Two days later, Johnson worked 6⅔ innings of relief and lost on an 11th-inning single.

The Lincoln franchise also struggled, to stay out of last place and to stay in business. On July 7, 1909, Green sold an option to purchase the team to Don C. DeSpain and L.B. Stoner for $7,000 in cash.[17] On August 7 the new owners sold Johnson and traded Jude to Ducky Holmes's Sioux City Packers.[18] The players joined the team in Des Moines, where Johnson lost, 5-3. The "Chief" lost to Omaha four days later but got his first victory on August 18, a 9-1 mastery of Topeka that ended the Packers' five-game losing streak.

Johnson became the Sioux City stopper, shutting out Topeka and defeating Pueblo and Lincoln down the stretch. The Packers finished one game behind champion Des Moines in the Western League, losing twice to Omaha on the final day. Johnson had a combined record of 15-19 with Lincoln and Sioux City in 45 games with 133 strikeouts, 105 bases on balls and 14 hit batsmen. A fine fielder, Johnson recorded 105 assists. *Sporting Life* noted Johnson's deeds but also reported that he was "excessively overweight and did not train down while with the Lincoln club."[19] In August the *Lincoln Journal Star* reported that Johnson's weakness was "an ungovernable appetite" and that he was 20 pounds overweight.[20]

In November 1909, Holmes sold his controlling interest in the Sioux City franchise.[21] The following March, the St. Joseph Drummers bought Johnson and catcher Johnny Shea from the Packers for $750.[22] In spring training the Drummers learned that Johnson was "the best fungo hitter

in the league. … His swats from home plate drove outfielders to the fence. With the wind, the ball is said to have traveled two blocks.[23] Manager John "Jack" Holland is said to have taught Johnson the spitball that future major-league pitchers Red Faber and Fidgety Phil Douglas had mastered in the Western League. Johnson tried "different varieties of slippery elm" while adding a curveball and a slide-step pickoff move to his arsenal.[24]

Johnson posted a 19-19 record in 46 games for the 1910 Drummers, who finished sixth in an eight-team league. He saved his finest performance for last, shutting out Topeka, 2-0, on September 19.[25] According to the *St. Joseph Gazette,* Johnson was a hard-luck hurler who consistently held the opposition to fewer hits than his teammates collected. He became the clubhouse leader and received rousing cheers from home crowds. A film buff, Johnson was the team's movie critic and is alleged to have received offers to appear in Westerns but refused. Author Jeffrey Powers-Beck believed that Johnson would rather present an accurate image of himself in a white man's game than project a false image in a white man's film.[26]

The Chief opened the 1911 in grand style, pitching a no-hitter against defending 1910 Western League champion Sioux City. Eight thousand fans at St. Joseph saw Johnson strike out six, make three assists, and smash a double in a 7-0 victory. Only four of 27 outs reached the outfield.[27] In his next three appearances, Johnson lost twice. On May 2 the *Omaha Bee* boasted that St. Joseph was added to the Omaha's list of "scalps," as the "Winnebago Indian" was knocked out of the box in the third inning of a 6-4 defeat.[28] Johnson won bragging rights in his next start, a complete-game 7-1 victory over the Rourkes. This time, the subheadline read, "Johnson Proves Almost Invincible."[29] Johnson started and relieved when needed and struggled until he blanked Denver, 5-0, on June 27. Even in victory, teams hit Johnson hard as the summer dragged on. On July 30 he allowed 10 hits but benefited from five Sioux City errors and won, 14-7. Johnson seemed to regain form with eight scoreless innings August 5 against Sioux City but left for a pinch-hitter in St. Joseph's 1-0 win. Johnson finished 14-10 in 35 games, helping St. Joseph to jump from sixth to second in the standings.

Johnson's 1912 season punched his ticket to the major leagues. He won 23 games and lost 10, working 312 innings in a career-high 49 games. He won his first four games, shutting out Omaha, 4-0, April 29. As the victories piled up, so did scouts' interest in signing him. The Chicago White Sox acquired Johnson in July for cash and players but he remained with the Drummers for the rest of the season. Johnson won 14 of 21 games prior to his signing and pitched three shutouts in September.

The August 31, 1912, *Sporting Life* said White Sox President Charles Comiskey had found himself a rival to Charles Albert "Chief" Bender, another Carlisle product who became the ace of the Philadelphia Athletics. The magazine described Johnson as a "spit-ball pitcher" with "hurricane speed."[30] *Chicago Tribune* sportswriter Sam Weller wrote that Johnson "may not be as well-advertised as James Thorpe (a Carlisle alumnus who signed with the New York Giants) but in the opinion of many players here, he is more likely to make good in the big league than the famed Olympic athlete." Weller reported that Johnson began playing ball at 14 in Nebraska and wanted to succeed in the majors "not so much for the fame that goes with it as for the money because he is thrifty and claims to have splendid places to invest right in his home county."[31]

Johnson pitched his first game on March 2, starting for the White Sox number-2 squad that defeated Santa Maria, 11-2, showing "consistent speed and a good slow ball."[32] On March 17 he lost a 5-1 rain-shortened game against Sacramento at Marysville, California. As the rain pelted down, Johnson allowed three runs in the bottom of the fifth, though the players believed the game should have been called after 4½ innings.[33] Four days later, Johnson lost a 4-2 complete game to the San Francisco Seals. In a 9-0 win at Yuma, Arizona, he pitched four scoreless innings in relief "so the Indians present could have an opportunity to see a man of their own race performing."[34] After the White Sox concluded spring training at El Paso on March 31, Johnson got a telegram saying that a son, Joseph, had been born back home in Nebraska, the third child of George and Margaret Le Mere Johnson.[35] Elaine Marguerite was born on December 2, 1905, and Catherine on September 12, 1910. Margaret, a three-fifths Ho-Chunk Indian with a Canadian father, Joseph, and a Wisconsin mother, was born in Nebraska in 1882. She ran a lodging house and raised the children while George played baseball and, in the offseason, barbered at Walthill and tended the family homestead.[36]

Johnson returned to Nebraska on April 4 and lost, 3-1, to his old Western League foes from Omaha. "Chief Johnson, the Indian hurler, probably will be left here to put in another season of minor leaguing on the slab," Weller wrote. "Manager Callahan will not announce the deal officially, but it looks like a sure thing." Weller expected Johnson to join another major-league team within the next two days, possibly Joe Tinker's Cincinnati Reds.[37] The White Sox eventually dealt Johnson to the Reds but the "Winnebago Ban" may have been the reason. Apparently White Sox manager Nixey Callahan learned that Johnson was a Winnebago Indian. The tribe had a reputation for alcoholism so Callahan decided to get rid of Johnson. In "Chief Johnson and the Winnebago Ban," author Thom Karmik quoted a 1913 *Milwaukee Journal* article that said Winnebago Indians had been blacklisted from performing in circuses, Wild West shows or for film companies. "(The) reputation of the tribe for love of firewater has been such that managers shun their reservation," the paper said.[38] Johnson was the only Winnebago in the major leagues at the time.[39]

If the White Sox could not use Johnson, the Reds sure could. Johnson, described as "strong as a bull, broad-shouldered and sturdy," pitched a 5-0 three-hit shutout against the St. Louis Cardinals on April 16. (The game was called after seven innings so the Reds could catch their train to Pittsburgh.) "It was his first game in the big ring, and he acted as if he had pitched as often as Chief Bender," wrote the *Cincinnati Enquirer's* Jack Ryder. "Never rattled, always there with the first ball over the plate, and following it with a spitter that broke a foot or more, he outguessed the enemy."[40] Clearly the strongest pitcher on a weak team, Johnson pitched the last four innings of a 12-inning 5-5 tie at Pittsburgh on April 18 that was called on account of darkness.[41] On two days' rest, he worked all 11 innings on April 21, but lost, 7-6, to the Chicago Cubs. In his second relief appearance in three days, Johnson failed to retire a batter and allowed three runs to turn a 5-3 lead into a 6-5 loss at St. Louis. Starting the very next day, Johnson held the Cardinals to four hits but lost, 2-1, walking Miller Huggins, who scored the winning run.

On May 1 Johnson's victory over the Cubs – with relief help from Three Finger Brown – gave the Reds their third win in 15 games. After a week off, Johnson's slippery-elm ball baffled John McGraw's defending National League champion Giants, 4-0, at the Polo Grounds. "The Chief is as cool as a chunk of ice and does his best work with runners on the bases," Ryder wrote.[42] The one-run bug returned on May 12 when Johnson lost, 4-3, at month-old Ebbets Field to the Brooklyn Superbas' Nap Rucker. The Chief finally got some support when the Reds scored 11 runs and beat the Boston Braves, giving Johnson a 4-4 record. That turned out to be an aberration as Johnson lasted three innings and lost, 12-0, at Philadelphia, then took a 12-4 defeat from the Cardinals. He got the first of two straight victories, 13-10, at St. Louis May 29 in relief of Gene Packard, then beat the Redbirds, 6-2, with a complete-game six-hitter on May 31 with Johnny Kling, his favorite catcher, calling the pitches. The streak ended on June 5 with a complete-game loss to Rucker that put the Reds back in the cellar.

"Johnson cannot hold the club up all by himself," wrote Ryder, who criticized the Reds for sloppy, inconsistent play.[43] Johnson took 11 days off, pitched two innings in relief, then lost two starts before being sent back to the bullpen. He returned to the rotation in mid-July and pitched a complete-game victory over the Phillies on July 17. On one day's rest, Johnson pitched another nine innings against the Phillies, did not allow an earned run, but was tossed for arguing balls and strikes with umpire Cy Rigler (and fined $25). Red Ames took the loss in 6⅓ innings of relief.[44]

Johnson did not win again until August 4, when he "had the spitter working just right" in seven innings of relief and beat Boston, 13-4.[45] After a 5-4 loss to the Giants in which Johnson allowed 12 hits in nine innings, the Chief got Tinker's permission to visit relatives. It turned out that Johnson had food poisoning but was fined $25 for missing a start.[46] On August 19 Johnson became an ace again. He beat Boston, 4-2, to end the Reds' seven-game slide, then extended a winning streak to five games, finally beating Rucker, 7-2, on August 22. Perhaps his greatest game was a 1-0 loss to Christy Mathewson on Fred Merkle's seventh-inning triple, which hit the baseboard of the right-field grandstand at the Polo Grounds, a ball "easily caught at Redland Field or any other open lot." Johnson's spitter "was a wonder and in perfect control." He allowed just three hits compared with eight for Mathewson in a classic duel that lasted 1 hour and 27 minutes.[47] Johnson won his last three games of the season at home, the 14th and final victory a 2-0 shutout of the Giants. Johnson "made monkeys of the champs for nine swift rounds," Ryder wrote. "He likes nothing better than to seize hold of a one or two run lead and grip it like grim death until he has scalped the enemy."[48]

Johnson (14-16) led Cincinnati in wins (14), games (44), starts (31), innings (269), strikeouts (107), complete games (13), and shutouts (3) in an amazing rookie campaign for a seventh-place team. But he and Tinker would join the new Federal League and become two of many controversial figures in the legal battle involving players jumping to a league that promised better pay and working conditions.

SECTION 7 AND THE OUTLAW LEAGUE

Tinker had openly criticized the Reds for not providing the players he needed for a winning team, then retracted the statement later. The National League cited him for saying, "I would rather go out to my fruit farm in Oregon than try to handle a club when I am not backed up by the owners."[49] Cuban outfielder Rafael Almeida and catcher Harry Chapman had been sent to the minors and a thin pitching staff put more work on Johnson's broad shoulders.

The Reds traded Tinker to Brooklyn after the 1913 season but he demanded a $10,000 salary and threatened to join the Federal League for the right price. The *Chicago Daily News* called the league "a joke from start to finish" and doubted Tinker would get the $40,000 he wanted from the new Chicago franchise. Tinker signed a $36,000 three-year deal, with $10,000 up front.[50]

Johnson took a three-year deal with the Kansas City Packers for $5,000 a season and $3,000 up front on the advice of Tinker and Reds clubhouse boy Johnny Schickel, who was fired for demanding a raise. Schickel had worked for the Reds for 10 years and reportedly got $500 from Tinker to get Johnson to jump to the new league. Johnson had threatened to leave after new Cincinnati manager Buck Herzog fined him $100 for being out of shape for his first start of the 1914 season against Pittsburgh, and another $50 for violating training-camp rules. "Cincinnati is well rid of Johnson," wrote Reds beat writer Ren Mulford Jr. "but it's hard to see where Kansas City gained much in the addition of a man who puts love of firewater ahead of earnest desire to win."[51]

Johnson vowed to never play for the Reds again, saying Herzog had it in for him. The Chief practiced with the Reds on April 20, then left early to meet with Packers President C.C. Madison. At 9 o'clock that night, Johnson left for Kansas City and met his new team in St. Louis.[52] On April 23 Johnson received an infamous first: he lost the first game ever played at what is now Chicago's Wrigley Field. Tinker's Chicago Chifeds christened brand-new Weeghman Park with a 9-1 victory with 21,000 fans celebrating. While Tinker received pregame flowers from well-wishers, Johnson received a court order to leave the game. He lasted two innings and was removed not by his manager, George Stovall, but by local authorities enforcing an injunction that Reds President August Herrmann had filed to prevent Johnson from pitching for the Packers.[53]

Johnson and Reds teammates outfielder Armando Marsans and pitcher Dave Davenport claimed that Section 7 of the major-league player contract – allowing teams to release players with 10 days' notice – was reciprocal, that players were free to leave their teams with 10 days' notice and join the Federal League. Cook County Circuit Judge George M. Foell ruled that Section 7 regarding the 10-day release notice had been general practice for more than 20 years and did not void player contracts. "It seems improbable," Foell said, "that (Johnson and Marsans) would sign such contracts voluntarily if they inflicted unconscionable hardship upon the players." Foell added that Cincinnati had made "repeated efforts to secure a baseball pitcher of the same comparative skill and ability as Johnson but that such efforts had been unavailing." The judge concluded that the terms of the clause "neither deprive the contract of mutual obligation, nor render it so unconscionable that equity should deny its aid to the complainant … (that) has complied fully and faithfully with all its terms." Herrmann pointed out that Johnson had been given a raise after 30 days in 1913, from $1,650 to $2,250 a year, and that the Reds had offered an increase to $3,250 for 1914.[54]

Johnson remained idle for nearly three months while Federal League attorneys appealed. The Baseball Players' Fraternity expelled Johnson on May 5 for jumping his contract.[55] On July 16 a three-judge federal appellate court reversed the decision, calling the provisions of Section 7 "a fatal objection to the right of the club to enforce by injunction the performance by Johnson of the negative covenant not to play or perform for any other than the club." The opinion essentially challenged baseball's reserve clause.[56] On July 16 federal appellate judge Frank Baker denied Cincinnati's appeal, saying the 10-day release clause voided Johnson's contract.[57]

Johnson returned on July 25 and lost the first game of a doubleheader at Buffalo, 3-1. The *Buffalo Evening News* reported that he looked like an elephant, apparently unable to control his weight during his three-month layoff.[58] Five days later, Allegheny County Common Pleas Court Judge Joseph M. Swearingen ruled that Johnson would be in contempt of court if he pitched anywhere before September 1, the date for a hearing on an injunction filed July 30. Swearingen noted that Johnson had signed a contract with and accepted bonus money from the Cincinnati Reds, then jumped leagues without returning a bonus that he did not earn.[59] Johnson failed to appear in court, instead traveling to Baltimore, where he lost, 9-7, to the Terrapins. The Packers ignored the injunction and Johnson pitched on August 6 at Brooklyn, losing 2-0 to another Indian pitcher, Jim Bluejacket.[60] After six consecutive losses, Johnson won his first Federal League game on August 13, scattering 11 Baltimore hits in a 4-2 victory at Kansas City.

That started a seven-game winning streak – all complete games – that concluded with back-to-back shutouts of St. Louis on September 4 and 6. Meanwhile the Federal League won a legal victory when an Illinois judge stopped all legal proceedings against Johnson until the league's appeal of the Cincinnati Exhibition Company's original injunction was decided.[61]

Johnson lost four of six decisions to conclude the season at 9-10, but avenged his legally aborted April defeat at Chicago in his last start, a 5-3 victory at Weeghman Park, striking out eight in a seven-inning complete game that was called on account of darkness. Johnson "had the Tinx at his mercy in every round except the sixth, when four large swats yielded all the local runs."[62] The victory completed a doubleheader sweep that dropped Chicago from the league lead. Indianapolis won the title while Johnson's Packers finished sixth.

Baseball Magazine predicted a record season for Johnson in 1915. Manager George Stovall had his number-3 starter hoop-rolling to stay in shape and Johnson "took it up with such zest that he began the season in the best condition of his career." Just add the training-camp activity to Johnson's other interests – wolf-hunting in Iowa, playing lacrosse, and chasing and catching wild horses.[63]

Johnson pitched three complete-game victories before imploding at Chicago, 13-1. A 7-0 shutout of Newark brought his record to 5-2, but the Chief lost three straight home starts and five of six games before blanking Pittsburgh's Rebels, 4-0, on June 2. A slump sent Johnson to the bullpen but he started at Brooklyn on June 30, facing 35 batters over nine innings, striking out five and scattering eight hits for his eighth victory. Tinker's Whales continued to frustrate Johnson, who lost a 4-0 shutout to former Chicago Cubs hurler George McConnell (Federal Judge Kenesaw Mountain Landis and his family saw the contest but he did not comment on the Federal League's antitrust suit filed against Organized Baseball). Three days later, Johnson was out in the fifth inning and lost, 7-2, to ex-Reds teammate Mordecai Brown.

A four-game personal winning streak followed, raising Johnson's record to 13-11. Another three-game streak in mid-August included 6-0 shutouts of Buffalo and Baltimore. His rain-shortened seven-inning shutout of Baltimore put Kansas City in first place with a 64-50 record. An apparently weary Johnson had a 1-4 September record with one save. His 2.75 ERA belied his 17-17 record. He pitched four shutouts, started 10 games in which Kansas City scored one

or no runs, and led in strikeouts with 118 on a staff featuring Nick Cullop (22-11) and Gene Packard (20-12). The Packers finished 81-72 in their second and final season.

Johnson headed west to the minor leagues for the final three seasons of his professional baseball career. Reds President August Herrmann initially claimed that Johnson belonged to Cincinnati but Ed Maier, owner of the Vernon (California) Tigers of the Pacific Coast League apparently paid money Johnson owed the Reds and Herrmann decided he did not want the Chief to return.[64] Johnson went 8-14 as the seventh pitcher on a staff with six starters with 13 to 23 wins, including Art Fromme (23-14) and Jack Quinn (16-13). In July Johnson and shortstop Don Rader were in danger of being released. In August, a Nebraska sheriff's deputy served Johnson with a warrant for nonsupport. Johnson met with Nebraska and Los Angeles County authorities and team officials and agreed to make regular payments to his family.[65]

Worse yet, Johnson became a laughingstock. Vastly overweight, he could no longer field his position. "The big Indian, the size of whose unie comes under the classification of tents and awnings, did everything but break a leg," the *Los Angeles Times* wrote. "The Bees found it impossible to hit him, but they got on occasionally through walks and then laid them down on him. Chief spiked himself trying to field one of them, fell down on one, threw one into the bleachers and finally sat down on another until members of both teams were almost convulsed with laughter."[66] Johnson did not finish the fifth inning and Quinn won the game, 14-7. Four days later, the *Times* reported that team owner Maier was to be kicked out of the league for breaking league rules, causing dissension that had two other owners ready to quit, and secretly overpaying players to stay under the league's $4,500 salary limit. Meanwhile, Philadelphia Athletics manager Connie Mack announced that Johnson was among eight minor-league players who would join his team.[67]

On August 30 Johnson beat former New York Giants hurler Doc Crandall, 2-1, in a 12-inning classic. On September 15 Johnson allowed two runs in the fourth inning and lost to Portland. The Beavers bunted on him three straight times during the third inning but two great catches behind him saved two runs.

The Chief had some victories in his 31-year-old arm as the 1917 PCL season opened. He shrugged off an Opening Day loss at San Francisco with three straight wins in which he allowed a total of three runs. On April 15 Johnson pitched a 6-0 no-hitter against the Portland Beavers, striking out nine, in the second game of a morning-afternoon home doubleheader. While Johnson was firing bullets, a $5,000 house fire raged outside the ballpark in full view of spectators, fire-engine bells and all. *Los Angeles Times* correspondent Harry A. Williams, likely in jest, wrote that the Vernon management set the blaze. "The day was unusually cold," Williams wrote. "Only by burning a house or two in the neighborhood is it possible to warm up the park. As the fire was back of the right-field bleachers the two-bit patrons got better service than those in the grandstand."[68]

Johnson's 7-5 victory on April 22 completed a doubleheader sweep for the Vernon Tigers, who trailed first place San Francisco by 1½ games. On May 5 he and Salt Lake City's Red Hoff pitched 14 innings before Johnson loaded the bases on a hit batsman, a single, and an intentional walk and eventually lost, 3-0. The personal losing streak reached three with two losses to Oakland, one of which Williams attributed to Johnson's failure to hold runners at first base and allowing three stolen bases.[69] Johnson won his next two games but Vernon's Tigers were in last place (19-29).

On June 7 Santa Monica police fined Johnson $5 for intoxication. He had partied at some beach cafés with Los Angeles merchant F.A. Head. Both were fined $5, Head paying an additional $25 for driving while intoxicated. The next night, Johnson lost to San Francisco and Williams assailed Johnson with Indian stereotypes, writing that he was "unable to bring home wampum," that his "scalp had been removed," and that Johnson's friends would "buy him a toupee to replace the lost article."[70] Stovall sent Johnson to the bullpen but he returned to the rotation on June 17, losing to Salt Lake City and Los Angeles. In the second game of a twin bill, Johnson missed a sign to cut off a throw to second, was struck in the ear and left the game. Williams wrote that Johnson thought he had been shot in the head with a gun. "For the moment he forgot that it was against the law to shoot Indians," Williams wrote, "although it is a possibility that (manager) Stovall would take the law into his own hands."[71]

On June 30, Johnson took his bad ear into battle and lost to Portland, 6-1. Four days later Stovall tried to sell Johnson to San Francisco. "It will take at least a week to have a couple of uniforms built for the Chief," the *San Francisco Examiner* commented.[72] Johnson faced the Seals in relief on the Fourth of July at San Francisco and expected to join them at the end of the series. Terms of the sale were not announced but the *Examiner* reported, "The Chief figures to be the biggest deal (Seals owner) Hen Berry ever made."[73]

In his farewell appearance for Vernon, Johnson beat his future teammates, 3-2. He faced 22 batters in seven innings, allowing two hits. In his first game for the Seals, the Chief allowed just four hits but lost, 2-1, to Portland. On July 22 his former Federal League teammate Duke Kenworthy walked and scored from first on a single in the bottom of the ninth, giving reliever Johnson another defeat. Victory finally came with a 4-1 two-hitter against Oakland that Johnson ended with three perfect innings. His 7-3 win in a drizzle at home made it two in a row. "The sprinkle sort of dampened his ardor in the late innings and he eased up," the *Examiner*'s Al C. Joy wrote, "but by that time the game had been securely tucked away and there was no reason for the chief to annoy his wide carcass with worry."[74] On August 8 Johnson held Vernon to three hits but his former teammates bunted their way to a 4-1 victory. Johnson drove

in the Seals' only run with a triple. An error pinned another loss on the luckless Johnson August 11 but his "wide carcass" produced a three-hitter and a 2-1 victory on the 17th over Salt Lake City.[75] Johnson split two starts against Portland and ended August by dominating Los Angeles, 9-1. He began September clipping the charging Angels twice by one run in consecutive starts, 2-1 and 4-3, but paid $35 in fines for harsh words with umpires.[76]

Next, San Francisco's Recreation Park at Fifteenth and Valencia Streets hosted a series between the Seals and Oakland Oaks. On September 13 Johnson bashed a triple and won, 5-3, "adding jazz to a slow game" and slimming down to "portly" in the local game story.[77] Three days later Johnson lost, 2-1, a ninth inning single and a safe bunt sealing a doubleheader sweep for the Oaks.

Johnson gave the first-place Seals some breathing room with a 4-2 victory over the Salt Lake City Bees. "The blood-sweating behemoth of the Seals," wrote Jack James of the *Examiner*, "displayed an ability to wriggle, roll and squirm out of tight places."[78] Johnson lost a rematch, 2-0, then allowed seven runs and walked six on a hot day in Los Angeles, 9-1, the *Examiner* writer calling him a "human walrus" because of his weight.[79] But the Chief clinched the PCL title for the Seals on October 28, beating Oakland, 3-1, for his 25th victory. "Chief Johnson," wrote the *Examiner's* Al C. Joy, "unwound from his mastodonic frame a variety of shoots that the Oakland batters could not solve."[80] The Seals (119-93) outlasted the Angels (116-94) by two games. The Winnebago Indian who vowed to make good was now a champion. Statistics show he earned it – 57 appearances, 398⅔ innings, a 25-23 record, a 10th-ranked 2.44 ERA and two shutouts.

The 1918 season got off to a bad start. Johnson allowed 10 hits and five runs in 4⅔ innings in a 17-4 loss to Oakland. His next two efforts may have been more painful, a 1-0 loss to the Oaks in which Lefty O'Doul pinch-hit for Johnson and popped out to end the game, and a 3-2 defeat at Sacramento. Visibly worried if he would ever get a win, the Chief blanked Los Angeles, 2-0, in 1 hour and 15 minutes without a strikeout.[81] On May 1 Johnson lost to Sacramento, 7-4. Ten days later, the Seals suspended Johnson for being out of shape. The *Examiner* first reported that it was for misbehavior but a May 20 article said he "took a rest for his health."[82] Johnson worked out while suspended and returned to make his second start in a week on May 24. He lasted one inning in a 12-2 loss at Los Angeles.

Johnson's decline and fall began on June 1. Described as "fat" and "rotund" in the press, he allowed three first-inning runs to Vernon in an 8-5 defeat.[83] At 2-6, he became a mop-up man with two extended relief appearances in lopsided losses. On June 16 Johnson failed to show up for the game and Seals President Charles Strub fired him.[84]

The Chief played occasional semipro baseball over the next four years in Nebraska and Oklahoma and became a promoter of Native-American patent medicines. On June 11,

1922, Johnson held a medicine show featuring a 200-year-old rattlesnake at the Blair and Haun Drug Store in Des Moines, Iowa. Afterward Johnson expected to return to his eastern Nebraska farms, where he raised pedigreed horses.[85] Instead he met his death and his murder has never been solved.

Described as an immaculate dresser of splendid physical appearance, Johnson went to a drinking party and dice game at the rented two-room framed cabin of Edward Gillespie and his wife in Des Moines. About a dozen people attended the party. Neighbors called police and officers reported a brilliantly lighted cabin inside of which they heard sounds of "drunken revelry."[86] Johnson had brought a Negro-Indian girl to the party and backed her in the dice game and refused to pay for a $2.50 bottle of liquor he got from Gillespie, who became angry when Johnson started to leave the party with the girl, who won the pot in the dice game and gave it to Johnson. The two men argued and Johnson threatened to "clean house" after the dice game broke up.[87] The argument moved to a vacant lot about 50 feet behind the cabin. Shortly, cabin owner Charles M. Haradon heard two gunshots from his home across the street and called police. The first shot from a .32-caliber weapon went through Johnson's right arm below the shoulder. A second shot went through his left lung above the heart. The Chief fell dead, flat on his back on a clump of weeds. There were no eyewitnesses.

On June 16, a grand jury indicted Gillespie for first-degree murder. At first, Gillespie asked for leniency in return for a complete statement to police, but later he denied shooting or even knowing Johnson.[88] The trial began on October 16. Haradon testified that he saw the flash of a gun but could not identify the shooter. A witness testified that he had bought the .32-caliber gun from a Mexican for 50 cents and had given it to Mrs. Gillespie. Another witness said Gillespie had tampered with Johnson's Ford coupe so he could not get away without paying for the bottle of liquor.[89] Gillespie testified that police coerced a confession from him and forced him to sign it.[90] The defense attorney claimed Gillespie suffered from mental illness going back to his service in the World War but Judge Lester L. Thompson threw out the insanity option for lack of evidence.[91] The jury deadlocked after 12 hours' deliberation. After another 30 hours' deliberation, the jury found Gillespie innocent.[92]

Johnson's body was held at a local funeral parlor. Mr. and Mrs. Levi Dupuis – the latter a sister of Johnson's – claimed the body and took it back to Thurston County, Nebraska, for burial.[93] A man who made his living on his strength and desire met his death when he could ultimately not control his weaknesses. Perhaps the same could be said of his baseball career, where Johnson made good but was not quite good enough because of his personal struggles. Yet Johnson's Winnebago pride and natural ability left a legacy that will live on in Native-American baseball history, though his life was tragically cut short.

SOURCES

In addition to the sources cited in the Notes, the author consulted Baseball-Reference.com and Retrosheet.org.

NOTES

1 US Federal Census, January 13, 1920.

2 Baseball Reference.com., "Chief Johnson – BR Bullpen," Biographical Information, baseball-reference.com/bullpen/Chief_Johnson. Accessed August 3, 2018.

3 "Kill the Indian, Save the Man – Native American Boarding Schools," youtube.com., video.search.yahoo.com/search/video?fr=yfp-t&p=youtube+carlisle+indian+school#id=44&vid=ce6d24ce7cfdf11fddfd9356d23408f6&action=view. Accessed August 21, 2018. "Carlisle Indian Boarding School – Lost Unto This World," youtube.com. video.search.yahoo.com/search/video?fr=yfp-t&p=youtube+carlisle+indian+school#id=3&vid=f9ea1867c3db8c775e2940e430650160&action=view. Accessed August 21, 2018.

4 Jeffrey Powers-Beck, *The American Indian Integration of Baseball* (Lincoln: University of Nebraska Press, 2010), 142.

5 "The Western League," *Sporting Life*, January 18, 1908: 10.

6 Powers-Beck, 124; "Where Will Ducky Go?" *Waterloo* (Iowa) *Daily Courier*, October 29, 1907: 9; Jeffrey P. Beck, introduction to Guy W. Green, *The Nebraska Indians and Fun and Frolic with an Indian Ball Team* (Jefferson, North Carolina: McFarland, 2010), xxxiv.

7 "NEBRASKA INDIANS Are Booked for a Trip To Florida, Cuba and Mexico," *Sporting Life*, October 5, 1907: 1.

8 "Locals Turn the Tables," *Lincoln* (Nebraska) *Star*, April 1, 1908: 3.

9 "A Year's Work," *Sporting Life*, January 23, 1909: 18.

10 "Lincoln Loses Red Hot Game," *Lincoln Star*, July 19, 1908: 9.

11 "Raps Bleacher Jokesters," *Sioux City* (Iowa) *Journal*, June 3, 1909: 9; Guy W. Green, xxvii.

12 "Turn About with Denver," *Nebraska State Journal* (Lincoln), September 10, 1908: 5.

13 Scratch, "Have Hard Time Getting Hip to Redskin Slang," *Lincoln Star*, April 24, 1909: 9.

14 "Lincoln Gets Opener," *Nebraska State Journal*, May 13, 1909: 5.

15 Scratch, "Prohibs Get Eye on Ball," *Lincoln Star*, June 15, 1909: 11.

16 Scratch, "Prohibs Split with Topekas," *Lincoln Star*, July 6, 1909: 10.

17 Scratch, "Option Taken on the Prohibs," *Lincoln Evening Star*, July 7, 1909: 6.

18 "Condensed Dispatches," *Sporting Life*, August 14, 1909: 2.

19 "The Western League," *Sporting Life*, September 11, 1909: 22.

20 "Diamond Gossip," *Lincoln* (Nebraska) *Journal Star*, August 12, 1909: 6.

21 "Western League Notes," *Sporting Life*, November 27, 1909: 6.

22 "Western Winnowings," *Sporting Life*, March 19, 1910: 6.

23 "Johnson Is Best Fungo Hitter in the League," *St. Joseph* (Missouri) *Gazette*, March 30, 1910: 7; Powers-Beck, 125.

24 Ancestry.com. *U.S., Professional Baseball Player Profiles, 1876-2004* [database online]. Provo, Utah, USA: Ancestry.com Operations, Inc, 2004; Powers-Beck, 126.

25 "The Western League," *Sporting Life*, October 8, 1910: 14.

26 "Sports Editor's Notes," *St. Joseph Gazette*, July 20, 1910; Powers-Beck, 126-7.

27 "Johnson Pitches No-Hit Game," *Omaha Daily Bee*, April 22, 1911: 18.

28 "Can't Be Beaten at Home," *Omaha Daily Bee*, May 2, 1911: 4; "Rourkes Still Winning; Drummers Are Victims," *Lincoln Star*, May 2, 1911: 9.

29 "Drummers Beat Rourkes, 7-1," *Omaha Daily Bee*, May 7, 1911: 29.

30 "A Bender Rival," *Sporting Life*, August 31, 1912: 5.

31 Sam Weller, "Indian Hurler of White Sox Team Promises to 'Make Good' in Majors," *Chicago Tribune*, February 27, 1913: 13.

32 "Sox II Beat Santa Maria, 11-2; Fournier Leads in Swatting," *Chicago Tribune*, March 3, 1913: 11.

33 "Sox Seconds Lose in Rain," *Chicago Tribune*, March 18, 1913: 15.

34 "White Sox Blank Yuma, 9-0, *Chicago Tribune*, April 1, 1913: 15.

35 "Sam Wellerisms," *Chicago Tribune*, April 2, 1913: 15.

36 "1920 United States Federal Census," Margaret L. Johnson, Elaine Marguerite Johnson, Catherine Johnson, Joseph Johnson. Ancestry.com. Accessed August 24, 2018; Powers-Beck, 124.

37 "Omaha Defeats White Sox," *Chicago Tribune*, April 5, 1913, 11; "Sam Wellerisms," *Chicago Tribune*, April 6, 1913, 29; Weller, "Drizzling Rain Keeps Sox Idle," *Chicago Tribune*, April 9, 1913: 15.

38 "'Chief' Johnson and the Winnebago Ban," *Baseball History Daily*, August 23 and August 30, 2012, baseballhistorydaily.com/2012/0823/chief-johnson-and-the-winnebago-ban/. Accessed August 2, 2018.

39 "Echoes from the Press Box," *Baseball Magazine*, July 1913: 84.

40 Jack Ryder, "First Red Victory Due to Indian's Fine Hurling," *Cincinnati Enquirer*, April 17, 1913: 8.

41 Ryder, "Two Chiefs Stopped the War Dance," *Cincinnati Enquirer*, April 19, 1913: 8.

42 Ryder, "Spitter Has the Giants Baffled," *Cincinnati Enquirer*, May 9, 1913: 6.

43 "All Sports," *Cincinnati Enquirer*, June 8, 1913: 49.

44 Ryder, "Broke. The Hoodoo's Buzzer," *Cincinnati Enquirer*, July 18, 1913: 6; Ryder, "Pass. In the Sixteenth Inning," *Cincinnati Enquirer*, July 20, 1913: 18.

45 Ryder, "Rambled Freely Over the Circuit," *Cincinnati Enquirer*, August 5, 1913: 6.

46 Ryder, "The Reds. Dropped Couple of Games," *Cincinnati Enquirer*, August 15, 1913: 8; Ryder, "First Ball. Pitched By the Indian," *Cincinnati Enquirer*, August 16, 1913: 8.

47 Ryder, "Quit It," *Cincinnati Enquirer*, August 23, 1913: 6; "Lucky Triple. Outpitched Mathewson," *Cincinnati Enquirer*, August 27, 1913: 8.

48 Ryder, "Outlucked, but Not Outplayed," *Cincinnati Enquirer*, September 22, 1913: 8.

49 Ryder, "The Reds. Dropped Couple of Games," *Cincinnati Enquirer*, August 15, 1913: 8.

50 The *Chicago Daily News* issues of December 24 and 27, 1913, were cited in Stuart Shea, *Wrigley Field – The Long Life & Contentious Times of the Friendly Confines* (Chicago: University of Chicago Press, 2014), 16-17.

51 Ren Mulford Jr., "Redland Dream Not Realized," *Sporting Life*, May 2, 1914: 25.

52 Ryder, *Cincinnati Enquirer*, April 21, 1914: 6.

53 Weller, "Chicago Welcomes Feds, Who Triumph Over Packers, 9-1," *Chicago Tribune*, April 24, 1914: 15; Handy Andy, "Enjoins Johnson and K.C. Federals," *Chicago Tribune*, April 24, 1914: 15.

54 "Johnson Cannot Play with Feds, *The Sporting News*, June 11, 1914: 3.

55 "Johnson Expelled," *Sporting Life*, May 16, 1914: 3; David L. Fultz, "The Baseball Players' Fraternity – Some Unfair Criticisms from the New York Evening Sun; Will the Fraternity Act?" *Baseball Magazine*, September 1914: 83-84.

56 "Another Turn of Wheel in the Usual Game of Judicial Reversals," *Sporting Life*, July 25, 1914: 3.

57 "The Law and Base Ball (Chief Johnson Free to Pitch)," *Sporting Life*, August 1, 1914: 2.

58 "It Was a Grand Rally in Last Two Innings, *Buffalo Evening News*," July 25, 1914: 1.

59 "Rejoice Over Big Victory," *Pittsburgh Press*, July 31, 1914: 24.

60 "Bluejacket Wins His First Federal Game," *Philadelphia Inquirer*, August 7, 1914: 12.

61 "Feds Secure Injunction to Stop Legal Proceeding," *Chicago Tribune*, September 1, 1914: 15.

62 Ryder, "Broke. The Hoodoo's Buzzer," *Cincinnati Enquirer*," July 18, 1913: 6; Ryder, "Pass. In the Sixteenth Inning," *Cincinnati Enquirer*, July 20, 1913: 18.

63 Who's Who in the Federal League – Brief Biographies of Some of the Leading Stars of the Younger Circuit," *Baseball Magazine*, June 1915: 64.

64 "In National League Camps," *Sporting Life*, April 15, 1916: 12; "National League Notes," *Sporting Life*, April 22, 1916: 11.

65 "The World of Baseball – A Weekly Digest of Most Important News," *Sporting Life*, August 19, 1916: 3.

66 "Play Game in a Wind Storm," *Los Angeles Times*, August 18, 1916: 16.

67 "Hen Knifes Eddie Maier," *Los Angeles Times*, August 22, 1916: 17; "Mack to Get Coast Players," *Los Angeles Times*, August 22, 1916: 17.

68 Harry A. Williams, "Chief Pitches No-Hit Game," *Los Angeles Times*, April 16, 1917: 5.

69 Harry A. Williams, "Some Random Remarks," *Los Angeles Times*, May 13, 1917: 91.

70 "Chief Johnson Draws a Fine," *Los Angeles Times*, June 8, 1917: 11; "Chief Johnson Minus a Scalp," *Los Angeles Times*, June 9, 1917: 6.

71 "Trim Tigers," *Los Angeles Times*, June 24, 1917: Part VI, 10.

72 "Hen Berry on Trail of Another Indian," *San Francisco Examiner*, July 4, 1917: 11.

73 "Baseball Notes," *San Francisco Examiner*, July 7, 1917: 11.

74 Al C. Joy, "Beavers Feel the Sorrows of Adversity," *San Francisco Examiner*, August 1, 1917: 13.

75 Al C. Joy, "Wienies Growl with Glee for the Bees Got the Wurst of It," *San Francisco Examiner*, August 18, 1917: 11.

76 "Baseball Notes," *San Francisco Examiner*, September 4, 1917: 14.

77 Al C. Joy, "Johnson Chief Event in Seal 5-3 Victory," *San Francisco Examiner*, September 14, 1917: 13.

78 Jack James, "Chief Johnson Encounters Frequent Troubles, but Wriggles Out, Aided by Spectacular Fielding and Timely Hitting; Score 4-2," *San Francisco Examiner*, September 21, 1917: 13.

79 Clyde Bruckman, "Angels Make Merry While Seals Falter," *San Francisco Examiner*, September 28, 1917: 13.

80 Al C. Joy, "Oaks Fall Twice in the Day's Pastiming," *San Francisco Examiner*, October 29, 1917: 11.

81 Al C. Joy, "Big Chief Johnson Victor in Slab Duel," *San Francisco Examiner*, April 25, 1918: 2.

82 Al C. Joy, "Finish Up Week with Streak of Victory," *San Francisco Examiner*, May 20, 1918: 13.

83 Al C. Joy, "Couple of Chiefs in Fray but Cats Win," *San Francisco Examiner*, June 2, 1918: 32.

84 "Chief Johnson Takes Count from the Seals," *San Francisco Examiner*, June 18, 1918: 13.

85 "Think Murderer of Ballplayer Escaped," *Des Moines Tribune*, June 13, 1922: 10.

86 "Ball Player Is Shot to Death," *Des Moines Tribune*, June 12, 1922: 1.

87 "Famous Indian Player Backed Gambling Negro Girl Before Shooting," *Des Moines Register*, June 13, 1922: 1.

88 "Negro Denies He Fired Shot Which Killed Ballplayer," *Des Moines Tribune*, October 20, 1922: 15.

89 "Says He Gave Death Gun to Mrs. Gillespie," *Des Moines Register*, October 18, 1922: 6.

90 "Death Gun Not Mine – Williams," *Des Moines Register*, October 22, 1922: 31.

91 "Chief Johnson Jurors May Not Agree," *Des Moines Tribune*, October 24, 1922: 1.

92 State of Iowa vs. Ed Gillespie, No. 17020, Thompson, Judge, October 24, 1922. "Gillespie Not Guilty, Verdict," *Des Moines Register*, October 25, 1922: 1.

93 "'Chief' Johnson Was Killed at Des Moines," *Brown County World* (Hiawatha, Kansas), June 16, 1922: 1.

ROY JOHNSON

By Bill Nowlin

Because he was born on an Indian reservation, Roy Johnson was considered a ward of the government. He and his younger brother Bob Johnson, who joined the Red Sox in 1944, were both born in Pryor, Oklahoma (some 35 miles east of Tulsa) – before Oklahoma became a state. Roy was the eldest of the two, born at home on the farm on February 23, 1903.[1] They had six siblings, two other boys and four girls. Robert Lee Johnson was their father; he'd moved to the area from Missouri. Anna Blanche Downing was half-French, half-Cherokee. There are different stories suggesting why the family moved to Tacoma, Washington, but by the time of World War I, move there they did.[2]

Both brothers enrolled in Irving School and playing sandlot ball. It's said they attended Tacoma High School, but biographers Patrick J. and Terrence K. McGrath report, "Nobody remembers the boys ever attending high school."[3] Roy himself completed a questionnaire for the National Baseball Hall of Fame and reported that he completed eight grades of school, and that's all.

Roy began playing ball in Tacoma, in the City League around 1922, and eventually came to the attention of scouts. Sonny Bailey, a former classmate of both Roy and Bob, saw them as opposites: "Roy was a hot-headed guy; Bob was real quiet. Roy could run like a rabbit. He was actually a natural right-handed hitter but his coaches always had him bat left-handed to take advantage of that great speed. Years later, when he made the big leagues, they made motion pictures of him running and bunting."[4]

Roy Cleveland Johnson is listed as batting left and throwing right, standing 5-foot-9 and weighing 175 pounds. He was an outfielder throughout his career. There may have been a brief interlude, his first appearance in pro ball, with Tulsa in 1925, for just 10 games and just one hit. For the most part, however, he seems to have played semipro ball in Everett, Washington and in the San Francisco area from 1922-25, initially mostly as a pitcher (pitchers were typically paid better in semipro ball.) When he arrived in California looking for work, he declared he was an outfielder. Johnson was with a Southwestern Washington League team in Ellensburg, Washington in 1923 and 1924. He reportedly spurned an offer from the New York Yankees in 1924, because he preferred to stay in Washington. He signed with Seattle late that year but stayed on the bench and when he went to California to play winter ball, Seattle relinquished their claim.

One the semipro clubs with which he played winter ball in San Francisco was the 23rd Street Skidoos, where he was managed by I. E. "Shouting Shorty" Couch, who helped him get signed by the Pacific Coast League's San Francisco Seals. In 1926 the Seals assigned his contract to Idaho Falls in the Class-C Idaho-Utah League. There he hit .369 with 19 home runs, and stole 17 bases. He scored more runs than there were games in which he played – 133 runs in 112 games. He was recalled to the Seals in August and got into 25 games, batting 260.

There had actually been some confusion before the 1926 season began, as to just who Johnson had signed with. He'd been playing with Everett, Washington, in 1924, but appeared in only two or three games. He was sent a contract for 1925 to the Tacoma address he had provided. It apparently never reached him, since he had gone south to play semipro ball around San Francisco. In any event, Couch seems to have helped him get signed by Seals scout Nick Williams. The problem was, he'd also signed a contract with Bill Cunningham of the Sacramento team.[5] The *San Francisco Chronicle* called him "the boy who is so anxious to play ball that he signs whenever he gets a chance."[6] This was somehow worked out relatively quietly, after a period of controversy. The *Chronicle* reported he was playing well in winter ball; his team, the Foresters, won the title.

The Seals didn't really need Johnson in their outfield in 1927; they had Lefty O'Doul, Earl Averill, and Smead Jolley.

Roy Johnson of the 1933 Red Sox at Fenway Park with brother Bob of the A's

The PCL played a very long schedule; the Seals played 196 games that year. (They finished second.) Jolley hit .396. O'Doul had 278 base hits. Roy hit .311 in 78 games. O'Doul was league MVP, and drafted into the major leagues, opening up a spot for Johnson in 1928. And O'Doul had good words to say for him: "This fellow Roy Johnson should be a wonderful ball player. He is as fast as a streak and as strong as a young bull. He has a wonderful throwing arm and has tremendous power. He has natural ability enough to be a major league star."[7]

Jolley won the Triple Crown and the Seals won the pennant. Jolley hit .404 and drove in 188 runs, with 45 home runs. Roy Johnson joined Jolley on the league All-Star team, though. Johnson hit .360, tied for the league lead in triples (again reflecting his speed), hit 22 homers, and scored 142 runs. And some seasoned observers, like columnist Bob Ray of the Los Angeles Times, felt that among Jolley and Averill, "Johnson…is the greatest prospect of the three… Johnson has the best arm in the league, is young and fast, and is now hitting above .350. What more could you ask of a young fellow in his first full season as a regular in AA ball?"[8] As to his speed, a story that ran in the Boston Sunday Advertiser dubbed him "an accomplished purloiner of the second hassock."[9] He had stolen 25 bases in 1928.

On October 19 Bucky Harris was named the manager of the Detroit Tigers for 1929. His very first act was to announce the signing of Roy Johnson, who had been acquired from San Francisco for a reported $75,000.[10] That was one of the highest amounts ever paid for one player at the time, and no doubt led to brother Bob looking to baseball as a way to make money. He'd been working as a fireman in Glendale, California.[11] He now started to look around for opportunities in baseball. Roy looked to get a piece of the purchase price and held out a bit in the spring. It appears that he was unsuccessful, and reported.

While Roy was due to break in during 1929, Bob meanwhile signed with Wichita (Western League) in February.

Roy joined the Tigers for spring training in Phoenix, the last Tiger to do so. He had a terrific season with the Tigers. His debut was on April 18 and he pinch hit, without a hit, that day and the next (though he scored his first run on the 19th, after reaching on a fielder's choice.) On the 20th, he started his first game and doubled in four at-bats, but committed two errors in the game. He made two more errors on the 23rd. He drove in his first two runs on the 26th. He drove in three more runs on the 27th, two of them on his first home run. As leadoff batter, his second homer was an inside-the-park one on May 18. Four of his homers in 1929 were leadoff ones; he hit eight of them in his career. An inside-the-park home run in the bottom of the 11th on August 11 won the game in a walk-off.

The 26-year-old rookie tied with Charlie Gehringer and Heinie Manush for the American League lead in doubles with 45. He hit for a .314 average, with 201 base hits (10 home runs), and scored 128 runs (second in the league).

He drove in 69. The Tigers had a .299 team average, and scored 926 runs, but finished in sixth place largely because of a 4.96 earned run average. Roy was named as left fielder on The Sporting News's All-Rookie team.

On November 9 he married Helen Lucille Fraser of San Francisco. Their first child, Marylyn, was born in 1932. They divorced later in life.

Sophomore slump? His average dropped in 1930, down to .275 in 125 games. He had eight hits in his first 15 at-bats, but then took 70 more at-bats (until May 24) to get his next eight. He had one RBI for the entire month of May. His RBI total dropped by almost 50%, down to 35.

Bucky Harris came close to trading him in 1931, and Johnson had to fight for his place in the outfield, but he came through and bumped things up a bit, leading the league in triples with 19 while hitting .279. Johnson stole 33 bases. Although never a very good fielder (his career fielding percentage was .938), he did have 25 outfield assists, matching his total in 1929.

He hit a "towering home run over the right-field fence" in Washington as the first batter on Opening Day in 1932, but Johnson declined sharply in June and was hitting only .251 when the Tigers traded him and Dale Alexander to the Red Sox for Earl Webb on June 13.[12] It was quite a good trade for Boston, but not for the Tigers. Webb had set the still-standing record for doubles in 1931 — 67 — while batting .333. He never approached those figures again, hitting 28 in '32 and just five in his final year, 1933. Alexander became the American League batting champion in 1932 and Roy Johnson hit .298 the rest of the year for the Red Sox. Even in doubles, Johnson (with 38) topped Webb (28). Interestingly, there was one day when Johnson showed he was indeed "a natural right-handed hitter." In the first game on August 14, facing the Athletics' Rube Walberg, Johnson batted right-handed and got three hits.[13] He talked about becoming a switch-hitter, but there is no evidence he ever did.

Johnson drove his stats higher with the Red Sox: in 1933; he hit .313 and drove in 95 runs. Several of his hits were game-winners. For instance, his home run beat the Yankees on June 15, 1933 (which brought the Sox out of the A.L. cellar) and his two-run triple with two outs in the 10th beat the Tigers a week later, 9-7, on June 22. On July 13, his 11th-inning single knocked in the only run of the game, bearing the Tigers again, 1-0 at Fenway Park. The Red Sox finished seventh, only the third time they'd not finished last since 1921.

Bucky Harris, Johnson's manager throughout his time with the Tigers, was hired as Red Sox skipper in 1934. Why did he think Johnson had started to hit again in 1933, showing the potential he'd first displayed in 1929?, Harris said he'd been a sucker for good pitching but "made great progress in the matter of picking good balls at which to hit. He taught himself to look them over."[14]

In 1934 he had his best season, batting .320 with 119 RBIs (sixth in the league). The Red Sox finished in fourth place, their best showing since 1918. Run production dropped off sharply in 1935 (for the team, but more so with Johnson, who suffered shingles early in the season); nonetheless, he was consistent with his batting average, hitting .315.

For a team that was the last to field an African American, it's of interest that the Red Sox in 1933, 1934, and 1935 had Native American Roy Johnson playing left field and Mexican Mel Almada playing center. Johnson played 26 games in left in 1933, but 95 in right field and 10 in center. In 1934, he played left field exclusively (137 in 1934 and 142 in 1935). Almada played sparingly in 1933 (13 games) and 1934 (23 games), but a full 126 games in center field in 1935. It was never a secret that Johnson was part-Cherokee. In reporting his 11th-inning homer that beat the Yankees on July 3, 1934, the Independence Day edition of the *Boston Herald* led by dubbing him "Cherokee Roy Johnson."[15] Almada was the first major leaguer born in Mexico. This fielding of the two was no commitment to diversity, but reflected an openness in signings that one wishes had been extended to other players of color.

Some of the newspapers, of course, played up the Indian angle. John Drohan of a Boston newspaper wrote about approaching Roy in the Red Sox dugout and holding up his right hand and saying, "How?" Then he asked, "How many base hits you ketchum today?" Roy, playing along (and it was in play), responded, "Injun no know, but him keep swingin' just the same. He like white man pitcher, but if white man pitcher get 'um mad, just too bad. Injun know you can't get 'em hit with tomahawk on shoulder. But if Injun swing 'em, ketchum base hit." How do we know this was all said in jest? After two more paragraphs of this farcical language, Drohan wrote: "'Say cut it out,' said Roy breaking into United States, 'you'll have me talking that way permanently.'"[16]

After four years averaging .313, Roy provided good trade bait and the Yankees were known to be after him. There were rumors during the fall of a three-way trade involving the Senators, Sox, and Yanks. On December 17, 1935, the Sox made a deal with the Senators, sending them Roy and Carl Reynolds for outfielder Heinie Manush. It was, per the *Boston Herald*, "the first player deal without money the dominating theme in which the Tom Yawkey-owned Red Sox have figured for a long time."[17] There was some thought that new Red Sox manager Joe Cronin wanted Manush, in part because the two had been roommates on the Senators. Of course, that Manush (a future Hall of Famer) had hit over .300 in 10 of his 13 years in the majors was no small consideration.[18]

It was another good deal for the Red Sox, because it proved out that Roy Johnson's best days were behind him. Johnson never played for Washington, though; one month to the day he'd been traded, the Senators swapped him to the Yankees as part of a four-player trade on January 17, 1936. He apparently wasn't pleased about the trades. Dan Daniel said he "was not one bit backward in expressing his chagrin over having been traded by the Red Sox."[19]

Johnson hit just .265 for the Yankees in 1936, with only 147 at-bats. That's the one time he saw postseason play, when the Yankees played against the Giants in the World Series. Johnson was used as a pinch runner in Game Three and reached second base as Frankie Crosetti singled in the go-ahead run in the bottom of the eighth, a 2-1 Yankees win. The inning ended when the next batter grounded out to first base. In Game Five, he pinch-hit but struck out.

He led the team in spring training and got in 12 games for New York at the beginning of 1937, mostly filling in for an ailing Joe DiMaggio, but once DiMaggio was ready, he was seen as surplus. Johnson was placed on waivers and picked up on May 11 by Boston's National League team, the Bees; he appeared in 85 games (.277) for the Bees, where one of his outfield teammates was Vince DiMaggio.[20] The sale provided an opportunity for Yankees prospect Tommy Henrich.

Johnson finished his time in the big leagues with the Bees in early 1938. His final appearance came on April 27. He was sold to the Milwaukee Brewers on May 12, four months before he would have become a free agent. The *Globe* said he'd come to spring training in excellent shape and torn it up during the exhibition season, but failed to hit as well once the regular season started. He was fortunate that the badminton "bird" which hit him in the eye during spring training with the Bees, only cost him four days in hospital. The *Globe* reported him as "disconsolate" and said he considered not reporting, but thought better of it.[21]

Roy's lifetime average was .296, but the Red Sox had him for his best years. For the Red Sox, these had been interesting times. When Roy came in, it was in the 43-111 season of 1932. Tom Yawkey bought the club in early 1933, renovated Fenway Park before the 1934 season, and by 1935 the team was over .500. Roy Johnson contributed. He hit over .300 the three full seasons he played for Boston, and .298 the year he arrived mid-season. His four-year totals were 611 hits in 1,954 at-bats, for an average of .313. He hit 31 homers and knocked in 327 runs.

BOB VERSUS ROY

Bob Johnson's first year in the majors was 1933. He had already played against the Red Sox for 11 seasons before he came to Boston, for Philadelphia and Washington. "Indian Bob" was three years younger than Roy, and entered the big leagues four years behind him. His two years with the Red Sox were the war years of 1943 and 1944. Bob was playing for the Athletics, though, for the three full years that Roy was playing for Boston — 1933, '34 and '35. Bob hit for more power (288 HR to Roy's 58, for instance) but, remarkably, both brothers wound up with identical .296 averages. If they really wanted to get down to it, though, Roy could lord it over his brother just a bit in batting average: Roy hit .2963982 and Bob came in second with .2963872.

Bob played 13 seasons compared to Roy's 10. He also held a very significant edge in another area, being named seven times to the American League All-Star team. Roy was never so honored.

The first time the two brothers faced each other in major league play came on April 23, 1933, when the Athletics visited Fenway Park. Bob played right field for Philadelphia and batted fifth in the order, following Jimmie Foxx. He was 0-for-5 on the day, batting against an unrelated Johnson, Red Sox pitcher Hank. Roy Johnson batted second for the Red Sox, playing center field. He had a 2-for-5 day, with one RBI and one run scored. He committed two errors. The Red Sox won. Both Johnsons had two RBIs the next day, with Roy enjoying another 3-for-5 day, and Bob settling for a double and three runs scored.

Their paths would cross more than a few times in the four seasons they both played American League ball. They never played for the same team at the same time, but after the June 17, 1933, doubleheader in Boston, the two teams shared the same train west — the Red Sox heading to Cleveland and the Athletics to Detroit.

The following year, Bob hit a pinch-hit homer that gave the Athletics the lead in a game they won, 12-11. The four RBIs that Roy drove in kept the Red Sox close, but it was Bob's hit that made the difference. There are numerous other times both played in the same game, but being on opposing teams didn't affect their closeness. The two often spent time together in the off-season hunting and fishing.

ROY JOHNSON WINDS UP HIS CAREER

In 1938 Roy batted .301 in 128 games for the American Association Brewers. In 1939 he played in 127 games for Milwaukee and hit .296. That December, he was traded to Buffalo, though he wound up with Syracuse. He hit .269, perhaps a sign that at age 37 he was starting to decline. In 1941, Johnson played with Syracuse for seven games and then, after May 15, Baltimore, hitting .300 in a combined 77 games.

There were a number of unfortunate matters that came to pass. His marriage had ended in divorce. His younger brother Cecil died in a motorcycle accident, and Roy's son took his own life in his early teens. His daughter also died at an early age.[22]

With World War II on in earnest, Roy Johnson spent 1942 and 1943 working in the San Diego Naval Shipyard. He also played some ball in the Shipyard League.[23]

His last two years in professional baseball were 1944, with the Seattle Rainiers (.260 in 111 games, an injured leg preventing him from getting started sooner in the season) and 69 more games in 1945, hitting .271. He was let go in June.

"Sadly, Roy Johnson's later years were not spent in splendor," write the McGraths. "Family members and acquaintances relate that Roy was not known to work and was not a stranger to alcohol." Friend Ed Zigsworth said, "He lived reclusively [in Tacoma]…I think Bob was somewhat

of a benefactor; very supportive." Martin Kibler added, "He was living in an old shack when he passed away."[24] Roy Johnson died on September 10, 1973, in Tacoma. His death was reported diplomatically as due to a heart attack in *The Sporting News*, but the cause of death entered on the State of Washington death certificate was blunt: "Chronic Alcoholism."

He had enjoyed one important recognition while still living. In 1960, he was inducted in the Tacoma-Pierce County Hall of Fame. Posthumously, he was inducted into the State of Washington Sports Hall of Fame in 1978.

SOURCES

In addition to the sources noted in this biography, the author accessed Johnson's player file and player questionnaire from the National Baseball Hall of Fame, the *Encyclopedia of Minor League Baseball*, Retrosheet.org, Baseball-Reference. com, and the SABR Minor Leagues Database, accessed online at Baseball-Reference.com.

NOTES

1   Roy Johnson reported being "farm born" on his Hall of Fame player questionnaire. Other accounts locate the ranch at Spavinaw, Oklahoma, about 24 miles from Pryor. Spavinaw itself is the birthplace of Mickey Mantle.

2   Most of the information about the Johnson family comes from the exhaustively researched *Bright Star in a Shadowy Sky: The Story of Indian Bob Johnson*, by Patrick J. and Terrence K. McGrath (Pittsburgh: Dorrance Publishing, 2002).

3   McGrath and McGrath, 3.

4   McGrath and McGrath, 2, 3.

5   The Staff, "Sportitorials," *Seattle Daily Times*, January 27, 1926: 23.

6   Ed R. Hughes, "Seals, At Boyes, Have Regular Game," *San Francisco Chronicle*, February 23, 1926: 25.

7   Ed R. Hughes, "Gordon Slade Signs to Play with Missions," *San Francisco Chronicle*, January 26, 1928: 23, 24.

8   Bob Ray, "Big League Scouts Have Eyes on Seals Gardeners," *Los Angeles Times*, September 23, 1928: A4.

9   Al Nickerson, "Al's Sports Sermonette," *Boston Sunday Advertiser*, undated clipping in Roy Johnson's Hall of Fame player file.

10 Associated Press, "Tigers Sign Harris, Former Washington Leader, As Manager," *New York Times*, October 20, 1928: 15.

11 Associated Press, "Brother Detroit Flash Signed By Westerns," *Dallas Morning News*, February 21, 1929: Part 2, 16.

12 The description of the home run was from the Associated Press. See *San Francisco Chronicle*, April 18, 1932: 13.

13 See Gene Mack cartoon, *Boston Globe*, August 15, 1932: 9, and "Play Against Walberg Makes Switch Batter of Detroit Gardener," *Dallas Morning News*, December 25, 1932: Section II, 2.

14 *Boston Herald*, January 12, 1934: 37.

15 Edwin Rumill of the *Christian Science Monitor* once called him "the Swedish Indian from Oklahoma." See Rumill, "Cubs Holding First Place by a Half-Game Margin as Series Opens Here Today," *Christian Science Monitor*, July 14, 1937: 16. Dan Daniel also called him a "Swedish Indian" and a "Scandinavian Cherokee," the latter perhaps being more accurate given his father's reported Norwegian ancestry. See Daniel, "Both Yanks and Senators Should Benefit by Trade," *New York World-Telegram*, date

unclear (clipping in Johnson's Hall of Fame player file.) On his player questionnaire, Johnson reported his ancestry as "Scotch, French, Cherokee Indian quarter breed."

16   John Drohan, "Cherokee-Swede Smote Ball for .571 Against St. Louis and Chicago Teams," unattributed, undated newspaper clipping, probably *Boston Herald*, in Bob Johnson's Hall of Fame player file.

17   Burt Whitman, "Bucky Harris Predicts Grove Will Win 20 Games for Sox, Pacing Weiland, Ostermueller," *Boston Herald*, December 18, 1935: 34.

18   James C. O'Leary, "Manush Gives Red Sox Batting Punch," *Boston Globe*, December 18, 1935: 21, provided a good assessment of how the Sox saw the trade.

19   Daniel, "Chapman's Job in Peril," *New York World-Telegram*, March 26, 1938.

20   Yankees manager Joe McCarthy said the price was "a little better than the inter-league waiver price of $7,500." Daniel, "Henrich Lands Yank Berth," *New York World-Telegram*, May 12, 1937.

21   "Roy Johnson Is Sold to Brewers," *Boston Globe*, May 13, 1938: 29.

22   McGrath & McGrath, 267.

23   McGrath & McGrath, 268.

24   McGrath & McGrath, 602, 603.

FRANK JUDE

By Terry Bohn

Like classmate Jim Thorpe, Frank Jude was one of many outstanding all-around athletes at the Carlisle (Pennsylvania) Indian Industrial School in the early 1900s. He was rushed to the major leagues before he was ready because teams hoped to uncover another American Indian star like the Philadelphia Athletics' Chief Bender. News features at the time assessed the chances for any Indian player of making it in the big leagues. Would they have the success of Bender or fail due to excessive drinking like Louis Sockalexis? John McGraw was being cautioned about a young catcher named Chief Meyers he was considering bringing up to the Giants.

When Jude first came up with the Cincinnati Reds, in 1906, he drew comparisons to Sockalexis, so when he didn't live up to expectations, moral failings like laziness or alcoholism (neither of which was true for Jude) were suggested. Even reports of his accomplishments were usually accompanied by racial stereotypes. Upon his arrival in Cincinnati, Jude "was welcomed in a chorus of warwhoops

Frank Jude

(public domain)

that were almost loud enough to arouse the bones of the aborigines cached in the far western hills…"[1] and, speaking of his promotion to the Reds, "was compelled to run the mid-season gauntlet from the teepees of the Mud Hens to the hunting grounds in Redland."[2]

By 1909, although Jude was only 24 years old, he was written about as a failed has-been. "Frank Jude … is now in the bush league class, and will probably never again play in even a Class A organization. … [J]ust as soon as he struck in the big league he seem to forget all he ever knew."[3] Jude played another dozen seasons in the minors, even winning a league batting title, but never got another opportunity in the major leagues.

Frank Donald Jude (Gay-Bay-Aush) was born on November 11, 1884, in Libby, Minnesota, a small community near the Mille Lacs Indian Reservation about 100 miles north of Minneapolis.[4] His father, William "Mickey" Jude, was White and his obituary described hm as "one of the last of the old-time lumberjacks."[5] Frank's mother, Mary Snetsinger, was an enrolled member of the Chippewa tribe. He had two sisters, Margaret and Elizabeth, and several step-siblings from his mother's subsequent marriages. Little is known of his early childhood other than that by the time of the 1900 US Census, when he was 16 years old, Frank was a student at the Carlisle Indian School.

An excellent all-around athlete, Jude set a school record in the pole vault and played left end on the school's celebrated football team. In the 1905 game against Army, played at West Point, Jude recovered a fumble and returned it 65 yards for a touchdown that won the game for Carlisle, 6-5. He also doubled as the team's placekicker, picking up the nickname "Golden Toe," and at one point converted 32 of 34 point-after-touchdown kicks.

He was a 5-foot-7, 150-pound fleet-footed outfielder on the school's baseball team and was elected captain for the 1906 season. Although he was small in stature, his best asset was always his speed. Like many students at Carlisle at the time, Jude usually went AWOL during the summers and played with area semipro teams. It is known that he played with an independent team in Washington, Pennsylvania, in 1905 and with the local Carlisle team, which may have also been called the Linder team, a member of the independent Pennsylvania League.[6]

As early as November of 1905, Jude and a Carlisle teammate, pitcher Charlie Roy, were being scouted by Garry Herrmann, owner of the Cincinnati Reds. However, he began his professional career when he was signed by Ed Grillo, manager of the Toledo Mud Hens of the Class-A American Association in January of 1906. After receiving his diploma from Carlisle in March,[7] Jude reported to Toledo and proved successful in fast company, batting .315 in 72 games. He was described as "crackerjack at the bat, like lightning on his feet, magnificent whip arm, as lithe as a cat."[8]

During the first half of the season, Jude was drawing attention from Jimmy Collins of the Boston Americans, who reportedly offered Grillo $5,000 for Jude.[9] However Herrmann continued to keep tabs on him as well and on July 7, 1906, the Reds traded pitcher Charlie Chech and outfielder Fred Odwell to Toledo to obtain Jude. Odwell had been the Reds' regular right fielder the previous two seasons but was mired in a slump, hitting just .223 at the time of the trade.

Only 21 years old, Jude made his major-league debut on July 9, 1906, against the Giants in New York, starting in right field and batting cleanup. In his first big league at-bat, he rapped an RBI single off Joe McGinnity, scoring Miller Huggins, to plate the game's first run. Two weeks later he hit a two-out, two-strike RBI single in the 10th inning, giving the Reds a 1-0 win over Philadelphia. Shortly after Jude's debut, the *Cincinnati Post* wrote, "He stands up to the bat all right and handles himself like a natural born sticker. He is fleet on his feet and the fearful sun glare in right doesn't seem to bother him a bit." But the article also noted an obvious weakness: "But can he throw? Is his wing O.K.? That's the question still to be settled. His two efforts to throw in Monday's game – which was his debut in Red – were pitfully [*sic*] weak. They weren't on a line, and they weren't in the air. Instead, they were more on the bounding grounder order. However, that weakness, if it exists, may not be vital."[10]

Jude made a positive initial impression on manager Ned Hanlon. After his first couple of weeks with the club, the skipper said, "I can see where he is going to be a star. ... His speed and good judgment on the bases is something that pleases me immensely." Hanlon added, "Jude is amenable to coaching and is looking for information all the time on the subject of improving his work." Hanlon predicted a bright future for his new outfielder saying, "[H]e ought to be good for 10 to 15 years in fast company, for he certainly has come to stay."[11]

After recording two singles in an 8-1 win over the Superbas in Brooklyn on August 7, Jude raised his batting average to a season-high .282 but faded badly after that, falling off to .208 at season's end. In his rookie, and what would turn out to be his only, major-league season, Jude played in 80 games, all of them starts in right field and committed four errors in 113 chances. At the plate Jude had 11 extra-base hits (6 doubles, 4 triples, and a home run) among his 64 total hits. He both scored and drove in 31 runs and stole seven bases.

By his own admission, Jude acknowledged that one reason for his lack of success, especially at the bat, was his inexperience and failure to adjust to big-league pitching after just half a season in the American Association. He recognized a phenomenon that was just as true then as it was more than a century later. In an interview shortly after his arrival in Cincinnati, Jude was quoted as saying "[T]he big league pitchers have so much better control. ... The [National League] pitchers can put the ball just where they want it, and while they don't drive you away from the plate except on rare occasions, they are always doing the unexpected by putting the ball where you're not looking for it."[12]

Sporting Life reported, "[Jude] has not impressed Redlanders as one whit better than Odwell. ... as a leather-rapper he has not been an impressive success."[13] *Sporting Life* echoed the comment: Jude "failed to hit as hard as Fred Odwell whom he supplanted."[14] However, there was one highlight to his otherwise mediocre rookie year. After the season, on November 6, he married Daisy Dyke, a young Indian woman he met while they were students at Carlisle. The couple made their home in Minneapolis, where he worked that winter as a typesetter in a print shop, a trade he learned at Carlisle.

In December 1906 the Reds sold Jude to the Columbus (Ohio) Senators of the American Association, beginning a 15-year odyssey through 13 minor-league teams in 11 leagues that lasted until 1923. In March 1907 he held out, demanding $50 a month more than Columbus was offering, but he eventually signed. Jude was put on waivers in August and sold to Youngstown of the Class-C Ohio-Pennsylvania League, but was later recalled by Columbus and placed on their reserve list.

Despite his hitting a solid .275 in 142 games for the Red Birds, including two five-hit games, there were stories that Jude's play had dropped off at Columbus. One report noted that he "has been suffering from lack of pepper and sleepiness on the sacks"[15] and another said that "Jude's worst fault of late has been his going into a trance during a game. He was forgetful on the bases and lacked ginger."[16] The cause was not noted but given the trials by other Indian stars such as Sockalexis, reporters felt the need to assure readers that this uncharacteristic change was not alcohol-related by emphasizing that "he remains steadfastly on the water wagon. ... [T]he redskin Jude clings to the vehicle."[17]

In the spring of 1908, Columbus set Jude to the Lima (Ohio) Cigarmakers, a club Red Bird owner Arthur Chalmers used as a quasi-farm for his excess players.[18] Jude was on Lima's Opening Day roster, even renting an apartment in town,[19] but by late April Columbus had sold him to the Lincoln (Nebraska) Railsplitters of the Class-A Western League. He spent the next three seasons with the team, the longest tenure he enjoyed with one club in his professional career. During spring training with Lincoln in 1910, it was reported that Jude was "showing surprising speed and pepper ... playing the best baseball of his career."[20] However, in the spring of 1911 he was on the move again as Lincoln sold him to Mobile of the Class-A Southern Association.

In March 1912 it was reported that Jude was signed by Utica of the Class-B New York State League. There is no evidence that he played for Utica, but he did appear with two other league teams, Albany and Syracuse. He was unconditionally released by Syracuse in July and hooked on with the Peoria (Illinois) Distillers of the Class-B Three-I (Indiana-Illinois-Iowa) League, for whom he hit .270 in 35 games the rest of the season. In 1913 Jude joined Dubuque in the Three-I League and hit a solid .288 in 137 games. He was reserved by Dubuque but after hitting just .201 over his first 45 games in 1914 was sent down to Class D, the Marshalltown (Iowa) Ansons of the Central Association.

Jude was signed by Winnipeg of the Northern League in April 1915, hit .277 in 128 games, and then disappeared from Organized Baseball. One report said he played for a time with an independent team in Chisholm, Minnesota.[21] At the time of his World War I draft registration he was employed with the Minnesota Steel Company in Duluth, Minnesota. He listed his wife, Daisy, as his nearest relative, but a Chicago address was given for her.

Jude enlisted in the US Navy in early 1918, was assigned to the Great Lakes Naval Training Station, near Chicago, and played baseball for the base team. He split the next couple of years between independent teams near his home in northern Minnesota and semipro industrial leagues around Chicago.

After a six-year absence from Organized Baseball, Jude was signed by the Saskatoon Quakers of the Class-B Western Canada League in 1921. Then 36 years old, he hit .335 and had the best season of his career since his debut with Toledo 15 years earlier. Because it was not clear if eligibility for the league batting title was based on plate appearances or games played, he and two other players were the subject of a disputed batting race.

Regina player-manager Bill Speas hit .350 but because the team folded late in the season, he played in only 74 games. Edmonton outfielder Floyd "Lefty" Herman – who would be known as Babe Herman during his career with the Brooklyn Dodgers – hit .330 in 107 games, and several sources, including *Spalding's Official Baseball Guide*, declared him the league batting champion. Jude's .335 average in seven fewer games than Herman played was determined to be the league's official batting leader by *The Sporting News* and the *Encyclopedia of Minor League Baseball*. One source reported that Jude struck out just nine times in 343 at-bats.[22]

Jude played the 1922 season with Ottumwa in the Class-D Mississippi Valley League and ended his professional career with Carrington-New Rockford in the Class-D North Dakota League in 1923. With the latter team, Jude hit an even .300 at the age of 39. Perhaps this was Jude's way of making a statement that he could have used his speed and

batting eye to help a major-league team during the prime of his career had he only been given another opportunity.

Little is known of Jude's life after he quit playing baseball. At the time of the 1930 and 1940 US Censuses he was divorced and living in International Falls, Minnesota, working as a truck driver for a mill. His World War II draft card from1942 indicated he was employed with the M&O Paper company in International Falls.

Sometime around 1950 Jude moved to Brownsville, Texas. At one point he and a partner were the proprietors of a nightspot, the 77 Club. He died on May 4, 1961, at the age of 76 and was buried at Roselawn Memorial Gardens in Brownsville. He was survived by two sisters and a brother but left no known descendants.

One incident demonstrated the way in which Jude was generally viewed by his teammates during his playing career, even while enduring slights and prejudice from baseball management. After the deal had been struck sending him from Toledo to Cincinnati in 1906, and before Jude had been informed of the transaction, Toledo President Grillo called a team meeting in his hotel room. The real purpose was "the boys [teammates] presented [Jude] with a testimonial to show their regard for him," but Grillo began to berate an unnamed player for rules violations and threatened a release for the offender. Then Grillo asked Jude to stand up, implying he was the guilty party. At that point, "The little Indian stammered, hemmed and hawed, and a tear rolled down his cheek." Only then did Grillo let Jude in on the joke and inform him he was going to the big leagues.[23]

Perhaps the best window into the character of Frank Jude came not from anything he did on the ball field, but from a poker game. While playing for Cincinnati in 1906, the Reds were in Brooklyn at the same time the Cubs were in New York to play the Giants. Cubs outfielder Frank Schulte, Orval Overall (who had been traded by the Reds to the Cubs that June), Reds left-handed pitcher Jake Weimer, and Jude got up a game called "eight-handed." Overall opened with two aces and filled a full house on the draw, while Schulte opened with three jacks and also filled his full house. Jude opened with two queens and Weimer folded. Both Schulte and Overall checked and Schulte, forgetting Jude was still in the game, showed his hand. Jude then filled his full house by drawing a third queen, beating Schulte's hand. However, Jude "wouldn't take advantage of Schulte's exposed hand" so he then checked and split the pot with the other players.[24]

SOURCES

Unless otherwise noted, genealogical information is taken from Ancestry.com and statistics from his playing career from Baseball-Reference.com.

Cook, William A. *Jim Thorpe: A Biography* (Jefferson, North Carolina: McFarland, 2011).

NOTES

1   Ren Mulford Jr., "Three New Redbirds," *Sporting Life*, July 21, 1906: 18.

2   Ren Mulford Jr., "37 Red Varieties," *Sporting Life*, November 17, 1906: 10.

3   "Indian Players Fail in Majors," *Duluth* (Minnesota) *News-Tribune*, January 17, 1909: 2.

4   "Jude Learns Real Name," *Cincinnati Post*, August 2, 1906: 6. Jude claimed he did not know his real name until he was presented the deed to an inherited tract of land in Minnesota in 1906 with the name Gay-Bay-Aush, the name of his maternal grandmother.

5   Mickey Jude obituary at https://www.findagrave.com/memorial/82427811/mickey-jude.

6   "Baseball," *Washington Times*, March 17, 1906: 6.

7   "Diplomas for Athletes," *York* (Pennsylvania) *Daily*, March 20, 1906: 3.

8   "Three Strikes – OUT," *New York Evening World*, January 30, 1906: 11.

9   "Jude Is Valuable," *Carlisle* (Pennsylvania) *Evening Sentinel*, June 11, 1906: 4.

10 "Dash Matty's Hopes That He's Now O.K.," *Cincinnati Post*, July 11, 1906: 6.

11 "Ned Hanlon Is Sweet on Jude," *Pittsburgh Press*, August 6, 1906: 10.

12 "Getting Next to the Game," *Washington Evening Star*, July 8, 1906: 9.

13 Ren Mulford Jr., "Garden Possibilities," *Sporting Life*, September 26, 1906: 25.

14 Ren Mulford Jr., "37 Red Varieties."

15 "Along the baselines," *Columbus* (Ohio) *Dispatch*, July 30, 1907: 3.

16 "Frank Jude Is Sold," *Columbus* (Ohio) *Dispatch*, August 1, 1907: 15.

17 "Big League Dope," *Fairmount* (West Virginia) *Virginian,* August 23, 1907: 6.

18 "Minor League Items," *Belleville* (Illinois) *News Democrat*, May 13, 1908: 6.

19 "Jude Likes Lima," *Lima* (Ohio) *Times Democrat*, April 4, 1908: 3.

20 "Baseball Notes-Lincoln News," *Topeka* (Kansas) *State Journal*, April 6, 1910: 3.

21 "Former Baseball Player Enlists as a Seadog," *Duluth News Tribune*, February 28, 1918: 3.

22 Jeffrey P. Powers-Beck, *The American Indian Integration of Baseball* (Lincoln: University of Nebraska Press, 2004), 22.

23 "Played Joke on Jude," *Dayton* (Ohio) *Herald*, March 19, 1907: 12.

24 "Three Fulls No Bets When Ball Stars Play Poker," *Dayton Daily News*, February 14, 1913: 28.

IKE KAHDOT

By A.A. Rubin

The diminutive Isaac Leonard Kahdot (Ike, Chief) was the first Native American to play for Cleveland after it changed its name to the Indians in 1915. The 5-foot-5½-inch third baseman's brief major-league career lasted just four games in the 1922 season. He went 0-for-2 at the plate. Though his major-league career was short, Kahdot enjoyed a long minor-league career, and would be, by the end of his life, the oldest living former Cleveland Indian, and for a brief time the oldest living ex-major leaguer. He also seemed to have a Forrest Gump-like penchant for crossing paths with Hall of Famers, including Tris Speaker, Babe Ruth, Walter Johnson, Ty Cobb, and Carl Hubbell.

Kahdot, a member of the Potawatomi tribe, was born on October 22, 1899, in Georgetown, a mostly Native American community in pre-statehood Oklahoma, to June (Curley) and Peter Kahdot.[1] The family, which included three younger brothers and a younger sister, lived near the Sacred Heart Mission and School in the Georgetown Community.[2]

Ike Kahdot

(Courtesy of Find-A-Grave)

Kahdot attended Sacred Heart briefly. "There were only two boys there at the time," he said. "I didn't like the priests, so I ran off every chance I got."[3]

When he was 6, he was kicked out of Sacred Heart when he was caught with another boy who was smoking. Kahdot said that he did not smoke himself but was considered guilty by association. Regardless, he was whipped for the incident and ran away from the school for the last time. His family then sent him to the Friends Missionary School, where he stayed until he was 13.[4]

Kahdot recalled baseball being a large part of his childhood. "My dad gave me a bat, and a ball, and a glove when I was growing up, and I always had that with me," he said. "We had an Injun team when I was a small kid, and my dad wanted me to play ball on it."[5]

At 13, Kahdot went to the Haskell Institute in Lawrence, Kansas, an Indian boarding school. Haskell was known for its nationally ranked football teams, but also produced a number of major leaguers, including Kahdot, Art Daney, and Ben Tincup, as well as Jim Thorpe, Louis Leroy, and George Johnson, who attended both Haskell and the Carlisle Indian Industrial School.[6]

Kahdot's love of baseball blossomed at the school, where he played third base for the baseball team. He could not, however, overcome his homesickness, and his time at Haskell was interrupted when he and a friend, Luther Snake, ran away from the school and took a two-day journey by train and foot back home. "We got lonely," he said.[7]

The Shawnee Indian Association gave Kahdot a job building a fence, but then sent him back to Haskell until he turned 18.[8]

At that time, he was starting to gain recognition for his baseball talent, and he was offered a job specifically to play baseball for the Empire Oil and Gas Company's semipro team, the Bartlesville (Oklahoma) Empires.

Kahdot hesitated to take the offer on account of his commitment to Haskell, but the school granted him permission to leave, and he soon joined the squad.[9]

Kahdot was described as "a performer who won the admiration of all who have seen him play," in a blurb about the hiring in the *Lawrence Daily Journal-World*. "He is the type who always believes there is a chance to field the ball until it touches the ground no matter how far away it's going to land."[10]

Although he was officially employed as a junior engineer, Kahdot said he was hired not to work, but to play ball. "We played about three games a week," Kahdot told the *Tulsa* World's Spencer. "They just paid me a salary, oh about $150 a month. And, well, I didn't work. I'd just go down to the ballpark and stayed there all day."[11]

He played for the Empires in 1919 and 1920.[12]

In 1920 Jimmy Hamilton, who managed the Joplin minor-league team, saw Kahdot play for the Empires and invited him to spring training. Kahdot was optioned to the Pirates in Pittsburg, Kansas, in the Class-D Southwestern League. He played there for a year and, despite hitting .322, was released after the 1921 season. He was then signed by the Coffeyville Refiners, for whom he hit .293 and led the league (the Southwestern had become a Class-C league) with 111 runs scored in 1921.[13]

Kahdot was called up to Cleveland as soon as the minor-league season ended in 1922, becoming the first Native American to play for Cleveland since it changed its name to the Indians in 1915.[14] Kahdot's major-league career was brief and relatively uneventful. He ran for Tris Speaker in the eighth inning in his first game, on September 5 in St. Louis, and was forced out at second on a groundball by Riggs Stephenson, the next batter.[15] He struck out in his first major-league at-bat the next day, after entering the game as a defensive substitute.

On the 21st, Kahdot was part of a stunt pulled by Speaker, the Indians' manager. As part of a "new act," Speaker subbed out his starters and inserted "an entirely new team onto the diamond," and, according to Francis J. Powers' game recap in the *Cleveland Plain Dealer*, "did not offend a soul by doing so." Speaker wanted to give fans a glimpse into the team's future because the Indians were out of contention. Kahdot was among a group of "youngsters the Indians' scouts dug up as prospects. Boys concealed beneath the oil derricks of [illegible] plucked from the plain towns of Kansas and Oklahoma … to make heroes for major league fans of next year and the years after."[16]

Kahdot acquitted himself well in the game, despite going 0-for-1 at the plate. "Ike Kahdot, the midget Indian third sacker, made quite the hit," the recap continued. "He had a putout and an assist. At the bat, he flied to Mike in left field."[17]

Over the course of the rest of the season, Kahdot played in two more games, running for Speaker in one and playing third base, going 0-for-1 at the plate, with a putout and an assist in the other.[18]

Although his career was brief, Kahdot crossed paths with a number of Hall of Famers. In addition to Speaker, he met Ty Cobb, and even shared a chew of tobacco with Babe Ruth.[19]

At the end of the season, Speaker gave each member of the team a baseball signed by every member of that year's team. Kahdot considered that ball among his prized possessions.[20]

"It was a Reach baseball, brand new baseballs," Kahdot recalled. "We got to take one with us, and that's what we got."[21] He kept the ball the rest of his life.

He never made it back to the major leagues. Kahdot's brief major-league career was typical of the early wave of Native American integration in baseball. Many of these players, including Kahdot, had long minor- and/or independent-league careers that indicated they could have been successful major leaguers if not for anti-Native-American prejudice that kept them from getting greater opportunities at a higher level.[22] Yet, in Kahdot's case, this narrative must be considered in light of the fact that he voluntarily bought himself out of his contract rather than accept the organization's assignment for the following season.

Cleveland wanted to send Kahdot to Grand Rapids, Michigan, a team to which the Indians would assign young players with promise, but he refused the assignment. He had moved back to Coffeyville, Kansas, married his first wife, Jenny Mae Brown, and wanted to start a family.[23]

"They said, '[Y]ou can make yourself a deal if you want to go up there and play ball,'" Kahdot recalled. "But I didn't want to go up there, So I bought myself from that team. It cost me, oh, about $2,500. That was some money in those days."[24]

He apparently never regretted the decision, and would often dismiss the idea that the sport was prejudiced against him because of his Native American heritage. "Baseball's been good to me," he said. "If I hadn't been playing ball, I wouldn't be here today. They took care of me."[25]

Kahdot continued to play ball after returning to Kansas. He played for 13 more years, hopping between minor-league and semipro teams for 15 more years in the Western League, Texas League, Western Association, Piedmont League, and South Atlantic League, appearing in 120-plus games each season but one.[26] Current records show he played in 1,726 minor-league games.

In 1924 Kahdot, playing for Oklahoma City of the Western League, roomed with Carl Hubbell three years before the future Hall of Famer made it to the big leagues.[27]

He also befriended Coffeyville's most famous resident, Hall of Fame pitcher Walter Johnson, with whom he enjoyed hunting, and played shortstop on the Big Train's barnstorming teams that toured Kansas and Oklahoma in the offseason.[28]

After he retired from baseball, Kahdot moved back to Oklahoma and worked in the Seminole oil fields. In 1941 he moved to Oklahoma City and for the next 15 years, he worked in various Oklahoma and Texas oil fields as derrick man, driller, and rope choker. Kahdot described his work schedule as "12 hours a day, 7 days a week." He claimed that he "never missed a day."[29]

In 1958, Kahdot left the oil fields for the Tinker Air Force Base water department, where he worked until he retired in 1969.[30]

During his retirement, he enjoyed hunting, fishing, and traveling in his motor home with his second wife, Lou.

Kahdot died at the age of 99 March 31, 1999, in Oklahoma City. He was considered by his tribe to be one of the last full-blooded Potawatomi.[31] He was also, for many years, the oldest living Cleveland Indian, and, for the last seven months of his life, the oldest living former major-league baseball player.[32]

NOTES

1   "Kahdot Isaac Leonard (IKE)," *Oklahoman* (Oklahoma City), April 3, 1999: 27. The 1900 United States census says that Peter Kahdot was a day laborer, and that Isaac had an older sister, Alen, born in 1897.

2   Gloria Thomas, "Baseball Was Good to Indian Boy from Sacred Heart," *Hownikan* (Shawnee, Oklahoma), March 1992: 1, 3. Accessed December 15, 2022.

3   Thomas.

4   Thomas.

5   Burl Spencer, "Oldest Cleveland Indian Remembers the Good Year: 1922," *Tulsa World*, September 22, 1993. http://tulsaworld.com/archive/oldest-living-cleveland-indian-remembers-the-good-year-1922/article_1a42d1f0-ef5b-5b87-9217-de429ba91b66.html Accessed December 26, 2022.

6   Jeffrey Powers-Beck, *The American Indian Integration of Baseball* (Lincoln: University of Nebraska Press, 2004), 12, 101-102.

7   Thomas.

8   Thomas.

9   Spencer.

10 "Haskell Star Here," *Lawrence* (Kansas) *Daily Journal-World*, December 26, 1919: 6. Accessed January 8, 2023.

11 Spencer.

12 Royse Parr,"Isaac Leonard 'Ike' 'Chief' Kahdot," in C. Richard King, ed., *Native Americans in Sports* (London and New York: Routledge, 2015), 167.

13 Spencer.

14 Parr.

15 "Kolp Falters in Sixth After Holding Indians to Four Hits in Five Innings," *St. Louis Post-Dispatch*, September 6, 1922: 20.

16 Francis J. Powers, "Red Sox Defeat Speaker's Army of Players, 15-5," *Cleveland Plain Dealer*, September 22, 1922: 19.

17 Powers. Information on Retrosheet and Baseball-Reference.com do not indicate the putout.

18 Spencer.

19 Parr.

20 Parr.

21 Spencer.

22 Powers-Beck, 100-101.

23 Parr.

24 Spencer.

25 Thomas.

26 Powers-Beck, 101.

27 Spencer.

28 Parr.

29 Thomas.

30 Thomas.

31 Thomas.

32 Email to author from Cassidy Lent, reference librarian, National Baseball Hall of Fame and Museum, December 21, 2022.

LOUIS LEROY

By Bill Nowlin

Louis Leroy was a Native American who almost became a charter player for the Boston Red Sox franchise. Leroy was born on February 18, 1879, in Omro, Wisconsin, as a Stockbridge-Munsee Indian, a group of Mohicans who relocated from New York's Hudson River Valley and Delaware to Wisconsin at the beginning of the nineteenth century. His parents appear to have been Frank and Susan (Bowman) Leroy of Richmond, Wisconsin, Frank a laborer and Susan keeping house. Frank was listed in the 1880 census as 40 years old and Susan 22.

Louis grew up hunting, fishing, and trapping in the Wisconsin woods of Shawano County near Red Springs with at least four younger siblings: Frank, Roy, John, and Lucinda. School records show him as "half-Indian," apparently on his mother's side, with his father, Frank, being French-Canadian.[1]

Louis was taught in reservation schools, and seems to have played his first baseball at age 15 in a team at the Keshena School in 1894. He's known to have pitched there. When he was 16, Louis was sent to the Haskell Institute in Lawrence, Kansas, for three years. He pitched for the Haskell team as well, but was dropped from the school for desertion.[2] After a year off, Leroy applied to continue his schooling at the Carlisle Indian Industrial School in Pennsylvania, and was accepted. The *Indian Helper* noted his arrival after a week as "a baseball player and a lover of athletic sports in general."[3] He had some degree of wanderlust, though, and was several times absent without leave even from Carlisle. It was apparently not uncommon for "Indian" boys to run off and join minor-league or semipro baseball teams during the summer in order to make extra money. Leroy's school training was in the blacksmith shop, which probably was not nearly as much fun. Carlisle newspapers show Leroy as the ace pitcher on the school squad.

Leroy played baseball under famous Carlisle coach Glenn "Pop" Warner for three years, 1899-1901, and began to become known to people in baseball. Jeffrey Powers-Beck, researching his book *The American Indian Integration of Baseball*, came across clippings in the National Baseball Hall of Fame files that indicate Leroy came to the attention of Boston ballplayer Jimmy Collins as early as his first year at Carlisle, 1899. After six seasons with Boston's National League team, the Boston Beaneaters, Collins became the first manager of Boston's new American League team in 1901. But Collins had signing power with the 1899 Beaneaters and offered Leroy a contract with the

team. Carlisle Superintendent Richard Henry Pratt denied the 20-year-old Leroy the opportunity; Warner explained that he was not free to accept outside work until graduation because "the U.S. government had a claim on the Indian."[4]

Every spring, Warner wrote, Leroy ran away from school as soon as Carlisle's baseball season was over: "His escape schedule was like clockwork. Leroy was crazy about playing baseball and was always trying to land a job with a professional baseball team. ... And every fall, like clockwork, Leroy would return to Carlisle and beg to be able to re-enter the Indian School."[5]

Warner dubbed Louis "the boy with the ten thousand dollar arm and the five cent head."[6] Were he caught, he would be arrested and returned to the school. In 1901 Coach Warner followed the again-missing Leroy to Boston, where he found that Jimmy Collins – now manager of the Boston Americans – had come to agreement with the young Carlisle pitcher. Warner convinced Collins that Leroy needed to complete his education and was – in any event – a ward

Louis LeRoy

of the school, without the rights any non-Indian American would have had at a similar age. With Leroy still recalcitrant upon his return, Warner had him placed in a cell at the school and kept on bread and water for 57 days, confined for a longer period overall from mid-June to early September 1901 – kept on the "reservation" when he could instead have been pitching for Boston. Given his age and his grade in school, Leroy would have been kept at Carlisle until he was 25. He ultimately did complete his course of studies, which qualified him as a college graduate.[7]

Leroy did play ball in Boston in 1901, as left halfback for Carlisle's football team. The Indians challenged Harvard at the college's Soldiers Field stadium, and were shut out by the Crimson, 29-0. Leroy made a number of small gains, a yard or two at a time, but the Harvard defense proved impenetrable. Leroy eventually did make it to the Red Sox, but it wasn't until 1910, and then only for the briefest of stays. His first major-league appearance came for the AL's New York Highlanders in 1905. Before that, he put in some time in the high minor leagues.

In 1902 manager George Stallings signed Leroy to a contract with the Buffalo Bison. Leroy pitched for the Eastern League team in 1902 (he was 13-5) and 1903 (a lesser 7-7), then for the Montreal Royals the following three years. (He was 14-10 and 18-12 in the first two seasons, before he had his first taste of major-league action.) A 1903 clipping reflects some of the attitudes of the day, referring to Leroy as "the little red man" and with a subhead saying the "Indian warrior cut down and scalped" the opposing team. Leroy was on the "warpath" – coverage of the "heap good injun" continued on in this vein. Powers-Beck said that Leroy suffered "crude caricatures and incessant war-whoops throughout his career."

Leroy worked hard at the craft of pitching, quickly realizing that he could not rely on his fastball alone. While working on control, he also developed some other pitches including a curve and a spitball. He enjoyed playing the outfield on days he wasn't on the mound, but even while pitching he was deemed a first-rate fielder. Leroy built up his pitching stamina, as well, and for the Royals in 1904, he won both games in two doubleheaders twice in the same week (September 10 and September 16.) A clipping from the day wrote that Leroy had gone through "a siege of trial to become a professional ballplayer, and his dogged persistence and determination are responsible for his being one of the stars of the diamond today."[8]

Late in 1905, the inevitably-nicknamed "Chief" Leroy was purchased by the New York Highlanders (later the Yankees), as announced on September 1, and he appeared in three games beginning on September 22. He won his first start, defeating the White Sox, 5-2, a six-hit complete-game effort against Nick Altrock at New York's Hilltop Park. Leroy walked one and struck out three.

He lost his second game, against the St. Louis Browns four days later, giving up three runs in the top of the first

and four more as the game progressed, surrendering 11 hits in all, two of them home runs. He walked no one and struck out three. He worked the first game of the September 30 doubleheader, against visiting Cleveland. The Highlanders won, but Bill Hogg had relieved Leroy after seven innings and New York scored twice in the bottom of the eighth, to win 7-5. Hogg got the win. Leroy had given up five runs on 10 hits, again walking no one and again striking out three.

With those three appearances, he closed the season with a 3.75 ERA and a record of 1-1. He had one base hit, a single, in eight at-bats.

In 1906 Leroy went to spring training in Birmingham with the New York team, and opened the season with them, too, winning his first game, 4-3, and his second one – more than six weeks later – 7-6. He saved another game, in relief. Leroy appeared in 11 games for the Highlanders – only two as a starter – and was 2-0 with a 2.22 ERA in 44⅔ innings, but his last game was on June 15 and he spent most of the year with the Montreal Royals. Why did New York give up on him? They had a strong pitching staff, and Montreal offered a considerable amount of cash. Powers-Beck writes, "The decision to return Leroy to Montreal for cash was almost entirely a financial one."[9] Leroy was perhaps dejected and pitched somewhat listlessly, compiling a 6-14 record for the Canadian ballclub, his one poor season.

From 1907 into 1913, Leroy pitched in the American Association for the St. Paul Apostles, with a brief excursion to Boston at the start of the 1910 season. St. Paul was A-ball, the highest level of Organized Baseball at the time other than in the major leagues. Only once in his seven seasons with St. Paul did the team have a winning record, but Leroy earned double-digit wins every year and three 20-win seasons (1907, 1909, and 1912). He won 28 games for St. Paul in 1907 – but lost 44. (The team finished in last place, with a record of 58-96. Leroy led the team in both wins and losses.)

In 1908 Leroy's batterymate with St. Paul was John Tortes "Chief" Meyers, the only Native American battery in baseball at the time. Red Sox scout Patsy Donovan had watched Leroy in a few games while on a visit to Minnesota in the summer of 1909; the pitcher was on his way to a 20-17 season and we see now that he posted a WHIP (walks and hits per inning pitched) of 0.976.

When Donovan was named manager of the 1910 Red Sox, he decided that he wanted Leroy. He was even quoted in the Boston Globe as envisioning Leroy as capable of becoming a second Chief Bender.[10] St. Paul manager Mike Kelley had promised Leroy that he'd help if any major-league team ever wanted him, and he was true to his word. The day after his signed contract was received, the Boston Globe reported that the contract of "Leroy, the Indian" was in hand. The paper headlined: "Boston Club Now Has Indian Sign on that Leroy Contract."[11]

Leroy was expert in pitching with expectoration, legal at the time. The spitballist was on his way to Boston, legitimately so this time. He joined the team for spring training in Hot Springs, and looked good at the start of spring training, but when the regular season arrived, he played in just one game for the Red Sox, and it was his last in major-league ball. Donovan may have worked him too hard early in the spring, and urged him to rely too much on the fastball, the pitch that had sometimes done him in due to the force with which he threw it and the strain it put on his arm. "My wing began to feel the strain, being unused to the hard work so early in the season," he told a sportswriter. His pitching suffered, and it produced at least one unfortunately stereotypical sports story, perpetuating the myth of the "lazy Indian." Leroy had told Donovan, "See here, Pat, I'm no spring chicken; I've pitched ball some time now, and there's still many good years of pitching in my arm if it isn't abused. I don't feel like throwing it away in these exhibition games; it isn't worth while." This prompted a newspaper headline: "La Roy [sic] Doesn't Like Hard Work in Spring" – the story also lamented that Donovan "didn't know how to handle the red man."[12]

Some of the stories Leroy had to endure included ones with headlines such as "La Roy, He Big Chief: He Had Heap Much Curves and Treated the Royals Like Squaws and Papooses" (referring to a 1903 game for the Bison against Montreal.[13])

Donovan apparently developed a lack of trust in the pitcher he himself had sought out, and used him sparingly for the rest of the spring. The sixth game of the 1910 season saw Leroy's one appearance for Boston. It was April 20, 1910, the day after the Patriots Day doubleheader. Charlie Smith started the game and gave up three runs in the first two innings, but Leroy's four innings of relief were disastrous. He gave up nine runs (to be fair, only five were earned) on seven hits and two walks. He struck out three. Ray Collins pitched the rest of the game without giving up a hit, but the final score was Washington 12, Boston 4. Leroy also misplayed two balls in the field, but the only errors charged were four committed by other Boston ballplayers.

After a couple of weeks of sitting on the bench, Leroy was returned to St. Paul on May 5. The *Boston Globe* observed, "Louis Leroy … was disposed of, yesterday, to the St. Paul club. … Leroy was perfectly satisfied to go back to his old wigwam in the far west."[14] He won 14 games and lost 16 with the 88-80 Apostles, including a July 15 no-hitter against Toledo for 9⅔ innings before a hit dropped in during the 10th inning. He recorded an official no-hitter just 12 days later against the Indians (the Indianapolis ballclub). Less than a year later, Leroy threw a no-hitter for the Bay City Cardinals in the Southern Michigan League on July 18, 1911, pitching against the Jackson Convicts. The *Washington Post* was among those who dubbed him "Chief" Leroy.[15] Brother Frank Leroy was a right-hander who pitched for three seasons in the minor leagues, two for Bay City and 1912 for Jackson. He threw a no-hitter on May 5, 1912.

Louis Leroy's Boston ERA was 11.25. Lifetime, he was 3-1, 3.22 in major-league ball. He had a perfect fielding record, handling all 27 chances he was presented without an error. He was 3-for-23 at the plate (.130), with one run batted in – on May 30, 1906, for the Highlanders, in a 7-6 win over the Washington Senators.

In the years that followed, Leroy pitched through 1913 with St. Paul, and for the Indianapolis Indians (when they signed him in 1913, a newspaper story called him "A Real Indian for the Indians"), Salt Lake City Bees, St. Paul again, Springfield Ponies, Muskegon Reds, Joplin Miners, La Crosse Infants, St. Paul for a fourth time, Seattle Giants, and Mitchell Kernels in South Dakota, the final team, which he helped lead to a championship in the 1920 Dakota League.[16] He won 236 games in minor-league baseball and lost 218, including at least 142 in the American Association.

After finishing his years in pro ball, Leroy lived in Gresham, Wisconsin, and played some semipro ball in the state while he farmed, did lumber work, and became involved in some of the tribal affairs of the Stockbridge. His first marriage, to Rose Poudry, had fallen apart in 1908, but he remarried at the end of the 1910 season, to Josephine "Joe" Hoffman. He had one son, Lee Daniel Leroy, from his first marriage, and two children (Louis Jr. and Arlene) from his second. In 1936 he moved to a two-story log cabin home on an expanded Indian reservation at Bowler, Wisconsin. There, he talked baseball and tribal politics, until he died of liver cancer on October 10, 1944.

SOURCES

The principal source for this biography is the chapter on Leroy in Jeffrey Powers-Beck's book *The American Indian Integration of Baseball* (Lincoln: The University of Nebraska Press, 2004).

Other sources are indicated in the text. The author also relied on the online SABR Encyclopedia, retrosheet.org, and Baseball-Reference.com.

NOTES

1   His 1942 World War II draft registration card provides the same birthdate but says he was born in Red Springs, Wisconsin.

2   Almost all the information about Leroy's early life comes from Jeffrey Powers-Beck's book *The American Indian Integration of Baseball* (Lincoln: The University of Nebraska Press, 2004), 97-119.

3   *Indian Helper*, April 7, 1899, per Powers-Beck.

4   As reported in Powers-Beck, 106.

5   Mike Bynum, ed., *Pop Warner: Football's Greatest Teacher: The Epic Biography of Major College Football's Winningest Coach, Glenn S. (Pop) Warner* (Canton, Ohio: Gridiron Football, 1993), 96-98.

6   Powers-Beck, 104.

7   "Pittsburgh to Secure Thorpe," *Washington Post*, September 15, 1912: S4.

8   Unattributed clipping from Leroy's personal scrapbook cited by Powers-Beck.

9   Powers-Beck, 112.

10 "Kittridge New Harvard Coach," *Boston Globe*, February 11, 1910: 4.

11 "LeRoy Now in Red Sox Fold," *Boston Globe*, February 22, 1910: 5.

12   Unattributed clipping in the Louis Leroy scrapbook.

13   Unattributed clipping from Leroy's personal scrapbook cited by
      Powers-Beck.

14   "Off Till Today," *Boston Globe*, May 6, 1910: 7. Powers-Beck rightly
      questions just how "perfectly satisfied" Leroy would have been to be thus
      "disposed of," but at least he got to pitch in St. Paul.

15   "Pitches a No-Hit Game," *Washington Post*, July 19, 1911: 9.

16   The "real Indian for the Indians" line is reported by Powers-Beck, 172.

KYLE LOHSE

By Allison Levin

"Arriving in Missouri at 29 with a lifetime's worth of rough outings in Minnesota and Cincinnati already behind him, Lohse was both not good and pretty old in ballplayer years – more flotsam than reclamation project."[1] Then he met Dave Duncan, who told him what to throw, most notably a new two-seam fastball, and Yadier Molina, who showed when and where to throw it, and Lohse put up the best numbers of his career and resurrected his career.[2]

Born in Chico, California, to Larry and Leslie Lohse on October 4, 1978, Kyle Lohse, who grew up on a farm, was a three-sport athlete, excelling at basketball, baseball, and football at Hamilton Union High in Hamilton City, California. He followed in the footsteps of his parents, who were also star athletes at Hamilton High. Baseball was the sport Lohse excelled at, being an all-conference pick all four years of high school. Upon graduating in 1996, he attended Butte Junior College a two-year institution in Oroville, California, where he met his first wife, Gabrielle.[3]

Heading into college, despite his mother's having ties to an indigenous population, Lohse considered himself "American" and did not focus on customs as a kid because his mother's Wintun-Nomlaki tribe did not reestablish itself until 1996.[4] However, despite his initial reluctance to identify as Indigenous, Lohse came to realize the impact he could have on youngsters and began to embrace his heritage. He explained that "when you get older, you start to realize there's possibly more kids out there with a Native American background. They kind of look towards you so it's good to try to set an example for them out there when you're on the field."[5] Lohse's heritage marks him as the first Indigenous person to play major-league baseball in the twenty-first century.[6] Lohse, while playing with the Milwaukee Brewers in 2013, explained that the Wintun-Nomlaki tribe was a small tribe and it seemed that everyone was a family.[7] After its reestablishment, his mother, Leslie, became known for her success as a businesswoman and tribal treasurer.[8] She discussed Lohse's impact on the tribe: "He truly is an inspiration. We don't live on a reservation; none of our people do. But I talk to our tribal leaders all the time and they are very excited. A lot of Indian country is watching him. It gives the kids something to aspire to."[9] Leslie eventually came to run the tribal casino. In that position, she was accused and later found guilty of lying to federal investigators about a $5 million line of credit she took out in the tribe's name. She also failed to report the embezzled tribal money on her tax returns.[10] Leslie was sentenced to three years and five months in prison and paid $902,208 in restitution for her transgression.[11]

Lohse was drafted by the Chicago Cubs in the 29th round of the amateur draft after his senior year of high school. However, he chose to attend college, spending one semester at Butte Junior College before joining the Cubs Rookie League team as a draft-and-follow signee.[12] A right-handed pitcher who stood 6-feet-2 and was listed at 215 pounds, Lohse was promoted in 1998 to Low-A and was known for throwing a lot of strikes and eating up a lot of innings.[13] He moved up to High-A for the 1999 season until he was traded to the Minnesota Twins on May 21, 1999, with Jason Ryan for Rick Aguilera and Scott Downs.[14] In High-A for the 1999 season and Double-A for the 2000 season, Lohse did not put up good numbers, and reports indicated "that his confidence was damaged by a series of poor early performances."[15] Lohse began in 2001 in Double A and, after a rebound from the 2000 season, was promoted to Triple A,[16] where he performed well enough to be called up to the majors after nearly six years in the minors.

Lohse made his major-league debut on June 22, 2001, when the Minnesota Twins played the Detroit Tigers. As a starter in that game, he threw 106 pitches and was pulled in the seventh inning of a 4-4 game. He gave up four hits and four earned runs, struck out five and walked one.[17] The Tigers went on to win the game 5-4. Lohse completed the 2001 season with the Twins, making 16 starts and going 4-7 with a 5.68 ERA and an 80 ERA+ in 90⅓ innings.

(Matthew Trommer/Dreamstime)

Kyle Lohse

In 2002, his first full year as a starter with the Twins, Lohse showed a glimpse of what would come, posting a 13-8 record with a 4.23 ERA and a 106 ERA+. Throughout his Twins career, he was known for eating up innings and putting up overall average numbers. Over his five years with the Twins, he went 51-57 with a 4.88 ERA and a 93 ERA+ in 172 games.[18]

After a poor start to the 2006 season, Lohse was traded to the Cincinnati Reds for minor leaguer Zach Ward on July 31, 2006. He completed the 2006 season with the Reds, appearing in 12 games and posting a 3-5 record. The Reds showed confidence in Lohse at the start of the 2007, giving him a spot in their starting rotation. After appearing in 21 games and posting a 6-12 record with a 4.58 ERA and a 101 ERA+, Lohse was traded on July 30, 2007, to the Philadelphia Phillies for Matt Maloney. He completed the season with the Phillies, appearing in 13 games, going 3-0 with a 4.72 ERA and a 97 ERA+.

Lohse was considered an average journeyman pitcher when he was granted his free agency after the 2007 season, but that changed when he signed with the St. Louis Cardinals and met up with pitching coach Dave Duncan. Lohse arrived in St. Louis for the 2008 season at 29, able to get only a one-year contract in free agency. Not signing until March 13, 2008, he was coming off two years of rough outings with the Reds and Phillies, along with average statistics from his years with the Twins. None of that mattered to the Cardinals because Duncan saw something in him. "Throughout the 2000s, Cardinals pitching coach/sage Dave Duncan and catcher Yadier Molina made a custom of shining up scuffed imports,"[19] and Lohse became a star pupil. Duncan had Lohse develop a two-seamer, Duncan's favorite pitch against the power hitters of the time, and in 2008 Lohse, riding that pitch, posted his best career numbers to that point.[20] He ended the season at 15-6 with a 3.78 ERA and a 112 ERA+. After it was clear that Lohse was adapting well to the tutelage of Duncan, the Cardinals and Lohse agreed to a four-year, $41 million contract extension. For the 2009 and 2010 seasons, Lohse appeared to return to his previous form and then came the 2011 season, after which he never looked back.

During the 2011 season, "Lohse and Molina practiced sleight of hand seven innings at a time, with strategies founded on an understanding of Lohse's weaknesses,"[21] and all the hard work paid off. During the regular season, Lohse led the Cardinals with a 14-8 record, a 3.39 ERA, and a 109 ERA+. On August 28, 2011, he won his 100th big-league game when the Cardinals beat the Pirates 7-4.[22] During the postseason, he struggled on the mound as the Cardinals made their improbable run to their 11th World Series championship, the only World Series of his career. Still, he played an instrumental role with his bat.

Lohse is touted as a hero of the miraculous Game Six of the World Series for his pinch-hit sacrifice bunt in the 10th inning. With the Cardinals out of position players, and with two men on, Lohse was called on to hit, though as he explained to sportswriter Rick Hummel, it was a total surprise as he had been told fellow pitcher Edwin Jackson would be getting the at-bat. "I was standing on the bench as Jackson was walking up to the plate thinking, 'Thank God I'm not the guy up there right now,' to be honest. There's a lot of pressure. There's a lot of things could go wrong in that situation."[23] However, things quickly changed. "When I was standing up in the dugout on those benches leaning over the rail, I see Pujols talking to Tony. I can read his lips and he's saying, 'Loshie,' and I'm thinking, 'Oh, my God, I might have to go up there."[24] Since he had left his bat in the cage, he went to the plate with Chris Carpenter's bat. Lohse felt all the pressure of the game ending on his at-bat. "Hitting into a double play was very likely. I'd been sitting there on the bench all night, and if I hit a hard bunt back to somebody, and if they get one of the runners out, I'm probably going to get thrown out, too."[25] Noticing where Texas third baseman Adrian Beltré was playing him, Lohse knew he had to push a bunt hard to the shortstop, which he did to advance the two runners, both of whom eventually scored, tying the game and setting up the game-winning David Freese leadoff home run in the 11th.[26] The Cardinals won the Series the next night, finishing an improbable World Series run.

In 2012 Lohse began the season as the Opening Day starter. He did not give up a hit until the seventh inning and ended the game giving up two hits, allowing one run, and striking out three. The outing made Lohse the first pitcher to win at the new Marlins Park.[27] That game was a precursor to his 2012 season – one of the best in major-league baseball. He finished with a 16-3 record, and his win percentage of .842 led the National League. He finished seventh in the NL Cy Young Award race and fourth in Win Probability Added with a 3.2 WPA. As he entered free agency again after the 2012 season, he had just completed the best five years of his career, where he went 55-35. Those years catapulted Lohse to become a top pitcher. In retrospect, Lohse wishes he had gotten to the Cardinals earlier. "Working with Dunc (pitching coach Dave Duncan) was huge. I can't say enough how he helped me realize the approach I needed to have on the mound as opposed to trying to throw four-seamers by everybody."[28]

On the strength of his time in St. Louis, on March 25, 2013, Lohse signed a three-year, $33 million free-agent contract with the Milwaukee Brewers at 34 years old.[29] In retrospect, Lohse, who signed eight days before the season's start, remembered his frustration. "There are days you wake up frustrated, there are days you wake up angry, there are days you feel down, there are days you feel all of that. You're property of a team for so many years, you get your shot for free agency, and then most teams don't want to talk to you. You try to stay positive, but it's hard. It's a gut-check."[30] Much of his wait to sign was because he was the guinea pig for the new draft-pick compensation in free agency for players who rejected qualifying offers that went into effect during that offseason.[31]

Despite the wait, that signing paid off for Lohse and the Brewers, as his numbers remained consistent from his 2011 and 2012 seasons with the Cardinals. From 2011 to 2014, he had an average ERA of 3.28 and while not a prototypical ace, he was highly dependable.[32] Lohse showed that he still had what it took to be an ace on September 25, 2013, when he threw a complete game in 89 pitches to beat the Atlanta Braves 4-0, completing a Maddux,[33] where the pitcher throws a shutout of at least nine innings in 99 or fewer pitches. The following season, 2014, Lohse threw another Maddux, the 12th in Brewers history, against the Cubs.[34] The 2014 season with the Brewers, when he was 35, was the last winning season of his career. He finished 13-9 with a 3.54 ERA and a 107 ERA+ and had optimism for the 2015 season. But Lohse's 2015 season, the third and final year of his contract with Milwaukee, was disappointing as he finished 5-13 with a 5.85 ERA and a 68 ERA+.

After his time with the Brewers, Lohse tried to prolong his career, signing a free-agent contract with the Texas Rangers on May 14, 2016. He pitched in just two games with the Rangers, going 0-2 with a 12.54 ERA and a 48 ERA+ before being granted free agency on August 1, 2016. After sitting out the 2017 season, Lohse, at 39 years old, made one more attempt at a comeback, signing a minor-league deal with the Kansas City Royals on April 3, 2018. He was released on May 10 after having pitched only at Triple-A Omaha. Lohse officially announced his retirement from baseball that day on Instagram by posting a picture of a beer in the stands at the Triple-A facility captioned, "It's been a hell of a ride! Baseball, you've taken me a lot of places I've never thought or even dreamed of. The highs. The lows. The people I've met. The teammates I've had the pleasure of battling alongside. The guys on the other teams I've had the pleasure of battling against. Time to take it to the house knowing I gave it all I had each and every time.'"[35]

Over his 16-year career, Kyle Lohse played in the majors for six teams but had the most success with the Cardinals. He retired with a 4.40 career ERA, a 96 ERA+, 1,615 strikeouts, and 2531⅔ innings pitched.[36] After his playing career, Lohse met and married his second wife, Nikou. Lohse has three children, Kameron and Alexis, from his first marriage, and Kai, from his second. He enjoys playing golf and is a frequent participant in celebrity golf tournaments.

SOURCES

In addition to the sources cited in the Notes, the author consulted Baseball-Reference.com.

NOTES

1   Robert O'Connell, "The Forgettable Career and Memorable Triumphs of Kyle Lohse," VICE, July 28, 2016, https://www.vice.com/en/article/gvavaj/the-forgettable-career-and-memorable-triumphs-of-kyle-lohse.

2   "The Forgettable Career and Memorable Triumphs of Kyle Lohse."

3   "Kyle Lohse," Kyle Lohse married, wife, Twitter, stats, salary • biography," https://bijog.com/biography/kyle-lohse.

4   Brendan Capria, "Kyle Lohse Brings Heritage and Work Ethic to Brewers," Milwaukee Journal Sentinel, March 21, 2014, https://archive.jsonline.com/blogs/sports/251610301.html. (Accessed June 24, 2024). Kyle Lohse himself is enrolled with the Paskenta Band of Nomlaki Indians. Communication from Rob Daugherty on March 17, 2025.

5   Capria, "Kyle Lohse Brings Heritage and Work Ethic to Brewers."

6   Royse Parr, "American Indians in Major League Baseball: Now and Then," https://www.readex.com/readex-report/issues/volume-4-issue-1/american-indians-major-league-baseball-now-and-then. (Accessed June 24, 2024).

7   Lori Nickel, "Brewers' Lohse Another Product of Chico," Milwaukee Journal Sentinel, April 15, 2013, https://archive.jsonline.com/sports/brewers/brewers-lohse-knows-all-about-his-location-q39n2rr-204787941.html/.

8   "Her Son Kyle May Have a World Series Ring, but Leslie Lohse Is an All-Star," Indian Country Today, June 20, 2013, https://indiancountrytoday.com/archive/her-son-kyle-may-have-a-world-series-ring-but-leslie-lohse-is-an-all-star.

9   Nickel, "Brewers' Lohse another product of Chico."

10 Nick Cahill, "Feds Accuse Tribal Casino Execs of Stealing Millions," Courthouse News Service, January 9, 2017, https://www.courthousenews.com/feds-accuse-tribal-casino-execs-of-stealing-millions/.

11 "Former Members of Tribal Leadership Sentenced for Multimillion Dollar Embezzlement Scheme," Eastern District of California | Former Members of Tribal Leadership Sentenced for Multimillion Dollar Embezzlement Scheme | United States Department of Justice, February 25, 2022, https://www.justice.gov/usao-edca/pr/former-members-tribal-leadership-sentenced-multimillion-dollar-embezzlement-scheme.

12 Baseball Reference, https://www.baseball-reference.com/players/l/lohseky01.shtml; John Sickels, "The Career of Kyle Lohse," Minor League Ball, October 22, 2012, https://www.minorleagueball.com/2012/10/22/3539354/the-career-of-kyle-lohse.

13 "The Career of Kyle Lohse."

14 Unless otherwise indicated, all career data comes from Baseball-Reference.com.

15 Sickels, "The Career of Kyle Lohse."

16 "The Career of Kyle Lohse."

17 "Major League Debuts as Minnesota Twins – June 22 – Kyle Lohse," Twinstrivia.com, June 22, 2017, https://twinstrivia.com/2017/06/22/major-league-debuts-as-minnesota-twins-june-22-kyle-lohse/. (Accessed June 26, 2024).

18 Sickels, "The Career of Kyle Lohse."

19 O'Connell, "The Forgettable Career and Memorable Triumphs of Kyle Lohse."

20 "The Forgettable Career and Memorable Triumphs of Kyle Lohse."

21 "The Forgettable Career and Memorable Triumphs of Kyle Lohse."

22 Derrick Goold, "Motte Closes Out Series Win vs. Pirates," STLtoday.com, August 28, 2011, https://www.stltoday.com/news/local/motte-closes-out-series-win-vs-pirates/article_d2024b50-d195-11e0-b0c4-001a4bcf6878.html.

23 Rick Hummel, "Lohse, Unsung Hero of 10th Inning in Game 6 of 2011 Series, Returns for the Party," STLtoday.com, September 17, 2021, https://www.stltoday.com/sports/professional/mlb/cardinals/lohse-unsung-hero-of-10th-inning-in-game-6-of-2011-series-returns-for-the/article_c0426a65-321d-5a2e-9938-571ca050a60e.html.

24 "Lohse, Unsung Hero of 10th Inning in Game 6 of 2011 Series, Returns for the Party."

25   "Lohse, Unsung Hero of 10th Inning in Game 6 of 2011 Series, Returns for the Party."

26   "Lohse, Unsung Hero of 10th Inning in Game 6 of 2011 Series, Returns for the Party."

27   Edgar Thompson, "On Opening Day, Marlins' Stadium Overshadows Their Play," New York Times, April 5, 2012, https://www.nytimes.com/2012/04/05/sports/baseball/on-opening-day-marlins-stadium-overshadows-their-play.html.

28   Hummel, "Lohse, Unsung Hero of 10th Inning in Game 6 of 2011 Series, Returns for the Party."

29   Justin Schultz, "Kyle Lohse Is the King of Consistency," Beyond the Box Score, July 2, 2014, https://www.beyondtheboxscore.com/2014/7/2/5858262/kyle-lohse-consistency-brewers.

30   Bob Nightengale, "While Blake Snell, Jordan Montgomery Remain Free Agents, Kyle Lohse Reflects on the Pain," USA Today, March 6, 2024, https://www.usatoday.com/story/sports/mlb/columnist/bob-nightengale/2024/03/06/kyle-lohse-reflects-on-mlb-free-agency-blake-snell-jordan-montgomery/72863083007/.

31   "While Blake Snell, Jordan Montgomery Remain Free Agents, Kyle Lohse Reflects on the Pain."

32   Justin Schultz, "Kyle Lohse Is the King of Consistency."

33   X.com, accessed February 25, 2025, https://x.com/SportsCenter/status/1883312382501372059.

34   Bill Berg, "Lohse Tosses 12th 'Maddux' in Brewers History," Reviewing the Brew, June 1, 2014, https://reviewingthebrew.com/2014/06/01/lohse-tosses-12th-maddux-brewers-history/.

35   Jessica Kleinschmidt, "Kyle Lohse Appeared to Announce His Retirement with a Picture of a Beer at a Ballgame," MLB.com, May 10, 2018, https://www.mlb.com/cut4/lohse-appeared-to-announce-retirement-at-baseball-game-c276180770.

36   "Kyle Lohse Announced His Retirement While Drinking Beer at a Baseball Game," Yahoo! Sports https://sports.yahoo.com/kyle-lohse-announced-retirement-drinking-beer-baseball-game-183631210.html

BOBBY MADRITSCH

By Jonah O'Callaghan

Robert Allen Madritsch, known as Bobby Madritsch, was a force to be reckoned with. He was born February 28, 1976, in Oak Lawn, Illinois, a Chicago suburb. Bobby was raised by his father, Ken, after his mother, Glenda Madritsch, left the family when he was just two months old. Glenda met Ken when she was in the US Army. Bobby never knew the reason why his mother left but told an interviewer he respected his father for not saying. "As a kid, you don't want to hear bad things parents might say about one another."[1]

Bobby, the youngest of three children in a poor family, loved baseball from an early age. When he was 6 years old, he would run to the corner newsstand and grab the Sunday paper for his father. It was worth it for Bobby because when his father was done reading the paper, he would take Bobby to go play T-ball. Ken coached Bobby in baseball up until high school.[2]

Bobby attended Reavis High School in neighboring Burbank, Illinois. Although there is not much information on his early childhood, he admitted to getting involved with gangs during his high-school years. "I more or less did it because it was the cool thing to do," he told a journalist.[3] But when one of his friends was killed, Bobby realized gangs were not so much fun after all and removed himself from them completely.[3] At Reavis High School, he won All-Conference honors and was offered a scholarship to pitch at Moraine Valley Junior College.[4]

After finishing high school, Bobby learned that his mother, Glenda, was 100 percent Native American and part of the Lakota Sioux tribe. His father, Ken, who worked on a loading dock for a Chicago company, gave Bobby his blue-collar work ethic.[5] He said he was grateful to have his father's work ethic but recognized how special it is to be Native American, especially a Native American baseball player.[5] "I'm just proud to be Native American, just because there are not many of us around," he said.[6]

During his first year at Moraine Valley Junior College, Madritsch found himself homesick and returned home. He found work as a laborer for a small Chicago business, rolling mats into boxes, a job he despised.[7] Then he heard about an opportunity to play baseball at Point Park College in Pittsburgh. He had a fantastic season (1997-1998) going 13-0 for a team that finished 46-6 and seventh in the NAIA World Series. The 6-foot-2, 190-pound left-hander's performance caught the eye of the Cincinnati Reds, and they chose him in the sixth round of the 1998 amateur draft.[8]

The Reds sent Madritsch to the Billings Mustangs, their affiliate in the rookie-level Pioneer League. While he pitched well, posting an earned-run average of 2.80 and a won-lost record of 7-3, Madritsch suffered a torn labrum in his pitching shoulder that put him out of action for the 1999 season.[9]

While he was recovering from surgery, Madritsch drew the sign of a Sioux medicine wheel, something he had seen in a book his brother gave him about their heritage. He decided to get the medicine wheel he had drawn tattooed on his body. He said, "If it worked for my ancestors, I thought it could work for me too."[10]

After coming back in 2000, Madritsch made eight appearances with the Reds' team in the rookie Gulf Coast League, and the Dayton Dragons of the Class-A Midwest League. After the season, he was released by the Reds.

(Courtesy of the Topps Company)

Bobby Madritsch's 2005 Topps Total card

Without a team, Madritsch headed south to pitch for the Rio Grande Valley White Wings and San Angelo Colts of the independent Texas-Louisiana League. Between the two teams he made nine starts. He finished off the 2001 season pitching for the Chico Heat in the independent Western League.

In 2002 Madritsch joined the Winnipeg Goldeyes of the independent Northern League for the 2002 season. Former major leaguer Hal Lanier was the manager of the Goldeyes and Madritsch felt that if he pitched well enough, he might be able to land a contract in the big leagues. Starting the season, Madritsch was not pitching well and was 0-3. Noticing Madritsch's "lack of confidence," pitching coach Rick Forney took the younger pitcher into the bullpen one day to have a conversation with him.[11] After that conversation, Madritsch's confidence grew and he wound up 11-4, 2.30 with 153 strikeouts in 125⅓ innings as the Goldeyes went to the league championship series. Madritsch was named the America's Independent League's Player of the Year.[12]

The Seattle Mariners and the Kansas City Royals expressed interest in Madritsch after his success with the Goldeyes.[13] Initially he leaned toward the Royals, but after a conversation with Lanier and the Goldeyes' owner, Sam Katz, he decided to sign with the Mariners.[14] But if it weren't for Mariners scout Charlie Kerfeld combing the minor league teams for talent, Bobby Madritsch might never have been found by the Mariners.[15]

In 2003 Madritsch was a starting pitcher for the San Antonio Missions, of the Double-A Texas League, posting a 13-7, 3.63 record. He started 2004 with the Tacoma Rainiers, the Mariners' Triple-A team, and in 12 starts was 5-2, 3.75 with twice as many strikeouts as walks.

Meanwhile the Mariners were struggling, and Madritsch's chances of playing in the big leagues were higher than they had ever been.[16] His opportunity came in late July. His manager at Tacoma, Dan Rohn, called Madritsch into his office and told him, "I got a call from the league, they said you can't play tomorrow."[17] Madritsch, assuming that he had been suspended for the time he hit a batter, slammed his fork down. Rohn then came clean: "You're on a flight to Seattle at 10 A.M. in the morning."[18]

On July 21, Madritsch made his major-league debut, against the Oakland Athletics at Seattle's Safeco Field. He entered the game in the 10th inning with the score tied, 5-5. A single and an error put runners at first and second with no outs. A sacrifice moved them up. But third baseman Justin Leone (who had made the error) snagged a line drive to end the inning with an unassisted double play. In the bottom of the 10th, Bucky Jacobsen swung at Justin Duchscherer's first pitch and homered to center field to win the game for the Mariners, 6-5.[19]

Now that he had become a major leaguer, Madritsch hoped the associated publicity would help connect him with his mother: "Maybe, if she hears about me, her and I can get in touch."[20]

August 5 versus Tampa Bay was another special game for him. Not only were some of his family members going to be there to watch him, but this game marked his first career start in the big leagues. He pitched eight innings, threw 105 pitches, gave up five hits, one run, and struck out six batters. The Mariners took the win over Tampa Bay 4-2. Mariners general manager Bob Melvin had good things to say about the type of player he was. "You just watch the way he competes out there… that's a lot of his success."[21] Madritsch believed his family watching helped him succeed as well and he is grateful they were there. "That's what gave me the extra oomph when I needed it, them being there."[22]

On September 29, Madritsch and the Mariners were up against the Oakland Athletics again. In the top of the ninth inning, Ichiro Suzuki—just two singles away from tying George Sisler's single-season record—was hit in the back by Oakland pitcher Duchscherer. Madritsch was furious and wanted to "drill that first guy up in the ninth."[23] But, with the help of his teammates, he was able to calm down. His competitiveness and care for his teammates was something to be admired. He had an impressive performance throwing 133 pitches and 85 of those were strikes. He was the first rookie to have a complete game for the Mariners since Freddy Garcia in August of 1999. Teammate Dan Wilson admired Bobby's competitiveness: "You've got to love his intensity, the way he competes."[24]

After the conclusion of the 2004 season, Madritsch was expected to continue as a starter for the Mariners in 2005. "We're going with a similar cast that we had last year," said pitching coach Bryan Price.[25]

Unfortunately, in his first start of the 2005 season, on April 6 against the Minnesota Twins, he felt "a twinge in his shoulder in the fifth."[26] He had to leave the game.

An MRI revealed that he had torn a ligament in his left shoulder and had to wear a sling for three weeks.[27] After getting the first MRI, the Mariners wanted to do a second one to get a more expansive idea of the injury.[28] Two weeks later, Bobby Madritsch was still in a sling, and was advised not to pick up a baseball for another four weeks.[29]

Madritsch never fully recovered from his left shoulder injury in 2005 with the Mariners. Pressed for roster space, the team released him, and he was picked up on waivers by the Kansas City Royals.[30] The Royals took Madritsch because—even though he was healing from an injury— "we believe he could help us in the long run" said general manager Allard Baird.[31]

In 2006, Madritsch was still working on getting his left shoulder healthy so he could get back out on the mound.[32] He even got another tattoo on his left hand, perhaps no surprise. "A crazy man," he said.[33] The man tattooed on his left hand looks like he wants to scream, yet nothing comes out.[34] Madritsch was frustrated he could not be out on the mound, pitching his heart out, and the tattoo shows that.

After the Royals released him in 2006, Bobby Madritsch's career in the major leagues was done.

He did play for the Long Island Ducks of the independent Atlantic League in 2008, starting in one game and playing a total of two, with one inning pitched.

After Bobby Madritsch retired from professional baseball, he founded a youth baseball program called the Burbank Knights with his brother Ken in his hometown of Burbank, Illinois. The Burbank Knights' first year of existence was in 2012 and it is unclear whether the program is still running today. As of 2025, Madritsch lived in Burbank, Illinois.[35]

ACKNOWLEDGMENTS

Thanks to Jason Levin for providing copious news clippings on Bobby Madritsch. Thanks to SABR member Carter Cromwell for providing some background information.

SOURCES:

In addition to the Notes, the author also consulted Baseball-Reference.com, Retrosheet.org, and Baseball-Almanac.com.

NOTES

1   "Madritsch," *Vancouver* (Washington) *Columbian*, July 27, 2004: B1.

2   Jeff Passan, "Royals: Madritsch Trying to Heal," *Kansas City Star*, March 5, 2006: C1, C12.

3   Bryan Borzykowski, "Seattle Prospect Bobby Madritsch Spells Out Native American Heritage," *Winnipeg Free Press*, December 18, 2002. https://www.angelfire.com/nc3/lakota/madritsch.html, accessed August 31, 2024.

4   Scott Taylor and Dr. Kris Row, *Home Run: The History of the Winnipeg Goldeyes and CanWest Global Park* (Winnipeg: Studio Publications, 2005), 121.

5   Bob Finnigan, "Benefits of Fame," *Vancouver Columbian*, July 27, 2004: B5.

6   Borzykowski.

7   Taylor and Row, 121.

8   Taylor and Row, 121.

9   Taylor and Row, 121.

10 "Injuries Have Taken Toll on More Than the Phillies," *Allentown* (Pennsylvania) *Morning Call*, August 15, 2004: C3.

11 Taylor and Row, 123.

12 Taylor and Row, 123.

13 Ken Wiebe, "Madritsch Switches Gears and Signs Triple-A Deal with Seattle," *Winnipeg Sun*, September 24, 2002: 53.

14 Wiebe.

15 Kirby Arnold, "Big Decision Due on Little Unit," *Bremerton* (Washington) *Sun*, September 5, 2004: C2.

16 Greg Johns, "Rookie Bobby Madritsch Bright Spot in Otherwise Dreary Year," *Olympia* (Washington) *Olympian*, September 20, 2004: 23.

17 Kirby Arnold, "Outfielder Bocachica Designated for Assignment," *Olympian*, July 22, 2004: D2.

18 Arnold, "Outfielder Bocachica Designated for Assignment."

19 Larry Larue, "Walk-Off Homer: 10th-Inning Blast Makes Madritsch Winner in Debut," *Tacoma* (Washington) *News Tribune*, July 22, 2004: C5.

20 Finnigan, "Benefits of Fame."

21 Chris O'Meara, "Bobby Madritsch Pitches Strong in His First Career Start," *Salem* (Oregon) *Statesman Journal*, August 6, 2004: 28.

22 Greg Di Cresce, "Madritsch Impresses in First MLB Start," *Winnipeg Sun*, August 7, 2004: 39.

23 Larry Larue, "Madritsch's three-hitter leads M's past A's, 4-2," *Spokane* (Washington) *Spokesman-Review*, September 30, 2004: 17.

24 Herald news services, "Suzuki 2 Hits from History," *Tri-City Herald* (Pasco, Washington), September 30, 2004: 21.

25 Kirby Arnold, "Mariners Take Their Chances," *Spokane Spokesman-Review*, April 3, 2005: 40.

26 Greg Johns, "Injury Underscores Fragility of M's Staff," *Bremerton Sun*, April 7, 2005: B2.

27 Corey Brock, "Madritsch Sidelined Indefinitely," *Tacoma News Tribune*, April 11, 2005: C7.

28 Larry Larue, "Starter Bobby Madritsch Is Eager to Learn More From a Second MRI on His Shoulder," *Tacoma News Tribune*, April 10, 2005: C5.

29 Corey Brock, "Lefty Bobby Madritsch Will Be Trapped in an Arm Sling for Another Three Weeks," *Tacoma News Tribune*, April 22, 2005: 37.

30 "Royals Claim M's Pitcher," *Kitsap Sun* (Bremerton, Washington), October 22, 2005: C3.

31 Bob Dutton, "Royals Claim Left-Hander on Waivers from Seattle," *Kansas City Star*, October 22, 2005: D5.

32 Passan, "Royals: Madritsch Trying to Heal."

33 Jeff Passan, "A Time To Heal," *Kansas City Star*, March 5, 2006: 27.

34 Passan, "A Time To Heal."

35 Jeff Sullivan, "Bobby Madritsch Update," *Lookout Landing*, https://www.lookoutlanding.com/2012/3/19/2884646/bobby-madritsch-update, accessed September 1, 2024.

BUCK MARTINEZ

By Curt Smith

Some baseball players evoke a position. Recall catcher Mickey Cochrane. Others define managing: Connie Mack comes to mind. Many broadcast as a color analyst or play-by-play man, like Bob Uecker and Bob Costas. Few have performed *all* of the above at one time or another as well as the Blue Jays' John Albert "Buck" Martinez, for whom the 2021 season marked his 53rd big-league year.

Before Buck became a Canadian fixture, his youth had a distinctly American lilt. According to Martinez, mother Shirley once served in the Women's Army Corps and made the cover of *Stars and Stripes* newspaper.[1] On December 7, 1941, his father John, a miner, was at Pearl Harbor in the midst of building a huge underground storage area to house fuel for the US Navy. Completing it, he enlisted in the Army in 1942.[2]

Buck was born on November 7, 1948, in Redding, California. He still has a picture of himself, at age 3, in a baseball uniform, near the site where his dad later built a diamond in their back yard. Martinez was in grammar school before learning that his real name was *John,* the sobriquet *Buck* hailing his Native American heritage as an enrolled member of Northern California's Karuk Tribe.[3] By 10, the family in South Sacramento, he played on Parkway Little League and Southgate Babe Ruth teams, enamored of the pastime from the start.[4]

At nearby Elk Grove, Martinez was a three-year All-Conference choice, batting .512 as a senior. In 1966, the 5-foot-10, 190-pound right-handed catcher graduated from high school. Not immediately drafted by a big-league team, he got an associate of arts degree at Sacramento

(*Courtesy Toronto Blue Jays*)

Buck Martinez

City College and studied at Sacramento State University. Meanwhile, Buck was signed by the Phillies as a 1967 amateur free agent, taken by the Astros in the December 1968 Rule 5 draft, and dealt later that month to Kansas City.[5]

The 1969 Royals began as an American League expansion team, Martinez debuting in the major leagues that June 18 at 20. In 1976 and 1977 he topped .990 in fielding percentage. Buck's best offensive season was 1976, tying 95 games, 267 at-bats, 61 hits, 13 doubles, three triples, five home runs, and 34 runs batted in.[6] Through 1977, his last year in Kansas City, he socked 13 homers, knocked in 104 runs, and averaged .222, including .333 in the then-best-of-five 1976 League Championship Series. By then, Martinez had met his future wife, Arlene, in San Juan, Puerto Rico in 1971 – Buck there for winter baseball; she, an American Airlines attendant, on vacation.[7]

"We had dinner, exchanged phone numbers, but then sort of lost touch for a few years," said Buck.[8] In 1974 they met again, began dating, and wed on July 14, 1975. In 1977, son Casey was born, later becoming a 47th-round pick by Toronto in the 2000 first-year player draft. A catcher like his father, he reached the Blue Jays' Triple-A Syracuse affiliate by 2001, his four-year playing career ending in the Phillies system in 2003.

Daily, baseball teaches humility. For Buck, November 1976 taught life's fragility. Arlene told him she was expecting their first child on the same day Martinez was shot in the left eye while hunting. After nine hours of surgery for a detached retina, his vision devolved from 20/15 to 20/250. "I went from playoff catcher to fourth-string catcher," he said, drolly, though the incident was no laughing matter. Martinez "needed to wear a contact lens in his left eye from then on," read the *Karuk Newsletter.*[9]

As a catcher, Buck upheld several long-held beliefs. One was the position's perceived weak-hitting bent. Thrice traded, Joe Garagiola, a .257 hitter from 1946 to '54, played for half of the then-eight National League clubs.[10] "I thought I was modeling uniforms," he joked.[11] Martinez may have felt that, too. On December 8, 1977, the Royals shipped him to St. Louis, which that day sent Buck to Milwaukee. On May 10, 1981, he was dealt again – to Toronto, for which he hit a career .222 but forged a single-year fielding percentage as high as .995.

Buck also affirmed catching's need to hang tough, "knocked out two or three times in collisions at home plate," he told CBS Sports.[12] In his first big-league start, Martinez collided with and tagged out the Twins' Bob Allison at the plate. "I threw the ball to third base, and I collapsed and I was unconscious. The trainers came out and gave me smelling salts, and I actually hit my first major-league home run in the next half-inning."[13]

At this point, Toronto still lacked a big-league franchise, Canada's largest city awarded an AL expansion team in March 1976.[14] "A nationwide contest chose the name Blue Jays. Fans came to our games from every province," Martinez said. "And we were aware of what we represented to the country."[15] The team's tricolor insignia fluttered in every province, even in the Montreal Expos' Quebec.

The Blue Jays' April 7, 1977, first opener remains parts fact and fable. Snow fell. "On the shores of Lake Ontario," Buck said, "people sat on aluminum chairs, the wind in force [wind-chill hit 10 degrees Fahrenheit]. Fans bundled up all year. So *Canadian!*"[16] The Jays beat Chicago, 9-5, before an overflow 44,649 in a 43,737-seat baseball capacity site. Doug Ault homered twice, becoming the club's first legend.[17]

In 1977 Buck's first visit to Toronto with the Royals, he saw how Exhibition Stadium resembled a "long, college football-style facility … converted for baseball use." Seats behind the plate and down each line "were really glorified bleachers." A left- to left-center-field football grandstand boasted the joint's "only covered seats."[18] In right field, a chain-link fence separated the outfield and vast "dead area," said Martinez. Behind it loomed a scoreboard, "far away from everything in the opposite end zone."[19]

Built on the Canadian National Exhibition's 350-acre fairgrounds, the makeshift *faux* grass park (née CNE Stadium) flanked "landscaped gardens, an amusement park, restaurants and concert facilities."[20] Frisbees and picnicking lent a down-home feel. A block away Lake Ontario brandished boats – and seagulls. Dave Winfield's 1983 warm-up throw accidentally killed one, prompting the Yankees outfielder's arrest.[21]

The first-year team drew 1,701,052, but lost 107 games. Between halves of the seventh inning, Exhibition crowds stood and stretched, yet invariably clapped softly – said Martinez, "the quietest in the league."[22] Once his wife, sitting with other Blue Jays wives, stood and implored spectators, "Come on, holler!"[23] To Martinez, noting how the park didn't sell beer, the stillness contrasted with his prior club in Milwaukee, where beer was appetizer, main course, and dessert.

"At first there was little reason to listen [or attend]," conceded 1977-2004 radio voice Tom Cheek, "except for the sheer novelty of big-league ball."[24] Blue Jays wireless/TV forged another. From birth, much of Canada has been isolated. The Jays wove a thread. Former Mets and Orioles Voice Gary Thorne once recalled how "Somewhere in a small town in the country [Canada or America], when you talked about the team, the broadcaster pictured the game

for them night after night"[25] – mic men like Cheek their link to the club.

Other links became Tom's 1977-81 and 1981-2005 partners Early Wynn and Jerry Howarth, respectively – and eventually Martinez. As a player, Buck had aired 1982 World Series, LCS, and All-Star Game color commentary on the Telemedia Radio Network across Canada, Cheek on play-by-play.[26] Martinez also frequently appeared on Canada's The Sports Network (TSN) television. "Up 'til about then I hadn't really thought of retiring or announcing," Buck said. He might not have, if not for a play that begs credulity, even now.[27]

Martinez's second career unfolded from a July 9, 1985, match in Seattle's Kingdome. Buck started in his frequent role as a reserve or platoon catcher to Ernie Whitt, as he had to the Royals' Darrell Porter and Brewers' Ted Simmons, said SABR's David Firstman.[28] In the third inning, a *Ripley's Believe It or Not!* moment occurred that led Jays vice president Bobby Mattick, a 1938-40 Cubs and 1941-42 Reds infielder, to hail "the greatest baseball play I'd ever seen."[29]

The Mariners' Phil Bradley led off by singling. With one out, pitcher Tom Filer balked him to second base. Gorman Thomas then singled to right field, Jesse Barfield – to Firstman, "possessor of one of the finest outfield arms in history" – charging the ball and "uncork[ing] a laser toward the plate."[30] The throw, slightly up the third-base line, arrived as Bradley crashed into Martinez and knocked him on his back in the right-hand batter's box. Somehow, he held the ball for the out, but Buck's spikes caught in the ground and "two bones came dislocated out of the ankle socket and in fact, I broke the fibula – the small leg bone – up to my knee," he told the Canadian Broadcasting Corporation's *Midday*.[31]

At first Martinez thought that his leg was asleep. "There was no pain involved, but I couldn't move my leg. I couldn't rely on it at all to prop me up or move about anymore. It was dead."[32] As play continued, Buck, sitting but unable to stand, saw Thomas running between second and third base and threw toward third baseman Garth Iorg, the toss sailing into left field. Picking it up, George Bell fired to the plate. Martinez nabbed the ball as the 210-pound Thomas plowed homeward, tried to score standing up, but instead felt the prostrate Buck's tag to complete a surreal 9-2-7-2 double play.

Out for the season, Martinez missed the Jays' LCS loss to Kansas City, his mental pain as bad as physical, but wrote a book, *From Worst to First: The Toronto Blue Jays in 1985*.[33] After Buck's collision, wrote ESPN senior writer Tim Kurkjian, "he endured five months of 50 hours a week rehab just so he could play one more year for the Blue Jays at age 37."[34] In 1986 he hit .181 in 81 games, penned his second tome, *The Last Out: The Toronto Blue Jays in 1986*, and that December called its title "my last out as a player, the way it looks right now."[35]

In 1981-86, Martinez had graced up to 102 games (1984), hit as many as 10 homers (1982 and 1983), batted as high as .253 (1983), and made only two errors in each of 1981, 1984, 1985, and 1986. Buck's career featured 1,049 games, 58 homers, 321 RBIs, a .225 batting average – his offensive peak the early 1980s – and a .984 fielding percentage. Torn, wanting to play again, Martinez thought he could. Blue Jays President Paul Beeston didn't, thinking the injury had dimmed Buck's skill. They met prior to the 1987 season, Beeston asking, "Albert, you want to do TV?" as a Jays "colour commentator" on TSN.[36]

Buck's wife, his agent and future actress, suggested he try, saying, "You can't play anymore. This is a great opportunity."[37] Direct, she was correct. Martinez signed with TSN, utilizing, as Kurkjian wrote, what a makeup woman termed his "great [facial] base" and "a marvelous tone."[38] Buck began a new life by practicing his delivery on the roof of the Jays' then-spring training park, Grant Field, in Dunedin, Florida. On the first-day ride home, he heard the tape and thought, "This is awful. I'm rotten."[39] Jerry Howarth added, "[Buck] always wanted to get better," amenable to criticism.[40]

Initially, Arlene told him, "You're trying to be [actor] Ted Knight," the formalized comic character Ted Baxter on TV's *The Mary Tyler Moore Show.* "Just be yourself."[41] She also persuaded him to take speech and acting classes. Ida Weedle, a speech pathologist, "got me [Buck] to start finishing my words."[42] Martinez's 1987-89 partner was play-by-play's Fergie Olver,[43] an ex-minor league and semipro Western Baseball League outfielder turned co-host of a CTV Television children's show, *Just Like Mom,* with then-wife Catherine Swing. Steadily improving, Buck never looked back.

On May 28, 1989, the Blue Jays bade Exhibition adieu: Toronto 7, White Sox 5. In 1963 John F. Kennedy recalled how as a boy the Irish writer Frank O'Connor and his friends would come to an arched wall while exploring the countryside. If it seemed too high or hard to hurdle, they removed their caps, flung them over the wall, and had to follow.[44] Domed stadiums kept out bad weather. Yet fans wanted to feel the sun and breeze. SkyDome became a solution, its first game June 5: the world's only stadium with a fully retractable roof,[45] which flung caps over the future, making baseball follow.

The 50,016-seat, five-tiered orb housed the 1991-92-93 AL East and 1992-93 World Series titlist. Its new digs helped lure a 1993 still-league record (as of 2022) 4,057,947 gate, averaging 50,098 per date. At SkyDome, Jim Hughson became TSN's Blue Jays play-by-play man in 1990, replacing Olver. He and Buck teamed through 1994, the British Columbia native calling each 1991-93 Jays division-clinching title.[46] (In 1995-2001, Toronto-born Dan Shulman succeeded him.) Martinez added 1994-95's ABC/NBC *The Baseball Network* – and 1992-2000's and 2002-05's ESPN,

its coverage of Cal Ripken Jr.'s record-breaking 2,131st straight game taking a 1995 Sports Emmy Award.[47]

In early 2000 ESPN enlarged Martinez's portfolio by hiring him for *Baseball Tonight.* "His first appearance looked like it could have been his 500th, it was that seamless," wrote Tim Kurkjian. Buck wasn't pleased with his preparation, thinking, "That won't happen again." It didn't. "One night," Tim noted, "he did a Blue Jays game on TSN, but because the game ran late, he missed his flight to Connecticut for a *Sunday Baseball Today* show."[48] Martinez drove 500 miles from Toronto to ESPN's Bristol, Connecticut, home, "using his cell phone for script updates and arriving 10 minutes before airtime." Buck minimized the effort, saying, "It was my job."[49]

That year attendance fell to 1,819,919,[50] helping induce another Martinez career – his November 3 hiring to replace Jim Fregosi as 2001 Jays skipper despite a lack of even coaching experience. Buck's sole managerial stint had been with "Martinez's Marauders" at the 1995-96 Blue Jays' Fantasy Camp. Former Padres and Astros skipper Preston Gomez told him, "Remember, the ball looks really small up in the booth. But down on the field, the ball is really big."[51] The populace cheered. Drivers left their cabs in the middle of the street to thank him. Martinez recalled season-ticket holders saying they hadn't been "so excited in five years."[52]

After Buck's signing, Kurkjian observed that "even as a player, [Martinez] was the guy from whom many of the Blue Jays players sought advice and went to," not "some self-infatuated gasbag who believes the team revolves around him."[53] GM Gord Ash said, "Sports is a people business. It's a business of communication and Buck is an excellent communicator."[54] He wrote letters to 32 players, telling them "he thought they could make up the five games that kept them from the [2000] playoffs."[55] Martinez phoned several personally, also speaking with big-league players-turned-managers Cookie Rojas, Don Zimmer, and, most famously, Joe Torre.[56]

Sadly, the 2001 Jays finished 80-82, had a home game postponed by metal siding and insulation falling from the roof,[57] and braved an adverse currency exchange rate: revenue in Canadian dollars, salaries in more costly US dollars. On June 3, 2002, the 20-33 Jays ditched Buck for minor-league skipper Carlos Tosca. "I don't know if [he] even knows what his philosophy or style is because he hasn't had a lot of time to manage," said new GM J.P. Ricciardi. "It's not so much the wins, the losses at this point, it's more the leadership."[58] Of Martinez he told CBC: "He's a class act. He handled this in a very professional manner."[59] Said Buck: "Gord Ash had been fired after my first season, never a good sign. I made mistakes, but … it made possible all that's happened since."[60]

Martinez managed Team USA in the 2006 inaugural World Baseball Classic, airing the next WBC tournaments in 2009, 2013, and 2017.[61] In 2003-09, Buck did Baltimore Orioles color with play-by-play's Jim Hunter, then Gary

Thorne, on TV's Mid-Atlantic Sports Network (MASN), taking a second Emmy for Best Analyst, Regional Sports Network.[62] He added TBS's 2008-09 postseason and *Sunday Afternoon Baseball* color with Chip Caray – and co-hosted 2005-09 XM Radio's *Baseball This Morning*; in 2009 substituted for the ill Jerry Remy on the Red Sox' New England Sports Network (NESN); and did the 2016-20 World Series and All-Star Game for MLB International.

In 2010, returning to the Jays, Martinez did play-by-play for 110 games on Canada's Rogers Sportsnet cable TV network, replacing Jamie Campbell,[63] and was hired to host the new pregame *Blue Jays Central*.[64] "I think it's a different challenge for me," Buck said. "Obviously, it's a different role but because I've been blessed with so many play-by-play partners – Tom Cheek, [previously noted] Jim Hughson, and Dan Shulman and the guys at ESPN – I think I can take something from all of them."[65]

By now, Jays radio/TV headliners largely differed from a decade earlier. In 2001 Cheek received the Canadian Baseball Hall of Fame's Jack Graney Award, named for the first Canadian major-league voice.[66] Tom broadcast 4,306 consecutive games, the streak ending with his father's death in 2004. Ten days later, he braved brain tumor surgery on his 65th birthday.[67] Cancer returned that offseason, demanding further treatment. On Opening Day 2005, Cheek aired an inning in person on the wireless at Tampa Bay, near his Florida home.

A nation grieved Tom's October 9 death at 66, ending the beloved "Tom and Jerry [Howarth] Show." In 2013 he posthumously became the 37th annual recipient of the National Baseball Hall of Fame and Museum's Ford C. Frick Award for "broadcast excellence."[68] Martinez recalled, "He was the voice and face of the Blue Jays."[69] Cheek often said, "Give me music with a message."[70] His message – inspiring other Toronto mic men – was that knowing baseball's heart could make its music soar.

Shulman, for instance, the first Canadian named National Sportscaster of the Year by the National Association of Sportscasters and Sportswriters and a 2020 Graney Award recipient, buoyed 2002-17 ESPN TV and 2016- Sportsnet Jays play-by-play with Buck.[71] In 1993 another contemporary, Pat Tabler, joined TSN's *Baseball Tonight* after a 12-year playing career.[72] Hired by Sportsnet in 2005, a decade later he inked an extension with Martinez through 2019 – "our soundtrack to a season of strikeouts, stolen bases, and home runs," said network vice president Rob Corte.[73]

Increasingly, their club bounced between poles. In 2003 Roy Halladay's 22-7 holiday earned a Cy Young Award. The '04-05ers then flunked .500. In 2005 SkyDome was renamed the Rogers Centre after its purchase by Jays owner Rogers Communications. Next season five Blue Jays made the All-Star team – the most since 1993. In 2008 nostalgia bloomed, 1989-1997 skipper Cito Gaston rehired to manage. Halladay won his 129th Jays game, behind only another big-game pitcher Dave Stieb's 175.

On October 3, 2009, Ricciardi was ditched for assistant general manager Alex Anthopoulos, Toronto having missed the playoffs in J.P.'s eight years as GM.[74] Next season the Blue Jays hit a franchise-high 257 home runs: Like 2000, seven smacked 20 or more, José Bautista (54) the 26th player with 50 or more.[75] "I was marking my scoreboard when suddenly I looked up to see the ball clearing the fence," said a surprised Martinez. "All I could say was, 'Fifty!'"[76] Halladay moved to Philadelphia, retiring in 2013 after signing a ceremonial one-day Toronto pact.[77]

At his 2015-19 Sportsnet signing, Buck evoked 2010: "[Then] I stepped into the unknown as the play-by-play guy but now, looking ahead for the next five years, I couldn't be happier." Reader critique included "Buck is a boring parrot" to "He's [equal to] Vin Scully."[78] Ending North America's longest active professional sports playoff drought, the '15 Jays took the AL East and erased Texas's 2-0 best-of-five Division Series lead on Bautista's last-game three-run homer succeeded by an "epic bat flip"[79] – to some, violating an unwritten code against disparaging the other team.[80]

In the melee's wake, benches twice cleared and garbage littered the Rogers Centre field. Toronto next advanced to the LCS, Game Six drawing Sportsnet's then-all-time largest audience – 5.12 million viewers for Kansas City's Game Six-clinching triumph.[81] On May 15, 2016, a pitch by the Rangers' Matt Bush hit José to repay his prior year bat flip. In turn, the Jays' slugger illegally slid into infielder Rougned Odor, who slugged Bautista in the jaw to start the first of two more brawls.[82]

On October 4 Toronto met Baltimore in the league's wild-card game. An average audience of 4.02 million viewers eyed Sportsnet's most-watched 2016 telecast, Edwin Encarnacion's three-run 11th-inning homer sealing a 5-2 Jays triumph.[83] Implausibly, almost as many Canadians as Americans watched, despite the huge disparity in population: an estimated 36,379,574 in Canada vs. the United States' 324,738,713.[84] Toronto again beat Texas in the Division Series before losing the LCS to Cleveland.

Thirty years earlier Martinez had released *The Last Out: The Toronto Blue Jays in 1986*. In 2016 he issued his third book, *Change Up: How to Make the Great Game of Baseball Even Better*.[85] "Current players make much more money than he did behind the plate," said CBC Sports, "but [Buck] thinks they're the ones missing out" – in part because money "has displaced team unity as the heart of baseball – and the spirit of the game has suffered as a result." How to revive it? Martinez had a thought.

"The money being made today is great," he began.[86] In his first year in Kansas City, Buck had made $10,000. In 2021, said Statista, the big leagues' *average* yearly wage was $4.17 *million*.[87] "I don't begrudge the players, most of 'em now a mini-corporation," Martinez said. "It's just that when you get more financially secure, you get more independent – it's a natural progression. That's why guys today miss a lot of what we had."[88]

Playing, he said, "we lived in the same spring training complex, had barbecues on the beach, most of us with only one car, so we car-pooled to the park. Our wives baby-sat for each other's kids. We looked after each other." Come April, "we lived in the same apartment complex – a place near Exhibition Stadium named the Palace Pier." Friendship fueled success "because you don't want to let your friends down."[89] Today, money made that feeling hard.

To Martinez, former Yankees captain Derek Jeter showed how money did not negate the reason "we played the game. Derek was in love with baseball, demanding respect from players *for* it."[90] After teammate Robinson Cano "had a great game," he sat reading a paper at his locker while giving an interview. Jeter told him, "We don't treat people like that in this clubhouse." Cano never read papers again, talking to a reporter.[91]

"Whenever I'd see Derek, he was messing with the guys, a great sense of humor,"[92] Buck continued. Chemistry was key – in or beneath the booth. He and Pat Tabler met at 3:30 before a night game "to talk about what we wanted to note," letting "one [broadcaster] know where the other was going before he said a word." It helped them accent how one player's strengths could enhance another's, "showing your audience in advance what they are."[93]

In 2017 polarity continued. Steve Pearce belted grand slams three days apart. Halladay was killed in a plane crash. Next season Tampa Bay bench coach Charlie Montoyo became the Blue Jays skipper. In 2019 several second-generation players made the team: Bo Bichette (his father, Dante), Cavan Biggio (Craig), and Vladimir Guerrero Jr. (Sr.)[94] A year later Halladay made Cooperstown. The Covid-19 virus forced the Jays to move most SkyDome games to Triple-A outlet Buffalo's home ballpark, Sahlen Field.

In 2020 Martinez was named president of a group founded in 1986 by former big-league players, especially 1991 Frick honoree Joe Garagiola: the Baseball Assistance Team.[95] At BAT's birth, the average major-league salary was $412,520.[96] "One pitcher didn't have the money to bury an 11-year-old son. A former Dodger had to consider a raffle to afford an amputated leg," Joe said. "There was no pension then to help."[97] BAT paid bills, bought insurance, preserved dignity: for Buck, a natural evolution. A profile of him asked, "What drew you to the game of baseball growing up?" Martinez said, "The San Francisco Giants and Willie Mays." He saw his first game in 1958 at Seals Stadium. "I can see the green grass as clearly now as I did then."[98]

In 2021 the Karuk Tribe descendant also went to bat for the Indigenous people "[who] did many great things that still aren't recognized as part of the overall culture of Native Americans," said Buck. He voiced video biographies for *The Indigenous Sports Heroes Education Experience,* a "multi-platform, web-based book, curriculum and celebration of 14 Indigenous Hall of Famers" from Colette Bourgonje and Bill Isaacs to Chief Wilton Littlechild and

Bryan Trottier, available to teachers and students from kindergarten to grade 12.[99]

That July 30, the Jays returned to Rogers Centre from Covid-19-dictated games in Dunedin and Buffalo. Robbie Ray became their fourth Cy Young Award pitcher, joining Pat Hentgen, Stieb, and Halladay. Toronto's power was as potent: eight homers in a game and a team and big-league season record 262. In 2021, Guerrero clubbed 48 to lead a franchise-tying seven Jays who for a third time hit 20 or more. Others: Marcus Semien, Teoscar Hernandez, Bichette, George Springer, Randal Grichuk, and Lourdes Gurriel Jr.[100]

Each Blue Jay helped fashion a 91-71 record, one game behind the Red Sox and Yankees in a wild last-week AL wild-card race. Since 1977 interest in the club has rarely failed, as John F. Kennedy said, to "throw [its] cap over" Exhibition Stadium's and Rogers Centre's "wall."[101] A reason is the man who as of 2021 had spent 17 years playing, two managing, and 34 in the booth.

Early in 2022, Buck was diagnosed with cancer, leaving the Blue Jays broadcast booth. "I'm grateful for a tremendous medical team, who has given me great optimism that I will come through this with flying colours,"[102] Martinez said, hoping to rejoin Sportsnet later in the year. Until then, Buck would be "watching from the sidelines."

Likely, he took solace from past experience, where good fortune had followed bad. After all, the 1985 collision that broke a small leg bone may have been the best break of Buck Martinez's career.

SOURCES

I wish to thank the sources cited under "Interviews by author," notably Buck Martinez. Grateful appreciation is made to reprint all play-by-play and color radio text courtesy of The Miley Collection. In addition to the sources cited in the Notes, most especially the Society for American Baseball Research, the author consulted Baseball-Reference.com and Retrosheet.org websites, box scores, player, season, and team pages, batting and pitching logs, and other material relevant to this history. FanGraphs.com provided statistical information. Beyond the sources cited in the Notes, the author consulted:

BOOKS

Elliott, Bob. *If These Walls Could Talk: Toronto Blue Jays: Stories from the Toronto Blue Jays Dugout, Locker Room, and Press Box* (Chicago: Triumph Books, 2020).

Martinez, Buck. *From Worst to First: The Toronto Blue Jays in 1985* (Toronto: Fitzhenry and Whiteside, 1985).

Martinez. *The Last Out: The Toronto Blue Jays in 1986* (Toronto: Fitzhenry and Whiteside, 1986).

Martinez, with Dan Robson. *Change Up: How to Make the Great Game of Baseball Even Better* (Toronto: HarperCollins, 2016).

O'Connell, Kevin, and Josh Pahigian. *The Ultimate Baseball Trip: A Fan's Guide to Major League Stadiums* (Guilford, Connecticut: Lyons Press, 2012).

Public Papers of the Presidents of the United States: John F. Kennedy 1963 (Washington, D.C.: Office of Federal Register, National Archives and Records Administration, 1964).

Shea, Stuart. Gary Gillette (ed.) *Calling the Game: Baseball Broadcasting from 1920 to the Present* (Phoenix: Society for American Baseball Research, 2015).

Thorn, John, Pete Palmer, and Michael Gershman, eds. *Total Baseball: Seventh Edition*, with Matthew Silverman, Sean Lahman, and Greg Spira. New York: Total Sports Publishing, 2001.

Ward, Geoffrey C. *Baseball: An Illustrated History* (New York: Alfred A. Knopf, 1994).

NEWSPAPERS

The *Globe and Mail* (Toronto), *Toronto Star*, and *Toronto Sun* have been primary sources of information about Buck Martinez and his playing, managing, and broadcasting career. Other key sources include the *Baltimore Sun*, *Kansas City Star*, and *USA Today*.

INTERVIEWS BY AUTHOR

Tom Cheek, 1994 and 2002.

Joe Garagiola, 1993.

Jerry Howarth, 2009.

Tim Kurkjian, 2010.

Buck Martinez, 2022.

Dan Shulman, 2009.

Gary Thorne, 2010.

NOTES

1   Buck Martinez interview, January 2022.

2   Martinez interview, 2022.

3   Martinez interview.

4   *Karuk Newsletter*, Spring 2017, 18. https://www.karuk.us/images/docs/newsletters/2017_Spring_Newsletter.pdf.

5   Martinez interview.

6   Thorn, John, Pete Palmer, and Michael Gershman, eds. *Total Baseball: Seventh Edition,* with Matthew Silverman, Sean Lahman, and Greg Spira. New York: Total Sports Publishing, 2001, 980.

7   https://dodoodad.com/buck-martinez/.

8   Martinez interview.

9   *Karuk Newsletter*, Spring 2017, 18.

10 Warren Corbett, "Joe Garagiola," SABR BioProject. https://sabr.org/bioproj/person/joe-garagiola/.

11 Warren Corbett, "Joe Garagiola."

12 R.J. Anderson, "Buck Martinez, Who Says He Was 'Knocked Out' Many Times, Still Opposes Posey Rule," CBS Sports.com, September 28, 2017. https://www.cbssports.com/mlb/news/buck-martinez-who-says-he-was-knocked-out-many-times-still-opposes-posey-rule/.

13 Anderson.

14 https://www.thecanadianencyclopedia.ca/en/article/toronto-blue-jays.

15 Martinez interview.

16 Martinez interview.

17 Ron Smith, *The Ballpark Book: A Journey Through the Fields of Baseball Magic* (St. Louis: The Sporting News, 2000), 294.

18 *The Ballpark Book*, 294.

19 Martinez interview.

20 *The Ballpark Book*, 294.

21 *The Ballpark Book,* 293.

22 Martinez interview.

23 Martinez interview.

24 Tom Cheek interview, 1994.

25 Gary Thorne interview, 2010.

26 Martinez interview.

27 Martinez interview.

28 David Firstman, "July 9, 1985: Catcher Buck Martinez Tags Out Two Baserunners on Same Play," SABR Games Project. https://sabr.org/gamesproj/game/july-9-1985-catcher-buck-martinez-tags-out-two-baserunners-on-same-play/.

29 Tim Kurkjian, "Buck Martinez Is About to Take On a Brand-New Role – One He's Been Rehearsing For His Whole Life," ESPN.com. https://www.espn.com/espn/magazine/archives/news/story?page=magazine-20010122-article38.

30 David Firstman.

31 "Buck Martinez's Broken Leg and His Journey into Broadcasting," CBC Archives, January 6, 2019. https://www.cbc.ca/archives/buck-martinez-s-broken-leg-and-his-journey-into-broadcasting-1.4963392.

32 "Buck Martinez's Broken Leg and His Journey into Broadcasting."

33 https://www.goodreads.com/book/show/3746572-from-worst-to-first.

34 Kurkjian.

35 "Buck Martinez's Broken Leg and His Journey into Broadcasting."

36 Martinez interview.

37 Martinez interview.

38 Kurkjian.

39 Kurkjian.

40 Kurkjian.

41 Martinez interview.

42 Martinez interview.

43 https://www.liquisearch.com/buck_martinez/broadcasting.

44 https://www.markholan.org/archives/2810.

45 www.pbs.org/wgbh/buildingbig/wonder/structure/sky.html.

46 https://icehockey.fandom.com/wiki/Jim_Hughson.

47 "Blue Jays Broadcasters." https://www.mlb.com/bluejays/team/broadcasters.

48 Kurkjian.

49 Kurkjian.

50 https://www.baseball-almanac.com/teams/toroatte.shtml#:~:text=Toronto%20Blue%20Jays%20Attendance%201977%20-%202020%20,%20A.L.%20Average%20%203%20more%20rows%20?msclkid=4da140dea5711ec8dac2f9a5f96cbd7.

51 Kurkjian.

52 Martinez interview.

53 Kurkjian.

54 Kurkjian.

55 Kurkjian. The deficit was actually 4½ games in 2000.

56 Kurkjian.

57 "SkyDome Roof Shreds," CBC Sports, April 12, 2001. https://www.cbc.ca/sports/baseball/skydome-roof-shreds-1.277009.

58   Associated Press, "Martinez Fired During Second Season with Jays," ESPN, June 4, 2002. https://a.espncdn.com/mlb/news/2002/0603/1390123.html.

59   "Blue Jays Fire Buck Martinez," CBC Sports, June 4, 2002. https://www.cbc. ca/sports/baseball/blue-jays-fire-buck-martinez-1.349252.

60   Martinez interview.

61   "Blue Jays Broadcasters."

62   "Blue Jays Broadcasters."

63   Chris Zelkovich, "Sportsnet Hits a Homer in Landing Martinez," *Toronto Star*, December 11, 2009. https://www.thestar.com/sports/baseball/2009/12/11/ zelkovich_sportsnet_hits_a_homer_in_landing_martinez.html.

64   https://www.imdb.com/title/tt4368002/characters/nm7061962.

65   Chris Zelkovich, "Buck Martinez Returns as Blue Jays TV Announcer," *Toronto Star*, December 10, 2009. https://www.thestar.com/sports/ baseball/2009/12/10/buck_martinez_returns_as_blue_jays_tv_ announcer.html.

66   "Tom Cheek," Canadian Baseball Hall of Fame. https://baseballhalloffame. ca/hall-of-famer/tom-cheek/.

67   "Tom Cheek."

68   "Tom Cheek."

69   Martinez interview.

70   Cheek interview, 1994.

71   "Blue Jays Broadcasters."

72   "Blue Jays Broadcasters."

73   Sportsnet staff, "Sportsnet Locks Up Blue Jays Broadcast Duo," Sportsnet. ca, September 25, 2014. https://www.sportsnet.ca/baseball/mlb/martinez-tabler-to-return-for-five-more-years/.

74   Associated Press, "Blue Jays Fire GM Ricciardi," ESPN.com, October 3, 2009. https://www.espn.com/mlb/news/story?id=4528183.

75   "Jose Bautista Becomes First Player Since 2007 to Hit 50 Home Runs in One Season," NESN.com, September 23, 2010. https://nesn.com/2010/09/ jose-bautista-becomes-first-player-since-2007-to-hit-50-home-runs-in-one-season/.

76   Martinez interview.

77   Matt Snyder, "Roy Halladay Retires as a Blue Jay," CBSports.com, December 9, 2013. https://www.cbssports.com/mlb/news/roy-halladay-retires-as-a-blue-jay/.

78   "Sportsnet Locks Up Blue Jays Broadcast Duo."

79   Howie Kussoy, "Jose Bautista's Epic Bat Flip Is Quite Polarizing," *New York Post*, October 15, 2015. https://nypost.com/2015/10/15/jose-bautistas-epic-bat-flip-is-quite-polarizing/.

80   Kussoy.

81   Sportsnet, "5.12 Million Viewers Watch Blue Jays vs. Kansas City ALCS Game 6 on Sportsnet; Delivers Most-Watched Broadcast in Network History," newswire.ca, October 26, 2015. https://www.newswire.ca/ news-releases/512-million-viewers-watch-blue-jays-vs-kansas-city-alcs-game-6-on-sportsnet-delivers-most-watched-broadcast-in-network-history-537260561.html.

82   SI Wire, "Watch: Blue Jays, Rangers Brawl after Takeout Slide," www. si.com. May 15, 2016. https://www.si.com/mlb/2016/05/15/watch-blue-jays-rangers-brawl-after-takeout-slide.

83   Ian Campbell, "Sportsnet reporting big ratings win with Blue Jays wild card game." *Calgary CityNews,* October 5, 2016. Sportsnet reporting big ratings win with Blue Jays wild card game | CityNews Calgary

84   Andrew Buckholtz, "Almost as Many Canadians as Americans Watched Jays-O's Despite Population Difference," AwfulAnnouncing.com, October 5, 2016. https://awfulannouncing.com/2016/almost-as-many-canadians-as-americans-watched-jays-os-despite-population-difference.html#.

85   CBC Radio, "Why Buck Martinez Feels Bad for Today's Baseball Players," cbc.ca, March 22, 2016. https://www.cbc.ca/radio/q/ schedule-for-tuesday-march-22-2016-1.3501928/why-buck-martinez-feels-bad-for-today-s-baseball-players-1.3501932.

86   Martinez interview.

87   https://www.Statista.Com/Statistics/236213/Mean-Salary-Of-Players-In-Majpr-League-Baseball/#.

88   Martinez interview.

89   Martinez interview.

90   Martinez interview.

91   Martinez interview.

92   Martinez interview.

93   Martinez interview.

94   Joon Lee, "Why Vladimir Guerrero Jr., Bo Bichette and Cavan Biggio Are Ready for the Next Step," ESPN.com, February 25, 2020. https://www.espn. com/mlb/story/_/id/28711372/why-vladimir-guerrero-jr-bo-bichette-cavan-biggio-ready-next-step.

95   Associated Press, "Joe Garagiola, Ex-Player Turned Glib Broadcaster, Dies at 90," Newschannel 5 Nashville, March 23, 2016. https://www. newschannel5.com/news/national/joe-garagiola-ex-player-turned-glib-broadcaster-dies-at-90#.

96   Edmund P. Edmonds, "MLB Minimum and Average Salaries, 1967-2012," Notre Dame Law School, February 2, 2012. https://scholarship.law.nd.edu/ cgi/viewcontent.cgi?article=1000&context=baseball_salaries.

97   Joe Garagiola interview, 1993.

98   https://www.mlb.com/baseball-assistance-team/director-profile-buck-martinez

99   David Giddens, CBC Sports, "Indigenous Sports Heroes in the Classroom," cbc.ca, August 9, 2021. https://www.cbc.ca/sportslongform/entry/indigenous-sports-heroes-heading-to-the-classroom.

100   Laura Armstrong, "A Look at Blue Jays Season, by the Numbers, Will Make Fans Wonder Why the Team Didn't Make the MLB Playoffs," *Toronto Star*, October 4, 2021. https://www.thestar.com/sports/ bluejays/2021/10/04/a-look-at-blue-jays-season-by-the-numbers-will-just-make-fans-wonder-why-the-team-didnt-make-the-mlb-playoffs.html#.

101   Mark Holan, "Remember J.F.K. – 3 – Caps Over Walls," n.d. https://www. markholan.org/archives/2810.

102   https://www.aol.com/mlb-broadcaster-stepping-away-following-165556490.html.

PADDY MAYES

By Phil Williams

A rich lineage lies behind Adair Bushyhead Mayes' memorable baseball name. His grandfather, Samuel Mayes (of Scots-Irish descent), married Nancy Adair (granddaughter of a full-blooded Cherokee woman) and was recognized as a Cherokee. In early 1838, the young couple joined a group of Treaty Party Cherokees (tribal members aligned with leaders who had signed the Treaty of New Echota in 1835, that led to an often-tragic Western resettlement) in a voluntary journey to Indian Territory. Samuel grew wealthy in the cattle business, held many slaves, and with Nancy raised 14 children.

The first-born was George Washington Mayes. In 1846 George married Charlotte Bushyhead, a daughter of the Baptist minister and esteemed Cherokee leader Jesse Bushyhead. The Reverend Bushyhead had opposed the Treaty of New Echota but volunteered to lead a large group of Cherokees westward and arrived in Indian Territory in 1839.

George and Charlotte's marriage produced eight children. Three years after her death in 1878, George married Sarah Taylor (of no apparent Cherokee descent), with their union producing three sons. The middle son, Adair Bushyhead, was born on March 17, 1885, in Locust Grove, a hamlet within the Cherokee Nation lands of Indian Territory. Today the town lies within Mayes County in northeastern Oklahoma.

Adair grew up in a prominent family. Two of his uncles, Joel B. Mayes and Samuel Houston Mayes, were chiefs of the Indian Territory's Cherokee Nation, as was his step-uncle Dennis Bushyhead. His father, George, served as superintendent of the Cherokee Male Seminary in Tahlequah, then as a district sheriff.[1]

Adair attended the Cherokee Male Seminary, making the first baseball team in March 1903 as a left fielder.[2] Later his classmates elected him president of their literary society, and he captained the school's football team.[3] The nickname Paddy found him in his youth and stuck.

Mayes played semipro ball with the Cherokee Indian team in 1907.[4] He made his professional debut in 1908 with the Class-D Oklahoma-Kansas League's Muskogee Redskins. Noting his speed in the outfield and on the basepaths, locals considered him "undoubtedly the best man on the payroll of the club."[5]

For the 1909 season, Mayes returned to Muskogee, although the renamed Navigators now played in the Class-C Western Association. In July he was sold to the Portland Beavers of the Class-A Pacific Coast League but hit only .114 in 16 games and was released.[6] Mayes returned to Muskogee. In 81 Western Association games, he hit .261 with 31 stolen bases.[7]

In 1910 Mayes began another campaign with Muskogee but in May was sold again, this time to the Shreveport Pirates of the Class-C Texas League.[8] "Mayes is fast as lightning," a local sportswriter soon noted. "He beats more scratch hits than anybody."[9] Mayes finished the season in Louisiana, mostly batting at the top of the order and hitting .260 (some 40 points over the league average) with 19 stolen bases.[10] A left-handed hitter, he was reportedly "helpless before left-hand pitchers."[11] Playing 55 games in center field, 18 in right, and 13 in left, the right-hander had only seven assists while his .922 fielding percentage was not particularly impressive.[12] Yet, with at least a sliver of justification, Shreveport manager Dale Gear marketed Mayes as showing greater potential than Zach Wheat, then one of the National League's brightest young outfielders, had shown in Shreveport two years earlier.[13]

This was enough to entice the Philadelphia Phillies, who purchased Mayes in August 1910.[14] He reportedly left Shreveport to head east on September 7, but somehow never arrived in Philadelphia, and a week later was playing amateur ball in Muskogee.[15] His failure to arrive was inconsequential. Philadelphia was out of the race, playing .500 ball, and its veteran outfield of Sherry Magee (in left), Johnny Bates (center), and John Titus (right) was performing well. In December the Phillies sent Mayes a contract for 1911. Mayes promptly returned it signed.[16]

Phillies skipper Red Dooin engineered a multiplayer trade with Cincinnati during the offseason that replaced Bates with Dode Paskert in center field. As 1911 spring training loomed, there was little belief that any of the ensconced flycatchers might be dislodged. Still, three outfield recruits hoped to make the team as a reserve: Mayes, Joe Mowry, a Texas Leaguer like Mayes, and Harry Welchonce, who hit .315 in South Bend the season before.

Mayes' speed impressed the Phillies at their Birmingham, Alabama, spring-training grounds while he made several fine plays in center field for the yanigan squad.[17] Nonetheless, a Philadelphia correspondent concluded that "[a]nother season in the 'bushes' will properly polish the Indian, Mayes, for major company."[18]

Yet Dooin and team President Horace Fogel sought a deep bench and kept the maximum league roster of 25

Paddy Mayes

players (plus Dooin as a player-manager).[19] Mayes and Welchonce made the team. "I am glad the Phillies have decided to keep me," Mayes said, "for I believe I can make good. This is my first trip to the east and I am not yet used to the climate. When the weather is warmer I'll be right for work."[20]

Titus turned an ankle on May 3. Dooin plugged Welchonce into the breach. On May 16 NL President Tom Lynch told the Phillies (who had added a couple more players since the season began) that they needed to trim their roster to 25 men.[21] Two days later, Fogel sent Mayes back to the Texas League, this time to Galveston.[22] Philadelphia was in first place with a 22-7 record. Leading the way was another 1910 purchase, Pete Alexander, on his way to one of the greatest rookie pitching seasons in baseball history.[23]

Mayes appeared in one game with the Galveston Sand Crabs, playing in left field and leading off in a loss at Fort Worth on May 23.[24] He then left the team, having found the club's salary offer unagreeable.[25] On the same day, the luckless Titus broke a bone in his ankle vs. St. Louis, forcing Welchonce back into the fray.[26]

After the Phillies lost their sixth game in a row on May 24, Fogel reportedly wired Mayes to return to Philadelphia immediately.[27] Yet when the squad embarked on a four-week road trip two days later, Mayes was not with them. Only after Dooin wired Mayes on June 8 to join the team in St. Louis, where the Phillies opened a four-game series two days after that, did the rookie return.[28] To that point, Welchonce and Jimmy Walsh, one of the better utility players in the league, had subbed for Titus.

In the series opener, Welchonce misplayed a fly ball in the ninth, enabling the Cardinals to rally in the ninth and snatch a 9-8 victory.[29] Dooin promptly announced Mayes would replace Welchonce in right field. Fogel then traded Welchonce to Nashville. Both Fogel and Dooin said Welchonce's poor play during the road trip had cost the Phils a handful of games.[30]

With temperatures rising into the upper 80s, Mayes had the warm weather he desired as he entered Robison Field on June 11 for his major-league debut. With Fogel having just announced that Philadelphia was after another outfielder, Mayes must have known that his opportunity to prove himself was limited. A raucous Sunday crowd of 17,000 was present.

Mayes did not distinguish himself, going 0-for-3. Dooin sent Walsh in to pinch-hit for him in the top of the eighth as the Phillies filled the bases with one out. Walsh grounded into a double play. St. Louis went on to win, 6-5.

The next day, with his team trailing and Mayes due up during a rally, Dooin again turned to Walsh. This time the move paid off. Walsh doubled to tie the score and Philadelphia triumphed, 8-4.

Walsh remained in right field for the next three weeks. Mayes pinch-hit for Phillies pitchers three times in the next five games, getting to base twice via a walk and being hit by

(March 28, 1911 Philadelphia Evening Times)

a pitch. After a four-game series in Chicago ended on June 18, Philadelphia released him. His brief major-league line: 0-for-5 with one run scored, while successfully handling two chances in right field. Philadelphia sportswriter James Isaminger wrote of Mayes, "[w]hile he was an improvement over Welchonce, his inability to hit placed him at a disadvantage."[31]

Mayes' cup of coffee would live in some fame, thanks an anecdote his fellow Cherokee Nation citizen, humorist Will Rogers, told for decades to come:

"I used to know an Indian ballplayer down my way in Tulsa, Oklahoma, by the name of Paddy Mayes. A few years ago, John Titus of the Phillies broke his leg and Dooin gave Mayes a chance. The first pitcher he faced was Slim Sallee of the Cards. [Mayes faced Bill Steele, not Slim Sallee, in his first at-bat.] Sallee struck him out on three pitched balls at which Mayes never lifted his bat from his shoulder and when he went back to the bench he asked Dooin what he should do next.

"'Sit on the bench,' yelled Dooin, 'before Sallee knocks the bat out of your hand.'

"A week later I asked Mayes what he thought of the big league.

"'Wall, Mr. Rogers,' he drawled. 'I heared a lot about how fast the big league was before I comed up here and by criminy, I wants to tell you it hain't been overexaggerated none.'"[32]

After his release from Philadelphia, the Class-A Southern Association's Mobile Sea Gulls purchased Mayes. Several weeks later he was hitting only .109 in 17 games and Mobile released him. Galveston repurchased Mayes, then traded him to their Texas League counterparts, the Oklahoma City Indians. Closer to home, Mayes hit .236 in 46 games.[33]

In 1912 Mayes played for his fourth Texas League team, the Beaumont Oilers, hitting .217 in 134 games, with only 10 extra-base hits. He began the 1913 campaign with the Class-D Cotton States League's Selma Centralites, but the circuit went under in late July.[34] The Class-C South Atlantic League's Macon Peaches then purchased Mayes, but there is no indication he played for them. Mayes concluded his professional career in 1914, playing for Augusta and Albany of the South Atlantic League, then with the Western Association's Muskogee Mets. For the next several years he played semipro ball with several Oklahoma teams.

As his baseball days faded, Mayes turned to farming in Locust Grove as a full-time career. In 1920 he married Estella DeMoss; a year later their sole child, Stella Marie, arrived. Mayes bought a butcher shop in town. Several years later the family moved some 140 miles northwest to Ponca City, Oklahoma, where Mayes began a lengthy career with Continental Oil as a refinery worker. Upon retiring in 1952, he and Stella moved to Fayetteville, Arkansas. On May 28, 1963, Adair Bushyhead Mayes died of coronary thrombosis. Survived by Estella, Stella Marie, and a grandson, he was buried several miles west of Fayetteville in Farmington Cemetery.[35]

SOURCES

In addition to the sources cited in the Notes, the author accessed the *Encyclopedia of Minor League Baseball* and the following sites: genealogybank.com/, newspapers.com/, and texashistory.unt.edu/.

NOTES

1   For family history, see John Barlett Meserve, "The Mayes," *Chronicles of Oklahoma*, Volume 15, No. 1 (March 1937): 56-65. Available online at: http://digital.library.okstate.edu/Chronicles/vo15/vo15po56.html. Ancestry.com also provides useful information.

2   "Male Seminary," *Vinita* (Indian Territory) *Leader*, March 19, 1903: 5.

3   Jack N. Leerskov, "Male Seminary News," the *Arrow* (Tahlequah, Indian Territory), October 26, 1907: 4; "Tahlequah Wins," *Vinita* (Oklahoma) *Daily Chieftain*, November 29, 1907: 1.

4   "Martins Win from Cherokees," *Little Rock Gazette*, May 8, 1907: 8; the *Clipper* (Pryor Creek, Oklahoma), June 21, 1907: 5.

5   "Carr's Breezy Bingles of the Leaguers," *Muskogee (Oklahoma) Times-Democrat*, August 19, 1908: 3.

6   "Additional Local," *Clipper*, July 15, 1909: 3. For his Portland statistics, see Francis C. Richter, ed., *Reach's Official American League Base Ball Guide for 1910* (Philadelphia: A.J. Reach Co., 1910), 307.

7   *1911 Reach Official American League Base Ball Guide for 1910*, 383.

8   "Tull Purchases Kahn's Stock in Ball Club," *Muskogee Daily Phoenix*, May 25, 1910: 1.

9   "Pirates Toyed with Dallas Yesterday," *Shreveport Journal*, June 3, 1910: 8.

10   For Texas League batting statistics, see Francis C. Richter, ed., *Reach's Official American League Base Ball Guide for 1911* (Philadelphia: A.J. Reach Co., 1911): 421-425.

11   "Short Talks with the Sporting Editor," *Muskogee Daily Phoenix*, August 5, 1910: 3.

12   For Texas League outfielder fielding statistics, see *Reach's Official American League Base Ball Guide for 1911*, 425-427.

13   "More Players Have Been Sold," *Shreveport Times*, August 18, 1910: 6. Wheat, with Shreveport in 1908, hit .268 (considerably over the Texas League average) while posting less than impressive defensive statistics. See *1909 Spalding Official Baseball Record* (New York: American Sports Publishing, 1909), 134-137.

14   "Shake-Up for Phillies," *Brooklyn Citizen*, August 20, 1910: 3.

15   Jim Nasium [Edgar Wolfe], "Mike Doolan's Clout Won Game," *Philadelphia Inquirer*, September 8, 1910: 13; "Phils and Cubs Double Up Today," *Philadelphia Inquirer*, September 14, 1910: 10; "Prior Creek Here Sunday," *Muskogee Times-Democrat*, September 21, 1910: 7.

16   "Phillies Sign Injun," *Philadelphia Inquirer*, December 17, 1910: 10.

17   "Three Missing Phils to Join Dooin Team," *Philadelphia North American*, March 13, 1911: 13.

18   "Manager Dooin Will Send Five Pitchers to Minors," *Philadelphia North American*, March 20, 1911: 13.

19   "Local Ball Teams Announce Rosters," *Philadelphia Press*, April 9, 1911: Sporting Section 1.

20   James C. Isaminger, "Athletics and Phils Lop Many Juveniles Off Lists; Mack Back," *Philadelphia North American*, April 9, 1911: Seventh Section 1.

21 James C. Isaminger, "Phils Score 21 Runs on Reds; A Season's Record," *Philadelphia North American*, May 16, 1911: 14.

22 "After Donahue as Crab Boss," *Galveston Tribune*, May 18, 1911: 7.

23 See Thomas E. Merrick's account of Alexander's one-hitter against Cy Young, "September 7, 1911: Rookie Pete Alexander Pitches One-Hitter, Tops Cy Young," SABR Games Project. https://sabr.org/gamesproj/game/september-7-1911-rookie-pete-alexander-pitches-one-hitter-tops-cy-young/.

24 "Ritter May Go to Cleburne as Manager; Robinson Today," *Fort Worth Star-Telegram*, May 24, 1911: 8.

25 "Hotly Contested Ten-Inning Game," *Galveston Daily News*, May 26, 1911: 8.

26 James C. Isaminger, "Still Slumping, Phils Lose to St. Looey, 12-4," *Philadelphia North American*, May 24, 1911: 12.

27 James C. Isaminger, "St. Looey Pulls Phillies Out of First Place; 4-2," *Piladelphia North American*, May 25, 1911: 12.

28 "Notes of the Game," *Philadelphia North American*, June 10, 1911: 14.

29 "Bresnahan Hits in Winning Run in Ninth Round," *St. Louis Post Dispatch*, June 11, 1911: Part Three 9.

30 "Fogel Releases Three; To Make Trade," *Philadelphia North American*, June 12, 1911: 12; James C. Isaminger, "Tips from the Sporting Ticker," *Philadelphia North American*, June 18, 1911: Second Section 16.

31 James C. Isaminger, "Tips from the Sporting Ticker," *Philadelphia North American*, June 25, 1911: Second Section 16.

32 The first telling found by the author: "Mixed Pickles," *Cleveland Plain Dealer*, April 11, 1914: 11.

33 For his Oklahoma City statistics, see "Averages of Texas League Players for Season 1911," *Galveston Daily News*, December 3, 1911: 8.

34 "High Loves Gets a Try-Out with Atlanta Bunch, *Selma (Alabama) Journal*, July 27, 1913: 1.

35 For his post-baseball life, see *Locust Grove* (Oklahoma) *Times*, November 17, 1921: 1; "Rites in Arkansas for Adair Mayes," *Pryor* (Oklahoma) *Jeffersonian*, June 6, 1963: 17; "Former Resident Dies in Arkansas," *Ponca City* (Oklahoma) *News*, May 29, 1963: 2; and Ancestry.com.

PRYOR MCBEE

By Joe Leisek

On May 22, 1926, in the bottom of the seventh inning at Fenway Park, Chicago White Sox manager and second baseman Eddie Collins just watched his bullpen turn a close game into a rout.

The *Chicago Tribune* described the inning as "too complicated and painful to bear narrating."[1]

Two relievers combined to surrender five runs, three on bases-loaded walks. After the third such walk and with the bases still loaded, Collins called on Eddie McBee, a young left-hander who had joined the club two weeks earlier.

For McBee, it was his debut – and the only appearance he would make in a major-league game.

Pryor Edward McBee was born on June 20, 1901, in Blanco, Oklahoma, a small rural community founded in the Choctaw Nation. Located in what would later become Pittsburg County, Blanco was established in 1901 with the opening of a post office.

A 1903 record of US Native American Enrollment Cards of the Five Civilized Tribes recorded McBee as one-eighth Choctaw.[2]

His parents, George McBee and Ella Duford, were both enrolled Choctaws. The 1900 US Census recorded George McBee as a farmer living in Township 4 in the Choctaw Nation Indian Territory.[3] George and Ella were married that same year in Krebs, Indian Territory.[4] The couple later divorced.

McBee had a younger brother, Joseph Lige McBee, born in 1907, and three half-brothers and a half-sister born several years later. (Joseph was killed in the Wheatley No. 4 coal mine explosion in 1930.[5])

McBee attended Jones Academy, a boarding school tribally controlled by the Choctaw Nation. Founded as a school for boys in 1891 and still open in 2025, the school is just north of Hartshorne in eastern Oklahoma, at the foot of the Pocahontas Mountains.

A 1926 newspaper article reported that at Jones Academy McBee "really mastered the game of baseball. He played the outfield and alternated on the mound."[6]

The article noted that McBee also played football and basketball in school and was an avid outdoorsman, particularly devoting himself to hunting and fishing and to owning hunting dogs.

As a youth, McBee played for sandlot teams around McAlester.

Nicknamed Lefty, McBee pitched in the minor leagues from 1922 to 1928, sandwiched around his 1926 appearance

with the White Sox. He was an imposing figure in his day, at 6-feet-1 and 190 pounds.

In 1922, at age 20, he pitched for two teams: the Oklahoma City Indians (Class-A Western League) and the McAlester Miners (Class-C Western Association). His combined record in 37 games was 6-19. He pitched 204 innings, giving up 221 hits and walking 64.

The next year McBee pitched for three teams: Oklahoma City and McAlester again, and the Henryetta Hens (Class-C

Indian Pitcher Signed by White Sox

PRYOR E. McBEE.

(*Brooklyn Eagle - January 7, 1926*)

Pryor McBee

Western Association). He pitched in only 22 games that year, with a 7-9 record in 125 innings pitched.

McBee married 19-year-old Lilly Neal in May 1924, when both lived in McAlester.[7] The marriage lasted just a few years.

From 1924 through 1926 McBee was on the roster of the Little Rock Travelers in the Class-A Southern Association. His most productive and durable professional season was in 1925, when he recorded 14 wins and 17 losses, with a 4.52 ERA in 42 games and 227 innings pitched.

News accounts reported that McBee was likely to make the White Sox roster in 1926. An article in the *Brooklyn Eagle* on January 7 contained refreshingly few Native American stereotypes. Reporter James J. Murphy instead focused on McBee's life and status as a promising White Sox pitching prospect, adding, "Manager Collins will give all of his recruits a thorough trial, but he is particularly interested in McBee, a southpaw curvist [*sic*] who was noted in the sticks last season for effective twirling."[8]

A brief report in March picked up by several newspapers, including the McAlester daily, said McBee was one of three Native American players with a chance to make the White Sox' 1926 roster out of spring training in Shreveport, Louisiana.[9] The report noted that the club's pitching coach was Native American great Charles Bender, a member of the Minnesota Chippewa Tribe who was elected to the National Baseball Hall of Fame in 1953.

One Oklahoma newspaper reported that McBee signed a contract with the White Sox on May 6 and was to report to the club immediately: "Eddie, who pitched for Little Rock in the Southern Association last season, went so good with the tail end club that he attracted the attention of the Majors and near the close of the season Comisky's [*sic*] White Sox were the best bidders, and the management at Little Rock received a good price for the portsider."[10]

The *Kingston* (New York) *Daily Freeman* reported that McBee, "an Indian pitcher from the Southern Association, cost the White Sox a 'fancy price,' according to owner (Charles) Comiskey."[11]

In fact, there's evidence that contract negotiations may have been difficult. The *Rockford* (Illinois) *Daily Register-Gazette* on May 15 reported that McBee was reinstated by Commissioner Kenesaw Mountain Landis after being placed on baseball's ineligible list when he refused to report to the White Sox.[12]

By May 22, the White Sox had a record of 19-17 on their way to a fifth-place finish in the American League. The game in which McBee pitched was the last in a four-game series at Fenway Park against the last-place Red Sox. Chicago won the first two games and Boston took the third.

Lineups for the fourth game, played before a crowd of about 10,000, included future Hall of Famers Collins and Red Faber of the White Sox and Red Ruffing of the Red Sox, along with Boston infielder and longtime major-league manager Fred Haney and White Sox third baseman Willie Kamm.[13]

By the seventh inning, Boston held a 7-6 lead. In the bottom of the inning, the wheels fell off for the visitors. The first run scored on a one-out bases-loaded walk issued by Sarge Connally, the second White Sox pitcher of the inning. Connally coughed up a single and a walk to the next two batters, then managed to coax a force play at home plate. He proceeded to walk two more batters, allowing two more runs to score.

McBee entered the game and retired the first batter he faced, Mike Herrera, on a popup to Collins. The inning was finally over.

McBee stayed in the game to mop up in the eighth. Unfortunately for him, the inning resembled the one before. Red Sox catcher Alex Gaston reached on a dropped throw by first baseman Harry McCurdy. Ruffing bunted Gaston to second base. McBee then walked the next two batters. Roy Carlyle singled to center field, driving in two runs. McBee got out of the inning two batters later after a walk, a caught-stealing, and a strikeout. In the ninth inning, Bill Barrett pinch-hit for McBee.

His pitching line for the day and his major-league career: 1⅓ innings pitched, one hit, two runs (one earned), three walks, one strikeout.

The *Chicago Tribune* observed: "With the bases full Connally gave a free passage to everybody in sight, three runs being forced over until McBee, the Indian southpaw, relieved Connally and ended the inning. Both sides scored some more in the eighth and ninth, but nobody cared."[14]

A week later the *Memphis Commercial Appeal* reported that McBee was "supposed to be" on his way back to the Travelers from the White Sox but had not yet reported.[15] He did report the next day, according to the *Arkansas Gazette*: "Eddie McBee, the Indian southpaw returned by the Chicago White Sox, arrived here yesterday and after taking a workout at Kavanaugh Field, left for Memphis to join the club."[16]

McBee replaced pitcher Phil Morrison on the Little Rock roster. Morrison had been recently returned to the club by the Pittsburgh Pirates.[17]

Less than two weeks later, in a start against the New Orleans Pelicans, McBee was lifted in the fourth inning after walking the first three batters. He had given up three runs the previous inning.[18]

Two months later, he was released to the Jacksonville Tars of the Class-B Southeastern League. McBee had pitched for 69 innings in 16 games. The *Arkansas Gazette* reported: "McBee came to the Travelers two years ago from the Oklahoma State League. Although with a tail-end club last year, the Indian had a good season, and was sold to the Chicago White Sox. He was returned here early this season and, although he pitched well, he had been unable to win."[19]

The Jacksonville sports press reported McBee's arrival enthusiastically. *Jacksonville Journal* sportswriter Walter

C. Lynch wrote: "Today, or at least upon the arrival of the new Indian pitcher, 'Chief' McBee, a southpaw, the Jacksonville Tars will place practically a Southern League caliber team in the field for the drive down the home stretch for the honors in the second half of the Southern League's split season."[20]

Lynch added: "The new comer is a flinger of real class and promises to become the ace of the local corps. He had a trial with the Chicago White Sox at the beginning of the season. It is being reported that the Pale Hose paid in the neighborhood of $10,000 for him. McBee possesses real pitching ability, a rare fast ball, clever change of pace and good curve."[21]

McBee finished with a 2-0 record in four games with his new club.[22]

In 1927 McBee was back with the Tars, making 36 appearances and ending up with a 10-13 record in 210 innings pitched.

He pitched for the Tars for part of 1928, throwing 74 innings in 14 appearances. He was released on May 23,[23] signed again on July 22,[24] then released again the next day.[25] His professional baseball career was over.

McBee had only three seasons with more than 30 appearances, so it seems likely he was injured for much of his career. Records and reporting are both sparse.

His last season did include an achievement few pitchers can claim. On March 31 the Tars hosted the Murderers' Row New York Yankees in a spring-training exhibition at Durkee Field. The *Jacksonville Times-Union* told the story under the subhead "McBee Fans Ruth, Gehrig":

"The Babe, Lou and all of the other boys, with the exception of Tony Lazzeri, who was sent back to New York with a touch of the grippe, were on display at Durkee Field. While Ruth was unable to hoist one of his noted home runs over the right field fence during any part of the encounter, he did edify the populace with one of his best strike out stunts, thereby being cheered to the skies. Gehrig came right behind him and watched a third one slink past, and Bob Meusel almost met with the same fate, though he ended up by poling a fly to Teen Gallegos. Chief McBee was tossing them when this strike out affair was going on, and had the distinction of whiffing the Sultan and the Crown Price in succession."[26]

In 1928 McBee married for the second time, to Gladys Wharton. The couple had a son and later divorced. McBee is listed in the 1929 Little Rock city directory as a machine helper for the Missouri Pacific Railroad.[27] The 1930 US Federal Census has a record of McBee and Gladys living in a boarding house with an infant son in Little Rock. McBee's occupation is listed as laborer.

In May 1938 McBee married Katherine Lea "Katie" Davis in Latimore, Oklahoma.[28] The 1940 US Federal Census records him as living in McAlester, married with four stepchildren.

Ten years later, the McBee family had moved west. A directory in Medford, Oregon, included an entry for McBee as a laborer.[29]

The couple eventually moved to Northern California, settling in Loomis and later Roseville, both in Placer County, for the last 15 years of McBee's life.

McBee died on April 19, 1963, at Roseville District Hospital. He was 61. The cause of death was cardiac arrest.[30] He was buried at Roseville Cemetery. Katie died two years later.[31]

An obituary in the *Roseville Press-Tribune* reported that McBee operated a lumber business for 25 years, though no location or dates are given.[32] McBee's death certificate stated that at the time of his death, he was a lumberman for the Placer Milling Company. In a baseball-related form McBee completed in 1960, he described his occupation as "piece work lumber" for Placer Milling Company.[33]

McBee spent nearly all his working life around lumber – as a pitcher trying to miss bats and as a worker in the mills.

The baseball questionnaire he completed in 1960 included the question: "If you had to do it all over, would you play professional baseball?"

Despite his career ups and downs, he answered: "Yes, gladly."[34]

SOURCES

In addition to the sources cited in the Notes, the author accessed a file provided by the Giamatti Research Center at the National Baseball Hall of Fame, as well as Retrosheet.org and Baseball-Reference. com.

NOTES

1   Irving Vaughn, "Boston Wins Over Sox in 14-8 Comedy," *Chicago Tribune*, May 23, 1926.

2   U.S., Native American Enrollment Cards for the Five Civilized Tribes, 1898-1914, Choctaw Roll, Citizens by Blood.

3   1900 United States Federal Census.

4   Oklahoma and Indian Territory, Marriage, Citizenships and Census Records, 1841-1927.

5   Associated Press, "Find 8 of 29 Mining Victims; Hope for Rescue Is Abandoned, Lethal Gas Is Obstacle," *Southeast Missourian* (Cape Girardeau), October 29, 1930.

6   James J. Murphy, "McBee Looks Best of Three Indians Signed by Collins," *Brooklyn Eagle*, January 7, 1926.

7   Oklahoma, County Marriages, 1890-1995.

8   James J. Murphy.

9   "Watching 'Em at Sox Camp," *McAlester* (Oklahoma) *News-Capital*, March 12, 1926.

10   "McBee Signs Contract, Will Leave Now," *Picher* (Oklahoma) *King Jack*, May 6, 1926.

11   "Prices Not Revealed by Clubs," *Kingston* (New York) *Daily Freeman*, May 3, 1926.

12   "Marquettes Will Meet R.L.A.C. Nine," *Rockford* (Illinois) *Daily Register-Gazette*, May 15, 1926.

13   "Errors, wild pitching and a great quantity of Boston hits did it, the fracas terminating with the Chicagoans losers 14-8 and 10,000 patrons ready to laugh themselves to death." Irving Vaughn, "Boston Wins Over Sox in 14-8 Comedy."

14   Vaughn.

15   "Travelers Here Today; Recent Changes in Club," *Memphis Commercial Appeal*, May 31, 1926.

16   "Little Rock Club Releases Hughes," *Arkansas Gazette* (Little Rock), June 1, 1926.

17   "Morrison Other Traveler to Go," *Arkansas Gazette*, June 2, 1926.

18   "Pels Win, 8 to 4, Sweeping Series With Little Rock," *Arkansas Gazette*, June 11, 1926.

19   "Eddie McBee Sent to Jacksonville – Indian Pitcher Leaves Travelers, Youngster to Be Tried Out," *Arkansas Gazette*, August 15, 1926.

20   Walter C. Lynch, "Tars All Set for Drive Down Home Stretch: Team Now Rates in Caliber with Southern Loop," *Jacksonville Journal*, August 16, 1926.

21   Lynch.

22   Irwin M. Howe, Southeastern League Pitching Records Seasons 1926," *Florida Times-Union* (Jacksonville), October 13, 1926.

23   Walter C. Lynch, "Sport Potpourri," *Jacksonville Journal*, May 23, 1926.

24   "Tars to Open Home Stay of One Week Today," *Jacksonville Journal*, July 23, 1926.

25   "By-Plays of the Game Yesterday," *Florida Times-Union*, July 24, 1926.

26   Sam Butz, "New York Yankees Are Extended in Nosing Out Jacksonville Tars, 2-1," *Jacksonville Times-Union*, April 1, 1928.

27   Little Rock City Directory, 1929.

28   Oklahoma, County Marriages, 1890-1995.

29   Medford City Directory 1948.

30   State of California Certificate of Death, from file provided by the National Baseball Hall of Fame.

31   "Katherine Lea McBee," *Roseville* (California) *Press-Tribune*, August 4, 1965.

32   "Deaths: Pryor Edward McBee," *Roseville Press-Tribune*, April 22, 1963.

33   Questionnaire from file provided by National Baseball Hall of Fame.

34   Questionnaire from file provided by National Baseball Hall of Fame.

CAL MCLISH

By Joseph Wancho

Indians fans in Cleveland awoke the morning of May 23, 1957, to the musings of columnist James E. Doyle of the *Cleveland Plain Dealer.* Doyle often wrote a small poem at the beginning of his column, and this spring day was no exception.

Soxcess with Cal *"That stuff served up by Cal McLish," The Red Sox say "was quite a dish." From homer hunger were the Sox –And then they gave poor Cal his knocks.*[1]

McLish indeed received his knocks, as Boston went deep against the Cleveland right-hander four times in the sixth inning at Fenway Park. With Cleveland trailing 3-0 and McLish pitching in relief, Gene Mauch homered, Ted Williams went deep to right field, Jackie Jensen walked, Dick Gernert smacked one to the screen atop the Green Monster, and Frank Malzone capped the barrage with a solo shot to left field. 8-0 Red Sox.

"I wasn't even supposed to be pitching that day," McLish recalled years later. "I had been pitching a lot. The writers asked our manager, Kerby Farrell, how come McLish wasn't starting in Fenway Park. Farrell said, 'I can't start McLish because I've been using him too much.'" Farrell started Bud Daley, a left-hander. McLish relieved Daley in the fifth inning, after the starter surrendered three runs. "I threw a changeup, a fastball, a curve and a slider and they all went out."[2]

In a career that spanned 20 years of professional baseball, McLish had his share of setbacks, ups and downs, and just plain bad luck. But through perseverance and resiliency, McLish was able to carve out quite a career for himself, both as a pitcher (with a half-season on the 1964 Phillies) and as a top-notch pitching coach.

Calvin Coolidge Julius Caesar Tuskahoma McLish was born on December 1, 1925, in Anadarko, Oklahoma, a small agricultural city. He was the seventh of eight children born to John and Lulu McLish. Of his unique name, McLish said, "Until I came along, my dad never got to name any of the kids. So I suppose he was into the firewater and he named me."[3] John McLish, who worked as a farmer, was part Choctaw and Lulu was part Cherokee. Cal's name has always been a bit of a mystery. Even though his father was a staunch Democrat and Calvin Coolidge was a Republican from Vermont, Cal took pride in being named after the 30th president. The reason behind the Julius Caesar portion of his name is unknown, at least to Cal. Tuskahoma, a Choctaw word meaning red warrior, is also the name of a tiny community in the southeast part of Oklahoma.

While at Central High School in Oklahoma City, McLish mostly played shortstop. In 1944 he was signed by Brooklyn Dodgers scout Tom Greenwade, who saw that the youngster had speed on his throws. Cal had made a pact with two of his high-school teammates: Any scout who wanted to sign one of them had to sign all three. So Greenwade signed McLish's teammate Bobby Jarvis, but conveniently forgot to sign Bobby Morgan. McLish and Jarvis didn't realize this until they got to the Dodgers' 1944 spring-training camp in Bear Mountain, New York. Learning that they'd been duped, they refused to play until all three returned to Oklahoma so they could see Greenwade actually sign Morgan.[4] McLish reported to the varsity as an 18-year-old, fresh out of high school with virtually no pitching experience. He received a bonus of $1,500 and was paid $150 a month.

Without any minor-league experience, the teenage McLish was on the Dodgers' roster to start the season. With the shortage of players because of World War II, the 1944 version of "Dem Bums" was a mix of players from opposite

Cal McLish

ends of their baseball careers. There were young, unproven players like McLish and Gene Mauch, and players whose better years were in the rear-view mirror, like Paul Waner and Johnny Cooney.

McLish won his first major-league game on May 31, beating the Pittsburgh Pirates 8-4. He hit a double and drove in a run to aid his own cause. As the season wore on, the possibility grew that McLish might be drafted into the military at any time. While the Dodgers were in St. Louis, he got the call and reported for active duty on August 21. At that point he had a 3-10 record with a 7.82 earned-run average. He served in the 3rd Infantry Division in Europe, earning two battle stars, before the Germans surrendered in May 1945. During that summer McLish pitched for the division baseball team in Czechoslovakia. He was discharged in August 1946. He had missed the equivalent of two seasons of major-league baseball.

McLish returned to baseball, pitching in one game for the Dodgers against the Cardinals in St. Louis on August 25, and facing just two batters. He didn't retire either, and allowed two earned runs. That was his only appearance in 1946, and after the season, he was part of a five-for-one deal when he was sent with four other players to Pittsburgh for outfielder Al Gionfriddo and $100,000.

When a player returned from the service in those days, he had to be kept on a major-league roster for one year. McLish pitched one inning for the Pirates on May 25, 1947, against the Cardinals and allowed two earned runs. After the year was up, McLish was optioned to the Kansas City Blues of the American Association, a Yankees Triple-A team, as part of a deal that sent pitcher Mel Queen to the Pirates from the Yankees. McLish compiled a 6-7 record in Kansas City, pitching 92 innings.

The next season, McLish pitched one inning in a game against the Cincinnati Reds on April 25 before he was sent down to the American Association, where he posted a 12-9 record for the Indianapolis Indians. Pittsburgh's top farm team, managed by Al Lopez, won the league pennant with a 100-54 record, but lost to the St. Paul Saints in the playoffs. McLish was called up by the Pirates in September and started a game on the 25th against the Reds in Pittsburgh. He pitched four innings and allowed five runs, seven hits, and a wild pitch, and didn't get the decision as the Pirates won, 8-6.

McLish changed addresses again in December 1948 when he was dealt to the Chicago Cubs. He pitched sparingly for the Cubs– 23 innings in 1949, with a 1-1 record– instead spending most of his days toiling on the mound for their top farm team, the Los Angeles Angels of the Pacific Coast League. Because of control problems (he issued more than six walks per game), McLish compiled an 8-11 record. Cutting his bases-on-balls almost in half in 1950, he won 20 games (20-11), while also leading the team in ERA (3.60) and innings pitched (260). McLish, a switch-hitter, proved to be adept at the plate as well as the mound; he hit .317.

He found the time to exchange "I dos" with his hometown girlfriend, Ruth Iris Lamer. They had five children: Cal Jr., John, Luanne, Ruth Ann, and Thomas.

McLish gained experience in 1951 at the back end of the starting rotation for the last-place Cubs (62-92). His only real highlight of the season occurred on May 5, when he pitched Chicago to a 2-0 victory over Johnny Sain and the Boston Braves. Though he struck out only one, McLish yielded just five singles and two walks. It was one of his four victories that season against 10 losses.

Back in Triple-A pitching for a mediocre (87-93) PCL Angels team again in 1952, he had a so-so, 10-15 year, but he began to turn things around by limiting his walks to 2.7 per game, thus giving himself a better chance for success. He won 16 games (16-11) in 1953, trailing Joe Hatten's 17 for the Angels' team lead. In 1954, he compiled a 13-15 record. Early in the 1955 season McLish was sold to San Diego, a Cleveland affiliate, for $5,000. There he blossomed under manager Bob Elliot, cutting his ERA to 2.86 with the Padres and winning 16 games (16-11), again finishing second for the team lead. "I was in Venezuela (playing winter ball) when I heard I had been bought by a big-league club. When I found out it was Cleveland, I couldn't believe it," he said in 1979. "Of all the places to try and make a ballclub! They had superstar pitchers."[5]

McLish was not only a switch-hitter at the dish, but he was also ambidextrous throwing the ball. Though he never threw left-handed in the major leagues, "There was one time in Venezuela [when] we were winning by six or seven runs," Cal recalled, "and we had one out to go. A left-handed batter was up, and all the guys had been trying to get me to throw left-handed. So I switched the glove to my other hand and threw one pitch left-handed. The manager of the other team came running out and argued for 15 minutes. Finally I said, 'Hell, it's not worth it.' [So] I went back to the other hand."[6]

McLish landed a spot in Cleveland. Though the Tribe boasted four solid starters in Herb Score, Bob Lemon, Early Wynn, and Mike Garcia. "Buster," or "Bus," as many teammates referred to McLish, competed for playing time with Art Houtteman, Bob Feller, Ray Narleski, and Hank Aguirre. He increasingly earned manager Al Lopez's trust as the Tribe finished in second place, nine games behind the Yankees. His record of 2-4 and his 4.96 ERA wasn't really indicative of his value to the team.

Lopez departed Cleveland after the 1956 season, and the front office promoted Kerby Farrell to replace him. The change of skippers did not much alter McLish's role on the staff, as he was again used mainly in middle relief, though his starts increased from two games to seven, and his innings from 61 1/3 to 144 2/3. He compiled a 9-7 record but more importantly he lowered his ERA to 2.97.

In 1958 Farrell was replaced by Bobby Bragan, who in turn was replaced by Joe Gordon on June 27. General Manager Frank Lane was anything but patient, changing managers and trading players at a brisk pace. Gordon, the former Yankees and Indians great, continued what Bragan had started – that is, keeping McLish in the starting rotation. At the age of 32, McLish had finally found a steady spot and responded to Gordon's confidence by winning the first five games he started for Gordon. After losing a game to the Senators, McLish strung four straight victories together. "Probably the best move I made all season," Gordon said.[7]

McLish ended the year with a 16-8 record and a 2.99 ERA. He led the team in wins, innings pitched (225?) and complete games (13). He was grateful to Gordon for the opportunity. "Joe Gordon is an ideal manager," McLish said. "He showed he had confidence in me after I won my first game for him. He didn't say so. He just kept starting me regularly and giving me a chance to prove that I could win. It was wonderful to know that I'd finally found a guy who didn't look at statistics. Joe saw me work, liked what I did and proved it by sending me to the box in my regular turn."[8]

The Indians' pitching staff had undergone a metamorphosis by 1959. Gone were Wynn, Lemon, and Bob Feller, and Mike Garcia was in the twilight of his career. McLish soon found himself as the ace of a staff that included youngsters Jim Perry, Mudcat Grant, and Gary Bell. Herb Score was trying to come back from various injuries, principally the effect of being struck in the eye by a line drive hit by the Yankees' Gil McDougald in 1957. McLish led the mound staff. He was 13-4 at the midseason break and was rewarded by being named to the All-Star Game on August 3 at the Los Angeles Coliseum. He pitched one-hit ball over the final two innings to earn the save as the American League topped the National League 5-3. The Indians fielded a good hitting team as well, and went toe-to-toe with Chicago for much of the season. The "Go-Go" Sox came into Cleveland in late August, nursing a 1½-game lead. The Tribe had won eight straight, but were swept in the critical four-game series. They never recovered, finishing in second place behind the White Sox. McLish led the team with 19 victories.

Yankees manager Casey Stengel had an answer for the sudden success of McLish: "Take this here McLish, which when he is a lot younger and stronger with the Dodgers, he doesn't make it. How do you figure that? Well, I will tell you. McLish has a slider and a sinker, which he does not have with Brooklyn. He still is called Cal McLish, but he ain't the same pitcher."[9]

McLish lost his chance for the magical 20 wins when it was decided that Score would pitch the season finale. "They wanted him to pitch without any pressure after coming back from his injury when he was hit in the eye. I said, 'That's okay with me.' I figured I wasn't going to set any records on winning 20 games."[10]

Despite having led Cleveland pitchers in victories over the last two seasons, McLish was dealt with Billy Martin and first baseman Gordon Coleman to Cincinnati for second baseman Johnny Temple after the 1959 season. "I was hoping I wouldn't be traded and I didn't want to leave the league," McLish said after the trade. "After you get used to it, it's like starting all over again to pitch someplace else. But since I'm going to have to go over to the National, I'm kind of glad it's Cincinnati because they've got a pretty good ball club."[11]

But McLish's season in the Queen City was horrendous. He posted a 4-14 record for the sixth-place Reds. He struck out a paltry 56 batters over 151 1/3 innings pitched. McLish did not enjoy the same run support he had backing him in Cleveland. The Tribe had supported him with 5.57 runs per game in 1958 and 4.94 in 1959. The Reds mustered only 3.38 runs an outing for McLish in 1960.

Again Cal was on the move after the season, this time traded to the White Sox with pitcher Juan Pizarro for infielder Gene Freese. On Chicago's South Side he was reunited with Al Lopez. Their new teammate, veteran Roy Sievers, was very pleased with the deal for the two pitchers, saying, "I believe that Juan Pizarro and Cal McLish will strengthen our pitching staff and that we'll win the pennant. ... It was pitching that prevented us from winning the flag last year and I think McLish and Pizarro will give us enough of a lift to make the difference."[12]

Sievers was half-right in his assessment: Pizarro led Chicago in wins in 1961, while McLish scuffled in mediocrity with a 10-13 mark. It was later learned that he had been suffering from a double hernia, which required surgery at the end of the season.

For the third straight season, McLish was swapped to another team. On March 24, 1962, he headed to Philadelphia, to complete a trade between the two clubs from the previous December. Again he was reunited with a familiar face, Phillies skipper Gene Mauch. "I don't know exactly how much Cal can help us, but he should be pretty good insurance in case some of [our] kids get off badly," said Mauch. "He's been a winning pitcher in the past, and I like that. I know on good days he can throw 25 or 30 curveballs or breaking balls in succession and get them over the plate."[13]

On the surface, it appeared that McLish pitched well for the Phillies, going 11-5 in 1962. But Mauch picked the spots for him to pitch, and of those 11 victories, six came at the expense of the two expansion teams, the Houston Colt .45s and the New York Mets.

McLish pitched well in 1963, winning 13 games with 11 losses and enjoying separate streaks of five and four games. But soreness at the top of his right shoulder ended his season two weeks early. The same soreness, which was later diagnosed as tendinitis, developed again the following season. After two appearances in 1964, the 38-year-old McLish ended his playing career when he was released by the Phillies in July.

But he did not stray far from the game of baseball, or the city of Philadelphia, for that matter. Mauch added McLish to his coaching staff, naming him as the Phillies' pitching coach, replacing Al Widmar. "Widmar and McLish are both real good men," said Mauch. "But we think the organization will benefit more with Cal working with the Phillies and Al with the kids in the minors."[14]

McLish's second career took hold as he followed Mauch to Montreal after Philadelphia, serving as pitching coach from 1969 to 1975. He joined the staff of Alex Grammas in Milwaukee in 1976, and served under managers Grammas, George Bamberger, Buck Rodgers, and Harvey Kuenn. In 1982, McLish's last season as pitching coach, the Brewers won the American League pennant, besting Mauch's California Angels three wins to two in the American League Championship Series. Under McLish's tutelage, Milwaukee had two Cy Young Award winners, Rollie Fingers in 1981 and Pete Vuckovich in 1982.

In his retirement, Cal enjoyed playing golf and writing poetry. In 2009 he was inducted into the Jim Thorpe Oklahoma Sports Hall of Fame.

McLish died on August 26, 2010 in Edmond, Oklahoma after a long battle with leukemia. He was preceded in death by his daughter Ruth Ann, who had been killed in an automobile accident in 1972.

NOTES

1   James E. Doyle, "The Sport Trail," *Cleveland Plain Dealer*, May 23, 1957: 27.

2   Rich Marazzi, "Calin Coolidge Julius Caesar Tuskahoma McLish," *Sports Collectors Digest,* March 13, 1988, 90-91.

3   Marazzi.

4   Stan Baumgartner, "Morgan Shifts Into High Gear at Second for Phils," *The Sporting News*, April 20, 1955: 27.

5   "Sports World Specials," *New York Times*, April 16, 1979: C2.

6   "Sports World Specials."

7   Hal Lebovitz, "Back-Seat McLish Moves Up As Front-Liner," *The Sporting News*, May 13, 1959: 7.

8   Charles Dexter, "The Indians Time Bomb," *Baseball Digest*, July 1959: 80.

9   Dan Daniel. "Over the Fence," *The Sporting News*, June 10, 1959: 12.

10   "Temple Goes to Indians for McLish, 2 Infielders," *Cleveland Press*, December 16, 1959.

11   Allen Lewis, "Mauch Sees Mound Vet McLish as Valued Starter on Phil Staff," *The Sporting News,* April 4, 1962: 32.

12   Edgar Munzel, "Roy Stops Show with Quick Okay of Veeck's Offer," *The Sporting News*, February 1, 1961: 7, 12.

13   Allen Lewis, "Mauch Sees Mound Vet McLish as Valued Starter on Phil Staff," *The Sporting News*, April 4, 1962: 34.

14   Ray Kelly, "Phillies Name Cal McLish Pitching Coach," *Philadelphia Bulletin*, December 1, 1964.

JOHN TORTES MEYERS

By R.J. Lesch

As a Native American playing in the Deadball Era, Jack Meyers couldn't avoid being saddled with the nickname "Chief," but he did as much as any Native American of his generation to battle the stereotypes. Sportswriters who covered Meyers found him to be far more sophisticated than most of his fellow players. One reporter wrote in 1909, before Meyers had even played one major-league game: "A strong love of justice, a lightning sense of humor, a fund of general information that runs from politics to Plato, a quick, logical mind, and the self-contained, dignified poise that is the hallmark of good breeding – he is easily the most remarkable player in the big leagues."[1] On the field, Meyers was one of the top offensive catchers of the Deadball Era, retiring with a .291/.367/.378 slash line for his nine-year career, and was a deft handler of pitchers.

A member of the Cahuilla Band (pronounced *ka'-weeyu*),[2] John Tortes Mayer was born on July 29, 1880, in Riverside, California. His mother, Felicité, raised him, his brother, Marion, and his sister, Christine, alone after her

husband, John Mayer, died in 1887.[3] They lived for a time on the nearby Santa Rosa Reservation, where John and Marion learned baseball. (Marion, one year older, was a pitcher until an accident cost him sight in one eye.) Felicité moved her family back to Riverside when John was 11. He attended Riverside High School and caught for the high-school team. At some point, attributed to a school administrator's action, the surname of John and his siblings was changed from Mayer to Meyers.[4]

When John was 13, he was recruited for a company team for the Santa Fe Railroad. The organizer, John Lightfoot, hired most of the players to easy jobs with the railroad. John, now using Tortes as his surname, went to the boiler room. In a 1961 interview, he said, "I loved the work," and added that swinging a heavy sledgehammer built up his muscles.[5] Over the next decade, he built his 5-foot-11-inch frame to nearly 200 pounds.[6] He worked for a number of mining and copper companies in Arizona and California and, naturally, played baseball with the company teams. He

John Tortes Meyers with Brooklyn in 1916

(George Grantham Bain Collection, Library of Congress)

also played in the California winter leagues, which included experienced professional players.[7]

While catching for a Clifton, Arizona, baseball team representing the Phelps-Dodge Copper Company, he played in a summer tournament for semipro clubs, held in Albuquerque. There he met a Dartmouth College student, Ralph Glaze, who played for a rival team (auspiciously enough, named Big Six.) Glaze starred in both baseball and football at Dartmouth and would later make the major leagues as a pitcher. Thinking the big catcher could help Dartmouth in both sports, Glaze recruited John, pointing out that Dartmouth's charter provided for the education of Native Americans.[8]

After the tournament, Glaze returned to his hometown of Denver with the catcher in tow. There he enlisted the aid of businessmen and Dartmouth alumni, who equipped the new recruit with cash, railroad tickets, and clothing. John, though intelligent and literate, had not completed high school, and so they also provided an altered diploma for him under the name of Ellis Williams Tortes, combining his mother's maiden name with the name of a Clifton teammate. The ersatz diploma gave his birth year as 1883, making him three years younger than he actually was.[9]

With the assistance of a tutor, Meyers attended classes at Dartmouth during the 1905-06 school year. Meyers loved Dartmouth. He joined a fraternity and engaged in campus society. For the rest of his life, he spoke fondly of his time there, though he hated the New Hampshire winters, and his grades suffered due to his abbreviated early schooling and his worries over the health of his mother in California. He enjoyed putting his classmates on with fanciful stories of Indian life,[10] a pastime he indulged in for most of his years. It should be noted, as did one biographer, that Meyers "must be considered the suspect source of some of the inaccurate, even bizarre, published references to his ethnic origins."[11]

Eventually, the school administration discovered that Tortes' high-school diploma was false. The college president contacted the school that issued the original diploma, then summoned Tortes and Glaze to his office and confronted them with the deception.[12]

Dartmouth, however, offered to admit Jack after he completed a program at a preparatory school. He declined; he was already significantly older than his classmates. However, Tommy McCarthy, the former ballplayer and Dartmouth baseball coach, recommended Meyers to Billy Hamilton, manager of the Harrisburg (Pennsylvania) club of the Tri-State League.[13]

In a 1909 newspaper interview, Meyers said the Harrisburg team "certainly laid themselves to make me a happy Indian. I went to the clubhouse ... and nobody paid more attention to me than they did to the batbag."[14] It didn't help that the one person who knew Meyers, Hamilton, resigned on June 22, 1906, the day Meyers arrived. Meyers had a lone pinch-hitting appearance, before finally getting to catch in the second game of the Fourth of July doubleheader.

Unfortunately for him, he was assigned to catch spitball pitcher Frank Leary. Meyers had never handled a spitball pitcher before. "I was getting it everywhere but in my glove. I had five passed balls in two innings." However, Meyers, in that 1909 interview, continued: "Do you know, that did me more good than anything that ever happened to me? It made me mad. I had been timid and now I was mad enough to be brave." Meyers chewed out the manager, Jack Calhoun, for putting him into a game in that situation. The manager admitted Meyers was right, and after that, Meyers found the courage to stand up to the other players as well. "I had an easier time" after that point, he said.[15]

Things might have looked that way from his 1909 viewpoint, but the path to acceptance appears a little twistier than Meyers let on. For one thing, Harrisburg released Meyers on July 10, claiming a surfeit of catchers.[16] However, the Lancaster club snapped up Meyers right away, needing to replace a hospitalized backstop.[17] Meyers caught regularly and started hitting, doubling in the game-winning run against Williamsport on July 22.[18] When Lancaster released Meyers in August (presumably because its regular catcher returned to action), Harrisburg had a change of heart and signed him back to close out the season.

Meyers' copper company connections probably helped him land a berth in the Northwestern League with the Butte, Montana, club in 1907.[19] His play sparkled; a Seattle newspaper reported that Meyers "is about half the Butte team, for he keeps the runners hugging the bases and besides, he can clout the leather high and far away."[20] He returned to California for the winter ball season. With the Pickwicks of the Southern California State League, Meyers participated in a postseason series against the Los Angeles Angels. In this series, he caught Walter Johnson, who fanned 16 Angels and won 1-0 in the first game of the series.[21]

Meyers then moved to St. Paul in 1908 and caught fire there too. He was leading the American Association in batting on June 28, with a .319 average.[22] Three days later, the Giants shelled out $6,000 for his contract.[23] It would have been a record price except for the Giants purchasing Rube Marquard for $11,000 the same day. Meyers was called to New York but saw no regular-season action during the tumultuous end of the 1908 season.

Despite the price tag, Meyers was no shoo-in for playing time. It's true that Roger Bresnahan, the popular catcher of the 1908 squad, was traded that offseason to St. Louis, where he could be a player-manager. However, as part of the deal, the Cardinals got Admiral Schlei from the Reds and sent him along to New York. Schlei had been Cincinnati's regular catcher in 1908 and he and Art Wilson were supposed to do the bulk of the catching, with Meyers and Fred Snodgrass vying for the third spot and learning the ropes.

But Giants fans immediately took a liking to Meyers. He socked two home runs in the annual exhibition game with Yale, his Polo Grounds debut, on April 10, 1909.[24] His first official major-league appearance was as a pinch-hitter on Opening Day, five days later, a game in which hard-luck pitcher Red Ames pitched 12 innings of shutout ball only to watch the Giants batters post 12 goose-eggs of their own. Brooklyn took a 3-0 lead in the top of the 13th. Frustrated by their team's poor showing at the plate, Giants fans shouted, "Put in the Indian!" and "Give us Meyers. He can hit a ball." Pinch-hitting for Ames in the 13th inning, Meyers notched his first major-league hit.[25]

Two days after that, Meyers took his place behind the plate to catch Rube Marquard's second career start. The $17,000 battery held the Phillies to three hits and a run in their first victory together.[26] Giants manager John McGraw seemed to like the way Meyers caught Marquard, and paired them up for four of Rube's next five starts. All were one- or two-run losses except for a win over Chicago on May 12, in which Meyers earned more plaudits with his bat, driving in the game-winner in the bottom of the ninth. Ring Lardner naturally resorted to the soft-core bigotry of the time in his game story the next day: "Big Chief Meyers, he break up big ball game with heap big triple in big ninth inning. Yes. He shoot Cubs full of heap big holes today."[27] That sort of thing. By now, Meyers had worked his way ahead of Wilson, and Lardner thought it remarkable that Meyers would work two days in a row, even though Schlei was feeling all right. Meyers worked a third straight day on May 13, catching Christy Mathewson for the first time.

Meyers' defense and arm were not as good as Schlei's, true, but Meyers made up for it with his bat and his brains. In his first big-league season he hit .277 to the Admiral's .244. Schlei caught 89 games in 1909, but Meyers caught 64, including 20 of Mathewson's 33 starts. Mathewson liked working with Meyers. The two clicked in that May 13 game, which was just Mathewson's second start of the season. They clicked again four days later for a six-hit shutout. The two rarely quibbled over pitch selection. Meyers was, like Matty, an able student of opposing batters and the two got into a rhythm quickly. The other pitchers, reluctant at first to work with the unknown Meyers, took their cue from Big Six.

By 1910 Meyers was the regular backstop, catching 117 games and batting .285. The only pitcher Meyers did not catch was Bugs Raymond, the spitballer. After a pitch from Raymond split a finger on Meyers' throwing hand, McGraw said, "From now on, you don't catch spitballers. You're the catcher for Mathewson and Rube and anybody who throws regular pitches."[28] That season, Wilson and Schlei saw little action, and Snodgrass, with no future as a catcher, moved to the outfield.

The press, in New York and elsewhere, took an immediate liking to Meyers because he made more interesting copy than his teammates. During rainouts or offdays, while the other players holed up playing cards or billiards, newspapers reported that Meyers would go out to do some historical sightseeing or watch a local college football team practice. In Boston, wrote Bozeman Bulger, Meyers made

a point of visiting the art museums where he spent hours touring the exhibits. Several writers noted his favorite paintings: "Quest for the Holy Grail," the mural by Edwin Austin Abbey that hangs in the Boston Public Library; and "Custer's Last Fight" by Cassilly Adams. When asked why the latter, Meyers would say "[I]t was the only picture he ever saw where the Indians were getting as good as an even break."[29]

Meyers became so popular with the fans in New York and around the league that the vaudeville circuit took notice. Mathewson and Meyers received either $1,500 or $2,000, combined, to appear with actress May Tully on the vaudeville circuit. They opened at Hammerstein's Victoria on October 23, 1910.[30]

What must it have been like for Meyers, appearing on stage with the national idol Christy Mathewson after only two full seasons in the big leagues? Well, given the state of American entertainment in the early twentieth century, it was a mixed blessing.

Ballplayers routinely appeared on the vaudeville circuit during the offseason. For baseball fans around the country, in the days before television and radio, vaudeville brought their favorite ballplayers to them. Occasionally a player might actually have possessed some talent for the performing arts. This was unusual, however. Most players had about as much talent for acting or singing as actors and singers did for baseball. That was not the point; the point was to hold the ballplayers up for display, and for the public to pay to see them. On the other hand, American entertainment is a mirror of American culture. Blatant racism and sexism were taken for granted in print and on the stage during this period (and since).

And so, Mathewson and Meyers performed a half-hour sketch called "Curves," written by Bulger and produced by Tully. In this sketch, Tully plays an ardent spectator at the Polo Grounds. The *Variety* reviewer described the scene:

In "Curves," Matty and his star catcher appear first as themselves warming up to go into a game that Hooks Wiltse is seemingly about to lose – off stage. They are in the clubhouse, and Miss Tully rushes, as is customary for women rooters at the Polo Grounds, from the grandstand to get Matty to come out and get ready to pitch. Myers [sic] is the first to answer the call for assistance, and when he comes out of the clubhouse door with his uniform on carrying his mask and protector and shin guards, the fans in the audience almost raise the roof. Myers explains that Matty is playing checkers and can't be disturbed, but a moment later, 'Big Six,' ball in hand, shows himself, and the audience is off again. Later Mr. Mathewson, pitching to Mr. Myers, shows Miss Tully how to shoot over the different sort of curves. This little lesson is interrupted by Myers leaving the scene long enough to get into the game as a pinch hitter, and he goes off right to rap out a home run. Then he and Matty retire to the clubhouse to dress, and while they are gone Miss Tully springs some imitations of well-known actors and actresses at a ball game, which are remarkably clever and entertaining.[31]

Mathewson and Meyers then return to the stage in their street clothes, and Tully returns the favor by convincing Mathewson and Meyers to join her in vaudeville and by teaching them to act. This "brings out a travesty drama with Meyers as the 'bad Indian' ... Mathewson is the cowboy who comes to the rescue of the forlorn maiden and over comes the 'bad Indian' by hitting him in the head with a baseball."[32]

Meyers naturally felt silly in this role himself, although he enjoyed the experience otherwise. At the time, though, newspaper reviews of the performance were complimentary. After its debut at Hammerstein's Victoria in New York on October 23, 1910, the reviewer for *Variety* wrote: "A most satisfactory vehicle ... a little cutting is all the piece needs."[33]

The act toured the vaudeville circuit for several weeks. Meyers was amenable to other stage offers later, but did not receive any. Mathewson never appeared on stage again, apparently sensitive to criticism of his performance.

For each of the next three seasons, Meyers finished in the Top 10 in Chalmers Award voting for the National League's most valuable player. In 1911 he led the Giants in batting for the first of three consecutive seasons with a .332 average, third highest in the National League. "Meyers has become the deepest student of batting on the team," wrote a *New York Times* reporter after watching him correctly predict the pitches thrown by Pirates phenom Marty O'Toole.[34] The next year Meyers hit for the cycle on June 10 en route to a career-high 6 home runs and a .358 average, second in the NL behind only Heinie Zimmerman's .372. His hot hitting continued in the 1912 World Series, when he started all eight games and batted .357/.419/.429. Meyers remained one of the Giants' best hitters through the 1914 season, when he batted .286/.357/.354 in a career-high 134 games.

The workload took its toll. "I cheated a little on my age so they always thought I was a few years younger," Meyers recalled, "but when the years started to creep up on me I knew how old I was, even if nobody else did."[35] Playing in over 100 games for the sixth consecutive season, the 34-year-old Meyers batted just .232/.311/.311 in 1915, and the Giants placed him on waivers. Both the Brooklyn Dodgers and the Boston Braves claimed him, and Brooklyn won his rights on a coin flip. In Brooklyn Meyers was reunited with ex-Giants Rube Marquard, Fred Merkle, and his catching mentor, Wilbert Robinson, now his manager. He remembered the 1916 Robins as "just outsmarting the whole National League" on their way to the pennant but running out of gas in the World Series against the Boston Red Sox.[36]

Meyers split the 1917 season between the Dodgers and Braves, on the latter club replacing Hank Gowdy, the first active major leaguer to enlist for service in World War I.

In 1918 Meyers joined the Buffalo Bisons, managed by his former Giants teammate Hooks Wiltse,[37] and batted .328 in 65 games. After the war-shortened 1918 season, Meyers enlisted in the US Marine Corps himself. The war ended before he could be deployed, and he received an honorable discharge on March 17, 1919.[38] He returned to baseball as player-manager for New Haven in the Eastern League but was replaced in midseason by Danny Murphy, whom he had played against in the 1911 World Series. Meyers was catching for a semipro team in San Diego in 1920 when the crowd booed him and he decided to quit baseball altogether.[39]

As gregarious as Meyers was, and as freely as he could tell tales about himself (however fanciful they might be), he said little publicly about his family or personal life. Almost nothing is known of his marriage to Anna Meyers, other than that the couple lived in a home with an apple orchard in New Canaan, Connecticut,[40] and the marriage ended at some point without producing children.

Meyers invested his earnings prudently, but the stock market crash of 1929 wiped out his savings. In a 1961 interview, he told this story:

I had a Lincoln automobile. I traded it for a Ford and struck out for California – home to me. I went back to the reservation and slept out under a big pine tree. It was a far different life than I had known – pampered by masseurs and the easy life in the country's best hotels. The ground was hard.

On the third morning, I woke up and told myself a few facts. "You're not the only Indian that went broke," I said. "Get up and go to work." I went to Riverside and at the Mission Indian Agency, asked if they had a job I could do. They told me I was just the man they were looking for. They needed an agent to direct law enforcement on the Indian reservations of Southern California, some 30 in all. I stayed on that job until I retired at 65.[41]

The picturesque tale telescopes several details but appears true in essentials. Meyers was actually already in Southern California, working as a construction foreman for the San Diego gas company, when the crash occurred. He lost his job due to cutbacks in 1931, and held several other jobs before his appointment as chief of police for the Mission Indian Agency of Southern California in 1933.[42] "You see," he told a reporter, "that really makes me a chief now. I'm entitled to the name."[43]

His nephew, Jack Meyers, remembered his namesake performing "Casey at the Bat" for children's groups around the Santa Rosa reservation. "He could be very theatrical and entertaining," recalled his nephew. Meyers was a favorite at old-timers' games for both the Dodgers and the Giants for many years, especially after those teams moved to California. He was also a favorite of sportswriters looking for reminiscences of the game's earlier days, and told many colorful stories (often with an implied wink and nod) to new audiences throughout the years.

William A. Young, Meyers' biographer, emphasizes that Meyers's story "must be seen within the context of the struggles of Native Americans in general, and athletes in particular, to maintain their dignity and self-respect. ... Though it was not an easy passage, he did successfully negotiate the treacherous boundaries between the Native American and Euroamerican worlds. Though he entered the white man's world willingly and was able to compete on its playing fields, according to its rules, he was also intensely proud of his Native American identity and heritage. Throughout his life he drew on the Cahuilla values he learned as a child."[44]

Meyers died on July 25, 1971, in San Bernardino, California, just four days before his 91st birthday.[45]

SOURCES

An earlier version of this biography appeared in SABR's *Deadball Stars of the National League* (Brassey's, Inc., 2004), edited by Tom Simon.

NOTES

1   "How Chief Meyers Broke into Game," *Washington Post*, April 15, 1909: 3.

2   William A. Young, *John Tortes "Chief" Meyers: A Baseball Biography* (Jefferson, North Carolina: McFarland, 2012), 23.

3   Young, 10. It should be noted that a genealogy on Ancestry.com gives John Mayer's year of death as 1911. Mayer's 1910 census entry gives his birthplace as Germany and his immigration year as 1868.

4   Young, 9.

5   Earl E. Buie, "They Tell Me," *San Bernardino* (California) *Sun-Telegram*, April 5, 1961, 14.

6   Young, 17.

7   Henry C. Koerper, "The Catcher Was a Cahuilla: A Remembrance of John Tortes Meyers (1880-1971), *Journal of California and Great Basin Anthropology*. Vol. 24, No. 1 (2004): 21-40.

8   Koerper, 24.

9   A copy of the diploma may be found in Meyers' National Baseball Hall of Fame Library file.

10   Koerper, 25.

11   Koerper, 25.

12   Jim McGreal, "Ralph Glaze: They Called Him 'Pitcher,'" *Baseball Research Journal* (SABR), 1986: 79.

13   "How Chief Meyers Broke into Game."

14   "How Chief Meyers Broke into Game."

15   "How Chief Meyers Broke into Game." Neither the box score of the game in the *Harrisburg* (Pennsylvania) *Daily Independent*, July 5, 1906: 5, nor the game story charges any passed balls to Meyers, but he is charged with one throwing error that resulted in a run. A blurb adds: "Meyers started to catch the game, but he was not used to Leary's 'spit balls,' and retired at the end of the first inning."

16   "Catcher Meyers Released," *Harrisburg Daily Independent*, July 11, 1906: 2.

17   "Bits for the Fans," *Harrisburg Telegraph*, July 12, 1906: 8.

18   "Lancaster 5; Williamsport 4," *Harrisburg Daily Independent*, July 23, 1906: 8.

19   Koerper, 26. The president of the Butte club, Charles H. Lane, was a prominent Butte coal dealer and eventual mayor of Butte from 1915 to 1917. Lane's business interests were probably closely tied to Anaconda Copper, a dominant employer in Butte. See https://archive.org/stream/montanaitsstoryb02stou/montanaitsstoryb02stou_djvu.txt (as of February 6, 2025) for a biography of Charles H. Lane.

20   "Chit-Chat of the Diamond," *Anaconda Standard*, May 3, 1907: 2.

21   Carlos Bauer, *The Obscure History of Baseball in San Diego: Before the Padres Came to Town, 1870-1936* (San Diego: Baseball Press Books, 2024), 49.

22   "Association Batting Averages," *Minneapolis Sunday Tribune*, June 28, 1908: 39. Meyers finished with a .292 average.

23   "Paid $17,000 for Pitcher and Catcher," *Buffalo Enquirer*, July 02, 1908: 10.

24   "Giants Please Home Fans," *Washington Post*, April 11, 1909: S2.

25   "30,000 See Giants Lose to Superbas," *New York Times*, April 16, 1909: 7. The Giants, however, could not score and lost, 3-0.

26   "$17,500 [*sic*] Battery Defeats Phillies," *New York Times*, April 18, 1909: S1.

27   R.W. Lardner, "Heap Big Indian Scalps Bear Cubs," *Chicago Tribune*, May 13, 1909: 8.

28   John Lenkey, "Chief Meyers Hale and Hearty at 86," *The Sporting News*, January 14, 1967: 29.

29   Irvin S. Cobb, "Irwin [*sic*] Cobb Tells of the Giants Victory," *Buffalo Times*, October 26, 1911: 14.

30   "$2,000 For Baseball Act," *Variety*, September 24, 1910: 4. The article reports both figures.

31   Dash, "Curves," *Variety*, October 29, 1910: 16.

32   Dash, 16.

33   Dash, 16

34   "Giants Confident, Pirates Hopeful," *New York Times*, September 18, 1911: 9.

35   Lawrence Ritter, ed., *The Glory of Their Times: The Enlarged Edition* (New York: William Morrow, 1992), 179.

36   Ritter, 179.

37   "Bison Players Signed for 1918; Open Here May 17," *Buffalo Enquirer*, April 20, 1918: 10.

38   Young, 182-184.

39   Steve George, "Chief Meyers, Unrecognized and Almost Forgotten, Emerges from Out of Game's Early Memory Book," *The Sporting News*, March 26, 1936, 9.

40   Meyers' World War I draft registration card lists his address as New Canaan, and his occupation as "farmer."

41   Buie.

42   Koerper, 42.

43   George.

44   Young, 7.

45   "Ex-Big League Great, Chief Meyers, Dies," *San Bernardino County Sun*, July 27, 1971: D1.

EUEL MOORE

By Rory Costello

In the history of major leaguers of Native American descent, the first from the Chickasaw Nation was Euel Moore. The burly right-hander (6-feet-2, 185 pounds) pitched for the Philadelphia Phillies and New York Giants for parts of three seasons from 1934 through 1936.

Moore posted some strong performances during the 1934 season, and at age 26 should have been in his pitching prime. But arm problems stemming from mismanagement ruined his career. His final career totals in the majors: 9 wins, 16 losses, and a 5.48 ERA in 61 games.

Euel Walton Moore was born near Reagan, Oklahoma – just north of Tishomingo, the tribal capital, where he lived much of his life – on May 27, 1908. His father was Charlie Harley Moore, a full-blooded Chickasaw; his mother, Daisy Pearl Barger, was non-Indian.[1] According to Chickasaw tribal historian Richard Green's 1996 article about Euel Moore, there were nine children in the family. Findagrave. com reveals the names of the eight siblings. William, Viola, and Charles preceded Euel; Homer, Deloise, Netta, Lewis, and Dorothy followed.

As Richard Green observed, Charlie Moore "was a farmer and trader, just eking by, as were most of his friends and neighbors. He spoke Chickasaw, but like many tribal members in the 1920s, thought that speaking it would be an impediment to his children. The kids went to school for a few years but were needed to work on the farm. Euel completed the eighth grade, nicknamed himself 'Monk,' and headed into a life of hard work for little or no gain."[2]

Green noted, "Had Moore been born a few generations earlier, he might well have been a great player in the game of Chickasaw stickball. With his large muscular build, athleticism, and intensely competitive nature, he would have been a force to be reckoned with."[3]

The family moved to Walters, about 115 miles west in Cotton County, Oklahoma. There, by Green's account, Moore first pitched for pay at age 19. As *The Sporting News* reported when Moore made the Phillies roster in 1934, he played semipro ball for a year or so. Then in 1928, he joined an independent city league in Wichita Falls, just across the Red River in Texas. Green wrote, "A local scout recognized the raw talent and signed him to play for [the] Abilene [Aces in the Class-D West Texas League in 1929]. Moore was 7-6 when he broke his pitching arm on July 20 sliding into second base. Although he pitched no more that season, he battled back and won a spot with Wichita Falls in the Texas League."[4]

The *Sporting News* article continued, "[H]e was dropped by Wichita Falls before the 1930 season opened. Later that year Euel joined Muskogee and in 1931 bobbed up with San Antonio."[5] With the seventh-place San Antonio Indians, he had a 9-12 record and a 4.05 ERA. The highlight of his season was a no-hitter against the last-place Galveston Buccaneers on June 5.

Among other opponents that year, Moore faced Dizzy Dean and Joe "Ducky" Medwick – the stars of the 1934 Cardinals Gas House Gang were then farmhands in Houston. Family lore has it that Moore and Dean once squared off in a 13-inning duel before the future Hall of Famer prevailed. As his widow recounted more than six decades on, "Diz told me later that he didn't care who won just so the game would end," Moore said.[6] If ever that matchup took place, it would have been in this season or possibly an exhibition game. They faced each other as starters once in the National League regular season (on May 11, 1935), but it wasn't close.[7]

Euel Moore

Moore moved to Galveston in July 1932 when San Antonio could not pay all of its players' salaries. He won 3 and lost 8. But he established himself as a workhorse with the Buccaneers in 1933. He was 17-15, but six of his losses were by one run, and he pitched many no-decision games as he posted a 2.67 ERA in 256 innings. As Richard Green observed, starting pitchers then were expected to finish games.[8]

Moore started the 1934 season with the Baltimore Orioles of the International League; Double A was then the highest classification. On that cellar-dwelling club, his record of 8-10, 4.04 was actually quite good – allegedly aided by the old frozen-ball trick. In any case, major-league teams were interested in him. Rumors circulated until July, when he was dealt to the Philadelphia Phillies for George Darrow, Irv Jeffries, and cash. The Phillies were a perennial second-division team in the National League; although the offense was not bad, they sorely needed pitching. The club had a new skipper that season, Jimmie Wilson, a catcher with a reputation as a skilled handler of pitchers.[9] They had also obtained a new ace, 30-year-old Pacific Coast League veteran Curt Davis. However, the staff was still thin behind Davis, and hopes of improving on 1933's weak showing were quickly endangered by losing seven straight out of the gate, giving up nearly six runs a game on average. In early July, the Phillies were in seventh place (of eight) in the standings, as they had been in 1933.

A Moore scrapbook clipping noted that when he arrived, the team's publicist described the hurler as being 'built on the lines of an All American guard on one of Pop Warner's Carlisle teams. He has an arm like a leg, a build of a wrestler. Why, I couldn't get both hands around his forearm.'"[10]

Moore made his first major-league start on July 8, 1934 – and won, as the Phillies edged the Boston Braves, 5-3. The newspaper account said he had "hurled like a veteran," displaying a "great fastball, good curve and fair change of pace." He allowed 10 hits but no walks and "exhibited all the cool craftiness of his race."[11]

Indeed, as Richard Green noted, sportswriters trotted out the standard clichés of the times about Indians when covering Moore. From the beginning of his pitching career, he had been known as "Chief." The Philadelphia press said that he would "have on his warpaint" and "tomahawk the visiting team."[12] One photo in a Baltimore newspaper shows Moore in his uniform wearing a child's headdress and holding a hatchet over another ballplayer's head. The caption read, "Moore shows how his ancestors won ball games back in pioneer days."[13]

It was inevitable that "Chief" Moore would be compared to Charles "Chief" Bender," the Ojibwa who'd starred on the mound for the Philadelphia A's from 1903 through 1917. In July Moore won three more times and lost only once, 2-1 to the Chicago Cubs. Richard Green's research showed that after one of those victories, he complained to teammates about his inability to get a hit. He had been a reliable pinch-hitter throughout his career, having batted .316 in Baltimore. The reporter opined that Moore's hitting woes were "enough to annoy even a wooden Indian, and this Chickasaw is very much alive."[14]

As Green wrote, "Although Moore in 1934 was only 26 years old, this was still a little old for a rookie."[15] Thus, he told sportswriters that he was born in 1910, which would have made him only 24.[16] By the end of July, the Phillies, behind Moore's 4-1 start, were showing signs of life. Green added, "He was now being counted upon by his teammates and the fans. Still, he told a reporter that he was 'dead tired' after his first start and was more glad that the game was over than he was to notch his first big-league victory. In his next starts, he was pitching 'courageously,' which usually meant that his fastball had no pop but he was able to keep enough hitters off-balance with breaking balls and offspeed pitches to win three of four games.'"[17]

Moore finished with a 5-7 record and a 4.05 ERA in 1934. There were other signs that he was arm-weary: just 38 strikeouts in his 122⅓ innings, which included only three complete games in 16 starts. "Like most other pitchers of that era, he took pride in completing the job," Green wrote. "While finishing the task at hand was and is regarded as a virtue by most of society, pitching was and is an unnatural act." Sooner or later, nearly all arms will break down.[18]

By one account, Moore hurt his pitching arm early in spring training in 1935. He said it happened during an outing in cold weather that was scheduled to be three innings but lasted seven. Manager Wilson said it was poor conditioning on the pitcher's part. The press insinuated that he was not trying hard enough, that he was making too much money, and that this was a "damaging influence."[19] As Green put it, "He was making $850 per month, not a lavish amount, but excellent by Depression-era standards."[20]

When the season started, Moore was hit hard (1-6, 7.81 in 15 games, including eight starts). He was demoted to the Phillies' minor-league team in Class-A, Hazleton, Pennsylvania. Wilson felt that a few victories over minor leaguers would bolster his confidence and show him "there was nothing wrong with his arm." Moore continued to pitch in pain and ineffectively (4-3, 5.09). But as Richard Green put it, "he did not complain much about the pain; if they would not believe him, it was not his way to argue. He would work harder."[21]

On August 2, 1935, the New York Giants obtained Moore conditionally from Hazleton. Desperate for relief pitching, they told the Phillies they would take a chance on him, but only if his arm seemed in shape. Moore picked up a win in his first appearance as a Giant but was ineffective in the last two of his six outings; he was sent back to Philadelphia on August 29. His totals for the year were 2-6, 7.45.

That fall, Moore met Gwyndoline Gray, an Irish girl from Connerville, Oklahoma, a town just northeast of Reagan. They were married on February 29, 1936.[22] Soon thereafter, Moore reported to spring training.

The sportswriters noted that his marriage was just the incentive Moore needed "to reform." One wrote that Moore "is anxious to make a comeback," and has been "full of enthusiasm. The Chief tossed a few fast ones the other afternoon that made [manager] Wilson smile."[23] Moore said his arm was not sore and he expected to win between 15 and 20 games.

He was quoted as saying that he "cured" his arm problem by pitching to his brother every day during the off-season. One reporter noted, "At first, the flipper gave him intense pain, but he realized that he was 'on the spot' – that unless he showed something he was washed up in baseball, so he gritted his teeth and went ahead."[24] He was probably telling them what they wanted to hear, but the lack of pain was undoubtedly thanks to a rested arm.

Although Wilson brought Moore along slowly at first, he let Monk talk him into leaving him in for eight innings late in spring training. While his fastball and curve seemed better than ever, his injured arm apparently had not healed completely and the pain recurred. Subsequently, Moore learned that his injury involved the rotator cuff. Surgery to correct the problem was not available until the 1970s.

Years later, Phillies teammate Dick Bartell told another version of the story:

"There was one pitching prospect I thought Wilson didn't do right by. Euel 'Chief' Moore, an Oklahoma Indian, was a young righthander with a straight overhand delivery. Moore had been bought from Baltimore for about $10,000. According to the catcher, Bill Atwood, who was with the Orioles at the time, the Baltimore manager had used the old frozen ball trick to make Moore look like the greatest thing since Mathewson.

"But Wilson told him he couldn't throw overhand in [the Phillies' tiny old bandbox] Baker Bowl. He had to throw sidearm.

"Moore protested that he couldn't do it without hurting his arm. Wilson insisted. It was pitch that way or not at all. So poor Chief Moore threw sidearm and ruined his arm and never had a winning year. Two years later he was through."[25]

But in 1936, Moore only knew that he was not getting anybody out (2-3, 6.96 in 20 games) and again letting down his teammates. In late July, the Phillies released him.

Back in the minor leagues, Moore had another brief stop with Baltimore (0-1). In 1937 he played first for Dallas (6-10, 5.24), but the Steers released him on June 29.[26] He joined Atlanta for a while (although Baseball-Reference does not show this) and then became a player-coach for the New Orleans Pelicans (6-5, 3.64). There is an amusing anecdote from that season featuring Moore and hell-raising pitcher Sig Jakucki.

"According to Arthur Daley in the New York Times, Jakucki and Pelicans manager [sic; records show no sign of this] Euel Moore once went to see a wrestling match after a game. The hefty, playful Moore had the reputation of being the strongest man in baseball, and in Jakucki he found a kindred soul. The wrestling match turned out to be slightly on the boring side, so to provide some excitement, Moore 'picked up the 200-pound Sig,' Daley wrote, 'and tossed him into the ring. The startled grapplers thought Jakucki was merely part of the act and that someone had forgotten to tip them off. But the indignant referee took a swing at Jakucki, a sad mistake.' Jakucki flattened him. 'Thereupon the two wrestlers pounced on the interloper, also a mistake.' Moore joined in until the police broke up the free-for-all and carted Jakucki and Moore to the nearest jail."[27]

Moore was still affiliated with the Pelicans as of late March 1938, but the statistics show no signs that he pitched for them that year. He saw semipro action in 1938-39, including the 1938 national semipro tournament in Denver with the Hubbers of Borger, Texas.[28] He then quit playing ball. But when he joined the US Army in 1943, at age 34, he told a reporter that he had recently been pitching again and his arm "felt quite swell. I expect to play with service teams and when this war is over I'll be ready to go again."[29] His Army duties included serving with a selected unit of 110 men, mainly former athletes, at Camp Grant, Illinois. Moore and other major leaguers such as Bama Rowell and Heinie Mueller helped convalescent soldiers in physical rehab.[30]

Richard Green noted, "The war lasted longer than Moore expected. When he was discharged, all hope of a comeback had vanished. He and wife Gwen moved to Tishomingo." According to Gwen, state Senator Joe Bailey Cobb got Euel a job as a state game ranger, a position he held for 27 years.[31]

In February 1950, Moore had a feature role in a story that made national news. A leopard escaped from the Oklahoma City zoo, and in the resulting furor, "members of the police force, highway patrol, Marine reserves, Civil Air Patrol, and Air National Guard combed 100 square miles by land and by air – some 3,000 Oklahomans took part in the search."[32] The wild chase eventually made Time and Life magazines – and Ranger Moore landed on the front page of the New York Times after he helped capture the wildcat.[33]

In 1954 Monk and Gwen adopted a baby boy they named Larry Euel Moore. During Larry's childhood, as Richard Green recounted, Euel coached Little League and American Legion ball before retiring to his couch with Gwen to watch ballgames on TV on Saturday afternoons. "Euel enjoyed the games but usually didn't reminisce about his career or comment on modern baseball except to say that money was ruining the game," Gwen recalled. "It wasn't Euel's way to complain or talk about regrets. If he had any, you'd never hear about them. He was a happy person who had some setbacks, just like most folks."[34]

As Green related, Moore had inherited diabetes and heart disease from his father's side of the family. His father had died from a heart attack in his early 60s. Euel had his first heart attack in 1970, and two more in 1971 and 1973. By 1978, the angina was so bad that he could scarcely shower or shave despite taking increasing doses of nitroglycerine.

Finally, he agreed to heart bypass surgery in 1979. He wished that he'd had it sooner because the operation made him active again and gave him another 10 years of life.[35]

Larry Moore was killed in a traffic accident in February 1984. He was 31. Later that year, Euel Moore was nominated for induction into the American Indian Athletic Hall of Fame, but when it was discovered that he lacked a Certificate of Degree of Indian Blood, he was ruled ineligible. Inductions took place only every five years, so Moore had to wait. He was notified in December 1988 that he had been elected and was to be inducted in May 1989 – but it was just a bit too far in the future.[36] Euel "Monk" Moore died on February 12, 1989. His death certificate gave "acute coronary insufficiency" as the cause, noting that he also suffered from Parkinson's disease as well as diabetes. He was buried in Tishomingo City Cemetery.

Gwen and several relatives attended the induction ceremony, which was held in Tulsa. Allie Reynolds, who had been inducted in 1972, gave a speech praising Moore. Gwen accepted her husband's plaque from the leader of his tribe, Governor Bill Anoatubby.[37] The Chickasaw Hall of Fame subsequently enshrined Moore in 1996.

Gwen Moore died in June 2004, aged 90. Mrs. Moore was retired from her duties as deputy county clerk for Johnston County. (Tishomingo is the county seat.) She worked for many years as a voting precinct official.[38] Shortly before her passing, she donated all of her clippings, photos, and other memorabilia to the Chickasaw Council House Museum in Tishomingo.[39]

ACKNOWLEDGMENT

Acknowledgment to the work of Richard Green.

POSTSCRIPT

Three other men with Chickasaw heritage have subsequently made it to the majors. The paternal grandmother of Wyatt Toregas was Chickasaw, and Toregas became a citizen of the Chickasaw Nation.[40] Dallas Beeler is part Choctaw and Chickasaw on his mother's side; his family, especially his grandmother and aunts, are active in the tribe and community.[41] Brandon Bailey is one-eighth Chickasaw, is also enrolled as a member of the tribe, and had plans to learn the language.[42]

SOURCES

The main source for this biography is an article by Richard Green, "The Major Leaguer." It was originally published in *The Journal of Chickasaw History*, Vol. 2, No. 2, 1996.

Much information for Green's article was obtained through his interview in 1996 with Mrs. Gwyndoline Moore and by examining her scrapbook of Euel Moore's baseball press clippings and articles about him. Unfortunately, many individual sources cannot be cited because the clippings did not include either the name of the newspaper or the date.

Professional Baseball Players Database V6.0

Johnson, Lloyd, and Miles Wolff, eds. *The Encyclopedia of Minor League Baseball*. 2nd ed. (Durham, North Carolina: Baseball America, Inc., 1997).

www.retrosheet.org

www.baseball-reference.com

www.findagrave.com

Chickasaw Hall of Fame (https://hof.chickasaw.net/)

NOTES

1   Record for Charles, William, and Viola Moore, Dawes Rolls, Oklahoma Historical Society (https://www.okhistory.org/research/dawesresults?cardnum=908&tribe=Chickasaw&cardgroup=by%20Blood).

2   Richard Green, "The Major Leaguer," *The Journal of Chickasaw History*, Vol. 2, No. 2, 1996.

3   Green, "The Major Leaguer."

4   Green, "The Major Leaguer."

5   "Wilson Starts Philadelphia Moore Colony," *The Sporting News*, August 2, 1934: 3.

6   Richard Green, 1996 interview with Gwyndoline Moore (hereafter Green-Moore interview).

7   Moore gave up six runs and was pulled before the second inning was over. The Cardinals won, 15-6.

8   Green, "The Major Leaguer."

9   Gary Livacari, "Jimmie Wilson," SABR BioProject, https://sabr.org/bioproj/person/jimmie-wilson/, accessed June 29, 2025.

10   Clipping of unknown origin, circa July 1934, Gwyndoline Moore scrapbook.

11   Clipping of unknown origin, circa July 1934, Gwyndoline Moore scrapbook.

12   Clipping of unknown origin and date, Gwyndoline Moore scrapbook.

13   Clipping of unknown origin and date, Gwyndoline Moore scrapbook.

14   Clipping of unknown origin, circa July 1934, Gwyndoline Moore scrapbook.

15   Green, "The Major Leaguer."

16   Bill Dooly, "Indian Euel Moore Makes Hitters Do Tenderfoot Dance," *The Sporting News*, December 27, 1934: 3.

17   Green, "The Major Leaguer."

18   Green, "The Major Leaguer."

19   Clipping of unknown origin, circa early 1935, Gwyndoline Moore scrapbook.

20   Green, "The Major Leaguer."

21   Green, "The Major Leaguer."

22   "Gwyndoline G. Gray Moore," Oklahoma Cemeteries, undated (https://www.okcemeteries.net/johnston/tishomingo/mooreggg.html).

23   Clipping of unknown origin, circa early 1936, Gwyndoline Moore scrapbook.

24   Clipping of unknown origin, circa early 1936, Gwyndoline Moore scrapbook.

25   Dick Bartell with Norman L. Macht, *Rowdy Richard* (Berkeley, California: North Atlantic Books, 1987): 110.

26   *Galveston Daily News*, June 30, 1937: 8.

27   John Heidenry & Brett Topel, *The Boys Who Were Left Behind* (Lincoln: University of Nebraska Press, 2006), 37. Arthur Daley, "Back to Normalcy," *New York Times*, October 8, 1944: 58.

28   *Big Spring* (Texas) *Daily Herald*, July 25, 1938: 2.

29   Clipping of unknown origin, circa early 1943, Gwyndoline Moore scrapbook.

30   *Abilene* (Texas) *Reporter-News*, October 26, 1943: 17. See also Gary Bedingfield, writing on Rowell and Mueller in "Baseball in Wartime," https://www.baseballinwartime.com/player_biographies/rowell_bama.htm and Mueller in "Baseball's Greatest Sacrifice." at https://www.baseballsgreatestsacrifice.com/wounded_in_combat/mueller-heinie.html/.

31 Green, "The Major Leaguer."

32 Rod Lott, "After Escaping Zoo in 1950, Leapy the Leopard Held City in Fear," *Oklahoma Gazette* (Oklahoma City), October 3, 2007.

33 William M. Blair, "Leopard Recaptured After Drugging, Dies," *New York Times*, March 1, 1950: 1.

34 Green-Moore interview.

35 Green, "The Major Leaguer."

36 Green, "The Major Leaguer."

37 Green, "The Major Leaguer."

38 "Gwyndoline G. Gray Moore."

39 Richard Green, "Chickasaw Major Leaguer One of Select Few Ballplayers," *Chickasaw Times*, December 2007.

40 "Chickasaw Manager Leads MLB Pirates' Class A Affiliate," *Chickasaw Times*, January 2016 (http://www.chickasawtimes.net/Web-Exclusives/Chickasaw-manager-leads-MLB-Pirates%E2%80%99-Class-A-affil.aspx).

41 Kelly Bennett, "Dallas Beeler," SABR BioProject.

42 Joe Trezza, "Chickasaw Heritage Helps Drive Orioles Pitcher," MLB.com, February 26, 2020 (https://www.mlb.com/news/orioles-brandon-bailey-native-american-heritage).

JESS PIKE

By Zac Petrillo

Jess Pike's story isn't one of glory, fame, or the ascent to the top of the baseball world. Pike's story is, instead, about a persistent commitment to the game that paid off in small victories and one short stint in the spotlight. Born in a tiny Great Plains town to a large family of Native American heritage, Jess Pike's unlikely journey to the big leagues took him around the United States. His 14-year professional baseball career spanned over a dozen ballclubs in leagues from the West Texas-New Mexico League to the US Navy. In the middle of it all, Pike climbed to the highest level for 16 games with the New York Giants.

Jess Willard Pike was born on July 31, 1915, the third son of Henry Sylvester and Edna Alice (Smith) Pike, in Dustin, Oklahoma. Dustin sits roughly 70 miles south of Tulsa and has never had a population above 800.[1] Pike's mother, Edna, was born in Creek Nation Indian territory in 1887. Her parents, Rannie and John Smith, were each part Native, with Rannie born in Indian territory and John migrating to the region from Alabama. The small town where the family lived was named Spokogee, a Creek word for "exalted." Edna's native name was Pett.

The Fort Smith and Western Railway tracks reached the small town in the early 1900s. In September 1902, a gun battle between the Willis Brooks family and an outlaw gang led by Jim McFarland broke out in Spokogee. The feud had been simmering for years because Brooks held McFarland responsible for murdering his son. Willis Brooks was killed in the fight along with his brother Clifton. The marshal arrested McFarland and his gang, but they were later acquitted. Two years after the bloody battle, the town officially changed its name to Dustin (the Creek word for "prairie town").

Pike's father, Henry, worked in farming and later real estate. Henry and Edna married in 1903 when he was 24 years old, and she 16. A boxing fan, Henry named his son after the "Great White Hope," Jess Willard, the heavyweight who knocked out the champion Jack Johnson, three months before Jess Pike's birth.[2] Henry was of Irish descent, and Jess listed his nationality as Native and Irish on a baseball questionnaire in 1946.[3] Jess had two older brothers, two younger brothers, and three younger sisters.

A multisport youngster, Pike was nicknamed "Biddie" by friends. His time in school left much to be desired as he developed a reputation for "skipping study hall," and his classmates described him as "lazy bones."[4] At 16 years old, Pike was arrested and charged with second-degree burglary for stealing $23 from the Red Star garage in Weleetka, Oklahoma.[5] He was held on a $2,000 bond.[6] At 6-foot-2 and 170 pounds, Pike was a football star, playing quarterback as a "triple-threat man," successfully passing, running, and kicking for the Weleetka High School Outlaws.[7]

Raised in Weleetka, Pike attended the Connors State School of Agriculture in nearby Warner. In 1935 he joined the Yellow Cab baseball team of Oklahoma City. The "City Cabbies" won the *Daily Oklahoman* medal for winning the Class-B championship. Pike went south to Mount Pleasant, Texas.[8] On June 3, 1935, while employed by the Mount Pleasant baseball club, he married his former high-school classmate Dorothy Jean Allen.[9]

Pike joined the Monahans Trojans in 1937. He pitched in one game, going all nine innings and taking the loss. Also in 1937, Pike played at Seminole[10] under fellow Oklahoman Bennie Warren, who went on to spend six years in major-league baseball. Pike participated in the Denver Post

Jess Pike

Tournament along with fellow Muskogee player Allie Reynolds.

Pike started his professional career in 1939 with the Cedar Rapids Raiders of the Class-B Illinois-Iowa-Indiana (Three-I) League. He converted to the outfield, where he played 110 games, covering all three spots. About the move, Pike said, "Heck, right, left, center, what's the difference after you learn to play the outfield? You can play them all after a little while."[11] With the Raiders, he tied for the team lead in home runs with 13 while batting .304 and slugging .486.

In 1940 Pike split his time between the Buffalo Bisons of the Double-A[12] International League and the Winston-Salem Twins of the Class-B Piedmont League. With the Bisons, he played in 23 games, garnering 24 hits but little power as he hit just one double, triple, and home run. But over 119 games with the Twins, Pike clubbed 11 home runs and 11 triples, co-leading and leading his team respectively.

Pike next joined the Knoxville Smokies of the Southern Association in early 1941. On May 8 Smokies manager and future Hall of Famer Freddie Lindstrom announced that Pike had supplanted Hubert Shelley, though he remained uncertain which outfield position Pike would play. Two days later, a slide into second base landed Pike in General Hospital after the play knocked him unconscious.[13] Pike stayed with the Smokies for 32 games before moving on to the Elmira Pioneers of the Class-A Eastern League.

With Elmira, Pike's finest moment came on September 3 against the Wilkes-Barre Barons, who had Bob Lemon on their roster. After the Barons starter, Red Embree, took a no-hitter into the 10th inning, Pike hit a home run that won the game for his club.[14] Overall, Pike stuck in Elmira for 63 games, batting .259 with nine doubles. Pike finished the year with the Oklahoma City Indians for five games playing under Hall of Fame manager Rogers Hornsby. Pike's numbers, especially his power production, remained way down all year. Over 100 games across three leagues, Pike managed just two home runs.

For the 1943 season, Pike's contract was purchased by the Indianapolis Indians. With the Indians, Pike enjoyed his best season up to that point as a professional. Over 425 plate appearances, he recorded 113 hits, with 13 doubles, 6 triples, and 7 home runs, for a .318 batting average. Pike also walked 61 times, helping to bring his on-base percentage to a team-leading .422. Three years later, Pike commented that he most owed his baseball career to Donie Bush, the former major-league shortstop who managed Indianapolis during the 1943 campaign.[15] In late September 1943, the Philadelphia Phillies purchased Pike's contract from the Indians for an undisclosed amount of cash and two players to be named later. The Phillies expected Pike to report the following season.[16] However, in November Pike was called up for World War II military service.[17]

The general manager of the Phillies, future Hall of Famer Herb Pennock, signaled that Pike was a "promising outfielder … now in the Navy."[18] Pike spent all of the 1944 season and most of 1945 in the Navy. Stationed at the Bainbridge Naval Training Center in Maryland, Pike joined the base's baseball club. Dick Sisler, the son of George Sisler, future major-league All-Star, and later a hero for the 1950 pennant-winning Phillies, was also on the club. The Pike and Sisler pairing proved to be formidable for Bainbridge. On June 19, Pike's triple and run scored on Sisler's hit helped Bainbridge defeat the Boston Red Sox 5-2 in an exhibition game in front of 8,000 sailors.[19]

The war over, Pike rejoined the Indianapolis club, now the Boston Braves' Double-A affiliate, at the end of the 1945 season. To end the year, he played in 22 games and batted .333 with a .415 on-base percentage, continuing the success he saw with the club before his tour in the military. Both statistics would have put him in the top two on the team had he had enough at-bats to qualify.

In September 1945 the New York Giants purchased Pike's contract from the Indians for cash and two players.[20] On January 2, 1946, the *Ponca City News* reported that the Giants' 37-year-old player-manager Mel Ott intended to continue his playing career until minor leaguers showed him they could do better. He name-dropped Pike as a potential option, in addition to fellow minor-league outfielder Willard Marshall.[21]

Pike joined the Giants in April and made his major-league debut on April 18. He was 30 years old and had played pro ball for the better part of a decade, and he finally had his chance on the big stage at Ebbets Field in Brooklyn. In his first game, he went hitless against the Dodgers, but he did manage two walks in five plate appearances. Pike platooned for the next few games. His first big-league hit didn't come until the first game of a doubleheader on April 28, 10 days after his debut. He clubbed a three-run first-inning home run off Brooklyn's starter, Joe Hatten. In the second game of the doubleheader, Pike knocked in another two runs with a single off Ralph Branca. Over the two-game set, Pike drove in five runs for his best day as a big leaguer.

Pike failed to record a hit in his next start, on May 2, but on May 3 he tallied a hit and did the same in each of his next three starts, including his first double in Cincinnati on May 5 and his first two-hit game on May 7. Pike added his first triple and another RBI against Boston on May 11, but he also struck out three times. He didn't record another hit for the Giants, but he did manage one more run with the help of two future Hall of Famers when, on May 12, he reached on a first-inning fielder's choice, took third on Johnny Mize's single, and scored on Ernie Lombardi's bunt single.[22] After that, Ott plugged Pike in as a pinch-hitter three more times, but he failed to get on base.

At the end of May, the Giants optioned Pike to the Jersey City Giants, their Triple-A affiliate. In 16 games, Pike hit .171 with seven hits, including one home run, one double, and one triple, and 6 RBIs. By June 2 (according to the *Brooklyn Daily Eagle*), the Giants had started seven different players in right field in an ever-shifting outfield.[23] Pike was one of the seven and one of four who had appeared in left field for the club.

Pike remained with Jersey City for the duration of the 1946 season. He hit there like he couldn't in New York, and his power started to emerge. On June 9, his first-inning home run provided all the runs his team needed to defeat Buffalo.[24] A few weeks later, Pike's Giants headed to Montreal. In a 16-2 drubbing by the Montreal Royals, featuring Jackie Robinson, Pike provided the only Jersey City runs with a two-run homer over the scoreboard off African American pitcher Roy Partlow.[25] Over 96 games with Jersey City, Pike clubbed 9 home runs and 13 doubles. His OBP was .363, partly due to 48 walks. He had 11 stolen bases.

In early 1947 Pike was briefly obtained by San Diego before he moved to the South Atlantic League to play for the Charleston Rebels, managed by Chick Autry. In 86 games with the Rebels, Pike batted .291 and hit 8 home runs. He stayed on with Charleston the following year and posted similar numbers, though his homers ticked up slightly to 14, and he posted 113 walks.

By the late 1940s, Pike settled into a home in Sherman Oaks, California, where during the offseason, he worked as a carpenter for movie studios. Pike was a hunting enthusiast who indulged in the hobby, especially duck hunting, during his free time.

Now a 33-year-old minor-league journeyman, Pike signed on with the Bakersfield Indians of the Class-C California League in mid-April of 1949. At 10 years older than the average player in the league, Pike set career highs in multiple statistics, putting up his best season as a professional ballplayer. Soon after signing, Pike spearheaded the first of three consecutive wins over Visalia by hitting a two-run home run. The homers never stopped coming. A few days later, Pike thumped a 377-foot home run against the Ventura Yankees.[26] Three days after that, a Pike home run sparked yet another Bakersfield victory, this time against Santa Barbara.[27] By June 15, Pike brought his season total to 13 when he smacked two home runs in one game against Ventura.[28]

On August 2 Pike would have set the record for walks in league history (held by Bob DiPietro) in a season, but the game was ruled off the books.[29] and Pike had to wait some more before entering the history books. Pike was also on pace to break the record for runs in a season, held by Tommy Glaviano of Fresno (142). Pike had 134 at the time.[30] Pike wound up obliterating the record, taking an additional 60 walks before the season was out. The *Bakersfield Californian* announced that when Pike returned home from the team's August road trip, the elder statesman would hold three new records. He then broke the league home-run record of 31 on August 17. By season's end, Pike set new league highs for walks (194), home runs (37), runs scored (167), and RBIs (156) in one season.

Pike also defined himself as a fan favorite during his time with Bakersfield. On August 24 he and home-plate umpire John Yelovic devised to play a trick on the crowd. Pike played the entire ninth inning with a starter's gun in his hip pocket. They planned for him to get near enough to the Yelovic to stage a fake shooting. Both parties were in on the gag, but ultimately, they failed to pull it off.[31]

After the season, Pike's personal life was struck by tragedy. His wife, Dorothy, was killed in an automobile accident in Sherman Oaks when her car collided with another one. The couple had four children.[32]

In 1950, now the "California League's home run king,"[33] Pike moved up north and joined the Modesto Reds. On April 27 he returned to Bakersfield and the "fence-busting left-handed batter"[34] once again put on a show. He hit a double in the first inning, then homered in the fifth inning to drive in two runs. For the season, he hit .251 with 25 home runs and 100 RBIs.

In April of 1951, the night before Pike was scheduled to head to San Fernando with his Reds teammates, he was held for the investigation of a murder. Pike was arrested after Floyd Napoleon Smith tripped on a curb and split his skull in front of the 400 Club in Modesto. Pike and Smith argued inside the tavern before Pike followed Smith outside, and the two exchanged punches. The accident occurred when Smith stood up and started after Pike before falling over the curb. Pike told police he went to the club searching for the woman who had been babysitting his children.[35] Witnesses inside the club said Smith had been bothering Pike, saying, "[A]ll ball players are tramps." Smith allegedly threw the first punch. Police charged Pike with manslaughter[36], but the next day his lawyer declared he had been found "blameless."[37]

By mid-April Pike was back with the Modesto ballclub, where he joined forces with Dick Wilson, forming a combination that the year prior had produced 55 home runs between them, as Wilson had clubbed 30 (and 154 RBIs) of his own. Pike got into 93 games between Modesto and his old club in Bakersfield, swatting 14 home runs. He rounded out his career in 1952, playing 18 uneventful games with Bakersfield before latching on with the Mexicali Eagles of the Southwest International League. After 16 seasons as a pro, Pike hung up his spikes.

Pike aspired to become a manager when his playing days ended, but that dream never came to fruition. He never managed a professional club. Instead, Pike stayed in the Chula Vista area of Southern California. He spent 30 years breeding thoroughbred racehorses. He was a member of the National Left-Handed Golfers Association. Pike married Barbara Mary Todd, a lifelong resident of San Diego, who owned an import-export business.[38] Pike's sister, Chris, was married to Edgar McFadden,[39] a sports journeyman who pitched in the Cleveland Indians farm system, scouted for Cleveland and Cincinnati, and worked in the front office for the NHL's Washington Capitals.[40]

Pike died at 68 years old on March 28, 1984, in San Diego. He was survived by three brothers, three sisters, his wife, his son Gary, three daughters, Donna Jean, Catherine, and Jessica (all from his marriage to Dorothy), as well as 10 grandchildren and one great-grandchild. Pike was buried in Glen Abbey Memorial Park in Bonita, California.[41]

ACKNOWLEDGMENTS

Special thanks to Paul Proia for his research support.

SOURCES

In addition to the sources cited in the Notes, the author consulted Baseball-Reference.com and Retrosheet.org.

NOTES

1   Kathy Weiser, "Brooks-McFarland Feud," *Legends of America*, https://www.legendsofamerica.com/brooks-mcfarlandfeud/ (last accessed October 17, 2022).

2   "Willard Pike Plays with O.C. Indians," *Weleetka* (Oklahoma) *American*, April 16, 1941: 1.

3   Jess Pike, Publicity Questionnaire for American Baseball Bureau, March 26, 1946, https://www.ancestry.com/sharing/30479868?h=db30b7 (last accessed October 22, 2022).

4   Cornella Gaston, "Kitchen Favorites," *Weleetka American*, November 23, 1933: 6.

5   "Hold Weleetka Youth," *Okfuskee County* (Oklahoma) *News*, December 25, 1930: 1.

6   Details are unclear about how Pike's burglary charged was resolved.

7   "School Notes," *Weleetka American*, October 13, 1932: 4.

8   "Willard Pike Plays with O.C. Indians."

9   "Allen Announces Marriage of Daughters," *Weleetka American*, June 13, 1935: 5.

10   "Willard Pike Plays with O.C. Indians."

11   "Willard Pike Plays with O.C. Indians."

12   After World War II, the Double-A classification was elevated to Triple A.

13   "Pike Hurt in Slide," *Knoxville News-Sentinel*, May 10, 1941: 5.

14   F.X. Welsh, "Do You Know That?" *Wilkes-Barre Times Leader*, September 4, 1941: 26.

15   Jess Pike, Publicity Questionnaire for American Baseball Bureau.

16   Associated Press, "Phillies Purchase Jess Willard Pike," *St. Louis Globe-Democrat*, September 25, 1943: 4.

17   "70 County Men Ordered for Induction," *Okemah* (Oklahoma) *News Leader*, November 16, 1943: 1.

18   "Phillies Bill Lee Is Placed in 1-A," *Lima* (Ohio) *News*, February 10, 1944: 21.

19   Associated Press, "Bainbridge Beats Sox," *Wilkes-Barre Times Leader*, June 20, 1944: 15.

20   Associated Press, "Giants Buy Indianapolis Outfielder Jess Pike, *St. Louis Globe-Democrat*, September 27, 1945: 20.

21   Associated Press, "Ott Plans to Play With Improved Giants," *Ponca City* (Oklahoma) *News*, January 22, 1946: 8.

22   Associated Press, "Braves Take Double Win," *Rutland* (Vermont) *Daily Herald*, May 13, 1946: 6.

23   "Lefties Galore Set for Giants," *Brooklyn Daily Eagle*, June 2, 1946: 25.

24   Associated Press, "Little Giants Turn Back Bisons, 2 to 0, *Syracuse Post-Standard*, June 9, 1946: 46.

25   Associated Press, "Royals Parade to 16-2 Triumph On 22-Hit Attack," *Syracuse Post-Standard*, June 25, 1946: 12.

26   John Peri, "Hard Hitting in State Circuit," *Stockton* (California) *Evening Standard and Sunday Record*, April 27, 1949: 35.

27   United Press, "Indians Capture 6th Straight Win," *Oakland Tribune*, April 30, 1949: 10.

28   United Press, "Pike Hits Two Homers," *Stockton Evening and Sunday Record*, June 15, 1949: 28.

29   The *Bakersfield Californian* newspaper, reporting on Pike's new records, makes no mention of why the original record-breaking game in Modesto was ruled off the books.

30   Walter Little, "Little Quotes," *Bakersfield Californian*, August 18, 1949: 29.

31   Walter Little, "Little Quotes," *Bakersfield Californian*, August 25, 1949: 29.

32   "Hold Services for Mrs. Dorothy Pike, Victim of Accident," *Van Nuys* (California) *News*, November 10, 1949: 8.

33   John Peri, "Ports and Reds Clear Decks for Tomorrow," *Stockton Evening and Sunday Record*, April 20, 1950: 34.

34   "Tribe Faces Bruising Red Sox; Pike Is Rough for Former Mates," *Bakersfield Californian*, April 28, 1950: 27.

35   "Jess Pike, Modesto Outfielder, Jailed as Result of Fatal Fistic Altercation," *Stockton Evening and Sunday Record*, April 2, 1951: 32.

36   While no official court record was found, it's likely the case against Pike was dismissed.

37   "Manslaughter Charge Against Pike; Attorney Says He Is Blameless," *Stockton Evening and Sunday Record*, April 3, 1951: 23.

38   "Barbara Mary Todd Pike (Obituary)," *Chula Vista* (California) *Star News*, December 8, 1988: 7.

39   Edgar Burdette McFadden, *The Sporting News* Contract Card, https://digital.la84.org/digital/collection/p17103coll3/id/132646/rec/1 (last accessed October 22, 2022).

40   Edgar McFadden Obituary, https://www.legacy.com/us/obituaries/dayton/name/edgar-mcfadden-obituary?id=29178353 (last accessed October 17, 2022).

41   "Jess Pike, Horseman, Major Leaguer (Obituary)," *Chula Vista Star-News*, April 1, 1984: 24.

ED PINNANCE

By Martin Healy Jr.

At the turn of the twentieth century, Native American base-ball players found themselves becoming integrated into the professional ranks of baseball. Charles Albert "Chief" Bender, a member of the White Earth Band of Chippewa, became a Hall of Fame pitcher for Connie Mack's Philadelphia Athletics. Louis LeRoy of Stockbridge-Munsee, the boy with the "ten thousand dollar arm,"[1] went on to star with the St. Paul Saints of the American Association, after brief stints with the New York Yankees and Boston Red Sox. And perhaps most famously, due to his all-around athletic prowess, Jim Thorpe of the Sac and Fox played in the big leagues for the New York Giants, Cincinnati Reds, and Boston Braves. These three players were among a long list of First Nations players who proved their worth in baseball during the Deadball Era. They were all born in the United States. But the first full-blooded Native American to appear in a regular-season game in the major leagues was a member of the Chippewa tribe born in Canada. His name was Edward Pinnance.[2]

On September 22, 1880, Elijah Edward Pinnance, the first son of John and Martha Pinnance, came into the world at Walpole Island, Ontario, Canada. Walpole Island is a First Nation reserve located 25 miles north of the town of Chatham, Ontario. (Chatham is the birthplace of Hall of Famer Ferguson Jenkins.)

As a young child, Pinnance demonstrated great skill in athletics and excelled at traditional Native games. When he became of school age, Edward enrolled at the Shinkwat Indian Residential School in Sault Ste. Marie, Ontario. There, he was introduced to baseball and quickly became a

ATHLETICS AMERICAN LEAGUE BASE BALL CLUB OF 1904
THE PHILADELPHIA SPORTING BOILER SUPPLEMENT NO. 2 OF NATIONAL AND AMERICAN LEAGUE TEAMS.

Photo by H. S. Tarr, Phila

Top Row, Reading from left to right—M. Cross, Seybold, Hoffman, Pickering, Bender, Barthold, Pinnance, Schreckengost, Henley.   Lower
Row—Waddell, Lave Cross, Hartsell, Powers, Davis and Murphy

Lane Ed Pinnance with the 1904 Athletics

star player for the school.[3] The first accounts of Pinnance playing in fast company came in 1902 when he suited up for New Baltimore, a club in a local amateur league in Michigan. New Baltimore is on the American side of the St. Clair River, a mere 19 miles from Ed's birthplace. He played great ball in the amateur league, earning recognition from the Detroit Tigers. The *Detroit Free Press* wrote, "Phenoms for the Tigers are being dug up in Michigan one a day. The latest heard from is one Pinnance, a Walpole Island Indian wonder, who has been instructed to report for trial on Thursday."[4] There are no reports of Pinnance ever attending a tryout with the Tigers, but his splendid pitching for New Baltimore put him on the baseball map.

Pinnance did not end up playing with the Tigers. Instead he enrolled at the Michigan Agricultural College, today's Michigan State University. A pitcher, he helped MAC beat up on rival teams like the University of Michigan, Detroit College, and Depauw University in 1903. In a change of pace for the college men, MAC scheduled a game with the top nine from Walpole Island. In what must have been an exciting game for Pinnance, he got to play against his fellow Chippewa tribesmen. He likely knew his opponents. Pinnance retreated from the pitching box to play third base in the game. He went 2-for-5 at the plate in a 10-4 victory. The *Detroit Free Press* subheadline stated, "Walpole Redskins Trimmed Neatly by M.A.C."[5] As the school season ended, Pinnance easily found a baseball job with the Mount Clemens club of the Great Lakes River League. Nicknamed the Lawyers, Pinnance and his teammates laid down the law on all comers throughout the summer. In a late-season game, he pitched an 8-0 shutout against the Myrtles of Detroit. In this game he got his lucky break. Philadelphia Athletics superstar Harry Davis was in Mount Clemens to take advantage of the town's famous hot springs. He decided to take in a baseball match. Pinnance caught the eye of Davis, who recommended him to his boss, Connie Mack. Mack summoned the young Canadian to the City of Brotherly Love at once.

Before Pinnance could meet up with Mack's big-league club, the Athletics' leader rescinded his original order and instructed him to report to Lebanon, New Hampshire, for seasoning with that town's nine. Pinnance hopped on a train from Michigan to New Hampshire armed with a "suit case made from the skin of a large elk he killed himself with a bow and arrow."[6] His stay in Lebanon did not last long. On September 6, 1903, in his first game with the small-town club, he made it through only three innings. In the fourth frame, the big Native Canadian was hit by a pitch, which forced him to retire from the match. Notwithstanding the severity of the injury, Mack soon recalled Pinnance from the Lebanon independent nine.

Just a few days later, on September 14, Pinnance made his big-league debut at American League Park, home of the Washington Senators. "In the eighth Manager Mack trotted out the Indian, Pinnance, from the wilds of Michigan, and his first endeavors against the professionals cannot be said to have been a success," commented a *Washington Evening Star* columnist, who was wrong.[7] Edward Pinnance did not hail from the wilds of Michigan and, more to the point, he did not pitch poorly. Pinnance allowed only one run in two innings of work in his debut, and finished a 13-1 victory for his club. Hardly unsuccessful. The paper did relent later in the article and gave him a break: "He is only a youngster and very green, but he will do to farm out next season."[8]

On the lighter side of the diamond, the young pitcher earned a moniker from the Washington fans upon his arrival to big-league soil. "As soon as Pinnance stepped on the rubber he was christened 'Peanuts' by the bleacherites, and this nickname will probably stick with him for all time."[9] In his book *Over The Fence Is Out!*, baseball historian Jim Shearon explained the occasion further: "At the start of the eighth inning, the public address announcer stepped in front of the grandstand to call out, 'Pinnance now pitching for Philadelphia.' The bleacher crowd, straining to catch his name, couldn't quite hear. 'What's his name?' a man asked his neighbor. 'Peanuts, I think' was the answer."[10] Pinnance's teammates overheard the fans and adopted the moniker with glee. Days later, Pinnance was asked about his nickname, "Why should that name annoy me? I'll be roasted more or less, and from what I've been able to observe, the roasting process vastly improves the peanut."[11]

Pinnance stood 6-feet-1 and is listed as weighing 180 pounds. He threw right-handed and batted left-handed. On September 17, Philadelphia sportswriter Charles Dryden noted: "He has a low raise curve, said to equal [Joe] McGinnity's famous 'Old Sol,' and other effective slants and shoots. But the youngster lacks even a minor league experience. Mack thinks one season in a strong independent team would fix Mr. Pinnance about right."[12]

Despite not being in the pennant race, Connie Mack didn't use Pinnance down the stretch. His next appearance for the tall lanky manager came on the final day of the American League season. Donning his brand-new Athletics uniform, he pitched with excellence during his first career start. "In the five innings that Pinnance was in the box the Clevelanders made but three hits and scored one run," noted the *Philadelphia Inquirer*.[13] Unfortunately for Pinnance, manager Mack wanted to take a look at another rookie, Jim Fairbank. Fairbank proceeded to give up six runs to conclude the game, and the A's lost their season finale, 7-5. Although Pinnance failed to earn his first career victory, he did not fail in impressing his manager. Mack appointed him to pitch in the city series against the National League's Phillies. Another good performance there secured Pinnance an invitation to 1904 Athletics spring training in Spartanburg, South Carolina. A syndicated article picked up by the *Palatine Enterprise* suggested that Mack's 1904 squad would change its name to Indians, as the skipper signed three Natives to his roster: Chief Bender, Lou Bruce, and Ed Pinnance.[14] The name change never happened.

Spring training began well for Pinnance. Mack played him with the regulars and he had two strong performances in intrasquad games. The *Philadelphia Inquirer* spoke of the skipper's confidence: "Manager Mack is satisfied that Pinnance is possessed of the material of which great pitchers are made, and that it is only a matter of a little time when he will demonstrate his ability to be classed among the crackerjacks of the profession."[15] Then Pinnance's pitching started to deteriorate. He lost a game he should have easily won against the Princeton University Tigers. The *Inquirer* noted, "Pinnance did not show good form to-day, having no control and lack of his usual speed."[16] His troubles continued in a preseason series against the Phillies. Despite the Athletics' taking the series from the Phillies, the games that Pinnance pitched resulted in losses. The manager had no choice but to send him out for polishing. He ordered the young recruit to the Wilmington Peaches of the Tri-State League.

Tri-State League rivals were not happy that Wilmington received a player contracted to a major-league team. The Camden team filed an official complaint to the league president. Before any word came from the president, manager Mack put out his own statement: "Pinnance is a member of the Wilmington club. He has been signed by Manager Frysinger, of that club, for the season of 1904. ... I do not care to get mixed up in any Tri-State arguments, but this much is certain, Pinnance belongs to Wilmington."[17] After Mack spoke, Pinnance's appointment to the Peaches became official. He started well and in just his third start with his new club, "Pinnance of Wilmington Pitched a Remarkable Game."[18] The Lancaster team came to Wilmington and was beaten badly by the Peaches. Pinnance pitched a one-hitter in the 6-0 victory. "Pinnance was responsible for the calamity that befell the lads from the land of sauerkraut and onions [Lancaster had a large German population]. But thirty-one men faced him during the game and of that number but one hit the ball safely," the local paper observed.[19] In spite of his great pitching for Wilmington, the game of July 3 was his last with the team. He spent the remainder of the 1904 season as a vagabond baseball player. He pitched for Federalsburg of the Maryland Amateur League and Nashua of the New England League. In August he settled in to play for Amsterdam-Gloversville-Johnstown of the New York State League. He played well with the aptly nicknamed Hyphens, earning himself a contract with the team for 1905, a contract which he signed in mid-March.

By mid-May of 1905, Pinnance grew out of favor with manager Earl Howard. Not worried about future retaliation, Howard released Pinnance to the league-rival Troy Trojans. Pinnance joined fellow Canadians Alex Hardy and Abbie Johnson on the Trojan squad. His season highlight came at a game in Scranton, Pennsylvania, in mid-July: "Pinnance's Pitching Was More Than the Locals Could Solve With Success."[20] Pinnance pitched brilliantly in a 4-0 shutout of the Scranton Miners. For the following season Pinnance stayed in the New York State League but jumped to the Albany Senators. Late in the 1906 season, manager Mike Doherty inserted Pinnance to pitch against Scranton. The Miners batted the Canadian hurler hard, tallying 13 hits off him. Scranton won the game, 4-3 in 10 innings. Perhaps because Pinnance usually handled Scranton with relative ease, upon the defeat the *Scranton Truth* pelted Doherty and Pinnance with seemingly retaliatory, culturally insensitive slander. "[Doherty] uncaged his noble red skin, Hiawatha Strongheart Pinnance, but Poor Lo has been seen on parade here so often this summer that he was no more novelty than the average Indian who attends the park. The act fell flat. The red man carried neither tomahawk nor scalping knife, and caused no more uneasiness or shakes in the local camp than his wooden relative in the cigar business."[21] Pinnance was not oblivious to the callous chants he often heard, and stood stoic against them. Nonetheless, he left the New York State League at the end of 1906 and never returned.

In 1907 Pinnance returned home and played in the Southern Michigan League. He became a top contributor for the Bay City team. In September, for reasons unknown, he was transferred to the Flint Vehicles. His continued excellence with the Vehicles garnered him interest from around the nation. At the end of the 1907 campaign, manager Judge McCredie of the Portland Beavers drafted Pinnance as an insurance measure for the 1908 Pacific Coast League season. He made the team out of spring training but was not on the top rung of the ladder for McCredie's pitching staff. His first appearance for Portland came in a relief role during the team's fourth game of the season. Despite the team's 11-2 loss to the San Francisco Seals, the reviews were shining. "Pinnance was the only Beaver who showed any class at all. He worked during the last three spasms and the best the Seals did was a pair of hits," observed a sportswriter.[22] Pinnance struck out five batters. McCredie's Beavers lost their first seven games of the season. A Portland reporter wondered, "Why doesn't Mac send Pinnance in to pitch the first ball over? The Indian might scalp the Seals."[23] McCredie relented in his trepidation about using Pinnance, and allowed his new pitcher to make a start. The move paid off.[24] Pinnance threw a complete-game 5-0 shutout against San Francisco in his debut start in the Pacific Coast League. He allowed just five hits. "The Indian was a life saver," said a San Francisco sportswriter. "The way he twisted that ball around the necks of the Seals caused [San Francisco manager] Danny Long to throw at least fourteen fits. ... The red man struck the ball right over the plate all the time and put plenty of smoke behind it."[25]

Pinnance quickly became a fan favorite. He also earned praise, not just around Oregon, but across the country. Papers from Los Angeles to Wilkes-Barre to Brooklyn spoke of Pinnance's superlative pitching with the Beavers. The former Connie Mack student seemed destined to finally prove his worth after years of toiling in the minors. The *Oregon Daily Journal* of Portland wrote of Pinnance: "Of all the new ones McCredie has sprung on the San Francisco public this time, Pinnance, the Indian, looks the best. After that game he pitched last Saturday afternoon against the Seals he was voted all the candy by every one who saw him work. The way he twisted that ball around the neck of every hard hitter on the local lineup was awful for the admirers of the home team to stick around and look upon, and the steadiness that he displayed all the way through made the multitude sit up and take notice. The redskin has the most peculiar line of benders that any man has thrown from a box in this city for a long time. The curves seem to approach in a threatening sort of manner and then they break sharply at the plate. As Pinnance tosses every one of them with practically the same motion, none of the local batters ever could get jerry to his system."[26] But just as the accolades began to roll in, Pinnance found himself with the ultimate dilemma. Back home in Canada, the government began to allocate reservation lands to Natives. Pinnance, who was entitled to 160 acres of land in the Walpole Island area, "explained to McCredie that unless he is on hand when the allotment is made he will not get his farm."[27] The Portland bench boss reluctantly let his top pitcher go.

On June 12 Pinnance left for the East with every intention of returning to Portland to finish the PCL season after attending to his business matters in Canada. Pinnance never journeyed back to the West Coast, instead preferring to stay home and play for the local club in St. Clair, Michigan.

Pinnance received a telegram that asked him to return to Portland for the 1909 season. Perhaps because of his abrupt departure and failure to return, he found himself demoted to the city's number-two club, the Portland Colts of the Northwestern League. Judge McCredie of the PCL Beavers released his top pitcher from the first half of 1908 to manager Pearl Casey, who felt so confident of a pennant win for his Colts that he placed an order for a new flagpole before the season even started. Manager McCredie reserved the right to recall any of the Colts during the season, including Pinnance, whose play did not justify a call-up to the Beavers. He finished 1909 with 15 victories and 18 losses, and the team finished in fourth place in a six-team league. Pinnance fell out of favor with the management and fans of the West Coast leagues. His career seemed destined to return East.

Flint, Michigan, ended up being Pinnance's new baseball home. He found comfort in the Michigan League, but his pitching skill became needed elsewhere. The Native Canadian journeyed to the Midwest to play for the Davenport Prodigals of the Illinois-Indiana-Iowa (Three-I) League. Pinnance had a terrible go with the Davenport club and in midsummer the local paper sarcastically praised a win: "The unusual happened again yesterday. Pinnance won a game and pitched an average grade of good ball in doing so at that."[28] He won just five games in 1910. In 1911 Pinnance returned to the Michigan League to play for Bay City, the last stop in his professional baseball career. He continued to pitch in local exhibitions, but never returned to the form of his early career.

Edward Pinnance's son Parker later described his father's departure from baseball. "Dad finally quit baseball when he became a diabetic. He would not stay on his diet given by his doctor and manager. He liked his food and you know what a diabetic diet is like."[29] After he retired, Pinnance worked as a marine contractor. He built docks and seawalls on Lake St. Clair and the St. Clair River. He also worked as a blacksmith. His time on earth ended on December 14, 1944, after he suffered a heart attack at home on Walpole Island.

NOTES

1   Jeffery Powers-Beck, *The American Indian Integration of Baseball* (Lincoln: University of Nebraska Press, 2009), 188.

2   Robert Peyton Wiggins, *Chief Bender* (Jefferson, North Carolina: McFarland, 2010), 49.

3   Clipping file, National Baseball Hall of Fame, Cooperstown, New York.

4   "Local Baseball Talk," *Detroit Free Press*, August 26, 1902: 10.

5   "Scalped Indians," *Detroit Free Press*, May 31, 1903: 9.

6   "Gossip of the Diamond," *Topeka State Journal*, September 9, 1903: 2.

7   "Sports of All Sorts," *Washington Evening Star*, September 15, 1903: 9.

8   "Sports of All Sorts."

9   "Sports of All Sorts."

10 Jim Shearon, *Over the Fence Is Out!* (Ottawa, Ontario: Malin Head, 2009), 86.

11 Charles Dryden, "Athletics Must Win Nine Games to Beat Out Spiders," *Philadelphia North American*, September 17, 1903: 5.

12 Dryden, "Athletics Must Win Nine Games to Beat Out Spiders."

13 "Cleveland Takes the Final Game," *Philadelphia Inquirer*, September 30, 1903: 10.

14 "Odds & Ends of Sport," *Palatine Enterprise*, October 17, 1903: 3.

15 "Athletics Will Be Stronger Than They Were Last Year," *Philadelphia Inquirer*, April 3, 1904: 36.

16 "Princeton Puts Athletics Away," *Philadelphia Inquirer*, April 2, 1904: 10.

17 "Tri-State Troubles," *York* (Pennsylvania) *Dispatch*, May 13, 1904: 5. The newspaper article actually read: "I do not case to get mixed up in any Tri-State arguments …" but we have changed that to reflect what we believe was the intended wording.

18 "Lancaster Had One Hit," *Lancaster* (Pennsylvania) *New Era*, May 20, 1904: 2.

19 "Lancaster Got But One Hit Off Pinnance," *Wilmington* (Delaware) *Evening Journal*, May 20, 1904: 7.

20 "Troy Gave Us White Wash Coat," *Scranton Truth*, July 20, 1905: 8.

21 "Locals Win Again in Ten Innings," *Scranton Truth*, September 8, 1906: 9.

22 "Seals Pound Beaver Curve Artist," *San Francisco Call*, April 8, 1908: 9.

23 "Squeeze Plays," *Oregon Daily Journal*, April 11, 1908: 12.

24 "Beavers Break Seven Day Hoodoo by Indian's Good Work," *San Francisco Call*, April 12, 1908: 46.

25 "Beavers Break Seven Day Hoodoo by Indian's Good Work."

26 "Pinnance Looks Best of Beavers," *Oregon Daily Journal*, April 19, 1908: 36.

27 "Indian Twirler Released by Portland," *San Francisco Examiner*, June 12, 1908: 11.

28 "Pinnance Wins a Game," *Quad-City Times* (Davenport, Iowa) August 12, 1910: 6.

29 Clipping file, National Baseball Hall of Fame, Cooperstown, New York.

ALLIE REYNOLDS

By Royse Parr

Because of religious strictures imposed by his parents, Allie Reynolds did not play baseball in an organized fashion until after he left high school. He overcame that handicap and had an outstanding 13-year career in the 1940s and 1950s as a pitcher with the Cleveland Indians and the New York Yankees.

Allie Pierce Reynolds was born in Bethany, Oklahoma, a suburb of Oklahoma City, on February 10, 1917, to David C. and Mary (Brooks) Reynolds; he was the eldest of three sons. Allie was three-16ths Creek Indian, descending from his three-quarters-Creek grandmother, Eliza Root Reynolds. He grew tired of explaining the three-16ths and often told reporters he was one-fourth Creek.

Allie's father was born in Indian Territory in 1890, attended Chilocco Indian School, and became a Nazarene preacher. Allie's parents lived strictly by Nazarene doctrine, staying away from movies and dances. One doctrinal stand that affected their athletic young son was the prohibition of playing sports on Sunday. From an early age, Allie loved baseball. Because most sandlot and semipro games were played on Sunday afternoon, he did not play baseball on a team until after high school, but turned to other sports, including softball, track, and football.

Except for football in the sixth grade, Allie did not play any school sports until he entered Oklahoma City's Capitol Hill High School in the fall of 1933 for his senior year. He weighed 145 pounds and saw only limited action as a back on offense and defense. The Capitol Hill Redskins were an undefeated team that claimed the national high-school football championship by defeating Chicago's Harrison Tech, 55-13.

Allie had completed his high-school class work by going to summer school in 1934, but he returned to Capitol Hill High School for one more semester to play football. As the starting quarterback, he led the team to an undefeated season that was marred only by two ties.

His father's meager income as a Nazarene minister meant Allie would have to earn his own way if he wanted to go to college. He was disappointed to learn football coaches at the University of Oklahoma were not interested in him because of his light weight. However, in January of 1935, he accepted a track scholarship from Oklahoma A&M that paid $20 a month toward his tuition and room and board. Also, because of his Muscogee Creek heritage, he was granted a $400 loan by a foundation.

In May 1935 Allie was the Missouri Valley Conference's high-point man for Oklahoma A&M in the annual freshman track meet. His times in the 100-yard dash, the 220-yard dash, and his distance in the javelin throw were comparable to those of the great Jim Thorpe in the 1912 Olympics.

On July 7, 1935, Allie married his Capitol Hill High School sweetheart, Dale Earlene Jones. He had a summer job slinging a sledgehammer and playing baseball in the outfield for an Oklahoma City oil field equipment firm. Their first son, Allie Dale, was born on June 8, 1936. He died in an airplane crash in Wyoming in 1978.

In 1935, Reynolds was the leading ground gainer for Oklahoma A&M's freshman football team. For the next three seasons, he was the starting fullback and a tenacious defensive back on varsity teams that won only six games and lost 24.

Allie Reynolds

One afternoon in the spring of 1937, Oklahoma A&M's athletic director and basketball and baseball coach, Henry P. Iba, saw Reynolds throwing a javelin next to the baseball field. Iba asked the track and football star if he could help the baseball team by throwing batting practice. Allie agreed, and without any warm-ups, he started striking out batters, throwing as hard as he could. After a few batters, Iba called him in and told him to go to the equipment room and get a uniform.

Allie was used primarily as a relief pitcher at the beginning of the season. In his first start as a collegian, he pitched all nine innings and hit a home run in a 3-2 victory over the University of Oklahoma.

In late June 1937 the need for a summer job took Reynolds to Colorado to play on the Leyden Coal Company's semipro team. With Allie pitching the championship game, Leyden Coal won Colorado's first statewide semipro championship.

Reynolds had a 5-2 record as Oklahoma A&M won another state conference title in 1938. On May 20 of that year, he and Earlene became the parents of a daughter, Bobbye Kay Reynolds. In 1939, Allie was elected team captain. He was 5-1 in his final college season, including a May 15 no-hitter against Southwestern Oklahoma State University.

Coach Iba advised Reynolds to consider a career in professional baseball and set up a meeting for him with Cleveland Indians scout Hugh "Red" Alexander. The Indians signed Reynolds, paid him a $1,000 bonus, and assigned him to their Springfield, Ohio affiliate in the Class-C Middle Atlantic League. Plagued by control problems, he nevertheless compiled an 11-8 record.

Because he had not yet completed his college education, Reynolds returned to classes at Oklahoma A&M for the fall semester of 1939. Later, he took correspondence courses, completing a bachelor of science degree in June 1942.

Cleveland promoted Reynolds to the Cedar Rapids (Iowa) Raiders of the Class-B Three-I League, where he had a 12-7 record for the 1940 season. On March 8, 1941, Earlene gave birth to their third and last child, James David. Reynolds opened the 1941 season at Wilkes-Barre, Pennsylvania, in the Class-A Eastern League. He appeared in only three games with no decisions before being sent back to Cedar Rapids, where he had a 10-10 record.

As he had in 1941, Reynolds began the 1942 season with Wilkes-Barre. He became the Eastern League's premier pitcher with an 18-7 record, including 11 shutouts. He was named the right-handed pitcher on the league's all-star team (Warren Spahn was the left-landed pitcher). After the Eastern League season ended, Reynolds was called up to the Indians, and he made his major-league debut on September 17, 1942, as a reliever against the Washington Senators.

As the 1943 season began, Cleveland had high hopes for Reynolds to replace Bob Feller, who was in the Navy. The 1943 game that established the six-foot, 195-pound Reynolds as a coming star was a 12–0 shellacking of the Yankees on July 2 at League Park. He finished the season with an 11-12 record and a league-leading 151 strikeouts.

Pitching for a second-division ballclub in 1944, Reynolds posted an 11-8 record, which gave him the best winning percentage among Indians' pitchers. He was 18-12 for the fifth-place Indians in 1945, but led the league with 130 walks in 247 1/3 innings. Reynolds got off to a great start in 1946, but he had to win nine of his final 14 decisions to salvage an 11-15 record.

At the end of the 1946 season, Reynolds was the subject of trade discussions between the Indians and the Yankees. During a World Series game at Fenway Park, Larry MacPhail, the president of the Yankees, asked Joe DiMaggio which Cleveland pitcher would be best for the New Yorkers, Red Embree or Reynolds. DiMaggio said he could hit Embree but had never been successful against Reynolds. MacPhail made the trade, sending second baseman Joe Gordon to the Indians in exchange for Reynolds.

Reynolds started the 1947 season year with back-to-back shutouts, including a two-hitter against the Boston Red Sox on April 23. He duplicated the two-hit shutout against the Red Sox exactly a month later. He finished the season with a 19-8 record and a .704 winning percentage, the league's second best. The Yankees easily won the American League pennant and defeated the Brooklyn Dodgers four games to three in the World Series. Reynolds had a complete-game, 10-3 victory in Game Two and a no-decision in Game Six.

The Yankees acquired left-hander Eddie Lopat from the Chicago White Sox in 1948, and he, Reynolds, and Vic Raschi became a dominant pitching trio throughout most of Reynolds's remaining years in baseball.

Reynolds opened the 1948 season with five straight victories and finished with a 16-7 record for the third-place Yankees. He was 17-6 in 1949, as the Yankees edged Boston for the pennant on the last day of the season. In Game One of the World Series against the Dodgers, Yankees first baseman Tommy Henrich hit a ninth-inning home run off Don Newcombe to secure a 1–0, two-hit shutout for Reynolds. In Game Four, he came into the game in the sixth inning and retired all 10 batters he faced (including five strikeouts) to save Lopat's 6–4 win.

In the 1950 World Series, the Yankees swept the Philadelphia Phillies. The Game Two starters were Reynolds, who had a 16-12 record during the season, and 24-year-old future Hall-of-Famer Robin Roberts. The Yankees scored a run in the second and Reynolds yielded a single tally in the fifth. The score held up until the 10th when Joe DiMaggio homered against Roberts. Reynolds gave up a leadoff walk to start the bottom of the frame but then set down the Phils in order, winning 2–1. It was his third World Series victory without a loss

Going into the 1951 season, Reynolds was the Yankees' main pitching concern. Doctors had told him he had several bone chips floating in his elbow and an offseason operation might be needed, but Reynolds chose not to have the surgery. To combat the pain in his back and elbow, allergies, and a tired feeling that may have been pre-diabetes, he started eating a prescribed four oranges per game.

If the Yankees were concerned about Reynolds for the '51 campaign, they needn't have worried. The 34-year-old right-hander had one of his finest seasons, which included pitching two no-hitters. On the night of July 12, in Cleveland, he topped Bob Feller in a 1-0 squeaker. Yankees' center fielder Gene Woodling homered in the top of the seventh for the only score of the game. Reynolds ended it with a strikeout of second baseman Bobby Avila.

Going into the final weekend of the season, the Yankees led the Indians by 2 1/2 games. The Yankees had four games at home against arch-rival Boston including a Friday doubleheader. Reynolds faced 18-game-winner Mel Parnell in the opener and had an 8–0 lead with two outs in the top of the ninth inning. He had issued four walks but not a hit as he prepared to face Ted Williams. Williams hit a towering foul ball behind home plate that was muffed by catcher Yogi Berra. Reynolds threw a second fastball in the same spot, and Williams popped it up again. Berra caught it for the final out of the game, preserving the no-hitter. When Raschi won the nightcap, the Yankees clinched the pennant.

Reynolds became the first pitcher in the American League to pitch two no-hitters in a season. After the second one, Yankees broadcaster Mel Allen began calling him "Super Chief," a nickname that stuck.

Reynolds completed the 1951 regular season with a 17-8 record and a 3.05 ERA over 221 innings. He led the American League with seven shutouts and, showing his versatility, had seven (retroactive) saves. The Yankees met the New York Giants in the World Series. Riding the momentum of their amazing late-season surge capped by Bobby Thomson's storied home run off Ralph Branca, the Giants rolled over Reynolds and the Yankees in Game One, 5–1.

After the teams split Games Two and Three, Reynolds evened the Series by shutting down the Giants, 6-2, in Game Four. The Yankees took the last two games of the Series behind Lopat and Raschi to claim their third successive world championship. Reynolds won the Ray Hickok Award as the Professional Athlete of the Year. The award was an alligator skin, gold-buckled, diamond-studded belt, which Reynolds kept in bank storage for years because it was too expensive to insure.

The Yankees were confident they could win a fourth consecutive pennant in 1952, a feat accomplished only twice before. The team started slowly but finished two games ahead of the Indians. Reynolds had the only 20-victory season of his career at 20-8. He had a 2.05 ERA, six shutouts, and led the American League in strikeouts with 160. His second-place finish in the MVP voting was the highest of his career.

In the World Series, the Yankees and Dodgers squared off in Game One in Brooklyn. Reynolds pitched well but lost 4-2 to surprise starter Joe Black. Reynolds got revenge

against Black with a masterful 2-0 shutout in Game Four that evened the Series. The Dodgers won Game Five to go ahead three games to two. Reynolds relieved Raschi with two outs in the eighth inning of Game Six, and saved the Yankees' 3-2 victory. In Game Seven he relieved Lopat in the fourth inning. He gave up one run in three innings and was the winning pitcher in a 4-2 victory that gave the Yankees their fourth consecutive World Series championship.

Reynolds spent the winter in Oklahoma City building his oil business. As a prelude to spring training, he achieved a longtime ambition in mid-February by winning the National Baseball Players Golf Championship, beating Giants shortstop Alvin Dark, one-up, in Miami, Florida.

The Yankees won their 20th American League pennant in 1953. Reynolds, now primarily a reliever, had a record of 13-7 with 13 saves. The Yanks defeated the Dodgers in six games for their record fifth consecutive world championship. Reynolds was the winning pitcher in Game Six after relieving Whitey Ford in the eighth inning.

By winning his seventh World Series game, Reynolds tied a record held by Yankees pitcher Red Ruffing. It was his last World Series game. He went home to Oklahoma to trade his baseball glove for oilfield gloves. A successful winter in the oil business and an aging right arm combined to convince him that 1954 would be his last baseball season.

Reynolds continued to work as both a starter and a reliever in 1954. On September 23, he pitched his last major-league game, beating the Philadelphia Athletics at Yankee Stadium, 10-2. The Yankees closed the season with 103 victories, more than in any of their five previous seasons. But the Indians won 111 games for a new American League record. Reynolds finished with a 13-4 record and a .765 winning percentage, the best of his career. In his 13 major-league seasons he had started 434 regular-season games and relieved in 309.

At season's end, he had not made up his mind about retirement. He continued his representation of American League players in talks with baseball management on pension matters. In an interview on February 25, 1955, with sportswriter John Cronley of the *Daily Oklahoman*, Reynolds announced his retirement from baseball.

Living in Oklahoma and working in the oil business all of his retirement years, Reynolds became the sole owner and president of Atlas Mud Company. His active participation in Oklahoma civic and charitable causes was extensive. One of his favorite causes was the YMCA baseball program. In 1960 he headed a fund drive to build a new YMCA in his hometown of Bethany. On April 24, 1982, the new baseball stadium at his alma mater, now called Oklahoma State University, was dedicated in his honor.

On October 28, 1983, Allie's wife of 48 years, Earlene, died after a lengthy battle with cancer. On November 16, 1991, Allie was inducted into the Oklahoma Hall of Fame.

More than 1,200 people attended the black-tie event that was televised statewide.

Reynolds was a member of the Yankees All-Star team selected by former manager Casey Stengel. In 1989 he was honored with a plaque in Monument Park at Yankee Stadium.

Reynolds did everything he could to promote his Native American heritage. He served as president of the National Hall of Fame for Famous American Indians at Anadarko, Oklahoma. His last public appearance was on October 3, 1994, when he was in Anadarko for the dedication of a portrait in bronze of Kiowa Chief Stumbling Bear.

Suffering from lymphoma and diabetes, Reynolds entered Oklahoma City's St. Anthony Hospital in December 1994. He died on December 26, 1994, at the age of 77. He was buried at Oklahoma City's Memorial Park Cemetery after American Indian services celebrating his Creek heritage.

SOURCES

Bischoff, John Paul. *Mr. Iba: Basketball's Aggie Iron Duke* (Oklahoma City: Western Heritage Books, 1980).

Burke, Bob, Kenny A. Franks, and Royse Parr. *Glory Days of Summer: The History of Baseball in Oklahoma* (Oklahoma City: Oklahoma Heritage Association, 1999).

Bucek, Jeanine. *The Baseball Encyclopedia, 10th edition* (New York: MacMillan, 1996).

Golenbock, Peter. *Dynasty: The New York Yankees 1949-1964* (Englewood Cliffs, New Jersey: Prentice Hall, 1975).

Halberstam, David. *Summer of '49* (New York: William Morrow and Company, 1989).

Kahn, Roger. *The Head Game: Baseball Seen from the Pitchers Mound* (New York: Hartcourt, 2000).

Parr, Royse and Bob Burke. *Allie Reynolds: Super Chief* (Oklahoma City: Oklahoma Heritage Association, 2002).

Telephone conversation between Thomas Bourke and Allie Reynolds's daughter Bobbye Kay Ferguson on February 12, 2011.

http://www.okstate.com/trads/hall-of-honor.html

CHARLIE ROY

By Terry Bohn

As a star pitcher with the Carlisle (Pennsylvania) Indian School, Charlie Roy was favorably compared to a famous alumnus, and his fellow Ojibwe from Northern Minnesota, Charles "Chief" Bender. The right-hander attracted the attention of several major-league organizations and was the subject of a drawn-out contract dispute between two of those clubs. However, his big-league career consisted of only a few games with the 1906 Philadelphia Phillies. A deeply religious man, Roy said he would "never again sign a contract which required him to work on the Sabbath.[1] So after one more season in the minor leagues, and Roy, only 23 years old, quit baseball to become an evangelist among his American Indian people.

Robert Charles Roy was born on June 22, 1884, to Benjamin and Philomene Roy, the third of at least eight children.[2] In the 1900 Census, Benjamin listed his occupation as a steamboat laborer. Charles was born in the small town of Beaulieu, on the Ojibwe (Chippewa) White Earth Indian Reservation in north central Minnesota. Hall of Fame pitcher "Chief" Bender's birth date and birthplace are not certain but it is known that Bender's family moved to the White Earth Reservation when he was young and Roy and Bender were childhood friends.

Like many American Indian children at the time, Roy attended boarding schools while growing up. He first went to Flandreau, South Dakota, and later to the Morris Indian School in Minnesota, where he played on the school's baseball team. Because the school didn't have money to hire coaches, Charlie said, he learned to pitch from his older brother Louis, who was also a student at the school. (Later, in many of the independent and semipro games Charlie pitched in, Louis was his catcher.)

After graduating from the Morris school in 1904, Roy began study at the Carlisle Indian Industrial School in Pennsylvania. In addition to Bender (who was at Carlisle a couple of years before him), the school also produced professional players Frank Jude, Chief Johnson, and Jim Thorpe. Roy led the 1906 team in wins, but two game summaries suggest he may not yet have been ready for the major leagues. In April he dropped a 3-1 decision to the University of Virginia in Charlottesville and was beaten 8-1 by Georgetown University in Washington.

In addition to being the captain of the baseball team, Roy also played on the school's nationally prominent football team. In November of 1905, in the first-ever meeting between the two colleges, Carlisle defeated Army 6-5 with the 6-foot, 170-pound Roy listed in the lineup as a right tackle. Also, that fall, the football team traveled to Ohio to play the University of Cincinnati. While in town, Roy was approached by Garry Herrmann, owner of the Cincinnati Reds. They reached an agreement for Roy to pitch for Cincinnati the following season, but Charlie held off on signing a contract until he could get his parents' consent to play professional baseball.

Roy returned to Carlisle and then to his home at the White Earth Reservation during the semester break. That December Major William Allen Mercer, superintendent of the Carlisle school, said Roy "informed me that he does not intend pitching professional ball for at least two years."[3] However, the Reds continued to try to sign him, and at one point the frustrated Herrmann said, "I guess he'll lose as much or more as the Reds do. I'm tired of writing letters and getting no reply."[4]

In 1905 Charles "Togie" Pittinger won 23 games for the Philadelphia Phillies, or Quakers as they were sometimes called. He lived in Carlisle and that offseason worked out

(Courtesy of Find-A-Grave)

Charlie Roy

with and helped coach the school's baseball team to get in shape for spring training. After seeing Roy pitch, he recommended him to Hugh Duffy, his manager in Philadelphia, and Pittinger signed Roy for the Phillies organization in April 1906.[5] Roy was to join the Phillies at the completion of the Carlisle season.

For an inexperienced college pitcher, Roy was the subject of a great deal of hype. Pittinger and others touted him as being equal or superior to the great Chief Bender.[6] The Phillies were impressed with Roy's potential, but part of the reason for their interest was competition for fans with their crosstown rival, the Philadelphia Athletics of the American League, who had their own Indian pitcher (Bender). There was also interest from owner-manager Connie Mack of the Athletics and the Washington organization, but no serious effort was made by the Senators to sign him.

Although Roy had never actually signed a Cincinnati contract, Herrmann claimed that he and Roy had shaken hands and agreed on a salary during their meeting in Cincinnati. In May Herrmann filed a claim on Roy with the National Commission, arguing that based on that verbal agreement, Roy was the property of the Reds. Meanwhile, Roy and his Carlisle teammates had wrapped up their season and were guests of the Phillies for their May 31 game against New York. The next day he joined the Philadelphia club.

Roy made his major-league debut on June 27, 1906, pitching the final three innings of a 10-0 loss to the Brooklyn Superbas. A couple of weeks later, on July 10, a decision was reached on Roy's contract status. According to the July 14 *Sporting Life,* "In the matter of the appeal of the Cincinnati Club the Board of Directors of the National League for the services of Charles Roy claimed by the Philadelphia Club and now under contract to said Philadelphia Club, after a careful consideration of the evidence submitted, the Board is of the unanimous opinion, Mr. Dreyfuss of the Pittsburg club not voting, the Cincinnati club should be given to withdraw said appeal and that the contract of said Roy with the Philadelphia club be approved."

In one of Roy's pitching performances, an unusual play occurred in which the same man was called out twice on the same play. The Phillies were playing the Cubs in the second game of a doubleheader on August 3. Roy entered the game in the seventh inning and surrendered three hits to load the bases. After a foul out and a walk forcing in a run, Chicago shortstop Joe Tinker hit what looked to be a sure inning-ending double play ball to Philadelphia shortstop Mickey Doolin. Chicago's Harry Steinfeldt was forced out at second, but second baseman Kid Gleason threw wildly to first. Steinfeldt thought he was safe at second and kept running and was thrown out (again) on the relay home. When the umpires realized the mistake after the game, they took one of the Cubs' runs off the board, making it a 7-0 win, instead of 8-0.[7] In seven games with Philadelphia, one of them a start, Roy allowed 24 hits and 10 earned runs in 18 1/3

innings, striking out six and walking five. He was charged with one loss and had an earned-run average of 4.91. Roy also played part of one game at first base. That cameo was apparently enough for manager Hugh Duffy, who said, "Roy lacks the experience necessary to make him a success in the big league. He is still green, and until the greenness wears off, he will be of no value to a big league team."[8]

In August Roy was sent down to the Newark Sailors of the Eastern League and went 2-4 in 48 innings. He returned to Newark the next season but was released in June and signed by Wilmington of the Tri-State League. He finished the season with Steubenville in the Pennsylvania-Ohio-Maryland League. After the season Roy was drafted by Boston of the National League but refused to report. The *Washington Post* wrote that Roy "says he has had all the National League game he wanted."[9] He quit Organized Baseball and became an evangelist. In his regard he was following the footsteps of another former ballplayer who had become an evangelist, Billy Sunday.

Roy made no secret of the fact that he had played ball only to earn money to further his religious studies. When his pitching interfered with his objection to playing on Sunday, he quit baseball. Roy said, "I consider it no more of a sin for a ball player to play ball on the Sabbath than I do for an engineer to run a train on that day. It is a case of work for the ball player, as well as an engineer, both making their livelihoods in a legitimate way, but in different channels. For me personally, I prefer to cut out Sunday playing altogether."[10]

Baseball-reference and other sources show no other appearances in Organized Baseball, but over the next few years Roy continued to pitch near his home in Minnesota. In 1908 he pitched at least one game for Brandon, Manitoba, in the Northern League and in 1909 he pitched for an independent team in Fosston, Minnesota. In 1910 Roy played briefly Red Wing, Minnesota, in the Minnesota-Wisconsin League. He also pitched at least one game for a semipro team in Grand Forks, North Dakota. In 1912 he was with an independent team in Bemidji, Minnesota. In early 1913 it was reported that Roy would be signed by a team in Valley City, North Dakota, but no evidence could be found that he ever played there.

Roy's whereabouts over the next several years are unclear. It is not known if he served on active duty during World War I, but his draft card from September 1918 listed him as being employed with the US Indian Service on the White Earth Reservation in Becker, Minnesota. He was also still apparently single, as he listed his father, Benjamin, as his nearest relative.

By 1919 Roy was living in Bismarck, North Dakota, and working as a teacher at the Indian school in that city. He also pitched for the town's semipro team in 1920. In August of 1920 he married Mattie Johnson, an Indian who was a native of Idaho, and a fellow teacher at the Indian school. A brief wedding announcement in the *Bismarck Tribune* said Roy was an "accomplished instructor" and "a former ballplayer of note." The couple had three children, a daughter Philomene, born in 1922, and two sons, Robert, born in 1923, and Matthew a year later.

The Indian Service then sent Roy to the Flandreau Indian School in South Dakota, where he had been a student as a teenager. There he was placed in charge of the dairy operation, the trade he learned at Carlisle. In 1927 he was transferred to the Fort Hall agency in Idaho on an evangelical Christian mission and worked with the school's dairy herd. His last stop with the Indian Service was Fort Washakie, Wyoming, where he worked for three years.

Roy's wife, Mattie, died in 1927; the 1930 Census shows him as a widower with his three children living with him in Idaho. Around 1932 he took his family back to Minnesota but three years later returned to Fort Hall, Idaho, where he operated his own farm the rest of his life. Roy died of a heart attack in Blackfoot, Idaho, on February 10, 1950, at the age of 65.

A funeral service was held at the Howard Jackman mortuary chapel in Blackfoot under the direction of the Church of Jesus Christ of Latter-day Saints. Roy was buried in the Gibson Mission Cemetery. He was survived by his daughter, Philomene, and son, Robert, both of Blackfoot, and three grandchildren.

SOURCES

In addition to the sources cited in the Notes, the author consulted Ancestry. com, Baseball-reference.com, Laliberte, David J. "Winning Indians and Other Contradictions: The Morris Indian School Baseball Team, 1898-1908," in *NINE: a Journal of Baseball History and Culture,* 18 (2), 29-64, and Powers-Beck, Jeffrey. "The American Indian Integration of Baseball 1897-1945," in *American Indian Quarterly,* Volume 25, Number 4 (Autumn, 2001), University of Nebraska Press, 508-538.

NOTES

1   Jeffrey Powers-Beck, *The American Indian Integration of Baseball* (Lincoln: University of Nebraska Press, 2004), 190.

2   Roy's mother's name, and that of his daughter, who was named after her mother, were spelled many ways in census rolls and other historical documents. The most common spelling was Philomene.

3   "Redskin Twirler Charles Roy Is Lost To The Reds," *Cincinnati Post*, December 23, 1905: 6.

4   "Efforts to Get Indian Twirler Given Up," *Cincinnati Post*, February 12, 1906: 6.

5   At the time it was not uncommon for players to be given authority to sign new players for their teams.

6   "Charles Roy, Captain of Carlisle Indians, to Play with the Phillies," *Boston Herald*, April 2, 1906: 11.

7   "Spuds Take Two, Both Shutouts," *Chicago Tribune*, August 4, 1906: 10.

8   "Pitcher Roy Green Indian," *Pittsburgh Press,* June 9, 1906: 12.

9   "Baseball Briefs," *Washington Post*, September 7, 1907: 8.

10 "Follows Sunday," *Sporting Life*, August 10, 1907: 21.

LOUIS SOCKALEXIS

By David L. Fleitz

Louis Sockalexis, a member of the Penobscot Indian tribe of Maine, played in only 94 major-league games, but is remembered today as the first Native American, and first recognized minority, to perform in the National League.[1] He was signed by the Cleveland Spiders in 1897, 50 years before Jackie Robinson broke baseball's color barrier with the Brooklyn Dodgers. Sockalexis, like Robinson a multi-talented athlete who excelled in football and track as well as baseball, appeared destined for stardom, but alcoholism derailed his promising career. He is, however, at least indirectly responsible for the nickname "Indians" as formerly applied to the present American League team in Cleveland.

Louis Francis Sockalexis was born on the Penobscot reservation on Indian Island, near Old Town, Maine, on October 24, 1871. He was the son of Francis Sockalexis, a logger who later served as governor (formerly called "chief") of the Penobscot, and the former Frances Sockbeson. The Penobscot valued athletic prowess, and Francis Sockalexis was a fine athlete. But Louis, who grew

Louis Sockalexis

to be nearly 6-feet tall with straight black hair and a muscular build, became the best athlete in the tribe. As a teenager, Louis won footraces and throwing contests against all challengers, and his natural baseball ability led him to play semipro ball for various teams in Maine during his late teens and early 20s.

In 1894, after playing college ball at Ricker Classical Institute in Maine, Louis spent the summer at a popular resort, patrolling the outfield for a baseball nine sponsored by the Poland Spring Hotel. One of his teammates was Mike "Doc" Powers, a future major leaguer who, at the time, was the captain of the baseball team at the College of the Holy Cross in Worcester, Massachusetts. Powers was impressed with Sockalexis's talent, and persuaded Louis, a Catholic, to enroll at the Jesuit-run institution. This he did in the fall of that year.

Louis excelled on the diamond at Holy Cross, batting .436 in 1895 and .444 in 1896, and also starred as a running back on the school's first football team, in the fall of 1896. He ran track, specializing in the medium and long distances and reportedly winning five events in a single meet. However, it was as a baseball player that he shone most brightly. In 1895 an incredible throw he made against Harvard one day from deep center field to the plate was measured by a group of professors at 414 feet, an unofficial national record at the time. A few weeks later, he belted two home runs and stole six bases against Brown University. Legend has it that one of Sockalexis's homers shattered a fourth-floor window in a dormitory behind the right-field fence.

Sockalexis may have been the best college player in the country, and began to draw interest from National League clubs. The Cleveland Spiders had the inside track, as two members of that team, outfielder Jesse Burkett and infielder James "Chippy" McGarr, coached for Holy Cross during the spring months. Louis took hitting tips from Burkett, the two-time league batting champion, and looked forward to the day when he would compete at baseball's highest level.

In December 1896, Sockalexis and Mike Powers left Holy Cross and enrolled at Notre Dame University in South Bend, Indiana. Burkett and McGarr had recommended that the Cleveland team sign both Sockalexis and Powers, so in early 1897 Patsy Tebeau, manager of the Spiders, traveled to Indiana to acquire the two players. Powers turned Tebeau down, but on March 9, 1897, Tebeau signed Sockalexis to a contract. He agreed to report to the Cleveland club at the conclusion of the college season.

Sockalexis stayed at Notre Dame for only a few months, and never played baseball for the school. In March of 1897, he and another student were expelled from the college after a drunken disturbance at a local tavern. He then boarded an eastbound train and showed up, unannounced, at the Spiders' spring practice at an indoor gymnasium in Cleveland on March 19, 1897. Tebeau, who was surprised to see Sockalexis so soon, was impressed with the Native American ballplayer, and the local sportswriters were so enamored of the exotic newcomer that a headline in the *Cleveland Plain Dealer* on March 20 referred to the team as "Tebeau's Indians." By the end of the month, the Spiders' moniker was virtually forgotten, and the Cleveland club became the Indians. A few days later, the *Cleveland Leader* stated, "With four first-class outfielders, five infielders, eight pitchers, and four catchers, the 'Indians' of 1897 would seem as well equipped to start out for a pennant as any team in the League."[2]

The 25-year-old Sockalexis (who told the club that he was 23) arrived at practice in top condition. Despite his muscular build, he easily defeated all his new teammates in footraces. Tebeau organized handball contests to keep his players active, and Sockalexis had no trouble winning all his matches. He also displayed his talent at gymnastics. "Sockalexis, who is quite a gymnast, occasionally breaks out with some caper that would tear the ordinary man in two," reported the *Plain Dealer*. "Those things are all right in a circus, Louie," said Tebeau, "but you don't need 'em to win ball games."[3] In *Sporting Life*, former New York Giants manager John Ward, who saw the Penobscot star perform at Holy Cross, declared, "I have seen [Sockalexis] play perhaps a dozen games, and I unhesitatingly pronounce him a wonder. Why he has not been snapped up before by some League club looking for a sensational player is beyond my comprehension."[4]

The Spiders played their first intrasquad game on April 2. Tebeau divided the team into the "Indians" and the "Papooses," and Sockalexis, batting cleanup for the Indians, drilled three hits, scored three runs, and threw a runner out at the plate from deep right field. He kept up his fine hitting and outfield play, making a strong challenge for the starting right-field spot for the newly christened Indians. The national press began to notice Sockalexis, as Charles W. Mears explained in *The Sporting News*:

"Everybody in Cleveland as well as in other league cities, for that matter, are talking Sockalexis, and if the young Indian isn't the best advertised new man that ever entered the big organization then it will not be the fault of the baseball paragraphers of the press. They have discovered a novelty in it. The newspaper talk concerning the youngster has stirred up great local interest in the Red Man, and of all the young players on the Cleveland Club's list he is the most talked of, and it will be his appearance that will

Louis Sockalexis, the first Native American, and first recognized minority, to perform in the National League

draw the greatest number of curious people at the opening of the season."[5]

The newly named Indians knew that the Native American would draw plenty of attention, but they also saw Sockalexis as the answer to their long-standing problem in right field. The team had finished in second place in the National League in both 1895 and 1896, and many believed that it needed one more strong bat to finally win a pennant. The incumbent right fielder, Harry Blake, was an outstanding fielder but a weak hitter, and Tebeau gave Sockalexis every chance to supplant Blake in Cleveland's lineup.

Louis Sockalexis went hitless in his major-league debut, a 3-1 loss to the Colonels in Louisville, but singled twice and drove in two runs two days later in a 9-4 loss. The Indians then traveled to Cincinnati, where he belted two singles and a double as the fans cheered the newcomer with war whoops. The Cleveland club lost its first five games of 1897, but Sockalexis looked like a future star. The Indians finally broke into the win column on April 30, when he smashed a homer, the first of his career, against the Browns in St. Louis. Some of the fans claimed that the four-bagger, a high fly ball that easily cleared the right-field fence, was the longest they had ever seen in the city. On May 1, in another win against the Browns, he hit three singles and broke up the game with a bases-loaded triple in the ninth. He also thrilled the fans with long, running catches and powerful throws from the outfield.

Sockalexis lived up to his billing during the early months of the 1897 campaign. He hit his second home run, another long shot over the right field fence, against the Reds on May 5. After 20 games, his batting average stood at .372, and his presence in the lineup increased attendance both at Cleveland's League Park and on the road. He was a sensation, though many fans bought tickets to jeer at the first Native American ballplayer in major-league history. "Columns of silly poetry are written about him, [and] hideous looking cartoons adorn the sporting pages of nearly every paper," commented Elmer Bates in *Sporting Life*. "He is hooted and bawled at by the thimble-brained brigade on the bleachers. Despite all this handicap the red man has played good, steady ball, and has been a factor in nearly every victory thus far won by Tebeau's team."[6]

On May 13 Sockalexis belted a double and a triple off Boston's best pitcher, 30-game winner Kid Nichols, but the Indians lost the game by a 4-1 score. Sockalexis had trouble hitting curveballs from left-handers, and sometimes found it difficult to judge balls hit directly at him in right field. He also showed poor command of the strike zone and swung at balls in the dirt or above his head. But Patsy Tebeau expressed confidence that the rookie would correct his faults and become a more complete ballplayer. "He is a sensible fellow and sees his weakness, which is a good trait in a young player," said the manager.[7]

Perhaps the high point of Sockalexis's season, and of his career, came at the Polo Grounds on June 16, when he faced New York's strikeout champion Amos Rusie in the first contest of a four-game series. While more than 4,500 fans hooted and made Indian war cries at the Cleveland rookie, Sockalexis stepped into the box against Rusie in the first inning. He swung and missed at a Rusie fastball, spinning himself around, and before Sockalexis could get set, Rusie let fly with another fastball. Sockalexis made a "wild stab" at it, according to the next day's report in the *New York World*, and sent a liner to the outfield that split the gap in right-center field and rolled to the wall. By the time right fielder Mike Tiernan could retrieve the ball, Sockalexis had sped around the bases for a home run, his third of the season. He struck out in his next appearance, and misplayed a line drive hit by Tiernan for a three-base error later in the game, but Cleveland coasted to a 7-2 victory.

However, Sockalexis brought a drinking problem with him to the major leagues, and on July 3, disaster struck. He went out on the town in Cleveland that Saturday evening, and drank what onlookers recalled as a prodigious amount of alcohol. Sometime during the wee hours, Sockalexis either jumped or fell out of a second-story window, severely spraining his ankle. He managed to hide the injury from his manager and teammates on Sunday, an offday for the Indians, but when he showed up at the ballpark in Pittsburgh for a doubleheader on Monday, July 5, he was limping noticeably. Patsy Tebeau pulled him from the lineup and sent him back to Cleveland to have his injury treated.

A physician put his ankle in a cast and ordered him to bed, but Sockalexis reportedly spent the next several evenings in the local bars while his teammates carried on in Pittsburgh.

Sockalexis returned to the lineup on July 8, and although he was still limping, he hit well for the next few days. He suffered an embarrassing relapse four days later, when the league-leading Boston Beaneaters came to League Park. Sockalexis dropped a fly ball in the first inning, then let Fred Tenney's grounder get through his legs for a three-base error in the fifth. Two batters later, Jimmy Collins swatted a liner to right that Sockalexis did not appear to notice right away. It went for an inside-the-park home run, and the fuming Tebeau yanked the rookie from the game. Sockalexis was most likely intoxicated on the field, and his alcohol problem was now public knowledge, in Cleveland and around the league.

Sockalexis was losing his battle with alcoholism, and on July 29, when the Indians departed on a Western trip, he did not accompany them. He had been suspended without pay by team owner Frank Robison. "I think I can truthfully say," the owner told *The Sporting News*, "that I have done everything I could for Sockalexis, and he has repaid me, and the Cleveland club, by the basest ingratitude. I have waited as long as I could, and have given him every chance to do what is right, and only punished him when I felt that I must do so in justice to myself and the rest of the club."[8] Sockalexis expressed remorse for his actions, and although Tebeau left him behind on another road trip in late August, the rookie appeared to be sincere in changing his behavior. He played little in August and September, however, and ended his rookie season with a .338 average and 16 stolen bases in 66 games.

Though Sockalexis was arrested for public intoxication in September while his teammates were on the road, and spent a night in jail, Tebeau was not yet ready to give up on the talented athlete. He had played well, sometimes sensationally, when sober, and might yet prove to be a valuable player. Also, the Cleveland team suffered from poor fan support during the 1890s, finishing either last or next to last in the National League in attendance during each of the previous four years despite a string of winning seasons. A healthy and focused Sockalexis might still become the drawing card that the team needed.

Sockalexis told the papers that he kept out of trouble all winter. But in March of 1898, when Tebeau's team gathered in Cleveland for the journey to spring training in Hot Springs, Arkansas, Sockalexis fell off the wagon again. He missed the train to Hot Springs, much to Tebeau's disgust. "It's a pity [Sockalexis] doesn't keep straight," sighed Tebeau to the writers on the train. "If I can keep him in line this year he will strengthen us to a great degree. However, it looks as though Blake would start the season covering right field."[9]

The troubled outfielder arrived at Hot Springs two days later and immediately went in for a one-on-one talk with his disappointed manager. Sockalexis, to his credit, was honest about his behavior. "I did it again, Cap," he said sadly. "A crowd got hold of me and before I knew it they had loaded me. I had not taken a drop in so long that I did not know my capacity, and before I knew it they had me. I am through for good now. My friends in Cleveland are my worst enemies, I fear, even though they don't mean to be. After this I will defy anybody to get me started."[10]

Sockalexis had promised to stay out of trouble several times before, but with the right-field situation unsettled, Tebeau elected to believe him, at least for the moment. However, the *Plain Dealer* commented, "it is a known fact that the club will stand no more foolishness from Sockalexis. One more slip and he will be suspended, just as sure as there is a rule to provide for such suspension. … [T]here are too many good outfielders to put the club in any seriously embarrassing position by the suspension of one, and the rest are all conscientious workers."[11]

Although Sockalexis appeared to stay sober thereafter, he hit poorly in spring training and lost his starting position in right field to Harry Blake. He spent most of the season on the bench, appearing in only 21 games and batting .224. He played right field in a July 4 doubleheader in Chicago when Blake was called away by a family emergency, but Sockalexis hit only two singles in the two games. Worse, the Chicago fans entertained themselves by making derisive war whoops and yells, and by throwing firecrackers at him in the outfield. At times during the second game, Sockalexis could barely see the infield because of the cloud of blue smoke at his feet. He played the next two games and went hitless, and took to the bench again when Blake returned.

In August Tebeau sent Sockalexis to Mansfield of the Interstate League, though it appears he played in only one game there before returning to Cleveland. The Cleveland club, now known again as the Spiders with the decline of Sockalexis, played 39 of its last 42 games on the road, shifting many of its home games to other cities due to poor attendance at League Park. Because Tebeau did not trust his troublesome outfielder, he left him behind during the team's extended road trip in September and October.

Sockalexis spent the winter of 1898-99 in Cleveland, though he returned to Maine when his mother, Frances, died in February of 1899. But Sockalexis did not take care of himself during the offseason, and perhaps his mother's death sent him off the deep end once again. He surfaced in Cleveland in early March, but was so overweight and out of shape that Tebeau refused to take him to the training camp in Hot Springs.

At the same time, weak fan support and boardroom turmoil among the National League club owners threatened the future of baseball in Cleveland. Frank Robison was tired of losing money in Cleveland, so in early 1899 he bought the St. Louis Browns and transferred all the Spiders stars (including Tebeau, Cy Young, Bobby Wallace, Jesse Burkett, and more) to the Mound City. Robison now owned

franchises in both St. Louis and Cleveland, and rather than fold the Spiders, he decided to operate the Cleveland club on a shoestring. Tebeau had finally given up on Sockalexis, who was not invited to join the exodus to St. Louis. Instead, he remained in Cleveland with what historian Lee Allen called "the sorriest shell of a team ever seen in the major leagues,"[12] on a roster filled with rejects, prospects, and semipro players.

The 1899 edition of the Spiders proved to be the last chance for Louis Sockalexis. He told the local newspapers that he was sober and ready to play, but his appearance proved otherwise. Sockalexis, once so athletic and muscular, now weighed over 200 pounds and was "big as an alderman," in the words of teammate Dick Harley. Said the 38-year-old catcher Chief Zimmer, "I can give him twenty yards and beat him in a hundred. … You would not know the big Indian if you saw him now."[13]

The new manager of the talent-poor Spiders, third baseman Lave Cross, nonetheless put Sockalexis on the roster and hoped for the best, though he left Sockalexis at home in Cleveland during the team's season-opening road trip to St. Louis, Louisville, and Cincinnati. Not until May 1, during the second game of a doubleheader against Louisville at Cleveland's League Park, did Sockalexis make an appearance. He struck out in a pinch-hitting assignment.

He made his first start in right field on May 9 and managed a single against Cy Young in an 8-1 loss to St. Louis, but the next day Sockalexis appeared to be daydreaming on the field. Standing on third base, he got such a slow start on a clean single to the outfield that he was thrown out at home. He also allowed several fly balls to fall safely for hits, though he was charged with no errors. Although the *Plain Dealer* reported that "the big Indian seems to have come to his senses at last, and is doing his best to get back to his old-time form,"[14] it was obvious that Sockalexis was in no condition to play.

His last hurrah came on May 11. He belted five hits – four doubles and a single – against St. Louis and made an incredible throw from the outfield to retire a runner at third. But he also dropped two easy flies in right and was thrown out by a wide margin in a botched double steal. Two days later in Pittsburgh, Sockalexis went hitless and fell down twice in the outfield while fielding groundballs. Despite his claims to the contrary, it appeared that he was drunk on the field. A few days later, Sockalexis got into a drunken dispute at a theater in downtown Cleveland and spent the night in jail. The Spiders released him the next day, and his major-league career was over. He was dismissed after only seven games with the worst team in baseball history, as the hapless Spiders won only 20 of their 154 games in 1899.

Billy Barnie, manager of the Hartford club of the Eastern League, quickly signed the Penobscot as a gate attraction, but Sockalexis did not last long. He was overweight and painfully slow both on the bases and in the field, and most of his hits were weak singles. He batted only .198 in 24 games and drew his release after dropping an easy fly ball to lose a game. He then played for Waterbury and Bristol in the Connecticut State League. On this much lower level of competition, Sockalexis found his footing, batting .320 in 61 games and apparently keeping his drinking under control.

However, although the Waterbury club was interested in retaining him for the following season, Sockalexis was nowhere to be found when the spring of 1900 rolled around. A series of news reports during the next two years detailed several arrests for public drunkenness and disturbances, and it appears that the former baseball star was reduced to homelessness and vagrancy. He spent several short terms in jail during this period, and remained out of the game until 1902, when he signed with Lowell of the New England League. Now 30 years old, Sockalexis hit for a credible .288 average, though he still had problems in the field. He committed 29 errors that season, and his fielding percentage of .800 was one of the worst in all of organized ball. Nevertheless, he lasted the entire season for Lowell, and it appeared that his drinking days were finally behind him. He didn't return to Lowell for 1903, preferring to stay closer to his home in Maine, but at least he cemented a moderately successful return to the professional ranks.

Louis Sockalexis wound up back on the Penobscot reservation in Maine, and except for a stint with Bangor in the Maine State League in 1907, he never again played professional ball. He played for local town teams, served as an umpire for semipro games, and taught the game to young tribesmen. He piloted a ferryboat between Indian Island, home of the reservation, and the mainland, and enjoyed reading copies of *The Sporting News* and other papers that his passengers left behind. Although he had apparently stopped drinking to excess, he was not healthy, and caught colds and fevers easily. He also suffered from attacks of rheumatism, and appeared much older than his years.

In the fall of 1913, Sockalexis joined a logging crew that harvested trees deep in the Maine woods. While cutting down a massive pine tree on December 24 of that year, he suffered a heart attack and died at the age of 42. He was buried in the cemetery on the Penobscot reservation.

Ed McKean, the longtime Cleveland shortstop, paid tribute to his former teammate in an interview with the *Cleveland Leader*. "He was a wild bird," said McKean. "He couldn't lose his taste for firewater. His periodical departures became such a habit [that] he finally slipped out of the majors. He had more natural ability than any player I have ever seen, past or present."[15]

Cleveland's American League team (which began play in 1900) had been called the Naps in honor of playing manager Napoleon Lajoie, but when Lajoie left the team after the 1914 season, a new nickname was in order. In January 1915, team owner Charles Somers, after consulting with several local sportswriters, decided to revive the name that had defined the city's National League club 18 years before. Somers, perhaps recalling the all-too-brief period of

excitement that Louis Sockalexis had brought to Cleveland in 1897, dubbed his team the Indians, a name that remained for 107 years.

Though his career was short, Louis Sockalexis is remembered today while other great players of the 1890s are long forgotten. Sockalexis, directly or indirectly, inspired the nickname of the Cleveland baseball team. His athletic feats have been honored by many different organizations. The great Penobscot athlete was elected to the Holy Cross Athletic Hall of Fame in 1956, the Maine Baseball Hall of Fame in 1969, and the Maine Sports Hall of Fame in 1985. In April 2000 he was inducted into the American Indian Athletic Hall of Fame. In 2025, Holy Cross officially retired a baseball jersey in Sockalexis' honor.

In addition, research by Ed Rice, a Maine journalist who has spoken and written extensively on Sockalexis, shows that the ballplayer may well have been the model for "Frank Merriwell at Yale," the fictional baseball hero created by Gilbert Patten. Patten was a Maine resident and saw Sockalexis play in townball competition during 1894.[16]

He is not eligible for induction into the National Baseball Hall of Fame in Cooperstown, New York, because he played in the National League for only three seasons, and Hall of Fame candidates are required to have played in all or part of 10 major-league campaigns. Had he managed to stay away from alcohol, Louis Sockalexis might well have joined his Cleveland teammates Cy Young, Bobby Wallace, and Jesse Burkett in Cooperstown. Nonetheless, he has earned his place in baseball history. He is remembered not only as the original Cleveland Indian and as the first recognized Native American to play in the major leagues, but also as one of the greatest "might-have-beens" in the annals of the game.

SOURCES

In addition to the sources cited in the Notes, the author drew on two books:

Fleitz, David L. *Louis Sockalexis: The First Cleveland Indian* (Jefferson, North Carolina: McFarland, 2002).

Phillips, John. *Chief Sockalexis and the 1897 Cleveland Indians* (Cabin John, Maryland: Capital Publishing, 1991).

Also see:

Brian McDonald, *Indian Summer: The Tragic Story of Louis Francis Sockalexis, the First Native American in Major League Baseball* (Rodale Books, 2003)

Ed Rice, *Baseball's First Indian: The Story of Penobscot Legend Louis Sockalexis* (Down East Books, 2019)

Bill Wise, *Louis Sockalexis: Native American Baseball Pioneer* (Lee and Low Books, 2005), a children's book

NOTES

1   Several players with partial Native American ancestry had previously played in the National League, but Sockalexis was the first full-fledged member of a tribe, and the first recognized minority, to do so. The Penobscot Indian Nation lists Sockalexis in its records as a "100%" Native American.

2   "Like a Sphinx," *Cleveland Leader*, March 23, 1897: 3.

3   "At the 'Gym,'" *Cleveland Plain Dealer*, March 26, 1897: 3.

4   Elmer Bates, "Cleveland Chatter," *Sporting Life*, March 27, 1897: 3.

5   Charles W. Mears, "Good Drawing Card," *The Sporting News*, April 24, 1897: 3.

6   Elmer Bates, "Cleveland Chatter," *Sporting Life*, May 15, 1897: 5.

7   "Baseball Notes," *Washington Post*, June 9, 1897: 8.

8   "Fined and Suspended," *The Sporting News*, August 7, 1897: 6.

9   "Going South," *The Sporting News*, March 12, 1898: 4.

10 "Home Training," *Cleveland Plain Dealer*, March 14, 1898: 6.

11 "Hot Work," *Cleveland Plain Dealer*, March 11, 1898: 6.

12 Lee Allen, *The National League Story* (New York: Hill and Wang, 1961), 79.

13 "Caught on the Fly," *The Sporting News*, May 27, 1899: 5.

14 "A Warm Welcome," *Cleveland Plain Dealer*, May 10, 1899: 6.

15 Bob Dolgan, "Sockalexis a Tragic Figure," *Cleveland Plain Dealer*, April 24, 2000: 1D.

16 Email from Ed Rice to Bill Nowlin, July 9, 2025.

JIM THORPE

By Don Jensen

Jim Thorpe was the most outstanding all-around athlete of the Deadball Era. In addition to playing major-league baseball for six seasons, the 6-foot-1, 185-pound Thorpe was an Olympic champion in the pentathlon and decathlon and at one point was considered the greatest American football player in history, according to a 1977 *Sport* magazine poll. One sportswriter called Thorpe the "most marvelous creation fashioned in human likeness that has ever inhabited the earth," [1] but others – reflecting the ugly stereotypes about Native Americans a century ago – described him as simple-minded, lazy, averse to training, and unable to hold his liquor. Thorpe's disappointing baseball career – he played in 289 National League games and hit only .252 with 7 home runs and 29 stolen bases – demonstrated what multisport athletes like Michael Jordan have since discovered: that mere possession of superb natural tools doesn't guarantee success on the diamond. "I can't seem to hit curves," Jim admitted. "I believe I could hit .300 otherwise." [2]

Jim Thorpe, with the 1913 New York Giants

(George Grantham Bain Collection, Library of Congress)

Great-great-great-grandson of the famed Sauk warrior Black Hawk, James Francis Thorpe was born on May 28, 1887, on the Sac and Fox Reservation near Prague, in the Indian Territory (today's Oklahoma). His father, Hiram, was a blacksmith who married at least five Native American women and fathered more than 20 children. Because of his early athletic prowess, Jim received the Indian name Watho-huck ("Path Lit by Lightning") from his mother, Charlotte. He became a disciplinary problem after his twin brother, Charles, died at age 9. Jim's truancy finally angered his father so much that he sent the teenager to the Carlisle Indian School in Pennsylvania in 1904. Carlisle was a vocational institution operated by the federal government to teach Indians industrial skills and integrate them into society. According to one of its former athletes, "nothing but an eighth-grade school, but they called us a college." [3]

In the fall of 1907, legendary Carlisle coach Glenn "Pop" Warner persuaded Thorpe to try out for the football team. Jim excelled as a halfback, punter, and kicker, but in 1909 he withdrew from Carlisle (one of several times he left the institution) and worked on a farm in North Carolina. During the summers of 1910-11, he accepted $60 a month to play baseball for Rocky Mount and Fayetteville of the Eastern Carolina League. Encouraged by Warner – and with an eye toward the 1912 Olympics – Thorpe returned to Carlisle in 1911-12. He was sensational on the gridiron against major collegiate foes, and Walter Camp selected him for the All-America football team in both years. In a 27-6 road win in 1912 against a heralded Army team, Thorpe said later that "there wasn't a boy on that Indian team who didn't carry the scars of family feud with the Long Knives. … We beat [Army] hands down, and that night we felt we had done something for our fathers." [4]

With his triumphs at the Stockholm Olympics in 1912, Jim Thorpe's fame spread worldwide. "Sir, you are the greatest athlete in the world," declared Sweden's King Gustav. [5] After the Games, however, Thorpe was forced to return his medals and trophies when the Amateur Athletic Union discovered that he had played minor-league baseball. It was a crushing blow that Jim never overcame. "I did not play for money," he wrote in a letter to the AAU president. "I was not very wise in the ways of the world and did not realize this was wrong. I hope I will be partly excused by the fact that I was simply an Indian School Boy and did not know that I was doing wrong because I was doing what many other college men had done, except they did not use their own names."[6]

Stripped of his amateur status, Thorpe signed a three-year contract in February 1913 for the then-staggering sum of $6,000 per season to play baseball for the New York Giants, who beat out five other clubs in signing the "red-skinned marvel."[7] It was the most money ever paid to a major-league rookie. The agreement included a $500 signing bonus, and Pop Warner received $2,500 for steering Jim to the Giants. "There can be no denying that he is a great prospect," wrote one observer, "and many critics would not be surprised if, under [John] McGraw's careful tutelage, he developed into another Ty Cobb."[8] At the signing ceremony, however, the Giants manager admitted that he had never seen Thorpe in action; he didn't know what position he played or even whether he hit right- or left-handed. (Thorpe was right-handed.)

At the Giants' spring training in Marlin Springs, Texas, Thorpe got off to a rocky start by showing up late for an exhibition game. He received playing time at first base and the outfield, and it soon became evident that he had difficulty with breaking pitches. During the 1913 season, Thorpe was used primarily as a pinch-hitter and pinch-runner, compiling only 35 at-bats in 19 games and hitting .143 with two stolen bases. "I felt like a sitting hen, not a ballplayer," he said.[9] It wasn't a happy time. His roommate, Chief Meyers, remembered a night when Jim came in late and woke him up. "He was crying, and tears were rolling down his cheeks," Meyers recalled. "'You know, Chief,' he said, 'the King of Sweden gave me those trophies. He gave them to me. But they took them away from me, even though the guy who finished second refused to take them.'"[10]

On the 1913-14 World Tour, Thorpe brought along his first wife (he eventually had three), but McGraw viewed his behavior as inappropriate for a married man and lectured him on the dangers of drinking and playing cards. Thorpe spent most of 1915 in the International League, hitting a combined .303 with 22 steals for Harrisburg and Jersey City. While with the latter club, he was sued for his involvement in a saloon brawl. Harrisburg "released him because he had a 'disturbing influence on the team.'"[11]

In 1914 Thorpe appeared in 30 games for the Giants, batting .194. In 1915 he only got into 17 Giants games but hit slightly better – .231. Over his first three seasons, his major-league stats saw him produce only five RBIs in 66 games and 122 plate appearances.

Thorpe was back in Milwaukee in 1916. In the press, McGraw insisted that although Jim was still raw, he was a fast learner with excellent instincts and would eventually become a star. Privately, however, the Giants manager was beginning to have his doubts.

After Thorpe played in four mid-April games at the start of the 1917 season, McGraw loaned him to the Cincinnati Reds, then managed by Christy Mathewson. "Jim would take only two strides to my three," said teammate Edd

Roush. "I'd run just as hard as I could, and he'd keep up with me just trotting along."[12] Thorpe's last day with the Reds was August 18 and he returned to the Giants. He appeared in 23 more games for McGraw's club and in the only big-league season in which he played in over 100 games, he had a composite batting average of .237.

The Giants won the pennant. But Thorpe's only postseason appearance was an odd one. He was in the starting lineup for Game Five of the 1917 World Series, played at Chicago's Comiskey Park on October 13. He was to bat sixth in the order against southpaw Reb Russell. The Giants scored one run in the top of the first inning and had base-runners on first and second with two outs. McGraw wanted another run home and had the left-handed-hitting Dave Robertson pinch-hit for Thorpe against right-handed White Sox reliever Eddie Cicotte. Robertson singled the second tally home and replaced Thorpe in right field. Thus, Thorpe had not played a moment in the game. Ring Lardner wrote, "Jim stayed in the batting order until it was his turn to bat. Then he put his ugly brown sweater back on and resumed his habitual seat in the wigwam."[13]

In 1918 Thorpe appeared in only 58 games all year, batting .248 with 11 RBIs. The following season, he had appeared in just two as of May 2. After Jim complained about his lack of playing time, the Giants traded him to the Boston

Jim Thorpe, 1917 Cincinnati Reds

Braves for washed-up pitcher Pat Ragan. Thorpe hit .327 in 60 games for the Braves, by far his best major-league performance, but 1919 proved to be his last season in the majors. In each of his six seasons in the major leagues, his batting average improved over that of the prior year.

Thorpe played in 289 major-league games, with a career batting average of .252. He did not draw that many bases on balls (27); his career on-base percentage was .286. He struck out 122 times in 698 at-bats. Thorpe homered seven times, four while on loan to the Reds, and drove in 82 runs while scoring 91. As a fielder, he primarily played left field (89 games), right field (72), and center (38), with two games (13 innings total) at first base. His career fielding percentage was .951.

Over the next three years, Jim Thorpe played baseball for several minor-league clubs, putting up respectable statistics but focusing most of his energies on professional football, which he had been playing during the offseason since he founded the famous Canton Bulldogs in 1915, excelling at running back, kicker, and punter. In 1931 he was selected to the NFL's first all-decade team.

Thorpe had trouble adjusting to life after his career in professional sports. In 1928 he was playing semipro baseball at his home reservation in Oklahoma when he unsuccessfully sought a job with Waterbury of the Eastern League. Two years later, he traveled to Southern California as master of ceremonies for C.C. Pyle's cross-country marathon. Thorpe settled there, working as a ditch digger on a WPA project and as an extra and bit player in motion pictures. Though past the age of enlistment, he joined the merchant marine in 1945 and served on an ammunition ship.

Between 1931 and 1950, Thorpe appeared in 70 films, several of which are classics or well-remembered titles. He was a New York theatergoer in the original *King Kong* (1933); a pirate in Michael Curtiz's *Captain Blood* (1935); a "John Doe applicant" in Frank Capra's *Meet John Doe* (1941); an Indian in Raoul Walsh's *They Died With Their Boots On* (1941); a ship's passenger in the Bob Hope-Bing Crosby comedy *Road to Utopia* (1945); a convict in Walsh's *White Heat* (1949); and another Indian in John Ford's *Wagon Master* (1950). He wore baseball uniforms in Joe E. Brown's *Alibi Ike* (1935) and the Buster Keaton short *One Run Elmer* (1935). Thorpe even appeared as a Carlisle football player in *Fighting Youth* (1935), a curio involving communist agitators who infiltrate a college campus. Primarily, however, Thorpe played a range of roles in such B-Westerns as *Moonlight on the Prairie* (1935), *Treachery Rides the Range* (1936), *Cattle Raiders* (1938), *Frontier Scout* (1938), *Arizona Frontier* (1940), and *Beyond the Pecos* (1945).

Burt Lancaster played Thorpe in the 1951 biopic *Jim Thorpe, All-American*. The film depicts his being stripped of his medals for playing minor-league ball. Warner Bros., the studio that produced the film, paid Thorpe $15,000 for his services as a technical adviser. Additionally, Mort Blumenstock, the studio's head of publicity, donated $2,500

toward an annuity fund for Thorpe.[14] It was around this time that Thorpe also tried to develop a nightclub act. However, after he underwent an operation for lip cancer in November 1951, newspapers reported that he was penniless.

Jim Thorpe was 65 years old when he died of a heart attack in his trailer home in Lomita, California, on March 28, 1953. Though he'd been operating a nearby bar, his death certificate listed his occupation simply as "Athlete." Jim's third wife had his body interred in Shawnee, Oklahoma, before she moved it to Tulsa. In 1957 the body was transferred to Mauch Chunk and East Mauch Chunk, Pennsylvania – a place Thorpe had never been to. Hoping to transform themselves into a tourist center, the towns merged and renamed themselves Jim Thorpe in his honor. His surviving sons tried to use the courts to have his body returned to Sac and Fox land in Oklahoma. However, the Third US Circuit Court of Appeals ruled in 2014 that Thorpe's remains should stay where they were. Though disappointed with the decision, son Bill Thorpe said, "It's been a good place. They've taken good care of him and continued the name."[15]

In 1953 the Associated Press selected Thorpe as the greatest American athlete of the first half of the twentieth century. He is a member of the Pro Football, College Football, and National Track and Field Halls of Fame. After a long campaign led by Thorpe's daughter Grace, the International Olympic Committee reversed its 1912 decision on Thorpe's eligibility in 1983, reissued his Gold Medals and declared him the co-winner of the pentathlon and decathlon at the 1912 Stockholm Olympic games. In July 2022 the International Olympic Committee restored Thorpe as the sole winner of the two events.[16]

An earlier version of this biography appeared in SABR's *Deadball Stars of the National League* (Brassey's Inc., 2004), edited by Tom Simon. It also appeared in *From Spring Training to Screen Test: Baseball Players Turned Actors* (SABR, 2018), edited by Rob Edelman and Bill Nowlin.

SOURCES

For this biography, the author used a number of contemporary sources, especially those found in the subject's file at the National Baseball Hall of Fame Library.

NOTES

1   "Greatest Living Athlete," *Omaha World-Herald*, July 28, 1912: 18. Kate Buford attributes the original quotation to the *Philadelphia Inquirer* in her book *Native American Son: The Life and Sporting Legend of Jim Thorpe* (New York: Knopf, 2010).

2   Bob Hersom, "Thorpe Remembered for Baseball Prowess," *Oklahoman* (Oklahoma City), June 3, 2006.

3   Joe Guyon, quoted in Dave Anderson, "Jim Thorpe's Medals," *New York Times*, June 22, 1975: 199.

4   Andrew R. Graybill, "Path Lit by Lightning," *Wall Street Journal.* July 3-31, 2022. See also, David Maraniss, *Path Lit by Lightning: The Life of Jim Thorpe* (New York: Simon & Schuster, 2022), 538.

5   Associated Press, "Great Jim Thorpe Wants Sons to Follow Diamond, Not Gridiron," *Hartford Courant*, April 6, 1940: 11.

6   Robert W. Wheeler, *Jim Thorpe, World's Greatest Athlete* (Norman: University of Oklahoma Press, 1981), 145.

7   *Des Moines Register*, January 9, 1926: 8.

8   Hersom.

9   Ray Robinson, *Matty: An American Hero* (New York: Oxford University Press, 1993), 153.

10 William A. Cook, *Jim Thorpe: A Biography* (Jefferson, North Carolina: McFarland, 2011), 88.

11 Cook, 138.

12 Charles Einstein, *The Fireside Book of Baseball* (New York: Simon & Schuster, 1987), 322.

13 Ring W. Lardner, "In the Wake of the News," *Chicago Tribune*, October 14, 1917: A1. The White Sox won the game in the end, 8-5. They won Game Six as well, winning the World Series, four games to two.

14 Kate Buford, *Native Son: The Life and Sporting Legend of Jim Thorpe* (New York: Alfred A. Knopf, 2010).

15 Associated Press, "Pennsylvania Town Named for Jim Thorpe Can Keep Athlete's Body," CBS News, October 23, 2014. http://www.cbsnews.com/news/pennsylvania-town-named-for-jim-thorpe-can-keep-athletes-body/. Accessed September 5, 2022.

16 Jeremy Schaap, "IOC Reinstates Jim Thorpe as Sole Winner of 1912 Olympic Decathlon and Pentathlon," ESPN.com, July 14, 2022. https://www.espn.com/olympics/story/_/id/34245374/ioc-reinstates-jim-thorpe-sole-winner-1912-olympic-decathlon-pentathlon. Accessed September 5, 2022.

BEN TINCUP

By Joel Rippel

When the Philadelphia Phillies signed a pitcher from the Class-D Texas-Oklahoma League in August of 1913, it caused a sensation in Philadelphia newspapers.

While it was rare for a major-league team to sign a player from Class D, what created the stir was the player's background.

One Philadelphia newspaper raised two points in its story that made the Phillies' signing of Ben Tincup newsworthy – "Ben Tincup, Phils' original Indian, is one of the game's wealthiest players." A subheadline said Tincup "Belongs to Rich Cherokee Tribe and Will Come into Small Fortune Next April When He Reaches Voting Age."[1]

The article explained that Tincup owned land in Oklahoma where oil had been discovered and added, "[T]here are probably few wealthier ball players in the big leagues today than this Indian lad."[2]

Ben Tincup in Cuba

(SABR – The Rucker Archive)

As for his baseball abilities, "[U]nless all signs fail this Cherokee Indian lad is another natural born ball player like Sockalexis, the Penobscot."[3]

After he joined the Phillies in 1914, references to Tincup's wealth were often repeated. Tincup said the reports were partially true.

"Yep, I'm 100 percent Cherokee and I own 500 acres of Oklahoma land," said Tincup, "but I'm the Indian, who owns the land where they didn't find oil."[4]

Tincup said his father, who raised cotton, corn, wheat, oats, and livestock on his farm, wasn't rich either. He said, "Why shoot, if I'd hit oil, do you think I'd be here?"[5]

Tincup went on to spend nearly 50 years in professional baseball – as a player, manager, umpire, scout, and coach.

Tincup was born Austin Ben Tincup to James and Lucinda Tincup on April 14, 1893, in Adair, Indian Territory. The territory was set aside by the US government in what would become the state of Oklahoma in 1907.[6]

James Tincup was a farmer. Ben was the youngest of nine children; he had four brothers and four sisters. James Tincup was a Civil War veteran, having served three years as a member of Company H, Indian Home Guards, in Kansas. After the Civil War, he was a sheriff in Delaware County in Indian Territory.

Ben Tincup started his professional baseball career in 1912, about 50 miles from his hometown. Tincup, who had pitched for semipro teams in nearby Pryor, Adair, and Vinita, signed to play for Muskogee in the Class-D Oklahoma State League. It was the first year that Muskogee had fielded a minor-league team.

Tincup's season got off to a good start. On May 9 he allowed just one hit and struck out 13 to pitch Muskogee past Anadarko, 3-1, in Muskogee. He faced just 29 hitters.

The eight-team league disbanded on June 29, 1912. Muskogee was in sixth place with a 19-24 record, 16½ games behind first-place Okmulgee (38-10). Tincup had been a tough-luck pitcher for Muskogee. Despite posting a 2.61 ERA with a league-leading 163 strikeouts in 162 innings, he had a 7-13 record.

After the league disbanded, Tincup joined Sherman (Texas) in the Class-D Texas-Oklahoma League. In five starts with Sherman, he went 2-3 with a 1.29 ERA.

A 6-foot-1, 180-pound right-hander who batted left-handed, he returned to Sherman for the 1913 season. In 41 appearances, he went 17-11 with a 2.26 ERA and a league-leading

233 strikeouts (in 247 innings). When not pitching, he was used in the outfield. In 59 games, he batted .279.

Tincup had caught the eye of at least one scout. John Callahan, scouting for the Philadelphia Phillies, urged Phillies manager Charley "Red" Dooin to sign Tincup: "Grab this Indian, Tincup, with the Sherman team," Callahan wrote to Dooin. "He isn't a great pitcher, but take it from me, he's going to be a great ballplayer some day."[7]

After he pitched Sherman to a 9-1 victory over Bonham on August 15, it was reported that Tincup had been sold to the Phillies for $1,500. He reported to the Phillies in Philadelphia on August 20 and "was immediately sent to pitch to the batters in batting practice. Then he went to the plate in batting practice and that right-field fence got the walloping of its life."[8]

Tincup did not appear in any games for the Phillies, who finished the 1913 season in second place, 12½ games behind the first-place New York Giants.

In the offseason, the Phillies assigned Tincup to Lowell (Massachusetts) of the Class-B New England League. Tincup joined the Phillies for 1914 spring training in Wilmington, North Carolina, and made the Opening Day roster.

Tincup didn't make his first appearance of the season until the Phillies' 36th game – in the second game of a doubleheader against the New York Giants in Philadelphia on June 2.

With the Phillies trailing 4-0, Tincup replaced Phillies starter Elmer Jacobs to start the fifth inning. Phillies left fielder Josh Devore tried to make a shoestring catch of a ball off the bat of Giants second baseman Larry Doyle but it got past him and Doyle wound up on third. Doyle scored on a groundout. That was the only run allowed by Tincup in three innings in the Phillies' 7-0 loss to the Giants.

Tincup's next outing came on June 10, when he pitched six innings of relief, allowing six hits and four unearned runs in the Phillies' 8-2 loss to Cincinnati.

In his third outing, on June 25, he entered the game in the eighth inning with the Phillies trailing Brooklyn 6-4. He allowed an unearned run and then pitched a scoreless ninth as the Phillies rallied for an 8-7 victory, Tincup's first major-league win.

The next day Tincup struck out the only two hitters he faced in the Phillies' 7-4 loss to Brooklyn.

In the first game of a doubleheader in New York on July 4, he relieved Eppa Rixey in the bottom of the first. He finished the game, allowing two runs in 7⅓ innings in the Giants' 5-4 victory.

Five days later in Pittsburgh, Tincup made his first major-league start. He threw a five-hit, 1-0 shutout against the Pittsburgh Pirates.

For the rest of the season, Tincup was in the Phillies' rotation. He threw two more shutouts – 1-0 over the Cardinals in St. Louis on August 20 and 2-0 over the Pirates in Philadelphia on September 17. He finished the season with

an 8-10 record and a 2.61 ERA in 28 appearances (17 starts). In addition to the three shutouts, Tincup completed six other starts and had two saves. In 155 innings, he struck out 108.

In 1915 the Phillies' strength was their starting pitching. They added Al Demaree to their rotation of Grover Cleveland Alexander, Rixey, and Erskine Mayer. Along with George Chalmers, the five started 143 of the Phillies' 153 games and pitched 92 complete games. Alexander was 31-10 with a 1.22 ERA and 12 shutouts among his 36 complete games.

That left Tincup, who was with the Phillies all season, with few pitching opportunities. He appeared in just 10 games – all in relief – and pitched just 31 innings. He had no decisions and a 2.03 ERA.

Behind their starting pitching, the Phillies, who had won 74 games in 1914, went 90-62 to win the NL pennant, seven games ahead of the Boston Braves.

In a World Series preview story, Tincup said, "I don't expect to get in the series myself, but I am confident that the boys who do play will beat the Red Sox all right."[9]

The Red Sox won the World Series in five games. The Phillies used just one reliever in the Series, Rixey in the final game.

Tincup summed up his 1915 season: "The Phillies didn't really need me in 1915. Gosh, they had pitchers like Alec (Grover Cleveland Alexander), Al Demaree, Eppa Rixey, George Chalmers, George McQuillan, and my old roommate, Lefty Baumgartner. I could have spent the year in the grandstand."[10]

Tincup was with the Phillies in 1916 spring training, then was assigned to Providence of the International League. Phillies manager Pat Moran "told Tincup and (Stan) Baumgartner several days before the Phillies finished their spring training that he would have no use for them this season and would save expenses by farming them out."[11]

After going 16-11 with a 2.50 ERA for Providence, Tincup joined the Phillies in late September. He appeared in one game – as a pinch-hitter in the season finale. He was hitless in the Phillies' 4-1 loss to the visiting Boston Braves.

In 1917 Tincup pitched for Little Rock of the Southern Association, was 11-10 with a 2.50 ERA, and provided one of the highlights of the Travelers' 64-86 season when he threw a perfect game against the Birmingham Barons. Little Rock won, 3-0.

A newspaper account of the game said Tincup's outing, "with Tom Rogers' defeat of the (Chattanooga) Lookouts, 2-0, on July 11 last year, probably comprises the only two such games in the history of the Southern League."[12]

Tincup's outing stood out for another reason: "His achievement is the more unusual because of the fact that he had no rest prior to the game," the *Arkansas Democrat* reported. Tincup and the Travelers had played a doubleheader in Mobile, the previous day. Tincup played right field in both games. The Travelers then traveled all night (257 miles) to reach Birmingham.[13]

"Ben has shown it all along despite that he has worked steadily as an outfielder and has been pitched without rest. It was his third shut-out," the *Democrat* commented.[14]

After the season the Travelers sold Tincup to the St. Louis Cardinals, but the Phillies claimed Tincup was still their property. The National Association agreed and Tincup remained with the Phillies.

Tincup made the Phillies' Opening Day roster in 1918. In his first nine innings – over five appearances – he allowed 14 runs. In his next three appearances he threw 7⅔ shutout innings. After he pitched four scoreless innings in the Phillies' 6-3 loss to the New York Giants in Philadelphia on May 30, his season was interrupted when he was called up for US Army duty. At Camp Merritt in Hoboken, New Jersey, he was assigned to Motor Transport Company 801. He was discharged as a corporal on February 20, 1919.

After being discharged from the Army in February of 1919, Tincup resumed his baseball career, although the details are somewhat vague. He signed with the Phillies soon after his discharge, but at the end of February, it was reported that the Phillies had asked waivers on him.

After being waived by the Phillies, he accepted offers from both Louisville of the American Association and Little Rock of the Southern Association. In late April, he reported to Louisville and Little Rock appealed to minor leagues governing body.

While waiting for a ruling on which contract was valid, he did not play for Louisville. No announcement on a decision could be found and he made his first appearance for Louisville around May 12. Except for two appearances with the Chicago Cubs in September 1928, he spent the next 12 seasons in the American Association.

In 1919 Tincup was 11-8 with a 2.85 ERA in 24 appearances for the Colonels, managed by Joe McCarthy. The next season he was 15-12 with a 2.84 ERA in 34 appearances and 238 innings. When not pitching, he was regularly used in the outfield. For the season, he batted .331 and had a slugging percentage of .531 in 124 games. His batting average was 4 points shy of batting champion Goldie Rapp, who hit .335 for the St. Paul Saints.

In 1921 Tincup went 9-0 in 26 appearances and batted .284 in 102 games as the Colonels won the American Association pennant – their first of four between 1921 and 1930 – with a 98-70 record.

In the 1921 Junior World Series, the Colonels faced the International League champion Baltimore Orioles. The Orioles had gone 119-47 in the regular season to claim their third (of an eventual seven) consecutive International League titles. (Only one other minor-league team – the 1934 Los Angeles Angels, who went 137-50 – has won more games in a season).

Tincup played a big role in the Colonels winning the best-of-nine series against the Orioles in eight games.

The series opened with four games in Louisville. The Colonels won the opener on October 5, 16-1, but the Orioles evened the series the next day, when Jack Ogden, who was 31-8 during the regular season, outdueled Tincup, 2-1. The Orioles scored a run in the eighth to break a 1-1 tie.

On October 8 the Colonels outslugged the Orioles, 14-8, as Tincup pitched 2⅔ innings of relief.

The next day, the Orioles evened the series, 2 games to 2. With the Orioles leading 12-4 with two outs in the top of the ninth, fans rushed the field after a call went against the Colonels. The game was not completed and ruled a forfeit. One newspaper account said, "[T]he demonstration by local fans at yesterday's ball game at Eclipse Park between the Colonels and Orioles was one of the most disgraceful in the history of Louisville baseball."[15]

Tincup pitched 2⅓ innings of relief in the game.

The series shifted to Baltimore and resumed on October 13 as the Orioles won 10-5 to take a 3-2 lead. The Colonels evened the series on October 15 with a 3-0 victory as Tincup outdueled Lefty Grove. Tincup allowed just five hits and struck out nine.

The next day Tincup pitched 1⅓ shutout innings of relief to save the victory as the Colonels outlasted the Orioles, 7-6.

The Colonels defeated the Orioles, 11-5, on in Game Eight on October 17 to close out the series.

Manager Joe McCarthy summed up the series victory by the Colonels: "I was badly informed as to the strength of Baltimore against left-handers and when I saw Ben Tincup could throw them past the batters, I knew I had the righthander who could puzzle them."[16]

In 1922 Tincup won 20 games for the first time, going 20-14 for the Colonels, who slumped to 77-91 and a sixth-place finish in the eight-team American Association. He made 46 pitching appearances and threw 279 innings (both career highs). He batted .309 in 149 at-bats.

After the season, Tincup pitched in the Cuban Winter League. Pitching for Marianao, a franchise representing a suburb of Havana, Tincup was 2-3 in 11 appearances as Marianao went 35-19 and finished in first place.[17]

The 1923 season – his fifth in Louisville – saw him go 17-16 in 43 appearances and 252 innings.

In 1924 Tincup set new career highs for victories, appearances, and innings pitched as he went 24-17 in 49 appearances and 293 innings.

During the winter of 1924-25, Tincup returned to Cuba, going 6-3 with four complete games in 10 appearances for Marianao.

After back-to-back third-place finishes in 1923 and 1924, the Colonels won back-to-back pennants in 1925 and 1926.

Tincup was 14-16 in 1925. After the Colonels lost to the Baltimore Orioles in the Junior World Series, McCarthy was named the manager of the Chicago Cubs.

In 1926 Tincup went 18-7 for the Colonels, who were swept by Toronto in the Junior World Series. The next season, he tossed 265 innings and went 16-15. In 1928 he was 14-10 with Louisville before joining McCarthy and the Cubs in September.

On September 3 at Forbes Field in Pittsburgh, Tincup made his first major-league appearance in 10 years. With the Pirates leading 4-0 in the bottom of the second inning and two men on base, Tincup replaced Cubs starter Charlie Root. He gave up a two-run double to Pie Traynor before getting the final out of the inning.

After pitching a scoreless third inning, Tincup gave up six runs in the fourth before being replaced with two outs by Guy Bush. The Pirates went on to win 16-1.

Tincup made one more appearance for the Cubs, on September 15 in Boston. After the Braves scored four runs in the first inning off Root, Tincup entered the game in the second. He finished the game, allowing just one run in seven innings in the Braves 5-2 victory. It was his final major-league appearance.

Tincup returned to Louisville in 1929, going 7-16 in 33 appearances at the age of 36.

In 1930, he returned to the bullpen and went 14-3 in 43 appearances as the Colonels won their fourth pennant since Tincup first joined the team. The Colonels, 93-60 in the regular season, lost to Rochester, 5-3, in the Junior World Series.

The 1931 season was Tincup's last in Louisville. After going 1-4 in 11 appearances, he was released by the Colonels on July 23. He was 38 years old.

"Tincup's departure from the Colonels will tug many a heartstring," the Louisville Courier-Journal commented. "He had the respect and admiration of every opposing player in the league and every fan in the league. For years, he had been considered the smartest pitcher in the circuit and luck rarely entered in any of his mound triumphs."[18]

Over his tenure with the Colonels, Tincup had "toiled for the cause of the Louisville Colonels a greater number of years than any other player in the circuit has labored for any other club, and he has pitched more games in which he either won or lost by a margin of a single run than probably any moundsman in the history of baseball over the same number of years, 12."[19]

Two days after being released by the Colonels, Tincup signed with the rival Minneapolis Millers. He made three ineffective relief appearances for the Millers before being released by the Millers on August 11. For the season, he was a combined 1-4 in 14 appearances.

Tincup spent the 1932 season – his final season as an active player (at age 39) – with Sacramento of the Pacific Coast League. He went 9-12 in 28 appearances for the Solons.

In 1933 Tincup was hired by the American Association as an umpire. The season began on April 15, and on April 19 in Louisville with American Association President Thomas Hickey in attendance, Tincup worked behind the plate for the first time as the Colonels defeated the St. Paul Saints, 5-4.

After the first week of the season, a Minneapolis sportswriter wrote, "[T]hey say Ben Tincup is doing a good job of umpiring."[20]

Just two weeks later, the American Association released Tincup.

"Wily as he was as a pitcher, he could not be converted into a competent umpire in one season. … Ben took his assignment seriously and he had the well wishes of the players, but it is patent that umpires must progress by easy stages, just as do players," the Kansas City Star commented.[21]

Tincup returned to his farm in Oklahoma and was out of baseball until 1936, when he was named manager of the Cincinnati Reds' Paducah (Kentucky) farm team in the Class-D Kitty League.

Paducah – which won the league's first-half title – and Union City (Tennessee), which won the second half – met in the league's championship series. After Union City won the first game of the series, Paducah refused to play the remaining games because of a decision by the league president, Dr. Frank H. Bassett, that two Union City players, who Paducah claimed were ineligible, could play.

Union City was awarded the championship and Tincup and seven Paducah players were put on the ineligible list by National Association President W.B. Bramham. Tincup and the players were reinstated in early 1937.

Tincup began the 1937 season as manager of Cincinnati's Peoria (Illinois) farm team in the Class-B Three-I League. In mid-August, Cincinnati reassigned him to oversee a tryout camp in Muskogee, Oklahoma. Peoria was 42-54 under Tincup.

Tincup remained in Muskogee in 1938 and managed the Muskogee Reds to a 71-68 record in the Class-C Western Association. He returned to Paducah in 1939, managing the Indians to a 57-69 record.

In 1940 Tincup joined the coaching staff of the Brooklyn Dodgers. The Dodgers, managed by Leo Durocher, finished second in the National League with an 88-65 record.

Tincup began the 1941 season as a coach with the Milwaukee Brewers of the American Association, but in late July he returned to Paducah to manage for the remainder of the season.

In 1942, with World War II raging, Tincup took a job as a pipefitter at the Jeffersonville (Indiana) Boat & Machine Works. In early August he took over as manager of Fargo-Moorhead in the Class-C Northern League and managed the Twins for the final month of the season. Tincup, who was 49, made one pitching appearance (of three innings) for the Twins.

For the duration of World War II, Tincup was out of baseball. In 1946 he became a scout for the Boston Braves. After three seasons scouting for the Braves, Tincup switched to the Pittsburgh Pirates. After five seasons with the Pirates, he spent the 1954 and 1955 seasons as a minor-league pitching instructor for the New York Yankees.

From 1956 to 1958, Tincup scouted for the Philadelphia Phillies and in 1959 he was a minor-league pitching instructor for the Phillies.

In November 1960 Tincup returned to the Yankees as a minor-league pitching coach. He retired from baseball after the 1961 season and returned to Oklahoma.

For his playing career, Tincup appeared in 627 minor-league games as a pitcher. He won 250 games and had a 3.49 ERA in 3,738 innings. In 1,122 minor-league games overall, he batted .271.[22]

In parts of five major-league seasons, Tincup appeared in 48 games. He was 8-11 with a 3.10 ERA.

Tincup died on July 5, 1980, in Claremore, Oklahoma. One report said he "was survived by two granddaughters."[23]

Tincup married Hesper Lelia Rice in Louisville in 1930. They had two daughters – Virginia Colleen and Cecelia Annette – before divorcing. In April of 1952, Cecelia died from injuries suffered in an automobile accident near Frankfort, Kentucky. Cecelia, who was 16, lived in Louisville with her mother and stepfather, Asa McGinniss.

Tincup's brother, James Yeargin Tincup, briefly played professional baseball, and his nephew, Frank, who had nine seasons in professional baseball, spent his rookie season in 1939 playing for his uncle Ben in Paducah.[24] For three seasons, Frank Tincup played for teams in the American Association and the Pacific Coast League. His overall record was 91-72. Frank was the son of Ben Tincup's brother John Henry.[25]

Ben Tincup is a member of the American Indian Athletic Hall of Fame and the National Hall of Fame for Famous American Indians. When the Will Rogers Museum opened in Claremore, Oklahoma, in 1941, Tincup donated a baseball from his 1917 perfect game to be displayed.

SOURCES

In addition to the sources cited in the Notes, the author consulted familysearch. com, findagrave.com, Baseball-Reference.com, Newspapers.com, Retrosheet.org, the *American Association Record Book*, 1977, and the following:

Selko, James. *Minor League All-Star Teams, 1922-62* (Jefferson, North Carolina: McFarland & Co., 2007)

Wright, Marshall D. *The International League, Year-by-Year Statistics, 1884-1953* (Jefferson, North Carolina: McFarland & Co., 1998).

NOTES

1   Jim Nasium, "Ben Tincup, Phils' Original Indian, Is One of Game's Wealthiest Players," *Philadelphia Inquirer*, August 24, 1913: 46. Jim Nasium was the nom de plume of Edgar Forrest Wolfe, a sports cartoonist and writer for various newspapers, including the *Inquirer*.

2   Jim Nasium.

3   Jim Nasium.

4   Burr Van Atta, "Ben Tincup, 89, a Former Phillie," obituary, *Philadelphia Inquirer*, July 8, 1980: 16.

5   Van Atta.

6   Birth dates ranging from 1890 to 1894 can be found for Tincup. In the 1910 US Census he was listed as 17. In the 1920 Census he was listed as 26. His World War I registration card lists his birth year as 1893, while his World War II registration card, dated April 27, 1942, lists his age as 50. His entry in the Veterans Administration Master Index (1917-1940) and his Social Security Index list his birth year as 1892. His entry on www.findagrave.com lists 1894. Tincup's page on www.retrosheet.org has 1893, while baseball-reference.com has 1893 on his statistics page, and 1890 on his info page on baseball-reference.com/bullpen.

7   Jim Nasium.

8   Jim Nasium.

9   "World's Series Opens Here on Friday, Oct. 8," *Philadelphia Evening Public Ledger*, October 2, 1915: 13.

10   Van Atta.

11   "Moran Will Farm Pair of Hurlers," *Reading* (Pennsylvania) *Times*, April 12, 1916: 10.

12   "Tincup Pitches Perfect Game and Travelers Win It, 3 to 0, with Ponder Giving Up Five Hits," *Arkansas Democrat* (Little Rock), June 19, 1917: 9.

13   "Tincup Pitches Perfect Game."

14   W.H. Harley, "From the Coop," *Arkansas Democrat*, June 19, 1917: 9.

15   Charles A. Reinhart, "Crowd Stops Fourth Game," *Louisville Courier-Journal*, October 10, 1921: 6.

16   Charles A, Reinhart, "'I Thought All Time I Had Better Team,' Says Joe McCarthy," *Louisville Courier-Journal*, October 18, 1921: 10.

17   Stats are according to Jorge S. Figueredo's *Cuban Baseball, A Statistical History, 1878-1961* (Jefferson, North Carolina: McFarland, 2003). Tincup's page on baseball-reference.com says he was 2-4 in seven appearances.

18   Bruce Dudley, "Tincup Released Unconditionally After 12 Years," *Louisville Courier-Journal*, July 24, 1931: 17.

19   "Ben Tincup Has Hurled 106 One-Run Margin Tilts," *Minneapolis Sunday Tribune*, February 1, 1931: 27.

20   Charles Johnson, "Andy Hitting Leader, Fields Without Error," *Minneapolis Star*, April 22, 1933: 13.

21   "Between Innings," *Kansas City Star*, May 11, 1933: 15.

22   Lloyd Johnson and Miles Wolff, eds., *The Minor League Register*, 1st edition (Durham, North Carolina: Baseball America, 1994).

23   Van Atta.

24   "3 Honest Indians May Start Season in Tribal Attire," *Paducah* (Kentucky) *Sun-Democrat*, April 14, 1939: 8.

25   There may have been another ballplayer in the family, too. The 1920 US census lists Ben living at home with a brother Edmund. That brother's occupation is listed as "baseball."

WYATT TOREGAS

By Douglas Stark

Wyatt Reeder Toregas was a catcher who played 22 games over the course of two seasons with the Cleveland Indians (now Guardians) and the Pittsburgh Pirates. As a player, he was known for his defensive-mindedness as a catcher and his quick bat and short, compact swing that generated good power. He was born on December 2, 1982, in Fairfax, Virginia, to William and Laura Toregas.

Toregas is a member of the Chickasaw Nation, which is based in Oklahoma. He is the grandson of Jalna Wenonah "Maw" Wolf Toregas, who was a professional ballroom dancer and actress. Born in Norman, Oklahoma, in 1911, she lived to 103 years and died in March 2015. Her final resting place is in Virginia. His memories of her stories about the tribe led him to pursue official membership near the end of his playing career.

"She was very proud to be Chickasaw," Toregas said. "She would tell us stories and remind us we are Chickasaw."[1]

Before his grandmother's death, Toregas was moved by his Chickasaw blood to request citizenship with the tribe. "I've been a proud citizen of the Chickasaw Nation for about two or three years now," he said in January 2016.

As a child growing up, Toregas gravitated toward baseball and played Little League and local baseball before enrolling in high school.

He spent the first three years of high school at Park View High School in Sterling, Virginia, before moving to South Lakes High School in Reston, Virginia, for his senior season. He earned varsity letters four years in baseball and wrestling and three years in golf.

In his sophomore season, Toregas batted .491 with two home runs; as a junior, he batted .418 with a pair of homers. In each season, he earned all-county and all-district honors.

As a senior at South Lakes High School, Toregas earned the Concorde District player of the year and all Northern Region catcher honors. He batted .609 with three home runs, 12 doubles, and 15 runs batted in, which earned him all-district, all-region, and first-team Group AAA state honors. He was also named the MVP of the Virginia League High School All-Star Game.

During the summer after high school, Toregas participated in the Connie Mack Baseball League and led his team to second place in the Connie Mack World Series by setting a record with his .765 (13-for-17) batting average. He was selected second team Washington Post All-Metro.[2]

During his high school career, Toregas developed a strong work ethic and could be found each night hitting 500 balls in a batting cage. "He's a workaholic," said his father, Bill Toregas. "Since he was 13, he's worked every day: he either lifts or swings. Not a day goes by he doesn't work."[3]

Part of Toregas's training included wrestling in the winter to stay in shape. As a senior, he placed fourth in the AAA state wrestling tournament at the 171-pound level.

After his high-school career ended, Toregas continued to play baseball at Virginia Polytechnic Institute and State University (Virginia Tech), a Big East School. He played for three years with the Hokies and was a key contributor both offensively and defensively.

As a freshman utility player in 2002, Toregas played in 58 of the team's 59 games, starting 26 games as the designated hitter, 13 games in right field, and 12 games as the catcher. Offensively, he was an important part of the Hokies attack. For the season, he batted .347 and in Big East games he carried a .378 batting average. He batted .378 with runners in scoring position and .571 with the bases loaded. He collected 15 doubles, 4 triples, and 8 home runs. A run producer, he drove in 51 runs while scoring 38 runs. He led the team with 16 multiple-RBI games. For his effort, Toregas made third team All-Big East as a utility player. He was named honorable mention freshman All-America by Collegiate Baseball in 2002.[4]

Toregas's college career got off to a quick start as he collected two doubles against Western Carolina. His offensive success continued throughout the year. Against Western Michigan in a three-game series, he went 6-for-11. He hit a triple and had four runs batted in against Rutgers University. In a 10-inning affair against Villanova, he doubled in the winning run. Against the Virginia Military Institute, he

Wyatt Toregas

was 4-4 with two doubles, a triple, and two RBIs, while scoring two runs. In a matchup against the University of Connecticut, he collected three hits and three RBIs, and scored two runs.

In one game against Georgetown University, the Hokies broke or tied 12 Big East records and 11 school records in a 35-4 win over the Hoyas. In that game, Toregas, playing in the outfield, batted nine times, breaking conference and school records. In his nine at-bats, he had seven hits, including three doubles, which tied Big East and Virginia Tech marks. He scored five runs while driving in two.[5]

Toregas finished his freshman campaign on a high note. Over the final two months of the season, he averaged .400 (58-for-145) and won the Big East Player of the Week honors the final week of the regular season when he went 10-for-18 with 4 home runs, 10 runs batted in, and 5 runs scored. Virginia Tech, with its 18-8 Big East record, tied Notre Dame for first place in the conference during the regular season.

In 2003 Toregas's sophomore season began slowly with an elbow sprain the week before the season opener. He opened the season with two starts in right field before moving to designated hitter for 13 games, then switching to catcher. He eventually played 41 games as a catcher and was a first-team All-Big East catcher. Offensively, he picked up where he left off as a freshman. He batted .319 for the season, leading the team with 60 runs batted in, which was good for second in the Big East. He was second on the team with 10 home runs, while also contributing 14 doubles and 2 triples. In Big East games, his batting average was .337.

Throughout the season, Toregas continued to have strong offensive games, including a double and home run vs. Campbell University, four RBIs against James Madison University, a double, triple, home run, and four RBIs against Liberty University, 4-for-4 with three runs scored and two runs batted in during a win over St. John's, and 3-for-4 with two RBIs, two runs scored, two doubles and a home run against Virginia.

Defensively, though, Toregas made his mark, particularly with his strong arm which was the reason Virginia Tech was the toughest team to steal against in the Big East. The team allowed just 36 steals in 64 attempts.

After his sophomore season, Toregas was invited to play for the Harwich Mariners of the Cape Cod Baseball League. In 36 games that summer, he collected 33 hits for a .236 average.

Returning for his junior year in 2004, Toregas slumped offensively as compared with his sophomore season. He batted .280 with 4 homers and 39 RBIs. However, he was again an all-state team selection. During his three seasons as a Hokie, he had a .316 batting average with 22 home runs and 150 RBIs in 167 games.

After his junior season, Toregas elected to make himself available for the 2004 major-league draft. At the time of the draft, he was ranked as one of the top 100 college prospects by *Baseball America.* Toregas was drafted by the Cleveland Indians in the 24th round as the 707th pick. He felt that he should have been taken in the first round. The snub bothered him. "I wanted to go really high, and the fact that I didn't, it does kind of upset you. You want to do well not only for yourself now, but you want to show these guys that they made a mistake. Because of my batting statistics this year, they're going to take guys with better statistics. They don't want uncertainty. I had a bad year."[6]

Toregas, a right-handed batter who stood 5-feet-11 and weighed 210 pounds, rose to the big leagues by working his way through the minors. From 2004 to 2009, he played with the Mahoning Valley Scrappers, Lake County Captains, Kinston Indians, Akron Aeros, Buffalo Bisons, and the Columbus Clippers, steadily progressing from Class A to Triple A.

In 2004 he played with the Mahoning Vallery Scrappers of the short-season New York Penn League. In 59 games, he collected 63 hits and 48 RBIs while posting a .294 batting average. In 2005, he played in 104 games with the Lake County Captains of the South Atlantic League, batting .231.

In 2006 with the Kinston Indians, Toregas was a in the Carolina League all-star. In 44 games, he had 49 hits, 23 RBIs, and a .336 average. During the season, he was promoted to the Double-A Akron Aeros, for whom in 48 games he had a .258 average.

During the winter of 2006-07, Toregas played for Azucareros of the Dominican Winter League, where he batted .320 in 16 games. During that offseason, he also participated in the Indians' winter development program in Cleveland in January.

In 2007 Toregas he was a nonroster invitee to the Indians spring training. He spent the 2007 season with the Double-A Aeros and was one of the Eastern League's better defensive catchers, throwing out 52 percent of would-be basestealers (32 of 62). Toregas hit .250 with 6 home runs and 39 RBIs in 86 games. He was named as an Eastern League all star, but due to an injury, he was replaced by Altoona catcher Brian Peterson.

Toregas was optioned to the Buffalo Bisons of the International League in March 2008, and began the season as the starting catcher. He struggled to hit with the Bisons and was sent down to Akron in late June. "I just need to hit; no one has to tell me that," Toregas said. "There's no need to sugar-coat it. I know why I got sent down."[7] He spent the remainder of the season with Akron. He improved his hitting with a .296 average in 47 games with 12 home runs and 35 RBIs. For the week of July 7, he was the Eastern League Player of the Week.

Back with Buffalo in 2009, Toregas was hitting .284 with 7 home runs and 29 RBIs and had been named an International League all-star when he was called up by the Indians on July 31. He made his major-league debut for manager Eric Wedge on August 1 and got his first major-league hit in his first at-bat, a line-drive single to left field off Detroit's Rick Porcello to lead off the bottom of the third inning at Progressive Field. He went 1-for-5 and collected an RBI in the bottom of the 12th inning as the Indians came up one run short and lost 4-3. He played 19 games for the team during August and September while compiling a .176 batting average.

Shortly after his debut, Toregas started to experience a series of injuries, all of which eventually led to the end of his playing career.

"I had three injuries that did me in," Toregas said. "The first was an elbow injury in a collision with another player. The second was more serious – a dislocated shoulder after a slide into second base. That one really slowed me down, but I fought through it."

The injury "that tied the bow," as Toregas recalled, was when he pulled a groin muscle running to first base.

"My body never healed to the point where I could run or have any confidence in running. Every time I ran, I could feel it trying to pop again."

He fought through it, but ultimately he could not hide the injuries from the staff. "[Scouts] are really good. They can tell when you're hurt. I tried to trick them as long as I could. The smallest injury can be so devastating because at the professional level you're playing against elite opponents. When an injury slows you down, it shows."[8]

After spring training in 2010, Cleveland designated Toregas for assignment. He elected to stay with the Cleveland organization and was assigned to Akron before moving to Mahoning Valley and then to Columbus, where he finished out the year.

After the season Toregas elected free agency and on January 18, 2011, the Pittsburgh Pirates signed him and invited him to spring training. At its conclusion, he was sent to the Triple-A Indianapolis Indians, then to the Double-A State College Spikes and then back again to Indianapolis. On June 9 the team added him to the major-league roster. At the time, he was batting .034 (1-for-29) in Indianapolis.

Upon his call-up, Pirates manager Clint Hurdle said, "He has been a pretty solid catch-and-throw guy. We saw him, he's just a bat-handler, move the ball around and hit you a double, but he is pretty much a defensive ... a second catcher, an organizational-type catcher who has a small volume of big-league games."[9]

It did not take Toregas long to display his arm strength to his new Pirates teammates as he gunned down the New York Mets' José Reyes trying to steal second base in his first inning with the Pirates.

Toregas played three games and did not get a hit in four at-bats. Four days later, June 13, the Pirates designated him for assignment, and he played out the rest of the 2011 season with Indianapolis.

During his eight-year playing career, Toregas competed in 22 games at the major-league level. In those games he batted .164 with 6 RBIs.

After the season Toregas signed with the Pirates as a player-coach. He was the first-base coach for Indianapolis before being invited to join Hurdle's major-league staff for the 2013 and 2014 seasons doing video work scouting future opponents.

In January 2015, Toregas was named as the first-ever manager in the franchise history of the West Virginia Black Bears, the Pirates' short-season Class-A affiliate in Morgantown, West Virginia, which had relocated from Jamestown, New York. The team won the 2015 New York Penn League championship over the Staten Island Yankees. In that season, he guided the team to a 42-34 regular-season record. The next season, the team was 38-38.

"I thought I was a really good player, but I think I'm doing what I was meant to do as a manager. I believe I may be better at this than I was at playing," Toregas said.

"There is a great satisfaction I get when (a skill) we've been working on with a specific player ... shows up in a game. I just think I have a much better feel for this (managing)," he said. "Don't get me wrong, I loved having personal success on the field, but there is something very emotionally satisfying when someone else you've been working so hard with succeeds. I kind of like it more. There is nothing that compares to it."[10]

After spending two seasons with the team in Morgantown, Toregas was named manager of the West Virginia Power of the South Atlantic League, where he managed the team for two seasons, 2017 and 2018. In 2017 he guided the Power to a 69-67 record.

In 2019 Toregas became the manager of the Bradenton Marauders of the Class-A Florida State League. At the end of the season, he was fired after guiding the Marauders to a 73-62 overall record and missing the playoffs.

In March 2021 Toregas took over as manager of the Mississippi Braves of the Southern League, the Double-A affiliate of the Atlanta Braves. At the time of his hire, he had compiled a 293-263 (.527) record as a manager. He coached Mississippi to an 18-15 mark, two games out of first place, before resigning on June 11. No reason was given for his resignation.[11]

Toregas and his wife, Holly, have two children, Ava and Alexander, and live in Ashburn, Virginia.

SOURCES

In addition to the sources cited in the Notes, the author consulted Baseball-Reference.com and Retrosheet.org.

NOTES

1 "Chickasaw Manager Leads MLB Pirates' Class A Affiliate," *Chickasaw Times: Official Publication of the Chickasaw Nation.* Vol. LIV. No. 8. January 2016. https://www.chickasawtimes.net/Web-Exclusives/Chickasaw-manager-leads-MLB-Pirates%E2%80%99-Class-A-affil.aspx. All quotations from Wyatt Toregas not otherwise attributed come from this article.

2   "Wyatt Toregas" player biography, Hokiesports.com, Virginia Tech Athletic Department, Accessed [Accessed April 4, 2025], https://hokiesports.com/sports/baseball/roster/player/wyatt-toregas.

4   "Wyatt Toregas," Hokiesports.com.

5   "Wyatt Toregas," Hokiesports.com.

6   Mark Berman, "Indians Select Toregas," *Roanoke* (Virginia) *Times,* June 9, 2004: 9.

7   Stephanie Storm, "Toregas Returns for Work at Plate," *Akron Beacon Journal,* June 25, 2008: C1.

8   "Chickasaw Manager Leads MLB Pirates' Class A Affiliate."

9   Paul Zeise, "Reliever Battles His Way Back," *Pittsburgh Gazette,* June 12, 2011: 37.

10 "Chickasaw Manager Leads MLB Pirates' Class A Affiliate."

11 Jordon Gray, "Mississippi Braves manager Wyatt Toregas resigns," WLBT.com, June 11, 2021. https://www.wlbt.com/2021/06/11/mississippi-braves-field-manager-wyatt-toregas-resigns/.

JOHN VANN

By Tom Willman

In June of 1913, the St. Louis Cardinals were sinking in the National League's second division. Rookie manager Miller Huggins needed a lot of things, but just then he was fretfully looking for a short-term backup catcher. He settled on a youngster on loan from Indianapolis of the American Association. This was John Vann, a Native American just turning 23.

Vann (a Cherokee) puttered around the St. Louis bullpen for a week until a home game on June 11 against the Boston Nationals. Lefty Tyler was working for Boston and he carried a shutout into the eighth. Then both teams rallied, and by the bottom of the ninth Boston led 5-3 but the Cardinals were threatening. The tying run came to the plate in the person of pinch-hitter John Vann. Vann's time was at hand. It was his big-league debut – and it came and went in a Moonlight Graham moment. "Vann, batting for [pitcher Slim] Sallee, fanned, while Hug grounded to [Rabbit] Maranville." Game lost, 5-3.[1]

After the game, the *St. Louis Post-Dispatch* reported: "Catcher Vann, who helped out here while Wingo and McLean were on the sick list, will be sent back to Indianapolis Friday."[2] And that was it: John Vann never got another shot at the major leagues. More than a century later, his big-league-baseball record is as short as an epitaph. He's a one at-bat player, a lifetime .000 hitter.

That is a dismissive understatement of John Vann's life in the game. He was, by many measures, a baseball success: 17 years, 14 teams – college and pros – playing and managing. His real story, little more than a footnote today, is a saga of Deadball days in the American heartland.

People who saw Vann in his prime were surprised at his size – 6 feet tall, around 190 pounds – and at his athleticism. One sportswriter's first impression: "Vann is a graceful and easy moving receiver and he steps into the ball with a terrific cut when hitting."[3] He was also bright, college-educated, and the scion of a well-to-do Cherokee Nation family. A 1912 sports-page profile concluded that Vann was "in the game just for the love of it," adding that he "owns some plantations that would swallow all the ball parks in this circuit."[4] Writers often remarked on his winning personality and his good looks: One of Vann's teams seriously considered giving away his autographed picture on ladies day.[5] In short, in an age when every American city and town cheered its homegrown baseball heroes, Vann was a natural. One winter, his hometown paper found him greeting fans and friends on the street. "John is the only real base ball player

in all northeastern Oklahoma probably," the paper reported, "and when he comes to town he is like the circus elephant to the small boy."[6]

John Vann was born on June 7, 1890, in Fairland, a farm town in Indian Territory that became the state of Oklahoma. Many Indians were not US citizens, Oklahoma did not become a state until 1907, and in many ways it was still the Old West. The land run came in 1889. The first great oil boom began less than a decade later. The horseback Dalton Gang met its storied end in a blazing gunfight in the streets of Coffeyville, Kansas, barely 60 miles from Fairland. John Vann was 2 years old that year.

John Vann

But for Vann, Indian Territory would be a land of opportunity. Fairland was at the heart of the Cherokee Nation. The Vann clan had produced important tribal statesmen and canny business leaders going back generations.[7] Like other tribes, the Cherokee were repeatedly pushed off their lands, enduring broken treaties, punishing wars and the bitter Trail of Tears. But the Cherokees also had proven strikingly adaptive to legal systems and trade opportunities.[8] Cherokee leaders developed a framework for self-government modeled on the US Constitution which served their civil society for a half-century. The tribe had its own legislature, its own judiciary, its own Cherokee-language newspaper. The Cherokee were recognized as one of the "Five Civilized Tribes."[9] John Vann's father, David W. Vann, originally of Georgia, was both influential and successful: In Fairland there was a Vann Hall for community and tribal meetings, a Vann block of buildings where lawyers sought office space. The family holdings included modernized farms and an industrial brickyard serving regional growth.[10] There may have been an oil tract as well, and as "prominent and well to do farmers," the Vanns kept "a beautiful country home four miles southeast of town."[11] Wife and mother Martha Vann kept a bustling household: By 1910 there were extended family visitors and six siblings at home, John and five younger sisters. John Vann, heir apparent, who had his own acreage as part of the family holdings, was brought up in agriculture and the family business. But it was baseball that spoke to him.

He would have taken up the sport in the usual rural way: In Sooner Oklahoma that meant making a ball out of a green walnut wrapped in yarn and crudely covered with leather. There were plenty of open spaces inviting the game, and by 1904 there was a four-team area league. In his midteens, Vann's parents sent him to Drury College, a small private school in Springfield, Missouri. Drury, founded with Congregationalist roots in the 1870s, had traditionally welcomed students from Oklahoma Indian Territory. And it had a baseball team. Vann was hitting college pitching there in 1907 when he was just 16. By 1909 he had made the jump to the University of Arkansas and Razorback baseball. By 1910, he was being touted as "the sensation of the western college circuit," having hit .500 over a 32-game stretch.[12] That April the World Series champion Pittsburgh Pirates were training in the area and booked a game with Arkansas. Pirates manager Fred Clarke saw Vann play an errorless first base, handle two double plays, and pound one over the outfielders' heads off star pitcher Howie Camnitz.[13] By June the Pirates had signed Vann. He was sent to the Class-B Connecticut League, where he got into about 90 games for Hartford, drawing good reviews. His batting average for the season was then reported as .265, notably better than the .241 that survives in the spotty record.[14]

To this point, Vann had been a capable first baseman with a good bat. He played hard, he drove the ball and yet he was also a reliable contact hitter. He put the ball in play; he could sacrifice dependably. (One season, playing for Shreveport in the Texas League, he struck out just 14 times in 331 plate appearances, fewest of any regular in the league.[15]) But his hitting wilted after this rookie year. Vann was with Hartford for the next two seasons, and his average tailed off – dipping to just .226 in 1912. What happened?

At the start of the 1911 season, Hartford decided to make him a catcher. He took up the challenge to learn the new position in earnest – and to learn it on the job. He had done a little catching, back when he also thought he might like pitching or second base. But this was no small order, and Vann had just begun when a series of shocking personal developments derailed things. Early in May, his mother developed erysipelas on her foot and was hospitalized with serious complications. Vann prepared to rush home, but then was told his mother was improving, so he stayed with the team. To his lasting regret: Shocking news came in side-by-side news stories in mid-May: His mother had taken a turn for the worse and would ultimately lose her leg – and with almost no warning, his 22-year-old sister, Pearl, fell ill and died.[16] With somber apologies to his team, Vann said goodbye, closed out his Connecticut affairs and went home. He had played in just 60 games. He did come back for the 1912 season, but the team had adjusted to his absence. There was a new first baseman and a new catcher as well. This left Vann trying to learn the catching position while platooning behind the plate and backing up at first, too. Then in August he was "beaned" by a projecting grandstand in Holyoke. The next day he broke a bone in his hand and was declared out for the season. In 1912 he played in just 72 games.[17]

For all that, in the winter of 1912 the Indianapolis club of the American Association had purchased Vann from Hartford. It was an exciting promotion. Vann had some lingering issues on defense – in particular, handling bunts, and high pops around the plate – but his bat was seductive and he came into camp as the potential starter. The stage was set for the season of his single major-league at-bat. It proved to be a misbegotten year in other ways as well.

The spring 1913 plan for the Indianapolis team called for about two weeks of conditioning in West Baden, 100 miles south of Indianapolis, followed by a couple of weeks of exhibition play as the squad moved north for a final series with the Chicago Cubs and then Opening Day. On March 21 that plan was obliterated by the storm of the century, a powerful destroyer that roared up from the south, spawning nine tornadoes, smashing whole towns and killing at least 48. Incredibly it got worse, then worse again, spinning off more tornadoes and a blizzard across 20 Midwest states, dumping record amounts of rain, tearing away homes and bridges and levees as rivers overflowed. In Indianapolis, six square miles of the city flooded and the ballpark was "severely damaged." It was later reckoned that regionwide there had been 650 deaths and a quarter-million people left homeless. It would be recorded as The Great Flood of

1913, second only in death and destruction to the terrible Johnstown Flood of the previous century.[18]

On March 29 the "Homeless Hoosiers" straggled north to find a dry place "to start the spring training all over again." Opening Day was barely two weeks away. The Cubs, having trained farther south in good weather, were fit and ready to play. The Indians were anything but, and when they arrived in Chicago, they found soggy grounds, chill winds and scattered knots of huddled spectators.[19] They had two games against the Cubs.

With Vann watching from the frigid bench, the Cubs won the first game with a razzle-dazzle inning that featured a hit, a walk, a bunt, and a scratch hit with runners flying and two panicky throws by the Indians. Welcome to the big leagues. The next day John Vann was catching for Indianapolis. At game time, temperatures fell into the 30s. For two innings things went all right: Chicago scored one run. In the third, an infield error put a Cub on first. Wildfire Schulte then hit a high infield pop that came down almost exactly on the pitcher's mound. "The visitors let Catcher Vann go after it, but he muffed it squarely."[20] The runners were racing and it was a paralyzing moment on the infield: Neither runner drew a throw. There ensued an embarrassing replay of the first game's chaos – double steal, booted grounder, an umpire's bad call, Heinie Zimmerman stole third then went right on to score when the third baseman let a throw get away, etc. It was a three-run inning with just one hit. The Hoosiers settled down after that. Vann played the whole game. The box score charged him with one of his team's three errors; his fly ball in the eighth produced his team's first run. Final score, 7-3, Chicago.[21]

Abruptly after that game John Vann all but disappeared. The commonly accessible versions of the historical statistical record show no entries for him as a member of the 1913 Indianapolis Indians.[22] There's no hint that he ever played an inning with the team. His 1913 season is presented as 74 games with the Sioux City Packers of the Class-A Western League and his one mortifying at-bat with the St. Louis Cardinals. Likewise, Vann's name all but evaporated from sports-page coverage in the first half of 1913. This obscured the fact that as April turned to May, and then to June, John Vann suited up and rode the Indianapolis pine. It's not that he never got in. He merely fell so far down the depth chart, playing so briefly and infrequently, that as those gaps in the record suggest, he was all but beneath notice. The truth looks more like this: Two appearances in April, maybe just four in May, totaling a few innings catching and 2-for-6 pinch-hitting.[23] It may be that Vann hadn't faced live pitching in nearly three weeks when he stepped up to the plate for his lone at-bat as a big-leaguer. Afterward, on June 14, just returned to Indianapolis, Vann "celebrated" being back by striking out in a 3-1 loss to Kansas City.[24] Five days later he was sent down to Sioux City.

Sioux City must have been a joyous release. Vann arrived on a Saturday morning and started the afternoon game. It went 11 innings, his team won 6-5, and he caught the whole thing. Working with three unfamiliar pitchers, he was charged with a single passed ball. At the plate he was 3-for-4 with a sacrifice. In late July, the *Sioux City Journal* reported: "Another Indian has slugged his way to a place among the league's star stickers – Jack Vann. The handsome catcher has been clouting consistently on the road and now has the fine average of .354."[25] Vann also found himself batting behind another fine hitter, the young "Tioga" George Burns. Burns was destined for a star career – 16 years in the American League, an MVP season, 2,018 hits, a lifetime .307 average – but in this moment, he and Vann became a popular young one-two punch. As August began, Vann was hitting .324; Burns was at .330. By late September, it was Vann .316, Burns .315. By season's end in October, it was Vann .328, Burns .301.[26] So the season of John Vann's major-league at-bat ended.

In February 1914 Vann was sold to Terre Haute of the Central League. Terre Haute was part of a resilient Class-B league that this year had six franchises and a 133-game schedule. Vann was hailed as a star and a drawing card. Just turning 24, he was maturing as a team leader. One of his pitchers, two years younger, showed particular promise. This was Art Nehf. That year, Terre Haute finished fifth in the league. Art Nehf was 11-7. Vann hit .271 with a team-best 8 home runs. His fielding percentage was .971, but context is noteworthy. Vann "actually caught 131 games during the season, more than any other catcher in the league. He did not have a passed ball all season long."[27]

Both Vann and Nehf were back in Terre Haute in 1915. Vann played in 100 games and led the team in batting at .300. Nehf led the pitching staff, going 19-10 with a 1.38 ERA. Called up by the Boston Braves, he won another five games. It was the start of a 15-year National League career in which he would win 184 games, more than 100 of them for the New York Giants and John McGraw. Vann was going to the Pacific Coast League. His performance caught the eye of catching-starved Cliff Blankenship, manager of the Salt Lake Bees.[28]

Vann arrived at spring training highly touted. But he soon developed a sore arm. On orders he rested it and resumed play, but it recurred, to the point where by April Blankenship was talking openly about returning Vann to Terre Haute.[29] By May, Blankenship had relented; Vann's hitting was redeeming. But by June the issue was back. The word was out and runners were taking liberties. In July Vann was back on the bubble and now even a .330 batting average wouldn't balance the scales.[30] In mid-August, Vann was sold to last-place Oakland, where he played out the PCL season. Once again there are large gaps in Vann's statistical record. This conceals the fact that in 1916 he was one of only 10 qualifying PCL hitters to finish "in the charmed .300 circle."[31] Vann went into the last weekend of the season batting .306 and finished in a horse race with noted hitters Ping Bodie and Johnny Bassler. Filling more statistical blanks reaffirms that Vann was a top-flight hitter. Still, many of his real baseball moments would not be measurable that way. Rather, they are like faded scrapbook photos of the game as it was.

In the heyday of the Native American ballplayer, in 1915, a baseball story had been widely syndicated. In a Los Angeles paper, it was headlined "American Indians Star on Diamond."[32] It featured the usual standouts – Charles Bender (Chippewa), Jack Meyers (Cahuilla), Jim Thorpe (Sac and Fox) – as well as a dozen other Native Americans playing in the big leagues or high minors. Vann was among those mentioned prominently. In this time of national recognition for accomplished Native American ballplayers, he played in a spring game against the New York Giants and Jim Thorpe. He pinch-hit against spitballer George Johnson (Ho-Chunk) in the Coast League (and cracked out a double). And (in 1914, in camp with Indianapolis) he formed an all-Native American battery with Louis Leroy (Stockbridge-Munsee). They lost a memorable spring exhibition game, 2-1, to the Cubs. The game featured a two-rundown double-play and snow flurries.[33] In his own time – and in the company of distinguished Native American ballplayers – John Vann made a name for himself.

This was also the evolutionary age of the storied Negro leagues. Coming off his .300 season at Terre Haute in 1915, Vann was named to a Midwest all-star team of high minor leaguers. The team's primary postseason booking: the region's young Black powerhouse team, the Indianapolis ABCs. The Negro National League was not established until 1920, but the upstart ABCs were staking an independent claim to Western rivalry with the great Chicago American Giants. The ABCs' star was Oscar Charleston. A century on, consensus ranks Charleston as one of the four best baseball players ever, after Babe Ruth, Honus Wagner, and Willie Mays. In this moment he was a rising 18-year-old phenom. The ABCs' first baseman was Ben Taylor, a great fielder, hitter and baserunner. Both players were elected posthumously to the National Baseball Hall of Fame. There were other well-known names in the lineup: Bingo DeMoss, Dizzy Dismukes.[34] Vann was the starting catcher for the all-stars. The teams first met in a doubleheader with a short second game, and the ABCs ran wild on the bases, winning 12-1 and 7-0. It was a shock. The all-stars promptly retrenched, upgrading pitching and middle infielders; Vann, the only all-star to collect three hits in the doubleheader, kept his place. That formula provided an epic thriller in the third game. "The 3,000 or more fans present saw a spicy game. Swell stops and neat catches were frequent, while Johnny McCarty's wonderful throw to the plate in the ninth inning fairly set the white fans wild."[35] The score had been tied 3-3 since the sixth inning. There it stayed into the 10th, into the 11th, into the deepening twilight until the game was called for darkness in the 12th. Oscar Charleston was 3-for-5. Vann had a 1-for-5 day at the plate, but what he was remembered for was his part in an electrifying play

at the plate. Bottom of the ninth: First up was the speedy ABC right fielder Morten Clark. He hit a grounder to third, playable, but the throw went wild and Clark wound up on third base. Next up was catcher Russell Powell. "Powell lifted a fly to left center and after the catch Clark dashed for the plate with what he thought was the winning run. (Center fielder) McCarty shot the ball on the dead line toward home, and one neat hop put the pellet into Catcher Vann's glove ahead of the runner." Out! For the fourth game, the all-stars upgraded again, adding Detroit Tigers Donie Bush, Bob Veach, Hooks Dauss, and George Boehler. The all-stars won that matchup, 5-2, but it may have seemed anticlimactic. Dauss, who had won 24 this year for Detroit, and his teammate Boehler did all the pitching; Vann caught an error-free complete-game three-hitter and incidentally led the All-Stars in hitting across those four games.[36]

Vann left the team at that point. There would be two more games over the next two weeks. Both were won by the Major League All-Stars. The second game flared into a hot dispute over a close play on which Donie Bush, stealing second, was called safe. DeMoss and then Charleston rushed the umpire, fists flew, the umpire went down, spectators swarmed the field and "a race riot of serious proportions was narrowly averted."[37] After the two ABC players were removed from the field, peace prevailed and the game was concluded, after which the ABCs left immediately on a planned tour of Cuba. The *Indianapolis News* played its story as a brief with a box score at the bottom of the sports page and a headline like a benediction: "Scrappy Game Ends 1915 Baseball Season."[38]

The trajectory of John Vann's baseball career arc changed again in 1917. He was with Waco in the Texas League that season. Vann was one of two catchers named to the league's unofficial all-star team. But he had known for most of the season that he would not be playing in 1918. On April 6, 1917, Congress declared war on Germany. Vann soon registered for the draft in Waco. In February of 1918, the Waco club sent him a contract for the coming season but Vann's Cherokee-country draft group had already undergone physicals. These men all had taken a distinct Indian path. Historically, Native Americans have an extraordinarily high rate of service in the US military. Culturally, the warrior ethos and pride in defending the homeland run deep. About 12,000 Native Americans, a dramatic number, ultimately served in World War I. Vann was one. In the summer of 1918, Private John Vann entered Officers Training School at Camp Pike, Arkansas. It was not to be foreseen yet, but the war would be over within three months. Sixteen days after the guns fell silent, John Vann was discharged from service.[39]

Vann was looking for a team in 1919. He went to spring camp with Waco, was traded to Dallas, then moved again in late June to the Shreveport Gassers. This time he got lucky. Baseball has always had a special place in its heart for old-fashioned rivalry, those hoarse, hard-fought games with local pride and bragging rights on the line. That was the Texas League split-season showdown of 1919. The Gassers were dark-horse winners of the league's first half. They were serious underdogs against second-half winners Fort Worth. The playoff was to be best of seven. The trains and hotels were crowded, the stands were packed, the fans were primed to go wild. At home, Shreveport surprised Fort Worth in Game One, 7-2. Vann was one of the day's heroes. "The Panthers were playing Vann for a bunt and the entire infield was drawn in in the expectation that Vann would lay one down. Instead, he drove a hit to right field on which both Brown and O'Neill scored."[40]

Shreveport also won the second, but the games moved to Fort Worth and the Panthers rallied back. When they met on September 30, a Shreveport win would finish it. There ensued a classic 10-inning battle, called for darkness with the score 2-2. There were lots of heroics, but Vann was exorcising old demons. In the second inning, with one Fort Worth run already in, he killed a rally by throwing out a runner trying to steal second. In the seventh, score tied and bases loaded for a noisy Fort Worth, Vann caught a pop foul, ending that rally; in the ninth, with one on for Fort Worth, he did it again.

In the final game, with Fort Worth playing desperately, the Gassers were leading 6-0 into the seventh when their pitcher blew up. A walk and two singles loaded the bases, then another hit drove in two runs and Fort Worth was on a roll. By the time Gassers reliever Gus Bono put out the fire, it was 6-5 Gassers. That would be the final score, but here's how close it came to going a different way: With Fort Worth catcher Larry Woodall on third in the seventh inning and one out, rally adrenaline was pulsing. The batter grounded toward third baseman Emmett Cain and it looked like a chance to Woodall: He sprinted for home. "Gathering in the ball, Cain made a quick throw to the plate to nip Woodall. Although the Fort Worth catcher came in full tilt, Vann did not yield an inch and put Woodall out on a close play."[41] The sportswriter added that the moment "ranked with the best of the many spectacular feats performed in the series." The Shreveport sports pages were ebullient, in big bold type. Stories about that other series -- the 1919 White Sox being shocked by Cincinnati in Game One – were pushed aside. [42] Vann batted .288 for the season, and .261 in the series, third best among starters; he had caught all seven games flawlessly. He had helped to bring Shreveport its first (and only) Texas League pennant. And that, the *Shreveport Times* crowed, was "the 'world's series' in this part of the United States." [43]

And then came Ruth. It was the spring of 1921 and the Babe, just 26 years old, was the swaggering harbinger of the new era. In 1920 he hit 54 homers and batted .376. In 1921 the Yankees made Shreveport their spring camp – and when Babe arrived, throngs met the train and hundreds filled the Lions Club hall for the banquet and welcome speeches. [44] The real show, though, was at the ballpark,

where the Yankees were to meet a series of opponents. One of Shreveport's turns came on March 23. The fact that the Yankees won 8-2 was beside the point. Ruth went 3-for-4. His longest hit was to deep center, a high fly that was thrilling for an instant but caught. John Vann, in addition to his close-up look at Ruth, cracked a long triple off submariner Carl Mays, the best pitcher in the American League that year. [45]

The Gassers finished fifth in the eight-team Texas League in 1921; Vann hit .260. He remained a fan favorite. In September of 1920, he had married a Shreveport woman, Grace Prothro. The entire team attended, and before the game they presented the newlyweds with a silver set. A year later, after a series in Beaumont, Vann hurried home to meet his new baby boy. He was going on 32, and his baseball life was changing.

In 1922 Vann's numbers declined. The Gassers made a dismal start that year. At the end of May, venerable manager Billy Smith was fired. Vann, the senior player on the team, was handed the job. Personnel woes and health issues made the rest of the season a rolling crisis. (A dengue fever outbreak made road trips to Galveston cringe-worthy.) But Vann had the full-throated support of the local paper and managed to keep a promise not to finish last. Shreveport climbed to sixth place, but it was not enough. With no hard feelings, Vann did not return.[46]

In 1923 Vann played about half-time, splitting the season between the Little Rock Travelers and the Birmingham Barons of the Southern Association. His final three seasons were spent as playing manager of the Corsicana Oilers of the Class-D Texas Baseball Association. In 1924 Vann won the pennant but lost a showdown Lone Star Series to the Tyler Trojans, the powerful East Texas League champs. In 1925 he won the pennant again, this time over the Palestine Pals, but the Series was canceled over a schedule wrangle. Still, it was an interesting year: Under Vann's management, a modestly successful pitcher named Smead Jolley was converted into a misadventure-prone outfielder who could play every day and hit .362. In 1926, with Jolley gone to the Pacific Coast League, Vann's team finished fourth. He obviously still found the game fulfilling, but he was coaching, teaching teammates who were just out of high school. His own son was turning 5.

In 1926 Vann went home to Fairland. For a while he considered taking a majority interest in a team in Joplin, Missouri. He reported being a baseball scout for the 1930 Census.[47] But this is the moment when he turned to his private business and ranch life that had always been running in the background; to wife and family (a son and a daughter). He seems in this way to have always lived a compartmentalized life. How else to explain his final profession: In 1934 Vann joined the Shreveport Police Detective Bureau. He retired from that work after 19 years. When he died in 1958, his final team – the entire Detective Bureau – stood for him as honorary pallbearers.[48]

SOURCES

In addition to the sources cited in Notes, the author consulted various sites under the auspices of the Smithsonian's National Museum of the American Indian. https://americanindian.si.edu

In particular, see "Nation to Nation: Treaties Between the United States and American Indian Nations: Treaty with the Western Cherokee, 1828."

https://americanindian.si.edu/nationtonation/treaty-with-the-western-cherokee.html

and "Why We Serve: Native Americans in the United States Armed Forces."

https://americanindian.si.edu/why-we-serve/

NOTES

1 "It was Ed Koney's Day Off at Bat So Braves Broke Even with Cards," *St. Louis Post-Dispatch*, June 12, 1913: 17.

2 "Redding Returned to Cardinals; Vann Goes Back to Indianapolis," *St. Louis Post-Dispatch*, June 13, 1913: 14.

3 "Bees Show Pep in First Local Workout," *Salt Lake Telegram*, March 30, 1916: 4.

4 "It Happened in Fanland," *Hartford Daily Courant*, July 25, 1912: 18

5 F.C.L, "The Dictagraph," *Sioux City Journal*, July 20, 1913: 10.

6 "A Fairland Star," *Fairland* (Oklahoma) *News-Herald*, November 14, 1913: 1.

7 "Drawn from Archives of the Historical Society," *Daily Oklahoman* (Oklahoma City), April 5, 1908: 21; "Three Cherokees Living Who Once Ruled as Chiefs," *Daily Oklahoman*, June 22, 1919: 17.

8 "Cherokee People: Dealings with the Early United States," https://www.britannica.com/topic/Cherokee-people.

9 "The Cherokee Nation: The History of the Cherokee Nation," https://www.cherokee.org/about-the-nation/history/.

10 "Fairland 15 Years Ago," *Fairland News-Herald*, April 25, 1913: 2.

11 "Six O'Clock Dinner at Vann's," *Fairland News-Herald*, July 4, 1913: 1.

12 "Dutch Vann Is Making Good," *Arkansas Democrat* (Little Rock), June 25, 1910: 2.

13 "Collegian Fans Mighty Wagner," *Daily Arkansas Gazette* (Little Rock), April 9, 1910: 8.

14 "Johnny Vann Visits Friends in City," *Springfield* (Missouri) *News-Leader*, September 30, 1910: 10.

15 "Kraft and Eibel Put Thrills into Texas League; Panthers Well-Balanced Aggregation," *Shreveport* (Louisiana) *Times*, October 2, 1921: 9.

16 "Removed to the Hospital" and "Mrs. Dillon Holt Dead," *Fairland News Herald*, May 19, 1911: 1.

17 "Double-Header Is Stopped by Rain," *Hartford Daily Courant*, August 22, 1912: 16.

18 "Vandalia Bridge Goes Down with a Roar; White River Flood Is Receding Slowly; Bitter Gale Brings Intense Suffering to Refugees," *Indianapolis Star*, March 27, 1913: 1.

19 "Indian Refugees Find More Rain at Chicago," *Indianapolis News*, April 4, 1913: 20.

20 "Cubs Again Down Hoosier Nine, 7-3," *Chicago Tribune*, April 7, 1913: 17.

21 "Sol Meyer Sees Indians Beaten," *Indianapolis Star*, April 7, 1913: 8.

22 John Vann entry, baseball-reference.com, https://www.baseball-reference.com/register/player.fcgi?id=vann--001joh.

23 "Story of Indians' Defeat in Final Contest on Road," *Indianapolis Star*, April 23, 1913: 8.

24 "Vaughan Holds 'Em in Rubber of Series," *Indianapolis Star*, June 15, 1913: 25.

25 "Sioux Fielding Improved," *Sioux City Journal*, July 20, 1913: 11.

26 "Final Western League Averages," *Sioux City Journal*, October 12, 1913: 11.

27 "Holderman Leads League," *Fort Wayne* (Indiana) *Daily News,* September 22, 1914: 4.

28 "Tots in Demand," *Indianapolis Star*, January 26, 1916: 10.

29 "Diamond Dust," *Salt Lake Telegram*, April 2, 1916: 8.

30 "Coast Batting Averages" and "Utes Must Let Out Player to Cut Down List," *Salt Lake Herald-Republican*, August 1, 1916: 8.

31 "Goodbye Baseball; Players Scatter," *Oakland Tribune*, October 30, 1916: 10.

32 "American Indians Star on Diamond," *Los Angeles Evening Herald*, February 1, 1915: 6.

33 "Polar Cubs Beat Indianapolis, 2-1," *Chicago Tribune*, April 4, 1914: 15; "Indians Lose by 2-1 Score," *Indianapolis Star*, April 4, 1914: 8.

34 SABR's Negro Leagues Research Committee and its annual Jerry Malloy Negro League Conference. https://sabr.org/research/negro-leagues-research-committee/ https://sabr.org/malloy.

35 "Stars and A.B.C.s in a Drawn Battle," *Indianapolis Star,* October 4, 1915: 8.

36 "Large Crowd Sees Bush's Stars Win," *Indianapolis Star*, October 11, 1915: 12.

37 "Race Riot Is Balked By Police," *Indianapolis Star,* October 25, 1915: 1

38 "Scrappy Game Ends 1915 Baseball Season," *Indianapolis News*, October 25, 1915: 12.

39 Native American Soldiers in World War I, *National Archives*: https://visit.archives.gov/whats-on/explore-exhibits/honoring-native-american-soldiers-world-war-i-service. John Vann's service records assembled with the assistance of Erin Fehr, assistant director of the Modern Warriors of World War I database at the Sequoyah National Research Center, the University of Arkansas at Little Rock. https://ualr.edu/sequoyah/wwi/.

40 "Gassers' Easy Victory in First Game of Series Lowers Morale of Chesty Atzmen," *Shreveport Journal*, September 25, 1919: 7.

41 "Panthers Give Gasmen Real Scare But Bono Checks Rally In Time to Save '19 Pennant," *Shreveport Journal*, October 2, 1919: 7.

42 "Shreveport Fans Delirious with Joy as Gasmen Give City First Baseball Pennant"; "Victory in First Game Gives Cincinnati New Confidence; White Sox Not Discouraged," *Shreveport Journal*, October 2, 1919: 7.

43 "Shreveport Wins Texas League Flag," *Shreveport Times*, October 2, 1919: 1.

44 "Hope We Can Come Back Every Year,' Ruth Tells Lions," *Shreveport Journal*, March 21, 1921: 7.

45 "Massey's Homer Saves Gassers from Shutout," *Shreveport Journal*, March 24, 1921: 7.

46 "Club Owners May Shake-Up Pilots in 5 T.L. Cities," *Shreveport Journal*, September 14, 1922: 8.

47 Fifteenth Census of the United States, 1930: Ottawa County (Council House Loop), Oklahoma. John Vann.

48 "Detective Here 19 Years Dies," *Shreveport Journal*, June 10, 1958: 1.

TOMMY WARREN

By Sean Kolodziej

Tommy Warren lived a complex life. He was the first player with overseas combat experience in World War II to appear in a major-league baseball game.[1] Known for his pitching skills, he could also swing the bat quite well. Prideful of his indigenous heritage, he would often be stereotypically referred to by the press as "the Indian" or "Wahoo Tommy." He worked with children with disabilities in his free time. He was also so heavily addicted to gambling that it led him to stealing money from friends and, eventually, taking his own life.

Thomas Gentry Warren was born on July 5, 1917, in Tulsa, Oklahoma. His mother, Maud Jones Warren, was of Muscogee (Creek) heritage. Most of the Muscogee people were forcibly moved from the Southeastern United States to Oklahoma with the passing of the Indian Removal Act in 1830. This Act, better known as the "Trail of Tears," saw the relocated peoples suffer from exposure, disease, and starvation during the journey to their newly designated Indian Territory.

Tommy's mother and grandmother, Lydia Childers Madison, are both listed in the Dawes Rolls. These rolls, created by the US government to accept applications for tribal enrollment, are used in determining individuals' degree of Indian blood. His grandmother is listed as full-blooded Muscogee, while his mother is listed as half-blood. Although the 1930 census lists Warren as "½ Creek Indian," he would eventually write on his World War II draft card that he was "¼ Indian."

Tommy's father, Fay, was of Irish heritage. He played semipro baseball for many years in his hometown of Springfield, Missouri. Later he managed the Frisco Railroad team in Tulsa. Tommy was the team's "bat boy, mascot and fly shagger."[2] Tommy and his younger brother, Larry, grew up without their mother around. Their father "pretty much raised them, and he worked on the railroad. He'd take off and would be gone for five or six days," Tommy's son said in a 2016 radio interview. "When they had to scrounge their own food, (Tommy) was particularly good at finding good, hard rocks off the railroad tracks, hitting something and (Larry) would club it to death, and they would take it home, skin in, and eat it."[3]

Warren went to Central High School in Tulsa. He was an all-state athlete in football and basketball. Playing baseball as a pitcher, he was never beaten in three seasons.[4]

By 1936 Warren was playing for the Tulsa Safeways, a semipro team that made it to the finals of the state sandlot baseball tournament, sponsored by the *Oklahoma City Daily Oklahoman* newspaper. 1937 saw him playing for the Texas Oil Co. baseball team. He also found time to play for the Sapulpa Gas softball team.

In 1938 Warren signed his first professional contract, to play for the Midland Cardinals of the Class-D West Texas-New Mexico League. In 24 games started, he went 13-11 with a 4.61 ERA. He was also used as a pinch-hitter and hit .228 in 101 at-bats.

The next season, Warren's contract was assigned to the Abilene Apaches of the same league. In April, he "didn't get the raise he thought should have been forthcoming and because he was under age, he demanded and obtained his release."[5] He then returned to semipro baseball with a team in Perry, Oklahoma, where he could make more money. Now known as a double threat because he could not only pitch but also hit well, he made the league all-star team as a utility player.[6]

Tommy Warren, with the Tulsa Oilers

Around this time, Warren went to play in the Denver Post Tournament for a team from Louisville. In one game, he smacked a pinch-hit grand slam that gave his team the victory. "'It made me an outfielder for the rest of that tournament,'" he said.[7]

In 1941 Warren was still playing semipro baseball, with a team in Elk City, Oklahoma. Near the end of the season, Claude Jonnard, manager of the Amarillo Gold Sox in the West Texas-New Mexico League, brought Warren in to help his team get into the playoffs. He hit .321 while playing the outfield and also pitched two games, winning both.

Just as Warren's baseball career was on the rise, Pearl Harbor was bombed on December 7, 1941. He enlisted in the Navy the next day. He told *The Sporting News*, "I wanted to get in because I knew my young brother, Larry, was on the aircraft carrier *Saratoga*, at Pearl Harbor."[8] On January 21, 1942, "he was informed that he qualified for a trade school, it was medical, but also, he qualified for the baseball."[9] He started practicing baseball again.

It was not long before Warren reconsidered his decision to play baseball. In a diary he kept during the war, he wrote: "Changed my mind at the last minute and decided to go to sea. Baseball manager doesn't like it."[10] In the 2016 radio interview, Tommy's son David said, "This is a man who could have sat there in a uniform and play baseball to entertain people. He was talented enough, and they wanted him to do that. But this Indian boy went to war."[11]

Warren trained as a pharmacist's mate at the Norfolk (Virginia) Naval Training Station, and later served on the battleship *USS Texas*. In October of 1942, he sailed on the Navy transport *Elizabeth Stanton* to support the US invasion of North Africa. He volunteered to go ashore with the Marines. Warren "tended to a wounded officer during the Battle of Casablanca, when a grenade landed in his foxhole. He covered the grenade with his helmet, and fell on it." Warren's medical records in the archives don't mention any injury suffered in that battle, but a month later he fell off a 15-foot ladder while on active duty and suffered a serious head injury. That was the official reason for his return home."[12]

Warren returned to the United States to recover and ended up spending 10 months at St. Albans Naval Hospital in Queens, New York. He was honorably discharged from the Navy in September 1943. Soon after, he was signed by the Brooklyn Dodgers. This time he chose baseball over the military. "I've been in some hot spots, and served with a lot of the men who are fighting this war," Warren told *The Sporting News*. "If I thought they wanted me to go into a defense job after getting my discharge, that is what I would do. But I know them, and I know how much they want baseball to go on. That is why I am doing my part to help the game carry through."[13]

In March of 1944, Warren reported for Dodgers spring training at Bear Mountain, New York, drawing a lot of attention to himself. He arrived wearing a pair of red leather cowboy boots. "He talks as fast and free as Dizzy Dean," wrote J.G.T. Spink in *The Sporting News*. "To prove he can run, he has bet Branch Rickey, Jr. he can beat any Dodger in spring camp, to prove he can hit and pitch, he offers a scrapbook full of newspaper evidence that he has out-pitched Satchel Paige and has hit homers with the bases full."[14]

While pitching during spring training, Warren did not give up a single earned run. He made a good impression on manager Leo Durocher. *The Sporting News* reported: "At the drills indoors over at West Point, Wahoo Tommy never rests. When he isn't pitching to the hitters or hitting himself, he's running footraces with the other players. Durocher thinks he can find a place for him on the club, perhaps not as a pitcher, but Warren would make a good replacement for Max Macon, as a pinch-hitter and part-time outfielder."[15]

Warren did eventually earn a spot on the team, and made his major-league debut on Opening Day, April 18, 1944, against the Phillies in Philadelphia. He pitched the eighth inning, giving up no runs and one walk, in a 4-1 Dodgers loss. In doing so, he became the first player with overseas combat experience in World War II to appear in a major-league game.[16]

A couple of weeks later, on April 30, Warren had perhaps the worst pitching outing of his career. After four Dodgers pitchers gave up 11 runs in four innings to the New York Giants, Warren was called in to pitch the rest of the game. He proceeded to give up 15 runs in five innings pitched, including a three-run homer by Phil Weintraub, who finished the game with 11 RBIs, one shy of the single-game major-league record.

Shortly thereafter, Warren was sent down to the Montreal Royals of the Double-A[17] International League. He played quite well there, posting a 7-2 record with a 1.83 ERA in 13 appearances. He quit the team in mid-June and tried to reenlist in the Navy. After some persuasion by Branch Rickey, general manager of the Dodgers, Warren was back in Montreal on July 2 and ready to play ball again.

On July 15, he was recalled by the Dodgers during the All-Star break. He had a pinch-hit infield single in the eighth inning, but the team lost to the Boston Braves, 6-3. On the 22nd he made his debut as a starting pitcher, against the Pittsburgh Pirates. He failed to get out of the first inning, giving up three runs and recording only one out.

By July 30, the Dodgers were in last place in the National League and were set to take on the first-place St. Louis Cardinals in a doubleheader. The Cardinals were red-hot, winning their last nine games. Warren got the nod to start game one. He pitched all nine innings, earning his first and only win, as the Dodgers won 10-4. He also helped himself at the plate, going 2-for-3 with a walk and a run scored. Warren was also called in to pitch in game two, getting out of a ninth-inning one-out, bases-loaded jam. He had a chance to win the game, but an 11th-inning throwing error by catcher Mickey Owen allowed Stan Musial to score, giving Warren the loss.

NATIVE AMERICAN MAJOR LEAGUERS

The Dodgers finished in seventh place in the National League in 1944. Warren's final pitching stats were unimpressive: a 1-4 record with a 4.98 ERA. In 68⅔ innings pitched, he walked 40 batters while striking out 18. His ERA+ was 71. (100 is equivalent to the league average.) His batting stats were just as unremarkable: a .256 batting average with two RBIs and one run scored in 45 plate appearances. After the season, he was sent back down to Montreal.

The Montreal Royals finished first in the International League in 1945. Warren put up good numbers when batting, including a .330/.376/.564 slash line, but struggled on the mound. He ended up 9-7 with a 5.63 ERA. The Royals released him at the end of the season. Because of this, he missed out on being Jackie Robinson's teammate by a year. Robinson played for the Royals in 1946, before making his debut with the Dodgers in 1947.

When not playing baseball, Warren lived in Tulsa and was a sheriff's deputy. It was here while doing a publicity tour in an aircraft factory that he met his wife, Frances. Tommy Warren and Frances Hammond were married on May 11, 1945. Their only child, David, was born on July 13, 1947, in Tulsa.

No longer affiliated with the Dodgers, Warren ended up playing for the Tulsa Oilers of the Texas League from 1946 to 1948. He won 20 games with a 2.86 ERA in 1946 and 14 in 1947, but in 1948 he won only 6 games and was released after the season.

At this point in his life, Warren's gambling problem started to cause problems in his personal life. His son David described life growing up as Tommy's son: "He loved kids, not particularly me. He was beloved by my friends. He could be himself when he was with children, especially if there was a baseball involved. He tried to be a good father, the best he could be with what he knew, but there were problems. By the late '40s he had a noticeable gambling problem and it really hurt his baseball career. The bad times were when he was on losing streaks and he would strike out. The only time he ever really beat me, he beat me so bad that blood ran down my legs and stained my tennis shoes and my socks. My mother broke the door open and laid a sawed-off 12 gauge on the back of his head and said, 'Next time you touch him, I'm firing both barrels, and I will kill you.' He never touched me again."[18]

Early in 1949, while still a deputy sheriff, Warren set up a scheme to try to get money to pay off his gambling debts. He got friends, including Tulsa Sheriff George Blaine, to give him money to purchase new automobiles. He told them he knew someone in Detroit who could get the vehicles at wholesale cost. Warren never delivered the cars; the money was gambled away. When this finally caught up with him, he said, "Never did I have any thought of doing anything dishonest or taking a cent from my friends. I got in a jam, and when I got the money, I thought I would try it once again, hoping to recoup. But every time it went the same way."[19]

In mid-February of 1949, Warren's wife handed in his resignation to the sheriff's department. She said he "left their home Saturday 'acting like a wild man' after losing a reported $7,200 on the Willie Pep-Sandy Sadler fight in New York and the Oklahoma A&M-University of Oklahoma basketball game Friday night."[20] Sheriff George Blaine was aware of Warren's gambling problem for quite some time. "I told him he'd have to stop and he promised he would," the sheriff said.[21]

For a while, after agreeing to help the police in exposing Tulsa's gambling rackets, it looked as if Warren would get out of jail time. But on March 11, it was reported that four used-car dealers and a tavern owner planned to seek new charges against him. Ted Wilmot, president of the Tulsa Used Car Dealers Association, said, "We won't be satisfied to see some judge slap Tommy on the wrist and say, 'Poor Tommy, he did wrong, but he didn't mean to,' and then turn him loose. We want to see him put in jail where he can think about what he did to fellows who thought of him as a friend."[22]

On May 4, 1949, Warren was found guilty of larceny by fraud and sentenced to three years in prison. He appealed the decision and posted bail. Knowing that there was too much bad publicity about him in the United States, Warren asked permission to go play baseball in Canada. His request was granted.

Warren wound up playing in Ontario for the Galt Terriers of the Intercounty Baseball League. His former teammate on the Dodgers, Goody Rosen, was a teammate. He started the season strong, getting the win in a 9-1 victory over the Guelph Maple Leafs. By June he was leading the league in both home runs and RBIs. In early August, Warren broke a bone in his foot while sliding into second base. After a couple of weeks off to recover, he was back in time to help his team win the pennant.

Controversy started as soon as the playoffs began. Warren and a few other veterans on the team had signed contracts that guaranteed them 10 percent of the gate for playoff games. Now, with the playoffs soon to start, they were demanding 25 percent of the gate. The team owner refused and eventually the whole thing seemed to blow over. In the fifth inning of the final game of the semifinals, against the Brantford Red Sox, a ball was hit between the shortstop, center fielder, and left fielder. Warren, playing left field, called off everyone and then hesitated and let the ball fall in front of him. Umpire Johnny Kumornik later said, "I could have caught that ball in my jockstrap. Warren was no bush leaguer, for chrissakes. He had been up in the majors. The bloody Indian had short-legged it."[23] To make matters worse, the day after the game Warren deposited a large sum of money in the local bank. The rumor among the other Galt players was that Warren had placed a large bet on the underdog Red Sox and then threw the game to collect on his bet.[24]

Warren returned to Tulsa and was still awaiting his appeal to be heard. Granted permission to once again leave the country, he played in the Venezuelan Winter League for the Sabios de Vargas team. The team was managed by Cuban hall of famer Pelayo Chacón and featured Negro League Hall of Famer Ray Brown. Warren played center field and sometimes pitched. The team did not do well, however, finishing with a record of 17-31.

In 1950, while Warren's appeal was still being considered, he was once more granted permission to leave the country to play baseball. This time he played for the Sultanes de Monterrey in the Mexican League. The team finished three games out of first place.

In December of 1950, the Oklahoma State Criminal Court of Appeals ordered a new trial for Warren. The court ruled that he should have been accused and tried on a charge of obtaining money under false pretenses instead of larceny by fraud. While he awaited the new trial, Warren began the 1950 baseball season managing and playing for the Miami Eagles of the Class-D Kansas-Oklahoma-Missouri League.

In late June 1951, Warren was found guilty of obtaining money under false pretenses and sentenced to three years in prison. He appealed, was released after posting bond, and returned to the Eagles. On July 4 he pitched a no-hitter against the Iola Indians in the seven-inning opener of a doubleheader. Warren struck out nine batters and walked one. He then came on in relief in the second game, allowing just two hits in three innings of work. A few weeks later, he made the KOM League All-Star team as a reserve.

On February 15, 1952, Warren dropped his appeal. Explaining why, he said, "I want to start serving my sentence. I want to get this thing off my mind. I have a boy who will soon be five and I want this out of my life before he grows older and tragedy drapes around his shoulders."[25] Warren started serving his sentence in April.

While an inmate at the Oklahoma State Penitentiary, Warren pitched and managed for the McAlester Outlaws. The Outlaws were a part of the prison's competitive sports program, which Warden Jerome Walters, a retired Army colonel, thought was "a great thing for the prisoners."[26] Their baseball, "about a caliber of a Class C league,"[27] was played both in and outside the confines of the prison walls. The convicts would play about 10 games a month during the season. Their opponents came from "Oklahoma college teams, the Class D Sooner State League and semi-pro outfits."[28] Traveling for a "road" game would leave the team at a disadvantage: "Two of its infielders have escape records and are forbidden to leave the gates."[29] Warren won at least 22 games on the mound[30] and the Outlaws were invited to participate in the annual Oklahoma state sandlot baseball tournament. Warren made the sandlot all-star team as a pitcher.

On February 23, 1953, after serving 10½ months of a three-year sentence, Warren was granted parole. His baseball skills may have helped him get parole early: He had been offered a job with Temple of the Class-B Big State League. "Robert Conwell, manager of the Temple team, appeared before the board personally on Warren's behalf," a newspaper reported.[31]

After appearing in 42 games for the Temple Eagles, Warren was traded to the Corpus Christi Aces of the Class-B Gulf Coast League. The Aces struggled to a record of 61-83; Warren posted a record of 6-5 with a 3.62 ERA.

Warren was named player-manager of the Seminole Oilers in February of 1954. The Oilers, playing in the Class-D Sooner State League, were in financial distress. Even though Warren was 10-1 on the mound and hitting .298 as an outfielder, the team released him in June to save money. He quickly signed as player-manager with the Borger Gassers of the Class-C West Texas-New Mexico League. The team folded on July 17 and was taken over by the league. Warren was released to save money. By July 25, Warren signed with the Wichita Indians of the Class-A Western League. Finishing the season for the Indians with a 3-1 record and a 2.10 ERA, Warren finally found stable ground and continued to pitch for Wichita in 1955, his last season in Organized Baseball.

Warren played semipro ball around the Wichita area for the next two years. After finally retiring from baseball, he stayed close to the game by working with children with physical disabilities and young aspiring baseball players. He told a Canadian author, "[T]he late Bill Skelly of Skelly Oil Co. got me interested in the little ones in 1947 when he asked me to visit the Tulsa Children's Home, and I have tried to work with them ever since."[32]

But gambling was still a big part of Warren's post-baseball life. His son, David, said, "After dad got out of baseball, he just had to have the gambling, and he had to have the big-time gambling, it had to be dangerous gambling. I remember that last year in 1967. I went to spend three months with him. [The gambling] was so serious that he wouldn't have me in his apartment. He had me in another apartment because he was afraid something violent was going to happen. I didn't see him again until Christmas that year. I was at my grandfather's with my mother. They were divorced by this time, and my uncle was there. Normally, my dad would stay the whole time that (uncle) Benny was there, and he just came in, had dinner, and left, which was really strange. I knew something was really, really wrong."[33]

Warren bet on three games on New Year's Day. He lost all three and he didn't have the money to pay off the bets. He checked into the Ramada Inn that same day. The next day, he shot himself in the chest with a shotgun. He left behind a short note, saying he intended on taking his life. He was 50 years old. He is buried in Memorial Park Cemetery in Tulsa.

In spite of his flaws, Warren made a positive impact in many people's lives. His son, David, observed that "it wasn't until my father's funeral that I realized how much he was really loved by the people of Tulsa. I've got pictures of him taking kids in wheelchairs to the games and setting them on the field so they actually felt like they were part of it in their wheelchairs, and lean against the wall with their crutches. That funeral, it was unbelievable of all the people that were in wheelchairs. Those were the kids that he took to that field. He didn't know that all those kids he took to the ballpark remembered him and cared."[34]

NOTES

1   Gary Bedingfield, "Baseball in Wartime," https://www.baseballinwartime.com/player_biographies/warren_tommy.htm. Accessed August 16, 2022.

2   J.G.T. Spink, "Looping the Loops: Dodgers Casanova Cowboy," *The Sporting News*, March 16, 1944: 14.

3   WBUR radio interview with David Warren, interviewed by Greg Echlin, May 21, 2016. Tommy Warren: A WWII Veteran Turned MLB Pitcher | Only A Game (wbur.org). Accessed August 16, 2022

4   "Tommy Warren, Former Gold Sox Star, Is Most Colorful Hopeful of Dodgers," *Amarillo* (Texas) *Globe-Times,* March 31, 1944: 15.

5   Spink.

6   "Enid Fielder Is 'Most Valuable' of Semi-Pros," *Blackwell* (Oklahoma) *Daily Journal*, July 23, 1939: 5.

7   Spink.

8   Spink.

9   WBUR interview.

10 WBUR interview.

11 WBUR interview.

12 WBUR interview.

13 Spink.

14 Spink.

15 Harold C. Burr, "Dodger Outlook Murky Without Arky, Says Lip," *The Sporting News*, March 30, 1944: 4.

16 Bedingfield.

17 Double A in 1944 was the equivalent of today's Triple A.

18 WBUR interview.

19 "Tulsan Admits Gaming Loses," *Miami* (Oklahoma) *News-Record*, February 16, 1949: 1.

20 "Tommy Warren Is Expected Back in Tulsa Today," *Sapulpa* (Oklahoma) *Herald,* February 16, 1949: 4.

21 "Tulsan Admits Gaming Loses."

22 "Ex-Baseball Star Warren Faces Criminal Charges," *Bartlesville* (Oklahoma) *Examiner-Enterprise*, March 11, 1949: 1.

23 David Menary, *Terrier Town: Summer of '49* (Waterloo, Ontario: Wilfrid Laurier University Press, 2003), 252.

24 Menary, 256.

25 "Tom Warren Asks to Start Prison Term," *Bartlesville Record*, February 16, 1952: 1.

26 "There Is One Team Free from Holdouts – It's from State Pen," *Oil City* (Pennsylvania) *Derrick,* May 10, 1952: 10.

27 "There Is One Team Free from Holdouts – It's from State Pen."

28 "There Is One Team Free from Holdouts – It's from State Pen."

29 "There Is One Team Free from Holdouts – It's from State Pen."

30 "McDaniel vs. Warren in Saturday's Contest," *Durant* (Oklahoma) *Daily Democrat*, August 5, 1952: 4.

31 "Tommy Warren Receives Parole," *Durant Daily Democrat*, February 24, 1953: 2.

32 Menary, 339.

33 WBUR interview.

34 WBUR interview.

BILL WILKINSON

By Bill Lamberty

Bill Wilkinson's arm talent was easy to spot, even when he was throwing snowballs.

"In the winter time, before the spring (season) started, this kid came into the gym and said, 'Coach J, you've got to get outside," said legendary Cherry Creek High School baseball coach Marc Johnson. "They've got a snowball fight going and Billy Wilkinson's going to kill somebody because he's throwing snowballs so hard and guys are pinned on the brick wall."[1]

The incident began innocently but served as the introduction of Wilkinson's left arm to the baseball program at Cherry Creek in suburban Denver. "I actually hit a guy in the head and knocked him out," Wilkinson recalled. "I was just standing there, standing around, and all of a sudden these guys started throwing snowballs. Nobody knew who I was, so I pick up a snowball and start rifling at people, and it went dead silent because I was throwing so hard."[2]

Wilkinson's success in the ensuing months arrived as startlingly as that snowball. The move-in from Montana

Bill Wilkinson, with the 1987 Mariners

(1987 Topps Traded, courtesy of the Topps Company, with thanks to Sam Dolson)

led his school to an undefeated state championship season, Cherry Creek's first title, and that dominant campaign vaulted him into the fourth round of the 1983 major-league draft. He punctuated a nine-year professional career with parts of three seasons with the Seattle Mariners, linked with his great-grandfather Jim Bluejacket as the first great-grandson of a big-leaguer to pitch in the majors.[3]

William Carl Wilkinson was born on August 10, 1964, in Greybull, Wyoming, the third of Jim and Patti (Bluejacket) Wilkinson's five children. The family's roots in north-central Wyoming ran deep, and in baseball ran deeper. Patti Wilkinson's grandfather, Jim Bluejacket, a native Oklahoman and member of the Cherokee Nation, played for the Brooklyn Tip-Tops of the Federal League in 1914-15, then for Cincinnati a year later, one of an early wave of talented Native Americans to play in the major leagues.[4]

In 1920 Bluejacket traveled to Wyoming to play with Greybull of the Midwest League (organized by the Midwest Refinery rather than a nod to geography) while awaiting an opportunity with Columbus of the International League. While he was "[n]ot much impressed with the possibilities at Greybull" upon arrival, a visit to the town's ballpark changed his mind. Upon seeing several players he recognized from his time as a professional, he thought, "Somebody is paying for this and they must have money to land these players."[5]

After a memorable summer in Greybull[6] and the conclusion of his career, Bluejacket worked for Standard Oil, eventually living in and spreading the gospel of baseball in Aruba. After he retired, he and his family moved back to Greybull for two years after World War II before returning to his hometown of Pekin, Illinois. He died in 1947, but his son Jimmy remained in Wyoming to operate a dude ranch.[7]

Bill Wilkinson briefly discussed his family background: "I am a member of the Cherokee Nation of Oklahoma. As far as my native heritage, I really didn't think much about it until the last 15 years or so. My mother did mention it from time to time but we never really were involved in it. I am not sure what to include about my heritage other than the fact that my great-grandfather was one of the first natives to play major-league baseball."[8]

While Jim Bluejacket found athletic success across the nation, the Wilkinson clan became a sporting dynamo in Wyoming. Bill Wilkinson's father, Jim, was a fine athlete in Greybull, and Jim's brother, Tom, gained fame on a larger scale. "The Greybull Rifle" earned All-Western Athletic Conference honors during each of his three seasons as Wyoming's quarterback and also pitched and played short-stop for the baseball team. After his college career he took his talents to Canada, eventually earning induction into both the Wyoming Athletics and CFL Halls of Fame.[9]

"Tom was a Wyoming native from Greybull known as 'The Greybull Rifle' and he was true to his nickname," according to Kevin McKinney, longtime University of Wyoming Athletics official who watched Wilkinson's Cowboy teams while growing up. "To that point in Cowboy football history, nobody had come along who possessed his arm strength and accuracy. A star on the baseball team as well, he was a very special Cowboy who was an excellent leader. He will always be considered one of the all-time Cowboy greats at quarterback."[10]

Jim Wilkinson worked in marketing for Amoco for a quarter-century, moving the family from Greybull to Billings, Montana, in 1965 when Bill was one year old, then north to Glasgow in 1968 and finally to Great Falls in 1970.[11] "That's what I consider my hometown," Bill said of Great Falls, where Jim was an important figure in the town's youth baseball scene and coached the Great Falls Electrics American Legion club for two years. But in 1982 the family moved on to Denver.[12]

Jim Wilkinson served as the family's advance party, arriving in Denver early "looking for a place to live, trying to decide where we were going to live (and) looking at schools," with the baseball program an important factor. Marc Johnson's reputation was catching up to his coaching acumen at that moment in time, and Jim Wilkinson's base-ball knowledge served him and his sons well. He decided on the district that included Cherry Creek High School, with Pomona High also receiving strong consideration, and it was Pomona that Cherry Creek topped for the state title the next spring.[13]

Wilkinson's presence became known immediately to Johnson, Cherry Creek's baseball coach. "I remember him coming into my physical education class and I'm talking to him, obviously a new student, and I said, 'Are you a pretty good athlete?' He said, 'I'd like to think that I am,' and then he took a basketball and dunked it backhand. He was like 5-9, and myself and my coaches just marveled."[14]

A self-described loner who mostly kept to himself during his early weeks at Cherry Creek, Wilkinson made the basketball team in November and that process helped him "feel like I started fitting in." While basketball was his first love, and he didn't recall any tide-changing events that pushed him toward baseball, small signs that his left arm was something special emerged along the way.

When he was 10 or 11, he innocently threw a snowball at a car and moments later the driver was on the front porch of the family house with the news that it had cracked her windshield. "My dad didn't tell me this at the time, but later he said that he thought, 'How in the hell did he do that with

a snowball?'" He was the only boy his age who could throw a rock or a baseball over the local water tower.[15]

And then there was his first indoor bullpen session in the winter of 1982-83, when Marc Johnson lined him up with a sophomore catcher. "I turned to (Johnson) and said, 'Are you sure he can catch me?' He said, 'What do you mean?' And I threw it right by him and put a big hole in the wall. He didn't even get a glove on it, and it went right by him."

To that point early in his senior season, Bill Wilkinson's left arm hinted occasionally at what was to come. "It was just a bunch of weird little things." But the ensuing months set him on the path that framed the rest of his life.

"I feel very blessed that he chose to come to our par-ticular school," Johnson said. "We had a lot of good years, won 10 state titles, but that was one of our very best. That team went unbeaten and I've coached a lot of very good teams but only two went completely unbeaten through the year, and his was one of them. We've had some very, very good players, pitchers and players that have gone to the big leagues, but I can honestly say that in my mind, to this day, that he was the best pitcher in high school that I have ever seen. Not what he did later, but in high school, he was the best."[16]

Wilkinson's new teammates noticed his presence, as well. "He could jump out of the gym, and basically what-ever he wanted to do in any sport he could do," said Reed Peters, a junior in 1983 who eventually enjoyed a long and successful college coaching career. "[Before him] we couldn't get over the hump and win big games," but Peters said that Wilkinson's arrival and the presence of a group of kids he'd grown up with helped generate the mentality of toughness needed to "finally get us over the hump."[17]

During the spring of 1983, Cherry Creek High made the hump a distant memory. The Bruins put the rest of the state on notice early, with Wilkinson throwing a no-hit-ter and striking out 14 in seven innings. That set the stage for a streak of 40 scoreless innings to open the season for Wilkinson.[18] He gave up just one earned run during the season[19] and was known within the Cherry Creek program as an intense competitor and tremendous teammate.[20]

A moment from that season's state championship game defined Wilkinson's competitive spirit for his teammates. Early in the game, a star player from Pomona High, a future University of Colorado football player named Don DeLuzio, hit a fly ball deep for an out. As he passed by the mound, he said to Wilkinson, "I like it, I like it a lot." After a short rain delay Wilkinson returned to the mound and "dominated the rest of the day," Peters recalled. "And (late in the game) Billy said the same thing to him, 'I like it, I like it a lot.' Billy won that day, and we ended up winning the state championship game. He was a fierce competitor."[21]

With his amazing senior season in the books, highlighted by state tournament and state MVP awards, all that was left for Wilkinson was the major-league baseball draft. He had signed to play at Nebraska, part of a star-studded class that included Brian Holman of Wichita, Kansas. When draft day rolled around, Holman was chosen by the Expos in the first round, and Wilkinson in the fourth round by Seattle. Holman informed Wilkinson during a phone call that he planned to sign, and Wilkinson's sentiments were the same "if the money was right."[22]

The money was right, and after the standard wrangling over the signing bonus, he was headed for Bellingham, Washington, to join the Mariners' short-season rookie league team. As the only prep draftee on the team, Wilkinson was the player whose arm was the most stretched out so he drew the Opening Day start. With his head spinning much of the season, one of the youngest players in the Northwest League[23] finished fourth in the loop with 87 strikeouts in 13 games, all starts, while posting a 3.39 ERA. His 54 walks led to a 1.696 WHIP, but the performance earned him a promotion to Wausau in the Midwest League.[24]

His first season as a professional, when he described himself as "wild as all hell just trying to throw the ball over the plate," included "a lot of ups and downs" and "doing some things I shouldn't have." The theme of the summer was adapting to the lifestyle of a professional athlete in his first time away from home while learning how to read, manage, and care for his body.[25]

It also set the stage for a strong 1984 campaign in the Midwest League. He logged a 3.31 ERA for Wausau, with 117 strikeouts in 103⅓ innings. While continuing the process of learning about life and baseball, Wilkinson posted a 6-4 record with Wausau, raising his strikeout-to-walk ratio to 2.25 and dropping his WHIP to 1.268. He allowed just 79 hits after he "realized I'm going to (have to) buckle down (and) understand how it works away from the field, how to prepare myself on the field for a start, what to do in between starts."[26]

After a 6-1 start in Salinas in the Class-A California League in 1985 and one game in which he struck out 17, Wilkinson was visited by Mariners minor-league field co-ordinator Bill Haywood with a simple question. "He said, 'Is this too easy for you?'" Wilkinson said. "I didn't know how to answer that at first, but then I said, 'I feel like I'm in high school again.' He started laughing, and the next day I got sent to Triple A."

That promotion came in early May, and after winning two of his first three starts for Calgary, he was called into manager Bobby Floyd's office for a meeting with him and pitching coach Bobby Cuellar. "(Floyd) says, 'We're making some moves.' I looked at him and said, 'Oh, am I going to Double A, or back to A ball?' He smiled and said, 'No, you're going to Seattle to pitch against the Royals.'"

The ascent was breathtaking to Wilkinson, and was compared to something out of a FedEx commercial by a national baseball writer.[27] "I went from A ball to the majors in a month," he said. "And I was just two years out of high school." He called his father, who, upon learning of the promotion, "just went nuts." The promotion from Salinas

to Calgary and then from Triple A to the majors in quick succession came due to a rash of injuries to the big-league staff. Jim Beattie, Mark Langston, Salomé Barojas, Mike Moore, and Mike Morgan each hit the disabled list for some period of time in this stretch.[28]

Wilkinson's major-league debut came against the eventual World Series champion Kansas City Royals in the Kingdome on June 13, 1985. The opening inning was a rough one. After he struck out Willie Wilson and Lonnie Smith, Frank White singled and Wilkinson walked Steve Balboni. One of that fall's World Series heroes, Darryl Motley, followed with a three-run homer. Wilkinson then retired Hal McRae, and cruised until he surrendered a homer to Jim Sundberg in the fifth. He made it into the sixth before departing with a final line of 5⅔ innings pitched, four runs and five hits allowed, with five strikeouts and four walks.

While the opening-inning barrage by the Royals was momentarily unnerving, the young southpaw fared much worse five days later when he was knocked out of the game in the first inning for the first time in his career.[29] After retiring the Texas Rangers' Oddibe McDowell on a fly out to lead off the bottom of the first, he walked Toby Harrah and Buddy Bell and allowed a double to Pete O'Brien and back-to-back singles to Gary Ward and Larry Parrish. "I got the shit kicked out of me," Wilkinson said.

That start earned Wilkinson a ticket back to Calgary, where he pitched well for about a month before a bizarre incident ended his season. On July 12,[30] with the team caught shorthanded, Wilkinson was forced to hit for himself. After one swing, "I felt a twinge in my back and thought, 'That doesn't feel right.' So I went out after that half-inning and couldn't even throw the ball to the plate. I'd tweaked my back so bad that I actually pulled muscle away from the rib cage." His first season with a taste of big-league baseball was ended by his only plate appearance as a professional. That injury was also the first in what would become a cascade of physical setbacks that would eventually end his career and alter his life.

Wilkinson spent the 1986 season in the rotation at Calgary, posting an 8-8 record with a 4.78 ERA. Pitching at altitude (Calgary's elevation is just over 3,400 feet) in an offensive environment, he struck out 86 batters while walking 51 in 143 innings with a 1.38 WHIP. While the statistical portfolio was in line with the rest of his career, Wilkinson said his focus wasn't.

"For whatever reason I didn't take 1986 seriously," he said. "I don't know why. I look back on my career and try to pinpoint certain things as to why I did this and why I did that, but 1986 was a huge learning experience for me in that I [figured out that I] still have to work to get to Seattle. They're not just going to give me an opportunity, I have to prove that I deserve it. In '86 I was just kind of nonchalantly half-assing it, and sure enough I spent the whole year [in the minor leagues]."

For the second straight year, Wilkinson's season ended on the operating table. After throwing a pitch late in the season he felt numbness in two fingers and his elbow, precipitating surgery to move the nerve back into its proper canal. The injury healed over the winter, and he entered spring training in 1987 with a healthy arm and rejuvenated attitude.[31]

While 1986 proved stagnant for Wilkinson, it was one of turmoil for the Mariners. Seattle opened the season with Chuck Cottier at the helm, but after 29 games handed the reins to eventual Hall of Fame manager Dick Williams. The team finished last in the AL West for the first time since 1983 but assembled a solid roster heading into 1987. The lineup featured Harold Reynolds, Alvin Davis, and Phil Bradley, while a talented group of young starters featuring Mark Langston, Mike Moore, Mike Morgan, and Scott Bankhead anchored the rotation.

Wilkinson cruised through spring training "getting everyone out," but late in the spring faced the reality of a role change. "We get into late March and I'm still [with the big-league club], so Dick Williams, the manager, said, 'If you're going to be on this team you're going to pitch out of the bullpen.' 'I want to start,' that's what I told him. And he said, 'If you're going to be here, you're going to be in the bullpen.'"

With spring training nearly complete, Wilkinson found himself in the middle of a team scheme. Unknown to him, pitcher Mark Langston and a couple of other moundsmen approached Williams to ask about Wilkinson's status on the team. Williams answered in the affirmative, and a prank was hatched.

"Dick Williams calls me in with Billy Connors, the pitching coach, and they said, 'We decided we're going to keep so and so and we're going to send you back to Triple A,'" Wilkinson said. "And I said, 'Are you kidding me? Will I at least get to start down there?' He says, 'No, we want to keep you in the bullpen. But you're going to pitch today so you're going to pitch here today.'"

During the pitchers' pregame routine, teammate Domingo Ramos "kept egging me on" about his demotion, and Wilkinson felt his aggravation rising. "I was pissed," he said. Before the game, "Dick Williams calls a huddle and he goes, 'Does anybody know what today is?' He looks at me and says, 'Wilkie, what's today?' And I said, 'I don't know, what's today?' He goes, 'Does April First mean anything to you?' Everyone was laughing, the whole team knew about it, so I said, 'April First is April Fool's Day.' He said, 'April Fool's, you made the team.'"[32]

It took Wilkinson "a couple of months" to figure out life in the bullpen. The vagaries of when and how much to warm up, how to stay tuned up during long stretches without action and how to care for his arm during busy stretches sorted themselves out eventually, and when they did he enjoyed his new role. During his only full season in the big leagues, he compiled a 3.66 ERA, second-best on the team among pitchers with at least 20 appearances. He posted an impressive 1.074 WHIP, allowing 61 hits and 21 walks in 76⅓ innings. He struck out 73, and his strikeouts-to-walks ratio of 3.48 was the best of his career. His rate of 8.6 strikeouts per nine innings was the best rate he posted above Class A.

A Mariners catcher from 1986-92, Scott Bradley remembered being impressed with Wilkinson's arm action. "He was a little undersized but his arm was just so loose and his fastball really exploded," said Bradley, who later became the longtime head baseball coach at Princeton. "He was deceptive, guys would see the delivery and didn't think he was throwing that hard. We didn't have TrackMan and Hawkeye and everything back then, but I'm sure, as a former catcher, his fastball had a very pure spin and a very high rate on it. The ball had life."[33]

Bradley said Wilkinson relied on a "swing-and-miss" fastball and a "short little cutter," a simple repertoire befitting a reliever. Bradley also liked Wilkinson's aggression and said that in 1987 the rookie benefited from a smart usage plan.[34]

"When we first brought him up, he had a lot of success early on, really, really pitched well," Bradley said. "We did a nice job when we first brought him up starting him out in nonleverage situations just to get his feet wet. He pitched in some situations where maybe we were behind quite a bit, pitched well, then pitched in some situations where we were ahead quite a bit. Then gradually we got to the point where we used him in some pretty leveraged situations as a setup guy, seventh-, eighth-inning type guy."[35]

Mariners radio play-by-play broadcaster Rick Rizzs remembered a light moment during the season. During a game with his command faltering and pitch count elevated, Wilkinson received a mound visit from pitching coach Connors.

"Bill was struggling on the mound," Rizzs recalled, "and Billy went out to make a visit. I'm watching the conversation and all of a sudden Bill started laughing. Here he is in the middle of a mess with runners on base and the game is really speeding up on him and he's out there laughing."[36]

"I was going full count on every hitter," Wilkinson recalled with a chuckle, "so he walked out to the mound, he looked at me and smiled and blew me a kiss and said, 'I love you.' I started laughing, I actually had to put my glove up, and I said, 'Billy, you're a sick man.' Then he turned around and went back to the dugout. I got the next two guys out and we won."

Wilkinson had 10 saves. He enjoyed playing for both Williams and Connors. He said Connors' ability to keep things light was a good counter to Williams's old-school toughness. "He was a hard-ass," Wilkinson said of Williams. "A lot of the guys on the team didn't like him. He was tough. I loved him."

Williams's ability to get to the heart of the matter showed itself during one mound visit in 1987. "He said, 'Do you like pitching here?' I said, 'What, in Seattle?' He goes, 'No, in the big leagues.' I said, 'Yeah, why?' And he goes, if you don't get your shit together you'll be in Triple A tomorrow.' And I said, 'Yeah, but I'm here now.' He told me later that no one had ever said anything like that to him before, and that I was the smallest guy on the team but I had the biggest balls."

Wilkinson's successful 1987 season set the stage for a 1988 campaign that would send his career spiraling toward its eventual end. "Once again, I took it for granted," he said. His season began with a whimper in 1988: He allowed six hits and two walks in his first 2⅓ innings. After those four outings he didn't allow a run through his next six, covering 4⅔ innings. He gave up four runs on four hits and a walk to the Blue Jays on May 3, and his ERA ballooned to 7.88. The early months of the season were one long yo-yo ride, and May 12 was his last major-league appearance until August 12.

Bradley saw a slight decrease in velocity during his time in the majors that season. "Because he was a little smaller when he lost that extra life on his fastball, he wasn't throwing fastballs by people," Bradley recalled.[37]

Wilkinson's 21 games in Triple A led to a 9.13 ERA, but he returned to pitch fairly well in the season's final two months in Seattle. He allowed five earned runs in 21⅓ innings. He allowed 12 hits and nine walks in that stretch. At some point in 1988, Wilkinson damaged his shoulder, and he pitched in 1989 with a partially torn rotator cuff. He opened that season with Calgary, but in late April was traded to Pittsburgh and spent most of the season with Buffalo in the Pirates chain.

By this point, a drinking problem that began "getting pretty bad in '88 toward the end (of the season)" facilitated weight gain which in turn led to a breakdown in his muscles. He finished 1989 with a 3.69 ERA for Calgary and Buffalo in 102⅓ innings over 23 appearances, 20 of them starts. He struck out 52, walked 60, and at the end of the season he was chosen by Kansas City in the Rule 5 draft. His shoulder gave out the next spring, leading to shoulder surgery. "I missed the whole year, so I got paid just to sit at home in Seattle and drink."

That led him to rehab for alcohol in 1991, and although Wilkinson returned to sobriety in 1992, a brief comeback in the Oakland A's system lasted only to July 4. He was released and his career was finished at age 28.

After his playing days Wilkinson returned to the site that had truly launched his baseball career, Cherry Creek High and the watchful and caring eyes of Marc Johnson. He coached with his mentor until 1997 with an eye toward coaching in professional baseball, but "the real world got in the way." While he was pursuing coaching he also taught himself accounting without the benefit of a formal education.

He worked as a staff accountant for a firm in Denver for seven years, then returned to Montana. He worked as an accountant for Helena Sand and Gravel until 2017, then took a position as a tax auditor for the State of Montana. He retired in 2024. He's kept his hand in sports with occasional private pitching lessons, and in 2024 began exploring the possibility of working with Fellowship of Christian Athletes and as a speaker to educate young athletes to the perils of alcohol and drug abuse.[38]

SOURCES

In addition to the sources cited in the Notes, the author consulted baseballalmanac.com, Baseball-Reference.com, and Retrosheet.org.

NOTES

1   Marc Johnson, telephone interview, June 5, 2025.

2   Bill Wilkinson, telephone interview, July 14, 2025. All direct quotations attributed to Bill Wilkinson come from this interview, unless otherwise indicated.

3   Bill Wilkinson interview; also Baseball Almanac, https://www.baseball-almanac.com/family/fam4.shtml. Wilkinson said he learned of that historical fact when ESPN used it as a trivia question and friends called to ask if he'd seen the telecast or knew of the information.

4   Bluejacket was a contemporary of American Indian players including Charles Bender, Jim Thorpe, and John Tortes Meyers.

5   "Beating Casper Was Job Given Greybull Hurler/Jim Bluejacket, Former Midwest League Star, Visits Here on Return from Aruba," undated article from *Casper Tribune-Herald* cited on Genealogy Trails website, https://genealogytrails.com/wyo/bighorn/bios_bluejacket.html.

6   "Beating Casper Was Job Given Greybull Hurler/Jim Bluejacket, Former Midwest League Star, Visits Here on Return from Aruba."

7   "Beating Casper Was Job Given Greybull Hurler/Jim Bluejacket, Former Midwest League Star, Visits Here on Return from Aruba."

8   Bill Wilkinson, email correspondence, July 31, 2025.

9   "UW Intercollegiate Athletics Class to Induct Class of 2020-21," gowyo.com, https://gowyo.com/news/2021/7/12/general-uw-intercollegiate-athletics-hall-of-fame-to-induct-class-of-2020-21.aspx.

10   Kevin McKinney, text interview, July 16, 2025.

11   *Billings Gazette*, May 12, 2002. https://www.legacy.com/us/obituaries/billingsgazette/name/james-wilkinson-obituary?pid=198216394.

12   Wilkinson cited the help of his mother, Patti Wilkinson, in reconstructing his family's timeline.

13   Wilkinson interview.

14   Marc Johnson interview. Wilkinson is listed as 5-feet-10, weighing 160 pounds. He threw left-handed, but batted right-handed.

15   Wilkinson interview.

16   Johnson interview.

17   Reed Peters, telephone interview, June 12, 2025.

18   Wilkinson interview.

19   Johnson interview.

20   Peters interview.

21   Peters interview.

22   Wilkinson interview.

23 Wilkinson interview.

24 *1985 Seattle Mariners Media Guide*, 96.

25 Wilkinson interview.

26 Wilkinson interview.

27 Bill Plaschke, "Wilkinson Makes Great Leap to M's," *The Sporting News*, July 1, 1985.

28 Plaschke.

29 Plaschke.

30 *1988 Seattle Mariners Media Guide*, 60.

31 Wilkinson interview.

32 The same incident is referenced in an unidentified news clipping from Wilkinson's file at the National Baseball Hall of Fame library. See Jim Street, "There's No Fool Like..." April 13, 1987. Some details in that account differ from Wilkinson's account, but the story lines up. "It was a big-league deke," Wilkinson told Street of the prank.

33 Scott Bradley, telephone interview, June 24, 2025.

34 Bradley interview.

35 Bradley interview.

36 Rick Rizzs, email interview, June 26, 2025.

37 Bradley interview.

38 Wilkinson interview.

JIM WILLOUGHBY

By Jon Daly

James Arthur Willoughby was a right-handed pitcher perhaps best known for his contributions to the 1975 Boston Red Sox (including being pinch-hit for in Game Seven of the World Series). Willoughby also pitched for the San Francisco Giants and the Chicago White Sox.

"Willow," as he was often called, was born in Salinas, California, on January 31, 1949 (the same date as Fred Kendall, briefly his Red Sox teammate in 1978), the son of James Roger Willoughby, a noted scuba diver, and Marlene Dickison Willoughby. He had two younger sisters, Marcy and Beverly. Willoughby had three-eighths Potawatomi blood in addition to British ancestry. His great-aunt Mamie Echo Hawk was the tribe's chief lobbyist in Washington for years. (A later Red Sox hurler, John Henry Johnson, also had some Potawatomi blood.)[1]

Willoughby was raised in the San Joaquin Valley town of Gustine, California, and grew up a Yankees fan because his mother came from Mickey Mantle's home state of Oklahoma. He also also particularly admired Jim Thorpe and Satchel Paige.

Jim Willoughby pitched for Boston in the 1975 World Series.

(Courtesy of the Boston Red Sox)

Jim played both Little League and Colt baseball. While attending high school in Gustine, he played four years of varsity baseball and American Legion ball and also played basketball and football (split end), and participated in one year of track. The University of California at Berkeley recruited Willoughby for football, but the San Francisco Giants drafted Jim out of Gustine High in the 11th round of the June 1967 draft.

Willoughby faced a tough decision. Under NCAA rules at the time, he would forfeit his eligibility to play football for the Golden Bears if he played baseball professionally. His family was of modest means and he wanted to attend college; a football scholarship would have afforded him the opportunity to do so. When Giants scout Dick Wilson offered him participation in the Professional Baseball Scholarship Plan as part of his signing package, Willoughby signed with San Francisco.

Willoughby pitched for Salt Lake, Fresno, Medford, and Phoenix in the Giants' system, all the while pursuing a degree in electrical engineering. As part of his scholarship plan, he spent the 1967-1968 offseason at Cal-Berkeley; he also took classes at Fresno State, Phoenix College, and the College of San Mateo.

It was an interesting time to go to college in the Bay Area. Willoughby would sometimes drive his convertible with a roommate to Golden Gate Park and see bands such as Creedence Clearwater Revival, Jefferson Airplane, Big Brother and the Holding Company, and Country Joe and the Fish. He never finished his degree work, remaining a few credits shy of a bachelor's degree.

Willoughby was also a chess player – at one point, a rated member at the Burlingame Chess Club in California. During his baseball career, his opponents included fellow pitcher Steve Stone and sportscaster Dick Stockton. Asked to compare Willoughby's chess-playing style to that of Boston Celtics guard Paul Westphal, Stockton replied, "Willoughby is a gambler. Westphal is very conservative."[2]

For 1967 Willoughby was assigned to the Salt Lake City Giants in the Pioneer League, where he appeared in 17 games. He was still in school at the start of the 1968 season. After he finished his finals on a Friday, he was married to high-school sweetheart Mary Ann Ryan on Saturday, started his honeymoon on Sunday, and got into a car accident on Monday. "I smacked my face on the windshield (I reported with two shiners!), but strained my pitching arm (both arms) by absorbing the impact with the steering wheel,"

Willoughby said. He was assigned to Fresno for 1968, but was ineffective, so the Giants demoted him to Medford for most of the season.

In June 1969, again pitching for Fresno, Willoughby was named the California League player of the month, and was named to the circuit's year-end all-star squad. He injured his right elbow with several weeks left in the season and had to see Dr. Frank Jobe in Los Angeles. When the Giants knew he was healthy, they added him to their 40-man roster. But he wound up pitching for Phoenix in the Triple-A Pacific Coast League in 1970. Willoughby had always been fascinated by spaceships – both the real and science-fiction varieties – and got into model rocketry during his Phoenix years. After the season, Willoughby pitched in the autumn Arizona Instructional League. He returned to Phoenix in 1971, and made the Pacific Coast League all-star squad that year with a 14-9 record. Best of all, he was called up to the Giants on August 30.

It's a treat for any player when he first makes the majors. In Doug Hornig's *The Boys of October*, Willoughby recalled arriving in the dugout for his first major-league game. There were two coolers. One had water, but the other one had "red juice," a liquid amphetamine concoction. He tried to take a drink from the wrong cooler and was quickly chastised. "Red juice" was for veterans, not rookies. He pitched in two September games for San Francisco; the first was a start against Houston on September 5, which he lost, giving up three runs in three innings.

The next season, 1972, saw Willoughby's third tour of duty with Phoenix, but he was called up again to San Francisco on August 3 when a sore shoulder placed Sam McDowell on the 21-day disabled list. Three days after his arrival, Willoughby extracted revenge on the Astros for that debut-start loss the year before by recording his first major-league victory against them, a 6-2 Giants win. Willoughby started 10 more games for San Francisco and finished the season with a 6-4 record and a 2.36 ERA. The Giants finished the season in fifth place in the National League West Division, 17 games below .500.

Willoughby was a groundball pitcher who relied on a sinker and a slider and was more effective when he threw from a three-quarters arm slot or side-arm instead of overhand. He used a slow curve 10 percent of the time as well. He had what was described as a "herky jerky" motion. He had small hands for a pitcher, despite a 6-foot-2, 185- to 205-pound frame.

During the offseason the Giants harbored high hopes for Willoughby and penciled him into a five-man rotation in 1973 along with Juan Marichal, McDowell, Tom Bradley, and Ron Bryant. Obeying the new rule of Giants manager Charlie Fox, Willoughby shaved off the mustache he wore in 1972. Wearing number 42, Willoughby indeed began the season in the starting rotation, but in mid-May the Giants moved him to the bullpen. Fox and pitching coach Don McMahon were trying to get him to throw harder; this

caused him to throw more over the top. While Willoughby got more velocity, he lost movement on his pitches, making them flatter – and more hittable. Willoughby worked most of the rest of 1973 out of the bullpen, compiling a 4-5 record and a 4.68 ERA. Toward the end of the year, he studied film of his delivery and corrected it by dropping down more. "There's so much Cinderella in this game," he said. "When I was going bad with the Giants and had changed my whole way of throwing, I had to get work. But when you're in the bullpen, you often aren't in the best throwing shape and the whole thing snowballs. One bad outing and you don't work for a couple of weeks, and when you get back, you're completely out of whack."

After the season Willoughby pitched winter ball in Venezuela with the Maracay club, managed by Giants scout Ozzie Virgil. He had wanted to go to Venezuela the previous winter, but he'd worked a combined 250-plus innings between Phoenix and San Francisco. In 1973 he had pitched only 123 innings, and felt he needed more work. After finishing in Venezuela with an 8-7 record and an ERA under 3.00, Willoughby wanted another shot at the San Francisco starting rotation in 1974. According to the March 3, 1974, *New York Times*, Willoughby said, "They can have all that long relief stuff they want. After I fell out of the rotation last year, they tried me 'long' and during one spell I went 18 days without getting close to the mound."[3]

But Willoughby got only four starts and 40 innings of work in San Francisco in 1974 (1-4, 4.65 ERA) before being sent outright to Phoenix once more. After the season, the Giants traded him to St. Louis in a minor-league deal for infielder Tom Heintzelman. He expected to be invited to spring training with the Cardinals, but wound up starting the season with the Tulsa Oilers in the American Association under manager Ken Boyer. This proved beneficial because minor-league pitching instructor Bob Milliken helped straighten out his delivery.

Willoughby was thrilled to meet one of his idols in Tulsa. Satchel Paige served as both a part-time pitching coach and a greeter at Oiler Field. Willoughby pitched well in Tulsa; well enough for Boston Red Sox general manager Dick O'Connell to select him on July 4 as the "player to named later" to complete a springtime deal in which the Cardinals had received shortstop Mario Guerrero. Boston was on the way to its first pennant since the 1967 Impossible Dream season, but the team needed bullpen help. Dick Drago was having shoulder problems from overwork and Dick Pole had recently been hit in the face by a line drive. Oilers manager Boyer recommended Willoughby and when Red Sox executive scout Eddie Kasko visited Tulsa in 1975, he was impressed with the right-hander.

Willoughby had never been a short man out of the bullpen before, but he took to it like a duck to water. In 24 appearances with 48⅓ innings pitched. Willoughby compiled five wins, two losses, eight saves, and a 3.54 ERA. His first outing with the Red Sox was rocky, though. In the July 6 nightcap against Cleveland, he gave up a three-run homer to Oscar Gamble. Jim was fortunate in that Boston's bullpen was depleted at the time. They needed live arms and didn't have the option of burying him.

Willoughby did not pitch in the American League Championship Series against Oakland, but he appeared in Games Three, Five, and Seven of the World Series against the Cincinnati Reds. Willoughby was on the mound in the 10th inning of Game Three when Ed Armbrister bunted and may have interfered with Carlton Fisk's throw. In a controversial decision, the umpiring crew did not call Armbrister out for interference. This allowed Cesar Geronimo, who was on first, to advance to third and Armbrister to advance to second. Roger Moret replaced Willoughby and intentionally walked Pete Rose to load the bases. After Merv Rettenmund struck out, Joe Morgan hit a single over center fielder Fred Lynn's head to win the game for the Reds and tag Willoughby with the loss. After a mopup assignment in Game Five, Willoughby was called on to put out a fire in the Game Seven. The score was tied, 3-3, in the top of the seventh inning. The bases were loaded and there were two outs with Johnny Bench at the plate. Willoughby retired Bench on a foul pop to catcher Fisk. Willoughby then pitched a 1-2-3 eighth inning. In the bottom of the inning, though, with none on, two out and the score still tied, manager Darrell Johnson pulled Willoughby for a pinch-hitter, the rusty Cecil Cooper. Cooper popped out to Pete Rose in foul territory.

Jim Burton, the rookie hurler who succeeded Willoughby, wound up giving up a run in the ninth and losing both the game and the Series. A story that has grown into a piece of urban folklore among Red Sox fans tells of a sportswriter going into a Boston area watering hole sometime after the World Series and encountering a solitary drinker mumbling to himself about Darrell Johnson, "He never should have hit for Willoughby." Peter Gammons also has spun that tale.

Johnson would not have had to pinch-hit for Willoughby had there been a designated hitter during the '75 Series. In fact, l'affaire Willoughby-Cooper-Burton may have led major-league baseball toward adopting the designated hitter in the World Series in alternating years. This rule was in place until 1985, when it was modified so that the DH was used in American League parks but not in National League parks.

In 1976, after the Red Sox sent Dick Drago to California, Willoughby was the main short man out of the Boston bullpen for the whole season. While his record was an unfortunate 3-12, Willoughby pitched well. He recorded 10 saves and his ERA dropped to 2.82. The Red Sox failed to defend their American League East pennant and Darrell Johnson was replaced in midseason by third-base coach Don Zimmer. As Willoughby's teammate Bill Lee recounted, most notably in his book *The Wrong Stuff*, there was a culture clash between baseball lifer Zimmer and some of his players – a group of unconventional types known as the Buffalo Heads,

whose number included Lee, Willoughby, Ferguson Jenkins, Rick Wise, and Bernie Carbo. These young players came of age in the turbulent and countercultural 1960s and held a distinctly different worldview than that of Zimmer, a product of the Depression era. Zimmer rarely, if ever, drank and liked to spend his free time at the racetrack. The Buffalo Heads were more educated, were fans of rock music (which hadn't then achieved mainstream acceptance), drank, and experimented with drugs. Willoughby himself smoked pot and drank heavily, although he never took the mound drunk or stoned.

Willoughby was upset at the end of the 1976 season when assistant general manager John Claiborne acknowledged that the Red Sox had private detectives tailing their players that season. But what really upset him was learning from a coach about the existence of written reports that anyone with access to the locker room could have stumbled upon. Claiborne left after the 1977 season. The bicentennial of the Declaration of Independence was in 1976; the year also marked the independence of baseball players from the reserve clause. It was the dawning of the age of free agency. In the offseason, the Red Sox signed Bill Campbell to be their bullpen ace. Campbell had been with the Minnesota Twins and made it from Vietnam to a factory league to the majors. With Campbell on board in '77, Willoughby's role with the team was reduced. He also spent time on the disabled list for the first time in the majors. On May 22 he slipped on the outfield grass during pregame drills and broke his right ankle. He returned in August, but was not as effective, posting a 4.94 ERA, his highest ever in the majors (not counting those four innings in 1971). Although the Red Sox finished only 2½ games back of the Yankees in an exciting pennant race, they decided to clean house over the winter.

Before the first pitch was thrown in 1978, the Red Sox had traded Fergie Jenkins to the Texas Rangers for pitcher John Poloni and cash, Rick Wise was traded with prospects to the Cleveland Indians in a deal that netted Dennis Eckersley, and Willoughby was sold at the end of spring training to the Chicago White Sox for a figure barely over the waiver price. (Bernie Carbo was sold to Cleveland in midseason and Bill Lee, who staged a walkout after the Carbo sale, was traded to Montreal for infielder Stan Papi, prompting a graffiti artist in Boston area to paint, "Who the hell is Stan Papi?" on the Lansdowne Street side of the Green Monster.) According to Willoughby, he was never officially informed by the Red Sox of his sale to Chicago. Peter Gammons of the *Boston Globe* was the one who broke the news to him.

The popular perception is that Don Zimmer broke up the Buffalo Heads because he didn't like those players. Zimmer was also perceived as not liking pitchers as a class due to the several beanings he suffered during his playing days. While there may have been some truth to this, there may have been other reasons that the Red Sox shook things up.

NATIVE AMERICAN MAJOR LEAGUERS

Longtime Red Sox owner Tom Yawkey died during the 1976 season. After his estate was settled, the team was purchased by a partnership consisting of his widow, Jean R. Yawkey, former trainer Buddy LeRoux, and scouting director Haywood Sullivan. One result of this was the October 4, 1977, firing of general manager Dick O'Connell, whom Mrs. Yawkey disliked. Another was an attempt to maximize short-term profits at the expense of long-term success. LeRoux, for example, borrowed money to buy his stake in the team and needed profits from the Red Sox to cover his debt service. Also, the ownership group received tax-depreciation advantages for a limited number of years and looked to hold down expenses during that time frame. The front-office staff was slashed. Veteran players were let go in favor of players who were not eligible for salary arbitration and could approximate their production at a lower cost. While some were traded for other players, others were merely sold for cash to better the bottom line. In Willoughby's case, he was a Buffalo Head pitcher, relatively expensive for a middle reliever, and a Dick O'Connell acquisition, so he had three strikes against him.

In any case, Willoughby joined Bill Veeck and Roland Hemond's 1978 White Sox squad. After winning 90 games in 1977, the White Sox proved disappointing, losing 90 in 1978. Willoughby started the season as the ace out of the bullpen, but as the year went on he appeared less frequently as Lerrin LaGrow took over that role. Frustrated with his lack of playing time, Willoughby asked the White Sox to play him or trade him. They obliged, sending him to the Cardinals organization once again for outfielder John Scott on October 23.

The Cardinals released Willoughby during spring training and he signed on with Wichita in the Cubs system. His contract allowed Jim to request his release if he wasn't called up to Chicago by the trade deadline. After the Cubs traded for Dick Tidrow, Willoughby asked for and was granted his release. He searched for another pitching job and found one in Portland, Oregon, with the Pittsburgh Pirates' Triple-A affiliate. Willoughby eventually wound up getting summoned to the parent club as bullpen insurance, but never got into a game. He did, however, receive a $250 World Series share from the "We Are Family" Bucs. Willoughby pitched the entire 1979 season with undiagnosed Type I diabetes, the type that usually strikes people much earlier than in their late 20s. He was unaware of it until he went to Venezuela to play winter ball and wound up in a diabetic coma. It was neither lengthy nor deep, but he was briefly in the hospital. At this point, Willoughby retired from playing. He said he could have continued, but he was tired of the journeyman ballplayer's life.

After his baseball career, Willoughby did a stint in sports radio. He hosted a talk show in Waltham, Massachusetts, but he didn't care to invest the amount of time required to properly prepare for the broadcasts. In December 1980 he was named baseball coach at Suffolk University, but didn't last a whole season. He resigned in April after he was suspended for a bat-throwing incident during practice. He also said he found the politics at Suffolk worse than in any major-league clubhouse he experienced.

Willoughby moved back to his native California, where he worked in construction until he got his contractor's license. He embarked on a career building houses on the western slope of the Sierra Nevadas.

Willoughby did get the opportunity to return to the pitcher's mound. In 1989 and 1990, he participated in the Senior Professional Baseball Association. First, he had a chance to reunite with some of the other Buffalo Heads with the Winter Haven Super Sox. Bill Lee was the player-manager, Fergie Jenkins was the pitching coach, and Bernie Carbo was a teammate. In 1990 Willoughby pitched for the San Bernardino Pride. It was the first time in his professional career that he pitched sober; by his own admission Willoughby was a recovering alcoholic and stopped drinking in 1983. Because of this, he felt an affinity with one of his boyhood idols, Jim Thorpe, who, in addition to being a fellow Native American, also had a drinking problem.

Willoughby and Mary Ann were divorced in the late 1970s. She was the mother of his two sons Trevor and Ryan. It was what Willoughby called "a classic case of baseball divorce." He was married for six years to Boston area attorney Cathy Cullen, but his alcoholism ended that marriage. In 1984 he married Sandra Aubert.

Son Trevor played baseball at California State-Fullerton. Ryan played basketball in high school but suffered from bad knee injuries.

In describing himself at his website (jimwilloughby. com), this is what Willoughby had to say: "I played professional baseball for 15 years spanning 4 decades. I drank enough, smoked enough, snorted enough stuff to kill me. I lost several dear friends like that. Yet, like one of my idols, Ozzy (Osbourne, not Nelson), I survived. Here I am today: 20 years of total sobriety thanks to my friends in AA. I am building houses, riding motorcycles, shooting guns, voting Republican. I'm happy, some say crazy. My buddy Bill Lee, The Spaceman, used to say it's better to be crazy than insane. I agree."[4]

SOURCES

Hornig, Doug, *The Boys of October* (New York: McGraw-Hill, 2003).

Lee, Bill, with Dick Lally, *The Wrong Stuff* (New York: Penguin, 1988).

Stout, Glenn, with Richard Johnson, *Red Sox Century* (Boston: Houghton Mifflin Company, 2000).

Willoughby, James Arthur, personal Interview, July 11, 2004.

baseball-reference.com

retrosheet.org

jimwilloughby.com

NOTES

1   Unless otherwise notes, family information and all quotations attributed to Willoughby come from the author's July 11, 2004 interview.

2   Peter Gammons, "Willoughby, suddenly order in a bullpen," *Boston Globe*, August 26, 1975: 29.

3   It was actually 15 days, from May 18 to June 3. See "What They Are Saying," *New York Times*, March 3, 1974: Section 5: 11.

4   Willoughby's website, active at the time it was accessed in 2005, was no longer active when sought in 2014.

MOSE YELLOWHORSE

By Todd Fuller and Thomas Kahle

Though Mose YellowHorse toed the rubber for two under-achieving Pittsburgh Pirates teams in 1921 and 1922, he left an indelible mark on the club and its fanbase. Because of his off-the-field antics and on-the-field accomplishments, YellowHorse was a longtime fan favorite. Those in executive and administrative positions with the Pirates were not so quick to share the fans' enthusiasm for the Pawnee Nation citizen. Ever the competitor, YellowHorse fully embraced the role of athlete-entertainer and enjoyed putting on a good show for paying customers.

Born on January 28, 1898, to Thomas YellowHorse and Clara (Ricketts) YellowHorse in Pawnee, Oklahoma, Mose grew up on or near the Pawnee Nation during most of his childhood.[1] Those exceptions included going "on the road" with his father to perform for Pawnee Bill's Wild West Show and attending Chilocco Indian School, from which he frequently fled during his teenage years.[2]

In the 1870s, after the Pawnee Nation was forced to cede their traditional homelands in Nebraska, YellowHorse's parents, then children, were among those who walked 400-plus miles to present-day Pawnee, Oklahoma. Once there, chaos and dysfunction were the order of the day. Pawnee Agency officials were slow to comprehend or meet the needs of the displaced population. Supplies and resources promised to the tribe by treaty agreement were often late arriving and usually short on required inventory. Some quartermasters in charge of doling out food rations and other goods were not typically sympathetic to those they thought of as "vanishing." That is, many non-Natives believed or perpetuated a prevailing myth that Indigenous populations were going to disappear or assimilate completely into the mainstream. Regardless, during the mid- to late nineteenth century, and even into the early twentieth century, numerous instances of theft and/or fraud by Indian agents and others within the system were documented and even prosecuted on rare occasions.[3]

Despite such challenges, Clara and Thomas eventually met, courted, and had a son who entered a world of future uncertainties: At the end of the nineteenth century, the so-called "Indian Wars" had reached a conclusion, at least according to settler-colonial ways of thinking; the Spanish-American War was fought (April to August 1898), bringing an end to Spanish presence in the Americas; and, in Russia, Vladimir Lenin established the Communist Party, which would have worldwide ramifications.

As a youngster in the Oklahoma Territory, Mose and his parents struggled. In a photo, Mose and his father are shown in Native regalia, a Pawnee father and son with stoic expressions – similar to many others during the same period. Since father and son performed in Pawnee Bill's Wild West Show, it is possible the photo was taken for such an occasion. It is also possible Thomas farmed on his allotment (#76) land in Pawnee County; as for Clara, she is documented helping with traditional female Pawnee domestic work.

While Indian agents and other corrupt officials were often skimming off the top, other economically-minded businessmen were developing different ways to exploit both

Mose YellowHorse, a citizen of the Pawnee Nation, worked mostly as a sharp-shooting relief specialist for the Pittsburgh Pirates in 1921 and 1922, pitching to an 8-4 major-league record.

Native labor and non-Native audiences. The evolution of Wild West shows began near the close of the Civil War (or shortly after, depending on one's source). The shows were a theatrical mix – usually outdoors, usually traveling – of vaudeville, historical reenactments, and staged performances. They provided romanticized depictions of outlaws, Natives, cowboys, wild animals, and military scouts. Three prominent shows included those by Buffalo Bill, Pawnee Bill, based in Pawnee, Oklahoma, and the Miller Brothers 101 Ranch, which was located outside of Ponca City, Oklahoma.

According to oral histories, YellowHorse developed his strong pitching arm by throwing rocks while hunting for small game. Several elders recounted how he often filled his rucksack with squirrels, rabbits, and other animals with strong throwing and good aim. Early on, he also developed a lifelong love of fishing.[4]

As part of the country's assimilationist policies, YellowHorse attended the Pawnee Industrial School for several years before going to Chilocco Indian School, where he studied carpentry. Eventually, he went out for the baseball team and played for several seasons, often sitting on the bench and participating in practices, before starring on the team in 1917. That year, he pitched to a 17-0 record, beating such competition as the University of Tulsa (then Henry Kendall College), Oklahoma State (then Oklahoma A&M), and other small schools, including Friends University and Bethany College. YellowHorse's success at Chilocco did not occur overnight, nor easily.[5]

Numerous records at the Oklahoma Historical Society indicate that YellowHorse often left Chilocco – interpret: ran away – to return to Pawnee, a distance of about 60 miles.[6] It's not difficult to imagine YellowHorse the young outdoorsman making his way from the northernmost and central part of the state to Pawnee County, crossing the Arkansas River along the way. He certainly wouldn't have had much fear making such a journey on foot. Not surprisingly, such impulses were common for Native youngsters who were taken from their communities and missed their parents as well as the comforts of home. His mother, Clara, had died in 1916, aged 52 – a year before Mose last attended Chilocco. She is buried in the North Indian Cemetery, which is adjacent to Highland Cemetery outside of Pawnee.

After YellowHorse's stellar season with Chilocco, he garnered the attention of area coaches and scouts and signed with the Des Moines Boosters of the Western League, which he did for a short time in 1918 – before the league folded operations because of World War I. YellowHorse then returned to Pawnee and kicked around with a few sandlot and semipro teams, getting work when and where he could.

Then, in the spring of 1920, YellowHorse received an unexpected invitation by mail, which also included ample train fare from Pawnee to Little Rock, Arkansas.[7] The note from Norman "Kid" Elberfeld requested YellowHorse's presence for a tryout. Elberfeld also noted YellowHorse's former

teammate at Chilocco, Bill Wano, highly recommended the Pawnee flinger for the opportunity. Though the tryout went well and YellowHorse made the team, the beginning of the season was unbalanced for the new starter. After tossing to a 7-7 mark and getting sick, he traveled home to Pawnee. Once he returned to Little Rock, YellowHorse dominated the Southern Association, winning 14 consecutive games and concluding the season with a 21-7 record (.750, the best in the league).

The Travelers then faced the Fort Worth Panthers from the Texas League in the inaugural Dixie Series. Much ado was made of the competition, especially in both cities. For his part, YellowHorse was actively engaged in helping the Travelers win two games, though they dropped the series four games to two. In the third game of the series, YellowHorse threw nine innings of five-hit ball, allowing two runs and striking out seven. He also lined a single to right, had one putout, two assists, and retired 12 in a row at one point. His performance prompted Fort Worth sportswriter Pop Boone to proclaim, "Too much Yellowhorse! That tells the story of Fort Worth's defeat today at the hands of Little Rock in the third game of the Dixie Series."[8]

Even as the Dixie Series was unfolding, YellowHorse signed with the Pirates. Announcements of the transaction occurred from Pittsburgh to Pawnee and points well beyond. There was even talk, at least in newspaper circles, of YellowHorse joining the team to close the season, but the minor-league postseason series intervened, and he would have to wait his turn until the spring of 1921.[9]

The Pirates brought in 48 players for 1921 spring training, an unusually high number for a team picked to contend. Early on in camp, manager George Gibson, a former big-league catcher, took a shine to YellowHorse and spent a lot of time working with him. A 14-year veteran who caught over 1,200 games, Gibson had much to teach the young pitcher.[10] The team's plan was to bring him along slowly, mostly out of the bullpen, and eventually ease him into a starter's role.

On April 15, 1921, YellowHorse made his major-league debut, against Cincinnati at Redland Field, which the Pirates won 3-1. In two innings of work, YellowHorse struck out one, walked none, and gave up no hits. Retrospectively, he earned a save.[11] An unattributed scribe writing for the *Pittsburgh Press* noted, "Yellowhorse finished for Pittsburg [sic] and although war whoops reverberated through the stands and all sorts of tricks were resorted to in an endeavor to rattle the Pawnee, Mose came thundering through – winner."[12]

Thus, YellowHorse was greeted with an unfortunate yet unsurprising dose of racism during his first major-league outing. *Pittsburgh Gazette Times* writer Charles "Chilly" Doyle stated, much more ambiguously, "Yellowhorse proved a big magnet to the fans who were all abuzz when the Indian walked to the hill. Mose had a fine fast ball and he was handled cleverly by Schmidt."[13] Though Cincinnati had a strong Klan presence at the time, it is likely that such excited behavior by fans had more to do with the lack of Native representation at the highest level of professional baseball.[14] It's quite likely the last Indigenous ballplayer the fans in Cincinnati would have seen was John Meyers, the sharp-hitting catcher for the New York Giants from 1909 to 1915, who retired after the 1917 season.

On April 21, YellowHorse returned to the mound, once again facing the Reds – this time in Pittsburgh and once again in relief. Over 3⅔ innings, he gave up one run, four hits, and one walk. When the Pirates rallied to win, he also earned his first major-league victory, the first rookie in Pirates history to win a home opener. Then, on Memorial Day, as the Forbes Field faithful filled the stands, with an attendance of nearly 30,000, YellowHorse entered a game against the Cubs in the second inning, the home team down 3-0. One sportswriter described it this way:

"The cries for Yellowhorse were drowning [out] every other noise as Gibby began to warm up relief pitchers. Ponder walked out to start the second inning, but Elmer experienced trouble after he had retired the first batter. The next two Cubs singled and once more the noisy enthusiasts shouted for the Redskin. The protracted yelling broke into a spasmodic riot of approval when the vast audience recognized the athletic boy of the dark visage as he walked coolly from the bullpen toward the mound. Gibby had heard the appeal of the fans and the Chief was going to the firing line."

He continued with the same energy:

"And what an exhibition the Indian gave from that early period of play through to the finish. Taking the ball with first and second occupied and only one out, the youthful brave seemed to forget the presence of almost 30,000 men, women, and children to go about the task at hand."

Finally:

"From then on through the warm innings the Indian held the Cubs' attack runless. Moses went to the pitching post with the Pirates trailing by three runs, but the fourth saw the game deadlocked and the sixth saw [the Pirates] out in front. And all the time the dark-skinned aborigine was handing Walt Schmidt the ball in such a manner as to mystify the hitters of the Chicago club. Truly it was a great day in Moses' life."[15]

Thus was born the long-standing cry of the Pittsburgh faithful to "Put in YellowHorse!" when they wanted a struggling Pirates pitcher to be relieved. The derisive chant stood the test of time, long outlasting YellowHorse. As late as the 1980s, sportswriters continued to reference the YellowHorse cheer.[16] With this, YellowHorse became a cultural phenomenon, a spectacle, a wonder, and not just in Pittsburgh.

A week before his Memorial Day game, while the team was in New York taking on the Giants, *Pittsburgh Gazette Times* writer Doyle noted: "The Giant officials do not give out the exact attendance figures, but Secretary Joe O'Brien informed me that today was the biggest in the history of the field [the Polo Grounds]." He continued, "Mose Yellowhorse was the center of picturesque interest with the early arrivals. The Indian was noted as soon as he walked on the field and the fans were shouting his name with enthusiasm."[17]

After the Memorial Day showing, YellowHorse wrote a letter to Pirates fans as a hand-written gesture of gratitude. It was published in the *Gazette Times*:

Dear Fans,

I was certainly glad to be able to please you after the fine reception you gave me on Memorial Day and trust that I should win many games for Gibby and the Pirates.

It makes one work better to realize the fans are pulling for him. Yours to the finish,

Chief Moses YellowHorse (signed)

Pawnee Tribe[18]

The article that accompanied YellowHorse's letter began with the phrase: "Put Yellowhorse in!!!" (exclamations included), in tribute to the team's fans.

For the next month, YellowHorse appeared in seven more games, winning three and losing three. He was out of commission because of an injury about two months, until mid-September, pitching his last game against the Giants at Forbes Field. The Pirates team treasurer, S.W. Dreyfuss, provided the following update to C.E. Vandervort, who was YellowHorse's "guardian," in a letter dated July 12, 1921: "You have probably seen in the papers that Moses Yellow Horse underwent an operation a few days ago. ... During a recent game he strained a ligament and our doctor felt that unless there was an operation to relieve the trouble Yellow Horse would be useless to our club for the balance of the season."[19] Such was not the case, however, as YellowHorse pitched one more inning to close out his rookie season. He finished with five wins, three losses and an ERA of 2.98.

During the season YellowHorse twice met the new commissioner of baseball, Judge Kenesaw Mountain Landis. The first time was on May 2 in Chicago. According to one account, Pirates manager Gibson took YellowHorse to Landis's office in Chicago for what was described as "an interesting meeting," during which Landis "seemed pleased with the appearance of the aborigine and soon was engrossed in asking chief some personal questions."[20] The second time was in Pittsburgh on June 20, when Landis attended a Pirates game against Philadelphia. YellowHorse pitched eight innings of seven-hit ball, giving up two runs and striking out seven, helping lead Pittsburgh to a 3-2 victory and outdueling veteran Lee Meadows.[21] By all accounts, Landis was impressed by YellowHorse's personal demeanor and his pitching performance.

As the 1921 season unfolded, the Pirates remained more than competitive, consistently holding a modest lead in the

National League over the Giants. At one point, the Pirates were 36 games over .500. However, a five-game sweep to the Giants in late August reversed the Pirates' fortunes. They eventually finished in second place.

Once the season was over, YellowHorse, along with other major-league players, played in what was then dubbed the "World Series of Oklahoma" in Oilton, one of many barnstorming tours across the country. The game was to be played on October 30, featuring YellowHorse for the visiting Pawnee-Cleveland team and Walter Johnson for the home team, Oilton. It was rained out. Instead, on November 9 YellowHorse defeated White Sox veteran Dickey Kerr, 8-2.[22]

During the offseason, YellowHorse returned to Pawnee, rested, and recuperated, healing from his surgery as well as in-season tonsillitis. His teammates voted him a full share of the team's second-place money. (It was standard practice at the time for the second-place teams in each league to receive payment from the Series.[23]) The prevailing sentiment among sportswriters anticipated a more positive outcome for 1922.

As 1922 spring training commenced in West Baden, Indiana, manager Gibson hoped to build off YellowHorse's shortened rookie season. Shortly after reporting to camp,

(George Grantham Bain Collection, Library of Congress)

YellowHorse became a sensation around the league, especially in Pittsburgh, where fans would begin chanting "Put in YellowHorse," when they wanted to see the fastball flinger squelch a rally. The rally cry could be heard at Forbes Field for 40-plus years.

YellowHorse was teamed with the other frontline pitchers. Charles Doyle wrote, "Gibby showed his high regard for Moses Yellow Horse's ability at the outset. ... Chief drew a first-squad uniform ... and was told to limber up with the aces of the mound." Doyle added that Gibson thought "the Indian has one of the fastest balls in baseball and he has no hesitancy in saying so."[24] Once the late-arriving YellowHorse reported to camp, he "took occasion to deny a rumor ... to the effect that he had taken unto himself a squaw."[25]

Once the season commenced, the Pirates performed well enough, getting off to a 27-19 start by June 10. At that point YellowHorse's ERA stood at an unremarkable 5.01. From June 11 through June 30, the Pirates greatly underperformed as well, going 6-14, and once again getting beat up by the Giants along the way. On June 30, Gibson resigned and team owner Barney Dreyfuss appointed coach Bill McKechnie to succeed him. After McKechnie took over, the team went 53-36-1, good enough to tie for third place in the league. For his part, YellowHorse's line was fairly uneven: He pitched in 28 games and was 3-1 with a 4.52 ERA. More telling, in 77⅔ innings pitched, YellowHorse gave up 92 hits, with a WHIP of 1.442.

YellowHorse's off-the-field shenanigans with future Hall of Famer Rabbit Maranville dominated too much of his season. One instance promulgated by sportswriter Frederick Lieb but contradicted by the Pittsburgh press, allegedly occurred when the Pirates were on the road facing the Giants. Lieb wrote that new manager McKechnie "held a [team] meeting before the first game with the Giants and laid down his disciplinary law. He was emphatic about bootleg liquor, the hour the men should be in bed, [which was midnight] and that sort of thing."[26]

Lieb wrote that Maranville and YellowHorse, bored in the early afternoon in New York, decided to squelch their restlessness with some high-rise antics:

"When the team checked in, McKechnie shared his suite with [Maranville and YellowHorse, who were roommates].

McKechnie started to undress. He opened a closet door and almost toppled over as a flock of trapped pigeons flew into his face. Bill recovered and, madder than a hornet, he shouted so loud that he awakened Maranville. 'What goes on here, Rabbit?'

"Rabbit blinked and replied: 'Hey Bill, don't open that other closet. Those pigeons that got out belong to the Chief – mine are in that one over there.'

"With popcorn and other tempting goodies, the two Pirate zanies had coaxed many pigeon residents of the district from a perch high up on the hotel into Manager Bill's apartment.[27]

Near the end of the season, on September 26, the Pirates traveled to Detroit for an exhibition game against the Tigers, a contest YellowHorse started and lost. During the game, the Pirates pitcher plunked Ty Cobb so hard he had to be carried off the field.[28] Decades later, Pawnee Nation citizen, Norman Rice, alleged YellowHorse beaned Cobb because the latter decided to dance mockingly around home before a plate appearance.[29]

On another occasion, about a month later, well after the season and World Series were completed, YellowHorse and Babe Ruth played in a barnstorming game in Drumright, Oklahoma. According to one account, which was published in *The Pawnee Chief* 70-plus years after the fact, YellowHorse supposedly struck out Ruth twice, once with the bases loaded.[30] However, newspaper accounts of the day do not mention any such heroics by YellowHorse. Once again, it seems YellowHorse's legend stretches beyond verification.

By December of the same year, the Pirates traded YellowHorse to the Sacramento Senators of the Pacific Coast League. The Pawnee hurler relished the situation and stated as much. He imagined the change in teams, situations, and scenery might allow for more pitching opportunities. According to the *Los Angeles Evening Post-Record*, YellowHorse's new manager, Charlie Pick, a former big-leaguer himself, "promised the Oklahoma tribesman all the work he can handle." Pick was quoted: "The way he is showing up in spring practice indicates he is going to be up among the pitching aces in the circuit."[31]

During the 1923 season, YellowHorse pitched in 53 games, earned 22 wins against 13 losses, and threw 311 innings – this for a Senators team that finished second in the league, 11 games behind the San Francisco Seals. Such a workload represented his most sustained campaign since pitching for Little Rock, when he logged 278 innings of work in 46 games.

After being among the PCL leaders in pitching wins the previous season, optimism regarding YellowHorse's potential in 1924 permeated the sport pages in Sacramento. Such hopefulness was quickly squashed when, in mid-May, he "hurt his arm during practice," while he "was in the outfield and he cut loose with a vicious peg to the plate," and "something snapped in his right arm and the big Indian was through for the day." The article goes on to state, "Later in the afternoon Colonel [Charlie] Pick tried to use Moses as a relief twirler, but after warming up the Chief threw his glove away in disgust. His arm bothered him so much that it was impossible for him to bear down."[32]

A different account by Bob Lemke, writing in *The Bleacher Bum* (in 1994), suggests YellowHorse permanently injured his arm during a game in Salt Lake City. According to Lemke, Sacramento was playing in Salt Lake City and doing so with a comfortable 18-5 lead heading into the bottom of the ninth. The Bees then rallied to score 10 runs, during which manager Pick told YellowHorse to warm up quickly. The article continues:

With only three warm-up pitches, Yellowhorse [sic] was called to the mound with the bases loaded, the tying run on first base. He reminisced later, 'I went in and I threw just nine pitches, striking out in order John Peters, Tony Lazzeri and Duffy Lewis,' and nailing down the victory."

"'That was the finest job of pitching I ever did,' Yellowhorse [sic] said, 'But I couldn't raise my arm the next day. Jack Downey was the trainer but he couldn't stop the pain.'[33]

Unfortunately, there are no citations in Lemke's article, so source verification is difficult and attempts to find either stories or quotations related to the incident via newspapers. com and other resources were not specific. One account in the Salt Lake City *Deseret News* provides the following snippet: "Mose Yellow Horse finished up and with his fast ball [sic] he turned back the ambitious Bees."[34] Suffice it to say, if YellowHorse pitched an immaculate inning, which included striking out a future Hall-of-Famer in Lazzeri, and two former major leaguers, it certainly would have been some of his best work as a professional.

Regardless of which account is true, YellowHorse's physical demise from the game was instigated. He pitched in a few more games for the Solons but ended the season with one win and four losses and an ERA of 6.07. By mid-June, Sacramento released him to Fort Worth of the Texas League, where he did not pitch and was then returned to Sacramento. YellowHorse then went AWOL and was suspended by his former team.

YellowHorse's 1925 and '26 seasons were equally disappointing. He pitched sparingly for teams in Mobile, Alabama (in the Southern Association, again, and reunited with Kid Elberfeld), Sacramento, and Omaha in the Western League. He pitched in a game for Omaha on May 1, giving up five runs off six hits in 2 1/3 innings. Seven weeks later, YellowHorse was back in Oklahoma playing semipro ball for the Fairfax Indians and Ponca City Oilers among others, his professional playing days finished.[35]

YellowHorse returned to Pawnee, played lots of semipro ball with an assortment of teams, and spent the next decade in survival mode. He continued to drink – probably too much for his own good – and held odd jobs, living with relatives and others, getting by as he could. One notable event from this period included the creation and appearance of a cartoon character, "Chief Yellowpony," in the *Dick Tracy* comic on March 27, 1935.[36] Since both hailed from Pawnee, with *Tracy* creator Chester Gould two years YellowHorse's junior, it was no surprise that such a character would show up. Gould often used settings and developed characters he knew from his hometown.

Otherwise, YellowHorse regularly played semipro and pickup baseball, even in city leagues, as often as he could, or cared to do so, through the mid-1930s. Local reports indicate he quit pitching for the most part and became an outfielder. In 1927, he even won the Muskogee City League batting title, hitting at a .412 clip.[37] By 1931, YellowHorse was also coaching baseball, managing Pawnee Bill's Indians in a number of area tournaments. Numerous stories from area newspapers clearly specify he stayed active as a player/manager though 1935.

As noted in *60 Feet Six Inches from Home: the (Baseball) Life of Mose YellowHorse*, several other noteworthy activities and events which took place include: serving as an umpire in the Kansas-Missouri-Oklahoma League; working as a groundskeeper for the Ponca City Drillers minor league club; presenting Pawnee war bonnets to the competing World Series managers during the 1954 fall classic between the Cleveland Indians and New York Giants;[38] having one of his gloves put on permanent display at the National Baseball Hall of Fame and Museum; receiving tributes in Little Rock; and, attending "Chief YellowHorse Night" in Sacramento.

YellowHorse later worked a steady job with the Oklahoma State Highway Department in the construction department. In January of 1964, the Pawnee Nation held a dinner in his honor. Three months later, on April 10, he passed away at the age of 66 of heart failure and complications from diabetes. With his passing, a unique and humorous hard-throwing sharp-shooter crossed over. Many tributes appeared across the country, including in Pittsburgh, where former teammate Charlie Grimm remembered YellowHorse "had a good fast ball. A very good fast ball," and went on, saying former Pirates catcher Walter Schmidt "thought Yellowhorse [sic] threw harder than any pitcher he ever caught."[39] More than 40 years after he played for the Pirates, Steel City fans continued to chant "Put in YellowHorse!" as the *Pittsburgh Gazette Times* noted in its obituary.[40]

Other posthumous honors occurred as well: induction in 1971 into the Oklahoma Sports Hall of Fame (strangely enough, this organization existed in theory only, and a location was never secured); in 1994, he was inducted into the American Indian Athletic Hall of Fame; and, having a street in Pawnee named in his honor, Mose YellowHorse Drive.

To be sure, Mose YellowHorse was one of the most revered short-timers to play the game. In Little Rock, Pittsburgh, and Sacramento, he went in blazing, made his mark, and left long-lasting and (mostly) positive impressions with fans, writers, and teammates (management was a different story). His wit was classic, his timing impeccable. Take this one: of his frustration regarding his relief role with the Pirates, YellowHorse quipped "just call me Chief Sitting Bull Pen." Also, a story published in *The Seattle Star* shared:

> One night last summer in Oakland Moses Yellowhorse, the Pawnee Indian pitcher with the Sacramento team woke up Charley Doyle, the club secretary and told him that a taxi driver was holding him up for a $37 dollar fare for a short ride.

Doyle dressed and went down to see about it.

"How about charging this man with a $37 dollar fare?" asked Doyle, in none too good a humor for having been awakened."

"Sure boss," said the driver, "Thirty-five dollars for liquor and $2 for taxi."[41]

"Charley" Doyle was, of course, Charles Doyle, one of the beat writers for the Pittsburgh *Gazette Times*, who also wrote a column, "Chilly Sauce," in which he wrote about YellowHorse a number of times.

Though YellowHorse had a sustained period of sobriety the last fifteen-plus years of his life, he apparently started drinking again, right at the end of his life, according to anthropologist Martha Blaine. She attended and recorded Mose's birthday honor dance and later went to his funeral. Mose, ever the showman, had a legendary fastball and a quicker sense of humor with a unique ability to fascinate and entertain while tossing pitches. His was a life quenched and full – a one-of-a-kind self-promoter who rarely lacked confidence in his skills and never hesitated with a story, as is the Pawnee way.

SOURCES

In addition to the sources cited in the Notes, the author relied on Baseball-Reference.com.

For a more complete biography of Mose YellowHorse, see the Todd Fuller's mixed-genre work, *60 Feet Six Inches and Other Distances from Home: The (Baseball) Life of Mose YellowHorse* (Duluth, Minnesota: Holy Cow! Press, 2002).

NOTES

1   From YellowHorse's "Delayed Certificate of Birth," which was issued December 27, 1951, by the State of Oklahoma – Department of Health. Some sites incorrectly state his birth as March 28, 1898.

2   A faint photo of little Mose (three or four) and his dad, which the author saw in a Pawnee Homecoming annual after *60 Feet Six Inches and Other Distances from Home: the (Baseball) Life of Mose YellowHorse*, can be found in the Oklahoma History Center holdings.

3   See William Unrau's article "The Civilian as Indian Agent: Villain or Victim?" in the *Western Historical Quarterly*, Vol. 3, No. 4 (October 1972), 405-420.

4   Todd Fuller, *60 Feet Six Inches and Other Distances from Home: the (Baseball) Life of Mose YellowHorse* (Duluth, Minnesota: Holy Cow! Press, 2002), 72.

5   "Base Ball," *The Indian School Journal* 17, no. 10 (June 1917): 521.

6   In December of 1999, as a graduate student (PhD in English), the author visited the Oklahoma History Center and read several letters between the Chilocco superintendent and C. E. Vandervort, in which the head of the school informs Mose's "guardian" he has run away, again.

7   "Yellow Horse Looms Up as Best Prospect in League," *Pawnee* (Oklahoma) *Courier-Dispatch*, June 24, 1920: 7.

8   Pop Boone, "Elberfeld's Indian Phenom Hits Stride and Travelers Win Third Game from Cats," *Fort Worth Record-Telegram*, September 24, 1920: 10.

9   "Pirates Collecting Big Squad of Rookies," *Cincinnati Post*, September 21, 1920: 14.

10 https://www.baseball-reference.com/players/g/gibsoge01.shtml.

11 Saves were not a baseball statistic in 1921.

12 "Ponder to Likely Hurl Final Contest at Redland – Bucs Begin Series with Cubs Tomorrow," *Pittsburgh Press*, April 16, 1921: 8.

13 Charles Doyle, "Buccaneer Bingles," *Pittsburgh Gazette Times*, April 16, 1921: 9.

14 The *Cincinnati Enquirer* published advertisements for Ku Klux Klan apparel during this period. For more detail, see: *Cincinnati Enquirer*, January 16, 1921: 26.

15 Charles Doyle, "Pirates Beat Chicago Twice, 13-0 and 6-3," *Gazette Times*, May 31, 1921: 3.

16 Joe Browne, "She Could Be Bucs Ace in the Hole," *Gazette Times*, June 23, 1983: 18.

17 Charles Doyle, "Chilly Sauce," *Gazette Times*, May 23, 1921: 7.

18 Drew Rader, "Chief Yellowhorse and His 'Roomie,'" *Gazette Times*, June 5, 1921: 23.

19 Moses YellowHorse player file, National Baseball Hall of Fame and Museum. It was common practice by the U.S. government during this period to appoint so-called non-Native guardians to "protect" Native people with potential means. In YellowHorse's case, a prominent banker in Pawnee, C.E. Vandervort, was this individual.

20 Charles Doyle, "Yellowhorse Holds Confab with Landis," *Gazette Times*, May 3, 1921: 11.

21 See https://www.baseball-reference.com/boxes/PIT/PIT192106200.shtml.

22 "Oilton Lost in Ball Game Last Sunday," *Oilton* (Oklahoma) *Gusher*, November 10, 1921: 6.

23 Moses YellowHorse player file, National Baseball Hall of Fame and Museum.

24 Charles Doyle, "Bucs Gingery in First Outdoor Session," *Gazette Times*, March 4, 1922: 9.

25 Charles Doyle, "Adams and Whitehill Absentees from Pirates Training Camp," *Gazette Times*, March 3, 1922: 32.

26 Frederick G. Lieb, *The Pittsburgh Pirates* (New York: Putnam's Sons, 1948), 195.

27 Lieb, *The Pittsburgh Pirates*, 196. Lieb's account conflicts with newspaper stories of the day, which were published in two Pittsburgh papers and clearly state YellowHorse was in Pittsburgh during the first series in New York, which took place from July 29 – August 1, a four-game sweep for the Pirates. Both papers also state YellowHorse was in Pittsburgh recovering from tonsillitis.

28 "Cobb Is Shelled by Yellowhorse," *Reading* (Pennsylvania) *Times*, September 27, 1922: 10.

29 Fuller, 102-103.

30 Fuller, 110.

31 "From Majors to Sacs – and Glad of It!" *Los Angeles Evening Post-Record*, March 12, 1923: 17.

32 John H. Peri, "Seals – Sac Battle Will Draw Fans Sunday Morning," *Stockton* (California) *Daily Evening Record*, May 15, 1924: 17.

33 Bob Lemke, "Pirates Pawnee Pitcher went 'way of all bad injuns,'" *Bleacher Bum* (Iola, Wisconsin), March 4, 1994: 62.

34 Les Goates, "Locals Drop Doubleheader Saturday and Lose Hectic Series," *Deseret News*, May 12, 1924: 8.

35 See https://www.baseball-reference.com/register/player.fcgi?id=yellow001mos. The author also has a record that shows YellowHorse won two games for Mobile in 1925, neither of which is included on his reference page.

36 Chester Gould, "DICK TRACY – Indian Call," *Chicago Tribune*, March 27, 1935: 18.

37 "City Loop Slug Title Goes to Yellowhorse," *Muskogee Daily Phoenix and Times-Democrat*, August 28, 1927: 6.

38 "Pawnee's Mose YellowHorse Attends World Series Games, Presents War Bonnet to Cleveland and New York Managers," *Pawnee* (Oklahoma) *Chief*, October 7, 1954: 1.

39 Lester J. Biederman, "Grimm, Cub Official, Recalls Playing Days with Yellowhorse," *Pittsburgh Press*, April 16, 1964: 50.

40 "Yellowhorse, Former Buc Pitcher, Dies," *Pittsburgh Post-Gazette*, April 14, 1964: 26.

41 "Today's Giggle: Some Taxi Fare," *Seattle Star*, August 6, 1924: 10.

TODAY'S NATIVE AMERICAN BALLPLAYER: IDENTITY AND RESILIENCE

by Joe Leisek

Brandon Bailey takes immense pride in his Native American heritage. A Chickasaw citizen, he has ancestors who walked the Trail of Tears and attended Indian boarding schools.

"My Chickasaw identity is part of who I am every day," he said.

Bailey, pitching coach for the Los Angeles Dodgers Class-A affiliate in Rancho Cucamonga, California, pitched briefly in the majors for the Houston Astros.[1]

Heritage underscores a foundational belief he applies to his baseball career: "Representation matters."

Some Natives who play and coach professional baseball today were born and raised in communities close to their twentieth-century predecessors, particularly those from rural Oklahoma and other areas in the Southwest and Southeast with Native tribes and communities. Others, like Bailey, were raised in more suburban environments.

Ryan Helsley

In addition to their success in baseball, they're keenly aware of their Indigenous backgrounds and are comfortable speaking out on the topic – with colleagues and reporters and in social media. They plan to become involved in their Native communities when their careers wind down. These players and coaches also recognize the cultural complexities of race in baseball.

This article includes perspectives from five such major leaguers – Ryan Helsley, Jon Gray, Adrian Houser, Anthony Seigler, and Bailey – along with Tyler Gillum, head coach of the Savannah Bananas, a popular barnstorming team. Their stories share some common elements, especially how their Native identities inform their personal beliefs.

Some recent Native American major leaguers, such as Jacoby Ellsbury and Joba Chamberlain, have full SABR biographies. Dylan Bundy, a Cherokee Nation citizen from Oklahoma, retired after the 2022 season and does not yet have a full SABR biography.[2] He did have a substantive career as a starting pitcher who won 54 games for the Baltimore Orioles, Los Angeles Angels, and Minnesota Twins.

Ellsbury was profiled in a Florida newspaper about his involvement with a baseball camp for young Natives:

> Baseball plays an important role in his life, but serving as a role model to Native American kids does as well. Ellsbury combined those passions and teamed up with Nike in 2011 to run the N7 Jacoby Ellsbury Baseball Camp on the Sale Rover-Maricopa Indian Community in Scottsdale, Arizona.

> "This is a way to give back," Ellsbury said. "If the kids take one thing from camp, it's that they can work hard, go to school, get good grades and have a dream and goal in mind."[3]

The article also includes a section about the modern player's experience with racial stereotypes, with observations from Helsley, Bailey, and *New York Times* correspondent Kurt Streeter.

NATIVE AMERICAN MAJOR LEAGUERS

RYAN HELSLEY, CHEROKEE

New York Mets reliever Ryan Helsley gets most of his Native heritage from his mother's side, though his father is also Cherokee.

Helsley was born and raised in Tahlequah, Oklahoma, a city that is the capital of the state's two federally recognized Cherokee tribes, the Cherokee Nation and the Keetoowah Band of the Cherokee Indians.

Helsley, a right-handed flamethrower who set a Cardinals franchise record while leading the National League with 49 saves in 2024, said Cherokee culture was more in the background during his childhood.

"My grandma would watch us during the summer when we were kids," he said. "We didn't have a lot of Cherokee culture in our daily lives, but we did attend powwows. My grandma spoke the language fluently and taught us a few phrases."[4]

He attended local schools, including Sequoyah High School, a boarding school for Native Americans. He played multiple sports but did not attend showcases, so was not noticed much.

"I was a late bloomer," he said. "I didn't throw crazy hard back then. I threw hard enough for local colleges. I wanted to play football, but my college coach encouraged me to focus on baseball."

Helsley attended Northeastern State University in Tahlequah, not planning to play professional baseball. About a quarter of NSU's student population identifies as Cherokee, and the school offers many Cherokee linguistics courses — including a major in the Cherokee language. Some courses are taught in Cherokee.

"My plan was to get a degree – NSU was a four-year school. My mom works in radiology, reading MRIs, and I always thought that was cool growing up. I admired her work helping people. Initially, I wanted to go to medical school, but I changed my path to physical therapy. My next thought was helping athletes recover from injuries."

Those plans changed when he began to bloom on the diamond.

"Going to college allowed me to focus on one sport and train my body. I was athletic enough to play multiple sports and be decent at all of them, but once I focused solely on pitching, I improved significantly," he said.

After two years at NSU, he was drafted by and signed with the Cardinals in 2015. He moved up through the farm system, eventually making his major-league debut in 2019.

As a major leaguer, Helsley frequently returns to Tahlequah to visit family and friends. "I try to show my face in the community because it's important for people to understand that I'm not a celebrity," he said. "I'm just like them, trying to make it day by day."

Helsley is a good friend of Adrian Houser, a major-league pitcher who was also raised in Tahlequah.

Helsley and his family were profiled in an article in *The Athletic* during his rookie season.[5] The article notes that the

Jon Gray

morning after he was drafted, Helsley helped run a baseball camp for kids in his hometown.

"I try to be the best I can be, live in the moment, and make the most of every opportunity," he said.

JON GRAY, CHEROKEE

Texas Rangers pitcher Jon Gray was born in Shawnee, Oklahoma, and raised in Chandler, less than 30 miles away. His Cherokee roots come from his mother's side. He cites his grandfather, who grew up near Tahlequah, in Cherokee County, as a major influence on his Native awareness.[6]

"My grandfather grew up with four brothers. His father was an Irish immigrant, and his mother was a full-blooded Cherokee. They had a small farm near Tahlequah, where the boys were raised," Gray said.[7]

After serving in the military, his grandfather bought land near Chandler.

"A lot of my learning came later, but my grandfather spoke a little Cherokee and told us stories about growing up in Tahlequah," he said. "He shared what he knew, and I always appreciated that."

Gray took several Native studies courses in college, including Cherokee language classes.

"I feel like language is so important – if you keep it alive, it will stay forever," he said.

Before that, Gray played American Legion baseball in Ada, Oklahoma, and high-school baseball in Chandler, along with wrestling, football, and basketball.

"I also played against great Native American ballplayers," he said. "They were amazing athletes. I grew up not far from the Sac and Fox Nation, where Jim Thorpe was from. In eastern Oklahoma, we often played against them in football and basketball."

He recalled games against Sequoyah High School, a Cherokee boarding school in Tahlequah, being "fun matchups."

From there, Gray attended Eastern Oklahoma State College before transferring to the University of Oklahoma for two seasons. He was drafted by the Colorado Rockies in the June 2013 amateur draft and made his major-league debut for the Rockies two years later. In 2023 Gray appeared in two games, winning one, for the Rangers in the World Series.

Raised in the heart of Cherokee country, Gray said he feels his heritage played a role in his development as a professional baseball player.

"I do feel like my heritage has given me an edge – playing on North American soil, or just instinctively. I've always seen it as a positive thing. Plenty of teammates have asked me about Cherokee language and culture."

"Getting financial help for my college books made a big difference – we didn't have much money. That support meant a lot to me, and now I want to find ways to give back," he said. "After baseball, I want to get involved – whether in sports, health, or something else within the community. That's a big goal of mine."

Gray has a message for young Native ballplayers: "If you have a dream, you can achieve it."

"Sometimes it might feel like you can't escape your circumstances – but you can go out into the world, chase your goals, and bring that success back to your community. I'm living proof of that."

He added: "I want to see more Cherokee athletes rise up. The talent is there, and I want young players to know they shouldn't feel held back at all."

ADRIAN HOUSER, CHEROKEE

Pitcher Adrian Houser was born in a Cherokee Nation hospital in Tahlequah, Oklahoma. He is Cherokee through his mother's side of the family.

"I grew up in Locust Grove, about 25 minutes north of Tahlequah," he said. "Locust Grove is a small town with only two stoplights, while Tahlequah has 20 times as many. My high school had a graduating class of about 100 students."[8]

Houser described Locust Grove as a quiet, close-knit town where everybody knows everybody else. "Through my mom's side alone, I'm related to half the town," he said. "I spent a lot of time outside, playing in the dirt, running through fields, hanging out with friends, and playing sports. I had an awesome childhood, riding my bike to my friend's house – that's how small the town was."

Houser said that for most of his childhood, his Cherokee identity remained in the background.

Adrian Houser

"When I was young, I attended Cherokee Nation Head Start, which was similar to preschool. All the kids there were Cherokee. My grandma and aunt had Cherokee Nation photos on the walls, and we learned how to count and speak a little Cherokee. I didn't keep up with the language, though."

Baseball was a big part of his upbringing. Throughout his elementary-school years, he played baseball on a team coached by his father that traveled to nearby states and even Puerto Rico. He joined a travel team in high school, then in his junior year he played for a team based in Dallas, about five hours away.

"That's when we started playing in bigger tournaments and getting attention from scouts and agents," he said.

He was friends with Ryan Helsley and Dylan Bundy as they played against each other in youth tournaments and high school.

Houser was drafted in 2011 by the Houston Astros and broke in with the Milwaukee Brewers, debuting in 2015. He last pitched in the majors for the New York Mets in 2024. In 2025, he was signed by the Chicago White Sox and traded to the Tampa Bay Rays.

Houser's heritage drives many of his personal beliefs, especially those connected to baseball.

"Sometimes, I think about the fact that I'm representing more than just myself," he said. "Being a small-town kid, I want to show that you don't have to come from a big city to reach your dreams. And as a Cherokee, some kids in Oklahoma know about my background and can look up to that – they can see that someone with their heritage has reached their dreams too."

BRANDON BAILEY, CHICKASAW

To Bailey, baseball is a game of resilience – a word that resonates with every Indigenous community.

"Growing up, as far back as my memory can take me, my Chickasaw heritage has always been a part of my life," Bailey said during spring training 2025. "My grandfather is half Chickasaw and my great-grandfather was full-blooded.

My grandfather frequently talks about this – getting involved in the tribe, going to reunions."[9]

Though Bailey was born and raised in Colorado, he feels deeply connected to the Chickasaw Nation in Oklahoma.

"My family's history is tied to the Trail of Tears – some of my ancestors walked it. My great-grandfather attended an Indian boarding school in Oklahoma, where he met his future wife. They eventually planted their roots in Colorado," Bailey said.

"Because of his experience in boarding school, my great-grandfather swore he would never return to Oklahoma. That has always stuck with me. Even though I didn't experience that firsthand or grow up on the reservation, I strive to be an example for young Indigenous children interested in sports."

He added: "I want to learn more about Chickasaw culture. As I made my way through the minor leagues, I had big dreams of being involved with the community. Injuries led me to retire, but staying in baseball allows me to make an impact – teaching youth the game and helping them grow."

"I'd love to work with Chickasaw youth and other tribal communities to help make baseball a sport of interest for Native American kids."

Bailey believes sport is medicine.

"Movement is one of the greatest things we can do as human beings. Baseball is truly special. You play outdoors, run on dirt and grass under the sunshine – it lifts your spirits, makes you feel healthy and alive."

Bailey has conversations about this heritage with colleagues.

Anthony Seigler

(Courtesy of the St. Louis Cardinals)

"These conversations come up often. I frequently discuss my background with coworkers. My boss knows how proud I am to be Indigenous, and I'm always happy to share my perspective."

ANTHONY SEIGLER, NAVAJO

On July 1, 2025, Anthony Seigler became the second Navajo (Diné) player in major-league history.

That's the day the 26-year-old switch-hitting infielder was selected by the Milwaukee Brewers from the team's AAA-affiliate, the Nashville Sounds of the International League.

When he got the call, the Brewers were in New York for a series against the Mets — a long way from the Navajo reservation where Seigler was born.

Seigler was chosen by the New York Yankees in the first round of the 2018 draft, out of Cartersville High School in Cartersville, Georgia. A year earlier, he played catcher for the USA team that won the U-18 Baseball World Cup. Nearly all his teammates eventually played professional baseball, including several in the major leagues.

Seigler learned about Jacoby Ellsbury — the first player of Navajo descent to make the major leagues — only after being drafted. Now, he is fully aware of being one of the few Native American players in professional baseball.

"I carry it as a badge of honor," he said shortly after joining the Brewers. "There aren't a lot of Native Americans in professional sports, and the ones who are there are not

Brandon Bailey with Corpus Christi in the spring of 2019.

(Courtesy of Wikeah Vigil)

always widely known. So for us, especially being on the stage I'm at, it's awesome to be able to represent and play for my Navajo Nation."[10]

Seigler was born in Fort Defiance, Arizona, a small community of fewer than 4,000 people located in the Navajo Nation on the border with New Mexico. Over 90 percent of the population of Fort Defiance is Native American, according to the 2010 U.S. Census.

"Everyone calls it *The Fort*," said Seigler's mother Alysia Webb, herself born and raised on a reservation in Window Rock, Arizona, capitol of the Navajo Nation. Webb speaks the Navajo language, Diné bizaad, as do her parents. Her grandfather was a Navajo code talker in World War II.[11]

Webb said her family, including Anthony and his three siblings, have always focused on basketball.

"On the rez, basketball is *it*," she said. "We probably have nine or 10 state high school basketball championships in our family."

In fact, Webb had never been off the reservation until she went to college, where she played basketball. As Seigler said: "We're a love-to-hoop family."

But Webb knew her son was a gifted athlete in baseball too. "We knew he was a good ballplayer but for us it felt normal, as crazy as that may sound," she said.

It wasn't until Seigler entered professional baseball that he began to understand how much his heritage meant — not just to him, but to others. Messages started to come in from family, community members, even strangers on Instagram.

"They tell me how I'm representing the Navajo Nation really well," he said. "Kids on the rez started playing baseball when they heard about me. It gives them hope, whatever situation they're in."

His identity often sparks curiosity, especially in a sport where Native American players are few and far between. "Usually if I show up somewhere new, the Latino guys start talking Spanish to me because of how I look," he said. "My teammates usually get curious when they learn I'm Native American. If they ask, I talk with them. It does come up."

Though he moved off the reservation as a child, he doesn't take for granted the challenges others still face. "Native Americans who live on the rez have harder lives — I can't speak fully to that. But I do believe in understanding where people come from and treating them how they want to be treated."

Seigler never set out to be a symbol—but as his profile has grown, so too has his sense of responsibility. What began as a love for sports has become a way to carry his heritage with him, everywhere the game takes him.

That connection became especially clear during his time with USA Baseball.

"I remember my mom bringing the Navajo Nation flag," he recalls. "When I went out on the field, I was representing Team USA, but I wanted the Navajo community to know I was there for us."

Tyler Gillum

"It's awesome to have a community, a whole big Navajo Nation, cheering for me, pulling for me, praying for me."

TYLER GILLUM, CHICKASAW

Chickasaw citizen Tyler Gillum is head coach of the Savannah Bananas, a barnstorming team that in 2024 drew more fans than one major-league team.

Gillum was born in 1986 in a Chickasaw hospital in Ada, Oklahoma.

"Growing up in Ada, I was surrounded by Native American culture all the time. There were so many aspects of Chickasaw heritage that I took part in," he said shortly after kicking off the 2025 Bananas tour.[12]

In 2024 the team played in 29 cities, drawing more than one million fans – more than the home attendance of the Oakland Athletics. In 2025 the team expected to play in 18 major-league ballparks, two NFL stadiums, and one college football stadium, with overall attendance expected to double.[13]

The Chickasaw Nation played a major part in Gillum's baseball journey.

"It started with Chickasaw baseball camps in high school. The first one I attended was in Ardmore, Oklahoma, at Ardmore High School," he said. "That camp was one of the best I've ever been a part of – high-level coaching with former major-league players, scouts, crosscheckers, current players, and college coaches from Division I schools."

That experience was a huge stepping stone for Gillum – it inspired him to want to play college baseball. He ended up attending Seminole State Junior College in Seminole, Oklahoma.

"While I was in college, I started coaching at Chickasaw baseball camps," he recalled. "Along that route, the Chickasaws provided multiple opportunities for me. They helped pay for my school, clothing, and full Pell financial aid. Their support made a huge difference in helping me chase my baseball dream.

"If it weren't for the Chickasaws investing in me, I wouldn't have had the same opportunities."

Gillum transferred to East Central University in Ada, where he earned undergraduate and graduate degrees in education. He did not play baseball after college — instead, he pursued his passion for coaching.

"I started coaching at East Central University, but they didn't have paid assistant positions – only two graduate assistant roles. I was making about $5,000 a year while working 100 hours a week.

At 23 years old, I was the recruiting coordinator, infield coach, and working in the office too," he said.

"It was an incredible opportunity. I wasn't in it for the money – and I still am not. I do it for the experience and the impact."

Gillum's personal motto is "Bet on Yourself," and his goal is to make a positive impact on one single person every day. He surpassed that goal by about a million in 2024.

"Whenever I think about the Chickasaw Nation, I come back to one of their main principles – servant leadership," Gillum said. "I always view myself through that lens – how can I serve? How can I make an impact?"

OLD STEREOTYPES, NEW OUTSPOKENNESS

Generations ago, Native players were commonly nicknamed "Chief" and cultural stereotypes were the norm for sports reporters covering Native athletes in baseball and other sports. While today's Native ballplayers aren't subjected to those caricatures, others persist — mascots, team names, and more.

One example: The 2021 World Series between the Atlanta Braves and Houston Astros averaged over 11 million television viewers per game. (The Braves' Series-clinching win in Game Six drew over 14 million viewers.[14]) During the three Braves home games, television viewers saw thousands of fans doing the "tomahawk chop" and chanting a supposed war cry, accompanied by thumping, Native-sounding music.

The old trope isn't as acceptable as it once was; today's players and those who write about them are at ease sharing their perspectives.

In the *New York Times*, columnist Kurt Streeter called the chop a "spectacle of ignorance."[15] In a conversation more than three years later, Streeter added: "It's crazy that we're still doing that and that it's still considered acceptable."[16]

Streeter's article and other coverage noted Commissioner Rob Manfred's statements that local Native communities support the chop, despite widespread opposition from those who find it a stereotypical and offensive representation of Native culture.

"It wasn't hard to find people within these tribes who were disgusted by their connection to the Braves," Streeter said. "There's nothing uniform about the way Native communities view these affiliations and imagery. There is a range of opinions."

At least two of today's Native ballplayers reflect that range.

Ryan Helsley, then pitching for the Cardinals, was widely quoted about the chop during the 2019 National League Division Series, when the Cardinals played the Braves. Reporters asked him about the chant after the first two games, both played in Atlanta. He called it "a misrepresentation of the Cherokee people or Native Americans in general."[17]

It was his rookie season and his first visit to Atlanta. He looked back on the experience two years later in a conversation during a Cardinals visit to Boston.

"I understand why they do it for the fans, but there are better ways to honor Native culture," Helsley said. "Mascots and teams often use regalia and headdresses – which are deeply important to our culture – as costumes. Many people don't understand the meaning and think it's harmless, but there needs to be more respect for people's wishes. The narrative painted by this imagery isn't who we are."

Helsley credits the Braves for hosting an all-Native baseball camp and for educating fans about Natives. "They're doing some good things to show who Native Americans are," he said.

Brandon Bailey noted that Native race and culture are often uncomfortable topics and added that he feels schools do not teach enough about Indigenous history. He said he tries to understand both sides of the issue.

"There's some shame, honestly, in how the federal government treated Native peoples – cultural genocide happened at the hands of the government," he said. "History matters so that it doesn't repeat itself. None of us today made those decisions, but we are in control of our actions now. Treating people with respect is something we can all commit to."

He added: "I appreciate when teams, like the Cleveland Guardians, take a step back and acknowledge the effect on people. They ask, 'How can we still be proud of our colors, our team's energy, and history, while finding common ground to make changes that matter?'"

"Pride shouldn't come at the cost of traumatizing people who've endured hardships."

Streeter concluded: "Sports are more transcendent and saturated now – more visible and powerful than ever. The imagery is stronger because sports are cathedrals, players are celebrities, and with the internet, access to these symbols is everywhere."

"When you see the chop and hear the chants, they carry a greater influence."

NATIVE PROGRESS, NATIVE TERMS

As heritage continues to be important to Ryan Helsley, Brandon Bailey, Jon Gray, and others, today's players and coaches can continue to speak out and participate in programs to gather cultural influence, helping to shape goals for Native progress on Native terms. They may not achieve these goals soon, but they can help set the track and maintain progress.

"I love the word *unconquerable*," said Gillum. "Move the needle, impact the world, and do good things – so you can keep moving forward."

SOURCES

In addition to the sources cited in the Notes, the author accessed a file provided by the Giamatti Research Center at the National Baseball Hall of Fame, Retrosheet. org, and Baseball-Reference. com.

NOTES

1 Andy McCullough, "Baseball's 2020 Club: Five Years Ago They Realized a Dream, but COVID-19 Stopped Anyone From Seeing It," *The Athletic*, March 12, 2025.

2 A player must be retired for five years before becoming a subject for a SABR biography.

3 Beverly Bidney, "Indian Country Profile: Jacoby Ellsbury," *Seminole Tribune* (Florida), April 29, 2014.For more on Ellsbury, see Jon Schwartz, "Yankees Magazine: In His Blood," MLB.com, April 3, 2017. https://www.mlb.com/news/ellsbury-honors-his-native-american-heritage-c222040346, accessed July 6,2025.

4 Ryan Helsley's perspectives shared in conversation with the author, June 2023.

5 Mark Saxon, "Cardinals Pitcher Ryan Helsley and His Family Work to Keep Cherokee Heritage Alive," *New York Times*, August 29, 2016.

6 Thomas Harding, "Gray Humbled by Cherokee Nation Roots," MLB.com, August 25, 2016.

7 Jon Gray's perspectives shared in conversation with the author, January 2024.

8 Adrian Houser's perspectives shared in conversation with the author, January 2023.

9 Brandon Bailey's perspectives shared in conversation with the author, February 2025.

10 Anthony Seigler's perspectives shared in conversation with the author, July 2025.

11 Alysia Webb's perspectives shared in conversation with the author, July 2025.

12 Tyler Gillum's perspectives shared in conversation with the author, February 2025.

13 Benjamin Hoffman, "The Savannah Bananas Needed a Bigger Stage," *New York Times*, October 4, 2024.

14 Jabari Young, "14.3 million people watched the Atlanta Braves win the 2021 World Series," CNBC.com, November 3, 2021.

15 Kurt Streeter, "M.L.B. Commissioner Can't Hear Native Voices Over Atlanta's Chop," *New York Times*, October 29, 2021.

16 Kurt Streeter's perspectives shared in conversation with the author, January 2025.

17 Alan Blinder, "Braves Pivot from 'Tomahawk Chop' Chant After a Cardinal's Criticism," *New York Times*, October 9, 2021.

THE CARLISLE INDIAN SCHOOL: BASEBALL AS A 'CIVILIZING' INFLUENCE

By Roger and Deena Parmelee

Children played baseball at the United States Training and Industrial School at Carlisle Barracks. On one level, they were children like any others, playing a game, having fun running about. But to the children, their teachers and coaches, school administration, the federal government, and even the nation, that same baseball was also so much more, as was every activity these children undertook. To understand the impact of their baseball we must understand the nature and significance of the school; we must know the children themselves: who they were, where they came from, and what the school meant to them and their families. We must also understand its founder, Captain Richard Henry Pratt. Jim Thorpe, "Chief" Albert Bender, and Glenn "Pop" Warner may be the names most commonly associated with the school, but there is much more to the story.

The United States Training and Industrial School at Carlisle Barracks, more often referred to as the Carlisle Indian School, was not the first boarding school for Native American children. It was, however, intentionally the first one to be well removed from the children's homes and families. In 1879, when the school was founded, the US government was still in the process of relocating Native nations onto reservations, but south-central Pennsylvania, where Carlisle is located, is nowhere near any of those reservations. The chronological context is important here; in 1879, George Armstrong Custer's "Last Stand" was only three years in the past, and the 1890 massacre at Wounded Knee was still to come. Warring between the US military and various Indian Nations was not history, but very current events.[1] The Civil War had not yet been over for 20 years, and it was during that conflict that Richard Henry Pratt began the set of experiences that would culminate in his idea of a different kind of boarding school for Native American children.

Today, Pratt is perhaps most infamous for being the originator of the phrase "Kill the Indian, save the man," but to use that phrase as the only lens through which to view the man is a drastic simplification. Historian Robert Utley wrote that "Carlisle [Indian School] was the institutional embodiment of Richard H. Pratt, as he was its personification."[2]

So, who was Richard Henry Pratt? A native Indianan, he tried his hand at the trades of printing and tinsmithing. He was 21 when the Civil War broke out and he enlisted in a volunteer regiment. Achieving some success in the Army, he rose to the rank of first lieutenant of cavalry by the time the war ended. Having acquired a bride, he and his bride opened a hardware store in Indiana, but an unsuccessful business made him yearn for Army life. He applied for a commission in the regular Army and was appointed a second lieutenant in the 10th US Cavalry. The 10th was a unit of "Buffalo Soldiers," made up of African American enlisted men but led by White officers.

Assigned to Fort Gibson in Indian Territory [now Oklahoma], Pratt worked well with the enlisted men and with the "Indian Scouts" and found himself attached to the scout units with greater frequency. Pratt described himself (writing in the third person) as looking "upon them as men and brothers, lacking in attainment only, and that through no fault of theirs. His contention ... was that the Indians were entitled to a full, fair chance for development in every way, and until they had that, our people had no right to form adverse opinions of them, or to condemn them as incorrigibly savage."[3]

In the mid- through late 1870s Pratt had further encounters with Native Peoples being held as prisoners of war at Fort Marion in St. Augustine, Florida. He found "three years of imprisonment resulted in English speaking, in the adoption of civilized dress and habits and in a hungering on their part for a career in the larger life of the nation."[4]

1885 Carlisle student baseball team

A school at Fort Marion provided the prisoners "with daily training in industries" and the opportunity to meet "multitudes of our own people."[5] Pratt took the initiative to organize the younger men along military lines into a company. He armed them and made them into a guard unit, allowing him to assign the regular soldier guards to other duties.

This combination of experiences caused Pratt to conclude: "In Indian civilization I am a Baptist, because I believe in immersing the Indians in our civilization and when we get them under holding them there until they are thoroughly soaked."[6] That meant removing them from reservations so they could be immersed in the culture of which they were to become a part. And what better way to achieve a complete cultural conversion than to start with the young? Pratt got permission and private funding for 17 of "his" young Indian men to attend the Hampton Normal and Industrial School, but it was a school intended for Black Americans; Pratt felt the Native American students should have one of their very own.[7]

What we now refer to as the Progressive Era was just getting underway by the time Pratt founded the school. Changes in social attitudes that accompany the period are inherent in the philosophy underlying not only Pratt's desire to found the school, but the support it received from the government and certain public sectors. Not that late nineteenth-century racial views mirrored our own; Europeans and Euro-Americans believed deeply in their own superiority, whether it was socioculturally, politically, or religiously. But they had come to believe that at least some of the non-White peoples could (and should) be taught to live/act/function "like whites did." In urban centers along the East Coast, this attitude was increasingly apparent when it came to views on Native Americans living within the country.[8]

Physical distance from sites of violence between the military and Native communities or settlers and Native communities allowed Easterners the freedom to sympathize with those Native communities, usually in a paternalistic way. That colonial paternalism was important to the success of the school, which was funded in part by the federal government; however, the funding never seemed sufficient. Pratt and his successors made tours to raise funds, entertained wealthy visitors who could be appealed to for donations. They also employed the students themselves whenever possible to save money, and earned income for the school by renting out student labor to farms and businesses across Pennsylvania.[9] The program was not referred to as "renting"; it was called "putting out" and was intended to provide the students with the opportunity to use and grow their vocational skills in real environments such as shops, offices, and farms.

The space that became the school's campus had inadequate facilities when the students arrived in the fall of 1879, so while local businesses and labor were employed to get things started, the school always relied on student labor. Permission and cooperation from the federal government – specifically the Bureau of Indian Affairs, then under the War Department – had come with the stipulation that girls be educated at the new school as well as boys.[10] Newspapers and newsletters to donors were printed in the school's print shop; girls were taught laundering by washing their schoolmates' clothing, but also worked in the print shop. The girls were taught how to "keep house" as defined by Euro-American standards, which saved the school more money since the girls could then also clean and cook.

Pratt seems to have been the one to suggest the Carlisle Barracks as the location for his school when he proposed the idea to the secretaries of the interior and war, with whom he met in person for that purpose. He liked it in part because it was far from any reservations, meaning the children would be removed from their homes and families and those influences. Additionally, it was good farming country, and the current generations of residents had never personally experienced perceived threats to their homes by regional Native communities, and so were "long free from the universal border prejudice against the Indians."[11]

Over the life of the school, children were brought from dozens of Indian nations from across what we know as the United States: as near to Carlisle as upstate New York, and as far away as Alaska and the Southwest. They carried with them an equal array of languages and customs, and varying degrees of previous exposure to the English language, Euro-Americans, and Christianity. The journey alone exposed them to a whirlwind of new experiences, such as train or steamship travel, and complete isolation from family and loved ones.

Once the children arrived at the school, they were forbidden to use their own languages or practice their traditions. Play became one of the universal languages; there is evidence that the children played with local Carlisle children sometimes. Pickup teams formed in open areas on the school grounds during free time after supper. Baseball may not have been entirely new to at least some of the children, depending on where they had lived prior to their arrival at the school. Baseball was played at most, if not all, US military facilities across the West; we know of teams consisting of Native American scouts and POWs at Fort Sill, in Oklahoma, playing teams made up of various cavalry units, from the 1880s through the end of the century.[12] It was, apparently, quite popular with the children themselves: "Ball, back of the hospital; ball, back of the schoolhouse; ball, in front of the Girls Quarters; ball, all around, has been the order of the hour after supper, this week."[13]

Teams were formed from the trades' schools and residence halls, and some of the most enthusiastic students were on more than one team. There were both boys' and girls' teams, though they didn't mix (it *was* the Victorian era), and it wasn't long before there were varsity and junior varsity teams as well as intramural teams with such societally approved names as the "Unions," "Young Americans," "Union Reserves," and "Unions Carlisle."

Pratt was not a sportsman or athlete by nature, but anything that could be seen as an "Americanizing force" was worth trying. By June of 1886, Pratt provided official recognition of a baseball program by authorizing the purchase of uniforms. Baseball was seen to be making citizens of the students, and uniforms were emblazoned with "C.I.T.S" for Carlisle Indian Training School. "Citizenship" was considered equivalent to assimilation into the broader culture. As the superintendent pointed out in a speech for the 1890 Decoration Day game with the team from the Educational Home (of) Philadelphia, "See how near that (C.I.T.S.) comes to being an abbreviation of 'citizens,' which they are all aspiring to become?"[14]

By 1888 Carlisle had a baseball coach, in the model of later coaches whose main responsibilities were elsewhere; Fisk "Tim" Goodyear was a teacher and also doubled as a clerk, overseeing the students who were part of the school's summer outing program. He was the 19-year-old eldest son of a local merchant and sheriff and left the school after six years, in 1893, when his father turned the family business over to Tim and his brother. Lacking the background or prestige of later coaches like Glenn "Pop" Warner, he was described as well-liked by the boys.[15] In the early days of his tenure in the spring of 1888 his teams played a mostly intramural schedule and also played nearby town teams and the Dickinson College freshman squad. As of 1890, they played a wider schedule that included the Dickinson College varsity in Carlisle, as well as Bucknell, Gettysburg, the University of Pennsylvania, and Pennsylvania State.

Carlisle had a highly esteemed coach in Warner as well as coaching from some major-league players – Charlie Bender, Harry L. Taylor, and Charlie Pittinger.[16] Eugene Bassford had no major-league coaching experience but was an experienced college coach. The team's record never rose much above the .500 level and for the period from 1895 till the end of the program in 1909, their overall record was 124-142-5 (.466). Bassford had the distinction of being Carlisle's final baseball coach but, curiously, was described in a *New York Times* report of January 31, 1909, as the first.

"The athletic officials of the Carlisle Indian School have engaged for the first time a baseball coach. He is Eugene E. Bassford, who coached Fordham College at baseball for the last four years. The Carlisle baseball schedule will contain nearly thirty games. Practice will begin about the middle of February."[17]

Whatever hair-splitting criteria were used to name Bassford the "first" baseball coach, he was definitely the last. Pop Warner preferred to concentrate on the more famous football program in the fall and on track and field in the spring. After an 11-16 baseball season in 1909, that was it: The baseball program was ended.

While baseball was the unwanted stepchild in Warner's athletic program, the school turned out seven major leaguers in its 23 years of competition with college, semipro, and town teams. Jim Thorpe was Carlisle's most famous athletic product, and Hall of Famer Charlie Bender was the best-known alumnus in baseball, but there were five others who matriculated at Carlisle and went on to play in the major leagues. (The SABR BioProject includes biographies of all seven.) The lives and careers of Thorpe and Bender are well documented, so we'll focus on George Johnson, Louis LeRoy, Mike Balenti, Frank Jude, and Charlie Roy.

Three of the five – Johnson, LeRoy, and Roy – were pitchers, and Robert Charles Roy had a background quite similar to that of Charles Albert Bender. Both were from northern Minnesota, and they are known to have been childhood friends. Roy's career was also the shortest, consisting of seven games with the Phillies in 1906. He also pitched for Newark of the Class-A Eastern League in 1906. In 1907 he was back at Newark, but he was released in June and had subsequent trials at Class-B Wilmington, Delaware, and Class-D Steubenville, Ohio. Charlie Roy is described as a deeply religious man, and he decided to quit baseball at the age of 23 to become a Christian evangelist.

Louis LeRoy's career in the major leagues wasn't much longer. He pitched three games for the New York Highlanders in 1905, 11 games for them in 1906, and one game for the Boston Red Sox in 1910. However, his minor-league career was extensive; only Hall of Famer Charlie Bender, with 4,292 innings across all levels, pitched more innings than LeRoy did with 3,621. Beginning in Buffalo in 1902, LeRoy's career took him literally from coast to coast, Boston to Seattle, across the border to Montreal, and to St. Paul, Indianapolis, and Salt Lake City before he finished up in Mitchell, South Dakota, in 1920.

George Johnson pitched 10 years at all levels and carried a heavy workload in his three years in the majors, at Cincinnati in 1913 and 1914. During the 1914 season he jumped to Kansas City of the Federal League, for which he also pitched in 1915. Relying mostly on a fastball and a spitball, Johnson went 14-16 in 269 innings with the Reds in 1913. In 1914 he was idled for three months while courts worked out whether he was to pitch for the Reds or the Federal League's Kansas City Packers, but turned in a 9-10 record in 138 innings. With Kansas City in 1915, Johnson went 17-17 while pitching 281⅓ innings.

Johnson pitched 200 innings for Vernon of the Pacific Coast League in 1916 and an astonishing 398⅔ dividing his time between Vernon and San Francisco of the Pacific Coast Lague in 1917. Described as "rotund" in the press of the time, George Johnson failed to show up for a game on June 16. 1918, and was "fired" by San Francisco Seals President Charles Strub. He played some semipro ball over the next few years and his life ended abruptly when he was shot to death after a dice game. He was 36.

There were two stars in the backfield of the Carlisle Indians in 1908. One was Jim Thorpe; the other wasn't.[18] Mike Balenti was the quarterback at Carlisle when Jim

Thorpe was the running back. Balenti was also captain of the baseball team in 1908 and '09 and went on to play 10 years in professional baseball.

Balenti signed with the Philadelphia Athletics and reported to them after Carlisle's 1909 season. The A's assigned him to the Milwaukee Brewers and the Brewers optioned him to Dayton of the Class-B Central League. He was released in July but caught on with El Reno of the Class-C Western League. Balenti spent 1910 with Savannah of the South Atlantic League, and a .326 season at Macon in 1911 resulted in his being purchased by the Cincinnati Reds in July. He appeared in only eight games for the Reds and spent 1912 having a good season batting .288 for Chattanooga of the Class-A Southern Association, who sold his contract to the St. Louis Browns in September.

Balenti played in 70 games for the Browns in 1913, hitting only .180, and St. Louis sent him back to Chattanooga after the 1913 season. Another year at Class-A Chattanooga in 1914, when he hit only .157, meant he spent 1915, 1916, and part of 1917 with San Antonio of the Class-B Texas League before drifting down to Tulsa of the Class-D Western Association. He made appearances again in 1923 and 1926 with lower-classification clubs before calling it a career.

Frank Jude's SABR biography tells that he caught the attention of Cincinnati Reds owner Garry Herrmann and Boston Americans manager Jimmy Collins with his play at Carlisle. He signed with Toledo of the Class-A American Association and began his professional career there, forgoing his senior year at the Indian Industrial School.

According to Baseball Reference.com, Jude began the 1906 season with the Toledo Mudhens and was hitting .315 after 72 games when the Reds traded two major leaguers to Toledo to acquire the speedy outfielder. In 80 games with the Reds, he managed only a .208 batting average. It was to be his only opportunity in the majors. After the season he was sold to Columbus of the American Association. His minor-league odyssey from 1907 to 1923 included stops from Columbus, Ohio, to Albany, New York, and from Mobile, Alabama, to Saskatoon, Saskatchewan.

Union Reserve baseball team, ca. 1891

(*Carlisle Indian School Digital Resource Center*)

Jude hit .261 for Lincoln of the Class-A Western Association in 1910 when he played in 167 games. He hit .335 for his best season while with Saskatoon of the Class-B Western Canada Association; that was in 1921, when he was 36 and after he had taken five years away from professional baseball. The numbers are incomplete but with what we know, he is computed to have hit .275 in 1,329 minor-league games.

Regardless of who was coaching, a few factors impacted how the Indian School's teams fared against their collegiate rivals. While educational structures were different in the nineteenth century than they were before educational standardization became the norm in the twentieth, the boys on the Indian School teams may well have been several years younger than the opposing players.[19] Further, a majority of the opposition came from the middle and upper-middle classes and had time to dedicate to athletics as a hobby or leisure pastime. The Indian School boys were still required to fulfill the vocational aspects of their education, despite their roster spots. It seems unlikely that Bucknell or Yale students also learned and spent time on bricklaying or masonry for school buildings the way the Carlisle boys did.

Those requirements didn't mean the school community, or the larger community, was any less interested in how the teams did. Both the *Indian Helper* and the *Red Man*, newspapers put out by the school's own printing office (one of the few vocations taught to both boys and girls), often included mentions of and stories about the teams and how they fared. The *Indian Helper* even included results of games played by other Indian schools from across the country. The *Philadelphia Times* covered the 1901 Carlisle season in some depth, including the hiring of former major leaguer Harry Taylor to coach the team as well as box scores and analysis of the games.[20]

The conscious use of organized athletics as a tool to Americanize children was implemented across the country with Native American children, as well as immigrant children in overcrowded urban slums. The late nineteenth and early twentieth centuries also saw an improved understanding of the health benefits of athletic play for children, especially as increasing numbers of them were slowly taken out of industrial environments and provided with educations.

There are indicators that Carlisle students who were athletes may have had a better or easier time at school than those who were not. Letters sent to the school after a student had left, alumni questionnaires, and attendance at reunions, provide evidence that some students retained good memories of their time at the school, and valued the education and training they received there.[21] Charlie Bender chose to stay in Pennsylvania even after retiring from baseball, although he certainly could have gone back to Minnesota.

And yet Jim Thorpe and others ran away from the school and from their assigned "putting out" work locations. The school's guardhouse doubled as "jail," in which such students were sometimes held when they were returned to the school. Countless miles from everyone they knew and loved, forbidden to speak the language of their very thoughts, forced into clothing completely foreign – and often associated with an "enemy" – made to participate in classes, activities, and religious observation in a language they didn't know or understand: These experiences can only have been bewildering and frightening. Some children arrived at the school as young as 3 or 4 years old. Boarding school was an individual experience as well as a collective one, and some children fared better than others, depending on countless factors.

The same was true after the children left the school; some got the few federal jobs available on their home reservations or neighboring ones, some taught at the Indian schools proliferating across the country. Most, however, went home to their communities and tried to fit in again. The duration of their absence could contribute to that success or failure; if you no longer speak the language or know the customs, how will you fit in? Your food ways, speech, dress, appearance (especially for boys) have all changed – how will you fit in? Returning students had to learn all over again, just as they had when they went off to school in the first place. Some were able to support themselves with the skills they had been taught at the school, such as building trades like masonry, carpentry, and bricklaying. For others, there was no market for those skills if they went back to the reservation.

As this article was completed in 2024, there were small red plastic flags at a dozen or so of the markers in the graveyard at the Carlisle Indian School, now the Army War College, indicating this year's group to be disinterred and taken home to their relations and communities. Native families and communities still battle with bureaucracy, the courts, and the Army's Office of Army Cemeteries to be permitted to receive their ancestors' remains from the school grounds.[22] Those battles symbolize the extent to which the damage done by boarding schools is a factor for families and communities to this day. The loss of the family members who died at the school, and the impact of the separation and education to the ones who returned, permanently changed the shape of Native lives and communities across the continent.

Fannie Charging Shield, Oglala Lakota, was 16 when she arrived at the Carlisle Indian School. It was early in 1891, only a couple of months after the December 1890 massacre at Wounded Knee, South Dakota. It must have disconcerting, if not terrifying, to arrive at a place run by the very same agency that had so recently killed people you knew. In June 1891 she was sent to a work assignment with a family near the Delaware border and did not return to school until January 1892, by which time she had probably already contracted tuberculosis. Not long after, the school sent for her father, which was unusual. Chief Charging Shield arrived with his good friend Chief American Horse, who may have visited the campus previously. Chief Charging Shield

was able to be with his daughter when she died but was dismayed to learn that because the school had funded his trip to be with her, there was no money to allow him to take her body home with him. He returned home without her and Fannie was buried at the school, but he always hoped that someday her body could be returned to her home. Fannie Charging Shield was one of the students disinterred in the late summer of 2024. Her remains and those of two other Lakota children were taken back to their lands for reburial.[23]

Perhaps it is naïve, but it would be nice to hope that watching or playing baseball while at school, or teaching it to others after school ended, was a small bright spot for the children at the Carlisle Indian School.

POSTSCRIPT:

On October 25, 2024, President Joe Biden formally apologized for the federal government's role in operating or promoting the operation of boarding schools for Native American children. During the speech in which he made the apology, the President called for a moment of silence for the children and the generations traumatized by the boarding school abuses.[24] In December Biden took another significant step in promoting generational healing in Native communities by declaring the grounds of what was the Carlisle Indian School a National Monument. Just over 24 acres are protected by this new status, including buildings and gateposts built by the students learning their trades at the school.[25] Together, these steps will hopefully help ensure that the boarding school experiences of the Native children and their families and communities will not be forgotten or swept aside.

SOURCES

In addition to the sources cited in the Notes, the authors also consulted

PRINT SOURCES:

Boston Post. "Indians Played a Weak Game," June 16, 1901.

Callow, Colin, ed. *First Peoples: A Documentary Survey of American Indian History*, Second Edition. Boston: Bedford/St. Martin's, 2004.

"Indian Education at Hampton and Carlisle," *Harper's New Monthly Magazine* 62, no. 320 (April 1881): 659-675.

Iverson, Peter. *"We Are Still Here," American Indians in the Twentieth Century*. Wheeling, Illinois: Harlan Davidson, Inc. 1998.

Maraniss, David. *Path Lit by Lightning: The Life of Jim Thorpe*. New York: Simon & Schuster, 2022.

Standing Bear, Luther. *My People, The Sioux*. Kindle Edition. Hegne Publishing, August 2017.

Weeks, Philip. *Farewell, My Nation: The American Indian and the United States in the Nineteenth Century*. Wheeling, Illinois: Harlan Davidson, Inc, 2001.

Weeks, Philip, ed. *"They Made Us Many Promises,": The American Indian Experience 1524 to the Present*. Wheeling, Illinois: Harlan Davidson, Inc., 2002.

DIGITAL SOURCES:

Rubinkama, Michael. "Native Children's Remains to be Moved from Army Cemetery," in *The Hill*, June 14, 2022.

https://thehill.com/homenews/ap/ap-u-s-news/native-childrens-remains-to-be-moved-from-army-cemetery/.

Virtual tour of Carlisle Indian School video: Barbara Landis, 2017, https://www.youtube.com/watch?v=hL8pa1ZDSGY.

History of the Carlisle Indian School: Dickinson College, 2021

https://www.youtube.com/watch?v=tfOKRglt8e8.

Carlisle Indian School Digital Resource Center

https://carlisleindian.dickinson.edu/.

Yu, Jane. "Kill the Indian, Save the Man," Spring, 2009, Pennsylvania Center for the Book

https://pabook.libraries.psu.edu/literary-cultural-heritage-map-pa/feature-articles/kill-indian-save-man.

PBS Newshour broadcast segment June 23, 2021

https://www.youtube.com/watch?v=gRNcCCgnauI.

Hedgpeth, Dana, "'12 Years of Hell': Indian Boarding School Survivors Share their Stories," *Washington Post*, August 7, 2023.

NOTES

1   On at least one documented occasion, teenage prisoners of war captured by the US military in ongoing conflicts with Native nations were sent as students to the school. *The Indian Helper* (Carlisle, Pennsylvania), Vol. 3, No. 47, July 6, 1888, 3.

2   Robert M. Utley, introduction to *The Indian Industrial School, Carlisle, Pennsylvania*, by Brig. Gen. R.H. Pratt, 1979 reprint of the 1908 text, Cumberland County Historical Society Publications, Volume 10, No. 3, 3.

3   Richard Henry Pratt, *The Indian Industrial School, Carlisle, Pennsylvania*, 1979 reprint of the 1908 text, Cumberland County Historical Society Publications, Volume 10, No. 3, 10.

4   Pratt, *The Indian Industrial School, Carlisle, Pennsylvania*, 11.

5   Pratt, *The Indian Industrial School, Carlisle, Pennsylvania*, 11.

6   Pratt, *The Indian Industrial School, Carlisle, Pennsylvania*, 5.

7   Richard Henry Pratt. *Battlefield and Classroom: Four Decades with the American Indian, 1867-1904* (New Haven: Yale University Press, 1964), 190. In 1868, General Samuel Chapman Armstrong founded the Hampton Normal and Industrial School in Hampton, Virginia, for the express purpose of educating freed slaves.

8   The April 1881 issue of the popular *Harper's Magazine*, for example, included a lengthy, illustrated article on "Indian Education at Hampton and Carlisle." *Harper's New Monthly Magazine* 62, no. 320 (April 1881): 659-675.

9   There are buildings on the campus today that were built by school students as they learned construction trades.

10 Pratt, *The Indian Industrial School, Carlisle, Pennsylvania*, 15.

11 Pratt. *Battlefield and Classroom*, 216.

12 https://klaw.com/events-lawton/historic-base-ball-game-set-at-fort-sill/23-july-2011/, accessed August 19, 2024.

13 *Indian Helper.* Volume 3, No. 36, April 20, 1888: 3.

14 *Indian Helper,* Volume 3, No. 36, April 20, 1888: 39.

15 Jeffrey Powers-Beck, *The American Indian Integration of Baseball* (Lincoln: University of Nebraska Press, 2004), 40.

16 https://sabr.org/bioproj/person/charlie-pittinger/.

17 "Carlisle Baseball Coach," *New York Times.* January 31, 1909, Section 4, 3.

18 Think of Mike Balenti as Carlisle's Lou Gehrig to Jim Thorpe's Babe Ruth.

19 For example, during the 1901 season, Charlie Bender was only 17. Many of the players on the opposing college and town teams would have been well older – although it is also true that in the nineteenth century boys often went to college at a much younger age than is common today.

20 "Indians Won Opening Game," *Philadelphia Times*, April 13, 1901: 8.

21 Dickinson College is the principal digital repository for Carlisle Indian School records, including student records: https://carlisleindian.dickinson.edu/

22 https://ictnews.org/news/obscure-government-agency-at-center-of-carlisle-repatriation-dispute accessed September 1 and 2, 2024. Families of children who died at Carlisle Indian School have a particularly complicated maze to navigate for the return of their kin's remains because the property remains an active military facility.

23 Charles Fox, "Home From Carlisle: A Father's Wish Fulfilled After More Than 130 Years," *Indian Country Today*, September 18, 2024. https://ictnews.org/news/home-from-carlisle-a-fathers-wish-fulfilled-after-more-than-130-years.

24 Gabriel Pietrorazio, "Biden Apologizes for Government's Role in Running Native American Boarding Schools," NPR.org, October 26, 2024. https://www.npr.org/2024/10/26/nx-s1-5165427/biden-apologizes-for-governments-role-in-running-native-american-boarding-schools.

25 Cecily Hilleary, "Biden Designates National Monument at site of Carlisle Indian School," VOANews, December 10, 2024. https://www.voanews.com/a/biden-designates-national-monument-at-site-of-carlisle-indian-school/7896427.html

"ONWARD, HASKELL"

By Luis Blandón

The idleness and rhythm of baseball were a spring rite at the federally-operated Indian boarding schools of the late nineteenth century. Played passionately by the students on fields carved out of forests, the schools used baseball as another tool to impose the federal assimilation policy to teach values of the American White society like teamwork and discipline. For the boys, it was a chance for fun, an escape from the harsh conditions. Many Native students excelled in baseball, achieving recognition and pride through their athletic prowess.

PART I. THE CEMETERY AND THE PAST

Behind a foul-smelling sewage plant, adjacent to woods and wetlands that had been sliced by the South Lawrence Trafficway, lies a half-acre cemetery abutting the campus of the Haskell Indian Nations University in Lawrence, Kansas. Buried are the remains of 103 Native American children/students who perished at Haskell from 1885 to 1943.[1] Each grave is marked with a name, a tribe, an age, and little else. In that bygone era, runaways made their escape through the cemetery, woods, and wetlands toward safety. Haskell students interred here died of diseases such as consumption (tuberculosis), influenza, and typhoid, buried with their memories and little to acknowledge their journey. None went home again, individually buried with a Christian Mass in a Christian cemetery, though a portion were not Christian. Many had been subjected to the American policy of forced assimilation.

Strewn throughout are remembrances left behind by Native Americans. Spiritual symbols atop the burial sites such as the Native handmade willow dreamcatchers hung to protect the buried from evil. "I was thankful to have a beautiful place to pray. Who would I be if I didn't fight to protect it," said Pemina Yellow Bird in 2014 when she discovered the grounds.[2] She believed, as many do, that a spirituality existed in the cemetery.

Each interred child may never have had a chance to play with new toys, thrive in their culture, grow to adulthood or even play a game of pickup baseball on a barren field. The cemetery has been vandalized and burials lost over time. In 2017 Haskell built an eight-foot iron fence around the grounds, restored vandalized stones, and gave the grounds a sense of security and protection. "We had a case of vandalism in the cemetery going back a year or a little more where an individual pulled up some of the headstones and just tossed them in the corner of the cemetery," said Haskell spokesman Stephen Prue.[3]

On October 25, 2024, President Joseph Biden issued an apology to the Native American tribes and communities for the federal government's role in operating the Native American boarding schools, including Haskell. The apology was for the forced assimilation and abuse of Native American children that separated them from their families and cultures in an attempt to eradicate their individual tribal identities.

Biden said, "[T]he Federal Indian Boarding School policy and the pain it has caused will always be a significant mark of shame, a blot on American history. It's a sin on our [Nation's] soul."[4] In the effort to right a wrong, the apology was a step in the process of acknowledgment and healing that was welcomed by some tribes and viewed with skepticism by others.

PART II THE HASKELL INDIAN NATIONS UNIVERSITY

As of 2025 Haskell was a public tribal land-grant university operated by the United States Bureau of Indian Affairs. The school is the only federally operated four-year university for Native American students, accepting students from all federally recognized tribes.[5] The evolution of Haskell has been pockmarked with good intentions, self-determination efforts by Native tribes, and the sins of American policy.

Upon the conclusion of the American Civil War, the expansionary focus of the nation focused on the Plains and the West. The dilemma of whether to coexist with the Native American population occupied lawmakers and religious figures. What resulted was a period of American history focused on the eradication of Native American culture, lands,

Haskell Institute team, ca.1910.

and independence. The US government viewed education as the best method of achieving that end with a particular focus on making Native children into "Americans." Army Captain Robert Henry Pratt founded the Carlisle Indian Industrial School for the purpose of "civilizing" Indigenous children and implementing his theory of assimilating Indigenous peoples. His 1892 speech at the National Conference of Charities and Corrections in Denver used the wording that became the mantra of assimilation: "Kill the Indian in him, and save the man."[6] In 1882 Congress authorized three new boarding schools to be established in Nebraska, Kansas, and the Indian Territory[7] with Carlisle as the model. Haskell was one of the three.

Congressman Dudley Haskell (1842-1883), chairman of the House Committee on Indian Affairs, was instrumental in opening a boarding school in his hometown of Lawrence, with $10,000 from Lawrence citizens to "educate" Indigenous boys and girls under the age of 10.[8] He secured the legislation for the Indian school that still bears his name. Haskell was also responsible for the origins of baseball at the school. A local shoe merchant and player for the local Kaw Valleys, Haskell was known for his prodigious home runs.

Initially known as the United States Indian Industrial Training School, Haskell opened its doors on September 17, 1884, with 22 students from the Ponca, Sac and Fox, Shawnee, Kiowa, Comanche, and Chippewa Munsee tribes. Training focused on agriculture and vocational trades such as blacksmithing, textiles, farming, and sewing in a curriculum rooted in the era's English-only movement, enforced by corporal punishment.

The students who attended Indian boarding schools were primarily Indigenous children, often forcibly removed from their families and communities by the federal government.[9] Each student who arrived at Haskell was required to stay for a minimum of one four-year term. The children arrived by train. All semblance of the children's lives were stripped away, including clothing, photographs, toys, and keepsakes. Children were not allowed to speak their native languages. Contact with family was forbidden. The children were required to take English names.

By 1894 Haskell had transitioned from elementary education to advanced schooling, offering eight grades of "industrial training" for boys and girls.[10] By 1927 the school taught both high school and postsecondary courses.

At the start of the New Deal Era in 1933, Haskell chose its first Native Indian superintendent, Dr. Henry Roe Cloud (1884-1950), a full-blooded Ho-Chunk enrolled with the Winnebago Tribe.[11] With the racist language of the era, Cloud was described as a man "who rose from a bark wgiwam [sic] on the plains of Nebraska to recently become the superintendent of Haskell Institute, the largest institution of its kind."[12] Reportedly he "early showed a desire for further learning in the white man's school."[13] Cloud was a Mason, Rotarian, Elk, and Presbyterian minister. Most

importantly, he was a reformer and educator. Dismantling the assimilation curriculum and policies, he instituted a traditional style of schooling focused on arts, skills, advanced trades, and Native culture. Haskell became an Indigenous leader and advocate. In 1906 Cloud married Elizabeth Bender, a White Earth Chippewa. She was the sister of Albert "Chief" Bender, who was a Hall of Fame pitcher for the Philadelphia Athletics.[14]

In 1970 Haskell began offering junior-college degrees and became known as the Haskell Junior College. The college then became Haskell Indian Nations University in 1993, offering a four-year baccalaureate degree program with a mission dedicated to Indian cultural preservation, research, and education.

By 2024, Haskell offered bachelor's degrees in Indigenous and American Indian studies, business administration, elementary education, and environmental science along with nine associate degrees. The average enrollment at Haskell is 900, with multi-tribal representation. To apply for admission, one must either be an enrolled member of a federally recognized tribe eligible for education benefits from the Bureau of Indian Affairs or at least a one-fourth total degree Indian blood direct descendant of an enrolled member of a tribe.[15]

Athletics is a pivotal component of the Haskell community. The university competes in 11 intercollegiate varsity sports. Men's sports include basketball, cross-country, golf, and track and field (indoor and outdoor); women's sports include basketball, cross-country, softball, track and field (indoor and outdoor), and volleyball. Club sports include baseball; varsity baseball was dropped in 2015. The school colors are purple, gold, and white. Haskell is home to the American Indian Athletic Hall of Fame.

PART III. HASKELL'S AFFAIR WITH BASEBALL

A passion for baseball and other stick-and-ball games has long existed among Native American tribes, who created the game of lacrosse. The Choctaw developed an ancestral form of stickball called "Ishtaboli" that has been its national sport for centuries.[16] Those who attended Haskell were familiar with such games.

Many Indigenous athletes at Haskell played both baseball and football. In the first part of the twentieth century, Haskell had a dominant football program, competitive against the powers of the time like Yale, Brown, Missouri, and Creighton. After the 1931 season, the school shifted the team to a high-school status and eventually dropped football in 1938. Sport was a "serious and integral part of [Native] life and as an important developmental activity of young people."[17] At Haskell and elsewhere, Native Indian students accepted and excelled at "new" sports like baseball that were introduced to them.

A handful of Haskell baseball players briefly made it the major leagues; Jim Thorpe, George Johnson, Ben Tincup, and Louis LeRoy went to Haskell. A host of Haskell athletes also played in the minor leagues.

NATIVE AMERICAN MAJOR LEAGUERS

Haskell Institute's 1921 baseball team, Lawrence, Kansas.

While Native American baseball players did not face "official" segregation as did African American players, the arrival of Native Americans into professional baseball was marked by racism, hazing, and hostility. The common practice of racially tinged nicknames like Chief or Injun marked Native athletes as different. The number of Native Americans playing major-league baseball ebbed after World War I, reviving only recently.[18]

The words that Cahuilla Band John Tortes Meyers, a former New York Giants catcher, wrote about his teammate Jim Thorpe can be applied to any Native players in any sport: "It would be false modesty on my part to declare that I am not thoroughly delighted with the fact that my race has proven itself competent to master the White man's principal sport."[19]

Haskell student Isaac "Ike" Kahdot (1899-1999) mastered the game to become a major leaguer in 1922. Kahdot grew up in Georgetown, near present-day Konawa, Oklahoma. A Potawatomi Indian, he attended Sacred Heart School as a little boy. He was mistreated: "I didn't like the priests, so I ran off every chance I got."[20] Accusing him of smoking "tobacco," the priests whipped him as punishment. He attended the Friends Mission School, then his father enrolled him at Haskell. He excelled at baseball. He told the *Tulsa World* in 1993, "My dad give me a bat and a ball and a glove when I was growing up. And I always had that with me. We had an Injun team when I was a young kid, and my dad wanted me to play ball on it."[21] When he finished

high school, Kahdot advanced in the minor leagues before Cleveland acquired his rights from the Coffeyville, Kansas, team he played on.

As a shortstop and third baseman, Kahdot had a brief stay with the Cleveland Indians, from September 5 to 21, 1922, appearing in four games with two at-bats and no hits. In his first game, on September 5 against the St. Louis Browns, Kahdot came in to run for player-team manager Tris Speaker in the sixth inning. His final appearance in the major leagues was on September 21 in a 15-5 loss to Boston.[22] Speaker had Kahdot come into the game in the eighth during the blowout loss, substituting for Larry Gardner at third. He faced Jack Quinn and went 0-for-1, flying out to left in the bottom of the eighth. He had a putout and an assist executing a double play.[23]

Upon the completion of the 1923 minor-league season, Cleveland wanted Kahdot to play for its Grand Rapids minor-league team, where the Indians sent their top prospects. Kahdot lived in Kansas and "had a new wife, and a possible major league career didn't seem worth the move."[24] He paid the Indians $2,500 to release him from his contract.

Kahdot played baseball for 15 years in several minor leagues until 1935.[25] Then he was a derrick man, driller, and rope choker in oilfields until 1958, when he went to work at Tinker Air Force Base until his retirement in 1969.[26]

In 1993 *Tulsa World* wrote that "'Chief' Kahdot's only mark on the major leagues may have been but a line in four box scores. But his journey from a small community before statehood through the major and minor leagues, touched a part of the game, and America, that has long been forgotten except in history books."[27] He lived to almost 100 and was the oldest living major leaguer when he died in Oklahoma City on March 31, 1999.

Khadot's solitary reminder that he was a major leaguer, other than memories, was a memento he received: a brand-new Reach baseball signed by his Cleveland teammates and treasured until his death.[28]

PART IV. HASKELL BASEBALL STORIES

APRIL 15, 1901

Haskell's 1901 season began with a 5-5 tie with the University of Kansas in Lawrence. Haskell jumped to a 5-0 lead with four runs in the first and a run in the second. The contest "was devoid of features of great interest and would have been won by the Indians had they not got badly rattled and allowed the university boys to run five scores on errors."[29] The bottom of the ninth was not played "as the university boys thought they had won the game, and left the field."[30]

SEPTEMBER 4, 1903

During the 1903 season, the *Howard* (Kansas) *Courant* wrote several colorful statements about the Haskell baseball team, reflecting the period's simplistic attitudes toward Native Americans: 1) "They are a peaceable lot of braves, those Haskell boys, and they play fast ball." 2) "There is nothing especially aboriginal about the names of the Haskell Indian boys as they appear on the hotel register." 3) "Lots of ball players could learn good manners of the noble red men from Haskell."[31]

APRIL 18, 1905

An Oneida Indian, Chauncey Archiquette (1877-1949) was a unique athlete. It was announced that "the Indian star football half-back and base ball man, has left the Haskell Institute and has followed the two more of the best athletes Haskell ever had."[32] He left the school on April 17, 1905, to "join Green's Nebraska Indian base ball team."[33] He followed Chas. Guyon and Joe Rapp to Green, both of whom had played with Archiquette on Haskell's baseball and football teams. Archiquette, who graduated from high school at Carlisle before attending Haskell, was a popular figure who "won many honors for the Indian institute[,] and the people of the town as well as the students of Haskell dislike to see him go."[34] At Haskell, Archiquette was the baseball team's catcher and leading hitter.

In the fall of 1898, an impressionable 11-year-old Sac and Fox student watched the Haskell football practice in awe of Archiquette. He told himself, "I'm going to be as tough as Chauncey."[35] Archiquette asked the scrawny kid if wanted to play football and whether he wanted a football. Together, they went to the Haskell harness shop. Archiquette made him a makeshift football to play with.

Thus began Archiquette's mentoring of Jim Thorpe; they played football and baseball together at Haskell.[36]

Archiquette played football and baseball on barnstorming squads and later worked as a clerk for Carlisle in the book department and then went in 1906 to the Osage Indian Agency, for whom he worked until his retirement in 1942.[37] The agency described Archiquette as a member of a musical quartet and "as one of the most competent men around the agency."[38]

Archiquette was an American Olympian at the 1904 St. Louis Olympic Games. He participated in Haskell's two football games at Francis Olympic Field as part of the demonstration event of American football at the 1904 Summer Olympics.[39]

MARCH 31, 1909

Spring was dawning on the Haskell campus and baseball coach Maurice Kent thought his was going to be one of the best teams in the region.[40] During the previous two seasons, "the Redskins through indifferent management, allowed the team to take the toboggan."[41] Most of the games were taking place "on the opponents' diamonds ... because the Indians couldn't make expenses when they bought visiting teams" to Haskell.[42] In past seasons, there was little interest in the baseball team and there "seemed to be little enthusiasm among the Haskell students. This year, "Kent proposes to stir up enthusiasm."[43]

AUGUST 23, 1910

A death resulted from a game against Lecompton. Haskell's Henry Rigert was badly injured playing his first game for a "Cherokee Indian ball team."[44] A star football and baseball player, Rigert attempted to slide into home plate when he "struck his head against the catcher's knee, paralyzing him from the neck down."[45] Rigert was "conscious, ... awaiting death realizing that there is scarcely one chance in a thousand for his recovery. ..."[46] Two doctors who treated Rigert concluded that he suffered "a dislocated vertebra pressing on the spinal cord."[47] In early September, a press article noted that Rigert "was killed at a baseball game."[48]

MAY 7, 1915

Played in Emporia, Kansas, the Haskell Indian team defeated State Normal 6-2 on Normal's home turf. Haskell's lefty pitcher Delorme scattered three hits "while the Indians connected with nine of the Norman's twirler's offerings."[49] The field conditions were poor and as the players fought the muddy grounds and "the bunting in which the redskins indulged brought a victory.[50] The fifth inning was "when the Indians annexed half their runs."[51]

MAY 17, 1916

Haskell was about to play the Kansas Aggies in Manhattan when the team suffered a serious blow. Its 1916 prospects declined dramatically as it "received a serious bump by the 'withdrawal' from school of Pitcher McCloskey and Catcher James White Bull."[52] The school superintendent announced that the two Sioux Indians went back home to "Dakota." Rumors circulated among the student body "that the two have gone to join an Indian baseball team which will tour the middle west this summer."[53] The duo were "an interesting feature of the game this spring has been their native talk which they pulled as battery mates."[54] According to their teammates, the pair "intend to tour the country with an Indian baseball aggregation."[55]

SEPTEMBER 21, 1918

Like all parts of the country during World War I, "every Indian at Haskell engaged in war work."[56] Out of 832 students enrolled, 141 were registered for the draft; 325 graduates and current students ended up in the armed forces, and "one Haskell boy has been reported as a casualty."[57] The Miami tribesman and former Haskell baseball player Sandy Timothy "now holds the championship for hand grenade throwing in a Georgia cantonment."[58] In a photograph in full uniform, Timothy demonstrated his grenade-throwing form in an advertisement for Americans to "buy bonds till you sacrifice" since "backing up the Brave is the noblest duty of an American today."[59]

APRIL 8, 1925

John Thomas Levi (1898-1946) was a major-league outfield prospect with a rare mix of power and speed.[60] Considered the school's greatest recruit, Levi graduated from Haskell in 1924. Levi was awarded more letters than any other student who attended Haskell up to that time.[61]

A full-blooded Arapaho, Levi was an elite athlete with a great talent not only in baseball, but in football and track as well.[62] Jim Thorpe called Levi "the greatest athlete I have ever seen."[63]

A leg injury playing baseball quashed any desire to be like his hero Thorpe and fulfill his potential as a decathlete in the 1924 Paris Olympic Games. On December 1, 1924, "the charging buffalo" signed a contract with the New York Yankees based on reputation, since the Yankees scouts had never seen him play.[64] The Yankees believed Levi could "approximate the style of Bob Meusel, the Yankees' left fielder."[65]

Levi played with the Yankees during the 1925 spring training and joined them on a barnstorming trip. On April 8, the Yankees boarded a players' train in Nashville to Asheville, North Carolina to continue their money-making tour. Babe Ruth, though not feeling well physically, had been playing in the games. On the train, Ruth complained of chills, fever, and a headache. The trainers gave him medicine to relieve his symptoms, but it did not work. The train arrived in Asheville and as Ruth climbed off the train, "he collapsed in the arms of John Levi, the Haskell Indian."[66]

Yankees manager Miller Huggins never offered Levi an opportunity in spring training to demonstrate his skills. Levi was sent to the Harrisburg Senators of the Class-B New York Penn League on April 14 for further "seasoning." Levi became homesick for his people and never made it the majors, playing through 1930 for low-level minor-league teams and also played professional football.[67] Levi was an assistant football coach at Haskell for 10 years and was head coach in 1936, going 0-7-1.

In 1946 Levi was employed in a Denver packing house at 70 cents an hour.[68] On January 22 the Denver police found him mortally wounded in a hotel room. A newspaper account said that during a heated argument, Fannie Stabler stabbed Levi with a six-inch knife as she tried to leave. Levi slapped her when she screamed at him, "[T]ake your hands off me or I'll kill you."[69] Levi died at Denver General Hospital within an hour. Stabler was convicted of involuntary manslaughter.[70] At the time of his death, Levi was divorced from his wife Helen who was living in Wahpeton, North Dakota, with a son and daughter.[71]

During a 2012 interview about his father, Levi's son, John Jr., observed that whenever visiting Haskell, "I feel his spirit and Haskell means an awful lot to our family. … I'm proud to have his name. …"[72]

APRIL 23, 2000

Once a Haskell baseball pitcher, William Mehojah (1917-2000), the last full-blooded Kaw Indian, died at 82 on Easter morning, April 23, 2000, of lung failure.[73] In the seventeenth century, about 2,000 Kaw flourished on the Plains.[74] "The reality of being the last full blood to me is sad and lonely," he said in the Kaw newsletter in 1997.[75] As a child he had spoken his native language with his father, Jesse, losing the skill after Jesse died in 1935. However, he always understood his people's language.

Born in 1917 on a land allotment in Washunga, Oklahoma, Mehojah received an associate's degree in business administration from Haskell. His mission in life was to help Native Americans.[76] "He was a living treasure," said his son William Mehojah, Jr., "because he represented a people that have been eradicated."[77] His mother decided he needed to go to college so "he could work in an office somewhere," her son recalled.[78]

Mehojah served in the Army in World War II and later worked for the Veterans Administration's regional office in Muskogee, Oklahoma, and then for the Bureau of Indian Affairs. In 1964 he became the superintendent of the Bureau of Indian Affairs Turtle Mountain Agency in Belcourt, North Dakota.[79] He retired in 1976.

In 1987, Mehojah was elected Chairman of the Kaw Nation for a three-year term.[80] In 1995 Haskell named him alumnus of the year. "He spoke to the graduating class in his simple, measured way and from his heart," his son said.[81] Oklahoma Governor Frank Keating proclaimed August 6, 1999, as William A. Mehojah Day. Fredericka Mehojah, his wife of 57 years, said he was an avid golfer and had always been a good athlete.[82]

V. CONCLUSION

The Indian Boarding Schools began in 1819 when Congress appropriated the funding under the Indian Civilization Act of March 3, 1819.[83] The peak enrollment for Indian Boarding Schools occurred in the 1970s.[84] The schools exist to this day. The landscape changed after 1933 when the tribes increasingly had more say over the schools and students were no longer forced by the Federal government to go to boarding schools.

The Indian Reorganization Act of 1934 – called the "Indian New Deal" – attempted to improve the lives of Native Americans as it halted the policy of forced assimilation and promoted greater tribal self-governance.[85] Led by Bureau of Indian Affairs Commissioner John Collier (1884-1968), it was an era of advocating for tribal rights, preserving Native American cultures and traditions and ending the policy of forced assimilation.

Boarding schools like Haskell were created as an instrument to "'whiten' Native Americans and supplant their culture and language with American ideals and English."[86] Countless Native Americans were forced to attend the boarding schools, forbidden to speak their native languages, forced to renounce native beliefs and to abandon their native identities.[87] History may never fully account for what the students who played baseball and other sports for Haskell - all the students- suffered due to the assimilation policy of the federal government.

From its creation as boarding school designed to erase all vestiges of Native American life, Haskell has come to be a beacon of such life and in the vanguard of research, preservation, and celebration of Native American culture and history.

Since its beginning, the insatiable appetite for achievement in sports like baseball has been strong at Haskell. Each year, as spring marches onto the campus, the traditional sounds of the game are still heard from the Haskell club baseball team.

ACKNOWLEDGMENTS

With deep gratitude to my wife, Teri, for putting up with the author.

Much thanks and appreciation to noted and award-winning Native American Indian historian Dr. Edward Angel, for his review of this essay and consultations offering his expert opinion and advice.

SOURCES

In addition to the sources cited in the Notes, the author consulted Haskell University, the Kaw Nation, the Choctaw Nation of Oklahoma, the Cheyenne and Arapaho Tribes, the National Museum of the American Indian, Library of Congress, The Archival Collection of Gustavus Elmer Emanuel Linquist Native American Papers in the Missionary Research Library Archives at the Burke Library, Columbia University, National Archives and Record Administration, the Department of the Interior, Bureau of Indian Affairs, the National WWI Museum and Memorial, baseball-reference.com, retrosheet.org, mlb.com, and youtube.com.

NOTES

1 For more information about Haskell Cemetery, including a list of the 103 buried there, see https://www.haskellhistory.com/cemetery. In addition to the 103 marked graves in the Haskell Cemetery, there are eight individuals who are believed to be buried there, but whose graves are not marked.

2 Brenna Daldorph, "US Freeway to Pave over History of Native American Suffering," france24.com, January 28, 2014. See https://www.france24.com/en/20140128-us-freeway-pave-over-history-native-american-suffering, accessed November 26, 2024.

3 "Haskell Installs New Fence Around Cemetery After Vandalism," *Lawrence* (Kansas) *World Journal*, January 2, 2018. See https://www2.ljworld.com/news/2018/jan/02/haskell-installs-new-fence-around-cemetery-after-s/, accessed November 26, 2024. Efforts began in 2024 to clean each headstone, replace the faded historical marker and discover more about the lives behind those interred.

4 National Council of Urban Indian Health press release: "President Biden Formally Apologizes for Federal Government Involvement in Indian Boarding Schools," October 28, 2024. https://ncuih.org/2024/10/29/press-release-president-biden-formally-apologizes-for-federal-government-involvement-in-indian-boarding-schools/, accessed May 15, 2025.

5 The Southwestern Indian Polytechnic Institute in Albuquerque, New Mexico, a two-year college, is the other federally operated institution. Native American tribes also operate 35 colleges that received federal funding.

6 Carlisle Indian School Digital Resources, "'Kill the Indian in Him, and Save the Man': R. H. Pratt on the Education of Native Americans," https://carlisleindian.dickinson.edu/teach/kill-indian-him-and-save-man-r-h-pratt-education-native-americans, accessed May 16, 2025.

7 The Indian Territory became the State of Oklahoma on November 16, 1907.

8 Natalie Vondrak, "Haskell Institute: The Roots From Which We Bloom 1884-1930)," Watkins Museum of History online exhibit. https://www.watkinsmuseum.org/online-exhibits/haskell-institute-the-roots-from-which-we-bloom-1884-1930/, accessed November 6, 2024.

9 The federal government used various methods to bring/lure Native children to the boarding schools:

a) forced attendance: In many cases, government agents would forcibly remove children from their homes and reservations to attend these schools; b) government pressure and coercion: Federal agents were responsible for gathering children and getting them to schools using tactics like withholding food or other vital supplies from parents who resisted sending their children; c) seizure by authorities: If parents were unwilling to comply with the demand to send their children to boarding school, the police were sent to seize the children; d) compulsory attendance laws: Congress in 1891 made it mandatory for Native children to attend school, giving federal officers the authority to forcibly take them from their homes; e) families choosing to send children (often out of necessity). Some Native parents chose to send their children to boarding schools because there were no other educational options available in their tribal communities.
Research released in February 2025 by the National Native American Boarding School Healing Coalition says there have been 526 Indian boarding schools in the United States. See https://boardingschoolhealing.org/list/, accessed June 30, 2025. By 1900 there were 20,000 children in Indian boarding schools. By 1925, this number had more than tripled, reaching 60,889 children, according to the National Native American Boarding School Healing Coalition. By 1926, over 80 percent of Indigenous school-age children (more than 60,000) were attending federal or religiously run boarding schools. See "US Indian Boarding School History," *National Native American Boarding School Healing Coalition,* https://boardingschoolhealing.org/education/us-indian-boarding-school-history/, accessed June 30, 2025.

10 Keith A. Sculle, "The New Carlisle of the West: Haskell Institute and Big-Time Sports, 1920-1932," *Kansas History,* Autumn 1994, Vol. 17, No. 3, 195.

11   Dr. Cloud was the first full-blood Native American to attend Yale University. He graduated with a bachelor of arts in psychology and philosophy from Yale College in 1910 and earned a master of arts degree in anthropology from Yale University in 1914.

12   Associated Press, "Indian Climbs From Tepee to Exalted Office," *Washington Post*, August 13, 1933: 10.

13   "Indian Climbs From Tepee to Exalted Office."

14   "Indian Climbs From Tepee to Exalted Office."

15   The verification of tribal enrollment can be presented by one of the following means: a) Student is an enrolled member of a federally recognized tribe. Provide an official Certificate of Degree of Indian Blood (CDIB) card or other official tribal enrollment information with the student's name, other identifying information such as date of birth or social security number, and an enrollment (membership) number from the BIA agency or federally recognized tribe. b) Direct descendant of an enrolled member of a tribe eligible for BIA education benefits. Provide official documentation of at least one-fourth degree Indian blood descendant of an enrolled member of a federally recognized tribe eligible for BIA education benefits, signed by the appropriate BIA agency or federally recognized tribe.

16   Ishtaboli served as a social and diplomatic tool for the Choctaw. The Tribe used the game to train their warriors. "Stickball," *Choctaw Nation of Oklahoma*. See https://www.choctawnation.com/about/culture/traditions/stickball/, accessed June 7, 2025. Jeffrey Powers-Beck, *The American Indian Integration of Baseball* (Lincoln: University of Nebraska Press, 2004), 17.

17   David Oxendine, *American Indian Sports Heritage* (Lincoln: University of Nebraska Press, 1995), 181.

18   In 2014, there were only three active non-Hispanic Native American players in the major leagues: Joba Chamberlain (Ho-Chunk/Winnebago), Kyle Lohse (Nomlaki), and Jacoby Ellsbury (Navajo). See Vincent M. Mallozzi, "The American Indians of America's Pastime," *New York Times*, June 8, 2014: SP11.

19   Charlie Vascellaro. "The Real Indians of Baseball," *NMAI Magazine*, Summer 2012, Vol. 12, No.2. See https://www.americanindianmagazine.org/story/real-indians-baseball, accessed November 18, 2024.

20   "'Chief' Kahdot – A Real Cleveland Indian," Potawatomi Nation, October 20, 2021, https://www.potawatomi.org/blog/2021/10/20/chief-kahdot-a-real-cleveland-indian/, accessed December 3, 2024.

21   Burl Spencer, "'Chief' Was an Indian in Ruthian Age of Dreams," *Tulsa World*, September 22, 1993: Sports-1.

22   See box score in https://www.baseball-reference.com/boxes/SLA/SLA192209050.shtml/.

23   See box score in https://www.retrosheet.org/boxesetc/1922/B09210CLE1922.htm/.

24   Burl Spencer, "Oldest Living Cleveland Indian Remembers the Good Year: 1922," *Tulsa World*, September 22, 1993: Sports - 6.

25   "'Chief' Kahdot – A Real Cleveland Indian."

26   C. Richard King, *Native Americans in Sports* (New York: Routledge, 2015), 167. Burl Spencer, "'Chief' Was an Indian in Ruthian Age of Dreams." Tinker Air Force Base is in Oklahoma City.

27   Burl Spencer, "'Chief' was an Indian in Ruthian Age of Dreams."

28   "'Chief' Kahdot – A Real Cleveland Indian"; "Oldest Living Cleveland Indian Remembers the Good Year: 1922."

29   "The Game at Haskell," *Lawrence Daily World*, April 16, 1901: 3.

30   "The Game at Haskell."

31   "Clippings," *The Indian Leader* (Lawrence, Kansas), September 4, 1903: 2. "Base Ball Talk," *Howard* (Kansas) *Courant*, August 28, 1903: 1.

32   "Archiquette Leaves Haskell," *Topeka* (Kansas) *Daily Herald*, April 18, 1905: 1.

33   "Archiquette Leaves Haskell." Green's Nebraska Indians was early pro all-Indian touring team for which Archiquette played as a catcher.

34   "Archiquette Leaves Haskell."

35   Lars Anderson, *Carlisle vs. Army: Jim Thorpe, Dwight Eisenhower, Pop Warner, and the Forgotten Story of Football's Greatest Battle* (New York: Random House, 2008), 91.

36   Anderson. Jim Thorpe attended and played baseball, track and field, and football for Haskell before going to the Carlisle Indian Industrial School.

37   "C.E. Archiquette, Early Grid Star, Dies in Claremore," *Tulsa World*. March 13, 1949: 80.

38   "C.E. Archiquette," *Osage Journal and County News* (Pawhuska, Oklahoma), December 17, 1926: 29.

39   "Chauncey Archiquette," *olympedia.com*, https://www.olympedia.org/athletes/892472, accessed May 18, 2025.

40   A University of Iowa football star in 1905 and 1906, Kent was also Haskell's football coach. See "Haskell Athletics: Indian School Has Got an Instructor from Iowa," *Lawrence Daily Gazette*, February 14, 1908: 2.

41   "Will Have Good Nine," *Leavenworth* (Kansas) *Post*, March 3, 1909: 3.

42   "Will Have Good Nine."

43   "Will Have Good Nine."

44   "Indian Hurt in Ballgame," *Topeka State Journal*, August 25, 1910: 7.

45   "Indian Athlete Will Die," *Leavenworth Post*, August 25, 1910: 1.

46   "Indian Hurt in Ballgame."

47   "Indian Hurt in Ballgame."

48   "Intercollegiate," *Bethany Messenger* (Lindsburg, Kansas), September 9, 1910: 6

49   "Beat Normalites," *Leavenworth Daily Gazette*, May 8, 1916: 3.

50   "Beat Normalites."

51   "Beat Normalites."

52   "Gone to Join Indians," *Lawrence Daily Gazette*, May 17, 1916: 1.

53   "Gone to Join Indians."

54   "Gone to Join Indians."

55   "Haskell Baseball Team Weakened, Stars Quit," *Topeka Daily Capital*, May 18, 1916: 11.

56   "Every Indian at Haskell Engaged on War Work," *Lawrence Daily Journal-World*, September 21, 1918: 2.

57   "Every Indian at Haskell Engaged on War Work."

58   "Every Indian at Haskell Engaged on War Work."

59   "Are You With Us?" *Lawrence Daily Journal-World*, October 12, 1918: 2.

60   Levi was born on June 14, 1898, in Arapaho Indian country in the Bridgeport Territory (now Oklahoma).

61   "John Levi," *Kansas Sports Hall of Fame*. See: https://www.kshof.org/team/john-levi, accessed May 15, 2025. Levi graduated from Chilcco (Oklahoma) Indian School in 1917. He arrived at Haskell in 1921. "Skee" was Levi's nickname while he was at Haskell.

62   Levi was a first-team Walter Camp All-American in 1923 as a fullback.

63   Kansas Sports Hall of Fame. Levi was posthumously indicated into the American Indian Athletic Hall of Fame (1972), the Oklahoma Athletic Hall of Fame (1973), and the Kansas Sports Hall of Fame (1975).

64 "Flashback Friday: John Levi," *Haskell Athletics*, https://www.haskellathletics.com/article/134.php, accessed August 22, 2022.

65 "Yanks Sign John Levi, the 'Charging Buffalo,'" *Washington Post*, January 1, 1925: S1.

66 "Ruth Is Laid Up with Grip," *Washington Post*, April 8, 1925: 17.

67 Levi played in Harrisburg in 1925-26. He also played in the Class-A Western League in 1929 and 1930 for Topeka and St. Joseph respectively.

68 "Woman Admits She Slew Levi," *Webb City* (Missouri) *Sentinel,* May 24, 1946: 4.

69 "Woman Admits She Slew Levi."

70 "Levi, Ex-Haskell Indian Ace, Found Stabbed to Death," *Washington Post*, January 24, 1946: 12. Stabler, a Native American, was ultimately given a one- to five-year sentence. She was 38 years old in 1946 and a mother of three children. See Associated Press, "Convicted in Levi Death," *Kansas City Times*, May 24, 1946: 6.

71 United Press, "Levi, Once Haskell Grid Star, Slain," *Fargo* (North Dakota) *Forum and Daily Republican,* January 23, 1946: 1. Levi's first wife, Helen Hilda Levi, died in 1995 at the age of 90.

72 "Flashback Friday: John Levi."

73 Douglas Martin, "William Mehojah, a Kaw Leader, Dies at 82," *New York Times*, May 5, 2000: 24. Mehojah's Indian name was Little Star and he was a member of the Night Clan of a Plains tribe known as the Wind People. Before his death, the last other four remaining purebred Kaws passed away; all were related to him.

74 Also known as Kanza, Kansa, or Kona.

75 Martin, "William Mehojah, a Kaw Leader, Dies at 82."

76 Kaw Nation, "Last Kanza Full Blood," October 19, 2002. See https://www.kawnation.gov/last-kanza-full-blood/, accessed June 3, 2025.

77 Stacy Downs (New York Times News Service), "Last Full-Blooded Kaw Indian Buried," *Wichita Eagle*, April 30, 2000: 22A.

78 Downs. The land allotments were distributed to individual Indians after the Kaw reservation was dissolved in 1902.

79 "Kaw Indian Named Superintendent of Turtle Mountain Agency," United States Department of Interior, Indian Affairs, November 12, 1964. See https://www.bia.gov/as-ia/opa/online-press-release/kaw-indian-named-superintendent-turtle-mountain-agency, accessed November 25, 2024.

80 During his tenure, Mehojah ordered a new tribal constitution drafted that enabled the Kaw to develop a variety of businesses such as a bingo parlor, a motel, and a truck stop. Under his leadership, the Kaw brought $13.5 million in assets and an additional 1,000 acres of commonly-held land. See Douglas Martin, "William Mehojah, a Kaw Leader, Dies at 82," *New York Times*, May 5, 2000: 24.

81 Downs. William Mehojah, Jr. is a member of the Kaw Tribe of Oklahoma and was the director of the federal government's Office of Indian Education Programs.

82 Fredericka L. Mehojah died on July 26, 2022. She and her husband were married in 1943 in Tulsa. She also attended Haskell.

83 "American Indian Boarding Schools," *Georgia State University Library,* https://exhibits.library.gsu.edu/health-is-a-human-right/displacement/american-indian-boarding-schools/, accessed June 18, 2025.

84 Tens of thousands of American Indian children attended the boarding schools, peaking in the 1970s, with an estimated enrollment of 60,000 in 1973.

85 To review the Indian Reorganization Act, see National Archives and Record Administration's record https://catalog.archives.gov/id/7873515.

86 Howard University School of Law Research Guides, "A Brief History of Civil Rights in the United States: The Allotment and Assimilation Era (1887 - 1934)," https://library.law.howard.edu/civilrightshistory/indigenous/allotment, accessed May 27, 2025.

87 Equal Justice Initiative, "'Cultural Genocide' and Native American Children," September 2, 2014, See https://eji.org/news/history-racial-injustice-cultural-genocide/, accessed May 27, 2025.

THE OLD BALL GAME: SHERMAN INDIAN BASEBALL, EST. 1903

By Tom Willman

On February 21, 1903, a warm and sunny Saturday, the baseball team of the nation's newest Native American boarding school played its first game. The Sherman Institute was set among citrus groves outside Riverside, California, 60 miles east of Los Angeles. The Institute was the 25th and last major link in a federal Indian-school chain spanning the nation. The first school in the system, Carlisle in Pennsylvania, had opened in 1879. It had taken five years to string the chain westward to midcontinent Lawrence, Kansas, and Haskell.[1] But it had taken almost 20 years more to cross the rugged Southwest and create the line's Southern California terminus. Sherman's basic mission, though, was the same as the first schools: prepare Indian students for assimilation into mainstream American life and culture, at the expense of tribal languages, customs, and even family. The approach was to nestle into a supportive community, impose

a reassuring discipline model, and build college-town pride with sports as an entry point. On this Saturday, Sherman had been open barely five months. It had beaten a college team at football. Now its athletes were out to show they could play baseball.[2]

Sherman wasn't exactly a new team. It had a strong core of mature ballplayers from a resource-challenged rural school serving the Mission tribes of Southern California. It also had a remarkable young point man. Joe Scholder (Diegueño, Mesa Grande) had flourished at an Indian school in the San Diego back country. His superintendent nominated him to transfer to Carlisle, spend a year studying its success, and come home to emulate it. Scholder turned out to be just the man for the job.[3] He became a starter on Carlisle's nationally recognized football team, played baseball, studied coaching, honed a natural flair for promotion

Color postcard view of Sherman Institute, c. 1903.

and leadership, and even recruited his football mentor to return with him.[4] This was a sensational coup. Bemus Pierce (Seneca, New York) was a famous Carlisle captain and All-American in the decade before Jim Thorpe. In California, Pierce became a celebrity football player-coach. Scholder would energetically fill many roles: athletic director, promoter, player-coach in both football and baseball. For this day's inaugural baseball game on Sherman's home grounds, he was playing second base.

Another notable athlete on the diamond for Sherman was Ben Neafus, a multisport star from Northern California (Round Valley confederation, Klamath). In November 1902 Neafus starred in Sherman's 34-0 football victory over Occidental College. For the first baseball game, he was in center field.[5]

The opposition was Riverside's fast town team. It had one name player: catcher Jack "Chief" Meyers (Cahuilla). Still six years away from the major leagues and stardom with John McGraw's New York Giants, Meyers was a local role model for the Sherman players (and kinsman to several of them). The Riverside paper noted that "among the locals Jack Meyers is as sure with the bat as ever." In this hastily arranged game, Sherman started an untested pitcher and lost, 14-8. But everybody noticed Ben Neafus. "He knocked the only three-bagger tapped out," the *Press* reported, "and covers nearly the whole field from center. He never misses." Neafus was also the pitcher Sherman should have started. He worked the last two innings, giving up just one run (likely unearned).[6]

By summer, Neafus's baseball reputation was outgrowing Sherman. He was recruited to be "the regular 'twirler'" in weekend games for the crack Santa Fe Railroad team in neighboring San Bernardino. His regular catcher with Santa Fe was Jack Meyers.[7] Imagine: A marquee semipro team with a battery of two rising Native American stars. But it was not to be. Neafus's first commitment was to Sherman football, and his burst speed and long kicks were key to Sherman's game. He refocused. That fall, in quick succession Sherman beat Stanford, St. Vincent's, USC, Occidental, and Pomona to claim bragging rights as Southern California college football champion (though Sherman did not even confer high-school diplomas).[8] Yet by 1905, Ben Neafus was in his 20s and aging out of Sherman. There were responsibilities back home, there were absences, and by 1906 he was gone. A decade later, Los Angeles sportswriters were still recalling his gridiron exploits. But how good a baseball player might he have been? That can only be imagined.

What might have been: This is a theme that plays out over and over in the baseball stories from Sherman's glory years. There were plenty of big baseball games, big exhibitions. Before the Golden Age of Native American sport began to play out – before the Thorpe Olympics controversy, the onset of World War I and the closure of Carlisle – Sherman would produce a steady stream of solid, even prospect-grade ballplayers. Yet in all that time, no prominent Sherman players ever got a foothold in either the major leagues or the Pacific Coast League (established the same year as Sherman baseball). What accounts for that? The back story.

In 1900 the sprawling Southwest was still an American frontier. Arizona, New Mexico, and Oklahoma were sparsely populated territories, not states. For Native Americans, there were misbegotten federal Indian policies, broken treaties, conflicts, and reservation dispossessions. Most Native Americans were not citizens. California's context was equally dark. In the rapacious chaos of the Gold Rush, native tribes were decimated by epidemic, violence, fraud, legal snares, and high-handed servitude. The state's indigenous population, perhaps 150,000 before the Gold Rush, had shrunk to an estimated 25,000 by the turn of the twentieth century.[9] And this was not in the past. On May 12, 1903, speculators with court authority evicted the Cupeño Indians from their ancestral lands at Warner Hot Springs. They were wagon-trained 35 miles west to Pala and left to start a new life from scratch. This was Sherman's own Trail of Tears. Some students from these evicted families had played in Sherman's inaugural baseball game less than three months earlier.[10]

But Sherman was putting fans in the stands. In May of 1905, Sherman recorded its first victory over a college baseball team. In Los Angeles, Sherman beat USC 7-4 in 10 innings. Barely two weeks later, Sherman was back in LA for a well-publicized contest with the touring team of Japan's Waseda University. Waseda played the steadier game and won, 12-7, but Sherman prompted wild cheering with an explosive six-run sixth inning. With that, Sherman had hit a remarkable milestone. In its third year of baseball, the Indian school had won a populous fan base in Los Angeles as well as Riverside.[11]

July 1905: In this moment another Native American team passed through Riverside. "The famous Sioux Indian Baseball Club" had contrived to blend baseball, the ginned-up novelty of an Indian semipro team, and a flickering glimpse of the future, and it sold. The Sioux meandered the West by train (apparently with soldier chaperones). At each stop they set up with circus efficiency. They shrouded the ball field with a 12-foot-high canvas fence and played a twin bill against the locals. The promotional kicker was that they played a real nightcap under their own jury-rigged portable lights. "With the great lights burning at intervals over the entire field," promoters promised, "the diamond and outfield is made as light as day."[12] The Sioux had been doing this for seven years, averaging about 190 games a year. In Riverside they played a town team and lost the first game by one run in extra innings. "As little will be said of the night game as possible," the Riverside paper huffed. A big crowd had paid 50 cents a seat and the game was played with an oversized ball. "In reality, the field was very poorly lighted with some 25 or 30 gasoline lights, hung from five poles placed about the diamond. It was too dark to catch, too dark to hit and almost too dark to run the bases. But it was unique, don't forget that."[13]

As Sherman became a baseball success, its top players began to be noticed. One of the first was Lou Lockart (Sherwood Valley, Pomo), a right-hander with a surprising fastball. "Lockie" had a breakout year at Sherman in 1907 and played a while in the frenetic, all-season world of California semipro baseball. In 1911 he made spring camp with the Pacific Coast League Angels. This was his boyhood dream. "I used to read about Bender and Sockalexis in the papers and determined that I would be like them if I could," he recalled.[14] Lockart pitched decently in two games that spring but was let go with two other rookie pitchers. Manager Cap Dillon went with his veterans. Unhappy call. The Angels finished last, 39½ games out. Lockart would become a regular in circuits like LA's Trolley League, pitching another seven years before his arm gave out.[15]

But Lockart was an exception at Sherman. A career on the endless professional road, away from family and culture, did not fit with baseball's place in the cosmos of most Sherman athletes. It was true that some Sherman students, new to a jarringly regimented existence, endured wrenching cultural deprivation, homesickness, fear, anxiety. Imagine family separation.[16] But Sherman also reflected a generation of change. Modern historians of the boarding school experience have recognized that many Sherman students learned to subtly adjust. In historian Clifford Trafzer's phrase, students learned to "turn the power" of their own culture to live blended lives; they adapted to school and new possibilities even as they refused to abandon tradition and their people in a zero-sum exchange.[17] Sherman Museum curator Lorene Sisquoc (Fort Sill Apache/Mountain Cahuilla) caught the sense of it. Remembering her own years in the multitribal mix of Sherman students, she observed that Sherman became "our reservation."[18] In that evolutionary pan-Indian environment, the diamond was common ground.

Sherman students could embrace baseball because in its component skills it was like their own ancient games of shinney or lacrosse.[19] Students played baseball joyfully, for release. They played it hard, as a competitive outlet; in a telling phrase, they played to show what an Indian could do.[20] At big games, student fans rocked the home stands like a cheer squad, with Sherman's famous band booming a Sousa soundtrack. Sherman's vocational teams played for intramural pennants. Back home, reservation teams played one another, and the game became an integral part of traditional cultural events like fiesta.

Sherman was in its element in those years. A free Sherman education started with English as a second language and up to eight grades of instruction. By 1908, 550 students were enrolled. By 1909, 48 tribes were represented. Academics were taught in the morning; in the afternoon there was vocational instruction; there were extracurricular offerings from music and literary societies to sports. Advancement was by exam, and students could persist into their early 20s. By today's sensibilities, this may seem like a low educational bar. In its time, it was not. In 1900, according to the US Department of Education, only 6.4 of every 100 American 17-year-olds had a high-school diploma. And census data in this period found that 1.75 million American children were not in school at all but were working in mines, mills, and factories. Sherman's educational model was destined to fall out of step with regulated high-school sports. But until then, Sherman had a steady flow of mature students in their physical prime. That was how it could play head-to-head with college teams, and show what an Indian could do.[21]

In 1909 Sherman had a young right fielder named Kenny Marmon (Laguna Pueblo, New Mexico). Marmon's parents had been educated at Carlisle, but for his education, they looked west to Sherman. There was rising awareness that Sherman was more than the last Indian school. It also gave life to a larger pan-Indian institution – a transportation network that stretched common-ground accommodations from coast to coast. It started with Joe Scholder's marriage to a Carlisle graduate. The Scholders would make their lifelong home in Riverside. Sylvas Lubo (Cahuilla), another early Sherman baseball star and career staffer, also married a Carlisle grad. So the ripples spread: Friends connected, there were marriages, families were begun. Carlisle sent out questionnaires to keep track of alumni, networking followed: jobs were sought and found, educational opportunities multiplied, students and alumni moved back and forth along this secure cultural line.

Sports recruiting followed, too, though 1909 also delivered an ominous sign: This was the year Carlisle's Jim Thorpe was paid to play baseball for the Class-D Rocky Mount Railroaders. Carlisle actually eliminated its own baseball program in 1910. (Too many Carlisle ballplayers were being lured off to play for pay.)[22] Thorpe was famously awarded his Olympic medals in 1912 and stripped of them in 1913. But traffic along the continental Native American highway was established. By 1918, a Seneca athlete from Oklahoma named Bert Jamison had become a multisport star at Haskell, in Kansas, had married a Sherman grad, and had come west to coach at a smaller Arizona Indian school. He was "discovered" there and came to the Pacific Coast League Los Angeles Angels spring camp as a pitching prospect. He was the last man cut, but things worked out. He took a long-term Sherman coaching job.[23] And that was the year they closed Carlisle. By then, Carlisle had carried many former Sherman students on its rolls, including 75 from Southern California Mission tribes alone. But now, like Kenny Marmon, students sought other options up and down the line.[24]

The year of 1913 would be long remembered by baseball fans in Riverside. On March 25 the Chicago White Sox came to town to play a spring-training game against Sherman. This was the A team: Big Ed Walsh, Ray Schalk, Buck Weaver, Shano Collins, Joe Benz, and Harry Lord.

The result was a real old-time baseball carnival. Town leaders hosted a ceremonial luncheon at the Mission Inn Hotel. Some of the White Sox got to teasing pitcher Joe Benz about something and he took umbrage and stalked out. Later, nobody wanted to take batting practice when Benz was throwing. But the giddy festivities were unaffected. The Sherman band marched and played at the head of an auto parade to the city park; downtown merchants all closed at noon and 3,000 fans filled seats and standing room while 280 Sherman students were infectiously noisy in reserved seating. The White Sox won 14-3. They scored five while Sherman's players were still awestruck. With one out in the top of the first, there was a walk and a balk and a hit and Harry Lord came rounding third. But the throw to the plate beat him easily. He stopped and strolled up to the catcher, then suddenly sprang past him and scored. Later in the game, when Buck Weaver got a sharp grounder with nobody on, he sent it around the horn anyway, Weaver to Morrie Rath to Babe Borton at first. But the excitement was undiminished. Sherman's players would remember it as the day they got to face Ed Walsh (he worked three innings, no hits), and Sherman did have its moments. Kenny Marmon, playing second this day, had two hits and stole two bases (here imagine Ray Schalk fuming); Saturnino Calac (Luiseño, Rincon) played airtight shortstop and had a booming triple. From the locals' perspective, it was My Greatest Day in Baseball.[25]

In 1914 Emil Benson (Mono) emerged as both a notable student and arguably the finest pitcher to come out of Sherman in this Golden Era. This year, he threw a 13-strikeout no-hitter against the University of Redlands.[26] He also edited the *Sherman Bulletin*, participated in the literary society, and was the only male in the small graduating class of '14. He next pitched for Riverside High School. In the spring of 1917, when America entered World War I, Benson dropped out of school and enlisted in the US Army.[27] Almost overnight, on a broad coastal plain north of San Diego, the Army built Camp Kearny for the urgent processing of Doughboys. The parade ground was laid out with space for 43 baseball diamonds. On October 30, 1917, Emil Benson made himself a star, pitching and winning both games of a doubleheader.[28] In mid-1918 he was sent to France. In April 1919 he came back a sergeant, mustered out in San Diego and went directly to Sherman. That weekend Sherman happened to have a home baseball game with the University of Redlands. The *Sherman Bulletin* reported, "Emil Benson, a former student who has just returned from France, was here, and helped win the game." Benson struck out seven in relief and Sherman collected a walk-off win, 8-7.[29] Benson shortly took a staff position at Sherman. It was the beginning of a long career in the Bureau of Indian Affairs that would take him and his wife (a former Sherman staffer) to Keams Canyon Indian School in remote Hopi country east of the Grand Canyon. In 1934 (at age 39) Benson played shortstop and batted cleanup for a Keams Canyon team that went 19-2

Sherman Braves team warming up before a spring 2024 game on Sherman's home diamond. Foreground is Sherman assistant coach Raymond Tarin.

and finished third in the Northern Arizona baseball tournament. The team was notable, the papers said, because the players all had been educated at Indian schools, including Sherman and Haskell.[30]

The postwar career of Wallace Newman (Luiseño, La Jolla) is a useful marker for the eclipse of the Golden Era. Newman entered Sherman in 1913 at age 12. As he grew, he was seen to be an all-sport natural. He graduated from Sherman in 1919, but he continued to reside there while suiting up for Riverside High School and Junior College. The competition complained. So Newman took a two-sport scholarship to USC, starred as a passing quarterback, graduated, and became coach at a suburban LA high school. There he arranged to adopt two Sherman football stars so they could play for his high-school team. Newman's team went to the state championships, but the competition cried foul again. Which is how Wallace "Chief" Newman wound up coaching at Whittier College from 1929 to 1964, winning 10 conference championships in baseball (and seven in football), and being elected to both the NCAA Coaching and American Indian Athletic Halls of Fame.[31]

POSTSCRIPT

On May 29, 1919, the *Sherman Bulletin* published a memorial list of Sherman students who had served and died in World War I. There were 10 names. There would be others. The list included an Olympic-class distance runner and four baseball players.[32] (A University of Arkansas database lists 126 Native American World War I veterans with some connection to Sherman.[33])

By the 1920s, an alumni-varsity ballgame was a perennial feature of Sherman's commencement week. In May of 1939, the "Sherman Institute All Stars" defeated the Soboba reservation nine (Luiseño), 10-2, to win the third annual Southwest Indian baseball tournament. The umpires were Jim Thorpe and Jack Meyers. The game was played on the home field at Sherman where Meyers had helped inaugurate baseball nearly four decades earlier.[34]

As for Kenny Marmon: At Sherman he won the shortstop job and established himself as a top student. He graduated from Sherman in 1911. In 1912 he helped Riverside High School win a championship and was, emphatically, all-league at shortstop. "There has never been an infielder in the Citrus Belt League who could approach the Indian," the *Riverside Enterprise* declared.[35] When World War I began, Marmon was at New Mexico State. He was another who left school, joined the Army, and served in France (as a sergeant).[36] Like Emil Benson, he returned to Sherman, where he taught for a decade before leaving for promotion within the Bureau of Indian Affairs. By 1940 Marmon was one of just six Native American field agents on special assignment with the bureau to help tribes write constitutions, hold elections, and promote economic development. He was superintendent of the Seminole Indian Agency in Florida when he retired in 1958.[37]

And so to 2024. Sherman had survived through many iterations. Budgets were chronically tight. Its student population ballooned, then shrank back in the Great Depression. For some years it was a dedicated Navajo institution. Its baseball team remained in small-school competition. In time Sherman won accreditation. It struck a career-pathways partnership with the San Manuel Band of Mission Indians. It persevered.

In June of 2024, US Secretary of the Interior Deb Haaland – the first Native American to attain Cabinet rank and, like Kenny Marmon, a Laguna Pueblo – reflected on the legacies of Native American character in a guest essay for *Native News Online*. A child of a military family, she remarked on how military service among Indians honored the tradition of defending lands that had been theirs long before the coming of the Mayflower. She recalled a grandfather who "galvanized his peers around pastimes like coaching an all-Indian baseball team, which he led to the state championship."[38]

And on a sunny spring day in 2024, longtime coach Matt Townsend brought the Sherman Braves out for another home opener on the Sherman diamond. While ball fields may have shifted around the grounds across the decades, tradition was still at work here. On a part of this same spreading acreage where Jack Meyers and Joe Scholder and Ben Neafus played the first Sherman ballgame 121 years before, Sherman's students were still playing baseball. Still celebrating their own Native American pastime.

ACKNOWLEDGMENTS

I wish to thank to Lorene Sisquoc, curator of the Sherman Indian Museum, for her indispensable hospitality, guidance, and assistance to this project. As usual. The museum invites research inquiries. For more information, see https://www.facebook.com/shermanindianmuseum.

A growing archive of Sherman images and documents is now available on the web, through a partnership with the library of the University of California, Riverside. Visit Calisphere.org at

https://calisphere.org/collections/27124/?start=912&q=&sort=a.

Thanks for all assistance, as well, to Richard Tritt, archives and library photograph curator of the Cumberland County (Pennsylvania) Historical Society. Among other collections, the Historical Society is the keeper of the rich historical archive and image collection of Carlisle Indian Industrial School.

For information on other boarding schools in the national chain, see https://carlisleindian.dickinson.edu/teach/locations-reservation-indian-boarding-schools-us.

To access teaching and research guides on the history of Indian education, with links to the National Archives and Library of Congress, see https://carlisleindian.dickinson.edu/teaching.

NOTES

1   Haskell's original title was the United States Indian Industrial Training School.

2   "Indians Defeated in a Good Game of Baseball," *Riverside* (California) *Daily Press*, February 23, 1903.

3   "The Perris Indian Boys Downed Berdoo," *Riverside Enterprise*, October 28, 1900.

4   "Ambitious Red Men: Indians Start Their Football Campaign With High Hopes," *Philadelphia Inquirer*, September 10, 1899.

5   "Indians on the Warpath," *Los Angeles Times*, November 9, 1902.

6   "Indians Defeated in a Good Game of Baseball."

7   "Neafus Will Twirl," *San Bernardino Sun*, June 7, 1903; "Foul Tips," *San Bernardino County Sun*, July 17, 1903.

8   "Analysis of Sherman Team," *Riverside Press and Horticulturalist*, December 2, 1904.

9   Estimates vary. Contemporary ethnographer C. Hart Merriam thought low ebb was closer to 15,500. See "Nation to Nation: Treaties Between the United States and American Indian Nations," exhibit at the National Museum of the American Indian, Washington, DC. See https://americanindian.si.edu/explore/exhibitions/washington.

10 Phil Brigandi, "In the Name of the Law: The Cupeño Removal of 1903," *Journal of San Diego History*, San Diego History Center Quarterly. Winter 2018, Volume 64, Number 1. Accessed at https://sandiegohistory.org/journal/2018/august/in-the-name-of-the-law-the-cupeno-removal-of-1903/.

11 "Jap Team Scalps Sherman Braves," *Los Angeles Herald*, May 21, 1905.

12 "Sioux and Locals Break Even at Ball," *Riverside Enterprise*, July 28, 1905.

13 "Sioux and Locals Break Even at Ball."

14 "Berry's New Indian Pitcher Is Making Good with the Angels," *Los Angeles Times*, March 9, 1911.

15 "At the Training Camps," *Los Angeles Times*, March 16, 1918.

16 On August 4, 2023, Interior Secretary Deb Haaland took daylong testimony at Sherman as part of her "Road to Healing" Tour of Indian schools. The day's full transcript is accessible at www.doi.gov/sites/default/files/rth-ca-sherman-indian-high-school-transcript.pdf.

17 Diana Meyers Bahr, *The Students of Sherman Indian School: Education and Native Identity Since 1892* (Norman: University of Oklahoma Press, 2014), 7.

18 Bahr, 61.

19 For shinney, imagine field hockey as it might have been approximated by joyful children at recess, or in a twin-ball variant, played more like lacrosse by women's teams. "Games Bring Us Together," 2024 exhibit, the National Museum of the American Indian, Washington, DC. Also 2024, Sherman Cultural Director Lorene Sisquoc included shinney instruction and play in "Native Toys & Games" summer workshops at the school. She first introduced the sport at Sherman in 1995, in competitive play with area reservations. Accessed at www.shermanindianmuseum.org.

20 John Bloom, *To Show What an Indian Can Do: Sport at Native American Boarding Schools* (Minneapolis: University of Minnesota Press, 2000), 64. Phrase turned by an unidentified Navajo boxer of the 1930s.

21 "The Subtle Evolution of Native American Education," www.shermanindianmuseum.org; Thomas D. Snyder, ed., *120 Years of American Education: A Statistical Portrait* (National Center for Education Statistics, 1993), table 19, 55.

22 "Baseball Teams at the Carlisle Indian School," *Smithsonian Collections Blog*, July 12, 2010. Accessed at https://si-siris.blogspot.com/2010/07/baseball-teams-at-carlisle-indian.html.

23 "Tigers Brace Up and Win," *Los Angeles Times*, March 29, 1918; Sherman Institute column, *Riverside Daily Press*, March 26, 1928.

24 "Records of the Carlisle Indian School at the National Archives and Records Administration," Carlisle Indian School Digital Resource Center, Archives & Special Collections, Waidner-Spahr Library, Dickinson College, Carlisle, Pennsylvania. Accessed online at https://carlisleindian.dickinson.edu/additional-resources/records-carlisle-indian-school-national-archives-and-records-administration.

25 "White Sox Defeat Red Skins 14 to 3," *Chicago Inter Ocean*, March 26, 1913: 10; "Play Y.M.C.A. Benefit Ball Game: The Largest Crowd in the History of Riverside's Big Ball Park See the Chicago White Sox Defeat Sherman," *Sherman Bulletin*, March 26, 1913: 1.

26 "Riverside Wins in Three Games," *Riverside Enterprise*, March 16, 1914.

27 "Sherman Institute Notes," *Riverside Daily Press*, May 16, 1917: 14.

28 "Indian Benson Mainstay in Box," *San Diego Union*, October 31, 1917: 6.

29 "Sherman Wins from Redlands," *Sherman Bulletin*, April 24, 1919: 2.

30 "Twenty-Eight Entered in State Tournament," *Arizona Republic* (Phoenix), July 26, 1934: 8.

31 John S. Dahlem, PhD, "History of the California Interscholastic Federation Southern Section (CIFSS): Sherman Indian High School." https://cifss.org/wp-content/uploads/2015/06/CIFSS-History-31-Sherman-Indian-School.pdf.

32 "In Memoriam," *Sherman Bulletin*, May 29, 1919: 6.

33 "Modern Warriors of World War I," Sequoyah National Research Center (Little Rock: University of Arkansas, 2008). Database identifying 12,000 American Indian and Alaska Native veterans of World War I. Searchable at https://www.worldwar1centennial.org/index.php/american-indians-in-ww1-modern-warriors-of-world-war-i/5565-american-indians-wwi-servicement.html.

34 "Soboba Nine Drops Titular Game to Sherman All-Stars," *Hemet* (California) *News*, May 26, 1939: 12.

35 "All Star Team of Citrus Belt Picked," *Riverside Enterprise*, June 7, 1912: 6.

36 US World War One Centennial Commission, database.

37 "Harrington to Take Over as Seminole Agency Superintendent," press release, May 6, 1958, US Department of the Interior, Indian Affairs. https://www.docsteach.org/documents/document/photograph-of-kenneth-marmon-who-was-a-pueblo-indian-and-bureau-of-indian-affairs-field-agent.

38 "Interior Secretary Deb Haaland: Native Americans Have Always Been Citizens," *Native News Online*, June 2, 2024. https://nativenewsonline.net/opinion/interior-secretary-deb-haaland-deb-haaland-native-americans-have-always-been-citizens.

AMERICAN INDIAN BARNSTORMING TEAMS

By Jeffrey P. Beck

To understand why America's first peoples joined exhibition baseball teams that toured the country from the 1890s through the 1930s, it helps to review the US government's boarding schools for native children. The stories of these exhibition teams and the federal boarding schools are closely intertwined. The boarding schools offered baseball, among other sports, as a means of assimilating native children into American culture.

The so-called Progressive era of American history continued the federal government's legacy of violence against native peoples. This violent legacy, recognized by generations of scholars, has been documented officially now through the Federal Indian Boarding Schools Initiative, commissioned by former Interior Secretary Deb Haaland and conducted by Assistant Secretary for Indian Affairs Bryan Newland.[1] Newland's study cited extensively the US Senate's subcommittee report on Indian Education in 1969, known as the Kennedy report, which stated: "Beginning with President Washington, the stated policy of the Federal Government was to replace the Indian's culture with our own."[2] That forced separation of American Indians from their lands, families, languages, and cultures and forced assimilation into Anglo culture was the goal of the government from the founding, but it was implemented systematically starting in 1878 with the federal boarding school system. In 1879, Army Captain Richard Henry Pratt founded Carlisle Indian Industrial, the first such federal residential boarding school, in Carlisle, Pennsylvania, with his often-quoted slogan, "Kill the Indian in him, and save the man."[3] The first native inhabitants of the school were principally Chiricahua Apache children, whose parents were imprisoned after the surrender of *Goyaalé* (Geronimo), although Pratt's boarding school soon took on hundreds of children forcibly separated from their families from many native nations. At least in Pratt's eyes, Carlisle became the Bureau of Indian Affairs model for more federal boarding schools that removed children from their families as well as from their indigenous languages and cultures.[4]

Green's Indian Baseball Team, 1898.

NATIVE AMERICAN MAJOR LEAGUERS

The boarding school system was promoted by Pratt and others as an exemplary solution of "the Indian problem," and athletics were one featured component of the program. As Bentley, Bloom, and other scholars have noted, the success of Carlisle Indian Industrial School athletes on sports fields, especially celebrity athletes like Jim Thorpe, hid the violence of the system.[5] In her biography of Thorpe, Kate Buford likewise explains how native scholars describe the cultural destruction of the boarding schools as a "soul wound."[6] While Pratt and fellow superintendents trumpeted the athletic successes of Thorpe and his native classmates as epitomes of assimilation, the true stories of these athletes merit telling, starting with the traumas. Stripping Thorpe of his Olympic medals is only the most memorable trauma.[7] On September 25, 2024, at Gila River Indian Community in Chandler, Arizona, President Joseph Biden formally apologized to generations of American Indians for the federal boarding school system, calling it "a sin on our souls."[8]

As detailed in *The American Indian Integration of Baseball* and as this volume makes clear, native athletes were successful as major-league, minor-league, semipro, and college players, starting with baseball games on federal boarding school fields. The semiprofessional part of the story connects the trauma of the boarding schools with other exploitation of native athletes especially on native barnstorming or exhibition teams. The most famous of these teams, the Nebraska Indians, was inspired by the popularity of the Genoa (Nebraska) Indian Industrial School's baseball team.[9] Guy W. Green, as the manager of the Stromberg baseball team in 1895, witnessed the crowds that the Genoa team drew, and like other Progressive era entrepreneurs, he was eager to exploit the spectacle of native athletes. Green wrote, "When I counted my money after that game [Stromberg vs. Genoa Indian School], the idea of the Nebraska Indians was born."[10] He reasoned, "If an Indian base ball team was a good drawing card in Nebraska, it ought to do wonders further east if properly managed. I accordingly determined to organize 'The Nebraska Indians.'"[11]

The Nebraska Indians, which began touring in 1897 and continued, with an ownership change, into the 1920s, were not the first or last such team – in fact, their success led to many imitations. Because Green wrote two short books about the team and because it was often featured in newspaper stories, features, and postcards, it was certainly one of the best-documented such teams. And almost all these teams depended on federal boarding schools and local reservation schools for recruiting athletes. In their heyday, these exhibition teams played across the United States and Canada, and they featured talented native athletes who later signed minor-league and major-league contracts. These teams included Green's Nebraska Indians (c. 1897-1912), James and Oren Beltzer's Nebraska Indians (1912-1918), the Nebraska Indians of the 1920s (c. 1921-1928), Harry Homewood's Sioux Indians Baseball Team (c. 1896-1906), John Olson's Cherokee All Stars of Watervliet Michigan (c. 1904-1912),

Gus Whitewing's "All-Indian Baseball Team" (c. 1907), the Oxford (Nebraska), Indians (c. 1910), the Indian Ball Team of Bradley, Michigan (c. 1910), the All-Indian Baseball Team of Guthrie (Oklahoma, c. 1912), Kate J. Becker's Carlisle Indian Baseball Club, not affiliated with the boarding school (1916), the Mayetta (Kansas) Indian Baseball Team (c. 1925), Moses Poolaw's Indian Baseball Team (c. 1933), the Dakota Eagles of Flandreau (South Dakota, c. 1933), and Ben Harjo's Oklahoma Indians or All-Indian Baseball Club (1932-1933), which included Jim Thorpe in 1933. Some of these teams played only for a partial season, but the longest tenured teams, the Nebraska Indians, the Sioux Indian Baseball Team, and Cherokee All-Stars, drew large crowds across the country for years.[12]

In many ways, the native barnstorming teams, like the Wild West shows of the era, thrived on popular fascination with and exploitation of native stereotypes. This fact is clear in Green's account of the formation of the team as well as in photos and postcards of the team as well as the illustrations of Green's books. His *The Nebraska Indians: A Complete History* and *Fun and Frolic with an Indian Ball Team* were illustrated with grotesque cartoons of the native players in headdresses and loincloths lofting bats like spears. Ensuing illustrations show native figures in leather riding horses, pointing long rifles, and performing carnival tricks.[13] Similarly, press coverage of the games in many local newspapers usually included frequent mentions of "red men," "Poor Lo," "redskins," "braves," scalps and scalping, tomahawks, bows and arrows, braves, blows, bloodshed, and war chants – the sensational imagery of Western novels and Wild West shows. Baseball team owners like Guy Green and Harry Homewood trucked in these stereotypes to sell tickets, and obliging local newspapers promoted the games with all the grotesqueries.

Green's anecdotes of his players are replete with Western stereotypes. One clear example is his portrait of Juzicanea, a Pascua Yaqui man, apparently from Arizona. Green wrote:

In all my experience, I have had but one Yaqui ball player. The Yaquis are a savage tribe living in the extreme southwestern part of the United States, and I hesitated a long time before I added Juzicanea to my team. He was the meanest looking Indian I have ever seen. He wore his hair long, surveying everything suspiciously with piercing black eyes, and when he came down the street people moved to the edge of the sidewalk and apprehensively watched him pass. Juzicanea would not sleep in a bed. He could rest comfortably on the floor or the ground. …

Another of Juzicanea's peculiarities was his craving for raw meat; he demanded one to two pounds of this delicacy each day, and unless he obtained it, he was surly as a caged tiger. I used to fill my pockets with raw meat when we went out to the grounds, and after Juzicanea made a particularly brilliant catch or a long hit, I fed him a liberal chunk of the succulent delicacy, which invariably caused him intense delight and greatly amused the natives who watched him perform. I was compelled to line my pockets [with] oilcloth in order to provide suitable receptacles for Juzicanea's gory lunches. ...

At Burlington, Kentucky … the savage tossed his tangled hair out of his eyes, growled ominously, and in broken English cried, "Bring me a pound of raw meat."[14]

Here, Juzicanea's long hair and "broken English" are associated with his character as a "savage," his lunches are "gory," and he is described as a "caged tiger" and is fed treats like an animal, inspiring both popular fear and fascination. That combination of native stereotypes and intense emotions was gist for the coverage of the Nebraska Indians, Sioux Indians, Cherokee All-Stars, and other exhibition teams of the era.

Guy Wilder Green (1873-1947) was the founder and most successful owner of the Nebraska Indians, although later owners included James Beltzer, Oren "Buck" Beltzer (James's brother and a Nebraska Cornhusker legend), Pat Kelsey, and Ed Hamman.[15] As the most successful promoter of the team, Green also provided the most extensive documentation of American Indian exhibition teams in his two books and many newspaper interviews from 1897 to 1912, when he sold the team to the Beltzer brothers. In the team's first season, 1897, the season was short, the team was ill equipped to succeed, and the travelling arrangements were rugged at best. In "Experiences with an Indian Ball Team," a feature that Green wrote for *The Nebraska State Journal* in 1908, he recalled:

We took to the rocky trails of public amusement in wagons. I had two lumber trucks, six horses, a bale of hay and a dog as my traveling outfit. Four of the horses were hitched side-by-side to one wagon.[16]

In its first season, the team was hastily recruited from Genoa Indian School, the Winnebago reservation in Nebraska, and Sioux reservations in South Dakota, and Green recalled that the team lost its first game against the town baseball team in Wahoo, Nebraska, in late June by a score of 10-5. He noted: "Our disastrous experience at Wahoo is easily explained. Most of my players had come directly from their reservations to the place of opening. They were stiff from travel, were out of condition and lacking in practice. I was surprised to see them make as good a showing as they did."[17] And the going did not get easier in 1897 for the first team, as the team travelled and slept in wagons, as they ventured from town to town in Nebraska and Iowa, and as Green sent letters and telegrams to arrange games and drum up crowds. Green reflected that the first season "was only moderately successful whether surveyed from an artistic or from a financial standpoint," as the team disbanded on August 14, having won 21 games and lost 28. He observed that "[t]he boys were literally worn out" by the travel conditions.[18]

Starting in 1898, Green made several changes that contributed to greater success for the team. First, he abandoned the horse-and-wagon travel and began taking the team by train from town to town, followed by a livery wagon. That season the team also brought tents, to sleep on baseball fields at night. Green also worked relentlessly to recruit more players and to promote the team with photos, postcards, and the team's frequent monikers, "Green's Nebraska Indians: Greatest Aggregation of Its Kind," and "Green's Nebraska Indians: Only Ones on Earth" The team's season expanded to four states (Nebraska, Iowa, Missouri, and Illinois), and its record improved markedly to 81-22.[19] Green remarked that "the Indians were nervous and ill-at-ease while cooped up in hotels. But the minute they were furnished with tents they felt at home and gave me their best efforts."[20] The tent dwelling was also characterized by local press according to the stereotypes. *The Headlight* (Stromsburg, Nebraska) commented: "They camp right on the grounds where they play and live in true savage style."[21]

In fact, ironically, while the native barnstorming businesses thrived on the use of anti-Indian stereotypes, Green also expressed considerable sympathy for the mistreatment his players suffered. This mistreatment included his players being barred from hotels, accused by local citizens of crimes, ridden by local constables and shopkeepers, and constantly mocked by crowds. Some typical allegations leveled against players included fraternization with White women, thefts of clothes, food, watches, and baseball equipment, and accounts of a holdup and even a kidnapping.[22] While Green defended his players against such bogus charges, he also expressed a weary acquaintance with the rough treatment: "Strangers are always safe objects of suspicion."[23]

The raucous crowds that hooted at players were a constant fixture of the games played by the Nebraska Indians, Cherokee All-Stars, and other exhibition teams of their time. In an interview with the *Sioux City Journal* in 1909, Green described the typical treatment endured by his Winnebago (Ho-Chunk) pitcher George Howard Johnson (who would later pitch in the major leagues). Green stated:

He has never stepped to the mound to pitch a game anywhere on earth that three things have not happened. Numerous local humorists have started what they imagine to be Indian war cries, others have yelled 'Back to the reservation,' and a third variety of town pump jester has shrieked, 'Dog soup! Dog soup![24]

Of course, Green's three examples were not the only barbs and epithets hurled at the native players. They were also typically called "Chief (Johnson was one of many in the major and minor leagues), "Heap Big-Injun," "Poor Lo," "Redskin," "Savage," and so on.[25]

In keeping with the practices of owners of native exhibition teams, Green often recruited players from the leading federal boarding schools, Carlisle and Haskell, as well as smaller schools nearby such as Genoa. Some of his boarding-school recruits included Jean Baptiste, a Winnebago from Nebraska, who pitched for Carlisle in 1891-92; Jacob Buckheart (or Buckhardt), a powerful Shawnee from

Oklahoma, who caught for both Carlisle and the Nebraska Indians; George Green, a Sac and Fox pitcher and speedy infielder for Carlisle, who also pitched for the Nebraska Indians; George Howard Johnson, the talented Winnebago pitcher from Walthill, Nebraska, who briefly attended Carlisle, Haskell, and Flandreau, before starring as a pitcher with the Nebraska Indians; Walter Nevitt, a Delaware who pitched at Haskell before joining Green's team as a third baseman; Thomas Reed, an Ojibwe, who played second base at Haskell before joining the Nebraska Indians as an infielder; White Boy, a Winnebago of Nebraska, who pitched for Genoa before joining Green's team; and Jessee Youngdeer, an Eastern Cherokee, who played center field for Carlisle before joining Green's team for its 1911 season.[26] This preference of the exhibition team owners for boarding-school players was practical, as these talented athletes had been trained by experienced coaches and tested against college-level competition. However, it was also in keeping with the Progressive era agenda of assimilating native youth into American culture.

While Green's preference for boarding-school athletes was clear, the most emphatic champion of the assimilationist model was Harry Homewood, owner and manager of the Sioux Indian Baseball Team, which toured the United States and Canada from 1896 to 1906. A feature story on the team appeared in the *Marysville Daily Appeal* in 1905, when the team was touring California, and it specified Homewood's enthusiasm for the assimilation of indigenous youth. The terms used in the feature are strikingly like the vision of Carlisle Superintendent Pratt. According to M.T. Clark, a contracting agent for the team interviewed for the article:

To educate the Indian in the ways of civilized life, therefore, is to preserve him from extinction, not as an Indian, but as a human being.

Mr. Homewood says there seems to be only two phases of the Indian question. One, that the American Indian should remain in the country as a survival of the aboriginal inhabitants, a study for the ethnologist, a toy for the tourist, a vagrant at the mercy of the State, and a continual pensioner upon the bounty of the people, the other that he shall be educated to work, live, and act as a reputable, moral citizen, and thus become a self-supporting member of society.

The latter is the policy of the management of the Sioux Indian baseball club, and if it would be followed out by those in direct charge of the Indians, he will then pass out of our national life as a painted, feather-crowned hero of the novelist to add the current of his free American blood to the hearts of this great nation.

Manager Homewood will not allow any Indian literature on the sleeper in which they travel, and each week gives a prize to the Indian writing the best article on What I would do if I were President and other subjects which will have a tendency to educate and elevate the Indian.[27]

This emphasis on eliminating native culture to "educate and elevate the Indian" could have been written by Pratt himself. The essays that Homewood asked his players to write were like Carlisle and Haskell lessons, and the forbidding of native languages and cultures ("any

Phoenix Indian School Baseball Team c. 1910.

NATIVE AMERICAN MAJOR LEAGUERS

OLSON'S CHEROKEE INDIAN BASE BALL CLUB.

Olson's Cherokee Baseball Team c. 1905

Indian literature") were standard practices at the boarding schools.

Homewood's Sioux Indian Baseball Team included some Sioux players, but was constituted of players from many indigenous nations, and was well-funded, traveling by train across the US and Canada. The team boasted a roster of 17 players from 1904 to 1906, two Pullman cars with showers, and extensive equipment. Like the Nebraska Indians, they maintained team records and boasted a record of 1,263 wins vs. 304 losses (an astounding .810 winning percentage) from 1898 to 1905.[28] To draw larger crowds, the team was an early innovator of night baseball games. Accounts of the Sioux Indians team noted that they played day games and night games differently, with the team often erecting a large canvas circus tent along with a portable grandstand for the night games. The team carried its own electric generator, which powered a circuit of incandescent bulbs at the top of the tent, and players used a larger, softer ball (more like a modern softball) and narrower bats for the evening games. The double novelties of native players and night games proved popular with the crowds. The night games also made for frequent newspaper accounts, and the native players' familiarity with baseball in semi-darkness also provided them with a competitive advantage. A few quotations from the press accounts in 1905 and 1906, intended to draw interested spectators to the games, suffice to explain the novelty:

In a novel, exciting, and interesting baseball game here by electric light at night the Exeter Clippers defeated the Sioux Indians. This was the first game ever played here at night. It was enjoyed by a large crowd.[29]

This will be a baseball game at night. The game will be played with a team of Sioux Indians who are touring the state. They carry a generator and all the paraphernalia for lighting up the grounds as light as day and from papers where the Indians have played it describes the bleachers as being in twilight while the grounds are illuminated with 50,000 candle power arc lights.[30]

The ball used at night is about twice the size of the regular baseball. It is soft and bouncy, and it sounds like a pumpkin when it hits the bat. The bat is as small as the ball is large, and this combination prevents the ball being batted too far beyond the circle of electric lights. The electric lights look like a lot of railroad lanterns, and they hang so low that if the ball is thrown or batted very high it is very difficult to see it.[31]

While the idea of night baseball came soon after Thomas Edison's invention of the lightbulb in 1880, the attempts in the nineteenth century were few and halting.[32] The development of new arc lights early in the twentieth century led entrepreneurs like Homewood to develop the concept, but night baseball as we know it now would wait until the 1920s, when General Electric developed more powerful floodlights, which were adopted first by minor-league teams, before they came to the major leagues on May 24, 1935, at Crosley Field. President Franklin Delano Roosevelt switched on the stadium lights from the White House, affirming the importance of electrification for sports and entertainment in the United States.[33]

Although baseball was included in the athletic programs of the federal boarding schools as part of their assimilation efforts, there is another chapter of the story worth telling. The success of native students as athletes in football, track, baseball, and other sports gave opportunities that exceeded the manual and vocational labor available to the students through the boarding schools' "summer outings." Those summer outings were manual labor employment (e.g., farm work, ditch digging, lumbering, livestock and dairy work, sewing, carpentry, cooking, etc.) intended to provide vocational training to the students while supporting the boarding schools financially. *The Federal Boarding School Initiative Report* found that manual child labor was an entrenched feature of the schools, which "[predominantly] utilized manual labor of [the students] to compensate for the poor conditions of school facilities and lack of financial support from the Federal Government."[34] The talented young athletes at boarding schools, like Jim Thorpe, Louis Leroy, Charles Bender, Joe Libby, Jesse Youngdeer, and George Howard Johnson, found better paying and more enjoyable opportunities playing summer baseball for minor-league and exhibition teams, often playing under pseudonyms. Some of them also, including Thorpe, nursed dreams of major-league careers, and all of them found playing baseball in the summer preferable to the work they would do on summer outing programs.[35] As scholar Wade Davies observed: "Native people gravitated to ... Indian school sports, not only because it allowed them to express their indigenous athleticism, but also because they could exert some personal and collective control over this activity in otherwise authoritarian environments."[36]

Likewise, Alan J. Caldwell, the director of the Menominee Cultural Center in Kenosha, Wisconsin, and the son of James J. Caldwell, who played third base for the Cherokee All-Stars in 1912, described his father's baseball career with pride. Caldwell wrote about his father's stint with Olson's Cherokee All-Stars:

My father was not the type of person to talk much about his past. What little he told us about his baseball playing days was about the part of the country he traveled to such as the southeastern region. He didn't say anything that I recall about how they were treated or received in the towns that they played in. I think my father played for the pleasure of playing baseball and as a source of income. I think he may have also joined the team as a way to satisfy his sense of adventure. I envied my father. Though he only played semi-pro baseball he was a terrific player based on stories I heard from his peers.[37]

Evident in this account and other interviews done with other native players from the 1930s and 1940s was joy in playing baseball and pride in athletic accomplishment. This pride was also expressed by Lumbee athlete and scholar Joseph Oxendine, who wrote in his foreword to *The American Indian Integration of Baseball*: "Baseball is a noble game, a game of tradition, of allegiance and camaraderie. ... The character of baseball is consistent with traditional American Indian traits and attitudes toward sport. Consequently, young Indians 'took' to the game as soon as it was introduced to them in boarding schools."[38] While Oxendine was under no illusions about the injuries done by federal boarding schools, he also spent a career celebrating the athletic heritage that native players created in the twentieth century.

A related part of this athletic heritage was the teams of native players organized by the players themselves. While relatively few native players had the financial and social support to launch exhibition teams on extended tours, there were certainly native teams that deserve recognition. The most famous Oklahoma example of a native baseball team under native ownership was Ben Harjo's All-Indian Baseball Club of 1932-1933. Harjo founded the team in Wewoka, Oklahoma, equipped it for long tours and signed some major-league and minor-league players including Ike Kahdot, Bill Wano, Lee Daney, Williston Bohannon, Israel "Izzy" Wilson, Ben Tincup, and Harry "Rip" Collins. The team was financed generously by Ben and his wife, Susey Walker Harjo, who had inherited lucrative Seminole oil fields in Oklahoma. The team had its own customized touring bus, and after tryouts and practice in Holdenville, it began a well-publicized tour in May of 1922 from Oklahoma into Texas and Louisiana.[39]

Starting auspiciously, the team achieved its first major victory, a 4-1 win against the Muskogee Tigers of the Western Association, and it continued to win in Texas (playing at Temple, Killeen, Bartlett, Taylor, and Austin) and in Louisiana (Lakes Charles, Deridder, Arcadia).[40] Led by the strong pitching of Collins, by late June the team had recorded 41 wins against only 4 losses and was invited to the *Denver Post* Tournament, known by some as the Western World Series.[41] The team continued its torrid pace in Denver. On July 28, the *Denver Post* reported:

With 6,000 palefaces chanting the call to victory, the All-Indians of Holdenville, Oklahoma reached baseball's happy hunting grounds Wednesday night when they defeated the Sioux Falls Canaries, 6 to 5, in a great 12-inning game to win the championship of the *Denver Post* tournament.[42]

And with this success at Denver, the All-Indians received a championship check of $4,167. The team would finally disband for 1932 with an impressive record, but a debt of $1,800 from touring. In cases like this, Ben and Susey Harjo depended on the superintendent of the Five Civilized Tribes of Oklahoma (A.J. Landman) to release Susey's funds to pay the debts.[43]

In 1933 the Harjos' All-Indians planned a much larger tour, up to 140 games, from Oklahoma through the Midwest to New York City, and they also recruited new players for the team, including Earl Huckleberry, Rudy Jones, and, most famously, Jim Thorpe. When Thorpe joined the team, Ben Harjo's announcement of his hiring made newspaper headlines and led to a Jim Thorpe Day celebration and parade in Holdenville on May 11.[44] As in 1932, the team played well against local and Western League competition and determined to find larger crowds and fiercer competition in the East. As they traveled to Kansas City, they faced some of the strongest competition possible against the Kansas City Monarchs. That tough competition would continue as they faced strong teams in Pittsburgh and Philadelphia before reaching New York. Thorpe, who served as a player-manager for much of the season, occasionally played the field and often pinch-hit. A. Grant Carrow, a young fan who watched Thorpe play against the Lowell Lauriers, a Massachusetts minor-league team, admired his "beautifully executed fade-away slide" for a double, accentuated by Thorpe's wide grin at second base.[45] The *Holdenville Daily News* reported on September 14 that the team had played 128 games in 15 states, amassing a record of 87-41, with Thorpe leading the team in batting with a .341 average in 93 games.[46] However, by the end of the tough 1933 season, Ben and Susey Harjo were over $6,000 in debt, and Susey requested the agent of the Five Nations to release $10,000 to pay the players and also to pay debts related to the death of the Harjos' young daughter. The agent refused, leading Thorpe to send a telegram to Bureau of Indian Affairs Commissioner John Collier and a letter to California Senator William Gibbs McAdoo. Susey Harjo was only able to pay Jim Thorpe $500 of the $2,050 owed to him for the 1933 tour, and other players, such as Huckleberry, had to return their uniforms to the Muskogee agent before receiving partial payments. As in so many other cases, despite the athletic prowess on which they prided themselves, native managers and players were at the mercy of a federal system that treated them with condescension.[47]

Another outstanding example of a native touring team is Moses Edward (Mose) Poolaw's All-American Indian Baseball Team of 1933, which toured from Texas into Mexico, from September through December of 1933. Mose Poolaw (whose name also appears as Poolah) was a Kiowa from Mountain View, Oklahoma. He apparently attended Haskell Indian Industrial School and may have played for Beltzer's Nebraska Indians in 1917 before serving with the US Army in World War I, reaching the rank of sergeant.[48] Soon after his Army service, he joined Chickasha in the Western Association, playing infield. His greatest strength was as a pitcher, and he amassed a record of 60-53 in the Western Association, including a 20-win season in 1924.[49] Poolaw was listed as the manager, pitcher, and booking agent for the All-American Indian Baseball Team, and its itinerary included Houston, Monterey, Laredo, and Mexico City. Other players listed on the team included Tommy Cussens, Spencer Thomas, Woodrow Arketa, and Bill Collins.[50] Most of these players lived in Oklahoma, giving the team a local character, and some press accounts refer to the club as the Harjoche All-American Indian Baseball Team. Perhaps Poolaw saw the team as a fitting sequel to Harjo's team, given the team's Southern tour (like Harjo's in 1932), or perhaps he hoped to capitalize on the excitement recently generated by Harjo's team.

The story of native baseball players on touring exhibition teams begins with the boarding schools and agency schools that taught baseball as a means of assimilation, a history imbued with trauma. While that trauma persisted in the experiences of native youth from the 1890s through the 1930s, the athletic successes those players enjoyed were savored by them and their communities. For both the record of the trauma the native players endured and the record of athletic triumph they achieved, the stories of these barnstorming teams are worth preserving.

NOTES

1   Bryan Newland, *Federal Boarding School Initiative Investigative Report*, May 2022, volume 1, https://www.bia.gov/sites/default/files/dup/inline-files/bsi_investigative_report_may_2022_508.pdf.

2   Committee on Labor and Public Welfare, *Indian Education: A National Tragedy – A National Challenge*, United State Senate Report (1969), 143.

3   Henry Louis Pratt quoted in Matthew Bentley and John Bloom, *The Imperial Gridiron: Manhood, Civilization, and Football at the Carlisle Indian Industrial School* (Lincoln: University of Nebraska Press, 2022), 1.

4   Jacqueline Fear-Segal and Susan D. Rose, eds., Introduction, *Carlisle Indian Industrial School: Indigenous Histories, Memories, & Reclamations* (Lincoln: University of Nebraska Press, 2016), 2-3.

5   Bentley and Bloom, 2.

6   Kate Buford, *Native American Son: The Life and Sporting Legend of Jim Thorpe* (Lincoln: University of Nebraska Press, 2010), 41.

7   Buford, *Native American Son*, 159-168; James Ring Adams, "The Jim Thorpe Backlash: The Olympic Medals Debacle and the Demise of Carlisle," in *American Indian: The Magazine of Smithsonian's National Museum of the American Indian*, 13.2 (2012). Online. Accessed Dec. 23, 2024. https://www.americanindianmagazine.org/story/jim-thorpe-backlash-olympic-medals-debacle-and-demise-carlisle.

8   Mary Annette Pember, Shondiin Mayo, and Mark Trahant, "Historic Apology: Boarding School History 'a Sin on Our Souls.'" *ICT News*, October 25, 2024. https://ictnews.org/news/historic-apology-boarding-school-history-a-sin-on-our-soul.

9   Guy W. Green, *The Nebraska Indians and Fun and Frolic with an Indian Ball Team*, ed. Jeffrey P. Beck (Jefferson, North Carolina: McFarland & Co., 2010), 9-10.

10 Green, "Experiences with an Indian Baseball Team," *Nebraska State Journal*, December 20, 1908: C6.

11 Green, *The Nebraska Indians*, 10.

12 Jeffrey P. Beck, aka Jeffrey Powers-Beck, "'A Role New to the Race,': A New History of the Nebraska Indians," *Nebraska History* 85 (2004): 186-203, 198; Buford, 283-284.

13 Green, *The Nebraska Indians*, 9, 10, 33, 53, 66, 118.

14 Green, *The Nebraska Indians*, 117-118.

15   Jeffrey P. Beck, "Introduction," *The Nebraska Indians*, xii, xliii.

16   Guy Green, "Experiences with an Indian Baseball Team," C6.

17   Green, *The Nebraska Indians*, 11.

18   Green, *The Nebraska Indians*, 15.

19   Green, *The Nebraska Indians*, 145.

20   Green, *The Nebraska Indians*, 27.

21   "Other Locals," *Stromsburg* (Nebraska) *Headlight*, April 25, 1901: 4.

22   Beck, "'A Role New to the Race,'" 193.

23   Green, *The Nebraska Indians*, 115.

24   "Raps Bleacher Jokesters," *Sioux City* (Iowa) *Journal*, June 3, 1909: 9.

25   Beck, *The American Indian Integration of Baseball*, 125.

26   Beck, *The American Indian Integration of Baseball*, 182, 209-212.

27   "Not All Sioux Indians," *Marysville* (California) *Daily Appeal*, August 26, 1905: 3.

28   "Indian Team May Come," *Vancouver* (British Columbia) *Daily News Advertiser*, August 5, 1906: 6.

29   "Games at Night," *Boston Globe*, quoted in the *San Luis Obispo* (California) *Morning Tribune*, July 26, 1905: 3.

30   "Baseball at Night," *Salinas* (California) *Daily Index*, August 4, 1906: 3.

31   "Sioux Indians Scalped Local Players Again," *Bakersfield* (California) *Morning Echo*, August 26, 1906: 5.

32   Tim Wiles, "Night Games Gave Access to Baseball to Millions," National Baseball Hall of Fame, Cooperstown, New York. Accessed Oct. 24, 2024. https://baseballhall.org/discover/night-games-gave-access-to-baseball-to-millions.

33   Peter Morris, *A Game of Inches: The Story Behind the Innovations that Shaped Baseball* (Chicago: Ivan R. Dee, 2010), 378-379; General Electric Company, *The Light That Started Sports at Night* (Schenectady, New York: GE, 1930), 4-10. Thanks to Cassidy Lent, library director of the National Baseball Hall of Fame, for providing information on the history of night baseball.

34   Newland, *Federal Boarding School Initiative Report*, 92.

35   Buford, *Native American Son*, 92; Fear and Seagal, eds., *Carlistle Indian Industrial School*, 2, 97-98.

36   Wade Davies, *Native Hoops: The Rise of American Indian Basketball, 1895-1970* (Lawrence, Kansas: University Press of Kansas, 2020), 29.

37   Caldwell quoted in Beck, *The American Indian Integration of Baseball*, 61.

38   Oxendine, Foreword, *The American Indian Integration of Baseball*, ix.

39   Buford, *Native American Son*, 290-293.

40   Royse Parr, "Ben Harjo's All-Indian Baseball Club," *Nine: A Journal of Baseball History and Culture*, 17.2 (2009): 90-91.

41   Parr, "Ben Harjo's All-Indian Baseball Club": 92.

42   Quoted in Parr, "Ben Harjo's All-Indian Baseball Club": 93.

43   Parr, "Ben Harjo's All-Indian Baseball Club": 93.

44   Parr, "Ben Harjo's All-Indian Baseball Club": 94.

45   Lauriers quoted in Buford, *Native American Son*, 285.

46   Parr, "Ben Harjo's All-Indian Baseball Club": 98.

47   Buford, *Native American Son*, 284-285.

48   Bob Lemke, "Photos Evoke Minor League Time Travel," blog, August 21, 2014, https://boblemke.blogspot.com/2014/08/photos-evoke-minor-league-time-travel.html. "Sgt. Moses Edward 'Mose' Poolaw," *Find a Grave*. Website. Accessed December 1, 2024. https://www.findagrave.com/memorial/25013152/moses-edward-poolaw.

49   "Mose Poolaw," Baseball Reference. Website. Accessed December 1, 2024. https://www.baseball-reference.com/register/player.fcgi?id=poolawoo1mos.

50   "Indian Ball Players to Visit Old Mexico," *Anadarko* (Oklahoma) *American Democrat*, September 28, 1933: 1.

THE RELATIONSHIP OF LEGENDARY MANAGERS CONNIE MACK AND JOHN MCGRAW WITH THEIR NATIVE AMERICAN PLAYERS

by William A. Young

Without question two of the greatest managers in the history of major-league baseball were Connie Mack (1862-1956) and John McGraw (1873-1934).

Cornelius McGillicuddy, better known as Connie Mack, piloted 7,466 games in a 50-year career as Philadelphia Athletics skipper. He managed an additional 289 games for the Pittsburgh Pirates for a total of 7,755 games, by far the most of any major-league manager.

John McGraw managed the Baltimore Orioles for 2½ years and the New York Giants for 31 years, for a total of 4,769 games.

Connie Mack, 6-feet-1 and 150 pounds, was known as The Tall Tactician for his stature and his baseball acumen, and "the grand old gentleman" for his quiet reserve and dignity. He always wore a business suit rather than a uniform in the dugout during games. He guided the Mackmen to nine American League pennants and five World Series titles. He was famed for developing young players and then, after their A's teams had won championships, selling their contracts to keep the club solvent. Then he would repeat the cycle, building another winning team. One of the young players he tried to lure was Christy Mathewson. Mack succeeded in signing the Giants pitcher, but probably influenced by John McGraw, Mathewson broke the contract and returned to the Giants.

Mack is best remembered for his longevity and civility. His entire career as a journeyman catcher, manager, and owner lasted 71 years. He addressed his players by their given names, not nicknames, and they invariably called him "Mr. Mack." As the *New York Times* observed in Mack's obituary, "The old-time leaders ruled by force, often thrashing players who disobeyed orders on the field or broke club rules off the field. ... [Mack] always insisted that he could get better results by kindness. He never humiliated a player by public criticism. No one ever heard him scold a man in the most trying times of his many pennant fights."[1]

Players on other teams applauded Mack's approach to managing. Writing just before the 1913 World Series, Christy Mathewson compared the A's to a college team, saying, "There is never any dissension. ... You never hear one member of the team knocking some fellow player." According to Mathewson, the A's harmony was due to Connie Mack, who was "a marvel at handling men." By contrast, Mathewson claimed, the hard-driving McGraw had the players wound up tight.[2]

In 1937, 13 years before he retired as A's manager, Mack was inducted into the National Baseball Hall of Fame. His Hall of Fame plaque calls him "Mr. Baseball." Outside Citizens Bank Park in Philadelphia there is a life-sized

For three years (1913-1915) John Tortes Meyers (left) roomed with famed Olympian Jim Thorpe (right) while both played for the New York Giants. Unlike Meyers, Thorpe had a tempestuous relationship with their manager, John McGraw.

statue of Mack, wearing a business suit, waving the rolled-up scorecard he invariably held during games.

In contrast to the lanky Connie Mack, the pudgy John McGraw was only 5-feet-7. However, his reputation far exceeded his size. McGraw has been praised as the epitome of "what a baseball manager was supposed to be: smart, shrewd, pugnacious, tough and demanding with his players."[3] After McGraw's death, Commissioner Kenesaw Mountain Landis called him "one of the greatest natural leaders any sport has ever known," adding, "Baseball to him was more than a game. It was a religion and war combined. … He was emblematic of the fire and dash that belongs to the national game. He knew ballplayers and he knew how to handle them."[4]

From 1902 to 1932, McGraw led the New York Giants to 10 National League pennants, three World Series championships, and 21 first- or second-place finishes.

Known as Mugsy and Little Napoleon (both nicknames he resented), McGraw developed his reputation for pugnaciousness as an infielder for the Baltimore Orioles and perfected it as a manager. As Arlie Latham, one of his coaches, said of McGraw's famous irate charges across the diamond to confront an umpire, he "eats gunpowder every morning and washes it down with blood."[5] He was ejected from 118 games as a manager and 14 as a player during his career, a record for total game ejections that stood until it was surpassed by Atlanta Braves manager Bobby Cox in 2007.

Connie Mack (with scorecard), manager of the Philadelphia Athletics, had a close relationship with his Hall of Fame pitcher Charles Albert Bender.

(Bain Collection, Library of Congress)

McGraw was an innovator. He introduced what has been called the inside game or scientific baseball, a style of play that emphasized strategy and deceit over raw power. The Giants manager stressed solid defense, situational hitting, and aggressive baserunning

McGraw was known to keep such close tabs on players that he would review hotel meal checks to see which of his players might be overeating. One of his heavier players once convinced a waiter to write down "asparagus" on his check when he had actually ordered pie a la mode.[6]

At first many of McGraw's players were in awe of him, even afraid of him, but they often grew to admire him. As Josh Devore said of McGraw, "He was this gruff, angry guy sometimes, but the reputation was worse than the reality. How do you think he got so many different kinds of players to play so well for him through the years?"[7]

McGraw was posthumously elected to the National Baseball Hall of Fame in 1937 and inducted with the class of 1939. Though flamboyant as a manager, his Hall of Fame plaque read simply "For 30 years manager of the New York Giants. … Under his leadership the Giants won 10 pennants and 3 world championships."

Connie Mack, whom McGraw recognized as an outstanding manager, called the Giants skipper in 1927 more effusively "the greatest baseball manager of all time."[8]

Both Mack and McGraw managed Native American ballplayers who were among the stars of the Deadball Era.

On a pitching staff that included greats like Lefty Grove, Herb Pennock, Eddie Plank, and Rube Waddell, Connie Mack considered Charles Albert Bender (1884-1954) his ace.[9]

A member of the Chippewa nation (also known as the Ojibwe, and in their own language Anishinaabe, for "original people") Bender spent part of his childhood on the White Earth Reservation in Minnesota. His mother was Chippewa and his father was of German-American ancestry. Bender learned to pitch at the famed Carlisle Indian School in Pennsylvania, where he spent five years, graduating in 1902. He also developed at Carlisle a sharp mind, applying his acuity to the craft of pitching. However, like other Carlisle students, he experienced the disparaging of his Native American heritage, which had a lasting effect on him.

Bender was signed by Connie Mack to a contract with the Philadelphia A's in 1903. In his rookie year he had an impressive 17 wins. Although various ailments limited his pitching stamina, Bender developed a reputation as a reliable and effective hurler. He especially excelled in his World Series performances. In the only game the A's won in the 1905 Series, Bender outdueled Joe McGinnity in a four-hit 3-0 shutout. Facing the New York Giants in the 1911 World Series, Bender pitched brilliantly, winning two of three starts, posting a 1.04 ERA, and striking out 20 batters in 26 innings.

Over a 16-year major-league career, Bender won 212 games and posted a .625 winning percentage. He "led the American League in winning percentage three times, tossed a no hitter in 1910, and was one of the early World Series stars, posting a 2.44 earned run average in five career Series."[10]

Like other Native American ballplayers, Bender had to endure constant, sometimes vicious, racism. For example, during the 1905 Series against the Giants, Bender was bombarded with racist taunts like "Back to the tepee for yours." John McGraw even joined in, saying, "It will be off the warpath for you today, Chief."[11] Bender resented the bigotry, as evident in the moniker "Chief" given to virtually all American Indian major leaguers. When applied to all Native American ballplayers, "Chief" "assumed the same patronizing overtone as the term 'boy' when applied generically to all African American males."[12]

Bender always signed autographs with "Charles" rather than the racist nickname he rejected. "I do not want my name to be presented to the public as an Indian, but as a pitcher," he told *Sporting Life* in 1905. However, he was called "Chief" so often during his career that he even allowed the nickname to be etched into his tombstone. Bender's obituary in *The Sporting News* carried the headline, "Chief Bender Answers Call to Happy Hunting Grounds."[13]

In an October 1905 article in *Sporting Life,* sportswriter Charles Zuber praised Bender for a World Series shutout victory over the Giants, but then added that the success was due to the influence of his manager Connie Mack, for "like the negro on stage, who … 'will work himself to death' if you jolly him, the Indian can be 'conned' into taking up any sort of burden."[14]

For the most part, despite journalists' assumptions, Bender enjoyed a positive, respectful relationship with Connie Mack. Although other players and coaches, including his own teammates on the Philadelphia Athletics, invariably called Bender "Chief," Mack never used the label when talking to Bender. Instead, the A's manager called Bender by his middle name "Albert." Mack said of his ace pitcher, "If I had all the men I've ever handled, and they were in their prime, and there was one game I wanted to win above all others, Albert would be my man."[15]

Mack called Bender "the greatest money pitcher the game has ever known," at a time when the phrase, commonly used in sports, meant "one who excels when the pressure is greatest."[16] That perspective was put into practice when Mack surprised observers by bringing Bender back to pitch the sixth and deciding game of the 1911 World Series against the Giants. In the 1913 World Series, Mack cited Bender's "baseball smarts" when the pitcher repositioned Athletics outfielders. It was a move, Mack said, that few in the stands would have recognized but which was crucial to winning the game and the Series.[17]

Connie Mack was not the only one to recognize Bender's contributions. Christy Mathewson, who faced Bender in the World Series, said of the A's pitcher that he was "a student of baseball and a deeper student than many fans and writers are willing to admit. His presence on the bench or coaching lines would naturally mean much to a ball club, for I have never met a player who could grasp situations as quickly as the Indian."[18] Mathewson observed that Bender had "a cool head and a fine arm and plenty of courage."[19]

John Tortes Meyers also paid tribute to Bender, calling him "one of the main dependencies of Connie Mack's wonderful Athletics" and adding, "Fandom has endorsed him as one of the greatest pitchers of the age."[20]

At a time when one of the stereotypes often applied to Native American athletes was that they were lazy and lacked the will to win, Albert Bender was a consummate competitor. He "did not simply want to win baseball games, he burned with a white heat to win them." Sportswriters often described Bender's demeanor on the mound as "stern," "cool," "stoical," and "impassive," but there was no doubting his intensity in crucial games. What made him such a competitor was not only "a blazing fastball, a very good slider and change-up, and an ardent desire to win, [but also] keen intelligence." Sometimes reporters would set aside their racial prejudice and note, as one wrote, that Bender pitched "with brain and nerve rather than brawn."[21]

However, it is important to note that Connie Mack's relationship with Bender was not always positive. After the 1908 season, one of Bender's weakest on the mound, Mack was told that his starting pitcher was contemplating leaving the A's to devote himself to trap shooting, another sport at which he excelled. Mack responded by saying, "[H]e did very little work for us last year and it is immaterial to me whether he pitches for the Athletics this season."[22] Bender relented and signed a contract with a 50 percent pay cut, but it left a bitter taste in his mouth.

Bender's pitching also faltered during the 1912 season, in part as a result of his abuse of alcohol, which some believe began after the sudden death of his younger brother, John, who was also a baseball player.[23] Reporters took notice that Bender was at times so obviously inebriated that Mack had to respond. Drawing on common stereotypes, sportswriter F.C. Lane wrote in *Baseball Magazine* that Mack blasted Bender when his star hurler "blew in [to the team hotel] after a somewhat prolonged dalliance with the fire water which the soul of the red man craveth."[24] Mack tried tolerating Bender's drinking, but after more incidents, he suspended Bender and his drinking buddy, outfielder Rube Oldring.[25]

Before the 1913 season, Bender apologized to his manager for his behavior during the 1912 campaign and promised to remain sober. Mack once again cut Bender's salary in half and wrote into his contract that he would receive his full salary only if he "refrains from intoxicating liquors."[26] Bender's stellar record during the 1913 season suggests that he kept his promise, and his relationship with Mack improved.[27]

NATIVE AMERICAN MAJOR LEAGUERS

World's Championship Base=Ball Series
First Game

Giants in the field, Mathewson pitching first ball. Lord of Athletics at bat
1 Mathewson, delivering his famous "Fadeaway"
2 Big Chief Bender in action.
3 Manager McGraw and Mack shaking hands just before the game.

(SABR – The Rucker Archive)

Before the first game of the 1911 World Series, legendary managers John McGraw (left) of the New York Giants and Connie Mack (right) of the Philadelphia Athletics are pictured shaking hands. Also shown are the pitching aces of the two teams, Hall of Famers Christy Mathewson (left) of the Giants and Charles Albert Bender (right) of the Athletics. Bender was a Native American popularly known by the nickname "Chief," but Mack always addressed him as Albert. Not shown is the star catcher of the Giants, John Tortes Meyers, also a Native American known as "Chief." Like Mack and Bender, McGraw and Meyers had a good relationship.

Before the 1913 World Series, Mack called Bender into his office and told him, "Albert, I'm counting on you to win this Series." Bender won two games against the Giants in the Series and in so doing became the first pitcher to win six World Series games.[28] After the Series Mack called Bender once again into his office and handed him a check for $2,500 to pay off what the pitcher owed on his mortgage. The bonus may have been Mack's way of repaying the salary cut in the 1913 season.[29]

The next year tension between Mack and Bender re-emerged. The A's manager told Bender to scout the Boston Braves, whom the A's would face in the 1914 World Series. Instead, Bender went on a fishing trip. When Mack confronted him, Bender's excuse was that the Braves were just a "bunch of bush leaguers."[30] The "Miracle" Braves," as they were known, proved him wrong, sweeping the A's four games to none in the Series.

During the 1930s, after his playing career had ended and he had overcome his drinking problems, Bender reconciled with Mack.[31] He was named a scout for the A's and continued in that role into the 1940s. In 1951 he served as the team's pitching coach.[32] Mack and Bender remained

friends for the rest of their lives. A clearly emotional Mack attended Bender's funeral in 1954.

Charles Albert Bender knew both Connie Mack and John McGraw, as a player and coach. He summarized their styles well, saying, "They were different types, but both were real leaders. Mr. Mack was the fatherly, soft-spoken type while Mugsy was the hard-boiled, swashbuckling hell-for-leather type."[33]

John McGraw also managed several Native Americans during his career, including Jim Thorpe. However, the best ballplayer among the Indians for whom McGraw was skipper was John Tortes Meyers of the Cahuilla tribe of Southern California. He was also known by the racist moniker "Chief." McGraw signed Meyers, who was playing for the St. Paul Apostles (later the Saints), for $6,000 in 1908, a substantial sum for the time. Connie Mack had tried to trade with the Apostles for Meyers but lost in the bidding war to McGraw.

The investment paid off as Meyers, a catcher, became a power hitter and trusted batterymate of the great Christy Mathewson from 1909 until Meyers left the Giants to join the Brooklyn Dodgers in 1916.

Early in his professional career, when playing for the Harrisburg, Pennsylvania, minor-league team, Meyers demonstrated that he was willing to challenge his manager, a man named Calhoun. Meyers was sent into a game to catch a pitcher who threw a spitball, a pitch Meyers had at the time never seen. He couldn't handle it and Calhoun pulled him. Instead of retiring meekly to the bench, Meyers confronted his manager and, in Meyers' own words, "balled [sic] him out like a veteran." Calhoun apologized and from that point on Meyers was accepted by his manager and teammates.[34] This was a story Meyers often told, because it illustrated in his mind that he was being harassed not only because he was a rookie, but because he was an Indian. A half-century later he told Lawrence Ritter, "I don't like to say this, but in those days, when I was young, I was considered a foreigner. I didn't belong. I was an Indian."[35]

Meyers' relationship with John McGraw was different. He was among the players who respected the Giants manager. The Cahuilla catcher credited McGraw with changing the way ballplayers were viewed and how they were paid. At a time when baseball players were considered ruffians and second-class citizens, forced to stay in inferior hotels, Meyers claimed, "Mr. McGraw was the one who changed all that. He was the one who paid the price, and even more than the price, to get his ball team into the best hotels. Now, the ballplayer is respected."[36]

According to Meyers, McGraw's insistence upon respect was not only for members of his own team, but for other players as well. On one occasion the Giants manager chewed out fans during a game played in Pittsburgh, shaming them for booing the Pirates shortstop Honus Wagner when he made a fielding error. Meyers said that McGraw "stood up in front of the stands, held up his hands and gave those babies a piece of his mind. McGraw was a commanding figure, you know, and when he got through telling 'em about Wagner they were cheering instead of booing."[37]

Meyers also admired McGraw as "a master of invective and irony." He couldn't stand a player telling him "I thought." According to Meyers, "Mr. McGraw didn't use cuss words. He could cut you down without them." Once when McGraw questioned Meyers' pitch selection, the catcher responded, "I thought ..." Before he could finish, McGraw said scornfully, "What with?"[38]

Meyers sometimes got the better of his manager in these feisty exchanges. On one occasion the Giants catcher noticed that a Dodgers pitcher with a great pickoff move to first base was tipping the throw. On the bench Meyers asked his manager if he could steal second base the next time he reached first. McGraw fumed, "Don't ever steal a base. That's not your job." Meyers said he could not resist taking advantage of the opportunity and stole second anyway. McGraw fined him $10, but then asked the slow-footed catcher how he was able to steal the base so easily. Meyers responded by asking if the fine would be dropped if he told him. McGraw agreed and Meyers explained how the pitcher was tipping the throw. "After that," Meyers remembered, "we ran the poor guy out of the league."[39]

What did John McGraw think of Meyers? In a 1912 article, when Meyers was at his peak, McGraw called him "a vicious hitter ... the greatest natural hitter in the game." He also described him as "one of the best catchers in the National League," "a quick thinker," "a team leader," and "all around a very valuable man."[40]

On another occasion, after Meyers had caught George Wiltse in a one-hitter against the Pirates, the Giants manager gave his catcher nearly as much credit as he did Wiltse, saying, "It was one of the greatest exhibitions of outguessing skilled batters that [I] ever saw." He went on to praise Meyers as a hitter, commenting, "[H]e is the only man that [I] ever saw who is more likely to hit that ball when a hit will bring in runs than he is when the bases are clear."[41]

All things considered, Meyers' relationship with McGraw was enigmatic. Like many other players and managers at the time, McGraw could act in a racist manner. He was the Baltimore Orioles' third baseman in 1897 when Louis Sockalexis, one of the first Native Americans to play in the major leagues, signed with Cleveland. The first time Sockalexis appeared in Baltimore, McGraw took the field before the game "wearing a war bonnet with feathers reaching down below the seat of his baggy pants" and chanted "war whoops." The crowd got the point. "Every time Sockalexis came to the plate, ear-splitting war whoops erupted in the stands. For the remaining games in the series many Baltimore fans wore feathered headdresses."[42]

In 1901 McGraw was still managing the Orioles. In a scheme to circumvent the "gentleman's agreement" that banned Blacks from playing major-league baseball, he signed Charlie Grant, an African American who played in the Negro leagues. McGraw gave Grant the moniker "Charlie Tokahoma," a play on "poke a homer," and passed him off as a "full-blooded Cherokee." The ploy was discovered by Chicago White Sox owner Charles Comiskey, who recognized Grant and put out the word that he was not an Indian, but a Negro "fixed up with war paint and a bunch of feathers." McGraw would not have objected to Comiskey's stereotypical description of Grant's garb, for he had used it himself in demeaning Sockalexis.[43] Meyers had to endure some of the fallout of the Grant incident. Because of his dark skin, Meyers often heard shouts of the "n-word" from the stands.[44]

Meyers's Native American teammate Jim Thorpe rebelled against McGraw's overt racism and abusive tactics while playing for the Giants. Once, after Thorpe missed one of McGraw's signs, the manager yelled at him, "You dumb Indian!" It took half the team to restrain Thorpe from physically attacking his manager.[45] On another occasion, after learning that Thorpe had visited a New York bar, McGraw said to him, "A young fellow like you shouldn't ever drink. Besides no Indian knows how to drink." A clearly irked Thorpe responded, "What about the Irish," to which

McGraw, sensitive about his heritage and his many barroom escapades, said, "Listen, don't get smart with me!" "I'm not," replied Thorpe. "It just happens I'm Irish too."[46]

Unfortunately, Meyers involved himself in an incident that showed McGraw's distrustful supervision of Thorpe. When Thorpe joined the Giants, McGraw instructed Meyers to open Thorpe's mail, even love letters from Thorpe's fiancée. When Thorpe found one of the intimate notes in Meyers' locker, he exploded and chased the catcher around the locker room. Thorpe couldn't catch him, and McGraw, who was observing the scene, chuckled and said, "Looks as though the wrong Indian competed in the Olympic games."[47]

In the final analysis, although certainly aware of McGraw's racist temperament and behavior, Meyers really believed that his manager looked for talent regardless of the player's ethnicity.[48] He also was convinced that in addition to imparting baseball knowledge and skills, McGraw cultivated in players willing to look beyond his bluster and bias "a professional attitude, maturity, and self-respect."[49] Although he was only seven years younger than his manager, John Tortes Meyers considered John McGraw a mentor from whom he learned not only baseball knowledge but valuable life lessons as well.

Meyers summed up his attitude toward his manager in his 1964 interview with Lawrence Ritter for *The Glory of Their Times*: "What a wonderful man he was. Honest and forthright and charitable in the deepest sense of the word. We always called him Mr. McGraw. Never John or Mac. Always Mr. McGraw."[50]

According to Meyers' grandnephew, the Cahuilla catcher's most precious possession was not the bat Babe Ruth gave him but rather a gold watch fob in the shape of a catcher's mitt with a diamond on the clasp and a pearl to represent a baseball. It was presented to him by John McGraw.[51]

ACKNOWLEDGMENT

An earlier version of this essay appeared in William A. Young, *John Tortes "Chief" Meyers: A Baseball Biography* (Jefferson, North Carolina: McFarland & Co., 2012).

Background information on Connie Mack is drawn from his SABR biography by Doug Skipper: https://sabr.org/bioproj/person/connie-mack/, on John McGraw from Don Jensen's BioProject biography: https://sabr.org/bioproj/person/john-mc-graw-2/. Baseball-reference.com was consulted for statistics.

NOTES

1   *New York Times*, February 9, 1956.

2   Norman Macht, *Connie Mack and the Early Years of Baseball* (Lincoln: University of Nebraska Press, 2007), 588.

3   Charles Alexander, *John McGraw* (Lincoln: University of Nebraska Press, 1995), 3-4.

4   *Los Angeles Times*, February 26, 1934, 10; cited in Richard Adler, *Mack, McGraw and the 1913 Baseball Season* (Jefferson, North Carolina: McFarland & Co., 2008), 39.

5   Tom Simon, ed. *Deadball Stars of the National League* (Washington: Brassey's, 2004), 39.

6   Frank DeFord, *The Old Ball Game: How John McGraw, Christy Mathewson, and the New York Giants Created Modern Baseball* (New York: Atlantic Monthly Press, 2005), 158.

7   Mike Vaccaro, *The First Fall Classic: The Red Sox, the Giants, and the Cast of Players, Pugs, and Politicos Who Reinvented the World Series in 1912* (New York: Doubleday, 2009), 114.

8   Norman Macht, *Connie Mack: The Turbulent & Triumphant Years 1915-1931* (Lincoln: University of Nebraska Press, 2012), 451.

9   Background information on Charles Albert Bender drawn from SABR BioProject article on Bender by Tom Swift. https://sabr.org/bioproj/person/charles-bender/.

10   Robert Peyton Wiggins, *Chief Bender: A Baseball Biography* (Jefferson, North Carolina: McFarland & Co., 2010), 6.

11   Jeffrey P. Beck, *The American Indian Integration of Baseball* (Lincoln: University of Nebraska Press, 2004), 74-75.

12   William C. Kashatus, *Money Pitcher: Chief Bender and the Tragedy of Indian Assimilation* (University Park: Pennsylvania State University, 2006), 59.

13   Tom Swift, SABR BioProject article.

14   Beck, 73.

15   Tom Swift, *Chief Bender's Burden: The Silent Struggle of a Baseball Star* (Lincoln: University of Nebraska Press, 2008), 252.

16   *Chief Bender's Burden*, 83.

17   Beck, 71.

18   *Chief Bender's Burden*, 251.

19   *Chief Bender's Burden*, 215.

20   John T. Meyers, "Meyers Lauds Jim Thorpe, Olympic Hero," *New York American*, May 25, 1913.

21   Beck, 70-71.

22   *Washington Post*, February 21, 1909; cited by Wiggins, *Chief Bender: A Baseball Biography*, 105, and Swift, *Chief Bender's Burden*, 46.

23   Kashatus, *Money Pitcher*, 95.

24   F.C. Lane, "Greatest by Manager in Organized Baseball," *Baseball Magazine*, May 1913, vol. X, no. 7; cited by Wiggins, *Chief Bender: A Baseball Biography*, 152.

25   Swift, *Chief Bender's Burden*, 222.

26   *Chief Bender's Burden*, 224.

27   *Chief Bender: A Baseball Biography*, 156.

28   *Chief Bender: A Baseball Biography*, 6; Swift, *Chief Bender's Burden*, 193.

29   Swift, *Chief Bender's Burden*, 208, 224; Kashatus, *Money Pitcher*, 102.

30   *Chief Bender: A Baseball Biography*, 175; Swift, *Chief Bender's Burden*, 209; Kashatus, *Money Pitcher*, 112.

31   *Money Pitcher*, 145-47.

32   *Chief Bender: A Baseball Biography*, 225.

33   Swift, *Chief Bender's Burden*, 194-95.

34   *St. Louis Globe-Democrat*, August 29, 1909.

35   Lawrence Ritter, "Chief Meyers," *The Glory of Their Times: The Story of the Early Days of Baseball Told by the Men Who Played It*, Enlarged Edition (New York: HarperCollins, 2002), 172.

36   *The Glory of Their Times*, 172.

37   Grantland Rice, "A Talk with Chief Meyers, February 4, 1947 (John Tortes Meyers File, National Baseball Hall of Fame, Cooperstown, New York).

38   Paul Zimmerman, "Sportscripts," *Los Angeles Times,* August 13, 1947, 10; Beck, *The American Indian Integration of Baseball*, 85-86.

39   Jim Dawson, "McGraw Rescinded Fine After Talk with Chief," *Riverside* (California) *Press-Enterprise*, June 25, 1969.

40   John McGraw, "Making a Pennant Winner," *Pearson's Magazine,* November 1912: 121.

41   Unidentified, unattributed, undated article, John Tortes Meyers file, National Baseball Hall of Fame, Cooperstown, New York.

42   Brian McDonald, *Indian Summer: The Forgotten Story of Louis Sockalexis – the First Native American in Major League Baseball* (Emmaus, Pennsylvania: Rodale Press, 2003), 131.

43   Kashatus, *Money Pitcher,* 58.

44   Beck, 81.

45   Kate Buford, *Native Son: The Life and Sporting Legend of Jim Thorpe* (New York: Alfred A. Knopf, 2010), 215.

46   Beck, 92-93.

47   Beck, 93.

48   Ritter, *The Glory of Their Times,* 174.

49   Alexander, *John McGraw,* 5.

50   Ritter, *The Glory of Their Times,* 174-75.

51   Colonel John V. Meyers, personal interview, September 22, 2008.

HOW WILLIAM "BIG CHIEF" WATKINS BEGAN HIS CAREER AS A JAPANESE: EARLY NATIVE AMERICAN AND JAPANESE BASEBALL INTERACTION

By Robert K. Fitts

Harry Saisho had a problem. He wanted to transform his Los Angeles-based Japanese baseball club from an amateur squad to a professional barnstorming team and he needed a pitcher.

In the first decade of the twentieth century, high-quality Japanese pitchers were rare in the US. In November 1908 Saisho and his team's president, Dr. Takejiro Ito, went to Oakland to recruit a pitcher. A long article in the *Reno Evening Gazette*, probably republished from a Bay Area newspaper, describes their elusive search:

For three years [Harry Saisho] has been developing a little squad of Nippon athletes until he has one of the fastest fielding teams in the southern part of the state. He has infielders that are above the ordinary, outfielders that are certain and a good catcher – but the pitcher is lacking. That is the weakness in the Japanese ball team that Saisho must overcome. He has brought pitchers from every town along the coast south of Vancouver and they have failed to develop a pitching arm. ...

Dr. Ito and Captain Saisho are in Oakland looking for a pitcher. ... When you ask Ito what is the matter with having a Japanese pitcher, he throws up his hands, bites his under-lip suggestively and ... gives an explanation of his native countrymen. "Japanese are not built for pitching. ... They haven't a throwing arm. One reason is that the arm is too short, another is that the shoulder is too close set against the body. Our people are the greatest contortionists in the world but they can't stand the strain of pitching for their shoulders always give out. The players can't curve the balls either like you Americans. I thought at first it was the height, but I have seen the boys play against white pitchers smaller than our own and he would beat us. We are simply not people adapted to play ball and I can't remedy the defect.

Furthermore, he never expects to develop a pitcher among his people. It is a hopeless task that he has been disappointed so many times that he will not attempt again. The team, which is known as the Nanka Japanese for Southern California will tour the state next spring and will appear in Oakland probably with an Indian pitcher in the box out of respect for a harmony of the complexion of the player.[1]

It was not unusual for Issei (first-generation Japanese immigrants) teams to recruit Native American players and have them pretend to be Japanese.[2] This chapter will examine early baseball interaction between Native Americans and Issei in greater Los Angeles and then focus on William "Big Chief" Watkins, who began his professional career as the ace of the Japanese Base Ball Association.

Between 1901 and 1908 over 100,000 Japanese entered the United States. Baseball had been introduced to Japan in 1872 and by 1900 was played at most of the high schools and colleges across the nation. Many Japanese immigrants had learned the game in their native land and some formed amateur baseball teams soon after arriving in the United

William "Naga" Watkins on the Japanese Base Ball Association, 1911.

States. The first known team was the Fuji Athletic Club, founded in San Francisco about 1903. The Kanagawa Doshi Club of San Francisco and a loosely organized club from the *Rafu Shimpo* newspaper in Los Angeles were formed the following year.

In 1905 the Waseda University baseball team from Tokyo visited the West Coast, playing 26 games against American college, high-school, amateur, and professional teams. It was the first time a foreign team came to the United States to challenge Americans at their national pastime. The games attracted thousands of spectators and were covered in nearly all of the West Coast newspapers.

On May 20 Waseda met a squad from the Sherman Institute of Riverside, California. The game was closely covered by the local and national press as, according to *Sporting Life,* it "marked an epoch in the history of our national game … [as] the first time a base ball game was played by teams whose players were from two races that have adopted a sport heretofore distinctively that of the white man."[3]

Founded and operated by the United States government in 1892, the Sherman Institute was the first "off-reservation" boarding school for Native Americans in California. It educated children from 5 to 20 years old with the explicit goal of assimilating them into White American society. Like many government-sponsored Native American schools, the Sherman Institute encouraged the boys to play football and baseball to help instill "American values." The school soon became known for its outstanding football squad and would produce a number of professionals, but its baseball team was weak. To bolster the lineup against Waseda, the school recruited local Native American John Tortes Meyers. The son of German-American former Union Army officer and saloon owner John Mayer and Felicite Tortes of the Cahuilla tribe, Meyers would be raised by his mother, partly on the Santa Rosa reservation and partly in Riverside, before becoming a local semipro star and eventually the star catcher known as Chief Meyers for John McGraw's New York Giants.

The game began at 3:00 and "the largest crowd of the [season's] series gathered at Fiesta Park ... and cheered loud and long."[4] The Institute team took the field in dark trousers, high white socks, and white jerseys. The visiting Japanese wore buff uniforms with maroon socks. Waseda scored a quick run in the first on an error by the Sherman shortstop Padillo and added three more in both the fourth and sixth innings. Meanwhile, Waseda starter Atsushi Kono shut out the opposition for five innings. "The teams formed a curious contrast," the *Los Angeles Times* noted. "The Red Men, burly and muscular, seemed to tear through their game. The Brown men, lithe and wiry, slipped around them and out-played them."[5]

In the bottom of the sixth, down 7-0, the Institute fought back, scoring six as Meyers "tried to remove the cover from the ball by knocking it to the score board."[6] But Waseda's slick fielding held the Native Americans. "The little warriors from Waseda dashed around the field, taking down the long drives of the red man with ease and grace that was surprising."[7] The Japanese padded their lead to win, 12-7. All the newspapers agreed that it was a sensational game "replete with lively hitting, speedy base-running and good and bad fielding."[8]

With the novelty of opponents from different races, the newspapermen could not resist racial stereotypes, allusions, and metaphors in their game descriptions. "Jap Team Scalps Sherman Braves," "Wiry Japs Wallop Reds," and "Japs Stop a Break from Reservation," declared the next morning's headlines.[9] Not surprisingly the articles were replete with references to scalping, reservations, and the Russo-Japanese war. Typical was the *Los Angeles Herald*'s lede: "determined to win against a team which they considered in every way equal in strength to a company of Russian soldiers, nine little Japs from Waseda college across the sea took into camp the scalps of nine of the hardiest braves from the Sherman reservation school of Riverside yesterday afternoon and sent the big bucks crashing back to defeat with a one-sided score of 12 to 7."[10]

Accompanying an article loaded with racial stereotypes and demeaning terminology, the *Los Angeles Examiner* published a large montage covering the top of the sports section under the headline "Orientals Win Ball Game From the Aborigines."[11] The centerpiece is a drawing of a Native American and a Japanese man in traditional clothing each holding a baseball bat (Figure 1). On either side of this centerpiece are the photographs of three players from the respective teams.

The game initiated a long relationship between Japanese ballplayers and the Sherman Institute. Harry Saisho recruited Native American players from the Institute to fill out his teams and in 1921 he organized and financed a tour of Japan for a Native American ballclub called the Sherman Indians, which contained a number of Sherman graduates. The team arrived in Yokohama on September 29 and spent the month of October playing eight games in Osaka and Tokyo. The squad did not do well on the diamond, winning only two games. Plagued by poor weather as well as a lack of talent, the tour lost money, bankrupting Saisho. The Native American players, however, returned home happy, having enjoyed their expenses-paid trip to Japan.[12]

Intrigued by the press coverage of the Waseda games and the large attendance, Guy Green, the owner of the famed Nebraska Indians Baseball Team, decided to create an all-Japanese baseball club to barnstorm across the Midwest. It would be the first Japanese professional team on either side of the Pacific, as pro ball would not come to Japan until the 1920s.

Although Green would claim that he had "scour[ed] the [Japanese] empire for the best players obtainable," he did nothing of the sort.[13] In early 1906 Green instructed Dan Tobey, the Caucasian captain of the Nebraska Indians, to form a team from Japanese immigrants living in California. The players congregated in Lincoln, Nebraska, in early April to practice with Tobey and assistant coach Sandy Kissell, a Native American who had played on Green's Nebraska Indians.[14]

After a few days, the Nebraska Indians joined the Japanese at the practice field. Although the Japanese recruits knew the Indians' reputation as top semipros, their skill surprised them. They were particularly impressed with the shortstop Juzicanea, a Yaqui from Arizona whom Guy Green described in *Fun and Frolic with an Indian Ball Team* as "the meanest looking Indian I have ever seen."[15] According to Green, Juzicanea "wore his hair long, surveyed everything suspiciously with piercing black eyes, and when he came down the street people moved to the edge of the sidewalk and apprehensively watched him pass."[16] "Although he was small like us," a Japanese player wrote, he could throw the ball "like an arrow" so hard that the receiver sometimes dropped the ball from the sting of the impact. "Knowing that a small man could play that well, gave us a motive to practice harder. In poor English, we told the Indians' captain that we were newcomers and inexperienced, and our skin color is very similar, so please teach us."[17]

It soon became evident that not all of the Japanese were skilled enough to play on a professional independent squad, so Green and Tobey decided to bolster the roster with Native Americans – hoping that most spectators would not be able to tell the difference. Dan Tobey stayed with the team as a player-coach and shared pitching duties with Sandy Kissell. Seguin, occasionally called Sego in box scores, would catch most of the games. Both Kissell and Seguin would play on Green's Nebraska Indians in 1907. Two other men, known only by their nicknames Doctor (first and third base), and Noisy (first base, third base, and catcher), joined the squad.[18]

In mid-April Green's Japanese Base Ball Team embarked on a 24-week tour that covered over 2,500 miles through nine Midwestern states. From April 15 to October 10, the team played about 170 games against town teams and independent clubs. Although the team did well, winning 122 of the 142 games with known results, Green disbanded the club at the end of the season.[19]

Green's Japanese players returned to the West Coast and formed their own amateur and professional barnstorming teams. Harry Saisho began by organizing the amateur Nanbu Karifournia (Southern California) Base Ball Club, known as Nanka. For several years the team played other amateur clubs in the Los Angeles area but Saisho longed to turn the squad into a professional barnstorming team. Despite not being able to find a strong Japanese pitcher in Oakland in the fall of 1908, the following spring he renamed his squad the Japanese Base Ball Association (JBBA) and readied to barnstorm across the country. They began with three games in Los Angeles. But after consecutive one-sided loses to the African American L.A. Giants, L.A. High

School, and a Riverside semipro nine, Saisho realized that the team was not ready and canceled the planned tour.[20]

In 1911 the JBBA was ready to try again. The team spent April and early May honing its skills with weekly games in the Los Angeles area. Still lacking a quality Japanese pitcher, Saisho recruited Louis Lockhart, a Native American who had attended the Sherman Institute, along with two other non-Japanese. Fans, however, became suspicious during the May 10 game against the University of Southern California when the three "appeared strangely bewildered when the manager forgot and gave them some instructions in the Japanese language. In order to quiet the suspicions of the onlookers one of these players addressed the umpire with a string of gibberish that had a strong Spanish accent."[21]

On May 11, 1911, the JBBA headed east to begin a 25-week tour across seven states during which they would play 128 games. After starting the first few games, Lockhart left the squad and Saisho turned the mound over to Lockhart's Sherman Institute teammate, 21-year-old William Watkins. A Shoshone Indian, born in Round Mountain, Nevada, on March 16, 1886, Watkins enrolled at the Sherman Institute on November 4, 1909.[22] The next spring, he was elected captain of the school's baseball team. He grew into a powerful young man for his time, standing 5-feet-10½-inches and weighing over 160 pounds.[23] Saisho gave Watkins the stage name Naga and attempted to pass him off as Japanese, but with his size and distinctive Native American features, few were fooled.

The JBBA was not a strong team. Playing mostly town nines and a few independent clubs, they won just 25 of the 87 games for which results are known. Although reporters often singled out Watkins, who played third base when he was not pitching, as the team's top player, he was not dominating on the mound. Few box scores survive from the JBBA tour, but the existing statistics and newspaper articles show that he won just four of his 21 known starts and surrendered 5.86 runs per game. He did, however, strike out an average of 7.69 batters per game.[24]

Pitching nearly every other day, Watkins matured as a pitcher during that summer. On July 10 the *Quincy* (Illinois) *Daily Herald* noted that he "was a real twirler. He had steam and he had control. His curves broke nicely and in a way that was bewildering."[25] By the end of the tour, he threw some gems, including a 1-0 shutout with 11 strikeouts in Centerville, Iowa.[26]

In his last start, Watkins faced the St. Louis Giants, one of the top African American clubs in the Midwest. Their lineup included future Hall of Famer Ben Taylor, his brothers Steel Arm Johnny and Candy Jim Taylor, captain Dick Wallace, and Tullie McAdoo. A tremendous crowd came out to Athletic Park, expecting the locals to demolish the visiting Japanese, but to everyone's surprise Naga baffled the Giants. The two teams were locked, 2-2, after nine innings before the Giants squeaked out a 3-2 victory in the 11th.

The outing may have changed Watkins' life as it drew the attention of St. Louis Cardinals manager Roger Bresnahan.[27]

Bresnahan signed Watkins to a professional contract and tested him against major leaguers in the annual post-season matchup between the Cardinals and the crosstown rival Browns. The Cardinals were already down 4-1 when Watkins came on in the fifth inning with no outs and runners on first and second. Pitching against the toughest hitters he had ever faced, Watkins set down the side, although the Browns did push a run across. Bresnahan decided to keep the young pitcher in for the remainder of the game but Watkins could not contain the Browns, who scored another in the sixth, three in the seventh, and one in the eighth. At day's end, Watkins had surrendered five runs on six hits with a walk and a hit batsman in four innings.[28]

Although his hometown newspaper, the *Riverside Daily Press*, proclaimed on December 30, 1911, that "Watkins will have no trouble in the big league. ... [H]e is looked upon as a second Bender and every fan in the country knows what that means," Bresnahan decided that Watkins needed more seasoning and sent him to the Erie Sailors in the Class-B Central League for the 1912 season.[29]

The Sailors had finished in third place in the Ohio-Pennsylvania League in 1911 and had just joined the Central League. Nonetheless, the town had high hopes for their team, and they yearned for their new phenom to appear. "Watkins ... is a descendant of the same tribe as Chief Bender," the *Erie Daily Times* incorrectly reported. He "is a young and powerful specimen of the aborigine race. ... Bresnahan wired him to start immediately for Erie and it is expected that he will put in an appearance in about five days."[30]

Watkins arrived on May 7 with a new name and a refined spitball.[31] He was now known as Chief Watkins or Big Chief Watkins. "The Chief is husky," gushed the *Erie Daily Times*. "He is an imposing specimen of the American Indian. He is about five feet, eleven inches tall with massive shoulders and athletic physique. He ... [is] said to have everything that is needed for a first class pitcher."[32] Over the next week, the newspaper reported on when the fans would get to watch their new hero.

Watkins finally debuted on May 16 against the Youngstown Steelmen but the fans were disappointed. The Chief was hit hard, giving up 10 hits including two home runs and two doubles, as the Steelmen won 7-1. Catcher Bobby Schang had trouble handling Watkins' spitter, which took "a quick, deceptive break right at the plate and are hard to judge."[33] The local newspaper was forgiving. "While the Chief was batted hard in his debut on the mound, it was not entirely his fault. ... We might say right now that the Chief looks like a real pitcher and we predict that he will stand more than a few of the batters in this league on their heads before the curtain is rung down. But you can't win a ball game without some runs to win as much as the red man's supporting cast was way below its high pinnacle of

William "Big Chief" Watkins on the Nebraska Indians, circa 1915.

perfection. ... The crew had four slipups which may be connected with the run getting and were over-zealous in their base running."[34]

Four days later Watkins was given a second chance as he came on in relief in the second inning and "pitched superb ball," shutting out the Wheeling Stogies for the remainder of the game.[35] The *Daily Times* predicted that "he will be one of the pitching stars in ... [the] circuit this season."[36] But it was not to be. Watkins remained erratic, alternating meltdowns with brilliant outings. The *Fort Wayne Weekly Sentinel* noted, "[H]is worst fault was lack of control, but when he got 'em over he was hard to beat."[37] At those times he dominated – striking out eight and throwing six no-hit innings in a 4-2 win over Dayton on June 14 and a three-hit shutout over Terre Haute on June 24. But on his wild days, opponents feasted – Watkins surrendered eight runs off nine hits and three walks against the Grand Rapids Black Sox on June 26. After a disastrous start against Akron on July 11, when he was knocked out in the third inning after already surrendering four hits, two walks, and a wild pitch, Erie released Watkins.[38]

Watkins returned to the West Coast and played for a few weeks with the Vancouver Beavers of the Northwest League before finishing the season with the semipro Richmond Clothiers in San Francisco.[39]

The Big Chief spent the next two years bouncing around the minor leagues. During the winter of 1912-13, he received a contract from the Fort Wayne Champs of the Central League but did not report until May 7. As a result, the Champs required him to train at his own expense until he could "demonstrate that he is ready to work."[40] They also withheld his pay until he officially made the squad.[41] Watkins debuted in relief on May 16 against the Springfield Reapers. "All Hail the Chief!" exclaimed a subheadline in the *Fort Wayne Journal Gazette* as Watkins gave up just two hits in five shutout innings.[42] The next game did not go as well as Watkins suffered one of his meltdowns. The Champs already trailed Springfield 2-0 when he came on in relief in the first inning on May 22. "Watkins' downfall came in the second when the visitors started bunting on him. He had his trouble holding his feet while racing about on the muddy infield and the first thing he knew he was forced into a deep dark hole."[43] Despite giving up three runs in the inning, manager Jimmy Burke left Watkins on the mound for the next seven innings and "it was awful."[44] By the end of the game, Watkins had allowed 20 hits and 4 walks, and threw four wild pitches in the 18-7 loss.

The next morning, the Champs cut Watkins and sent him to the Steubenville Stubs of the Interstate League. "He has never shown anything here that would justify keeping him, and is of no value to the pitching staff," concluded the *Fort Wayne Sentinel*.[45] Watkins' stay with Steubenville was short-lived as the franchise disbanded in mid-July and he was transferred to the Battle Creek Crickets of the Southern Michigan Association.[46] He began well in Class-D ball, winning his first start with a four-hitter against Jackson on July 21 and shutting out Jackson on five hits four days later.[47] But as the season continued, opponents began to rack up the hits. Nonetheless, Watkins persevered and maintained a spot in the rotation until season's end.[48]

Watkins spent the winter in Detroit, working in a post office, before signing with the Jackson Chiefs of the Southern Michigan Association on March 2, 1914.[49] His stint with Jackson did not last long as he was trying out for the Toledo Mud Hens of the same league by May 19.[50] Watkins did not make the squad and may have injured his arm in the process.[51]

By late July, Watkins found his home with the Nebraska Indians.[52] Founded in 1897, the Native American squad was one of the top barnstorming teams in the nation prior to World War I. Capitalizing on the American public's fascination with Native Americans and the rapidly disappearing Wild West, the Nebraska Indians would entertain spectators with ball tricks, gags, and stereotyped "Indian" behavior like war whoops. Green gave players "Indian names" and created stories about them. Often these tales were filled with gross exaggerations based on ethnic stereotypes. Naomas, an ancient outfielder, could regenerate limbs after injury, and Juzicanea slept on the ground and ate only raw meat.[53] When they arrived in town, captain Dan Tobey would dress as a clown and lead the players in buckskin and headdresses through the town streets in a parade to the ballpark. At

night they would pitch tepees and camp on the ballfields, living "in true savage style." Spectators loved the act, and the Indians became one of the most popular squads on the barnstorming circuit.[54]

But the squad was not just a circus show. The team contained some of the best Native American players in the country. Each season the Indians would travel throughout the US, playing about 150 games against town teams and other independent clubs. From 1897 until 1914, the team put up a record of 1237 wins, 336 losses, and 11 ties.[55]

In 1912 Green sold the team to James E. Beltzer. Beltzer attempted to make the team even more "Indian." His players went by stereotypical names, such as White Bull, Little Deer, and Sweetgrass. He adopted uniforms that looked like buckskin with fringe, and players would often wear full-feathered headdresses. Watkins, playing under the name Big Chief, became one of the team's top pitchers. He finished the 1914 season with the club and then, after an unsuccessful tryout with the Muscatine (Iowa) Muskies of the Central Association the following April, rejoined the Indians in May 1915. According to the *Muscatine Journal*, that season he started 37 games, winning 28. The records of the Indians after 1914 are not available, but newspaper advertisements and articles feature "Big Chief" as one of the club's marquee players. Watkins continued pitching for the Indians until the team disbanded in 1918.[56]

By 1920, Watkins had married Louise Galloy (1898-1971) and moved to Chicago.[57] The couple had two children: William L. (born 1921) and Charles (born 1924).[58] William L. served as a pilot in World War II and was killed in a plane crash off the island of Kwajalein in the Pacific Ocean on September 26, 1950.[59] Charles died in 2009 with no known offspring.

While in Chicago, Watkins worked as a machinist for the Acme Steel Company.[60] He continued to pitch for semipro clubs into the mid-1930s and, according to his obituary, barnstormed with Jim Thorpe (although the date and team of this tour is not yet identified).[61] William Watkins died on November 8, 1966.

NOTES

1   "Little Brown Men Cannot Put Twist on a Baseball and Abandon Great Game," *Reno Evening Gazette*, October 27, 1908: 6.

2   Besides the examples discussed in the chapter, William "Chief Chouneau" Cadreau pitched for the Seattle Nippon against Keio University on April 9, 1914. "Redskin Is a Good Jap," *Seattle Star*, April 10, 1914: 21.

3   R.S. Ranson, "A New Departure. An Epoch-Making Game of Base Ball," *Sporting Life*, June 10, 1905: 19.

4   "Orientals Win Ball Game from the Aborigines," *Los Angeles Examiner*, May 21, 1905: 41.

5   "Wiry Japs Wallop Reds," *Los Angeles Times*, May 21, 1905: III 1.

6   "Jap Team Scalps Sherman Braves," *Los Angeles Herald*, May 21, 1905: 6.

7   "Jap Team Scalps Sherman Braves."

8   "Orientals Win Ball Game from the Aborigines."

9   "Jap Team Scalps Sherman Braves"; "Wiry Japs Wallop Reds"; "Orientals Win Ball Game from the Aborigines."

10   "Jap Team Scalps Sherman Braves."

11   "Orientals Win Ball Game from the Aborigines."

12   Yoichi Nagata, Robert K. Fitts, and Mark Brunke, "The 1921 Native American Tours of Japan," in Robert K. Fitts, Bill Nowlin, and James Forr, eds., *Nichibei Yakyu: US Tours of Japan, Volume I: 1907-1958* (Phoenix: Society for American Baseball Research, 2022), 87-101.

13   "The Japanese Ball Players," *Covington* (Indiana) *Friend*, June 22, 1906: 4.

14   Robert K. Fitts, *Issei Baseball* (Lincoln: University of Nebraska Press, 2020), 83-85.

15   Guy W. Green (Jeffery P. Beck, ed.), *The Nebraska Indians and Fun and Frolic with an Indian Ball Team* (Jefferson, North Carolina: McFarland, 2010), 117-18.

16   Green, 117-18.

17   Masaru Akahori, *Nanka Nihonjin Yakyushi* [History *of Japanese Baseball in Southern California*] (Los Angeles: Town Crier, 1956), 17-21.

18   Fitts, 88-89.

19   Fitts, 109.

20   Fitts, 130-145.

21   "Japanese Baseball Star Proves to Be an Indian," *Los Angeles Times*, May 11, 1911: Sec. 3, 1.

22   "Death Notices and Funeral Arrangements," *South End* (Chicago) *Reporter*, November 16, 1966: 34; *Sherman Institute Registration Ledger (Number 7)*, Sherman Indian Museum Collection, Calisphere.org, 54, https://calisphere.org/item/ark:/86086/n20c4x81/.

23   "W.W. Watkins," *The Sporting News Baseball Players Contract Cards Collection*, LA84 Foundation, https://digital.la84.org/digital/collection/p17103coll3/id/175985/rec/7.

24   "Maroons Annex Opening Game of Season," *Las Vegas* (New Mexico) *Daily Optic*, May 17, 1911: 3; "Honorable Trinidads Bingo Honorable Cork Center Very Much Japanese Boys No Can Hit Same," *Trinidad* (Colorado) *Chronicle-News*, May 22, 1911: 1-2; "Japanese Will Never Beat Yankees at Ball," *Hutchinson* (Kansas) *Daily Gazette*, May 25, 1911: 3; "Japs Won Out," *Strong City* (Kansas) *News Current*, June 1, 1911: 8; "Greenfield Humbles Japan," *Greenfield* (Illinois) *Argus*, June 9, 1911: 7; "Base Ball at Pavilion Park," *Henry* (Illinois) *Times*, June 22, 1911: 1; "Base Ball News," *Cuba* (Illinois) *Journal*, June 29, 1911: 1; "Potters Gain Victory in Ninth," *Macomb* (Illinois) *Daily Journal*, July 3, 1911: 8; "The Japs Lost Out," *Quincy* (Illinois) *Daily Herald*, July 10, 1911: 5; "Company L Whips Jap Team 4 to 1," *Keokuk* (Iowa) *Daily Gate*, July 14, 1911: 6; "Japanese Trim Locals Sunday," *Fort Madison* (Iowa) *Evening Democrat*, July 17, 1911: 7; "Home Team Victorious," *Fairfield* (Iowa) *Weekly Journal*, July 19, 1911: 4; "[Illegible] Ball Team Versus Locals," *Washington* (Iowa) *Evening Journal*, July 22, 1911: 3; "Marion Win Game from Japs," *Cedar Rapids* (Iowa) *Evening Gazette*, July 28, 1911: 9; "Oelwein Won Over the Japs Sunday," *Oelwein* (Iowa) *Daily Register*, July 31, 1911: 4; "Base Ball Results," *Boone* (Iowa) *News Republican*, August 7, 1911: 5; "Suzuki Scores and Japs Win," *Centerville* (Iowa) *Daily Citizen*, August 19, 1911: 4; "Nipponese Are Given Trimming," *Council Bluffs* (Iowa) *Daily Nonpareil*, August 27, 1911: 6; "Semi-Pros and Amateurs," *Des Moines Register*, August 29, 1911: 9; "Japs Defeated by All Stars," *Des Moines Daily News*, September 4, 1911: 8; "Giants Meet Japs Today," *St. Louis Star and Times*, September 27, 1911: 6.

25   "The Japs Lost Out."

26   "Suzuki Scores and Japs Win."

27   "Giants Meet Japs Today."

28   "George Pitches in Clever Style Against Cards," *St. Louis Post-Dispatch*, October 15, 1911: 37.

29   "Sherman vs. Nine Stars," *Riverside* (California) *Daily Press*, December 30, 1911: 3; "Rain Prevented Crew from Playing Third Game with Akron Yesterday; Another Pitcher from Cardinals," *Erie Daily Times*, April 30, 1912: 20.

30   "Rain Prevented Crew from Playing Third Game with Akron Yesterday; Another Pitcher from Cardinals."

31   "Chief Watkins," *Erie Daily Times*, May 8, 1912: 12.

32   "Chief Watkins Arrived Today," *Erie Daily Times*, May 7, 1912: 6.

33   "Sport Notes," *Erie Daily Times*, May 16, 1912: 15.

34   "Youngstown Runs Off with First Game," *Erie Daily Times*, May 16, 1912: 15.

35   "Sailors Win Third of Series in Game Featured by Brilliant Fielding and Schang's Throwing," *Erie Daily Times*, May 21, 1912: 11.

36   "Sport Notes," *Erie Daily Times*, May 21, 1912: 12.

37   "Fort Wayne's Indian," *Fort Wayne Weekly Sentinel*, May 8, 1913: Sports 1.

38   "Champs Take Last Game from Sailors Very Easily," *Akron Beacon Journal*, July 12, 1912: 16.

39   "Spokane Put Indian Sign on Former Teammate," *Vancouver World*, July 25, 1912: 12; "Spokane Takes Last Two Baseball Games," *Vancouver World*, July 29, 1912: 15; Lou Schroeder, "Independent Games," *San Francisco Examiner*, August 25, 1912: 93.

40   "Burke Ready to Take His Place," *Fort Wayne Sentinel*, May 9, 1913: 5.

41   "Burke Ready to Take His Place."

42   "Bilikeners Suffer First Shut-Out of Season; Atkins Yanked in Favor of Chief Watkins, Who Goes Great," *Fort Wayne Journal Gazette*, May 17, 1913: 6.

43   "Springfield Crowd Does Murder and Downs Biliken Gang, 18-7: Chief Watkins Is Handed a Fierce Drubbing," *Fort Wayne Journal Gazette*, May 23, 1913: 14.

44   "Springfield Crowd Does Murder and Downs Biliken Gang, 18-7: Chief Watkins Is Handed a Fierce Drubbing."

45   Watkins to Get Another Chance, *Fort Wayne Sentinel*, May 23, 1913: 15.

46   "Interstate Men Are Getting Busy," *New Castle* (Pennsylvania) *News*, July 19, 1913: 9.

47   "Indian Pitcher Beats Vets," *Flint* (Michigan) *Journal*, July 21, 1913: 10; "The Figures," *Jackson* (Michigan) *Citizens Press*, July 25, 1913: 13.

48   "Senators Cannot Stop Crickets," *Kalamazoo Gazette*, July 30, 1913: 6; "Beavers Take Series From Battle Creek," *Kalamazoo Gazette*, August 6, 1913: 6; "Ducks Are Defeated by Crickets, 9 to 2," *Kalamazoo Gazette*, August 7, 1913: 6; "Vallandingham Holds Crickets to Three Hits," *Flint Daily Journal*, August 20, 1913: 10; "Double Header in Foodtown Divided," *Kalamazoo Gazette*, August 24, 1913: 10; "Errors Give Game to Battle Creek," *Kalamazoo Gazette*, August 27, 1913: 6; "Kazool Take Third Game From Adrian/Final Contest of the Year With Tots Sees Good Baseball," *Kalamazoo Gazette*, August 29, 1913: 6; "Sandlotters Are Again the Heroes," *Kalamazoo Gazette*, September 7, 1913: 7.

49   Associated Press, "Jackson Club Signs Watkins," *Bay City* (Michigan) *Daily Tribune*, March 3, 1914: 6.

50   "Myersmen Return Wednesday for Five Games at Keeley Park/Toledo and Flint Come for Series," *Jackson* (Michigan) *Citizen Patriot*, May 19, 1914: 7.

51   "Strong Team to Oppose Indians Next Sunday," *Montgomery* (Alabama) *Advertiser*, July 31, 1914: 9.

52   "Strong Team to Oppose Indians Next Sunday."

53   Green, 105-09, 117-18.

54   Jeffrey P. Beck, "Introduction," in Green, xviii.

55   Beck, xvii.

56   Beck, xxxvii-xliii.

57   1920 United States Federal Census, Enumeration District 604, Chicago Ward 9, Cook County, Illinois, Roll: T625_312: 1B.

58   1930 United States Federal Census, Enumeration District: 388, Chicago Ward 9, Cook County, Illinois, FHL Microfilm: 2340165: 6B.

59   "Local Nay Pilot Dies in Crash Off Kwajalein," *Suburbanite Economist* (Chicago), September 27, 1950: 1.

60   "William Watkins," U.S. World War II Draft Registration Cards, 1942, Ancestry.com.

61   "Heights Hammers Harvey to Sleep," *Chicago Heights Star*, August 24, 1922: 1; "Durand 11, Chalmers-Hamilton 2," *Chicago Heights Star*, May 31, 1923: 10; "Notes from the Diamond," *Chicago Star Publications*, August 2, 1923: 2; "H.P. Elks Defeat Evanston Giants," *Highland Park Press*, July 15, 1926: 7; "Baseball Extra!" *Riverdale* (Illinois) *Pointer*, June 18, 1926: 5; "St. Cyril Blank Colts in Final Game of Season," *Blue Island* (Illinois) *Sun Standard*, October 4, 1935: 6: "Death Notices and Funeral Arrangements."

INDIGENOUS BASEBALL IN THE NORTHEASTERN BORDERLANDS: FROM LOU SOCKALEXIS TO CHARLIE PAUL

By Colin Howell

In the late nineteenth and early twentieth centuries, baseball was a common pursuit among Indigenous peoples in the Northeastern borderlands. In Maine, competitive native clubs organized at Sipayik (Pleasant Point Reservation), near Old Town, at the Peter Dana Point Reservation and Indian Township, and elsewhere along the Penobscot River among Penobscot peoples. All-Maine Indian baseball championships date from the late nineteenth century. A regional cross-border championship including Maliseet clubs from New Brunswick became a fixture of the interwar years.[1] The Maliseets, who occupied territory on both sides of the border around Houlton, Maine, and in New Brunswick at Woodstock, Richibucto, and Tobique, fashioned a solid baseball reputation. The Richibucto Braves, for example, were regional champions on more than one occasion between the wars.[2] Farther east, the Mi'kmaq peoples in Nova Scotia and Prince Edward Island actively involved themselves in the game and occasionally played other Indigenous teams in New Brunswick, Quebec, and Maine.[3]

At a time when movement across the Canadian-American border was uncomplicated, Indigenous teams competed against semipro teams and town teams on both sides of the line. Traveling by large motorboat up the coast into New Brunswick, for example, the Dana Point Nine Red Aces were frequent participants in matches against Grand Manan Island during Canada's Dominion Day celebrations.[4] Even before the First World War, members of the Dana, Mitchell, Francis, Neptune, Sockalexis, Sabbatus, Ranco, Paul, and Sacobasin families were well known in semipro baseball in the Northeast, following in the shadow of the legendary Louis Sockalexis from Indian Island, Maine, who had a brief career with Cleveland of the National League.

One of the most iconic Indigenous athletes of the first half of the twentieth century – along with multisport star Jim Thorpe and Canadian long-distance runner Tom Longboat – Lou Sockalexis was part of a celebrity triumvirate of First Nations athletes in the years before World War I. A hard-hitting outfielder, known for speed in the outfield and on the bases and a powerful arm that could throw 350 feet on a line to home plate, he played college ball at Ricker College in Bangor before attending Holy Cross. Sockalexis had a brief major-league career with Cleveland, hitting .313 over three seasons.

For a dozen years after retiring from major-league baseball, Sockalexis continued to play semipro ball in Maine and New Brunswick. In 1911 he retired as an active player and joined the independent New Brunswick-Maine league's umpiring contingent. He continued to officiate through the 1913 season, when the league affiliated with Organized Baseball. Later that same year, Sockalexis suffered a fatal heart attack while working in a lumber camp near Old Town. He was 42 years old.

Although Sockalexis was the only Indigenous player from the borderlands to fashion a big-league career, there were others who went on to play in the minor leagues and on independent semipro teams in the Northeast. One of those was Joe Neptune, a nephew of the big leaguer from

(Photograph from Baltimore Sun, June 5, 1923)

A nephew of Lou Sockalexis, Joe Neptune played minor-league and semipro baseball for over three decades in the northeastern borderlands.

the same Indian Island community. In his teens Neptune attended the Carlisle Indian School in Pennsylvania and played with amateur teams throughout New England, including the highly regarded Lynn Amateur Athletic club. In 1907 he began his career in Organized Baseball with Lewiston of the Class-D Maine State League, playing alongside team captain Bill "Rough" Carrigan. Only 15, he was considered a "coming rival of Sockalexis," who also played in the league that year. Of their first encounter, the *Lewiston* (Maine) *Daily Sun* reported that "Big Chief Neptune swung hard, sending the ball out into right field where it was eaten up by Sockalexis."[5]

Despite his early entry into Organized Baseball, Neptune spent the next six years playing on semipro clubs in Maine, New Brunswick, and as far away as Glace Bay, Nova Scotia. He occasionally turned down opportunities to play for teams in the New England and Eastern Leagues since borderland teams in mill towns and fishing and mining communities often offered salaries that exceeded those in the minor leagues. Two other native performers – pitchers Sam Sacobasin and Henry "Chief" Mitchell – were also sought after by a number of clubs along the border. When a newly formed New Brunswick-Maine League, flooded with former and future big-leaguers, opened play in 1911, Neptune, Sacobasin, and Mitchell joined the border towns of Woodstock, St. Stephen, and Calais-St. Croix. The *Bangor Daily News* dubbed Mitchell a "real find" for the Calais club.[6]

Charlie Paul was one of the finest indigenous ballplayers in Canada during the 1920s.

(*Courtesy of the Nova Scotia Sport Hall of Fame*)

Although there were close connections between Indigenous baseball in Maine and New Brunswick, Mi'kmaq communities in Nova Scotia and Prince Edward Island had taken to the game as well.[7] As early as August 1877, the *Acadian Recorder* reported that a Mi'kmaw baseball team played a "white" team in Halifax.[8] Over the next quarter-century, baseball appeared on Nova Scotian reserves at Bear River, Eskasoni, Chapel Island, Barra Head, Shubenacadie (Indian Brook), Milbrook, Big Cove, and Lennox Island in Prince Edward Island.

Although baseball became the sport of choice, it existed alongside other bat-and-ball games that were more inclusive. One of these, Old Pussum or Old Fashion, resembled the British game of rounders with players running clockwise and being retired when hit by the thrown ball. This traditional game was played for decades, at least until World War II. Mi'kmaq elder John Basque recalled that when the war ended, "the year I got out, about '45 or '46, I had a team two years."[9] With the growing popularity of softball as a social game, Old Pussum was no longer the only alternative to the more competitive game of baseball on reserves in Nova Scotia and Prince Edward Island.[10]

Although there are few specific newspaper references before World War I to individual Mi'kmaq players, sport was a central component of life on the reserves, and traditional craftsmen produced necessary equipment. Already in the late nineteenth century, Mi'kmaq carvers were internationally acclaimed for producing both baseball bats and hockey sticks. In the 1890s the Starr Manufacturing Company in Dartmouth, Nova Scotia, began producing trademarked "Mic-Mac" handmade hockey sticks for the North American market, advertising in newspapers across the continent by 1900. Hockey and baseball clubs from Smith Falls, Ontario, to Vernon, British Columbia, adopted the name "Mic-Macs" as their team name.[11] Maliseet craftsmen also produced baseball bats, lacrosse sticks, and axe handles, but the reputation of Mi'kmaq bat and stick makers was unrivaled.

The Mi'kmaw reputation for sporting craftmanship likely explains why the A.G. Spalding Company published *Altjematimgeol. Spalding's Baseball Rules in Micmac* as part of its 1912 baseball publications.[12] Not only did the publication of baseball rules in the Mi'kmaq language clearly demarcate the game from more informal games such as Old Pussum, but furthered Spalding's mission to expand the reach of the game. *The Spalding Canadian Baseball Guide* that same year provided a cross-country survey of baseball with a substantial section on the Maritimes and its connections across the border in New England.[13] Although there was shared interest, there is no evidence of the Spalding Company's appropriation and distribution of Mi'kmaw-crafted equipment.

The most accomplished Indigenous player in Northeastern North America after World War I was Charlie Paul, a Mi'kmaq left-handed pitcher from Springhill, Nova

Scotia. Paul grew up playing for the Springhill town team during the war, but quickly developed a reputation as one of the most talented moundsmen in all of the Maritimes and New England. At the time he also worked in a colliery, going underground during the day, washing off the coal dust and heading to the ballfield for games late in the afternoon. Paul's exploits over the next decade rivaled those of Jimmy Rattlesnake, who subsequently fashioned a marvelous career on the Prairies during the 1930s and has been recently inducted into the Canadian Baseball Hall of Fame. It is fair to say that Rattlesnake and Paul were the two finest Indigenous players in Canada between the wars.[14]

In 1919 Paul began the season at home but was later recruited to play for Dominion Colliery in the semipro Cape Breton League. Paid on a game-by-game basis, he dominated batters and averaged a dozen strikeouts per game despite working a regular day shift as a coal miner. After an appearance in Halifax, a reporter for the *Halifax Evening Mail* wrote that Paul "had the 'Indian sign' on the locals," striking out the first five batters who faced him, and adding, "With his wonderful cross-fire [screwball] and fast ball he looked like a million dollars."[15]

For a while Paul's stuff was so dynamic that his catchers had difficulty holding on to his pitches, but this was remedied when Dominion recruited catcher Ralph Hall, who was playing in Detroit at the time. The two were batterymates for a number of years after that. Paul's subsequent success against barnstorming Black clubs and others from the Boston twilight leagues quickly attracted the attention of big-league teams. A scout who had closely followed his career urged Boston Braves manager George Stallings to offer him a contract, comparing him to former big-leaguer Rube Waddell from the mining districts of Pennsylvania.[16]

When Stallings resigned as Braves manager at the end of the 1920 season and took on the same job with the Rochester Colts, his first priority was acquiring Paul as his left-handed starter. Rochester business manager Harry Hapgood sent ace pitcher Jack Wisner to Cape Breton to get Paul's signature on a contract and accompany him to spring training in Darlington, South Carolina. After a few days, however, it became clear that Paul would not sign.[17] "Bright Light Is no Magnet for Indian Pitcher," read a headline in the *Baltimore Sun*. The best that Wisner could get was an agreement that if Paul signed to play professional ball in the future, it would be with Rochester. He played instead with New Waterford of the three-cornered Cape Breton professional league, winning 16 games against only 4 losses during the 1921 season.[18]

The following spring Paul was courted again, this time by new Braves skipper Fred Mitchell, who received glowing reports from former big-leaguer Andy O'Connor and other Boston-area players who played against him in Cape Breton.[19] Aware of Paul's reluctance to travel on his own, the Braves arranged for an escort to Boston, where he joined Braves executives, manager Mitchell and a half-dozen players for a train ride to spring training on the Federal

Express. Competing for a job as a left-handed specialist against veteran Rube Marquard and young John Cooney, Paul had a good spring. Mitchell was "greatly impressed with his style" but the Braves decided to keep Marquard and Cooney.[20] Paul asked for and was granted his unconditional release so that he could return home to play for New Waterford. Over the next decade, Paul played a starring role with a number of teams in the Maritimes and New England and was subsequently inducted into the Nova Scotia Sport Hall of Fame.[21]

After his baseball career, Paul continued working as a coal miner. In August 1953 a cave-in at the 11,800-foot level in a Springhill mine took his life along with those of six others.[22] By that time baseball had been largely eclipsed by softball on reserves in the Maritimes and was in decline among Indigenous communities in Maine.[23] Today the rich history of baseball in Indigenous communities throughout the region has faded into a dim memory.

NOTES

1   *Lewiston* (Maine) *Sun Journal,* June 20, 1927: 8.

2   *Ottawa Journal,* October 7, 1939: 13.

3   Colin D. Howell, *Northern Sandlots. A Social History of Maritime Baseball* (Toronto: University of Toronto Press, 1995) provides a more extensive look at Indigenous baseball in the Maritimes. See especially Chapter 9, "The 'Others'"; Jeffrey P. Powers-Beck, *The American Indian Integration of Baseball* (Lincoln: University of Nebraska Press, 2009), 18-19.

4   *Bangor* (Maine) *Daily News,* June 20, 1917: 8; July 4, 1925: 6; June 7, 1927: 16.

5   *Lewiston Daily Sun,* June 3, 1907: 6. The nickname "Chief" was widespread for players of Indigenous origin. Jeffrey Powers Beck, "'Chief.' The American Integration of Baseball, 1897-1945," *American Indian Quarterly,* Vol. 25 (Autumn, 2001): 508-38.

6   *Bangor Daily News,* July 15, 1911: 3.

7   In Mi'kmaq, the word Mi'kmaw is an adjective, while Mi'kmaq is the noun.

8   *Acadian Recorder* (Halifax, Nova Scotia), August 7, 1877: 4.

9   Howell, *Northern Sandlots,* 189.

10   Quoted in Howell, *Northern Sandlots,* 189. Basque's remarks are drawn from a series of interviews with Mi'kmaq people by anthropologist Trudy Sable as part of this project on Indigenous bat-and-ball games in the Maritimes.

11   See, for example, the *Halifax Herald,* December 29, 1900: 8; *Merrickville Star* (Merrickville-Wolford, Ontario), March 2, 1905: 8; *Vernon* (British Columbia) *News,* January 10, 1907: 5. Similar advertisements appeared in newspapers across Canada and the United States.

12   *Altjematimgeol. Spalding's Baseball Rules in Micmac* (Rimouskie, Quebec: Spalding Publishers, 1912).

13   *Spalding's Official Canadian Baseball Guide, 1912* (Montreal: Canadian Sports Publishing).

14   "Bright Lights No Magnet for Indian Pitcher. Charlie Paul Turns Down Offer from George Stallings," *Baltimore Sun,* March 20, 1921: 89.

15   *Halifax Evening Mail,* August 25, 1919: 8.

16   *Springfield* (Massachusetts) *Union,* December 1, 1921: 17.

17   *Rochester Democrat and Chronicle,* March 6, 1922: 20.

18   *Rochester Democrat and Chronicle*, March 6, 1922: 20.

19   *Tampa Bay Times*, March 7, 1922: 7; "Pro Baseball Thrives in Cape Breton. Imported Americans Are Bolstering Up Dominion, Waterford and Glace Bay Teams," *Halifax Evening Mail*, July 23, 1921: 8.

20   *Halifax Evening Mail*, March 8, 1922: 8; *Boston Globe*, March 30, 1922: 16.

21   Charles Elbert "Charlie" Paul, *Nova Scotia Sport Hall of Fame*. https://nsshf.com.

22   *Montreal Star*, August 25, 1953: 1.

23   *Bangor Daily News*, May 17, 1961: 23.

ALTJEMATIMGEOL: TRANSLATING THE SPALDING RULES OF BASEBALL INTO THE MI'KMAQ LANGUAGE

By Colin Howell

As was true in other Indigenous communities elsewhere, native peoples in the northeastern corner of North America played a wide array of traditional stick and ball games that celebrated "The Creator" while enhancing healthful recreation, physical skill, community solidarity and inclusiveness. In addition to lacrosse – by far the most ubiquitous Indigenous pastime – the native peoples in Quebec, Labrador, and farther north played games that were particularly suited to their environment. The Inuit, for example, played a form of baseball called Anaulataq on an often rocky landscape and sometimes on ice. To the south, the Mi'kmaq in Nova Scotia, New Brunswick, and Prince Edward Island played Oochamkunutk, a traditional stick and ball game, in the summer, and when the winter came switched to a form of hurley on ice that they called Alchamadijik.

Over the years Mi'kmaq and Maliseet craftsmen in the Maritimes and Maine became especially proficient in fashioning both hockey sticks and baseball bats. Before the end of the nineteenth century, Mi'kmaq carvers had already developed an international reputation for the sticks they carved from the roots of alder and yellow birch trees. These lightweight hockey sticks, trademarked as the "Mic-Mac" hockey stick, were distributed across North America along with skates by the Starr Manufacturing Company of Dartmouth, Nova Scotia. Mi'kmaq craftsmen and the Starr hockey skate developed a reputation of quality in hockey equipment that rivaled that of the Spalding Company and its wide array of sporting goods.[1]

This explains to some extent the 1912 publication of *Altjematimgeol: The Spalding Baseball Rules in Mic Mac*. They were printed in Rimouski, Quebec, with the acknowledged permission of J.E. Sullivan, president of the Spalding Company. There is little indication of the project's genesis, nor are there the names of those involved in the translation. The book was made available, however, by the manager of the Mi'kmaw baseball club in Rexton, New Brunswick, with the blessing of the Mi'kmaq chief at Burnt Cove.

Obviously a 31-page translation like this would have involved considerable time and effort, and it remains a wonderful resource for those interested in studying and maintaining the Mi'kmaq language and Indigenous sporting life.[2] For the Spalding Company, the project was clearly in keeping with its broader interest in widening the acceptance and development of the sport and expanding the market for its sporting equipment. It also enhanced its array of baseball publications that included the annual official Baseball Guides and Spalding's Baseball Rules. Spalding had an extensive sporting library at the time related to football, hockey, basketball, baseball, and beyond that to include physical culture, gymnastics, and healthful exercise.[3]

The publication of baseball rules in the Mi'kmaq language was important in delineating the difference between baseball and other stick and ball games that were played in Indigenous communities at the time. In the early 1990s, cultural anthropologist Trudy Sable was a research assistant on a project on Maritimes baseball funded by the Social Sciences and Humanities Research Council of Canada. Working from the Gorsebrook Institute at Saint Mary's University in Halifax, Sable undertook a number of

The Spalding Rules booklet in the Mi'qmak language

interviews with Mi'kmaq elders on traditional stick and ball games like Old Pussum (Old Fashioned).

Although the game's origins are obscure, it was notable for its inclusion of everyone in the community, young and old, male and female, and for its celebratory and informal quality. People could enter or leave the game whenever they wished, and it usually ended with a feast. The influence of the British game of rounders was evident in the game's development over time, with baserunners moving in a clockwise direction and being retired by being hit by the thrown ball.

As baseball became increasingly popular in the last half of the nineteenth century, it diverged from the traditional games like Old Pussum in a number of ways, becoming a competitive rather than communal practice, played by men rather than women and often involving competition with other Indigenous and subsequently non-Indigenous players. As Indigenous players increasingly showed up playing alongside non-Indigenous ballplayers, conformity to the standard rules of the game was absolutely necessary. For Mi'kmaq players, the publication of the Spalding Rules in their own language was a particularly important part of the game's development in Indigenous communities throughout Maritime Canada.[4]

NOTES

1   See Alan Downey, *The Creator's Game: Lacrosse, Identity and Indigenous Nationhood* (Vancouver: UBC Press, 2018); Colin Howell and Chris Fletcher, "Modernization Theory and the Traditional Sporting Practices of Native People in Eastern Canada," *Journal of Physical Education and Sport* 19 (2), 1997: 79-84; Garth Vaughan, *The Puck Starts Here. The Origin of Canada's Great Winter Game. Ice Hockey* (Fredericton, New Brunswick: Gooseland Publishers, 1996), 138-152.

2   *ALTJEMATIMGEOL. Spalding's Base Ball Rules in Mic Mac* (Rimouski, Quebec: Imprimerie Generale S. Vachon, 1912).

3   In the same year that *Altjematimgeol* appeared, *Spalding's Official 1912 Canadian Base Ball* Guide contained a lengthy section on baseball in the Maritimes and New England as well as playing rules and a diagram of a baseball field.

4   This project led to the publication of Colin Howell, *Northern Sandlots. A Social History of Maritime Baseball.* (Toronto: University of Toronto Press, 1995). Sable's research provides the foundation for much of Chapter Seven, "The Others," especially pp. 184-95, which deals with the history of baseball and native people in the Maritimes.

THE 1911 WORLD SERIES: "INDIAN VERSUS INDIAN"

By William A. Young

On October 12, 1911 – Columbus Day – a new reform group, the Society of American Indians (SAI), met for the first time in Columbus, Ohio. The gathering was in response to a call by six Native American activists and intellectuals. In their summons they wrote, "[T]he time has come when the American Indian should take the initiative in the struggle for his race betterment, and to answer in his own way some of the vital questions that confront him."[1]

Called "Red Progressives," SAI members were largely boarding school or university-educated "Indians." While there were other progressive organizations, like the Indian Rights Association, seeking to work for the betterment of Indians, the SAI was unique as a group led by Indians rather than Whites. While nonnatives could be associate members, only Indians were admitted to full membership.

The two themes put forward by the SAI were pan-Indianism, the belief that Indians should cooperate across tribal boundaries on a common political and social agenda; and assimilation of Indians to the culture and lifestyle of the dominant society while retaining pride in their own Indian identities.[2]

On October 14, 1911, with the SAI organizational meeting still in session, Charles Albert Bender, known as "Chief," the nickname given to virtually all Native American ballplayers, took the mound against the New York Giants in the first game of the 1911 World Series. Although Bender would win two decisive victories for the Philadelphia Athletics in the Series and give up only six runs, on that day he lost the game when Giants catcher John Tortes Meyers – also known as "Chief" – scored the winning run. The Athletics-Giants matchup was called in the contemporary press the "Indian versus Indian" series.

Both events represent responses to the profound changes through which Native Americans were passing in the first decades of the twentieth century. According to Philip Deloria, the SAI provided a context in which Indians were able to approach assimilation on their own terms. By contrast, Bender and Meyers and other Indian athletes at the time were expected to display the traits Whites associated with Indians in their "primitive" state before they were affected by their contact with "civilization."[3]

However, the distinction should not be overemphasized, especially when considering the perspectives of these two Indian athletes themselves. Despite the racial epithets others used to define them, Bender and Meyers did not see themselves as enacting primitive stereotypes. In their own quite distinct ways, they fought to rise above such expectations.

Charles Albert Bender (1883-1954), a Chippewa Indian,[4] grew up on the White Earth Reservation in Minnesota. His nonnative father was of German ancestry and his mother was Chippewa. Bender graduated from the Carlisle Indian Boarding School and spent time at Dickinson College. A lanky (6-2½), 185-pound right-hander, Bender was signed in 1903 to a contract with the Philadelphia Athletics. Bender spent 12 productive seasons with the A's, finishing his career with a record of 212 wins and 127 losses, with 1,711 strikeouts and a 2.46 ERA. He was elected to the National Baseball Hall of Fame in 1953 by the Veterans Committee.

Bender experienced racial stereotyping throughout his career. For example, Charles Dryden of the *Philadelphia North American* could not resist racist imagery in describing Bender's masterful performance in the second game of the 1905 World Series, shutting out the New York Giants 3-0. Dryden wrote that the "dusky child of the forest" "had won a new turkey feather for his head piece," although but "for a wind-up [he] came within half an inch of letting the champions scalp him."[5]

Bender found his own approach to resisting such stereotyping. When asked if his Chippewa background was

John Tortes Meyers (left) of the New York Giants and Charles Albert Bender of the Philadelphia Athletics (right) pose before the first game of the 1911 World Series, deemed the "Indian versus Indian" series by sports writers. Like other Native American players of the era they were given the nickname "Chief."

the reason for his amazing poise on the pitching mound that day, Bender responded, "I want to be known as a pitcher, not an Indian." However, a cartoon in the *Philadelphia Inquirer* the next day showed him dressed as a stereotypical Indian warrior using an "Indian sign" to hypnotize Giants batters. Other epithets Bender heard from the stands that day and throughout his career included war whooping and shouts like "Back to the reservation!" and "Giants grab heap big wampum!"[6]

John Tortes Meyers (1880-1971) was a Cahuilla Indian, the son of a Cahuilla mother and, like Bender, a nonnative father of German ancestry. He was also throughout his career tagged with the racist nickname "Chief." Meyers spent his early years on the Santa Rosa Reservation in the mountains of Southern California and in Riverside, California. He enrolled in Dartmouth College in Hanover, New Hampshire, for one year (1905-06) where he was called "Big Chief," before beginning his professional baseball career. In 1908 he was signed to a contract with the New York Giants. Beginning in 1909, Meyers spent seven years as the trusted batterymate of Christy Mathewson. He was a power hitter in an era better known for softer contact. Meyers finished his career with the Brooklyn Dodgers and Boston Braves.

Meyers had a .291 lifetime batting average, highest among all catchers of the Deadball Era and higher than that of most of the catchers in the National Baseball Hall of Fame. In a time when catchers were emerging as "field generals," Meyers was heralded as one of the best strategists and tacticians behind the plate.

Like Bender, Meyers felt the sting of racist taunts throughout his career. As he said to a reporter in 1909, he felt like "a stranger in a strange land."[7]

Reflecting the "savage warrior" stereotype, journalists often described Meyers coming to the plate not with a bat, but with a "war club."[8] Meyers was typically greeted when he batted with tomahawk chops and war whoops. In his 80s, Meyers was interviewed by Lawrence Ritter for Ritter's acclaimed book *The Glory of Their Times: The Story of the Early Days of Baseball Told by the Men Who Played It.* Meyers reiterated to Ritter that as an Indian he had always felt resentment for being treated like an outsider, a stranger.[9]

Meyers and Bender were competitors, but also friends who shared the common experience of being stereotyped because they were Indians. However, the two responded differently to the racism and prejudice they had to endure.

Bender sometimes responded overtly to racist taunts. On one occasion, when fans were heckling him with war whoops, the college-educated pitcher walked over to the third-base stands and yelled, "You ill-bred ignorant foreigners; if you don't like what I'm doing here, why don't you go back where you came from?"[10]

However, such outbursts were not typical for Bender. Most often in response to the most vicious heckling, he would "just smile, sometimes tip his cap." *New York Times*

sports reporter William C. Rhoden compared such accommodating to the "'tying oneself in knots' behavior of Jackie Robinson."[11]

On the whole, Bender chose denial, withdrawal, and stoic silence as his coping mechanisms. He largely and purposefully immersed himself in White society, both during and after his baseball career. He never returned to the White Earth Reservation or spent time in Indian country, choosing instead to live out his retirement years in Pennsylvania.

Bender and Meyers and other Native American major leaguers during the early history of baseball experienced a catch-22. If they released the tension, frustration, and estrangement, they felt, they risked being labeled "savage warriors." If they kept it in, it was assumed they were displaying the "naturally impassive and unfeeling" nature of all "primitive people."[12]

Although Bender sometimes expressed pride in his Indian identity, he largely kept his hostile feelings at being stereotyped inside. As one of his biographers has observed, Charles Albert Bender "pursued a major league career to distance himself from his Indian heritage. ... [I]t was a decision that haunted him the rest of his life."[13]

By contrast, John Tortes Meyers chose not to abandon his Cahuilla heritage. He remained connected to his Cahuilla homeland both during and after his baseball career, willingly involving himself in the affairs of his people. He drew for personal strength as a ballplayer on Cahuilla values. Among them was *?iva?a*, the Cahuilla belief in a creative force that, if treated respectfully, will be beneficial to the endeavors you are pursuing. In addition, he was influenced by the Cahuilla values of respect for elders and tradition, interconnectedness, industriousness, order, precision, dependability, moderation, dignity, and reserve.[14]

Perhaps the most effective of the Cahuilla values upon which Meyers drew was ironic humor, used to defuse tense situations and level social distinctions. For example, late in his career a reporter noted that although right-handed, Meyers signed autographs with his left hand. The actual reason was that his right hand was so gnarled as a result of being hit in his throwing hand that he couldn't write with it. With a twinkle in his eye, Meyers told the reporter, who dutifully reported the insight, that most Indians sign their names left-handed, because "when we were signing treaties with the white man, we had to hold the pen in the left hand and a tomahawk in the right, or they would whack us on the dome in their treacherous pale-faced fashion. With the right hand armed, we were ready to meet their wickedness halfway."[15]

In contrast to Bender and other Native American ballplayers, John Tortes Meyers was willing to speak out in defense of the rights of the Cahuilla people and other Indian nations. For example, in 1909, when he was just a rookie, Meyers risked his career by defending a group of Creek Indians in Oklahoma who were trying to retain tribal control over their traditional lands. They were led by Chitto Harjo, called by the White press "Crazy Snake." Harjo was vilified and charged with threatening to set the Oklahoma frontier ablaze with the "horrors of Indian massacre."[16]

When asked by a reporter to comment, Meyers responded by saying that Indians were being treated like "irresponsible children." They were being driven onto reservations which were then taken over by railroad or land companies, forcing the Indians onto worse reservations. Chitto Harjo was accused of an uprising, and his land was stolen "and he was driven into the cold," Meyers told the reporter, but "he never stirred a finger." Meyers emphasized that it was "the white men who are robbing him and other Indians [who] are believed by the public and not the Indian."[17]

Before the first game of the 1911 World Series, Charles Albert Bender and John Tortes Meyers posed for a photograph. The horde of reporters covering the game made sure their audiences knew that the two players were the game's two greatest American Indian ballplayers. As noted, before the first pitch had been thrown it was dubbed the "Indian versus Indian" Series. Commenting on the impact of Indian ballplayers on the sport, one reporter wrote in his preview of the Series, "[W]hen the Pilgrims landed on Plymouth Rock they first fell upon their knees, and then fell upon the aborigines. Things have changed. The aborigines now fall upon the whites and make short work of them."[18]

Inspired by the two Indians in the 1911 Series, in its extensive game coverage the New York Times described the scene with a string of "Indian images." The Times writer could not resist displaying his "knowledge" of various tribal religions. He claimed that Bender was using "the aboriginal sign language of all the separate tribes" to overpower the Giants batters. The signs included "the Apache omen, the Mandan magic, the Sioux sorcery, the Arapahoe evil eye and even the Siwash shibboleth." Presumably guided by John Tortes Meyers, the Giants batters neutralized Bender's signs, the Times writer offered, by boiling some snake root and rubbing it in their hair.

When Meyers faced Bender for the first time in the 1911 Series it was not the Giants' power-hitting catcher against the A's ace, but "Chief Meyers, the Mission Indian,[19] fac[ing] Chief Bender, the Chippewa." Times writer W.J. Lampton drew on General Philip Sheridan's famous comment, suggesting that "[s]omebody has said that the only good Indian is a dead Indian, but whoever he was, never saw Bender and Meyers play ball."[20]

In the seventh inning of the first game of the 1911 World Series, it was once again "Indian versus Indian." When "Big Chief Meyers" drove a Bender pitch for a double and scored, it was, the Times claimed, the "Witch Doctor" who crossed the plate. The Times further exuded that perhaps "these two Redmen" "wished they had tomahawks in their hands instead of a bat and a baseball."

In an article ghostwritten for Meyers in the same edition of the Times, the writer called Bender "my redskin friend

New York Giants manager John McGraw with catcher John Tortes Meyers at the 1911 World Series.

Albert" and said he was "glad to belong to the same race as that big fellow."

According to the Times, Bender and Meyers were not accomplished major-league ballplayers as much as "primitives" acting out their warlike instincts in the guise of a baseball game. The burning question reporters wanted to know was, "Now who's the best Indian, the Mission or the Chippewa?"

The Giants' ace, Christy Mathewson, was the winning pitcher of the first game because, the Times noted, he had his own "Redskin wizardry" that had "set the fans to ghost dancing."[21]

The New York Herald praised Mathewson's performance in the 1911 Series in doggerel that featured a racist reference to Bender:

You punched the Mack men full of holes;
You spiked their biggest gun;
You tore the scalplock off the Chief;
You put 'em on the run.[22]

After the first game of the 1911 World Series, players on both teams discovered that Giants President John Brush had swindled them out of a portion of their Series shares by undercounting the gate. Meyers was chosen to lead a protest and players from both teams, including Bender, formed a committee to protest Brush's action. Although the protest was rebuffed, the selection of Meyers to lead the group and Bender to serve on the committee showed how much, despite the racism they endured, both the Giants and A's players trusted them.

Nevertheless, stereotyping persisted in the other games of the 1911 Series. Bender's outstanding pitching performance in the third game, a 3-2 A's victory, was credited by one writer to "the cunning characteristic of his race" that enabled him to see things that "escape the eye of the Caucasian."[23] When Meyers batted in the 11th with a chance to win the game, the New York Times reported, "War whoops, yells, Indian talk, filled the air as [Giants fans] pleaded, begged, yes, implored the Redman to tear the cover off the ball and drive it into the wilderness. ..."[24]

In his 2005 book *The Old Ball Game: How John McGraw, Christy Mathewson, and the New York Giants Created Modern Baseball*, Frank DeFord demonstrated that twenty-first-century commentators were still capable of employing stereotypical descriptions of Native American ballplayers. He wrote that the "celebrated medicine man," Chief Bender, was on the mound in the fourth game of the Series, a 4-2 A's victory.[25]

In the sixth and final game of the World Series, Athletics manager Connie Mack surprised observers by tapping Bender for pitching duties after the hurler had only one day of rest. In the *New York Times* coverage of the game Bender was yet again assigned stereotypes: "the Redman" or the "red boy."[26] Bender and the A's blasted the Giants, 13-2.

The 1911 World Series marked a turning point in the way World Series were covered. The "media circus" was born: Before each game hundreds of photographers swarmed the field to snap every conceivable shot. The "human interest" angles were played up. As noted, before the first game the press made sure readers knew that this was the "Indian versus Indian" series, with a well-publicized photo of Albert Bender and John Tortes Meyers together, both labeled "Chief." The Series was covered by a large national, even international, press corps. In the press box was a pantheon of sportswriters, including Damon Runyon, Heywood Broun, Grantland Rice, Sam Crane, Fred Lieb, Bozeman Bulger, Sid Mercer, and Ring Lardner.

Alongside were 50 telegraphers ready to flash the game action, play by play, to sites from Havana to Los Angeles. After each game a summary was sent to Tokyo. Throughout the nation thousands followed the games in real time on various types of public scoreboards, including new electronic versions. The justices of the US Supreme Court had clerks slip them inning-by-inning reports, and the proceedings of the houses of Congress were interrupted when there was a change in the score.[27]

It was also the first World Series when daily reports, ghostwritten by sportswriters, appeared under the names of ballplayers (including Mathewson and Meyers).[28]

When the A's and Giants players learned that rights for showing movies of the 1911 Series in theaters were being sold, they protested. The Giants once again selected Meyers to represent them to petition for the players to receive a share of the $3,500 payment for the rights. The appeal was not successful.[29]

One feature of the coverage of World Series did not change in 1911, and to a disturbing degree continues today. As demonstrated here, stereotypical imagery dominated the press description of the two Native American ballplayers in the Series, and racist tropes characterized fan responses to them.

Despite requests by Native American major leaguers, including Ryan Helsley of the St. Louis Cardinals, a member of the Cherokee nation, that Atlanta Braves fans discontinue the frequent tomahawk chops and "war whooping," they persisted in 2022.[30] While Cleveland's major-league team responded to complaints from Native Americans by dropping its racist Chief Wahoo logo and changing its name from the Indians to the Guardians, Cleveland's fans continue to purchase and display the imagery.

Although the Society of American Indians was dissolved in 1923, its advocacy of citizenship for Native Americans was instrumental in the passage of the Indian Citizenship Act, signed into law on June 2, 1924. Furthermore, the positive influence of the SAI lives on in progressive organizations like the National Congress of American Indians and the American Indian Legal Defense Fund.

ACKNOWLEDGMENT

An earlier version of this essay appeared in William A. Young, *John Tortes "Chief" Meyers: A Baseball Biography* (Jefferson, North Carolina: McFarland & Co., 2012).

NOTES

1 Lucy Maddox, *Citizen Indians: Native American Intellectuals, Race and Reform* (Ithaca, New York: Cornell University Press, 2005), 9.

2 Donald Fixico, *Daily Life of Native Americans in the Twentieth Century* (Westport, Connecticut: Greenwood Press, 2006), 77.

3 Philip Deloria, *Indians in Unexpected Places* (Lawrence: University Press of Kansas, 2006), 227-8, 234.

4 Today many Chippewa, also called Ojibwe, prefer to be known as the *Anishinaabeg* (singular, *Anishinaabe)*, a self-designation in their own language that means "original people."

5 Cited in Robert Peyton Wiggins, *Chief Bender: A Baseball Biography* (Jefferson, North Carolina: McFarland & Co. 2010), 59-60.

6 William C. Kashatus, *Money Pitcher: Chief Bender and the Tragedy of Indian Assimilation* (University Park: The Pennsylvania State University Press, 2006), ix-x.

7 "Chielf [*sic*] Myers [*sic*] Sole Ambition to 'Make Good' in New York Team," *Nebraska State Journal* (Lincoln), May 2, 1909: C7.

8 "Cubs Take Giants into Camp Again," *New York Times*, July 28, 1912.

9 Lawrence Ritter, "Chief Meyers," in *The Glory of Their Times: The Story of the Early Days of Baseball Told by the Men Who Played It, Enlarged Edition* (New York: HarperCollins, 2002), 183.

10 Norman Macht, *Connie Mack and the Early Years of Baseball* (Lincoln: University of Nebraska Press, 2007), 314.

11 Cited in Kate Buford, *Native Son: The Life and Sporting Legend of Jim Thorpe* (New York: Alfred A. Knopf, 2010), 173.

12 Jeffrey P. Beck, *The American Indian Integration of Baseball*, (Lincoln: University of Nebraska Press), 75-76.

13 Kashatus, *Money Pitcher, xiii.*

14 William A. Young, *John Tortes "Chief" Meyers: A Baseball Biography* (Jefferson, North Carolina: McFarland & Co., 2012), 25-27.

15 "Clippings and Cartoons," *Baseball Magazine*, August 1917, 451.

16 For a full account, see Mel H. Bolster, *Crazy Snake and the Smoked Meat Rebellion* (Boston: Brandon Press, 1976).

17 J.W. McConaughy, "Indian Most Remarkable Player in Game: M'Graw Picks Meyers for Chief Catcher," August 5, 1909 (National Baseball Hall of Fame, Cooperstown, New York); cited in Beck, *The American Indian Integration of Baseball*, 78.

18   *(Rochester) Union and Advertizer*, as reprinted in *The Arrow*, December 1, 1911; cited by Buford in *Native Son*, 105.

19   The Cahuilla were often grouped with other Southern California tribes and labeled "Mission Indians." It was a misnomer that continues to plague the Cahuilla to this day. As Meyers' grandniece Shanna Meyers told the author, "We are not 'Mission Indians.' The missions were on the coast and we're not there. We're still having trouble getting [the Bureau of Indian Affairs] to remove 'Mission' from our name." (personal Interview with Shanna Meyers, September 29, 2008).

20   W.J. Lampton, "Hits and Misses," *New York Times*, October 15, 1911.

21   Rex Beach, "Giants Take the First Game, Score, 2-1," *New York Times*, October 15, 1911.

22   Cited in Frank DeFord, *The Old Ball Game: How John McGraw, Christy Mathewson, and the New York Giants Created Modern Baseball* (New York: Atlantic Monthly Press, 2006), 163.

23   Tom Swift, *Chief Bender's Burden: The Silent Struggle of a Baseball Star* (Lincoln: University of Nebraska Press, 2008), 187-88, 190.

24   "Giants Lose Again, 3-2," *New York Times*, October 18, 1911.

25   DeFord, *The Old Ball Game*, 167.

26   "How the Giants Lost," *New York Times*, October 27, 1911.

27   Young, *John Tortes "Chief" Meyers*, 93.

28   Young, *John Tortes "Chief" Meyers*, 93.

29   Macht, *Connie Mack*, 518.

30   Mark Saxon, "Cardinals' Ryan Helsley, of Cherokee Descent, Expresses Disappointment over Braves' use of Tomahawk Chop," *The Athletic*, October 4, 2019.

JIMMY RATTLESNAKE

By Ian Wilson

His pitches offered enough venom to rattle the most seasoned of hitters. And he did it all with a grin that was as warm in welcoming opponents to the batter's box as it was in sending them back to the dugout after another futile at-bat.

Jimmy Dummy Rattlesnake - an exceptional left-handed pitcher in the 1930s and 1940s - was born in the Indigenous community of Ermineskin Cree Nation, located about 100 kilometers (62 miles) south of Edmonton, Alberta, on an unknown date 1909, the son of Peter Dummy Rattlesnake and Marguerite Moignon Rattlesnake.

He played a lot of different sports growing up, including soccer and curling, but it was baseball that matched his skill set and his interest.

Jimmy's father was a sportsman in his own right, having developed a fondness for riding and training horses.[1] The elder Rattlesnake was also a relative of Chief Robert Smallboy, an Order of Canada recipient who founded the

(courtesy Wetaskiwin & County Sports Hall of Fame)

Jimmy Rattlesnake

Smallboy Camp near Jasper in the late 1960s in an effort to live off the land and commune with nature.

Chief Smallboy was a farmer who had a love of sport, especially baseball and hockey. When the day's work was done, he would often practice pitching in the evening. Jimmy Rattlesnake learned about baseball in school and Chief Smallboy encouraged him to pursue his love of the game.

"The Chief told him to keep at it 'cause maybe he could beat the white boys at their own game," recalled Dorothy Rowan Smallboy, the daughter-in-law of Chief Smallboy.[2]

Rattlesnake did keep at it, much to the detriment of the hands of his classmates and catching partners. Chief Smallboy's son, Joe, was one of the victims of Rattlesnake's friendly fire. He started out behind the plate and when the pitches got too hard to handle, Joe moved to first base. When he discovered that Rattlesnake could still sling the ball with authority to first base, Smallboy decided to field balls in the outfield instead, a development that amused Rattlesnake immensely. Smallboy carried a crooked finger with him for the rest of his life as a souvenir of his baseball days with Rattlesnake.

Rattlesnake's cousin, Louis P. Crier, suffered a broken finger during his battery sessions with the southpaw.

"I was wearin' a catcher's mitt, big mitt and the ball was comin' straight at me and I was gonna catch it. Then that ball went a different way, hit my finger right on the top. Jimmy come runnin' from the mound and he just pulled my finger. … He put it in place," said Crier.[3]

Laurel Harney, another catcher tasked with taming the "Smilin' Rattler," first met the pitcher in 1931 when the hurler was a 22-year-old poised for baseball breakout.

"A bag of bones he was, but out on that diamond it wasn't his bones that seemed to rattle," recounted Harney, who played with Rattlesnake on the Stockyard Bulls in Edmonton under manager Webb King.

"Jimmy fascinated the heck out of those baseball people. They wondered where he learned to throw like he did. I wasn't so much fascinated as worried what his next pitch was going to do. Not that I ever had to try to hit it. Always played on his side."

Harney described a "sawdust ball," which was Rattlesnake's signature pitch.

"It made hitters antsy. You'd swear it was never gonna get to the plate. Then, just as a hitter was swingin', the ball would do something crazy, tail or drop, and he'd miss by a country mile. Batters all felt Rattlesnake was dangerous; he made mortals out of heroes. But catchers used to feel like they was stickin' their hand in a sack full of rattlers."[4]

Jimmy made headlines in his first start for the Royals of the Edmonton Senior Amateur Baseball League in 1932. Rattlesnake – who was often referred to as "Chief" in newspaper reports – struck out 10 batters while allowing seven hits and three walks in an 8-4 complete-game win at Diamond Park.

"Despite his youth and playing before a big crowd for the first time, the Chief worked like a veteran on the mound. He possesses nigh-perfect poise, fields his position well, and, more important still, showed an effective curve ball, combined with some 'fast' to make him extremely effective," wrote reporter Bill Lewis in the *Edmonton Bulletin*.[5]

Rattlesnake looked even better during an early July victory over the Oilers. In that 5-3 triumph for the Royals, he struck out 11 and gave up just six hits. It was a matchup that "was keenly enjoyed by the thousands of rabid fans who taxed the seating capacity of the stands to the limit," according to the *Edmonton Bulletin*.[6]

Word soon got out about Rattlesnake's abilities, making him a ballpark draw for sports fans in Alberta.

The lanky hurler returned to the Edmonton Royals the following summer "popular as ever" and "much improved," as the *Bulletin* put it.[7] In addition to pitching for the Royals, Rattlesnake also suited up in a number of games with the Wetaskiwin club, for whom he made some brilliant appearances as a reliever and a starting pitcher. On two occasions – a 15-4 trouncing of Bawlf in June and a July exhibition against his usual teammates with the Royals – he struck out 12 batters in front of large crowds.

"He'd show up anywhere and everybody seemed to get a thrill out of it, just knowin' he could appear outta the woodwork," said Harney.[8]

"Rattlesnake roamed all over Alberta and Saskatchewan. He pitched over at Wetaskiwin, he pitched down at Lacombe, at Neilburg, you name it, he was probably there. Tournaments used to be the big thing in this country. You'd go from one money-tournament to another. I'd run into him here, I'd see him there. Sometimes, a team'd try to keep him a secret until the lineups were called, sort of like a secret weapon in reserve."[9]

The "Rattler" had continued success in 1934, which ended up being a true showcase season for the lefty, who was also a capable hitter.

He tossed a no-hitter against Fredricksheim in leading Wetaskiwin to a 9-0 Central Alberta Baseball League victory on July 9, collecting seven K's and walking just two.

At an exhibition tournament in Camrose at the end of that month, Rattlesnake logged a pair of complete-game wins to ensure that Wetaskiwin collected the first-place prize money.

Provincial playoffs put Wetaskiwin on a collision course with the Shastas, who claimed the Edmonton championship.

"Not a great deal was expected from the country boys in this series to determine the northern Alberta senior baseball champions," wrote the *Edmonton Journal*. "It was expected, and probably with some justification, that the Shastas, one of the most powerful clubs ever organized in this city, would go on to a crushing victory."[10]

Rattlesnake, of course, had other ideas. He pitched masterfully in the opening tilt of the best-of-five series, throwing a four-hitter and striking out seven during Wetaskiwin's 7-4 victory at Renfrew Park.

The Shastas evened the series at one win apiece in front of 5,000 onlookers in Edmonton, and even though Rattlesnake was not on the mound for the second game, he was still making plays.

"Probably the best catch of the day was made by Chief Jimmy Rattlesnake, who was playing in left field," said the *Journal*. "The Chief had a bad leg – he was injured in Friday's game – but no one would have guessed it the way he tore after a hard-hit fly ball by Ike Davis. The Chief ran over 50 feet before he pulled it down. It was a marvelous catch."[11]

Game three of the series took both teams to Wetaskiwin for a low-scoring and controversial result. Rattlesnake found himself on the mound yet again, and pitched eight frames of three-hit baseball. Both teams, and a full house of fans, were denied a ninth inning of play when the game was called due to darkness.

"It was one of the finest ball games witnessed in this central Alberta city in years, but the game, closely fought all the way, and witnessed by a record crowd, almost broke up in a riot," reported the *Edmonton Journal*.

Wetaskiwin scored the go-ahead run in the eighth inning to claim a narrow 2-1 victory.

"When the umpire made his announcement, there were immediate protests from the Shastas management, along with spectators, who milled about the baseball grounds, demanding an explanation," said the *Journal*.

When the dust settled, Rattlesnake had "figured prominently in the home team's triumph."

In addition to striking out eight batters and limiting the offense of the Shastas to three singles, he went 2-for-3 at the plate and stole a pair of bases.

"Nonchalantly and with clock-like regularity Chief Jimmy Rattlesnake mowed them down," the *Journal* said.[12]

The paper's sports editor, George Mackintosh, described a pitcher who was clearly in the zone.

"As the game had progressed, there was no evidence of the Shastas suddenly coming to life and collecting any worthwhile hits off Chief Jimmy Rattlesnake," observed Mackintosh.[13]

The Shastas bounced back with a 6-1 win in Game Four to send the series to a winner-take-all confrontation that pressed the "smoke-ball artist" back into action.

The third time was a charm for the Shastas, who finally broke through against Rattlesnake. Both teams allowed eight hits and one earned run in the 5-2 loss for Wetaskiwin that featured a handful of errors on both sides, five double plays for the Shastas, and some uncharacteristically wild pitching by Rattlesnake. More than 6,000 fans filed into Renfrew Park to take in the game.

Despite the series defeat, Rattlesnake had emerged as a star on Alberta's baseball scene.

He matched up against his playoff rivals again in early September for an exhibition game to benefit a hospitalized Shastas player, this time donning an Edmonton Royals uniform. Rattlesnake returned to form with a nine-strikeout performance that saw him permit just four hits and one earned run in a hard-luck 2-1 loss. At bat, he went 2-for-4 with a triple and drove in the Royals' only run.

"If ever a man tried to win a ball game, Jimmy was that person," the *Journal* observed.[14]

Rattlesnake that year got an opportunity to show what he could do against some of the best baseball players. When a contingent of stars announced plans to play a series of barnstorming games across Canada in October, Rattlesnake was chosen to represent the locals at Renfrew Park. In preparation, he strengthened his arm by throwing hay bundles into a threshing machine back home and playing catch regularly.

Rattlesnake started the first of two games against the American League squad on October 11 in Edmonton.[15]

"The starting pitcher of the Edmonton ball club had enjoyed considerable success. He had nice control and was throwing everything he had at the big leaguers. But it just could not last," wrote *Edmonton Journal* reporter Ken McConnell of the performance, which was umpired at home plate by future Canadian Baseball Hall of Famer John Ducey.[16]

The pro batters struck for eight hits, including a home run by future Hall of Famer Heinie Manush, en route to a 9-2 victory. It was a better result than the rematch, which saw the All-Stars cruise to a 20-2 win.[17]

Rattlesnake returned to Alberta's senior circuit with Wetaskiwin for the 1935 season and when playoffs rolled around, he met up against some familiar faces on the Shasta-Royals roster. He let his bat do the talking in eliminating Edmonton from the postseason, going 3-for-4 with a homer to center field.

"Rattlesnake was instrumental in the scoring of four Wetaskiwin runs and that's not a bad day's work," noted McConnell of the 5-0 win in the *Journal*.[18]

Rattlesnake was denied a provincial title due to a dispute that arose when Wetaskiwin squared off against the Ponoka Panthers. The Panthers filed a protest over Wetaskiwin's use of outfielder Harry Levinson, who up until that point had played for the Shasta-Royals.

During the best-of-seven series, Rattlesnake tossed a complete-game 4-0 victory to put his team within one win of the title, but the Alberta Baseball Association awarded the championship to Ponoka and disqualified Wetaskiwin when Levinson was deemed an ineligible player.

Newspapers across Canada published articles reporting that Rattlesnake would join Seattle of the Pacific Coast League in 1936. There were also reports that Rattlesnake played pro baseball in New York at some point.[19]

Crier ran into Rattlesnake in 1936 when the two boarded a train for Saskatchewan from Wetaskiwin.

"He was tellin' me got called up in (the) States, I forget where, anyway it was down the States," said Crier. "I remember when I got back he was already home from Saskatoon. From there he went for a trial in the big league."[20]

The induction page for Rattlesnake on the Wetaskiwin and County Sports Hall of Fame website describes a pitcher who was scouted by a New York team and invited to spring training. After playing a few games, he "didn't like the big city of New York" and returned home.

"For Jimmy Rattlesnake to go to New York for a tryout and make the team was quite an accomplishment. It is said that Jimmy was one of the first Canadian baseball players to turn professional in the U.S.A. and certainly he was the first Aboriginal baseball player from Canada to do so," reads the online account.[21]

In a story about Rattlesnake's Wetaskiwin induction for the *Alberta Sweetgrass* newspaper, reporter Sam Laskaris wrote that the New York team was the Yankees.

"Though club officials were allegedly interested in having him on their roster, the belief is he didn't like New York City and returned home," Laskaris wrote.[22]

In the book *Game Plan: A Social History of Sport in Alberta*, author Karen L. Wall wrote of "a brief interlude with the New York Yankees in the 1930s."[23]

Lawrence Rattlesnake, Jimmy's eldest son, was also told by his father about the baseball opportunity in the United States.

"If I can remember right, he told me Brooklyn. He said he made the team but only pitched a few innings before he got in shit with the manager and came back to Canada. He never mentioned it again," Lawrence said.[24]

Yet another account of Rattlesnake's American adventure came from a player who was mentored by the pitcher.

Ralph Vold, who pitched in the minor leagues in the 1950s, was enthralled by Rattlesnake's curveball. As a teenager, Vold trekked from Ponoka to Ermineskin Cree Nation, where Rattlesnake taught him a number of different ways to grip the baseball.

After he played professionally for several seasons in the United States, Vold ran into Rattlesnake again and the two chatted about baseball south of the border.

"I think he'd kinda been followin' my career in the States. He asked me how it was down there and I told him it was tough bein' a Canadian ballplayer, the odds of catchin' on with a major league team were so slim," recalled Vold.

"He said, 'I always thought so too.' He said he'd been out drinkin' when he was down there, he showed up late for practice and the manager sent him home. He regretted it, said he would like to have stayed a while longer. Told me in the hot weather down there the beer just tasted so good. I played in the minors from Georgia to Texas to California and I never come across his name. But I don't doubt he crossed the line. I come along a lot later."[25]

Regardless of the circumstances that brought him back to Canada, Rattlesnake ultimately returned to action with Wetaskiwin in 1936. He faced Ponoka in early June of that year and whiffed 12 Panthers while yielding only four hits in a 3-1 loss.

He once again proved to be a reliable and consistent player, both on the mound and with a bat.

Rattlesnake was a dependable presence on Western Canadian mounds through the 1940s, often opting to stay close to home in the Central Alberta Baseball League and play for Wetaskiwin, Ponoka, or Red Deer.

He also pitched for the Dodgers in the Edmonton Senior Baseball League, where thousands of fans would gather at Renfrew Park to watch him befuddle batters.

In the summer of 1942, Rattlesnake traveled west to suit up for the Victoria Machinery Depot Shipbuilders, a team he played for briefly in the regular season.

"I convinced our team to bring Rattlesnake out," said his catcher friend Harney. "I said he'd win big for us and he did. Got him a job in the shipyard and put him to work fannin' long-ball hitters. But workin' in the shipyard, it drove him crazy, just insane with the noise from the rivet guns."

"One night my wife and I found him walkin' down the street alone in Victoria. 'I gotta go home, Harney,' he said, and I said, 'Why? We don't want to lose you.' He said, 'I'm too lonesome. ... I have to go.'"

Rattlesnake did return for postseason action, however. His arrival coaxed large crowds to Athletic Park, and the 6-foot-2 hurler helped VMD capture the city championship.

"He won two big games for us in relief. Came in in a tricky situation and retired the side. After that, Jimmy went home. ... It was baseball brought us together. After those days were over, our paths just never crossed," said Harney.[26]

There was no doubt that Rattlesnake was an elite pitcher in his day, one who was sought after across Canada and capable of filling up the stands of the diamonds he played on.

When his time on big-city mounds came to an end, Rattlesnake returned to the Ermineskin Cree Nation reserve.

It was a difficult life, according to Dorothy Rowan Smallboy.

"Jimmy kept everything to himself," she said. "All his frustrations. He put everything into his ball game when he pitched, but even that wasn't enough for him in the end. All the hard work he had to do, we all had to do, just to stay alive. And when he couldn't pitch, then what? I remember hearin' him talkin' to my husband and Chief Smallboy once. He said, 'It's hard tryin' to be a white man 'cause their ways are so different.' He told them about the time he was tryin' to hold a fork like a white man. He kept droppin' it and he said, 'I could feel my face goin' red. They were nice,' he

said, 'they tried not to see what I was doin' wrong.' That's what I remember Jimmy talkin' about, the funny things he did, the little mistakes he said he made out in the white world. He used to joke he didn't even know how to operate a toilet when he first went away from here."[27]

One of Rattlesnake's wives, Isabelle Morin Rattlesnake, recalled turbulent years with her well-known husband. Tuberculosis ravaged Indigenous communities and claimed the lives of several Rattlesnake relatives. But that wasn't the only challenge of life on the reserve.

"It was really tough for me with 10 kids," she said. "Jimmy was a good guy when he wasn't drinkin'. He was good to us, a good worker and when the kids were sick he was really watchin' them at night. But most of the time he was away workin', all he did around here was sell the grain and see to the cattle once in a while. I had to raise the kids by myself."[28]

Isabelle, who died in 1993, said her husband's skill as a pitcher never translated to hunting, which was essential to surviving frigid Canadian winters.

"Jimmy sure had better aim with a baseball than a gun," she said.

"We used to laugh about that, Jimmy and me – what a hunter he turned out to be." [29]

Jimmy's oldest child, Sylvia Rattlesnake, shared memories of a hard-working father who cared deeply for his family.

"All I knew him as was my father and a loving grandfather to my first son. You know he'd come running whenever that baby cried and he'd be out chopping wood at 4 in the morning to keep the house warm for the baby," said Sylvia. [30]

Lawrence was only 20 years old when his father died on April 17, 1972, at Maskwacis, Alberta.

"I was with him until he died, right to the last minute," stated Lawrence.

"He'd been drinkin' all night, and when I woke up he was downstairs. I didn't really know what he was doin'. My wife and I left to get some groceries ... by the time we got to the house he was on the front step vomiting. He said, 'Take me to the hospital, son, I didn't mean to drink it, it was a mistake.'"

Added Lawrence: "We tried to hurry. Then there was no point hurryin'. His heart stopped for the last time, he was lying in my arms. My dad, he'd drank gasoline antifreeze. He used to have a hidin' place for his booze downstairs and he must have been pretty well drunk and he grabbed the wrong bottle. ... He had one downfall, that was it."

His passing was devastating to the Rattlesnake family and the community, but the circumstances of his death did not dominate the memories of him.

"I like to remember my late Uncle Jim as he was, as a gentle person and as an athlete. There are so many stories about him, like about him eating x-number of pancakes before a game. That number keeps getting bigger as the years go by. My Uncle Jim would like those stories; he was a humorous person. I can still see him smiling," said Lester Fraynn.[31]

After Rattlesnake's death, several efforts were made to honor him. Ron Hayter, a past president of the Alberta Baseball Association, pushed to have Rattlesnake added to the group's honor roll. That happened in December of 1974.[32]

In 1985 Baseball Canada created the Jimmy Rattlesnake Memorial Award, which honored Canadian players of outstanding ability and sportsmanship. Major-league players who went on to have their nameplates added to that award include Stubby Clapp, Ryan Radmanovich, Rob Ducey, Pierre-Luc LaForest, Shawn Hill, and Scott Thorman. More recently, that award has been given to outstanding members of the Canadian women's national squad who display leadership qualities and team spirit.

A building was named after Rattlesnake – the Ermineskin Cree Nation's Jim Rattlesnake Building in Maskwacis – in 1987 and a chapter of the book *To Run With Longboat* by Brenda Zeman focused on Rattlesnake's story.

Rattlesnake was inducted into the Wetaskiwin and County Sports Hall of Fame in 2011, an event that was attended by several of his children and relatives.

"On behalf of the Rattlesnake family, it's a great honor to be here representing our father's legendary life and to reflect on his acknowledgments and awards," said Jimmy's daughter, Phyllis Rattlesnake, at the induction. "Our father was a kind and humble man filled with laughter. Being the down-to-earth person he was, he spoke very little of his professional baseball career.

"Jimmy Rattlesnake, who was fondly known as the Smilin' Rattler, will always be remembered as a man of outstanding athletic ability combined with great sportsmanship. We lost our father in 1972 when we were all still very young, but as adults, my brothers and sisters, we all still run into elderly people who speak very highly of him."[33]

Phyllis also discussed her father on *Alberta Dugout Stories: The Podcast.*

"Jimmy loved baseball. He respected the people he played with and against," she told show host Joe McFarland. "My dad was one of the first Canadian and aboriginal Cree athletes to achieve success through his natural athletic ability as a southpaw baseball pitcher."[34]

Rattlesnake also left a legacy of emerging baseball players, who were inspired by what he achieved.

Vold idolized him, as did Harold Northcott, a longtime Team Canada baseball player and coach who was a boy when his father took him to games to watch the Rattler pitch.

Northcott's father, who played with Rattlesnake, considered him the best lefty pitcher he'd ever seen and encouraged young Harold to emulate the techniques of the slender southpaw. One of Rattlesnake's skills the elder Northcott was thoroughly impressed with was his pickoff move to first base.

The decision to add Rattlesnake to the Canadian Baseball Hall of Fame in 2021 was made by a six-person committee of baseball experts, who started with more than 100 possible candidates before reducing that number to 29. Of those selections, 17 were voted in, including Rattlesnake.

Baseball historian William Humber told *Alberta Dugout Stories* that Rattlesnake was a logical choice for the honor.

"There's enough factual commentary, later backed up by my own review of Edmonton and other newspapers, to confirm Rattlesnake's talent, ballplaying prominence and the demand for his services. One has to, of course, read through the lines in the depiction of his prowess, which is often surrounded by the murky and outright racist categorizations of the day. His significant place in baseball in Western Canada between the wars, and then beyond this period seemed undeniable," wrote Humber in an email to the author.

"In the case of Rattlesnake, I was struck by the comments of two notable eyewitnesses to his career. One was Ron Hayter, later inducted into the Canadian Baseball Hall of Fame for his baseball leadership in Alberta. In 1972, he argued forcefully for Rattlesnake's recognition in some form by baseball authorities in Alberta shortly after Rattlesnake's death. The other was Jim Coleman, the noted sportswriter, who at the time of the Canadian Baseball Hall of Fame's founding in the early 1980s argued for Rattlesnake's induction."[35]

SOURCES

In addition to the sources cited in the Notes, the author also consulted Baseball-Reference.com, baseball.ca, https://baseballhalloffame.ca/hall-of-famer/jimmy-rattlesnake/, and a number of publications.

See also Wilson, Ian. "The Smilin' Rattler," *Alberta Dugout Stories,* November 16, 2021.

NOTES

1   Brenda Zeman, *To Run With Longboat* (Edmonton: GMS2 Ventures Inc., 1988), 28. According to a disclaimer in the book: "This book is a collaboration between a number of people, including those who lived the events described and the author and editor who maintained a limited freedom to interpret and invent where necessary. As such, the work has its roots in oral history, but ultimately it should be read as docufiction."

2   Zeman, 28.

3   Zeman, 31.

4   Zeman, 23.

5   Bill Lewis, "Chief Rattlesnake Pitches Royals to Senior League Win," *Edmonton Bulletin*, June 13, 1932: 12.

6   "Royals Improve Playoff Chances in Senior Circuit," *Edmonton Bulletin*, July 4, 1932: 10.

7   Lewis, "Pats and Pans," *Edmonton Bulletin*, June 5, 1933: 14

8   Zeman, 23.

9   Zeman, 23.

10   "Wetaskiwin Earns Decisive 7-4 Victory Over Shastas," *Edmonton Journal*, August 25, 1934: 12.

11   "Shastas Tie Up Senior Baseball Championship Series," *Edmonton Journal*, August 27, 1934: 8.

12   "Near-Riot Occurs as Wetaskiwin Defeats Shastas 2-1," *Edmonton Journal*, August 29, 1934: 10.

13   George Mackintosh, "Sporting Periscope," *Edmonton Journal*, August 29, 1934: 10.

14   "Shastas Win Bitterly-Fought Benefit Ball Game 2-1," *Edmonton Journal*, September 10, 1934: 11.

15   The AL all-stars included Heinie Manush, Luke Sewell, Roger Cramer, and Pinky Higgins. Jimmie Foxx was supposed to play but he had been hit in the head by a pitch in Winnipeg and sat out.

16   For more on Ducey, see Brant Ducey, *The Rajah of Renfrew: The Life and Times of John E. Ducey, Edmonton's "Mr. Baseball"* (Edmonton: University of Alberta Press, 1999).

17   Ken McConnell, "Major League Battery to Play for Edmonton Senior Club," *Edmonton Journal*, October 12, 1934: 10.

18   Ken McConnell, "Wetaskiwin Advances Into Finals for Provincial Baseball Title," *Edmonton Journal*, August 31, 1935: 14.

19   No official records of Rattlesnake playing professionally in the United States could be verified, but the topic was discussed by his relatives, and it was referenced in newspaper reports, as well as his Wetaskiwin and County Sports Hall of Fame biography

20   Zeman, 32.

21   Wetaskiwin and County Sports Hall of Fame. Wetaskiwinsportsfame.com

22   Sam Laskaris, "Humble Pitcher Gets Third Hall of Fame Induction," *Alberta Sweetgrass*, March 10, 2011.

23   Karen L. Wall, *Game Plan: A Social History of Sport in Alberta* (Edmonton: University of Alberta Press, 2012), 214.

24   Zeman, 38.

25   Zeman, 34.

26   Zeman, 24-25.

27   Zeman, 29.

28   Zeman, 37.

29   Zeman, 37.

30   Zeman, 30.

31   Zeman, 38-39.

32   "ABA Honors Taylor," *Edmonton Journal*, December 5, 1974: 69.

33   Wetaskiwin and County Sports Hall of Fame.

34   Episode 157: Celebrating Jimmy Rattlesnake, *Alberta Dugout Stories: The Podcast*, November 19, 2021.

35   William Humber, email correspondence with author, November 3, 2021.

YOLANDE TEILLET

By Ryan Woodward

In 2022 the Manitoba Indigenous Sports Hall of Fame was launched as a project of the Manitoba Aboriginal Sports & Recreation Council to publicly document the countless ways in which Indigenous peoples have served as athletes, coaches, and builders in the province of Manitoba.[1] Among the inaugural class of inductees was a Métis woman, Yolande Teillet Schick, whose professional sports career had begun over 80 years before. Teillet's induction served as an important recognition not only for Indigenous and Métis citizens, but also for women in baseball as well as elite athletes throughout Canada.

She was born Yolande Marie Sara Jeanne d'Arc Teillet on September 28, 1927, to Camille Teillet and Sara Riel in St. Vital, Manitoba, a neighborhood just south of Winnipeg. Métis leader and Canadian politician Louis Riel was her great-uncle. Teillet's older brother, Roger J. Teillet, was later a politician who served as minister of veterans affairs from 1963 to 1968.[2] Teillet's father was French and

 is vertical text — *(Courtesy Manitoba Aboriginal Sports & Recreation Council)*

Yolande Teillet's publicity photo upon joining the Fort Wayne Daisies in 1945.

her mother Métis, an aboriginal group of people in Canada of mixed European and Indigenous ancestry.[3] Often politically marginalized throughout Canadian history, the Métis, including many of Teillet's family, have worked toward gaining proper legal recognition and protections. Despite the lack of opportunities for Indigenous women and girls in the 1930s, especially in sports, softball was growing in popularity in the Prairie provinces of western Canada. Girls' softball leagues were springing up everywhere, even in tight-knit Métis communities, attracting the attention of young athletic girls like Yolande Teillet.

Beginning in the early 1940s, the St. Vital Tigerettes softball team offered local girls the opportunity to compete at a higher level and soon attracted elite talent throughout the region. Teillet's strong arm earned her a spot as catcher with occasional outfield duties. The 5-foot right-hander was called "Yo Yo" by her teammates, among them future AAGPBL players Audrey Haine and Dottie Ferguson. The level of play increased in the regional senior girls circuit and by 1943, the Tigerettes were well known for being top competitors. On August 20 of that year, for example, it was reported that Audrey Haine "pitched St. Vital Tigerettes to a thrilling 1 to 0 victory over St. Boniface Athletics in a nine-inning contest in which Haines [*sic*] struck out 19 of the 32 batters which faced her."[4] Weeks later, "Teillet poled out a couple of doubles in four tries, while Haine hit two for four. Haine also distinguished herself by striking out 12 C.U.A.C. players, while only allowing two free trips."[5] Eventually, the C.U.A.C. Blues and the Tigerettes battled in a best-of-seven series for the Greater Winnipeg Girls' Senior Softball league championship. In addition to errorless fielding from Dottie Ferguson and Audrey Haine's dominant pitching, "Catcher Yolande Teillet surprised the fans in the sixth chapter when she threw a fast ball to second bag to catch Mary Shastel who was stealing from first."[6] The Tigerettes won the game, 6-0, along with the league title.

Away from the softball diamond, Teillet worked at Eaton's Department Store and like most everyone at the time, thought constantly about the ongoing World War. Her brother Roger, a member of the Royal Canadian Air Force, had been a prisoner of war in Germany since 1942.[7] He would eventually return home in 1945 just as Yolande was turning pro as a ballplayer. Contributions to the war effort became part of Teillet's duties with the Tigerettes. She was chosen to participate in an all-star game benefiting Chinese

War Relief. "The All-Star game will be seven innings and should be one of the treats of the season for followers of this sport," the *Winnipeg Free Press* reported in August of 1944. "It is hoped some 6,000 people will be on hand to give their aid to the valiant Chinese next Wednesday night."[8] As for regular league play, the Tigerettes continued to excel despite losing Audrey Haine to the All-American League earlier in the year. Pitcher Marg Sutton threw a no-hitter for St. Vital in July 1944. Truly a team effort, it was reported the next morning in local papers: "Sutton's no-hit game was made possible by two great plays in the last inning by Yolande Teillet and Dot Ferguson. Both drew rounds of applause from the fine crowd in attendance."[9] Increased competition prevented the Tigerettes from reaching the championship finals in 1944, although the program remained strong, winning several provincial titles heading into the 1950s.[10]

With this high level of play and other Manitoba softball stars having performed well professionally for two seasons in the United States, it was only a matter of time before scouts from the All-American Girls Professional Baseball League would take notice. A brief announcement in the *Winnipeg Tribune* on September 26, 1944, states, "Gals Get Offers: Dot Ferguson, Joan Henderson, and Yolande Teillet of St. Vital Tigerettes of the Senior Girls Softball league have received offers from the All-American Girls' Softball league. It is not known whether they'll accept or not."[11] Henderson would continue to have a storied career in Manitoba softball for many years. Ferguson and Teillet headed south to Chicago and embarked on a shared journey as professional ballplayers. As Teillet told a reporter decades later, "When I was working at Eaton's, I was making $18 a week," compared to the $55 a week she made playing in the All-American League. Not in it just for the money, however, she added, "I played because I loved baseball."[12] The decision to turn professional and play at a higher level was not a difficult one.

The league Teillet entered was relatively new and while each season brought changes – whether rules of the game, field dimensions, or relocated teams – 1945 proved to be a pivotal year in the league's history. First, the underwhelming response from expansion into the larger cities of Milwaukee and Minneapolis in 1944 caused league officials to focus on smaller industrial cities, expanding eastward to Indiana and, for the first time, Michigan. Second, during the offseason, ownership of the league changed hands from Philip K. Wrigley to his advertising director, Arthur Meyerhoff. Part of Meyerhoff's restructuring of the organization included a central governing board composed of representatives from each league city, meaning all teams now had a say in the direction of league operations and ideas about rule changes. Max Carey, manager of the 1944 league champion Milwaukee Chicks, served as league president. Finally, Meyerhoff's increased promotion of the players' athletic skills, along with the wholesome image conveyed in the previous two seasons, set the league up for what many

consider to be its peak year in terms of attendance, quality of play, and media exposure.

The All-American League's final tryouts and spring training took place at Wrigley Field in Chicago in 1943 and Washington Park in Peru, Illinois, in 1944. The league returned to Chicago in 1945 with a series of drills and exhibitions at Waveland Park in order to field six teams for the second consecutive year. A *Life* magazine article in June 1945, reintroduced the league to a nationwide audience with both staged photos and action shots of standout players.[13] Completing the article is a two-page spread photo of all six teams in which Teillet appears in the second row among her teammates, the newly minted Fort Wayne Daisies. The six teams paired off for tours of military bases en route to their home cities and played exhibition games for Stateside troops.

Eleven players from the Minneapolis Millerettes comprised the majority of the Fort Wayne roster when the franchise relocated there ahead of the 1945 season. Of the 20 players who appeared in a Daisies uniform that year, eight were from Canada, including Teillet's former Tigerettes teammate Audrey Haine. Fellow St. Vital alumna Dottie Ferguson was assigned to the Rockford Peaches, appearing with that team through the final season of 1954. Although the charm-school exercises famously reported during the league's first two seasons were no longer part of the players' spring-training agenda, rules on comportment and appearance standards were still enforced by each team's chaperone. The Daisies employed Helen Rauner in this role, a local woman only a couple of years older than most of her players.[14] Players typically stayed in private homes with regular check-ins from the chaperone. This level of guidance and responsibility often convinced parents that the league was a first-rate operation for their daughters, including Teillet, who at 17, was one of the youngest players in the league.[15] At the helm was first-year AAGPBL manager, Bill Wambsganss. A major-leaguer 20 years prior, Wambsganss is best known for being the only player to complete an unassisted triple play during a World Series.

By the time the Daisies played their first home game at Northside High School's football stadium, just a block from the St. Joseph River in Fort Wayne, the roster was set with eventual league stars.[16] Speedy basestealers and hard hitters Helen Callaghan and Faye Dancer patrolled the outfield. Haine, along with Annabelle Lee and strikeout queen Dottie Wiltse, anchored the pitching rotation. Solid defense was found in infielders such as Vivian Kellogg, Margaret Callaghan, and Lavonne "Pepper" Paire; and catching in 110 games that season was Ruth "Tex" Lessing, who would be honored as the league's All-Star catcher for the following three years. It was no doubt a difficult lineup to break into for a rookie, but Teillet still appeared in 10 games and hit a respectable .231 in 13 at-bats in 1945.[17]

The Daisies were an immediate hit with hometown fans when their season opened in May 1945. The team nickname had been chosen via a panel of judges tasked with selecting a name from thousands of submissions.[18] Like other All-American teams, the uniform featured the host's city seal on a patch affixed to the center of the chest. In this case, an outer ring reading "City of Fort Wayne Indiana" encompassed a smaller circle that includes typical municipal symbols – a caduceus, a sword, and scales of justice. The Fort Wayne seal also features the word "KE-KI-ON-GA" referring to the capital village of the Miami tribe, located at the center of what is now Fort Wayne. The Daisies also inherited the Millerettes' pink uniforms, of which a replica anchors the AAGPBL exhibit at the Canadian Baseball Hall of Fame.

New cities, talented rookies, and for the first time, bus travel for teams that previously used trains all made for an exciting season in which camaraderie among teammates flourished. Years later, former players might remember an exceptional play or a come-from-behind win, but most will reflect on the friendships made and fun they experienced. Teillet once recalled deliberately missing a pitch while catching so as to hit a disagreeable, tobacco-chewing umpire. "The pitcher threw the ball ... and it got him right in the stomach and you could see this snuff come out. The girls were laughing so hard we couldn't play for a few minutes."[19]

Another change in operations for the league's third season was the introduction of the Shaughnessy Series format for playoffs, in which the top four teams compete in a single-elimination tournament to declare a champion. The first two seasons relied on a first-half winner vs. second-half winner structure. Thanks in part to stellar hitting from Helen Callaghan, 1945's batting champion (.299), Fort Wayne remained in second place for much of the season, ensuring the team's spot in the postseason. Teillet recorded two at-bats in four games against Racine in the opening round and is credited with one putout in the championship finals, which Rockford won four games to one.[20] Still, 1945 was a successful season for the fledgling Daisies and a preview of what was to come as the league grew in popularity.

Season four of the All-American League introduced more changes for its players. In this season, the ball was slightly smaller, the basepaths and pitching distance slightly longer, and pitchers could now use a side-arm delivery in addition to the underhand that had been in use since 1943. The league again expanded to eight teams with new franchises in Muskegon, Michigan, and Peoria, Illinois. Also, for the first time, spring training was held outside of Illinois, in Pascagoula, Mississippi. Teillet personally encountered another adjustment to make for the new year, having been assigned to the Grand Rapids Chicks.

The Grand Rapids roster had several holdovers from the 1944 league champion Milwaukee Chicks, including infielders Doris Tetzlaff, Ernestine Petras, and Alma Ziegler; pitchers Jo Kabick and Connie Wisniewski; and, returning to the outfield after a year's absence, slugger Pat Keagle.[21] Making the move with Teillet from Fort Wayne was catcher

(Courtesy Manitoba Sports & Recreation Council)

The 1943 St. Vital Tigerettes softball team featured several players who turned professional. Yolande Teillet is at the far left of the front row.

Ruth "Tex" Lessing, embarking on her first season as an all-star. By midseason Teillet's former Tigerette and Daisies teammate, Audrey Haine, would join the Chicks' pitching rotation. Former player Dottie Hunter began her third season as the Chicks' chaperone and former major- and minor-player Johnny Rawlings joined as a manager for his first of eight seasons in the league.

The post-spring-training journey home featured more exhibition games throughout the Southern United States. Though World War II had officially ended months earlier, its effects and results were still evident all around. Having multiple brothers who served in the war, Teillet felt an odd sadness watching German POWs scrub mess-hall floors while her team, on an exhibition stop in Alabama, ate nearby.[22]

The Chicks' home stadium, South Field, was yet another football stadium with a baseball diamond cut into one corner during the summer months. A factory building next door resulted in a shortened right field that became a trademark of games in Grand Rapids. With limited appearances behind the plate, Teillet's strong arm gained her playing time in either the abbreviated right field or endless left field of the Grand Rapids ballpark. By season's end, Teillet was once again on the second-ranked team, although Grand Rapids lost in the first round of playoffs to Rockford, which eventually lost the championship to Racine.[23] With just five game appearances, Teillet finished the 1946 season with a .167 batting average.[24]

The 1947 season brought even more change to the AAGPBL, most notably league-wide spring training internationally in Havana. The same eight teams participated in the league's fifth season, with the same field dimensions and baseball circumference. This year, however, pitchers were exclusively required to use a full side-arm delivery. The league's spring training in Cuba attracted much attention from local baseball fans and media alike. With league teams becoming more established in their home cities, as well as increased – and now international – media coverage, the 1947 season was perhaps the apex year of popularity for the league before expansion, management decisions, and other forms of entertainment signaled its decline a year later.

Teillet joined her Grand Rapids Chicks teammates for spring training in Havana and is present in numerous pictures, both in organized team photos and casual shots from league photographers. By the end of spring training, however, she is seen seated front and center with the Kenosha Comets in their official team photo – the only one without a Kenosha patch on her uniform. Last-minute allocations were not uncommon during the spring-training process. Unfortunately for Teillet, 1947 was be the season Grand Rapids won its first championship while her new team, the Comets, spent much of the year in last place.

Another advantage of hosting spring training far from league cities was the opportunity for teams to pair up on exhibition tours on their way back home. This not only spread news of the league to those unfamiliar with its existence, but often benefited the hosting cities and local charities financially and also served as excellent recruiting tools as teams hosted individual tryouts with local players. Exhibition tours also afforded playing time for less experienced players. For example, on one such tour stop in Charlotte, North Carolina, Teillet, filling in for a regular starter, and pitcher Janice O'Hara, a utility player turned pitcher thanks to the new side-arm rule, dazzled the crowd in a game against South Bend on May 14, 1947. "O'Hara, one of the most spirited players on the Comets with a 'will to win' all the way, was effective throughout the game. She missed a shutout when Bonnie Baker hit down the third base line for a home run in the sixth inning," reported a Kenosha newspaper. The report continues, "With the exception of "Yo Yo" Tillay [sic] behind the bat for Dottie Naum and Martha Haines at second for Betty Fabac, the Comets presented their full strength and played impressive ball."[25]

A week later, as the Comets prepared for their season opener against the Belles in Racine, the "new Comets" were special guests at a number of civic functions as all of Kenosha was seemingly excited for the coming season. A photo caption on May 21 reads: "WELCOME NEW COMETS – The Kenosha Comets, 1947 combination, were guests of the Rotary club at a luncheon at the Elks' club Tuesday with Judge Edward J. Ruetz, president of the organization sponsoring the team, on hand with Shirley Jameson, who says she will retire this season extending the official greeting to new girls. From left; Mary Wood, Yolanda Teillet, Jameson, Ruetz, Claire Lobrovich, Martha Haines, Mona Denton, and Dorothy Naum."[26] Two days later, the same six players are featured as "Sensational New Players Added to Kenosha Comets Roster" in a full-page *Kenosha Evening News* ad promoting the team's home opener on May 25 at Lake Front Stadium against the Rockford Peaches.[27] For Teillet, the season was short-lived, however. An illness in the family and an aggravated thumb injury from the previous year resulted in her exit from the league. Her stats for 1947 reveal two games played with a career-high .333 batting average.[28]

Post-league life for Teillet meant a return to Canada, and for a while, to St. Vital Tigerettes softball. She married William Schick, a farmer and later proprietor of a service station, and the couple raised nine children.[29] The following years found Teillet bowling, coaching softball, volunteering, and being very involved in her children's education. Forty years after Teillet's professional baseball career ended, the All-American Girls Professional Baseball League entered a period of rediscovery among the public, and numerous accolades for all former players became routine. First, the league became the primary focus of a new Women in Baseball exhibit at the National Baseball Hall of Fame and Museum in Cooperstown, New York, in 1988. Redesigned as "Diamond Dreams: Women in Baseball" in 2006, the exhibit features a listing of all known AAGPBL players and years played, including Teillet and nearly 600 others. The

1992 film *A League of Their Own* introduced the league to generations of new fans and many former players found themselves celebrities again attending screenings and sitting for interviews. Evelyn Wawryshyn Moroz, Mary Kustra Shastal, and Yolande Teillet Schick all attended the Winnipeg premiere of the film and were introduced to the audience.[30]

In 1995, Larry Fritsch Cards produced its first AAGPBL Series, in which Teillet is card number 197. Her brief bio mentions the Tigerettes and the three teams for which she played. The card's front features a photo of her in a Grand Rapids uniform.[31] More honors followed in June of 1998, specifically for former players from Canada. First, all 64 former AAGPBL players from Canada were inducted as a group into the Canadian Baseball Hall of Fame in St. Marys, Ontario. Days later, the 11 "Manitoban All-American Girls" were likewise inducted as a group into the Manitoba Baseball Hall of Fame in Morden.[32] In addition to the Manitoba Indigenous Sports Hall of Fame induction in 2022, Teillet's name is included in a Fort Wayne memorial unveiled in June of 2023 listing all former Daisies.

Yolande Teillet Schick died on January 26, 2006, at the age of 78, survived by her nine children and 21 grandchildren.[33] She is buried next to her husband in St. Vital, where she was born and raised. Though her professional athletic career was brief, it is no less remarkable or surprising, given her accomplished family, that she rose to the height of her field through disciplined work matched only by natural talent. Teillet's unique participation in baseball and contributions made to each of her teams remain a model for Indigenous and Métis athletes and also women in baseball.

ACKNOWLEDGMENTS

Photographs of the 1943 St. Vital Tigerettes and Yolande Teillet in 1945 Fort Wayne Daisies uniform are courtesy of the Manitoba Aboriginal Sports & Recreation Council.

Special thanks to Mark Davis for preliminary research and gathering important sources needed for this project. For guidance and support, many thanks to Gary Belleville, Leslie Heaphy, Bill Nowlin, Barrett Snyder, and Kat Williams.

SOURCES

In addition to the sources cited in the Notes, the author consulted:

Davis, Pepper Paire. *Dirt in the Skirt* (Bloomington, Indiana: AuthorHouse, 2009).

Fidler, Merrie A. *The Origins and History of the All-American Girls Professional Baseball League* (Jefferson, North Carolina: McFarland & Company, Inc., Publishers), 2006.

Heaphy, Leslie A., and Mel Anthony May. *Encyclopedia of Women and Baseball* (Jefferson, North Carolina: McFarland & Company, Inc., Publishers), 2006.

Henderson's Winnipeg Directory (Winnipeg: Henderson Directories), 1948.

Kenow, L.J. "The All-American Girls Professional Baseball League (AAGPBL): A Review of Literature and Its Reflection of Gender Issues," *Women in Sport and Physical Activity Journal*, 2010, 19(1), 58-69.

Kinsley, Lesley. "From the Prairie Fields to the Glamor League: Women's Softball in Canada and the All-American Girls Professional Baseball League," *Journal of Canadian Baseball* 2 (1) (2023). https://doi.org/10.22329/jcb.v2i1.8340.

NOTES

1 "Manitoba Indigenous Sports Hall of Fame & Museum," Manitoba Indigenous Sports Hall of Fame, 2024, https://www.mishof.com/.

2 Lawrence Barkwell, "The Accomplished Teillet Family," The Virtual Museum of Métis History and Culture, accessed October 2, 2024, https://www.metismuseum.ca/resource.php?/07243.

3 Adam Gaudry, "Métis," The Canadian Encyclopedia, January 7, 2009, https://www.thecanadianencyclopedia.ca/en/article/metis.

4 "Yolande Schick," Manitoba Aboriginal Sports & Recreation Council Hall of Fame, accessed October 7, 2024, https://www.mishof.com/yolande-schick.

5 "St. Vital Squares Series With C.U.A.C.," *Winnipeg Free Press*, September 15, 1943: 12.

6 "Yolande Schick," MASRC Hall of Fame.

7 Barkwell.

8 "Chinese War Relief Show Appeals," *Winnipeg Free Press*, August 5, 1944: 12.

9 "St. Vital Girl Hurls No-Hitter," *Winnipeg Tribune*, July 19, 1944: 14.

10 "St. Boniface Squares Playoff," *Winnipeg Tribune*, September 9, 1944: 12.

11 "Gals Get Offers," *Winnipeg Tribune*, September 9, 1944: 12.

12 Paul McKie, "Field of Memories: Manitoba Women Fondly Recall Their Days as Pro Baseball Players," *Winnipeg Free Press*, July 3, 1992, sec. C, https://www.mishof.com/yolande-schick.

13 "Girls' Baseball: A Feminine Midwest League Opens Its Third Professional Season," *Life*, June 4, 1945: 65.

14 Larry Fritsch Cards, "AAGPBL Baseball Card Sets: Series 2" (Stevens Point, Wisconsin: Larry Fritsch Cards, LLC, 1996), 308.

15 Lynn Ruester, "No Crones in Girls League," *Evening Courier* (Urbana, Illinois), June 12, 1945,

16 Don Graham, *Daisies, Diamonds, & Dugouts: The Fort Wayne Daisies Story* (D.F. Graham, self-published, 2021), 29.

17 W.C. Madden, *The All-American Girls Professional Baseball League Record Book: Comprehensive Hitting, Fielding and Pitching Statistics* (Jefferson, North Carolina: McFarland & Company, Inc., Publishers, 2000), 229.

18 Graham, 28.

19 Judy Fostey-Owen, "The Girls of Summer," *Winnipeg Sun*, June 27, 1992, sec. Inside Sports, 48.

20 Madden, 105.

21 "List Girls' Loop Lineups: Reveal 1946 Rosters of 8 Teams in All-American Pro Ball League," *Kenosha* (Wisconsin) *Evening News*, May 9, 1946: 18.

22 Michael Petrie, "Female Talent Honored," *Winnipeg Sun*, October 21, 1997: 44.

23 Madden, 109.

24 Madden, 229.

25 "Jerry O'Hara Pitches Five-Hit, 4-1 Win: Comets Go One Up on Benders in Exhibitions," *Kenosha Evening News*, May 15, 1947: 16.

26 "Comets Open at Racine Tonight; Helen Fox on Mound: Three of Six New Kenosha Players Bow," *Kenosha Evening News*, May 21, 1947: 14.

27 "Kenosha Comets Open 5th Season," *Kenosha Evening News*, May 23, 1947: 16.

28 Madden, 229.

29 Madden, 238.

30 Fostey-Owen, "The Girls of Summer."

31   Larry Fritsch Cards.

32   "Diamond Girls Enter Baseball Halls of Fame," *Winnipeg Sun*, June 3, 1998: 57.

33   "Yolande Schick (Teillet) Obituary," *Winnipeg Free Press*, January 30, 2006, sec. Passages, https://passages.winnipegfreepress.com/passage-details/id-104844/SCHICK_YOLANDE.

THE BOYS OF BACONE: 1967 NATIONAL CHAMPION BACONE COLLEGE WARRIORS

By Doug Wedge

Although the 1967 Bacone Warriors had a track record of incredible success, winning 42 regular-season games and losing only two, the odds were stacked against this small school in Muskogee, Oklahoma, formed in 1880 to educate American Indian students, from making much of a splash at the National Junior College Baseball tournament.[1] Actually, the odds were stacked against the team even physically *reaching* the tournament in Grand Junction, Colorado. Toward the end of the regular season, Bacone's president told baseball coach Enos Semore that bus trips were expensive and the school didn't have the money to transport the team to the tournament.[2]

Resourceful, Semore organized a group of parents and volunteers with station wagons to caravan the players to the tournament.

"We drove my parents' '63 Fury," right-handed pitcher Gerry Pirtle recalled about making the trip from Muskogee to Grand Junction. "That was really something, you know. All these other teams like Miami Dade had these big buses, and here's this little team from Oklahoma come in driving all their cars."[3]

Even with Semore's coordinating his team's arrival at the tournament, both through the volunteer station wagons and by guiding the team to such a lopsided won-lost record to earn an invitation to play at the tournament, the Warriors weren't expected to do much. Their best player, Jim Dunegan, who led the team in home runs and RBIs

and possessed an 11-0 pitching record with four no-hitters, signed with the Chicago Cubs the week before the tournament.[4] No longer an amateur, he was ineligible to play. George Brooks, the team's best pitcher, suffered an arm injury and couldn't pitch.[5] In the last game of the regular season, catcher Bob Hudspeth separated his shoulder. He too would miss the tournament.[6]

Despite the setbacks, third baseman and right-handed pitcher Loyd Colson said, the team approached the tournament with optimism. "We didn't ever expect to lose," Colson said.

An extremely confident outlook for a team from a small school. Bacone's enrollment in 1967 was around 500, and its baseball facilities were spartan if not barebones.

"[The field] was kind of like a pasture that they threw a fence up around and drug some bleachers in," Colson said with a laugh. Pirtle compared the playing field to a Little League park with no lighting, no locker room (players dressed in their dorm rooms for games), and certainly no practice facility other than the field itself. First baseman Travis Washington remembered a barbed-wire fence in the outfield and no dugout, just a bench. Players chipped in to maintain the field, raking the mound and painting the foul lines before games. Sometimes, the team would play or practice at a park in downtown Muskogee that high-school and American Legion teams also used. Consistent with the modest facilities, the school couldn't offer players loads of equipment.

"We didn't have a lot of stuff," Colson said. "I had one glove. One pair of shoes with a hole in the toe. And I think pitchers got jackets."

The small size and the limited resources contrasted with some of their competition in the tournament. Miami-Dade (Florida) Community College, the favorite to win, had an enrollment of over 23,000 students with more freshmen than the University of Florida, Florida State University, and the University of South Florida combined.[7] Future big leaguer Kurt Bevacqua, who spent 15 seasons in the major leagues, was on its roster. The defending champion Nassau Community College of Long Island, New York, boasted a booming campus on 135 acres.[8]

Despite the disparity, Bacone racked up the wins under Coach Semore, who created a culture of personal best.

Bacone College in its early years when its name was Bacone Indian College.

Colson remembered a doubleheader during the regular season when the sophomore team won the first game, but the freshman team dropped the second. After the team returned to campus, Semore trotted the freshmen out to the field to run.

"I cannot stand mediocrity," Semore said.[9]

Said Colson: "He got our attention because we only lost three games that year."

Though stern and demanding, Semore got along well with his players.

"We respected him," Colson said. "And still do. And he knew the game. I mean, he *knew* the game."

Talent and good coaching resulted in Bacone being nearly unstoppable in 1967.

"We played everybody that would play us," Colson said. "OU and Oklahoma State would not play us. You know, what do you have to win? I think we would have beat them. I know for sure we could have played with them. We played Tulsa University, which was good at the time. And [Oral Roberts University], played them a couple of times. They didn't beat us. That was, I guess, the biggest school we played. All the others were junior colleges. We played Cameron, we played all the ones in the state. Missouri. Some in Kansas."

The talent was balanced.

"We had speed. And we certainly had power, and we had good pitching," Colson said. He pointed to his roommate and teammate since Little League days in Gould, Oklahoma, Travis Washington, as one example of the team's talent. Selected to the All-American team, Washington hit .383 and socked 13 home runs.[10] Washington attributed his strong hitting to growing up on a farm in southwest Oklahoma and mucking hay as early as seven years old.

"I'd throw it up on the truck. I'd unload it," Washington said. "I didn't know it at the time, [but I was] strengthening forearms. That was the key. That's where hitting was, was in your forearms and wrist."

While not performing farm chores as a child, Washington would get an old hoe handle, toss rocks in the air, and hit them with the handle.

"Just rock after rock I'd hit," Washington said. "I didn't know it at the time, but what you're doing is coordinating your hand/eye."

Growing up poor in southwest Oklahoma and a member of the only Native American family in the area, Washington didn't have a supply of bats and balls to play with. He and his brothers would scavenge the town dump for discarded dolls and use the heads as balls. Or plastic lemons that once held lemon juice. To perfect his skills, Washington instructed his brothers to move closer to the plate when they pitched the dolls' heads, plastic lemons, or balled-up socks to him.

"I might move them just 20 feet back, make them throw it real hard, and I'd try to get around on it," Washington said.

As a Native American growing up in a White world (he is one-quarter Choctaw), Washington said, his family was looked down on. Older people called him disparaging names until he reached high school and those strong forearms clubbed home runs at a rapid clip.

"When I got to hitting that ball out, it all changed," Washington said. "Oh, you know, I was the greatest thing that ever was but not until then."

Washington was drawn to Bacone both by its stacked roster of talent and by its Native American roots, with classmates from 48 tribes representing 50 states at the school.

Before the season began, Colson and Washington were excited to learn that Van Fixico, a fellow southwestern Oklahoman with Creek Indian heritage, whom they competed against in high school and American Legion ball, was transferring to Bacone for the 1967 season. Fixico, an infielder one year older than them, began college at Southwestern Oklahoma State in Weatherford, but wanted to move to Bacone.

Semore asked Colson and Washington what they thought of Fixico and whether he should join Bacone.

"Go get him," they said.

With that, the speedy Fixico joined the Warriors, a team with considerable depth. Semore divided the team into two teams, a sophomore team and a freshman team. Colson thought the freshmen were better than the sophomores, so even with the loss of some of their best players after the regular season, the freshmen stepped up and arrived at the national tournament ready to compete. They won their first game, 5-3, beating Phoenix College.[11] ("I remember hitting a double off the wall," Colson recalled. "I played third.") Next, they faced Nassau and won handily, 11-1.[12] Colson twisted his ankle during the game trying to steal second base.

"That night, I didn't get any sleep," he says. "I remember doing a lot of whirlpool on it. I think it lasted just about a week. You turn one that bad, you don't get over it in two or three days."

In the third game, Semore named Pirtle the starting pitcher against Miami-Dade. During the regular season, Pirtle pitched primarily in relief, but with the departure or unavailability of several sophomores, he had the opportunity to start. He took advantage, striking out 13 and helping Bacone to a 5-3 win.[13] Pirtle's catcher was Marvin Thouvenel, stepping in for the injured Hudspeth, and Thouvenel was enthusiastic about Pirtle's performance.

"Every time I struck some[one out] – or every time I threw a pitch for a strike – he would come out of there jumping up, really excited [and] give the ball back to me. And he did that the whole game, and the fans loved it," Pirtle said.[14]

"Gerald was just steady," Colson said. "He always threw a lot of innings as a starter. Had a *really* good curveball."

Washington agreed. From his vantage point playing first base, the drop in Pirtle's curveball was outstanding, he said, comparing the ball to "rolling off this table."

Setting high expectations, Coach Enos Semore led the Bacone Warriors in 1967.

(Courtesy of the Oklahoma Historical Society)

"It'd just go in there and just drop straight into the plate, and then they couldn't hit it," Washington said.

Winner of three straight games in the tournament, Bacone then faced Odessa. Bacone's bats went quiet, and Odessa won 3-0.[15]

"They had a little curveball pitcher who threw curveballs 90 percent of the time, and we just couldn't hit him," Colson said.

After the game, three teams in the tournament had one loss apiece: Miami-Dade, Odessa, and Bacone. A coin toss between Odessa and Bacone determined which team played Miami-Dade.

Odessa won the toss. Bacone had to face Miami-Dade again. Right-hander Lloyd Kingfisher, who earned All-American honors that season and pitched a perfect game during the regular season, started for the Warriors. He shut down Miami-Dade, 4-1.[16]

"I pinch-hit that game," Colson said. "I grounded out. It hurt to run."

For the sixth and final game, Semore looked to his hobbled third baseman Colson to pitch.

"You're all we've got," Semore told Colson. "Can you do it?"

"Give me the ball," Colson answered.

And against Odessa, Colson, the team's third- or fourth-best pitcher, wrapped his ankle and took the mound.

"I hadn't pitched in a while," Colson said. "And I was one of those guys, and I try to do that with my high-school team: I don't want to pitch them too much, but I don't want to give them too much rest. I always remember if I had like 10 days' rest, I come in, and I didn't have command of my ball. I could throw hard, and it would move, but unless they swung at it, it probably wouldn't be a strike."

Even with his arm rested more than he preferred, Colson pitched well. Mixing his fastball with his curveball, he gave up seven hits and two walks and struck out eight. Consistent with the balanced talent working well for Bacone that season, hitters in turn pounded Odessa pitching. All but one Bacone starter had a hit as the team collected 16 hits.[17] Travis Washington went 4-for-4 with three singles and a double. Center fielder Gary Ratliff had three hits, and short-stop Bob Tate was a home run shy of hitting for the cycle. Bacone scored a run in the first, then added three more in the second, and another three in the third. Meanwhile, Colson had things under control on the mound.

"I got a little tired in the seventh, and they got a couple of hits off me," Colson said. "But I was able to finish it up."

He threw a complete game. Bacone won, 10-4, and captured the National Junior College Championship. The team that cobbled together its ride to the tournament completed its trip by raising the championship trophy in Grand Junction – and by tossing Enos Semore into their motel's swimming pool.

"Going back to the motel, the first thing we were going to do is throw the coach in the pool," Colson said. "He's about six-five. And then he was 30-something years old and probably weighed about 240. He was bigger than anybody on the team. But we got him in there. It took the team to get him in there."

Years later, in a gathering at Semore's home to celebrate his 91st birthday, Colson asked Semore, "Coach, we were good, and we always thought we were going to win, but when you look at it on paper, how did we beat Miami-Dade?"

"Nobody thought we would win," Colson said. "They thought we were good because Bacone had been [to the national tournament] before. But what they didn't know: We were even better this time."

The champions returned to Muskogee and a hometown enthusiastic about the team's accomplishments. Citizens gathered to throw a parade for the Warriors.

"They was waitin' on us," Washington said. "Big parade and all that. They took us downtown on floats and such as that. Floats on the back of trailers."

The well-earned celebration included Muskogee Mayor Jim Egan, who summed up the success: "Bacone's baseball team is a credit to the college and to Muskogee. I believed that from the season's first game that they had in mind to win the national championship."[18] Which is exactly what the boys from Bacone did.[19]

NOTES

1. "Bacone Nine Will Start NJCO Tourney Friday," *Muskogee Sunday Phoenix*, May 21, 1967; https://www.bacone.edu/about/. To learn more about Bacone, both its past and present, visit its website at https://www.bacone.edu/. The site says Bacone College, "formerly the Indian University, was founded in 1880 to educate American Indian students. Today, Bacone College is transforming into a tribal college." (Accessed November 30, 2022).

2. Author interview with Loyd Colson, February 8, 2020. All direct quotations from Loyd Colson come from this interview.

3. Author interview with Gerry Pirtle, May 26, 2022.

4. "Bacone Begins NJUCO Title Bid," *Muskogee Daily Phoenix*, May 26, 1967: 13.

5. "Bacone Begins NJUCO Title Bid."

6. "Bacone Begins NJUCO Title Bid."

7. https://www.mdc.edu/about/history.aspx.

8. https://www.ncc.edu/aboutncc/fastfacts.shtml.

9. Colson interview.

10. "Bacone Begins NJUCO Title Bid"; Interview with Travis Washington (June 11, 2022). All direct quotations from Travis Washington come from this interview.

11. "Bacone Faces New Yorkers After Beating Phoenix 5-3," *Muskogee Daily Phoenix*, May 27, 1967.

12. "Bacone Dumps Nassau, 11-1 at Tournament," *Muskogee Daily Phoenix*, May 29, 1967.

13. "Bacone Whips Miami, 5-3," *Tulsa Daily World*, May 31, 1967.

14. Pirtle interview.

15. "Warriors Dump Odessa, Texas, 10-4 in World Series Finale," *Muskogee Daily Phoenix*, June 2, 1967: 10.

16. . https://jucogj.org/documents/2018/3/7/Scores_by_World_Series.pdf. (Accessed December 14, 2022).

17. "Warriors Dump Odessa, Texas."

18. Bobby Branan, "National Champions Get Royal Welcome on Return Home, unidentified newspaper clipping from 1967 team scrapbook shown to author.

19. After guiding Bacone to the National Junior College Baseball Championship, Enos Semore was the baseball coach at the University of Oklahoma from 1968 to 1989, winning 851 games and leading the Sooners to five consecutive College World Series appearances (1972-76). Loyd Colson played seven years of professional baseball and pitched for the New York Yankees in 1970 before embarking on careers in insurance, real estate, and coaching baseball. Gerry Pirtle played 14 years of professional baseball, including 19 games as a Montreal Expo in 1978. In 1989 he played in the Senior Professional Baseball Association, pitching for the St. Petersburg Pelicans and Orlando Juice. Travis Washington was drafted by the Atlanta Braves in the first round of the January 1967 draft. He worked for several years as a police dispatcher in southeastern Oklahoma.

SOMETIMES WE GET TO BE THE HERO JACOBY ELLSBURY AND THE IMPORTANCE OF INDIGENOUS REPRESENTATION

By Christopher D. Chavis

Representations of Indigenous people in sports and media have never been particularly robust. When we are depicted, it's usually through the usage of crude stereotypes that render us as caricatures, side characters to support the hero, or a villain for the heroic cowboy to overcome. It's rare that we are depicted as heroes. For any Indigenous baseball fan in New England in the late 2000s and early 2010s, Jacoby Ellsbury was our hero.

Jacoby Ellsbury celebrates, holding the 2007 American League Championship Series trophy. With a .438 batting average and .500 on-base percentage in the World Series, he was a key contributor to the team's championship victory, his first of two with the Red Sox.

(Steve Babineau/Boston Red Sox)

Before moving to New Hampshire in the fall of 2008 to attend Dartmouth College, I had grown up in rural southeastern North Carolina, far removed from any professional baseball team, in the Lumbee Tribal homeland. Perhaps ironically, the closest team for much of my childhood was the Atlanta Braves. (Though to a poor rural kid, that 300-mile distance may as well have been 3,000 miles.) I watched baseball with my grandfather growing up, but after he died when I was 9 years old, I quit watching. My connection to the game was through him, not through a love for any particular team.

It wasn't until I got to college that I finally found my team, just a two-hour drive down Interstates 89 and 93, the Boston Red Sox.

By then, Ellsbury was in his second full season in Boston. He had speed, talent, and an undeniable spark, and within Dartmouth's Indigenous community, he quickly became a shared figure of admiration. He was good and his promise to get better was evident. We organized trips to Fenway Park to see him play. We wore his jersey. We followed his stat lines.

He was a tribal citizen with ties to his Navajo community. He wasn't a caricature, he wasn't a stereotype, and he wasn't relegated to the bench. He was the starting center fielder and one of the best players on the team, with a bright future ahead of him.

He was also a player whose Indigenous identity was not central to his public perception. He showed that representation does not mean tokenism. He was not the "Indigenous Red Sox player," he was the "Red Sox player who happened to be Indigenous." He did not hide his heritage or try to downplay it, but it did not solely define him. Ellsbury stood on the shoulders of players like Charles Albert "Chief" Bender and Louis Sockalexis, who had faced relentless stereotyping in the early decades of professional baseball.

This resonated with Indigenous students at Dartmouth, an institution that has its own dark history with Indigenous people. Originally founded in 1769 to educate English and Indigenous youth, Dartmouth did not fully commit to its charter mission and begin actively recruiting Indigenous students until the early 1970s. Around the same time, it also retired its "Indian" mascot, a move that continues to spark controversy decades later. During my time on campus, a vocal minority of students still clung to the imagery, reprinting it on T-shirts or cheering it at games, even in the face of opposition from Indigenous students and faculty.

Our experiences on campus were a reminder that representation could never be taken for granted, that in some spaces we were still seen as symbols, not as students. In that context, watching Jacoby Ellsbury excel wasn't just a sports story. It was a counternarrative. It was a statement of a truth that was evident to us, that Indigenous people could perform at the highest levels while being our authentic selves.

But even our heroes face setbacks. Ellsbury missed all but 18 games of the 2010 season with an injury. It was a setback that made his epic return in 2011 all the more sweeter. He went from simply excelling to being one of the best players in the game itself. Most of us are familiar with his stat line – .321 batting average, 32 home runs, 105 RBIs, and 39 stolen bases, accolades that came with an All-Star selection and ultimately a Gold Glove and Silver Slugger. Disappointingly, though, he finished second in the American League MVP vote to Justin Verlander of the Detroit Tigers. I still argue that that was decided incorrectly.

I graduated from Dartmouth during the 2012 season and the less said about that season the better. However, I continued to follow Ellsbury and the Red Sox from law school in Michigan and cheered when they won the 2013 World Series. That World Series win was a crescendo and the end of Ellsbury's run in Boston. He left town for the New York Yankees, a path upon which I could not follow.

The last time I saw Ellsbury play in person was a warm summer afternoon in 2015. By then I had graduated from law school and taken a job in Augusta, Maine. I sat in the outfield bleachers at Fenway Park as Ellsbury came to bat in pinstripes. A sad sight to behold.

But even that sight can't change what Jacoby Ellsbury meant to both my college experience and baseball fandom. Jacoby Ellsbury was more than an athlete. He was a point of connection, a source of pride, and proof that representation, real, respectful, and rooted, matters.

For an Indigenous college student trying to find his place, Ellsbury offered more than inspiration. He offered affirmation. He showed that we don't have to be the caricature, the villain, or the side character. Sometimes we get to be the hero.

THE SPOKANE INDIANS: A COLLABORATION OF TEAM AND TRIBE

By Eric Vickrey

Native American-themed team names and mascots were commonplace in professional baseball during the twentieth century. Images such as an Indian chief in a feathered headdress or warlike caricatures were often used in logos and advertisements. These depictions were often considered derogatory and misrepresented the rich diversity of America's Indigenous people. Protests by fans and Native American groups that began during the civil rights movement resulted in the Cleveland Indians finally dropping their offensive Chief Wahoo logo a half-century later. Two years after the logo switch, the team changed its name to the Guardians. The minor-league franchise in Spokane, Washington, on the other hand, maintains the name "Indians" as a tribute to the Native people through a unique collaboration with the Spokane Tribe.

The city of Spokane has a rich baseball history. Since the turn of the twentieth century, a long list of the sport's luminaries have passed through the so-called Inland Empire, including Stan Coveleski, George Kelly, Maury Wills, Steve Garvey, Tommy Lasorda, Bill Russell, Davey Lopes, Bill Madlock, Zack Greinke, and Carlos Beltrán, just to name a few. Hall of Fame second baseman Ryne Sandberg was born and raised in Spokane, as was popular singer Bing Crosby, who played baseball at Gonzaga University. They all wore spikes on land first inhabited by the ancestors of the Spokane Tribe of Indians – the Native people for whom the city was named.

Signage at Avista Stadium in Spokane.

For thousands of years, the Spokanes lived in an area of northeast Washington that covered approximately 3 million acres.[1] They lived a seminomadic existence, sometimes hunting and foraging in parts of present-day northern Idaho and western Montana. The Spokane River and its tributaries provided their primary source of food, and the visually stunning Spokane Falls were considered sacred. The Spokanes and other regional tribes spoke a dialect called Interior Salish.

The nineteenth century was a period of significant change for the Inland Northwest. It began with the arrival of the first White settlers and ended with the westward expansion of the Northern Pacific Railroad and the establishment of a city first known as Spokane Falls, and later Spokane. Between 1880 and 1910, the city's population exploded from 350 to more than 100,000.[2]

Along with Spokane's growth came baseball. The city's first professional team played in 1890 as a member of the Pacific Northwest League, but the league folded in its third season.[3] After a pair of unsuccessful attempts to revive the circuit in the 1890s, Spokane's next professional entry was organized in 1901. Two years later, the *Spokane Spokesman-Review* held a contest to adopt an official team name. The name Inlanders was selected, but a few weeks later the local papers inexplicably began referring to the team as the Indians, and the name stuck.[4] By 1909, the Spokane baseball club had started using depictions of Native Americans on printed materials. A few years later, "a man dressed in Native American regalia is seen performing a ceremony on the baseball mound."[5]

Because of World War I and the Great Depression, there was no professional baseball in Spokane from 1921 to 1936. When Spokane became a charter member of the Class-B Western International League in 1937, the team was called the Hawks for two seasons before Bill Ulrich bought the franchise and restored the name Indians.[6] Spokane remained a part of Class-B leagues through the 1956 season.

Another iteration of Spokane Indians baseball was born in 1958 when the city was awarded the Los Angeles Dodgers' Triple-A franchise. With Pacific Coast League baseball coming to town, Spokane County built a new ballpark, first called simply Spokane Indians Ball Park and later Avista Stadium. Native American appropriations remained

Eric Vickrey photograph)

part of the landscape; tepee-shaped ticket booths were placed outside of the ballpark entrance and newspapers from the early 1960s show players wearing feather headdresses to opening day galas.

After 14 seasons as the Dodgers' top farm team, the Indians cycled through Triple-A affiliations with four other major-league teams over the next nine seasons. Since 1983 Spokane has been home to Class-A baseball. Former major leaguers George and Ken Brett, along with brothers John and Bobby, bought the team in 1985. As of 2024, the Indians were an affiliate of the Colorado Rockies and owned by Brett Sports and Entertainment.

The National Congress of American Indians, a coalition of tribes from across the US, launched a campaign to ban disparaging Native mascots in 1968. Four years later, students at Stanford University successfully petitioned to have Indians removed as the school's mascot. In the 1990s, protests of Native American mascots became more fervent. One of the leaders at the forefront of the movement was Spokane Tribe member Charlene Teters, who began protesting Chief Illiniwek, the mascot of the University of Illinois at Urbana-Champaign, while she was enrolled at the school. In 1991, Teters helped found the National Coalition on Racism in Sports and in the Media. By 1993, the Spokane baseball club had removed all Native American imagery from its logos and signage and adopted a dinosaur named Otto as its mascot. But the team was still called the Indians.

In 2005 Spokane's baseball executives explored the idea of a new team logo and engaged the Spokane Tribe for their input. In a meeting between team brass and the Spokane Tribal Council at the tribe's headquarters in Wellpinit, Washington, tribal elders expressed appreciation that the team had avoided using offensive imagery, chants, and mascots for many years.

"As we looked for a new logo, we wanted to make sure they were still okay with us using the name 'Indians' if we continued to stay away from Native American imagery," recalled then-team President Andy Billig, a team co-owner and the CEO of Brett Sports. "We told them we were also open to changing the team name if they thought it was problematic. In that meeting the idea was hatched collaboratively to keep the name and embrace Native American imagery but do so in a way that was collaborative, respectful, and educational. From there the idea picked up steam with a particular focus on using this partnership to further educate the community about the Spokane Tribe and the Salish language."[7]

When it became clear that the tribe's priority was to preserve a dialect spoken by only a handful of elders, the team came up with a way to incorporate the Salish language in its rebranding. Two new logos were designed. The primary logo was a red "S" over a baseball inside a circle with two eagle feathers to pay homage to the Native people. A secondary logo was a shoulder patch with "Spokane Indians Baseball Club" written in Salish. The new logos were

(Courtesy of Spokane Indians)

Salish jersey

unveiled at a 2006 ceremony at the Northwest Museum of Arts and Culture. "We wanted this new identity to show respect for the Spokane Tribe and honor the rich 104-year history of the team," Billig said at the time. "I think we accomplished both of our goals."[8]

Though regional tribes and the Spokane community overwhelmingly supported the ongoing use of the name Indians, there was objection from some national groups. "Any compromise short of dropping 'Indian' and any identifiable Native logos would be unacceptable to us and should be unacceptable to the Spokane Nation," said Vernon Bellecourt, president of the National Coalition on Racism in Sports and Media.[9]

In 2014 the collaborative partnership between the baseball club and the Spokane Tribe resulted in a new jersey design with Spokane written in Salish – Sp'q'n'i – across the chest. (There is an additional symbol at the end of the word not found in the English alphabet.) Players wore the Salish jerseys that season as an alternate uniform in a handful of games. A year later, they donned them for every home game, and since 2017 the Salish jerseys have been worn both at home and on the road. The National Baseball Hall of Fame has recognized the jersey's cultural significance by adding one to the museum's permanent collection.

In 2016 Spokane baseball executives wanted to come up with a new mascot to excite fans in the bottom of the sixth inning and again looked at ways of honoring the Spokane Tribe. They landed on the redband trout, a historically important part of the Indigenous people's diet. In conjunction with the new mascot, the team designed alternate jerseys, caps, and logos. The campaign was meant to connect with younger fans who will be responsible for caring for the river habitat in the future.

Today, many signs in Avista Stadium are written in both Salish and English. Outside of the ballpark entrance is an exhibit that informs visitors about the history and culture of the Native people. The only Native American imagery in the ballpark is the Spokane Tribe of Indians' logo, which is located next the right-field scoreboard.

The distinction between Cleveland and Spokane's use of the name Indians has to do with sanctioned versus unsanctioned Native mascots. "The mascot issue is one of tribal sovereignty and input from those whose traditional lands the team and the community occupy is of primary importance," said a spokesperson for the National Conference of American Indians in 2023. "NCAI supports the Spokane Tribe of Indians exercising their sovereignty to collaborate with the Spokane Indians baseball club in pursuit of imagery which honors their peoples and culture. Given the formal collaboration with the Spokane Tribe of Indians, the Spokane Indians mascot is considered sanctioned by the Tribal Nation. NCAI always defers to and supports tribal sovereignty in this space."[10]

"We want [the Spokane baseball team] to keep the name because of how they approached us," explained Carol Evans, a member Spokane Tribal Council, in 2020. "They listened to the elders, and that is what really developed the relationship over time, and it has grown into like a family partnership unit where we have a lot of respect for one another."[11]

"We are not their mascot," said Evans. "They're named after our tribe."[12]

ACKNOWLEDGMENTS

The author wishes to express gratitude to Spokane Indians co-owner Andy Billig for sharing his memories of the team's collaboration with the Spokane Tribe.

Additional thanks to the National Congress of American Indians for expressing their viewpoint on this topic.

NOTES

1   "The History of the Spokane Tribe of Indians," https://spokanetribe.com/history/, accessed July 30, 2023.

2   *Spokane Press*, May 7, 1920: 1.

3   Jim Price, "Birth of the Indians," *Spokane Spokesman-Review*, June 21, 2003: 64.

4   Price, "Birth of the Indians."

5   Larkin Marie Mullin, "Spokane's Other Indians, A Baseball Story," *Spokane Historical*, https://spokanehistorical.org/items/show/513, accessed July 30, 2023.

6   "Spokane Hawks 'Indians' Now," *Spokane Spokesman-Review*, March 18, 1939: 15.

7   Email from Andy Billig to the author, August 23, 2023.

8   Kevin Graman, "Baseball Team Consults with Tribe on Logos," *Spokane Spokesman-Review*, November 30, 2006: 1.

9   Graman, "Baseball Team Consults with Tribe on Logos."

10 Email from a National Congress of American Indians spokesperson to the author, August 15, 2023.

11 David Waldstein, "They're the Indians, with Native American Support," *New York Times*, August 4, 2020: B7.

12 Jon Mooallem, "I Had a Chance to Travel Anywhere. Why Did I Pick Spokane," *New York Times*, September 21, 2021, https://www.nytimes.com/2021/09/21/magazine/spokane-indians-minor-league-baseball.html, accessed July 28, 2023.

THE RISE AND FALL OF CHIEF WAHOO

By Vince Guerrieri

For more than 70 years officially – and even longer unofficially – a grinning Native American caricature named Chief Wahoo was the mascot for the Cleveland Indians.

He adorned the uniforms of the last Cleveland team to win a World Series, in 1948, and was part of the uniforms of every pennant winner in Cleveland since. A bigger-than-life-size statue guided fans to see him at Cleveland Stadium, grinning when a lot of Indians teams didn't offer much for fans to smile about.

Although the statue didn't make the move from Municipal Stadium to the Indians' new home, Jacobs Field,[1] in 1994, Chief Wahoo remained a mainstay of Indians' gear, then some of the most popular in the major leagues. But as the team's success attracted more notice and more fans, so too did Wahoo attract more protests.

Ultimately, the mascot – conceived without malice, its creator said – became untenable, and was stripped from the team's uniforms, an early step in what turned into an overall rebranding. But Chief Wahoo remained an undeniable part of the Indians' history. Some fans were more than willing to see him fade away, but many remained unwilling to let go.

In 1915 Cleveland's American League baseball team, known most recently as the Naps in honor of player-manager Napoleon Lajoie, and before that as the Blues or Bronchos, was renamed the Indians. Many theories for the name have been offered. It wasn't long before Indian visages were used on the team's uniform.

The first year the Indians sported an Indian caricature on their uniforms was 1928, initially as a main logo on home uniforms. For the better part of the next 20 years, an Indian head appeared in profile on sleeves.[2]

In 1946 Bill Veeck bought the Indians from Alva Bradley, who had owned the team for 20 years. The Indians' dynamic new owner started implementing changes immediately. The most notable one was the team's move full-time to Cleveland Stadium from League Park. Veeck also commissioned a local graphics company, J.F. Novak, to design a new mascot for the Indians. The company submitted several designs. One stood out.[3]

The design was made by Walter Goldbach, a 17-year-old senior at James Rhodes High School in Cleveland. It was a smiling Indian with orange skin, a hooked nose and a single feather. "I wanted him to be happy," Goldbach recalled in a 2008 interview with *Cleveland Magazine*. "As a 17-year-old kid, it was the last thing on my mind that I would offend someone."[4]

The Indian bore more than a passing resemblance to a caricature that had appeared in the *Cleveland Plain Dealer* for the previous 15 years. It was the handiwork of Fred Reinert, who'd sent back sketches to his hometown paper while he was in the Army during World War I, and later became the *Plain Dealer*'s sports cartoonist. "The Little Indian," as the character was called, was shown smiling after a team win and with a blackened eye after a loss. The Little Indian was so recognized and beloved that when Paul Brown became the namesake for a new football team in Cleveland in 1946, he asked Reinert to make a Brownie to serve as the team's mascot. Shortly thereafter, Cleveland's hockey team, the Barons of the American Hockey League, got a similar caricature for its mascot.[5]

For the first time in 1952, the mascot was referred to in the *Plain Dealer* as Chief Wahoo.[6] At the time, "Big Chief Wahoo" was a comic strip character known as a "topper," common in the Sunday comics, a smaller strip at the top of a

A 1990s photograph of Chief Wahoo taken in the parking lot at Cleveland Stadium.

larger comic strip, in this instance, "Steve Roper and Mike Nomad."[7] Big Chief Wahoo became a shorthand term for Native Americans in popular culture, and, indeed, the first baseball-related reference to Chief Wahoo in print was as a nickname for Allie Reynolds, a Creek Indian who played for the Indians and then was traded to the Yankees.[8] An ad in the July 14, 1954, issue of *The Sporting News* touted Indians merchandise, including a Wahoo bank, a Wahoo jacket insignia, and an official Indians cap with the new official marking of Chief Wahoo.

By then, Chief Wahoo had gotten a facelift. In 1951, his skin tone changed from orange to red, and his nose lost its hook.[9] The Chief remained part of the Indians' uniform, inside the wishbone C of the baseball cap until 1957, and as part of the jersey for decades to come. In 1962 a large neon-lit sign was placed atop Gate D at Cleveland Stadium.[10] The Chief, 29 feet tall, in a pose ready to swing at a pitch, was manufactured by Cleveland's Brilliant Electric Sign Co.[11] (Former Browns quarterback Milt Plum, who'd been traded to Detroit a month before the sign debuted,[12] had his offseason job at the Brilliant Electric Sign Co., and was the sales rep who'd sold the sign to the team.[13])

By the end of the 1960s, the civil rights movement was in full force, populated by militant organizations. The Black Panther Party was founded in Oakland in 1966. Two years later, the American Indian Movement was founded in Minnesota, and the Chicano Movement began for Latino rights. AIM attracted attention with a series of bold movements, including a takeover of Alcatraz Island in 1969 and an occupation of Wounded Knee in 1973.[14]

In 1970 the Cleveland American Indian Movement was formed.[15] The group demanded of Indians owner Vernon Stouffer that the team's name be changed, writing, "Chief Wahoo, your degrading and insulting caricature which stereotypes the native American, must and has to be eliminated."[16] The group also started protesting the Indians name and Chief Wahoo at the team's Opening Day game.[17]

In 1972 Russell Means, who founded the American Indian Movement and its Cleveland chapter, sued Stouffer and the Indians alleging "group libel." Means also sought an injunction ending the use of Chief Wahoo.[18] "Maybe Mr. Means is being overly sensitive," wrote syndicated sportswriter Ira Berkow. "Maybe, though, oversensitivity comes only after a segment of our population is shunted aside and put, for example, into reservations and at best, condescendingly considered 'noble savages.'"[19]

Stouffer, facing cash-flow problems unrelated to the lawsuit, started shopping the team around. After a deal with George Steinbrenner fell through, the team was sold to Cleveland sports impresario Nick Mileti, who already owned the Cavaliers of the NBA and a World Hockey Association team, the Cleveland Crusaders. In 1973 a new Wahoo logo debuted, showing the Chief in full figure batting, not unlike the statue atop Gate D.[20] Also that year,

new uniforms debuted, with the cap that's become known as the Crooked C.[21]

Means's lawsuit was settled in 1983, with results kept confidential. In 1986 Chief Wahoo became the logo on the Indians cap – a move not without its own controversy. The team was in a transitional state at the time. Owner Steve O'Neill had died in 1983, and his estate was fielding offers for the team, including those from out-of-town buyers. And Peter Bavasi had been hired as team president. The son of illustrious front-office man Buzzie Bavasi, Peter had worked as a consultant in Indianapolis and Tampa, both cities that were trying to lure a major-league baseball team.

The team's 1986 uniforms said "Indians" on both home and road jerseys. And Chief Wahoo had replaced the C on the baseball caps. What evidence was there that the team was from Cleveland … or would remain in Cleveland?

"That's simply paranoia," Bavasi said. "What does Chief Wahoo mean? It means the Cleveland Indians. As a matter of fact, the Indians' new baseball cap is the hottest selling baseball item nationally."[22]

In fact, in an era when the Indians didn't have star power, the most recognizable figure in Cleveland baseball was Chief Wahoo. "If Chief Wahoo is your main man, then the Stadium will have to be your summer hangout," wrote the *Plain Dealer*'s Joe Maxse in the Indians 1987 season preview, outlining 19 giveaway days including Wahoo Bike Cap Day, White Wahoo Cap Day, Barbecue Apron Day, and Helmet Day.[23]

The next year, the Indians were sold to brothers Richard and David Jacobs, Akron, Ohio, natives who had made their fortune in real estate development. Plans were made for a new downtown baseball-only ballpark, but the Chief Wahoo statue – a landmark on the Lakefront – would not be making the trip.[24] The statue was donated to the Western Reserve Historical Society. After a $50,000 restoration, it was put on display by the group.[25]

But Wahoo remained. In fact, under Jacobs' ownership[26] – which coincided with the most successful period for the Indians in 40 years – the team was steadfast in its loyalty to Chief Wahoo. "Mr. Jacobs has gone on record as saying as long as he owns the team, the nickname and logo will remain," said Indians vice president of public relations Bob DiBiasio in 1998.[27]

After the 1999 season, however, Jacobs sold the team, to the Dolan family. Patriarch Larry Dolan was partner in a local law firm, but made his money through stock ownership in Cablevision, a company founded by his brother Charles.[28] Dolan's son Paul was named counsel and vice president for the team, becoming chairman and CEO in 2013.

Initially, Larry Dolan was just as passionately in favor of Chief Wahoo, describing him in a 2005 interview as "a beloved figure."[29] But there were limitations.

In 2009 the Indians moved into their new spring-training facility in Goodyear, Arizona.[30] The logos on the facility were the script I – not Chief Wahoo. "I know there was some sensitivity involved on the outside of the complex" regarding the use of Chief Wahoo, said Paul Dolan, at the time team president. But Dolan added that at that point, there were no plans to phase out Chief Wahoo.[31]

However, it was progressively being deemphasized. In 2011 Wahoo disappeared from the road cap, and in 2013 from the home batting helmet. In January 2014 the team announced that the main logo would be a Block C similar to the logo on baseball caps in the 1980s.[32] The *Plain Dealer* said in an editorial that it was time for the Chief to go entirely: "The Indians – the baseball variety – defend the smiling Wahoo as a benign symbol of the great American pastime, yet they have tacitly acknowledged its offensive characteristics by reducing Wahoo's role in team marketing over the years. It's time for a clean break."[33]

In 2015, a federal judge in Washington, DC, ruled that Redskins could not be trademarked, since it was viewed as a disparaging name.[34] The implications in Cleveland – where protests and lawsuits against Chief Wahoo and the Indians name went back decades – were clear.

The following year, the Indians won the American League Central Division championship. Their opponent in the American League Championship Series was the Toronto Blue Jays, and an indigenous activist, Douglas Cardinal, filed suit in Canada seeking an injunction preventing the Indians from wearing their uniforms or using their team name or logo.[35] It was interpreted in Cleveland as a bit of gamesmanship, but to new Commissioner Rob Manfred, it was a sign that action needed to be taken.

When the Indians made their home debut in 2017, the *New York Times* reported that Manfred "had made clear his 'desire to transition away from the Chief Wahoo logo.'"[36] Earlier that year, Manfred announced that Progressive Field[37] would host the 2019 All-Star Game, the first in Cleveland in 22 years. Early in 2018, the Indians announced that starting in 2019 – the year the Indians hosted the All-Star Game – Chief Wahoo would no longer be present on uniforms, on the field or in any decorations at the ballpark.[38] Chief Wahoo merchandise would continue to be available for sale at the team shop. It didn't take long for fans to start to believe that the midsummer classic was the team's 30 pieces of silver for dropping Chief Wahoo.[39]

As it turned out, it was a prelude to an even bigger change. In 2021 the Dolan family announced that starting in 2022, for the first time since 1915, Cleveland's team wouldn't be the Indians. They would be the Guardians.

NOTES

1   In 2008 the ballpark became Progressive Field, after the insurance giant acquired the naming rights.

2   http://exhibits.baseballhalloffame.org/dressed_to_the_nines/uniforms. asp?city=Cleveland&league=AL&sort=year&increment=9&pos=28.

3   Bob Finnan, "Wahoo Designer Die-Hard Tribe Fan," *Medina* (Ohio) *Gazette*, April 11, 2017: 1.

4   Andy Netzel, "Life According to Walter Goldbach," *Cleveland Magazine*, July 23, 2008. In the interview, he noted that the name Chief Wahoo was a misnomer, because he had only one feather, and chiefs had full headdresses. https://clevelandmagazine.com/in-the-cle/people/articles/life-according-to-walter-goldbach.

5   Gordon Cobbledick, "Plain Dealing," *Cleveland Plain Dealer*, February 14, 1962: 29.

6   Brad Ricca, "The Secret History of Chief Wahoo," *Belt Magazine*, June 19, 2014. https://beltmag.com/secret-history-chief-wahoo/.

7   Allan Holtz, "Toppers: Indian Slango," *Stripper's Guide*, November 14, 2016. http://strippersguide.blogspot.com/2016/11/toppers-indian-slango.html.

8   Reynolds was a throw-in at the behest of Joe DiMaggio, who said he had a hard time hitting him when he faced the Indians.

9   Emily Bamforth (Associated Press), "Cleveland Indians' Chief Wahoo, from Inception to End: A Timeline," https://apnews.com/article/mlb-new-york-baseball-cleveland-ohio-75c97df1d3c04f29ade9b7a5b1ec49d2.

10 Joe Posnanski, who grew up in Cleveland, said the statue could be seen half a mile away. https://joeposnanski.substack.com/p/wahoo-from-2007.

11 "King-Sized Chief Wahoo Takes Stadium Post to Cheer on Tribe," *Cleveland Plain Dealer*, April 27, 1962: 37.

12 "Browns Trade Milt Plum to Lions; Ninowski, Cassady Go to Cleveland in 3-for-3 Deal," *New York Times*, March 30, 1962. https://www.nytimes.com/1962/03/30/archives/browns-trade-milt-plum-to-lions-ninowski-cassady-go-to-cleveland-in.html.

13 Gordon Cobbledick, "Plain Dealing," *Cleveland Plain Dealer*, April 28, 1962: 33.

14 American Indian Movement, Encyclopedia Britannica. https://www.britannica.com/topic/American-Indian-Movement

15 https://case.edu/ech/articles/c/cleveland-american-indian-movement.

16 Regis McAuley, "Militant indians [sic] do not like Cleveland's use of emblem," *Dover* (Ohio) *Daily Reporter*, April 3, 1970: 16.

17 Those were the doldrums for the Indians, and Opening Day turned out to be the only real crowd the team could count on through the years.

18 Russell Schneider, "Indians' Wahoo Symbol Facing a Legal Skirmish," *The Sporting News*, February 5, 1972: 43.

19 Ira Berkow, "Indians vs. 'Indians': A Matter of Sensitivity," *McKinney* (Texas) *Courier-Gazette*, February 1, 1972: 5.

20 That logo lasted until 1978, when the previous incarnation of Chief Wahoo returned. "Tribal Notes," *Cleveland Call and Post*, December 16, 1978: 19B.

21 The font, according to the Indians media guide at the time, was Neuland.

22 Paul Hoynes, "There Is Much Ado About Chief Wahoo," *Cleveland Plain Dealer*, April 24, 1986: 50.

23 Joe Maxse, "Indians Plan 19 Giveaways," *Cleveland Plain Dealer*, April 6, 1987: 65.

24 When Jacobs Field opened in 1994, ceremonial first pitches were thrown by President Bill Clinton, Ohio Gov. George Voinovich, and former Indians ace Bob Feller. Voinovich and Feller wore Wahoo caps. Clinton wore a 1980s era cap with a C on it. https://www.c-span.org/video/?55799-1/cleveland-indians-opening-day.

25 Mark Podolski, "Chief Wahoo Still a Divisive Symbol in Cleveland Sports," *Lorain* (Ohio) *Morning Journal*, May 5, 2013. https://archive.ph/20130615123415/http:/morningjournal.com/articles/2013/05/05/sports/doc51872254d53a3380784079.txt?viewmode=fullstory#selection-1459.0-1459.55.

26 Although both brothers bought the team, David died in 1992, leaving Richard as the team's primary owner until he sold to the Dolans.

27   Terry Pluto, "It's time to Say Goodbye to Chief Wahoo," *Lorain Morning Journal*, August 20, 1998. DiBiasio remains with the team today, a career of more than 40 years in Cleveland – broken only by a year in exile during Bavasi's reign.

28   Charles's son James – Larry Dolan's nephew – is the controversial Knicks owner.

29   https://www.clevelandseniors.com/people/larrydolan.htm.

30   The Indians first went to Arizona for spring training in 1947. Owner Bill Veeck had a ranch in Arizona, but not coincidentally, that was the year the National League integrated with Jackie Robinson in Brooklyn and then the American League when Veeck signed Larry Doby to play for the Indians 10 weeks later. https://www.azcentral.com/story/travel/arizona/2019/01/18/cactus-league-arizona-spring-training-history/2233075002/.

31   Paul Hoynes, "Wahoo in Decline? New Spring Base Latest Sign of De-emphasis on Old Logo," Cleveland.com, April 12, 2009. https://www.cleveland.com/tribe/2009/04/mlb_insider_wahoo_in_decline_n.html.

32   Craig Calcaterra, "The Indians Are Changing Their Primary Logo from Chief Wahoo to the Block C," NBC Sports. https://mlb.nbcsports.com/2014/01/08/the-indians-are-changing-their-primary-logo-from-chief-wahoo-to-the-block-c/.

33   "The Tribe Should Retire Chief Wahoo Once and for All," Cleveland.com, February 28, 2014. https://www.cleveland.com/opinion/2014/02/the_tribe_should_retire_chief.html.

34   Ian Shapira, "Federal Judge Orders Cancellation of Redskins' Trademark Registrations," *Washington Post*, July 8, 2015. https://www.washingtonpost.com/local/judge-upholds-cancellation-of-redskins-trademarks-in-a-legal-and-symbolic-setback-for-team/2015/07/08/5a65424e-1e6e-11e5-aeb9-a411a84c9d55_story.html.

35   Nicole Thompson, "Canadian Activist Seeking Injunction Against Use of 'Cleveland Indians' Name," *Toronto Star*, October 16, 2016. https://www.thestar.com/sports/baseball/2016/10/16/canadian-activist-seeking-injunction-against-use-of-cleveland-indians-name.html.

36   David Waldstein, "Baseball Urges Indians to Phase Out Caricature," *New York Times*, April 13, 2017: B10.

37   In 2008, Progressive Insurance bought the naming rights to Jacobs Field. https://www.espn.com/mlb/news/story?id=3191639.

38   https://www.cbssports.com/mlb/news/cleveland-indians-fully-phase-out-chief-wahoo-logo-unveil-new-uniforms-for-2019/.

39   https://www.cbssports.com/mlb/news/rob-manfred-refutes-idea-mlb-granted-cleveland-2019-all-star-game-in-exchange-for-removal-of-indians-chief-wahoo-logo/.

FROM BLUES TO NAPS TO INDIANS TO GUARDIANS: OVER 100 YEARS OF TEAM NAME CHANGES

By Stephanie Liscio

After the Cleveland Indians initiated a name change in time for the 2022 season, there were fans who applauded the decision and others who were upset that they were abandoning the identity they had held since 1915. However, this was a club that had already had four different names between its founding in 1901 and 1915. By the 1970s there was very vocal opposition to both the club's name and its mascot, Chief Wahoo.

This opposition continued for nearly 50 years before the club announced in 2018 that it would no longer use its logo Wahoo starting with the 2019 season. Before the end of 2020 the club announced it would abandon the name Indians and teased an announcement of what the new identity would be. In the middle of the 2021 season, the team announced that the new name was Guardians via a video narrated by actor Tom Hanks. Even though there was a name change, the team held onto some of the aesthetic from the Indians, name particularly the font on "Guardians" on the front of the uniform. The team incorporated an Art Deco theme on the scoreboards and throughout the ballpark to complement its neighbor, the stone "Guardians of Traffic" depicting various forms of transportation, on the Hope Memorial Bridge next to Progressive Field.

Cleveland's entry into the new American League in 1901 did not have a set nickname; mostly the team was just referred to as "Cleveland" in newspaper articles that first season. The team used Blues for a time, and eventually settled on Naps, named for second baseman-manager Napoleon Lajoie. When Lajoie was traded to the Philadelphia Athletics after the 1914 season, the nickname had to be changed. Club President Charley Somers, after "disposing of his star player to Philadelphia," asked the baseball writers for Cleveland's newspapers to select a new nickname that would be "short, expressive and appropriate."[1]

On January 15, 1915, the sportswriters announced their choice: Indians.[2] They sportswriters chose "Indians." The *Cleveland Plain Dealer* asserted that the name had been used for Cleveland's old National League team years before.[3] The writers seemed to imply that perhaps it would be just a temporary placeholder. "The nickname, however, is but temporarily bestowed, as the club may so conduct itself during the present season as to earn some other cognomen which may be more appropriate. The choice of a name

that would be significant just now was rather difficult with the club itself anchored in last place."[4] Toledo's American Association team was moving to Cleveland and planned to share League Park with the American League club. Around the same time, the nickname Spiders was bestowed on the American Association team; the moniker had not been used since the National League franchise left town after the 1899 season.

The next day the *Plain Dealer* called attention to a Native American "star player" of the old Cleveland Spiders club named Louis Sockalexis "many years ago." According to the article, he was so skilled and outshined his teammates by so much "that he naturally came to be regarded as the whole team." The article said "Indians" was "an honorable name," offering nostalgia for "a time when Cleveland had one of the most popular teams of the United States" as well as a reminder for an excellent player. (Much of the article was focused on Cleveland's American Association team adopting the name Spiders.[5] With such a minor notice of Sockalexis, and one that seemed sparked by the new name creating nostalgia, it did not seem the sole reason for the new name. A scholarly article published in 1998 said the initial announcement that the name might be temporary seemed to suggest that it was not offered specifically to honor someone.[6]

By 1931 the *Plain Dealer's* Gordon Cobbledick tied Sockalexis to the team's name, but then appeared to debunk it almost immediately. After positing that "so great was (Sockalexis's) popularity that the team's name was changed to Indians and has remained Indians ever since," Cobbledick wrote, "That is fiction, of course. The Cleveland team was called the Naps through the early part of the present century – after Napoleon Lajoie. The name Indians was selected through a newspaper contest when the late James C. Dunn bought the club from Charlie Somers in 1916."[7] There are several clear inaccuracies with that version of events, however. As already noted, the name was chosen "temporarily" by sportswriters in January 1915 while Somers still owned the team. While there were stories about the name being chosen in a fan vote, the *Plain Dealer* seemed to make it clear that sportswriters selected it. Boston's National League team had rebranded as the Braves just a few years prior, so they were not the only team to rebrand with a name connected to Native Americans. Staurowsky in her article argued that the Indians leaned on the Sockalexis story by the 1990s to essentially defend its continued use of the name. She wrote that the stories the team used to connect the name "Indians" to Sockalexis in the 1990s did not even include much about the man, other than to note that he was the first Native American to play professional baseball.[8]

The first high-profile protest to the name "Indians" came on January 18, 1972, when the American Indian Movement filed a $9 million lawsuit against the team and its owner at the time, Vernon B. Stouffer. The legal action was initiated by the Cleveland American Indian Center and its director, Russell C. Means, and specifically wanted the team to stop using the caricature of Chief Wahoo. While the focus of the lawsuit was Wahoo, Means was critical of the team's name as well, asking if it would be appropriate to have a team named the "Cleveland Negroes" or the "Washington Rednecks."[9] The suit against the Indians was settled out court in 1983 for about $35,000, and the team refused to abandon both the name and Wahoo.[10]

The late 1960s and early 1970s were a time of protest against inequality in society and Native American groups wanted to fight back against a federal government that had oppressed them and belittled their culture for more than a century. The fight against degrading team names and symbols became a part of this larger battle. Nationally, the first statement against these names and symbols came in 1968 from the National Congress of American Indians as they "began a campaign to address native stereotypes found in sports and media."[11]

During the 1990s there was a sharp uptick in protests about Native American team names and mascots, with a push to eliminate these names once and for all; in Cleveland this included both Chief Wahoo and the name "Indians." Clyde Bellecourt, the co-founder of the AIM and the spokesman for the newly formed National Coalition on Racism in Sports and the Media, said in 1992, "It is time to cleanse America's favorite pastime of these vestiges of racism." Referring to supporters of racist team names, Bellecourt objected to "suggestions by opponents that the fight against using Indian team names and mascots is coming at the eleventh hour after being in use for decades. ... In other words, the offender now tries to dictate to the offended when we can be offended. ... We have been trying to deal with this subject for decades."[12]

By 2001 the groundswell to remove Native American team names was accelerating. More than 600 high schools and colleges ditched team names and mascots connected to Native Americans, in part thanks to the work of Native anti-defamation groups. The US Commission on Civil Rights officially called upon non-Native schools, colleges, and universities to stop using any names or mascots connected to Native Americans. The commission said that in addition to likely violating antidiscrimination laws, the Native team names could be a violation of the Civil Rights Act of 1964.

According to the commission, these Native names and mascots "can create ... a racially hostile education environment that may be intimidating to Indian students."[13]

The Cleveland club faced challenges connected to the name and Wahoo. When the team returned to Arizona for spring training in 2009 after 16 years in Florida, Wahoo was nowhere to be found at the team's complex (other than on items in the team shop). But club owner Paul Dolan said there were no plans to eliminate Wahoo.[14] As the Indians prepared to meet the Toronto Blue Jays in the 2016 American League Championship Series, a lawsuit filed in the Supreme Court of Justice in Toronto sought to bar the club from using Indians and Wahoo during the series. Major League Baseball said it "appreciates the concerns" of people offended by the team's name and logo, but that these issues should be addressed outside of litigation. MLB cited time constraints and said, "Given the demands for completing the League Championship Series in a timely manner, MLB will defend Cleveland's right to use their name that has been in existence for more than 100 years." The court rejected the complaint, and the team used Indians and Wahoo during the series.[15]

However, Wahoo's days on Cleveland's uniforms were severely numbered. In 2018 the club announced that Wahoo would not appear on its jerseys and hats starting the next season, in the lead-up to the city hosting the 2019 All-Star Game. An AIM executive in Cleveland said the group still planned to protest outside of games, focusing on the team's name. He said, "The racism that happens at the stadium with the red-face and the people dressing up as natives and the whooping and hollering, somehow thinking that they're honoring us, that doesn't come because of Wahoo. ... Wahoo comes because of that."[16]

In the summer of 2020, the Washington Redskins of the NFL announced that it would drop the team's racist name after years of complaints. Several corporate sponsors and investors had threatened to cut ties with the team if the name remained. The nickname eventually was changed to Commanders.[17]

In December 2020 the Indians announced that they would change their name. Other prominent professional teams with Native imagery in their names and logos like the Atlanta Braves, Kansas City Chiefs, and Chicago Blackhawks had no plans to make any changes. The club said it planned to do a "thorough review" of the team's name and consulted with several Native American groups.[18]

According to the *New York Times*, the club now believed "the time was right to determine whether the name was still appropriate."[19] The team conducted research and interviews with what it referred to as "stakeholders" – fans, Native American groups, researchers, historians, psychologists, and religious and civic leaders "from a variety of backgrounds." When the team announced the change in December of 2020, it said it would go by "Indians" for one more season; 2021 would be the team's last season with a Native American name and imagery.[20] In July 2021 the club announced that "Guardians" was selected as the new name out of 1,100 possibilities after more than 100 hours "of brainstorming sessions with fans, community leaders, local influencers, staff and front office."[21]

The new name was in part inspired by large Art Deco statues named the Guardians of Transportation that adorn the Hope Memorial Bridge, which sits across from Progressive Field. Opened in 1932 with a span of 5,865 feet across the Cuyahoga River, the bridge has four double-sided, 43-foot-tall pylons or statues dubbed the "Guardians of Transportation" and carved from sandstone from suburban Berea, Ohio. Designed by Frank Walker, with sculpting by Henry Hering and local stonecutters, the bridge Guardians are meant to represent "technological advances made in transit," while each stands holding a different type of vehicle in its hands. Originally named the Lorain-Carnegie Bridge, after a 1983 rehabilitation it was renamed the Hope Memorial Bridge "in honor of actor Bob Hope and his family, English immigrants who came to Cleveland in 1908." Bob Hope's father, William Henry Hope, worked on the statues as a stonemason.[22]

Owner Paul Dolan stressed that the team was not named directly for the Guardians on the Hope Memorial Bridge, "but there's no question that it's a strong nod to those and what they mean to the community." *Plain Dealer* columnist Terry Pluto wrote that the new name fit with "Guard The Land," since sometimes Cleveland was referred to as "The Land." Shortly after the name was announced, the team faced a lawsuit from a local roller derby club named Guardians, which claimed trademark infringement and "deceptive trade practices." By November of 2021 the two teams reached an "amicable resolution" that allowed both to continue using "Guardians." The exact terms involved in the deal were not disclosed, but the resolution meant that the baseball Guardians could finally begin selling merchandise with their new nickname, something that had been on hold while the lawsuit progressed.[23]

While Native American groups as well as several state and city officials praised the change, some fans objected to the rebranding. The *Plain Dealer* wrote that it seemed less anger about "Guardians" specifically and more anger at the fact that the team rebranded at all. However, there were fans who supported the change, including one high-profile fan – Oscar-winning actor Tom Hanks. He originally came to Cleveland in 1977 to intern at the Great Lakes Shakespeare Festival and worked for three summers at what is now called the Great Lakes Theater and became a huge Indians fan. Over the years he has publicly expressed fondness for Cleveland and wore Indians gear in television appearances. When it came time to create a video introducing the new name, Hanks agreed to narrate it.[24]

The *Plain Dealer's* Guardians beat writer Paul Hoynes pointed to a comment from owner Dolan that "a professional sports team should bring a city together, not divide it," Instead "this is a way to bring peace to the situation. To give the organization a chance to do good things in the community while not constantly answering questions and defending itself about its own name."[25] He said the team knew the change might be difficult for fans at first, and it wanted to keep some common links between the old and new names. For example, the team colors of navy, red, and white would remain the same and the same font would be used on the team jerseys. "The fact that the last five letters in each name are the same is not an accident," Hoynes wrote.[26]

The formal unveiling of the new name was delayed by the offseason lockout imposed by the owners that pushed Opening Day back slightly. When the Guardians finally opened at home against the San Francisco Giants on April 15, 2022, Hanks threw out the first pitch. In July of 2025, President Donald Trump attempted to push the team to revert to the "Indians" moniker after more than three years as the Guardians. However, Chris Antonetti, the team's president of baseball operations, essentially said there would be no further changes to the name. [27]

The Guardians, and the country, have come a long way since the defiant name-change denials of the 1990s; hundreds of secondary and collegiate schools had stopped using names and logos connected to Native Americans by the 2020s. While some teams cling to imagery and names that offend Native Americans, two professional teams and hundreds of high schools and colleges have rebranded. Fans did not appear to abandon the teams due to these changes; in fact, in 2024 Cleveland saw its highest attendance at Progressive Field since 2017, a year in which they won an American League-record 22 consecutive games.[28] Some remain upset about the change, as evidenced by complaints on social media and Change.org petitions asking for the team's name to revert to "Indians," but overall the rebranding appears to be a success. Perhaps this name change should have come in the 1990s when the team moved from its longtime home of Cleveland Municipal Stadium to the brand-new Jacobs Field (now Progressive Field) and in response to the increasing number of protests. While the team cannot rewrite that history, they can start fresh under a new identity that will hopefully serve them well for their next 100 years.

NOTES

1   "Must Select New Name for Naps Now Larry's Out," *Cleveland Plain Dealer*, January 6, 1915: 11.

2   "Baseball Writers to Rename Naps Today," *Cleveland Plain Dealer*, January 15, 1915: 13.

3   "Baseball Writers Select 'Indians' as the Best Name," *Cleveland Plain Dealer*, January 17, 1915: 15.

4   "Baseball Writers Select 'Indians' as the Best Name," *Cleveland Plain Dealer*, January 17, 1915: 15.

5   "Looking Backward," *Cleveland Plain Dealer*, January 18, 1915: 8.

6   Ellen J. Staurowsky, "An Act of Honor or Exploitation?: The Cleveland Indians' Use of the Louis Francis Sockalexis Story," *Sociology of Sport*, 1998 (15), 299-316.

7   Gordon Cobbledick, "Half of Tribe to Get Boosts in '31 Salaries," *Cleveland Plain Dealer*, January 1, 1931: 24.

8   Staurowsky.

9   Amos A. Kermisch, "Sioux After Wahoo, Stouffer Scalps," *Cleveland Plain Dealer*, January 15, 1972: 1.

10   Paul Shepard, "Indians Say Team-Name Issue One of Respect," *Cleveland Plain Dealer*, March 1, 1992: 1B.

11   Jason Edward Black, "The 'Mascotting' of Native America: Construction, Commodity, and Assimilation," *American Indian Quarterly*, 26(4) Autumn 2002, 605-622.

12   Paul Shepard, "Indian Activist Explains Chief Wahoo's Offense," *Cleveland Plain Dealer*, February 28, 1992: 3B.

13   "Toward a Groundswell on Mascots," *Indian Country Today*, April 25, 2001, 21(45): A4.

14   Paul Hoynes, "MLB Insider: Wahoo in Decline? New Spring Base Latest Sign of De-Emphasis on Old Logo," *Cleveland Plain Dealer*, April 12, 2009 (https://www.cleveland.com/tribe/2009/04/mlb_insider_wahoo_in_decline_n.html). Accessed September 5, 2024.

15   Robert Higgs, Canadian Judge Rules Cleveland Indians Can Use Name, Chief Wahoo Logo in Toronto ALCS Games," Cleveland.com, October 17, 2016. (https://www.cleveland.com/metro/2016/10/canadian_judge_rules_cleveland.html). Accessed September 24, 2024.

16   Kevin Barry, "Cleveland Indians Start Home Opener without Chief Wahoo, but Will Continue to Sell Wahoo Merchandise," *News 5 Cleveland*, April 1, 2019 (https://www.news5cleveland.com/sports/baseball/indians/cleveland-indians-start-home-opener-without-chief-wahoo-but-will-continue-to-sell-wahoo-merchandise). Accessed September 24, 2024.

17   Jeff Kerr, "Here's A Timeline Detailing the Origins, Controversies and More," CBS Sports, July 13, 2020 (https://www.cbssports.com/nfl/news/ washington-redskins-name-change-heres-a-timeline-detailing-the-origins-controversies-and-more/) <Accessed November 20, 2024.

18   David Waldstein and Michael S. Schmidt, "After Years of Protest, Cleveland's Baseball Team Will Change Its Name," *New York Times*, December 14, 2020: 37.

19   Waldstein and Schmidt.

20   David Waldstein, "In Cleveland, a Path to Put the Past Behind," *New York Times*, December 15, 2020: B7.

21   Paul Hoynes, "Changing of the Guard," *Cleveland Plain Dealer*, July 24, 2021: 17.

22   Michael Rotman, "Lorain-Carnegie Bridge, Home of the Guardians," *Cleveland Historical*, published September 24, 2010, updated September 27, 2023 (https://clevelandhistorical.org/items/show/73). Accessed November 30, 2024. Sometimes the statues are referred to as the "Guardians of Traffic" as opposed to the "Guardians of Transportation."

23   "Cleveland Guardians Settle Lawsuit with Local Roller Derby Team over Rights to Name," ESPN.com, November 16, 2021 (https://www.espn.com/ mlb/story/_/id/32643793/cleveland-guardians-settle-lawsuit-local-roller-derby-team-rights-name). Accessed November 30, 2024.

24   Joey Morona, "Is That ... Is That Tom Hanks Narrating?" *Cleveland Plain Dealer*, July 24, 2021: 4; Cameron Fields, "Some Fans Are Not Fans of New Nickname," *Cleveland Plain Dealer*, July 24, 2021: 4.

25   Paul Hoynes, "Changing of the Guard," *Cleveland Plain Dealer*, July 24, 2021: 17.

26   Paul Hoynes, "Changing of the Guard," *Cleveland Plain Dealer*, July 24, 2021: 17.

27   Ryan Lewis, "President Donald Trump calls on Cleveland Guardians to restore former name," *Akron Beacon Journal*, July 20, 2025.

28   Terry Pluto, "An Inside Look at How 2 Million Fans Have Embraced the Guardians," Cleveland.com, September 28, 2024) https://www.cleveland.com/guardians/2024/09/an-inside-look-at-how-2-million-fans-have-embraced-the-guardians-terry-pluto.html). Accessed November 25, 2024.

OTHERING AT THE BALLPARK: ORIGINS OF THE ATLANTA BRAVES' 'TOMAHAWK CHOP'

By Steven Goldman

One of baseball's most absurd semiannual rituals takes place when the Atlanta Braves advance in the playoffs and a national audience is reintroduced to the "tomahawk chop," an impression of Native American "braves" striking with a foam reproduction of the eponymous weapon. The subsequent discussion often devolves into an accounting of who is offended and who is not, the argument being that if enough Braves fans like it and not too many Native Americans are offended, the team is good to go. Commissioner Rob Manfred said as much in 2021:

> The Braves have done a phenomenal job with the Native American community. The Native American community in that region is wholly supportive of the Braves' program, including the chop. For me, that's kind of the end of the story. ... Ours is an everyday game. You've got to sell tickets every single day to the fans in that market. And there are all sorts of differences between the regions in terms of how the teams are marketed.[1]

Manfred's approving Native Americans remain obscure; as an NBC News story noted, while he claimed to have spoken to "local Cherokees," none of the three federally recognized bands of Cherokees dwell in Georgia (in fact there are no federally recognized Native American tribes or nations in the state at all), the Cherokees having been forcibly removed from the state by the government in the nineteenth century. "The Eastern Band of Cherokee Indians remains in nearby North Carolina," wrote David K. Li and Graham Lee Brewer, "and Principal Chief Richard Sneed has said for years that the tribe doesn't support the Braves' cheer." Added Jason Salsman, a spokesman for the Muscogee Nation, "I think for us, with the tomahawk chop, you're not getting anything really authentic. You're getting something that's more of a caricature." In a statement, the president of the National Congress of American Indians, Fawn Sharp, rejected Manfred's remarks: "[T]he name 'Braves,' the tomahawk adorning the team's uniform, and the 'tomahawk chop' that the team exhorts its fans to perform at home games are meant to depict and caricature not just one tribal community but all Native people. ... Native people are not mascots, and degrading rituals like

the 'tomahawk chop' that dehumanize and harm us have no place in American society."[2]

This gets at the root of the "tomahawk" problem: If the gesture is meant to connect the Braves to the supposed actions of the Native Americans who, as we shall see, did *not* inspire the club's name, then it invokes a traditional one-dimensional depiction of violence that is not only simplistic and overly broad, but doesn't apply to Georgia's history in particular: the Cherokees forced onto the "Trail of Tears" to Indian Territory by President Andrew Jackson and his successors were more likely to wield a plow than an ax; they were primarily farmers whose lands were coveted by White settlers, gold prospectors, and, like the Georgia governor who announced in 1821 that it was his intention to swap "all the red for a white population," politicians who had a vision of an ethnically homogeneous state.[3]

Braves fans only began chopping in 1991, when outfielder Deion Sanders joined the team. Sanders had played college football with the Florida State Seminoles, a team with its own Native American-appropriated iconography whose fans did a version of the chop. Atlanta-Fulton County Stadium organist Carolyn King legitimized the activity by adding a two-note "tomahawk song" both accompanying and prompting the fans to chop. "My music teacher would be real proud of me," she said. "A and G: that's my life."[4]

The two-note chop is an example of an ethnic pastiche, a leitmotif that may bear limited resemblance to the actual music of the group it purports to signify, yet has been heard so often that it trains the ear to hear it as if it does. Consider the use of the instantly identifiable "Indian" musical trope that accompanies the opening titles of John Ford's 1948 *Fort Apache* (composed by Richard Hageman) or the themes by Max Steiner that accompany the Comanche scenes in Ford's *The Searchers* (1956), both of which bear similarities to the "chop" music and singalong. This use of this music is, if not overtly racist, then reductionist, because it isn't the thing it purports to be, and it comes freighted with all of the imagery it has underscored – in the case of Native Americans, generally attacks on White settlers and soldiers.

As Timothy E. Scheurer wrote in *Music and Mythmaking in Film: Genre and the Role of the Composer,* the use of these themes displaces the Native American from the American community as a whole even as they serve another,

NATIVE AMERICAN MAJOR LEAGUERS

more overt purpose (underscoring a dramatic scene or, in the case of the Braves, exhorting the crowd):

Kathryn Kalinak has astutely observed that because we always hear the main title when the stagecoach is traveling across the landscape, "it is the Indian music, ironically, that seems out of place in Monument Valley, and Native Americans who seem outside the natural order of things in *Stagecoach* [another Ford film]. Thus music positions Native Americans not only as Other, but as intrusive, as not belonging." That sense of otherness, from a musical standpoint, is the result of the marked musical elements used to underscore the presence of the Native American in the Western.[5]

King, the ballpark organist, was not immune to the power of these "native" leitmotifs, which occur in countless other Westerns. Indeed, in 1991 she said she had been playing the two-note theme, "about two years ago, because it sounded *as if it would go with a team called the Braves.*" (Emphasis added.)[6]

Manfred's comment seemed to suggest not only that there isn't an objective standard of appropriate conduct when it comes to ethnic appropriation and parody ("Is there harm?"), but that Braves fans are so invested in the club's Native American iconography that giving it up would hurt the team. One of the most perverse aspects of that stance – besides its capitulation to racial caricature in the name of profits – is that the Braves name originally had little to do with Native Americans, but was chosen by a carpetbagger owner pursuing an internecine rivalry with a fellow creature of New York's Democratic Party machine.

The National League team playing in Atlanta can claim a lineage going back to the foundational nineteenth-century Cincinnati Red Stockings, but it wasn't referred to as the Braves until well into its 1871-1952 Boston residency. As with many teams in the early twentieth century, the club's early nicknames were transient and informal, more often the invention of the press than a reflection of any effort at official branding by the team. The nascent Braves' team colors early on were red, reflecting their founding, and they were referred to as the Reds or Red Stockings. They were called the Beaneaters for a while, a lost chance at advertising synergy. There wasn't much imagination involved in coining these names: When the team was co-owned by Pittsburgh brothers George and John Dovey, the club became the Doves; when the team was held by New York lawyer William H. Russell, it was called the Rustlers.

This period of wavering nomenclature ended – with one brief exception – after Russell died in late 1911. On December 12 the team was purchased by the latest of a series of out-of-town owners when a partnership of former player-manager, Players' League organizer, and attorney John Montgomery Ward, New York construction-company owner and political barnacle James Gaffney, and other investors consisting "almost entirely of members and associates of New York's Tammany Hall."[7]

Ward was initially team president and Gaffney treasurer, but the arrangement didn't last long; tiring of conflict with his major partner, he sold out to him approximately eight months after buying in. The major legacy of his brief ownership may have been the Braves name. Ward biographer Bryan Di Salvatore suggested that the team "adopt[ed] the symbol of Democratic Tammany Hall: The Delaware Indian chief, Tammamend in 'full headdress'" [sic] as an enticement to Gaffney to join his group. Harold Kaese's *Boston Braves* assigns the impetus to Gaffney, saying he "let Ward pick the manager [Johnny Kling] but he selected the new nickname for his team. … They kept their white uniforms and red stockings, but instead of the Old English 'B' they bore on their bosoms, they now had the profile of a proud Indian. The new name caught on. It was not only original, it was aboriginal."[8]

Kaese's pun was inaccurate. The chief was a symbol of Tammany, not of North America's indigenous peoples, even if it was hard to distinguish the two without realizing what was meant by the addition of the chief's profile to the uniform (not initially on the breast but on the sleeve; it eventually gravitated to the uniform front and, in 1930, shrank to fit within the blouse's column of buttons but was blown up to terrific size on the players' backs). Tammany Hall invoked Native American iconography from its earliest days, but only in the insular, cosplaying way of fraternal organizations; they had no affinity or interest in actual Native Americans or their affairs.[9]

The origins of New York City's Democratic Party machine began with a semimythical seventeenth-century Delaware or Lenni Lenape chief named Tamanend. His name had many spellings and was soon Americanized to Tammany. In 1682 or 1683, William Penn, proprietor of the colony that would come to be called Pennsylvania in his honor, met with Tammany and other Delawares under a tree at Shackamaxon (a site near the Delaware River in present-day Philadelphia) and agreed to a treaty of amity, not to mention land. Tamanend reportedly proposed that the Delawares and the colonists would "live in peace as long as the waters run in the rivers and creeks and as long as the stars and moon endure."[10]

In a period in which expansion-minded White colonists often clashed violently with Native Americans, Tamanend became a symbol of the good Indian. "He never had his equal," a missionary wrote. "He was in the highest degree endowed with wisdom, virtue, prudence, charity, affability, meekness, hospitality, in short, with every good and noble qualification."[11] Early Pennsylvanians, in a practice that spread to other colonies, adopted him as a hero and celebrated May 1 as *Saint* Tammany's day. As John Adams later wrote, "The people here have sainted him and keep his day."[12] Tammany societies sprang up around the continent. One of them, the Society of St. Tammany or Columbian Order, was founded in Manhattan in 1788.[13]

NATIVE AMERICAN MAJOR LEAGUERS

Not initially an explicitly political organization except in its anti-aristocratic, pro-democratic leanings, Tammany (the "Columbian" aspect soon faded) immersed itself in Native American costume and jargon from the outset. The leader was the Grand Sachem; upper-level members were Sachems. The official who ran the meetings was a Sagamore, while the doorkeeper (that is, the sergeant-at-arms) was called a Wiskinskie. For a while, the president of the United States was granted the honorary title of Kitchi Okemaw, or Great Grand Sachem. Ordinary members were Braves. Tammany even had a bespoke calendar that divided the year into seasons and seasons into moons, and took its dates from Columbus's "discovery" of America, the Declaration of Independence, and the organization's founding. Thus July 1800 was, by Tammany's reckoning, "Season of Fruits, Seventh Moon, Year of Discovery three-hundred and eighth; of Independence twenty-fourth, and of the Institution the twelfth."[14]

Beginning around 1800, Tammany underwent a change reflecting national political conflicts between Federalists and the Democratic-Republican Party, or the Jeffersonian Democrats. Aaron Burr, that most controversial of the founding fathers, was one of the earliest and most effective political organizers in the nation's history. At this turn he was working to capture New York's electoral votes for the anti-Federalist Thomas Jefferson against presidential incumbent Adams. He found in the Tammany Society a group of like-minded politically engaged members. Gradually, Burr's "Little Band" of Democratic-Republican operatives became part of the Tammany Society and Tammany Society members become part of Burr's organization until the difference between the two evaporated.[15]

Due to the turbulence of his own career, Burr quickly gave way to others, but his acolytes remained in control of Tammany. As the Democratic-Republicans broke up and were supplanted by the Democratic Party, Tammany changed in turn. Its metamorphosis into one of the most perfect (which is not to say beneficent or productive) political machines in the country didn't happen all at once, but by the middle of the nineteenth century, something that would become legendary had emerged. The key was the nation's embrace of universal male suffrage and the concurrent influx of a great wave of immigrants, many of them fleeing the Irish potato famine. Tammany Hall, the Society's meeting place, often referred to in the press as "the Wigwam," became a byword for the organization itself. It originally had a mild nativist bent, but its midcentury leaders realized that in this increased democratization of the country came power if only they made themselves indispensable to these newly minted Americans. Richard Condon perfectly encapsulated Tammany's apotheosis in his 1969 novel *Mile High*:

All of them – Italians, Irish and Jews – had come from countries where they'd had to fight like tigers to defend themselves from the steady wars declared on them by their own governments. The Irish were bashed and starved by the English; the Jews got it in the head from the Cossacks and the Czar; the whole citizenry of the south of Italy, and particularly Sicily, were looked on like some dumb and wild beasts by all the Italians in the north. They had to be against authority to survive. And when they got out and made it to the City of New York, where Tammany offered nothing but help and shelter in exchange for their votes, their inward-supported leaders took the guidance and the dignity. ... It was a democracy contained and sustained by the politicians in good working partnership with the gangs who would man the polls on Election Day with knucks and clubs and knives and guns and guide their own ethnic groups through to vote the straight ticket. ... The gangs needed the politicians for protection against the courts and the police and the law, and the politicians needed the sure vote. It was to be a long and increasingly successful marriage, perhaps never to end.

[It was] the greatest democracy, all of it exquisitely organized precisely along the lines of the church itself by Honest John Kelly. ... The individual's vote was captured by the tenement captain, who reported it to the block captain. All the block captains were members of the election district committee and accountable to an election district captain ... who reported to [the] district leader, the equivalent of a cardinal. He reported to the executive committee of Tammany Hall, the city's Curia, together with thirty-three other district leaders, and directly to the Leader of Tammany himself, their pope. All of them along the chain handed out bail money, Christmas turkeys, coal, jobs, justice, and clothes in return for votes and loyalty.[16]

Beginning with Burr, the Tammany's hallmark was careful attention to the voters themselves. As historian Kevin Baker noted in *The New York Game*, "By the 1880s, Tammany was coming into its own as an organization, collecting payments and doling out favors and contracts with machinelike efficiency. Its power rested ultimately on the city's new immigrants and America's neglect of them. They went to Tammany for help in getting all the basic necessities of life, for jobs and bail money and shoes, and for the famous turkey at Christmas.

"In return, Tammany asked for their votes. These it used to wield power over everything in the public realm – street paving, garbage collecting, policing, firefighting, building inspection – and thus put itself in position to *provide* the jobs and the turkeys and the favors. The machine's reach extended everywhere. ... The machine was inherently conservative. Tammany might have been the only institution at the time that consistently cared for the poor, but it needed them to stay poor. ... In Tammany's New York, anything might be granted as a privilege, but nothing as a right." As Oliver E. Allen put it, "Though ostensibly a friend of the poor, Tammany was in bed with the rich."[17]

Tammany was, from an early date, in bed with baseball as well. It wasn't just that, as Baker noted, the notorious grafter William M. Tweed "ran his own club, the New York

Mutuals, who were reputed to have a payroll of $38,000 – all of it supplied by taxpayers, in the form of no-show jobs in the city's Street and Coroner's departments" or that Tweed's famous fire company gave Christy Mathewson his "Big Six" nickname, but that its members and hangers-on achieved such wealth through what member George Washington Plunkitt called "honest graft" that they bought teams. As the "Ode to Tammany" reminded the sachems and Braves,

> To public views he added private ends, And loved his country most, and next his friends.[18]

James Gaffney was one of those friends and practitioners of graft, though the "honest" aspect was debatable, at least to a few prosecutors. "A rather rough-looking, large and fleshy fellow wearing a loud suit and derby … the soul of shameless affability,"[19] Gaffney was referred to as "Tammany's mystery man" and "a power under cover" whose position has been unprecedented."[20] He was born on Manhattan's packed, impoverished Lower East Side and grew up in what was then known as the Gas House District (as hard as it is to imagine now, for nearly 100 years, Consolidated Gas once had huge storage tanks parked in the East 20s). As with another Tammany hack turned baseball owner, Big Bill Devery, Gaffney began his public career as a police officer. Unlike Devery, he didn't stay on but instead veered more directly into politics, becoming an election district captain under Grand Sachem Charles Francis Murphy's brother Billy. This put Gaffney in position to go into partnership with the leadership. In 1901 Gaffney became the part-owner and frontman for the New York Contracting & Trucking Company. Although the majority owner "wished to remain anonymous," it was likely Charles Murphy, appropriately nicknamed Silent Charlie.

Gaffney's chance at the big money came when Tammany advanced him to the Board of Aldermen. "Honest graft" meant using inside knowledge of government actions to steer public dollars one's own way. For example, if one knew the city was looking to condemn a parcel and take it for some civic need, he might buy himself a piece of the parcel before the news got out and caused the price of the land to skyrocket. The Murphy-Gaffney enterprise also practiced more direct, exploitative forms of self-dealing. In 1904 the Pennsylvania Railroad wanted to dig tunnels to their eponymous station. The Board of Aldermen, run by Gaffney, said no. The railroad then awarded the digging contract to New York Contracting, though its bid "had actually been $400,000 higher than that of a competitor, and whose owners had virtually no experience in the contracting business." With that, the board reversed its decision.[21]

Gaffney got into real trouble only once: In 1903 he was indicted for using his position as alderman to enrich New York Contracting, having in 1901 acquired a lease on a pier at West 79th Street for the company despite aldermen being prohibited from leasing any city property. Gaffney claimed

the case was politically motivated. The state Supreme Court ultimately vacated the charges on the grounds that the law was too vaguely written; surely the legislature had not intended to penalize someone who had "nothing more than a stockholder's relation to the corporation having contracted with the city," as Gaffney, to all appearances, had with New York Contracting. Multiply this sort of activity across all of the many city institutions in Tammany's tentacle-like grasp and the amount looted from the taxpayers quickly reaches stunning proportions. This is what the Braves chief represented – not Native American heroism or nobility, but low theft.[22]

What the Braves represented to Gaffney was an opportunity to front a more legitimate business than New York Contracting. In this he was similar to his Tammany rivals Devery and Frank Farrell, a gambler and the owner of an opulent but illegal casino (who among other things ran a casino-protection racket). The two found their positions threatened by a reformist wave and attempted to cultivate a more refined image by buying the rights to the American League's defunct Baltimore franchise, transferring it to New York, and founding the team that would come to be known as the Yankees. (Some of the money behind them belonged to Charles Murphy's son-in-law.) Gaffney also wanted to beat Farrell to success in the game. This he did within a few years – the Farrell-Devery Highlanders never won anything – and then got out.[23]

The Braves lost 101 games in Gaffney's first season of ownership and 82 in his second. Free of Monte Ward, he hired George Stallings as manager and in year two hit it big: the 1914 "Miracle Braves" won 94 games, ran away with the National League pennant, and swept Connie Mack's Philadelphia Athletics in the World Series. Inspired, Gaffney built Braves Field (unsurprisingly nicknamed The Wigwam), a ballpark so cold and expansive as to be both extravagantly pitcher-friendly and fan-unfriendly given the way it kept home runs at bay even after the introduction of the lively ball in 1920. Not only did this cripple the team in its long war with the Boston Red Sox, but Gaffney retained ownership of the ballpark even after he sold the Braves club in January 1916. His heirs continued to collect rent long after his 1932 passing, a burdensome expense for subsequent owners. The National League would be forced to take over the lease in 1935. Gaffney's widow and one of his former Braves partners finally sold the park back to the team in 1949.[24]

Thus Gaffney remained a direct influence on the team's fortunes for approximately eight times as long as he owned the team, but the name he selected has lasted even longer. The team abandoned it only once: After the disastrous 38-115 season of 1935, a year so bad it chased both Babe Ruth and owner Emil Fuchs out of baseball, the new proprietors, fronted by J.A. Robert "Bob" Quinn, changed the name. For the next five years, the Boston National League club would be called the Bees and its park the Beehive.

The club reverted to its old name in 1941, just as the actual braves of Tammany were beginning to go into eclipse, the result of failing to support Franklin Roosevelt in his run for the presidency, multiple corruption investigations, and 12 years of setbacks at the hands of reform-minded Republican Mayor Fiorello La Guardia.

Just as the chop itself is a Braves "tradition" that goes back only to 1991 when its adoption came about as the confluence of a tune played by the Braves' organist and the club's return to competitiveness after the mostly fruitless 1960s, '70s, and '80s (two division titles, two 100-loss seasons), the Atlanta baseball team's ethno-appropriation was not a matter of inevitability but choice. It was a hollow reference to Tammany Hall that was retroactively filled in with faux allusions to actual Native Americans, including the addition of a tomahawk to the uniform jersey in 1946, a revised (roaring) chief's head to the sleeve in 1957, and such cringeworthy episodes as the nearly 20-year run (1966-1985) of mascot Chief Noc-A-Homa, who came complete with a tipi in left field. Over time, the Braves took something that was general and made it very specific, adding a troubling component that emphasizes the violence of a people who, at the time Georgia and the federal government dispossessed them, did not wield tomahawks but were yeoman farmers and Christians, just like those who coveted their lands. Even in Boston the invocation of Native Americans as mascots was in questionable taste given New England's ethnic cleansing in the aftermath of the Pequot War (1636-1638), but at least that was an event that could be dismissed as colonial-era primitivism, whereas the removal of the Cherokee remains a stain on the United States of America.[25]

Going back to 1991, the Braves have been one of the most successful franchises in baseball, playing in one of the most dynamic cities in America. Conversely, the original "Braves" notion is archaic, the tomahawk chant is archaic – as Eastern Band Principal Chief Richard Sneed said in 2019, it's "so stereotypical, like old-school Hollywood."[26] Whether one approves of its branding or not, for so long as it remains the team will remain a contradiction, a club very much at the cutting edge of the present with iconography which is confusingly rooted in the past.

Portions of this article are adapted from Steven Goldman, "If You Have to Ask, It's Probably Racist," Baseball Prospectus, October 28, 2021, https://www.baseballprospectus.com/news/article/70791/ycliu-atlanta-braves-racist-chant-chop/.

NOTES

1 Chelsea Janes, "Braves Name and the 'Chop' Get Rob Manfred's Support Before Game 1 of the World Series," *Washington Post*, October 26, 2021.

2 https://www.nbcnews.com/news/us-news/tribes-push-back-against-mlb-claims-native-americans-approve-tomahawk-n1282516; https://sports.yahoo.com/national-congress-of-american-indians-rob-manfred-braves-tomahawk-chop-000709992.html.

3 Pekka Hämäläinen, *Indigenous Continent* (New York: Liveright, 2022), 392.

4 https://www.nytimes.com/1991/10/13/sports/sports-of-the-times-the-braves-tomahawk-phenomenon.html; Jeff Schultz, "Tomahawks? Scalpers? Fans Whoop It Up," *Atlanta Journal Constitution*, July 17, 1991: B6.

5 Timothy E. Scheurer, *Music and Mythmaking in Film: Genre and the Role of the Composer* (Jefferson, North Carolina: McFarland, 2008), 150.

6 Terence Moore, "Organist Carolyn King Encourages Tomahawking 'Wave' into a Ripple," *Atlanta Journal Constitution*, August 9, 1991: 71.

7 Bryan Di Salvatore, *A Clever Base-Ballist* (New York: Pantheon, 1999), 380.

8 Harold Kaese, *The Boston Braves* (New York: Putnam, 1948), 129.

9 http://exhibits.baseballhalloffame.org/dressed_to_the_nines/database.htm.

10 William Pencak, *Historical Dictionary of Colonial America* (Lanham, Maryland: Scarecrow Press, 2011), 233.

11 Alfred Connable and Edward Silberfarb, *Tigers of Tammany* (New York: Holt, Rinehart and Winston, 1967), 21.

12 Terry Galway, *Machine Made* (New York: Liveright, 2014).

13 Connable and Silberfarb, 21.

14 Gustavus Myers, *The History of Tammany Hall* (New York: Boni & Liveright, 1917), 5.

15 Oliver E. Allen, *The Tiger: The Rise and Fall of Tammany Hall* (Reading, Massachusetts: Addison-Wesley. 1993), 13.

16 Richard Condon, *Mile High* (New York: Dial Press, 1969), 5-6, 19.

17 Kevin Baker, *The New York Game: Baseball and the Rise of a New City* (New York: Knopf, 2024), 29, 51-52; Allen, *The Tiger*, ix.

18 Baker, 29; Connable and Silberfarb, 9.

19 Jill Jonnes, *Conquering Gotham: A Gilded Age Epic* (New York: Viking, 2007), 157.

20 "James E. Gaffney, Sportsman, Dies," *Brooklyn Times Union*, August 17, 1932.

21 Allen, *The Tiger*, 210.

22 "J.E. Gaffney Dies at East Hampton," *New York Times*, August 17, 1932: 17; Kaese, *The Boston Braves*, 128; "Alderman Indicted in Pier Lease Case," *New York Times*, July 22, 1903: 14; "Gaffney Wins on the Doubt," *New York Times*, September 22, 1903: 2.

23 Luc Sante, *Low Life: Lures and Snares of Old New York* (New York: FSG, 1991), 172; Baker, *The New York Game*, 113; Kaese, *The Boston Braves*, 128.

24 Robert S. Fuchs and Wayne Soini, *Judge Fuchs and the Boston Braves, 1923-1935* (Jefferson, North Carolina: McFarland, 1998), 26; "Fuchs Remains Braves' Head," *Boston Globe*, February 6, 1935: 1; "Perini Signs to Purchase Braves Field," *Boston Globe*, January 22, 1949: 5.

25 Jeff Schultz, "Tomahawks? Scalpers? Fans Whoop It Up," *Atlanta Journal-Constitution*, July 17, 1991: 14; Dave Anderson, "The Braves' Tomahawk Phenomenon," *New York Times*, October 13, 1991: 8:1.

26 Johnny Edwards, "Chiefs of Georgia Native Tribes Call Tomahawk Chop Inappropriate," *Atlanta Journal-Constitution*, October 13, 2019: A1.

RED SOX, GIANTS CELEBRATE NATIVE AMERICAN HERITAGE NIGHTS

By Joe Leisek and Bill Nowlin

FENWAY PARK NATIVE AMERICAN AND AMERICAN INDIAN CELEBRATION

On August 6, 2025, for the second year in a row, the Boston Red Sox welcomed all to what they called "our Native American and American Indian Celebration, where we recognize the resilience and beauty of this diverse and vibrant community." Just outside the ballpark, seven members of the Iron River Singers, an intertribal group based in New Bedford, Massachusetts, sang and beat drums. Among the members were two father/son pairs.[1]

Some 24 community members were recognized on the field just prior to the baseball game. Peoples represented included Eastern Pequot Tribal Nation, Hassanamiso Nipmuc Band, Herring Pond Wampanoag Tribe, Holton Band of Maliseet Indians, Mi'kmaw Nation, Natick Nipmuc, Mashantucket Pequot, Massachusett Tribe at Ponkapoag, Passamaquoddy Tribe, Penobscot, Wampanoag Tribe of Gray Head Aquinnah, as well as representatives from local university and community programs.

Greeting guests on the field was Jason Notermann, chief engineer for Red Sox Productions and a Chippewa Indian. Shortly afterward, he said, "I'm proud that the Red Sox continue to recognize and celebrate the diverse cultural communities that shape our region. Events like the Native American celebration raise awareness and help amplify voices that haven't always been heard. These moments are more than single-day acknowledgments, they reflect a growing cultural shift toward sustained advocacy and I look forward to seeing that commitment continue."[2]

SAN FRANCISCO GIANTS NATIVE AMERICAN HERITAGE CELEBRATION

On August 15, 2025, the San Francisco Giants hosted their annual Native American Heritage Night at Oracle Park, the team's home ballpark. The Giants have hosted the celebration since 2005 – with the exception of the 2020 season – to spotlight the rich history, culture, and contributions of Native Americans. The event included pregame

(Joe Leisek photograph)

(Bill Nowlin photograph)

The Iron River Singers outside Fenway Park on August 6, 2025.

The Paskenta Band of Nomlaki Dance Group performs for Giants fans in front of the main gate at Oracle Park in San Francisco on August 15, 2025.

cultural performances and a jersey designed by local Native American artist Jesse Hernandez.

Performers included the Nomlaki Weleaq Olkapna, which shared traditional dance and culture with hundreds of fans outside the ballpark's main gate, and a pregame, on-field performance from the All Nations Singers and Pow Wow Dancers.[3]

The Nomlaki Weleaq Olkapna are cultural bearers for the Paskenta Band of Nomlaki Indians, a tribe based in Corning, California.

"We are grateful to the San Francisco Giants for hosting the Native American Heritage event, a gathering that brings vital awareness that California Native peoples are still here — and have always been here," said Victor Alvarez, captain of the Nomlaki Weleaq Olkapna and a tribal member of the Paskenta Band of Nomlaki Indians.[4]

"Our culture is resilient and thriving, rooted in one of the most rich and diverse Native communities in the world, California. There is profound beauty in seeing our people come together in unity, reminding us that the strength of our ancestors lives on in every generation."

The All Nations Singers are a Northern-style pow wow drum group, founded in Oakland, California, over 30 years ago.

The ceremonial first pitch was thrown by Natalie Aguilera, citizen of the Choctaw Nation of Oklahoma and CEO of the Native American Health Center, which serves

(Joe Leisek photograph)

The All Nations Singers and Pow Wow Dancers perform on the field before the San Francisco Giants game.

people in more than a dozen sites in the San Francisco Bay Area.

NOTES

1   The group has a presence on Facebook: https://www.facebook.com/IronRiverSingers/.

2   Jason Nottermann email to Bill Nowlin, August 18, 2025.

3   See https://paskenta-nsn.gov and a video from the August 15 event at Oracle Park on You Tube: https://www.youtube.com/watch?v=ljIL-xyOCAY.

4   Victor Alvarez text message to Joe Leisek, August 21, 2025.

CONTRIBUTORS

Jeffrey P. Beck is the author of *The American Indian Integration of Baseball* (University of Nebraska Press) among other works. He currently serves as Director of the School of Humanities at Penn State Harrisburg. He is a member of the Mathewson-Plank chapter of the Society for American Baseball Research. He lives with his wife Marjorie and daughter Maddie in Palmyra, Pennsylvania.

Kelly Bennett is a southpaw author of many award-winning books for children, celebrating all that goes into being a kid…and baseball! These include *The House That Ruth Built*, about Yankee Stadium and Babe Ruth's big wish, and for fans of all ages *Out of the Mouth of Babe, Babe Ruth on Life: Pitching, Hitting, Striking Out and Coming Back Swinging!* a collection of photographs and quotes by the King of Crash. Kelly holds a master's degree from VCFA in writing for children and young adults. She is a two-wheeling bleacher warmer based in Westhampton Beach, NY. For more about Kelly and her books, visit her website: www.kellybennett.com

Luis Blandón, a Washington, DC native, is a producer, writer, and historical researcher. He has garnered numerous awards, including three regional Emmys® and Edward R. Murrow Awards. He served as the principal researcher for several authors recently *The Mysterious Mrs. Nixon: The Life and Times of Washington's Most Private First Lady* by Heath Hardage Lee. Luis has a Masters of Arts in International Affairs from the George Washington University.

Terry Bohn has been a SABR member for nearly 40 years and was an original member of the Halsey Hall chapter. He has written three books on baseball history in North Dakota, has been published in the *Baseball Research Journal*, and is a frequent contributor to the SABR BioProject. Terry's research interests are early baseball in the Dakotas with an emphasis on amateur, semipro, and the minor leagues. He is retired and lives in Western North Dakota.

Frederick C. "Rick" Bush wrote articles for over two dozen SABR books, the Biography Project, and the Games Project. Before his passing, Rick lived with his wife, Michelle, and their three sons – Michael, Andrew, and Daniel – in the Houston metro area. He had been an educator for almost 30 years, primarily teaching English at Wharton County Junior College's satellite campus in Sugar Land, which is home to the Astros' Triple-A franchise.

Christopher D. Chavis's love affair with the Boston Red Sox began as an undergraduate at Dartmouth College in New Hampshire, where his frequent trips to Fenway Park instilled in him a love of the Olde Towne Team that spawned a deep interest in baseball history. A public policy professional by day and amateur baseball historian by night, he can usually be found reading a book or watching a documentary about the Sox. He lives in Rancho Cucamonga, California with his wife, daughter, and two cats – Teddy and Yaz. He is a citizen of the Lumbee Tribe of North Carolina.

Carter Cromwell was formerly a sportswriter for daily newspapers, covering a wide variety of athletics at all levels. In a later life, he was a public-relations professional in the high-tech world. Since 2019, he has worked with an independent-league professional baseball team, the San Rafael Pacifics, doing the play-by-play and coordinating the in-game statistics. A SABR member, he also writes baseball-related articles for various websites and has contributed to multiple book projects. When not doing that, he has a passion for family, world travel, photography, and rescue dogs.

Rory Costello has written about Native American ballplayers in keeping with a long-held view that diversity is a big part of baseball's richness. He is co-chair of SABR's BioProject Committee and Chief Editor.

Jon Daly was born in Connecticut and is a lifelong resident of the Greater Hartford area. His father introduced him to baseball and the Red Sox during the 1975 season. Because he was a young lad at the time, he expected the Red Sox to play in the World Series every year. Boy, was he wrong! Jon has been able to combine two of his passions – writing and sports – and has contributed to numerous websites as well as a number of biographies for SABR's BioProject. In his free time, he works in the financial service industry.

Rob Daugherty is an Enrolled Citizen of the Cherokee Nation in Oklahoma. Rob is a retired educator from the Bureau of Indian Affairs and most recently from the Cherokee Nation of Oklahoma. A graduate of Haskell Indian Nations University. He has been a lifelong geek fan of Baseball, having played and coached collegiately. His passion for Native baseball players has evolved into one of the largest collections of Native American baseball cards. Focused exclusively on Indigenous players prior to 1947. Through extensive research 28 have been verified as Natives who played in what is now MLB from the years 1897 to 1947. Rob is a HUGE HUGE Yankees fan.

Robert Fitts's articles have appeared numerous journals, magazines, and websites. He is also the author of 10 books on Japanese baseball and Japanese baseball cards. Fitts is the founder of SABR's Asian Baseball Committee and a recipient of the society's 2025 Chadwick Award; the 2013 Seymour Medal for the Best Baseball Book of 2012 (*Banzai Babe Ruth*); the 2019 and 2023 McFarland-SABR Baseball Research Awards; the 2012 Doug Pappas Award for the best oral research presentation at the annual convention; and the 2006, 2021, 2023, and 2024 SABR Research Awards. He has twice been a finalist for the Casey Award and has received two silver medals at the Independent Publisher Book Awards. His latest book, *In the Japanese Ballpark*, will be released in November 2025.

David Fleitz, a web developer and baseball writer from Troy, Michigan, has written 11 well-received books on baseball history, including biographies of Shoeless Joe Jackson, Louis Sockalexis, and Cap Anson. David is a graduate of Bowling Green State University and is a lifelong Detroit Tigers fan. David's latest work, titled *Schnozz: The Baseball Life of Ernie Lombardi*, was published by McFarland and Company in 2023.

After a failed Little League career, **Todd Fuller** became a huge Cubs fan (an infliction he inherited from his dad's side of the family) while listening to Harry Caray and Steve Stone call play-by-play and commentary on WGN. In the early 1990s, quite by chance, he came upon an entry in the *Baseball Encyclopedia* which piqued his interest: Chief Yellowhorse (1898-1964), who was born and died in Pawnee, Oklahoma. Since then, he has written a book, co-authored a screenplay, and co-written an award-winning sitcom pilot loosely based, in part, on Mose YellowHorse's life. He currently serves as curator of the Western History Collections within the University Libraries at the University of Oklahoma, Norman, Oklahoma, where he lives with his wife, two kids, and a dog named Jake.

Steven Goldman has been part of Baseball Prospectus for much of the past 20-plus years and currently serves as Consulting Editor and columnist. He edited, co-edited, and contributed to multiple volumes of BP's best-selling annual and edited *Mind Game*, *It Ain't Over 'Til It's Over*, and *Extra Innings: More Baseball Between the Numbers*. He's also the author of *Forging Genius*, on the education of Casey Stengel, and *Baseball's Brief Lives: Player Stories Inspired by the Infinite Inning*. His work has appeared in numerous other places ranging from *Deadspin* to *The Daily Beast*. He's the host of the long-running *Infinite Inning* podcast, which sits at the crossroads of baseball, history, politics, and culture. He resides in New Jersey, where his wife, children, and cats total six.

Vince Guerrieri is a journalist and author in the Cleveland area. He's the secretary/treasurer of the Jack Graney SABR Chapter, and has contributed to the SABR BioProject, the SABR Games Project, and several SABR anthologies, serving as an editor for the book on the 1945 Cleveland Buckeyes. Additionally, he's written about baseball history for a variety of publications, including *Ohio Magazine*, *Cleveland Magazine*, *Smithsonian*, and *Defector*. He can be reached at vaguerrieri@gmail.com, or found on Twitter @vinceguerrieri.

The late **Martin Healy Jr.** was from Hamilton, Ontario. A lifelong Toronto Blue Jays fan and Canadian baseball historian, he published his first book, a biography of George "Mooney" Gibson, in March 2020. After his passing in September 2020, Richard Armstrong, his friend and co-author, submitted Marty's essay on Ed Pinnance, which previously appeared in *Our Game, Too: Influential Figures and Milestones in Canadian Baseball*, ed. Andrew North (SABR 2022).

Colin Howell is Professor Emeritus (History) at Saint Mary's University in Halifax, Nova Scotia. He is the author of *Northern Sandlots* (U of T Press, 1995) and *Hardscrabble Diamonds. Postwar Baseball in New England and the Maritimes* (McFarland Publishers, 2023).

John R. Husman has been a member of the Society for American Baseball Research since 1982 and is the Toledo Mud Hens Team Historian. He lives in Sylvania, Ohio. He watched Gene Conley pitch for the Toledo Sox in 1953.

William "Will" Hyland is a native of Searsmont, Maine and graduate of Colby-Sawyer College in New London, New Hampshire. In addition to his work with SABR, William manages an online sports media and podcast network and has written a novel published in 2024. He resides in Lisbon, Maine with his wife, Summer.

Don Jensen is vice chair of the SABR Deadball Era Committee and editor of *The Inside Game*, the committee's newsletter. He was formerly editor of the award-winning quarterly journal, *Base Ball: New Research on the Early Game*. His primary research interests are the Giants (in San Francisco and New York), the San Francisco Seals, baseball concessions, and the Sporting Life of the field. He lives in Alexandria, Viriginia,

Thomas Kahle is a PhD student at the University of Oklahoma. He pursued his first love – baseball – for as long as he could. After a four-year playing career at Coe College, he turned to his second love: history. He now researches Native American activism and federal Indian policy. He continues to root for his favorite team, the Chicago Cubs, and hopes that they might someday win another World Series.

Sean Kolodziej, a SABR member since 2018, is a lifelong Cubs fan. He was born, raised, and still lives in Joliet, Illinois, with his wife, Amy. His greatest moment at Wrigley Field was watching Glenallen Hill hit a home run onto the rooftop of a building on Waveland Avenue. Sean enjoys writing player biographies and contributing to other SABR projects.

Bill Lamb spent more than 30 years as a state/county prosecutor in New Jersey. He has been a SABR member for more than 30 years and is the 2019 winner of the Bob Davids Award, SABR's highest honor. Now retired, he lives with his wife Barbara in Meredith, New Hampshire.

Bill Lamberty, who joined SABR in 1983, has worked in athletic communications at Montana State since 1990. A graduate of Wyoming (1986, BS, Journalism) and MSU (2009, MA, History), he and his wife Lynn raised Nate, a catcher on two conference championship baseball teams at Whitworth, and Ellie, an official scorer there as an undergrad. The lifelong Royals fan was a founding member and the original newsletter editor of SABR's Deadball Era Committee, has written pieces for several SABR projects, and was co-editor of a book on Rosenblatt Stadium.

Joe Leisek lives in Petaluma, California, with his wife Tracy and Irish setter Liam. Joe is a citizen of the Chickasaw Nation.

R.J. Lesch is a business analyst living in Carlisle, Pennsylvania. He has been a White Sox fan since the Harry Caray days and a SABR member since 1998. He is delighted to be a member of the Deadball Era and Baseball and the Arts committee. R.J. was a co-founder of the Field of Dreams Chapter in Iowa and the Mathewson-Plank chapter in central Pennsylvania. He is also an avid fencer and certified fencing coach, his specialty being sabre. This can be confusing to family and friends.

Allison R. Levin is a Professor of Sports Communication at Webster University in St. Louis, Missouri. Her work explores the social and cultural issues of sports fandom, particularly baseball. She currently serves as Vice President of the SABR Board of Directors. Allison was born and raised in St. Louis, which resulted in her St. Louis Cardinals fandom. Despite that, her favorite player is Clayton Kershaw.

Len Levin is a longtime newspaper editor in New England, now retired. He lives in Providence with his wife, Linda, and an overachieving orange cat. He now (Len, not the cat) is the grammarian for the Rhode Island Supreme Court and copy-edits its decisions. He also copy-edits many SABR books, including this one. He is just down the interstate from Fenway Park, where he has spent many happy – and some not-so-happy – hours.

Stephanie Liscio is the author of *Integrating Cleveland Baseball: Media Activism, the Integration of the Indians, and the Demise of the Negro League Buckeyes*. She is a past president of Cleveland's Jack Graney Chapter and has contributed to a number of SABR publications. An avid Guardians fan, Stephanie currently works as the Director of Prospect Research for Hiram College in Hiram, Ohio. When she is not watching baseball, she likes spending time with her husband John, and shih tzu Izzy.

Chad Moody is a nearly lifelong resident of the Detroit area, where he has been a fan of the Detroit Tigers from birth. An alumnus of both the University of Michigan and Michigan State University, he has spent over 30 years working in various supply chain and finance roles within the automotive industry. Chad has contributed to numerous SABR and Professional Football Researchers Association projects. He and his wife, Lisa, live in Plymouth, Michigan, with their dog, Daisy.

Jack V. Morris is the head of a large pharmaceutical company's research library. He splits his time between suburban Philadelphia and coastal Delaware with his wife and is the father of two adult daughters. His baseball biographies have appeared in numerous books including *The Team That Forever Changed Baseball and America* (1947 Brooklyn Dodgers) and *Scandal on the Southside* (1919

Chicago White Sox). He is not the Jack Morris of World Series fame but, every once in a great while, wishes he was.

Bill Nowlin worked more than 50 years in the recorded music business and is a former college professor of political science. A Boston native and Red Sox fan, he has greatly enjoyed working with SABR members on many books and publications, writing a number of biographies and Games Project accounts.

Jonah O'Callaghan is a first-year undergraduate student studying biochemistry at the University of Washington. He became a SABR member in 2024 during his senior year of high school where he completed a capstone project on the "Contribution of Native American basketball players on the high school basketball culture." Eager to learn more about Native American athletes and their culture, he heard about an opportunity to write a biography about a Native American baseball player and took it. He plans to stay a member of the SABR community and continue to highlight the Native American culture and athletes of Native American heritage.

Roger and Deena Parmelee live in south-central Pennsylvania, only a few miles from the former campus of the Carlisle Indian School. Roger is retired and spends his days reading about or watching baseball and meticulously recording SkeeterSoft replays of entire seasons of historic games. He has been a SABR member for many years, and a Red Sox fan since Ted Williams, Jimmy Piersall and Jackie Jensen roamed the outfield at Fenway Park. Deena has a PhD in US history, formerly taught US history at the college level, and currently works for the Commonwealth of Pennsylvania. Roger taught Deena to appreciate baseball 40 years ago by telling her stories about Germany Schaefer and Bobo Newsom.

Royse Parr (1935-2018) was a native Oklahoman and Cherokee from Tulsa who attended Oklahoma State University when Jerry Adair was a star athlete in baseball and basketball. While attending a Chicago Cub fantasy camp with Jimmy Piersall as his manager, he decided to retire as an attorney and spend more time doing baseball research and watching his grandchildren play baseball. The co-author of two books published by the Oklahoma Heritage Association: *Glory Days of Summer: The History of Baseball in Oklahoma* and *Allie Reynolds: Super Chief.*

Zac Petrillo holds a Bachelor of Arts from Hunter College and a Master of Fine Arts from Chapman University's Dodge College of Film and Media Arts. His experience spans directing multiple short films and producing content for networks like Comedy Central and TruTV. In 2016, Zac played a pivotal role in the launch of Vice Media's 24/7 cable network, Vice TV. As an active member of the Society for American Baseball Research, he dedicates his research to international baseball and exploring the realm of baseball post the 1980s, particularly examining its intersection with the media industry. He has published articles on topics such as Jackie Robinson and Roberto Clemente, concerts at Dodger Stadium, and biographies of several players, including Hall of Famer Adrian Beltré and former MVPs Miguel Tejada and Terry Pendleton. He serves as the Director of Technical Operations at A+E Global Media and imparts his knowledge in television studies as a lecturer at Marymount Manhattan College. Zac is currently editing a book on Korean baseball and co-editing one on Australian baseball.

Alan Raylesberg is a mostly retired attorney who lives in the New York City suburbs. He has had a lifelong love affair with baseball, rooting for the Yankees going back to the days of Maris and Mantle. He was also a big fan of the Mets from the time of their birth, in 1962, through the 1980s. While he still follows them today, his allegiance lies primarily with the Bronx Bombers. Alan has written numerous biographies and other articles for SABR and especially enjoys writing about those he saw play and games that he attended. Before going to law school, Alan was the sports director of his college radio station and dreamed of a career in sports broadcasting or journalism. Now after many years practicing law, he is grateful for the opportunity that SABR has provided to allow him to realize at least some of that dream from many years ago.

Carl Riechers retired from United Parcel Service in 2012 after 35 years of service. With more free time, he became a SABR member that same year. Born and raised in the suburbs of St. Louis, he became a big fan of the Cardinals. He and his wife Janet have three children and he is the proud grandpa of two.

Joel Rippel, a Minnesota native and graduate of the University of Minnesota, is the author or co-author of 12 books on Minnesota sports history and has contributed as a writer or editor to SABR publications and has contributed to the SABR Bio project.

A. A. Rubin has the speed of a catcher, the power of a glove-first middle-infielder, and the eye of an umpire. His work has appeared recently in *Spitball, Pseudopod,* and *Ahoy! Comics.* He can be reached on social media as @TheSurrealAri, or through his website, www.aarubin.com. He hibernates through winter waiting for the smell of pine tar and glove oil to awaken him in time for the season when hope springs eternal.

Jason Scheller is a professor of history at Vernon College in Wichita Falls, Texas. He is a graduate of Texas Tech University. His graduate work has been featured in the books, *The Empire Strikes Out: How Baseball Sold U.S. Foreign Policy and Promoted the American Way Abroad*, by Robert Elias and *The Boys Who Were Left Behind: The 1944 World Series Between the Hapless St. Louis Browns and the Legendary St. Louis Cardinals*, by John Heidenry and Brett Topel. He joined the Dallas-Fort Worth Banks-Bragan chapter of SABR in 2018. His interests are in World War II baseball, the Negro Leagues, the minor leagues, the Texas Rangers, Los Angeles Dodgers, and the Boston Red Sox. He enjoys attending minor-league baseball games throughout the country with his wife and daughter each summer. A Red Sox fan since 1986, he follows them every season and relishes the opportunity to attend games at Fenway Park whenever he gets a chance.

Steven Schmitt is an award-winning author for his book, *A History of Badger Baseball – The Rise and Fall of America's Pastime at the University of Wisconsin.* He has been a SABR member since 2009 and has written several biographies for inclusion in various SABR publications. He has a bachelor's and master's degree in journalism and mass communication from the University of Wisconsin-Madison.

Curt Smith is the author of 18 books, including *Voices of The Game,* to *Esquire* magazine among "the 100 Best Baseball Books Ever Written." Other books *include Pull Up a Chair: The Vin Scully Story*; *The Presidents and the Pastime,* a history of baseball and the White House; and *Character at the Core,* a biography of George H.W. Bush, for whom Smith also wrote speeches during the President's time in office, including Bush's address at the 50th anniversary of Pearl Harbor. Smith has hosted or keynoted the Great Fenway Writers Series, Cooperstown Symposium on Baseball and American Culture, the NINE Conference, and series at the Smithsonian Institution and National Baseball Hall of Fame. *USA Today* calls him "the voice of authority on baseball broadcasting."

Douglas Stark is currently a museum consultant. He served as museum director at the International Tennis Hall of Fame in Newport, Rhode Island. He has also held positions at the United States Golf Association Museum in Far Hills, New Jersey and Naismith Memorial Basketball Hall of Fame in Springfield, Massachusetts. He has written several books about basketball history and is working on a multi-volume series about race and sports in Boston.

Mark S. Sternman was graduated from Dartmouth College, founded in 1769 to educate Native Americans (a mission that Dartmouth failed to fulfill for centuries, but that's a story for a different book). With this take on Slade Heathcott, Sternman, a fan of the Yankees for nearly half a century, has now profiled six New York American League players, an eclectic crew that in addition to Heathcott consists of Johnny Damon, Joe Girardi, Rich Hinton, George McConnell, and Chris Widger.

Tom Swift, M.S., M.F.A., is the Seymour Medal-winning author of *Chief Bender's Burden: The Silent Struggle of a Baseball Star*. He lives in Minneapolis.

Oliver George Tapaha (Ph.D.) is a citizen of the Diné/Navajo Nation from northeastern Arizona. He is a Postdoctoral Research Associate in the department of Education Policy, Organization and Leadership at the University of Illinois at Urbana-Champaign. He is an educational biographer who seeks and narrates the wisdom, lived experience stories, and life histories of Indigenous Peoples.

Stew Thornley joined SABR in 1979, served as the organization's vice president from 2002 to 2004, and was one of the founders of the Halsey Hall Chapter (Where the Action Is!) in 1985.

Since joining SABR in 2020, **Eric Vickrey** has contributed numerous articles for the Games and Bio Projects. His writing through SABR has spurred two books—*Runnin' Redbirds: The World Champion 1982 St. Louis Cardinals* and *Season of Shattered Dreams: Postwar Baseball, the Spokane Indians, and a Tragic Bus Crash That Changed Everything*. Eric is also co-editor on a forthcoming SABR book about the 2001 Seattle Mariners. He lives in Washington state with his wife, Gina, and their two cats, Edgar and Ralphie.

Joseph Wancho resides in Westlake, Ohio. He has been a SABR member since 2005 and he serves as co-chair of the Baseball Index Project. He is an occasional contributor to various SABR research committees.

An Oklahoma native, **Doug Wedge** has written three baseball history books, *Pinnacle on the Mound: Cy Young Award Winners Talk Baseball*, *Baseball in Alabama: Tales of Hardball in the Heart of Dixie*, and *The Cy Young Catcher* (co-author Charlie O'Brien). He lives in Oklahoma City.

Phil Williams lives in Oreland, Pennsylvania, and has been a SABR member since 2007. He has contributed numerous articles to SABR's BioProject and is working on a book on Philadelphia baseball during the Deadball Era.

Tom Willman, a Southern California native, spent 35 years writing for newspapers, including two decades of editorial page work. His earliest ballpark souvenirs (with memories attached) are the last yearbook of the Pacific Coast League Angels and the first yearbook of the Los Angeles Dodgers. He first joined SABR in 1986 and has been an occasional contributor to its products.

Born and raised in Alberta, Canada, **Ian Wilson** got his first glimpse of professional baseball from the Medicine Hat Blue Jays of the Pioneer League in the 1980s. The odd road trip to Calgary opened his world to the Cannons and the Pacific Coast League. He completed his Bachelor of Arts in Journalism & Communications from the University of Regina in Saskatchewan and returned to Alberta, where he worked as a reporter and editor at the *Calgary Sun* newspaper for a decade. Through the years, a love of baseball remained constant. Despite any failings of players or those involved in the game, Ian considers it the perfect sport and one that is above reproach. It requires no clock, just the best that Mother Nature has to offer and willing competitors. These basic ingredients unlock the poetry that W.P. Kinsella revealed to the world - a reminder of all that once was good and can be again. Ian is the co-founder of and a frequent contributor to Alberta Dugout Stories and Saskatchewan Dugout Stories. He is also the media coordinator for the summer collegiate Western Canadian Baseball League (WCBL).

Ryan Woodward created the inaugural Women in Baseball Week in 2017 and continues to develop projects commemorating women in baseball, including the Women's Baseball Heritage Trail. Ryan is a member of the Society for American Baseball Research and the International Women's Baseball Center and is currently the full time IWBC Project Coordinator. He lives in Rockford, Illinois.

William Young is Professor Emeritus of Religious Studies at Westminster College, Fulton, Missouri. The books he has written on baseball include *John Tortes Meyers: A Baseball Biography* and *J. L. Wilkinson and the Kansas City Monarchs Trailblazers in Black Baseball.* For the latter book, he received a SABR Research Award. He also contributed essays to the SABR volumes on Jackie Robinson and the Kansas City Monarchs. He is the author of *Quest for Harmony: Native American Spiritual Traditions* and several other books on religion. Young is a lifelong St. Louis Cardinals fan. He and his wife, Sue, also a retired educator and Cardinals fan, reside in Columbia, Missouri.

Society for American Baseball Research

Become a SABR member today!

If you're interested in baseball — writing about it, reading about it, talking about it — there's a place for you in the Society for American Baseball Research.

SABR members include everyone from academics to professional sportswriters to amateur historians and statisticians to students and casual fans who merely enjoy reading about baseball history and gathering online or in person with other members to talk baseball.

We hope you'll join the most passionate international community of baseball fans!

Check us out online at SABR.org/join

SABR Membership Benefits

- Receive two e-book editions (spring and fall) of the Baseball Research Journal, our flagship publication
- Receive e-book edition of The National Pastime, our annual convention journal
- New e-books published by the SABR Digital Library, FREE to all members
- "This Week in SABR" e-newsletter, sent every Friday
- Regional chapter meetings, which can include guest speakers, presentations, and trips to ballgames
- Participate in research committees and online discussion groups

- Contribute to books, the Baseball Biography Project, and the SABR Games Project
- Collaborate with SABR researchers and experts
- Publish your research in peer-reviewed SABR journals
- Discount on registration to our annual conferences and National Convention
- FREE online access to Historical Black Newspapers Collection via ProQuest, the Newspapers.com World Collection, and The Sporting News via Paper of Record
- Discounts with other partners in the baseball community

- -

SABR MEMBERSHIP FORM

Name _____

Email _____

Address _____

City _____ State _____ Zip _____

Phone _____

If you wish to pay by credit card, please contact the SABR office at (602) 496-1460 or sign up securely online at SABR.org/join.

We accept Visa, Mastercard & Discover.

	Standard	Young Pro.	Student
Annual:	❏$80	❏$55	❏$25
3 Year:	❏$215		
Monthly:	❏$7.95	❏$5.95	

Members who wish to be mailed a printed copy of the Baseball Research Journal should add $7 per issue (U.S.) or $11 per issue (international). Two (2) issues of the BRJ are delivered each year.

SABR memberships are available on an annual, multi-year, or monthly subscription basis. Memberships auto-renew for your convenience. Young Professional memberships are for ages 30 and under. Student memberships are available to currently enrolled middle/high school or full-time college/university students. Monthly subscription members are eligible for SABR event discounts after 12 months.

Mail to: SABR, PO Box 1715, Milwaukee, WI 53201

The SABR Digital Library

Available wherever books are sold

The SABR
Digital
Library
• • •
Print &
Ebooks

SABR.ORG
OR
WHEREVER
BOOKS ARE
SOLD

The Stars Shone on Philadelphia: The 1934 Phila. Stars
ISBN 978-1-960819-04-8 $9.99 ebook
ISBN 978-1-960819-05-5 $29.95 paperback
Biographies of Ed Bolden's 1934 Negro National
League champions, including Biz Mackie and Jud
Wilson.

Yankee Stadium: America's First Modern Ballpark
ISBN 978-1-960819-16-8 $9.99 ebook
ISBN 978-1-960819-21-5 $39.95 paperback
Essays about the history of Yankee Stadium and
recaps of over 50 historic games and other events
there, including papal visits, football, and more.

*Ebbets Field: Great, Historic, and Memorable Games at
Brooklyn's Lost Ballpark*
ISBN 978-1-960819-16-1 $9.99 ebook
ISBN 978-1-960819-17-8 $39.95 paperback
Relive Jackie Robinson's and Sandy Koufax's debuts,
and over 90 other heartbreaks and triumphs in
Brooklyn, plus essays on the ballpark.

Nichibei Yakyu: Volume II: 1960-2019
ISBN 978-1-960819-14-7 $9.99 ebook
ISBN 978-1-960819-15-4 $34.95 paperback
Fascinating recaps of the exhibition tours and
MLB games by US baseball teams in Japan.

Sox Bid Curse Farewell: The 2004 Boston Red Sox
ISBN 978-1-960819-18-5 $9.99 ebook
ISBN 978-1-960819-19-2 $34.95 paperback
Biographies of every player and coach on the 2004
World Championship team, as well as essays about
the season, effects of the win on fans, and more.

Dodger Stadium: Blue Heaven on Earth
ISBN 978-1-960819-20-8 $9.99 ebook
ISBN 978-1-960819-21-5 $29.95 paperback
Essays about the history of Dodger Stadium and
recaps of over 50 historic games there, from
Fernandomania to Vin Scully's bow.

One-Win Wonders
ISBN 978-1-960819-13-0 $39.95 paperback
ISBN 978-1-960819-12-3 $9.99 ebook
Biographies of 78 players whose entire major league
pitching record consisted of just one win, from the
tragic, like Nick Adenhart, to the improbable, like
catcher Brent Mayne.

Willie Mays: Five Tools
ISBN 978-1-960819-02-4 $9.99 ebook
ISBN 978-1-960819-03-1 $29.95 paperback
Twenty essays on Mays' life and career, plus
recaps of 30 historic games.